REALITY THROUGH THE ARTS

SECOND EDITION

DENNIS J. SPORRE

Ball State University

PRENTICE
HALL

Prentice Hall, Englewood Cliffs, NJ 07632

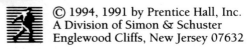

© 1994, 1991 by Prentice Hall, Inc.
A Division of Simon & Schuster
Englewood Cliffs, New Jersey 07632

10 9 8 7 6 5 4 3 2

ISBN 0–13–475286–4

This book was designed and produced by
CALMANN & KING LTD, LONDON

Designer Karen Stafford
Picture researcher Prue Waller
Artwork by Sarah-Jayne Stafford and David Kemp

Typeset by Wyvern Typesetting, Bristol
Printed in Hong Kong

Front cover: Julian Dupré, *The Reapers*, 1881. Photo: Fine Art
Photographic Library Ltd., London.

Back cover: Ando Hiroshige, *Maple Leaves at the Tekona Shrine, Mamma*,
1857. Polychrome woodblock print, $13\frac{3}{4} \times 9\frac{3}{4}$ ins (35 × 24 cm). British
Museum, London.

PICTURE CREDITS

The author, the publishers, and Calmann & King Ltd wish to thank the museums, galleries, collectors,
and other owners who have kindly allowed their works to be reproduced in this book. In general,
museums have supplied their own photographs; other sources are listed below:

INTRODUCTION
0.2 Archiv für Kunst und
Geschichte, Berlin
0.3 Photo: Geoffrey Clements
0.4A & B Photo: Wolfgang Volz
0.8 VAG (UK) Ltd
0.9 Alinari, Florence
0.10 © 1994 Pollock-Krasner
Foundation/ARS, New York

CHAPTER 1
1.8 © Est Thomas Hart
Benton/DACS, London/VAGA,
New York 1994
1.12 © ADAGP, Paris and
DACS, London 1994
1.14 © 1994 Pollock-Krasner
Foundation/ARS, New York
1.21 © DACS 1994
1.30 © DEMART PRO ARTE
BV/DACS 1994
1.31, 1.33 © DACS 1994

CHAPTER 2
2.6 Reproduced by kind
permission of the Henry Moore
Foundation
2.8 Alinari, Florence
2.9 © Christo 1976. Photo:
Wolfgang Volz
2.11 © DACS 1994
2.12 Giraudon, Paris
2.14, 2.17 © ADAGP, Paris and
DACS, London 1994
2.18 Rheinisches Bildarchiv,
Cologne
2.20 Alinari, Florence

CHAPTER 3
3.10, 3.11 Trudy Lee Cohen,
Philadelphia

CHAPTER 4
4.8 University of Arizona Theatre
4.9, 4.10 Old Globe Theatre, San
Diego
4.11 University of Arizona
Theatre
4.12 State University, New York
4.13 University of Arizona
Theatre
4.14 University of Iowa Theatre
4.15 University of Arizona
Theatre
4.16 University of Illinois

CHAPTER 5
5.1 © DACS 1993
5.2 Universal Pictures, a Division
of Universal City Studios Inc. All
Rights
5.3 B.F.I. London

CHAPTER 6
6.1–6.13 Linda Rich, Addlestone,
U.K.
6.14, 6.15 Roger Greenawalt,
Langhorne, PA
6.17 Linda Rich, Addlestone,
U.K.

CHAPTER 7
7.1 Britain on View (B.T.A.)
London
7.2 John Donat, London
7.5 Hirmer Fotoarchiv, Munich
7.12 A.F. Kersting, London
7.19 Library of Congress
7.20 Wayne Andrews/ESTO,
Mamaroneck
7.21 Ezra Stoller © ESTO,
Mamaroneck
7.22 Britain on View (B.T.A.),
London
7.26 Ralph Liebermann, North
Adams, MA
7.27 A.F. Kersting, London
7.28 Wayne Andrews, Chicago
7.30 Giraudon, Paris
7.31 A.F. Kersting, London
7.32, 7.34 Scala, Florence
7.35 Wayne Andrews, Chicago
7.36 Solomon R. Guggenheim
Museum/Robert E. Mates
7.37 Ezra Stoller © ESTO,
Mamaroneck

CHAPTER 9
9.2, 9.4 © DACS 1994
9.6–9.8 Novosti, London

CHAPTER 10
10.2, 10.4 Colorphoto, Hans
Hinz, Allschwil, Switzerland
10.15, 10.18 A.F. Kersting,
London
10.22 Hirmer Fotoarchiv,
Munich

CHAPTER 11
11.2, 11.3 Alinari, Florence
11.6 Hirmer Fotoarchiv, Munich
11.7 A.F. Kersting, London
11.9, 11.11 Alinari, Florence
11.14 A.F. Kersting, London
11.21 Calmann & King archives
11.22 Ancient Art and
Architecture Collection, London
11.29 Scala, Florence
11.30, 11.32 Alinari, Florence
11.33 Fototeca Unione, Rome
11.34, 11.35 Alinari,
Florence
11.38 Todaiji, Nara
11.41 A.F. Kersting, London
11.42 Alinari, Florence
11.45 Scala, Florence
11.46 Sonia Halliday
Photographs, Weston Turville,
U.K.
11.47 Hirmer Fotoarchiv,
Munich
11.60 Jean Dieuzaide, Toulouse
11.61 Clive Hicks, London
11.62 Bulloz, Paris
11.63 Scala, Florence
11.65 Britain on View (B.T.A.),
London
11.67 A.F. Kersting, London
11.68 Giraudon, Paris
11.69 © DACS 1994
11.70 Giraudon, Paris
11.74 Scala, Florence
11.75, 11.77, 11.78 Alinari,
Florence
11.79 Hirmer Fotoarchiv,
Munich
11.80 Scala, Florence
11.81 Alinari, Florence
11.86 Hulton-Deutsch, London

CHAPTER 12
12.12 Scala, Florence
12.13 Alinari, Florence
12.19 Robert Harding Picture
Library, London
12.20 A.F. Kersting, London
12.21 Ancient Art and
Architecture Collection, London
12.30 Bildarchiv Foto Marburg,
Germany
12.31 A.F. Kersting, London
12.36 Weidenfeld & Nicolson
Archives, London
12.50 G.E. Kidder-Smith, New
York
12.56, 12.57 A.F. Kersting,
London
12.59 Bridgeman Art Library,
London

CHAPTER 13
13.9 © ADAGP, Paris and
DACS, London 1994
13.13, 13.15 © DACS 1994
13.16 Succession H. Matisse
© DACS 1994
13.20 © 1994 Pollock-Krasner
Foundation/ARS, New York
13.22 © Roy Lichtenstein/DACS
1994
13.24 © 1994 Frank Stella/ARS,
New York
13.26 © ADAGP, Paris and
DACS, London 1994
13.27 Ralph Liebermann, North
Adams, MA
13.28 F.R. Yerbury Collection,
London
13.29 John Donat, London
13.30 Architectural Press,
London
13.31 Ezra Stoller © ESTO,
Mamaroneck
13.33 Cement and Concrete
Association, Slough, U.K.
13.34 Paschall/Taylor

CONTENTS

Preface 7

INTRODUCTION 11

The Work of Art 11
  The Humanities, Humanity, & the Arts 12
  What is Art? 13
The Functions of Art 16
  Entertainment 16
  Political & Social Commentary 16

  Therapy 17
  Art as Artifact 17
The Arts and Life 18
Aesthetic Perception and Response 21
  What Is It? 21
  How Is It Put Together? 21
  How Does It Stimulate? 21
What is Art Criticism? 22
  Types of Criticism 25
  Making Judgments 26

PART I: THE MEDIA OF THE ARTS 27
What Artists Use to Express "Reality"

ONE: PAINTING, PRINTMAKING, & PHOTOGRAPHY 29

What Are They? 29
How Are They Put Together? 29
  Media 29
  Composition 37
  Other Factors 46
How Do They Stimulate the Senses? 49
  Color 49
  Contrast 50
  Dynamics 51
  Trompe l'Oeil 53
  Line 53
  Juxtaposition 54
  Focus 54
  Subject Matter 54

TWO: SCULPTURE 57

What Is It? 57
How Is It Put Together? 57
  Dimensionality 57
  Methods of Execution 59
  Composition 63
  Other Factors 67
How Does It Stimulate the Senses? 68
  Texture 68
  Color 68
  Dynamics 69

  Line & Form 70
  Mass 70
  Lighting & Environment 71

THREE: MUSIC 72

What Is It? 72
  Sonata 72
  Symphony 73
  Concerto 73
  Suite 73
  Concert Overture 73
  Opera 73
  Oratorio 73
  Cantata 73
  Mass 73
  Motet 74
How Is It Put Together? 74
  Tone 74
  Melody 77
  Harmony 77
  Tonality 78
  Texture 79
  Rhythm & Beat 79
  Meter 79
  Tempo 80
  Structure 80
How Does It Stimulate the Senses? 81
  Opera 82

CONTENTS

FOUR: THEATRE 87

What Is It? 87
Tragedy 88
Comedy 88
Tragicomedy 88
Melodrama 88
Musicals 89
How Is It Put Together? 89
The Script 89
Plot 90
Character 91
The Protagonist 91
Thought 92
Visual Elements 93
Aural Elements 99
Dynamics 99
The Actor 99
Verisimilitude 99
How Does It Stimulate the Senses? 103

FIVE: FILM 105

What Is It? 105
Narrative Film 106
Documentary Film 106
Absolute Film 106
How Is It Put Together? 107
Magnitude & Convention 107
Editing 107
Camera Viewpoint 108
Cutting Within the Frame 109
Dissolves 109
Movement 109
How Does It Stimulate the Senses? 111
Crosscutting 112
Tension Build-up and Release 112
Direct Address 112
Structural Rhythm 113

SIX: DANCE 116

What Is It? 116
Ballet 116
Modern Dance 117
Folk Dance 117
How Is It Put Together? 117
Formalized Movement 117
Line, Form, & Repetition 123

Rhythm 125
Mime & Pantomime 125
Idea Content 125
Music 125
Mise en Scène 126
Lighting 127
How Does It Stimulate the Senses? 127
Line & Form 127
Dynamics 128
Sign Language 128
Color 128

SEVEN: ARCHITECTURE 129

What Is It? 129
How Is It Put Together? 129
Structure 130
Building Materials 138
Line, Repetition, & Balance 141
Scale & Proportion 144
Context 145
Space 147
Climate 148
How Does It Stimulate the Senses? 149
Gothic Cathedrals 149
Holy Family Church 150
United States Capitol Building 150
Guggenheim Museum 153
Zarzuela Race Track 154
Sears Tower 154

EIGHT: LITERATURE 155

What Is It? 155
Fiction 155
Poetry 156
Biography 156
Essays 156
Drama 157
How Is It Put Together? 157
Fiction 157
Poetry 158
Biography 159
How Does It Appeal to the Senses? 160
Fiction 160
Poetry 164
Biography 166
Essay 167

PART II: THE STYLES OF THE ARTS 169
How Artists Portray "Reality"

NINE: WHAT IS STYLE? 171

TEN: ANCIENT APPROACHES—
30,000 B.C. to 600 B.C. 179

Paleolithic Europe 179
    Our Earliest Art 179
    Venus Figures 181
    The Cave of Lascaux 181
Mesopotamia 182
    Early Sumerian Art 182
    The Archaic Period 183
Jerusalem 188
    The Temple of Solomon 188
    The Bible 188
Ancient Egypt 190
    Old Kingdom 190
    Painting 193
    New Kingdom 194
China 197
    The Shang Dynasty 198
Native American Culture 199

ELEVEN: ARTISTIC REFLECTIONS
IN THE PRE-MODERN WORLD—
600 B.C. to A.D. 1650 200

Classical Greece 200
    Classical Style 200
    Classical Theatre 203
    Classical Architecture 205
    Late Classical Style 207
    Hellenistic Style 208
Africa 211
China 214
    Confucianism 214
    Taoism 214
    Buddhism 214
    Buddhist Influence 216
    Chinese Theatrical Styles 218
Imperial Roman Classicism 219
    Roman Style 219
    Architectural Classicism 224

Japan 227
    Japanese Style: Painting and Sculpture 228
    Japanese Style in Theatre 229
Byzantium 230
    Byzantine Style 230
    Hieratic Style 234
Islam 236
    Islamic Style in Visual Art 236
    Islamic Style in Literature 238
    Islamic Style in Architecture 238
Native American Art 241
Medieval Europe 241
    Romanesque Style 242
    Gothic Style 247
    The Gothic Cathedral 248
    Gothic Sculpture 251
The Renaissance 253
    Flemish Painting 254
    Renaissance Painting in Florence 254
    Renaissance Sculpture in Florence 256
    Renaissance Literature 259
    Architecture 263
    The High Renaissance in Rome 265
    The Late Renaissance in England 271

TWELVE: ARTISTIC STYLES IN THE
EMERGING MODERN WORLD
1650 to 1900 273

The Ming Dynasty in China 273
    Ming Dynasty Styles 273
    Sculpture & Ceramics 275
    Imperial Architecture 277
India 277
    The Arya 277
    Alexander & Beyond 278
    Indian Painting Styles 279
    Muslim vs. Hindu Architecture 280
Baroque Style 281
    Counter-Reformation Baroque 282
    Aristocratic Baroque 283
    Bourgeois Baroque 285
    Baroque Music 286
    Court Baroque 287

CONTENTS

Japan 289
    Japanese Style in Painting 290
    Imari Porcelain 291
    Kabuki Theatre 291
    Japanese Style in Printmaking 291
The Enlightenment 293
    Rococo 293
    The Human Condition 299
    Landscape & Portraiture 300
    Genre & Social Comment 302
    Neoclassicism 305
    Architectural Neoclassicism 305
    Musical Classicism 307
Africa and Early Black America 309
    Art and Ancestor Worship 309
    Transportation to America 310
    The Music of Black America 310
Native American Art 312
    The Inuits 312
    The Northwest Coast Tribes 313
    Native American Literature 315
The Industrial West 319
    Classicism 319
    Romanticism 322
    Realism 330
    Impressionism 332
    Post-Impressionism 337
    Experimentation in Architecture 337

THIRTEEN: PLURALISM IN THE TWENTIETH CENTURY 340

Native American Styles 340
    Native American Fiction 340
    Native American Poetry 343
    Native American Ceramics and Painting 344
    Native American Music 345
African Styles 345
    African Sculpture 346
    West African Masks 347

    African Influence on Western Art 349
    African Tribal Music 350
African-American Styles 350
    Harlem Renaissance 350
    African-American Popular Music—Jazz 353
    African-American Dance 355
    Black Liberation in the Theatre 355
American and European Styles 356
    Expressionism 356
    Cubism 358
    Fauvism 359
    Futurism 361
    Abstraction 361
    Surrealism 365
    Realism 365
    Absurdism 366
    Abstract Expressionism 366
    Pop Art 368
    Op Art 370
    Hard Edge 370
    Primary Structures 371
    Environmental Art 371
    Photorealism & Conceptualism 372
    Art Nouveau 372
    Experimentation in Architecture 373
    Modern Classical Music 378
    Serialism 381
    Improvisation 381
    Mainstream 381
    Electronic Music 381
    Ultrarationalism & Beyond 382
    Modern Dance 383

FOOTNOTES 385

GLOSSARY 387

BIBLIOGRAPHY 393

INDEX 396

PREFACE

The purpose of this book is to teach basic principles and practices of the arts—painting, printmaking, sculpture, music, theatre, dance, literature, and architecture—of Western and other cultures. This text is an introduction to the humanities, and is designed for individuals who have limited experience in the arts. In addition, it attempts to provide the humanities instructor with a helpful textbook for courses that touch upon the arts in an inter- or multidisciplinary manner, and approach the arts from a world viewpoint. In order to meet those ends, I have been selective in the material included. My treatment of definitions and concepts in Part One is cursory: in order to stay within the bounds of practicality and the limited perspective of the intended audience, they are explained in general terms, making it simpler to apply them to the diverse cultural approaches examined in Part Two.

This book, of course, is not a self-contained humanities course. It cannot substitute for the classroom teacher, whose responsibility it is to shape and mold a course according to the needs of local curricula, and to assist the student to focus on what is important for the thrust of that particular course. No textbook can be relied upon to answer all the students' questions and include all key points. A good text can only suggest the breadth of what is available. This text should encourage the use of other source materials. The instructor should develop emphases or foci of his or her own choosing by adding lectures, videos, or field trips, and expansion of particular areas raised in the general overview presented here. I have aimed to provide a convenient one-volume outline, with enough flexibility to serve a variety of purposes.

In Part One we examine the various media of the arts—painting and architecture, for example—define and explain important terminology, discuss how works of art are composed, and suggest how various works of art effect responses in their viewers and listeners. The compendium approach used in Part One seems useful because it allows us to apply its terms and concepts as tools for perceiving, describing, and understanding the arts of the diverse cultures discussed in Part Two.

In discussing works of art, I have for the most part kept to description and compositional analysis. By so doing I hope to assist the readers in polishing their skills of technical observation. By avoiding forays into meanings and relationships, I have left room for the instructor to move discussions in whatever direction is deemed appropriate. As suggested earlier, the choice of what to include and exclude has been more or less arbitrary. This is not a comprehensive history of the arts; nor is it an introduction to aesthetic theory. Even the media discussed in the various chapters vary—for the simple reason that different cultures have left us different kinds of artifacts, some of which are better examples of the

culture than others. Thus, in organizing each chapter—particularly in Part Two—I have let the nature of the material suggest its own internal structure. In all cases I have tried to keep the focus of the discussion on works of art.

Part Two is arranged chronologically. Thus, with what I hope is a reasonably simple format, we are able to glimpse the arts from a variety of cultures that were occurring at relatively the same time in history. We must keep in mind, however, that the focus of Part Two is style, not history. In addition, not every culture has been represented—for example, I have not included Oceania, primarily because consultation with humanities instructors suggested priorities for inclusion. Given practical considerations, such as space and accessibility of illustrations, those priorities became imperative.

This book is based on the belief that art from whatever culture is a view of the universe, of human reality, that is, expressed in a particular medium and shared with others. Throughout time humans have struggled to understand the universe, and, though separated by centuries or cultures, our concerns and questions, as reflected in our works of art, are alike. By examining works of art we can enrich our own understanding of our existence. Therefore, as we proceed through the text, try to go beyond the facts and descriptions presented and seek the meaning of the works of art, if only from an individual perspective. Ask questions about what the artist may have been trying to accomplish, and seek to understand how you relate to these creative expressions in terms of your perception of human reality.

Finally, a work such as this does not spring entirely from the general knowledge or primary source research of its author. Some of it does, because of my long-term and close affiliation with the various arts disciplines. Much is the result of notes accumulated here and there, of travel around the world, and of research specifically directed to this project. In the interest of readability, and in recognition of the generalized purpose of this text, copious footnoting has been avoided. I hope that the method I have chosen for presentation and documentation of others' works meets the needs of both responsibility and practicality. The bibliography gives a comprehensive list of works used.

I am deeply indebted to many individuals for the completion of this project. A book is far more than the work of one author. Bud Therien at Prentice Hall, my friend and mentor for more than fifteen years, production editors, copy editors, and designers at Calmann and King in London, all played a key role in this project. Most of all, I am indebted to my wife, Hilda, whose patience, love, understanding, proofreading, note-taking, and research assistance provide me with a solid foundation from which to generate my part of the project.

D.J.S.

INTRODUCTION

This book is a story about us: our perceptions of the world as we have come to see it, to respond to it, and to communicate our understandings to each other. We have been doing this since at least the Ice Age, more than 35,000 years ago. At that time, we were already fully human. We have not "developed" into our humanity since then. Our human characteristics have been with us from the earliest times. Although we have learned a great deal about our world and how it functions, and we have changed our patterns of existence, the fundamental characteristics that make us human—our ability to intuit and to symbolize—have been with us from the beginning. Our art tells us this in terms which are inescapable. So a story of humankind's ventures is also our story.

We begin our story by drawing a brief and general picture of the arts. First, we will discuss what works of art are; then we will examine the functions of art, the arts and life, and aesthetic perception and response. Finally, we will look at how we evaluate works of art—that is, artistic criticism. We will in this way gain a clearer sense of how the arts relate to human understanding, the ways in which artists communicate human understanding, and how we describe, analyze, and judge works of art.

THE WORK OF ART

In order to function in the complex human relationships in which we find ourselves, and to understand human existence, we use a variety of vantage points. When, for example, we meet people, we usually choose several vantage points from which to perceive and relate to them: We can see them as organized systems of chemical components; as bundles of interacting psychological and social experiences; as spiritual entities; a combination of these, or something else altogether. How well we perceive and respond requires the development of certain skills. In a sense, these vantage points and skills are ways of "knowing" human reality or the "human condition." Humans have organized these ways of knowing into categories generally called *science*, *technology*, *social science*, *humanities*, and *fine arts*. We may say that science seeks to examine rationally; technology uses the discoveries of science to create tools for making life better; social science studies how people behave; and the humanities and fine arts try to describe what kinds of creatures we are, and how we got to be this way. Specifically, the arts try to understand the human condition by drawing upon "creative impulses" that sometimes communicate through mysterious channels. Very often the boundaries between science, technology, social science, and the humanities and fine arts are blurred. The scientist often depends as

0.1 Jackson Pollock, *Convergence*, 1952. Oil on canvas, 8 x 13 ft (2.43 x 3.96 m). Albright-Knox Art Gallery, Buffalo, New York.

much as the artist on intuition to sense or imagine that there is something to be discovered. For example, Sir Isaac Newton needed to use his creative intuition to deduce from being hit on the head by a falling apple that he could take that phenomenon and apply scientific methodology to it and thus prove the existence of gravity. This kind of creative intuition is much the same as that experienced by an artist who, having sensed some truth, may then invent a way of translating that insight into a painting, sculpture, musical composition, or theatrical artwork in order to convey it to someone else. None the less, the curiosity of the scientist, technologist, and social scientist is driven by a different expectation of outcomes than the curiosity of an artist. Although the demonstrable facts of science seem considerably different from the swirling globs of paint in a painting by Jackson Pollock (Fig. 0.1), for some people Pollock's painting portrays a universal truth more effectively than scientific fact. These different approaches allow each of us to enjoy different ways of understanding our world.

THE HUMANITIES, HUMANITY, & THE ARTS

The *humanities* and the field of the humanities called "the arts" both seek to understand what *humankind* is all about. Who are we? How did we get this way? How do we relate to each other? How do we behave? What do we believe? Sometimes, artworks try to answer such questions directly. At other times, they generate responses that indirectly reveal conditions of human existence. For example, is your reaction to the Pollock painting in Figure 0.1 a positive or negative one? Do you feel comfortable with it? Does it say anything to you—or is it just an incomprehensible swirl of colors and dots? Do you understand what the painting has done to make you feel the way you do? Do you understand how the painting has done this? Such revelations do not fall into neat packages that can be examined under a microscope. However, although those insights are less tangible, they may still be accurate.

As long as humans have existed, they have used artworks as a means for answering life's questions, and for revealing and communicating life's realities. Artworks may involve rituals, drawings, stories, dances, and songs—and thus become paintings, plays, novels, ballets, and symphonies. Although the first group is older than the second, it deals, remarkably, with the same issues that face us today. When Ice-Age humans painted scenes on the walls of their caves 15,000 years ago (Fig. **0.2**), they were probably expressing the same basic concerns and questions we have. When, in the fourth century B.C., Sophocles wrote a tragedy about a mythic king named Oedipus, who tried to escape the prophecy that he would kill his father and marry his mother, Sophocles was undoubtedly dealing with the same questions about human relationships that we have. Whether "capturing" a bison by describing it in paint, or dramatically portraying humankind's problems in a tragedy, our predecessors used art—as we do today—to express or deal with human concerns about the extent of our control of ourselves and the universe around us.

0.2 General view of cave chamber at Lascaux, France, from the early Stone Age (c. 15,000 B.C.).

WHAT IS ART?

In a broad sense, the arts are *processes*, *products*, and *experiences* that communicate aspects of the human condition in a variety of means, many of which are nonverbal. *Processes* are the creative thoughts, materials, and techniques artists combine to create *products*—the artworks. *Experiences* are the human interactions and responses that occur when people encounter the vision of the artist in the artwork. These are a few characteristics that identify the arts—as opposed to science, technology, and social science—as vantage points we use to understand reality.

But what is art? Attempts to answer this question have been made by scholars, philosophers, and aestheticians for centuries without yielding many adequate answers. The late Pop artist Andy Warhol reportedly said that "Art is anything you can get away with." (Fig. **0.3**) Perhaps we should be a little less cynical—and a little more specific. Instead of asking "What is art?", let us ask "What is a work of art?" A work of art is one person's vision of human reality, which is expressed in a particular medium, and shared with others. Now we can explore the terms of this definition.

0.3 Andy Warhol, *Green Coca-Cola Bottles*, 1962. Oil on canvas, 6 ft 10 ins x 4 ft 9 ins (1.97 x 1.37 m). Whitney Museum of American Art, New York.

Nonrestrictiveness

First, the definition is sufficiently nonrestrictive: an artwork is anything that attempts to communicate a vision of human reality through a means traditionally associated with the arts—drawing, painting, printmaking, sculpture, as well as works of music, dance, literature, film, architecture, and theatre. If the originator *intends* it as a work of art, it is one. Whether it is good or bad, sophisticated or naïve, profound or inconsequential matters little. A child's drawing that expresses some feeling about mother, father, and home, is as much an artwork as Michelangelo's Sistine Chapel frescoes. The music of the Grateful Dead and that by Mozart both qualify as artworks under our definition, even though the *qualities* we might ascribe to these artworks probably would be different. (We will discuss *value judgments* later in this chapter.)

Human Enterprise

The second implication of this definition is that art is a human enterprise: whenever you experience a work of art you are coming into contact with another human being. We experience human contact in works of art because artworks are intended to engage us and to animate a desire to respond. In the theatre, for example, we are exposed to a variety of visual and aural stimuli that attempt to make us feel, think, or react in harmony with the goals of the artist.

Our definition of a work of art, however, is not entirely nonrestrictive. The fact that art is a human enterprise places a certain restriction on it, for example, it eliminates objects in nature that may produce profoundly *aesthetic*—relating to the artistic or beautiful—experiences. Sunsets, oceans, mountains, clouds, rocks may all move us deeply. They are not, however, produced by a human being intent on sharing a vision of human reality—unless one wishes to apply such intentions to some power that created the world, which is why theology and philosophy have historical connections to art.

Medium of Expression

Among the problems some people have with an artwork is that of its medium. While we can readily accept the traditional media—painting, traditional sculpture, music using traditional instruments, theatre using a script and performed in an auditorium, and so on, sometimes, when a medium of expression does not conform to our expectations or experiences, we may reject the artwork. For example, Figures **0.4** A and B show two gigantic environmental installations of blue and yellow umbrellas in Japan and the United States respectively, created (and financed) by the artist Christo. For Christo, this work—which existed for only a short time—was an artwork. For other people, it most definitely was not. Even though the medium was unconventional, and the work transitory, our working definition would allow it because the *intent* of the work was clearly artistic.

Communication

Artworks involve communication and sharing. The common factor in all artwork is the humanizing experience, which needs another human being with whom the artist can share a perception of human reality. When artworks and humans interact, there is a wide spectrum of possibilities. Interaction may be casual and fleeting, as in the first meeting of two people, when one or both are not at all

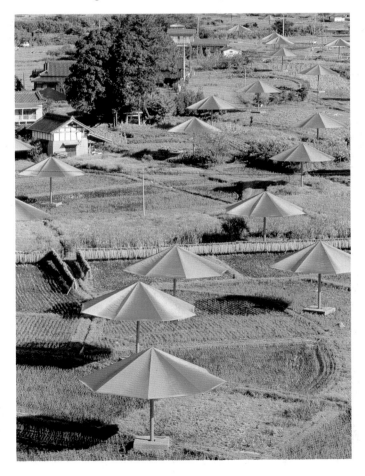

0.4A and B Christo, *The Umbrellas, Japan–USA, 1984–91*. (A) Valley north of Los Angeles, CA, 1,760 yellow umbrellas; (B) Valley in prefecture of Ibaraki, Japan, 1,340 blue umbrellas. Combined length: 30 miles (48 km). © Christo 1991.

interested in interaction. Similarly, the artist may not have much to say, or may not say it very well. For example, a play that shows little skill in its writing or production does little to engage the audience. In a similar fashion, the respondent may be ignorant, self-absorbed, preconditioned, or distracted. Take, for examples, an audience member whose preconceptions are rigid and not met by the production, or one who is so preoccupied by what may have occurred outside the theatre that he or she finds it impossible to perceive what the production offers—in such circumstances, the artistic experience fizzles. At the opposite end of the spectrum, all conditions may be optimum, and a profoundly exciting and meaningful experience may occur: The play may treat a significant subject in a unique manner, the acting, directing, and design may be excellent, and the audience may be receptive. Or, the interaction may fall somewhere between these two extremes. In any case, it is a human experience, and one that is fundamental to art.

In discussing art as communication, we need to note one important term, and that is *symbol*. Symbols are things that *represent* something else. They often use a material object to suggest something less tangible or less obvious. Symbols differ from *signs*, which suggest a fact or condition. Signs are what they denote. Symbols carry deeper, wider, and richer meanings. Look at Figure **0.5**.

0.5 Greek cross (?)

What do you see? You might identify this figure as a sign, which looks like a plus sign in arithmetic—it is what it seems to be. On the other hand, it might be a Greek cross, in which case it becomes a symbol because it suggests a wide variety of images, meanings, and implications. Artworks use a variety of symbols to convey meaning. By using symbols, artworks can relay a wealth of meaning that goes well beyond the surface of the work, offering glimpses of human reality that cannot be sufficiently described in any other manner. Symbols make artworks into doorways, through which we pass in order to experience, in limited time and space, more of the human condition.

THE FUNCTIONS OF ART

Art can function in many ways: As entertainment, political and social weapons, therapy, and artifact. One function is no more important than the others. Nor are they mutually exclusive; a single artwork can pursue any or all of them. Nor are these the only functions of art. Rather, they serve as indicators of how art has functioned in the past, and can function in the present. Like the types and styles of art we will examine later in the book, these four functions are options for the artist and depend on what the artist wishes to do with an artwork.

ENTERTAINMENT

Plays, paintings, concerts, and so on can provide escape from everyday cares, treat us to a pleasant time, and engage us in social occasions. Works of art that entertain us may also perform other functions as well. We can gain insights into the human experience through the visions of artists who primarily entertain us. We can also glimpse the conditions of other cultures, and we can find healing therapy in entertainment.

The primacy of any one function depends on the individual respondent. An artwork in which one individual finds only entertainment may function as a profound social and personal comment to another. A Mozart symphony, for example, can be relaxing and allow us to escape our cares—it may also comment on the life of the composer and/or the conditions of eighteenth-century Austria. Grant Wood's *American Gothic* (Fig. **0.6**) can amuse us, and/or provide a detailed commentary about nineteenth-century America, and/or move us deeply. The result depends upon the artist, the artwork, and the respondent.

POLITICAL AND SOCIAL COMMENTARY

When art is used to bring about political change, or to modify the behavior of large groups of people, it has political or social functions. In Ancient Rome, for example, the authorities used music and theatre to keep masses of unemployed people occupied, in order to quell urban unrest. At the same time, Roman playwrights attacked in their plays incompetent or corrupt officials. The playwright Aristophanes used comedy in such plays as *The Birds* to attack the political ideas of the leaders of Athenian society. In *Lysistrata*, he attacks war by creating a story in which all the women of Athens go on a sex strike until Athens is rid of war and those who would engage in it.

In late nineteenth-century Norway, Henrik Ibsen used *An Enemy of the People* as a platform for airing the issue of whether a government should ignore pollution. In the United States in the 1990s, many artworks act as vehicles to advance social and political causes, or to sensitize the viewer, listener, or reader to particular cultural situations.

THERAPY

In its therapeutic function, art can be and is used as therapy for individuals with a variety of illnesses, both physical and mental. Role-playing, for example, is used frequently as a counseling tool in treating dysfunctional family situations. In this context, often called psychodrama, mentally ill patients act out their personal circumstances in order to find and cure the cause of their illness. The focus of this use of art as therapy is the individual. However, art in a much broader context acts as a healing agent for society's general illnesses as well. Art-

works can illustrate the failings and excesses of society in hopes of saving us from disaster. The laughter caused by comedy releases endorphins, chemicals produced by the brain, which strengthen the immune system.

ART AS ARTIFACT

Art also functions as an *artifact*: A product of a particular time and place, an artwork represents the ideas and technology of that specific time and place. As we look back over history, we find in art striking, and in some cases, the only, tangible records of some peoples. The insights we gain into cultures, including our own, are enhanced tremendously by such artifacts as paintings, sculptures, poems, plays, and buildings. Artifacts connect us to our past, and to human relations sometimes as old as humanity itself.

In this text, the function of art as artifact—as an example of a particular culture—takes on a central role. In Part Two we will examine how artists reflect reality in their artworks. That reflection has much to do with the cultural perspective in which artists find themselves: We will go around the world to see and hear how reality in a variety of cultures found its way into works of art.

A common wisdom asserts that we cannot comprehensively understand or experience works of art from other cultures—we cannot grasp the nuances and subtleties of another culture's artistic expressions unless we have been nurtured in that culture. That wisdom is fundamentally true, but it does not and should not discourage us from attempting to develop as sensitive and sophisticated an awareness as our own cultural perspectives allow. Often art has a different function in some cultures. For example, African and Native American art has more to do with living in harmony with or controlling (super)natural forces than aesthetic appreciation. Part of understanding the art of various cultures is striving to understand other cultures' own view of art.

This book seeks to develop a positive response to this concern: there are things that we can do to come as close to these works as possible, with a resulting satisfying and culturally enriching experience. Sensitive and sophisticated awareness is the desired result.

Although those who have not grown up in Western, Asian, African, Islamic or Native American traditions will not have the intuitive understandings of those who have, studying art from various times and cultures acts as an introduction to further study and enhanced understanding. In turn, this can lead to a richly satisfying, lifelong experience. In one sense, you can say art is a complex social engagement that acts as a bridge to span impassabilities and to make connections. Thus, enhanced understanding of art from various cultures can connect us to other humans and to ourselves.

When we examine art in the context of cultural artifact, one of the issues we face is the use of artworks in religious ritual. We could consider ritual as a separate function of art. However, we may not think of religious ritual as "art,"

0.7 Scale drawing of an eighteenth-century highboy.

but in the broad context that we have adopted for this text, ritual often meets our definition of human communication using an artistic medium. Music, for example, when part of a religious ceremony, meets the definition, and theatre—if seen as an occasion planned and intended for presentation—would include religious rituals as well as events that take place in theatres. Often, as a survey of arts history would confirm, it is difficult to discern when ritual stops and secular production starts—for example, Ancient Greek tragedy seems clearly to have evolved from ritual. When ritual, planned and intended for presentation, uses traditionally artistic media like music, dance, and theatre, we can legitimately study it as "art," and see it also as an artifact of its particular culture.

In whatever way or ways art functions, it has the potential to affect and effect human response. Sometimes the response is superficial; sometimes it is profound—in either case, the function of the artwork depends upon numerous, complex interactions between artist, artwork, and respondent.

THE ARTS AND LIFE

Sometimes the arts are seen as being peripheral to real life—they are just frills. In part, the difficulty many people have in seeing the arts as important in life results from a lack of familiarity. This has perhaps been fostered by people both within the arts and without, who have tried to make the arts elitist, and the art gallery, museum, concert hall, theatre, and opera house privileged institutions open only to the knowledgeable and sophisticated. Nothing could be further from the truth. We live with the arts—the principles of artistic activity are everywhere in our lives. The use of artistic principles and elements of composition, whether visual or aural, govern the products we buy, the advertising we see and hear, and the attitudes we take or that others would have us take. Use of line, form, color, and sound attract us, calm us, manipulate us to do what others would have us do. Equally important, the artistic experience is a way of knowing and communicating. It forms a significant part of being human.

The arts and things related to them play an important role in making the world around us a more interesting and habitable place. When domestic objects are developed, practical matters like purpose and convention are taken into consideration. For example, electrical plugs fit every wall socket in the United States. The arts also have conventions: Western musical scales consist of precisely measured pitches that differ from each other by an established number of vibrations per second.

Often, artistic principles and practical conventions combine in everyday objects. Figure **0.7** shows a scale drawing of an eighteenth-century highboy. The chest was conceived for a practical purpose—the storage of household objects in an easily accessible, yet hidden, place. While designing an object to accommodate that practical need, the cabinetmakers also wished to provide an interesting and attractive—artistic—object. The result is a piece of furniture that is not only practical, but also challenges our perceptual acuity, and excites our imagination. The design is controlled by a convention that dictates a consistent height for tables and desks. Thus, the lower portion of the chest, from point A to B, uses space within a height that harmonizes with other furniture in the room. We can also see that the parts of the chest have been designed with a sophisticated and interesting series of proportional and progressive relationships: The distance from A to B is twice the distance from A to D, and is equal to the distance from B to C; the distances from A to F and

C to E are equal to each other, and to the distances from G to H, H to I, and I to J. In addition, the size of the drawers in the upper chest decreases at an even and proportional rate from bottom to top.

The design of the Volkswagen "Beetle" is also an example of artistic principles appearing in everyday life (Fig. **0.8**). Here, repetition of form—the oval—reflects a concern for unity, a fundamental characteristic of art. In the early VW, the front and rear show a variation on this theme in the windows, headlights, hood, and bumpers. Later models reflect the intrusion of conventions that broke down the strong unity of the original composition. As safety standards called for larger bumpers, the oval design of the hood was flattened to accommodate a larger bumper. The rear window was enlarged and squared for increased rear vision.

The previous discussion illustrates how artistic principles can affect practical as well as artistic objects. The more we realize what there is to see and hear, the greater is our potential for enhanced and exciting responses to the world around us.

0.8 Volkswagen Beetle, 1938. Courtesy of Volkswagen of America.

0.9 Hercules and Telephos (Roman copy of a Greek work), 2nd century B.C. Wall paintings from Herculaneum, 5 ft 7 ins (1.71 m) high. Museo Archeologico Nationale, Naples.

AESTHETIC PERCEPTION AND RESPONSE

The nature of the arts, artists, and their relationship to human reality involve complex issues. How we approach them, and how we study them, is nearly as difficult. A method of study must be used that can act as a point of departure from the familiar into the unknown. Inasmuch as we live in a world of facts and figures, it is logical to begin by looking at some of the characteristics that lend themselves to the kind of study with which we are familiar. This will be from a *cognitive* point of view: What devices and media do artists use as they seek to reveal reality?

It will be helpful in our examination to use a method that allows for consistency of observation as we pass from one art discipline to another. We will be asking three questions regularly in Part One—What is it? How is it put together? How does it stimulate the senses?—and study them in the general context of each of the art disciplines. These are also the basic questions we can ask of an individual work of art.

WHAT IS IT?

In response to the question *What is it?*, we use our perception of the two-dimensional space in a picture (Fig. **0.9**), the three-dimensional space in a sculpture or piece of architecture, or perhaps the design of time in sound, or of time and space in dance. We also recognize *form*—for example, a still life, a human figure, a tragedy, a ballet, a concerto, a narrative film, or a park.

HOW IS IT PUT TOGETHER?

When we respond to this question, we respond to the technical elements of the design, for example, that a picture has been painted in oils or made by a printmaking technique. We also recognize and respond to the elements and principles of composition—line, form or shape, mass, color, repetition, harmony—and the unity that results from these. What devices has the artist used, and how does each part relate to the others to make a whole? A concerto is composed of melody, harmony, timbre, tone, and more; a tragedy utilizes language, exposition, and complication; a ballet has formalized movement, line, idea, content, and so on.

HOW DOES IT STIMULATE?

Next, we examine how the work stimulates the senses—and why. In other words, how do the formal and technical arrangements of the artwork elicit a response from us? Here we must incorporate both physical and mental characteristics, and those that involve thought and intuition. Our response to sculpture, for example, can be physical: We can touch a piece of sculpture and sense its smoothness or hardness (Fig. **0.10**). Mentally, we experience responses that stem from the universal language—for example, we respond to upright triangles as having a quality of solidity. We perceive the colors green and blue as being cool; reds and yellows as warm. Pictures that are predominantly horizontal, or composed of broad curves are said to be soft or placid. Angular, diagonal, or short, broken lines are said to stimulate a sense of movement. Music that utilizes undulating melodic contours can be smooth; that which is highly consonant can be warm or rich. These and other sense responses tend to be universal: most individuals respond in a similar fashion to them.

We also can ask a fourth question: *What does the work mean?* We know, for example, that a painting is a seascape, done in oil with a particular palette. We discern how the artist has used technical elements like line and form, and how that affects our sense response—for example, predominantly harsh, broken lines inciting a feeling of movement and spontaneity. For us personally, however, the painting may elicit pleasant sensations

0.10 Dionysus (Herakles?) from the east pediment of the Parthenon, c. 438–432 B.C. Marble, over life-size. The British Museum, London.

caused by our own subjective experience or memory: perhaps a romantic encounter on a beach.

However, we cannot dismiss the question as a reference to purely personal experience. Meaning implies a certain level of communication from artist to respondent, as we will examine in Part Two. Because a work of art is a way of looking at the universe, and revealing human reality, the experience of an artwork goes beyond the personal. It is not sufficient to regard the disproportionate forms of a Mannerist painting as strange. Meaning implies understanding the circumstances that perhaps caused the strangeness. When we understand that, we may then understand why the paintings of that style appear as they do. As a result, the strangeness of the artwork may come to mean something entirely different. Meaning in an artwork can be enhanced by understanding cultural, historical, or biographical contexts.

0.11 Samuel Beckett, *Waiting for Godot*, Utah Shakespearean Festival, 1990. Director: Tom Marlens.

WHAT IS ART CRITICISM?

One of the questions we all seem to ask about an artwork is, "Is it any good?" Whether rock music, a film, a play, a painting, or a classical symphony, judgments about the quality of a work often vary from one extreme to the other, ranging from "I liked it" and "interesting," to specific reasons why the artwork is thought to be effective or ineffective.

Because the word "criticism" implies many things to many people, we must first agree what it means—or what it does not. Criticism is *not* saying negative things about a work of art. All too often we think of critics as people who write or say essentially negative things, giving their opinions on the value of a play, a concert, or an exhibition. Personal judgment may result from criticism, but criticism is not just passing judgment.

Criticism is a detailed process of analysis that is undertaken to gain understanding and appreciation. Identifying the elements of an artwork—learning what to look for or listen to—is the first step. We describe an artwork by

0.12 Jean-Baptiste Molière, *Tartuffe*. University of Arizona Theatre, 1990. Director: Charles O'Connor.

examining its many facets, and then try to understand how they work together to create meaning or experience. We then try to state what that meaning or experience is. Only when the process is complete does the critic offer judgment.

The critic, however, also brings a set of standards developed essentially from personal experience. The application of such standards is what makes value judgment a tricky task: Your *knowledge* of an art form can be shallow, your *perceptual skills* may be faulty, the range of your *experiences* may be limited. The application of standards may be especially difficult if one tries to judge an artwork as "good" or "bad" based on pre-established criteria: if someone believes that a plot is the most important element in a film or a play, then any film or play that does not depend heavily on a plot may be judged as being faulty, despite other qualities it presents. Such pre-established criteria account for much of the difficulty that new or experimental approaches in the arts often have in receiving critical acclaim.

History is full of examples of new attempts that received terrible receptions from so-called experts, whose ideas of what an artwork ought to be could not allow for experimentation or departures from accepted practice. In 1912, when Vaslav Nijinsky choreographed the ballet *Rite of Spring* to music by Igor Stravinsky, the departures from conventional music and dancing practice actually caused a riot: Audiences and critics could not tolerate the fact that the ballet did not conform to accepted musical and ballet standards. Today, both the music and the choreography are considered masterpieces. Similarly, Samuel Beckett's *Waiting for Godot* (1953) (Fig. **0.11**) does not have a plot, characters, or thoughts that are expressed in the conventional manner of the late nineteenth century. In it two tramps wait beside the road by a withered tree for the arrival of someone named Godot. They tell stories to each other, argue, eat some food, and are interrupted by a character named Pozzo leading a slave, Lucky, by a rope. After a brief conversation, Lucky and Pozzo leave. At the end of the first act a boy enters the stage to announce that Godot will not come today. In Act Two, much the same sequence of events occurs. Now Pozzo is blind and led by Lucky. The tree has sprouted a few leaves. The play ends as the young boy returns to indicate that Godot will not arrive that day either. If your standards indicate that a successful play must have a carefully fashioned plot, wrapped around fully developed characters, and a clear message, then *Waiting for Godot* cannot possibly be a good play. Some people agree with such an assertion, others disagree vehemently. What, then, are we to conclude? What if my criteria do not match yours? What if two experts disagree on the quality of a movie? Does that make any difference either to the movie or to our experience of it?

The easiest answer to such questions is that value judgments are intensely personal—but such an answer is not a satisfying one. Some opinions are more informed than others and represent more authoritative judgment. However, sometimes even knowledgeable people disagree. The best we can conclude is that value judgments simply may not be important or essential. Disagreements about quality, however, can enhance the experience of a work of art when they lead to thought about why the differences exist, resulting in a deeper understanding of the artwork. None the less, criticism can be exercised without involving any judgment. We can thoroughly dissect any work of art, describe what it comprises—describe and analyze, for example, plot, character, language, aural and visual elements, and thought—and how all of these factors affect an audience and its response. We can spend a significant amount of time doing this, and never pass a value judgment at all.

Does this mean that all artworks are equal in value? Not at all. It means that in order to understand what criticism involves, we must separate descriptive analysis, which can be satisfying in and of itself, from the act of passing value judgments. Analysis necessarily leads to enhanced understanding. We may not *like* the work we have analyzed, but we have understood something that we did not understand before. Passing judgment may play no role whatsoever in our understanding of an artwork.

As an exercise in understanding, criticism is necessary. We must investigate and describe. We must experience the need to know enough about the process, product, and experience of art if we are to have perceptions to share. One important value of criticism is the sharing process itself: our mutual agreement is less important than the enhanced perception that results from going through the process of understanding and sharing it with someone else.

Criticism without some form of summary judgment can leave people feeling the process is incomplete. Summary judgment, however, has many occasions and takes many forms. For example, a university art teacher must decide whether a performance, a painting, or a composition by a student has quality, and what kind of quality. Or, perhaps, someone wants to purchase a piece of art, as an investment or simply from appreciation. Is its quality in keeping with its price? Finally, people who write reviews may do so because their employers and the public expect judgment calls from them.

Certain judgments require higher levels of expertise than others, and the results of some judgments have wider-reaching effects than others. Media reviewers may or may not have significant impact. On the one hand, the combined weight of several negative reviews may spell doom for a production, with millions of dollars of investment lost. On the other, numerous plays and musicals have had long runs in spite of uniformly poor reviews. In the decision to buy a work of art or a ticket to a play, one's knowledge or wallet may or may not be important—one can simply fall in love with a piece of art and decide that living with it on a daily basis is worth the price. The effect of quality judgments can be minimal when compared with personal satisfaction. When applied to a student work, however, a teacher's inexpert judgment could lead to an unfair grade, or even affect graduation. The fact is that judgment is usually fairly personal and limited in impact. It is also probably not very important to predict the impact of a work of art on future generations: we will not be around to see the results. This is not to trivialize the impulse to make judgments, but rather to suggest that in wanting to understand a particular art form, we should put greater emphasis on the descriptive and interpretive aspects of criticism. Of course, we need to know the difference between trash and treasure. The idea that we are what we eat can be expanded into the idea that we are what we read and value. We need to know what is trash and what is treasure in order to choose where to invest our energy and resources, in order to avoid manipulation, and sometimes merely for the joy of knowing that we know. This is not a suggestion that some approaches to art are better than others, as such judgments are often like comparing apples and oranges—praising or condemning one because it is not the other. Rather, we should put our efforts into knowing what constitutes an apple or an orange so that we can discuss the relative merits of each. The more art we see and hear, and the more we practice criticism, the more confidence we will have in making judgments, and in finding artworks and art forms that have impact on our experience and that of others. Although we all develop preferences, they should not be confused with prejudices: one's ability to savor delicacies need not preclude one's love of hot dogs. The inability to distinguish one from the other, however, could have a number of unfortunate consequences. We need, therefore, some way of enhancing our understanding of those things in which we will invest our time and, perhaps, our money.

Now that we have examined briefly what criticism is and why we might do it, what criteria or approaches can we use?

TYPES OF CRITICISM

In general, there are two types of criticism. If we examine a single artwork at hand, it is called *formal criticism*. If we examine the same work in the context of the events surrounding it, and perhaps the circumstances of its creation, it is called *contextual criticism*.

Formal Criticism

Here, we are interested primarily in the artwork itself. We can allow the work to stand by itself, applying no external conditions or information. We analyze the artwork just as we find it: if it is a painting, we look only within the frame; if it is a play, we analyze only what we see and hear. Formal criticism approaches the artwork as an entity within itself. As an example, we will do a brief analysis of Molière's comedy *Tartuffe* (1664) (Fig. **0.12**, p. 23):

Orgon, a rich bourgeois, has allowed a religious conman, Tartuffe, to gain complete hold over him. Tartuffe has moved into Orgon's house, and tries to seduce Orgon's wife at the same time that he is planning to marry his daughter. Tartuffe is unmasked, and Orgon orders him out. Tartuffe seeks his revenge by claiming title to Orgon's house, and blackmailing him with some secret papers. At the very last instant, Tartuffe's plans are foiled by the intervention of the king, and the play ends happily.

We have just described a story. Were we to go one step further and analyze the plot, we would look, among other things, for points at which *crises* occur and cause important decisions to be made by the characters; we would also want to know how those decisions moved the play from one point to the next. In addition, we would try to locate the extreme crisis—the *climax*. Meanwhile, we would discover auxiliary parts of plot such as *reversals*, for example,

when Tartuffe is discovered and the characters become aware of the true situation. Depending on how detailed our criticism were to become, we could work our way through each and every aspect of the plot. We might then devote some time to describing and analyzing the driving force—the *character*—of each person in the play and how they relate to each other. Has Molière created fully developed characters? Are they types, or do they seem to behave more or less like real individuals? In examining *thought*, we would no doubt conclude that the play deals with religious hypocrisy, and that Molière had a particular point of view on that subject.

In this approach, information about the playwright, previous performances, historic relationships, and so on is irrelevant. It is thus useful for analyzing how an artwork works, and trying to decide why it produces the responses that it does. We can apply this form of criticism to any work of art and come away with a variety of conclusions. Of course, the critical process is enhanced by knowledge about how artworks are put together, what they are, and how they stimulate the senses. If we did not know that we could look for plot, character, language, thought, sound, and spectacle, we might not know where to begin.

Contextual Criticism

The other general approach to criticism seeks meaning by adding to formal criticism an examination of related information "outside" the artwork, such as the artist's life, his or her culture, social, and political conditions and philosophies, public and critical reactions to the work, and so on. These can all be researched and applied to the work in order to enhance perception and understanding. This approach tends to view the artwork as an artifact generated from particular contextual needs, conditions, and/or attitudes rather than from artistic necessity. If we carry our criticism of *Tartuffe* in this direction, we would note that certain historical events help to clarify the play. For example, the object of Molière's attention probably was the Company of the Holy Sacrament, a secret, conspiratorial, and influential society in France at the time. Like many fanatical religious sects—including those of our time—the society sought to enforce its own view of morality by spying on the lives of others and seeking out heresies—in this case, in the Roman Catholic Church. Its followers were religious fanatics and they had considerable impact on the lives of the citizenry at large. If we were to follow this path of criticism, any and all such contextual matters that might illuminate or clarify what happens in the play would be pursued.

MAKING JUDGMENTS

Now that we have defined criticism and noted two approaches we might take in pursuit of understanding and enjoying a work of art, we can move on to the final step—making value judgments.

There are several approaches to the act of judgment. Two characteristics, however, apply to all artworks: they are *crafted*, and they *communicate* something to us about our experiences as humans. Making a judgment about the quality of an artwork should address each of these.

Craftsmanship

Is the work well made? To make this judgment, we first need some understanding of the medium in which the artist works. For example, if the artist proposes to give us a realistic vision of a tree, does the artist's handling of the paint yield a tree that looks like a tree? If craftsmanship depended only on the ability to portray objects realistically, judgment would be quite simple. However, we must remember that judgments about the craftsmanship of the artwork require some knowledge about the techniques of its medium. Although we may not yet be ready to make judgments about all of the aspects of craftsmanship in any art form, we can apply what we do know. We can, for example, use clarity and interest as touchstones. Is the work clear or confusing? Has the artwork held our inter-

est? If the answer is no, we may wish to examine whether the fault lies in the artwork or in ourselves. Beyond that, we are left to learn the lessons that the rest of this book seeks to teach. Each chapter will give us more pieces by which we can evaluate the craftsmanship of a work of art.

Communication

Evaluating what an artwork is trying to say offers more immediate opportunity for judgment, and less need for expertise. Johann Wolfgang von Goethe, the nineteenth-century poet, novelist, and playwright, set out a basic, commonsense approach to communication. Because it provides an organized means for discovering an artwork's communication by progressing from analytical to judgmental functions, it is a helpful way in which to end our discussion on criticism and this introductory chapter: What is the artist trying to say? Does he or she succeed? Was the artwork worth the effort? These principles focus on the artist's communication by making us identify first what was being attempted, and then on the artist's success in that attempt. Whether or not the project was worth the effort raises other issues, such as uniqueness or profundity. This question asks us to decide if the communication was important. Was it worthwhile? We can see immediately that these principles may require some contextual information. Or the artist's purpose may be clear in the artwork itself. For some people, that basic clarity itself functions as a fundamental criterion for quality.

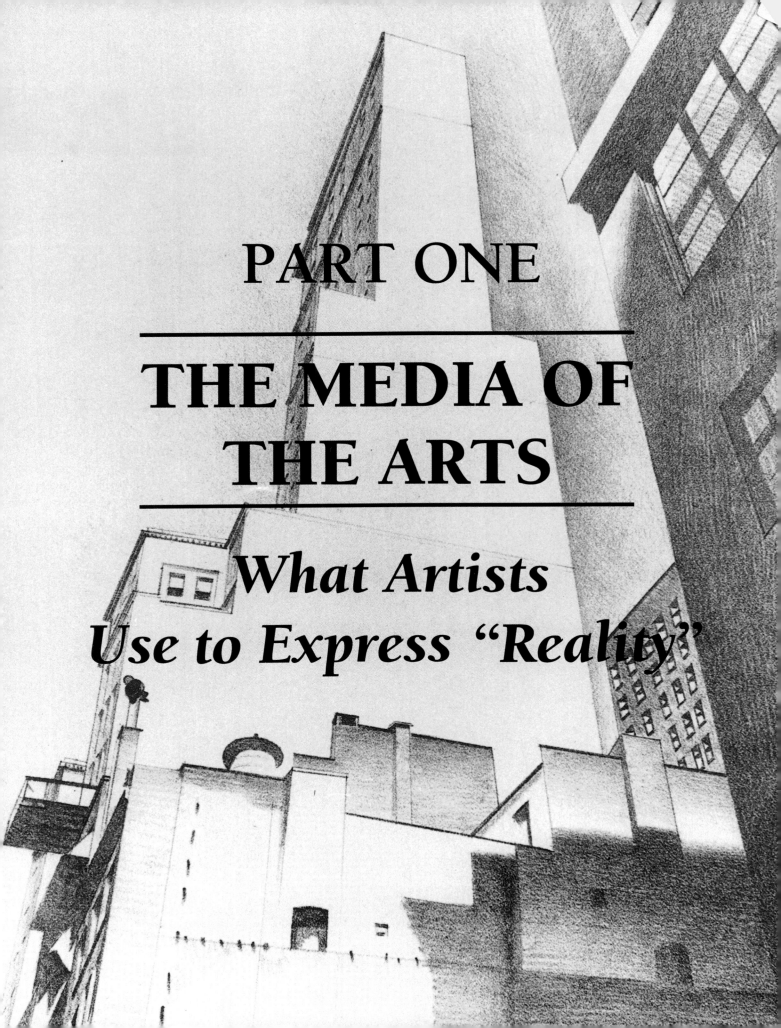

PART ONE

THE MEDIA OF THE ARTS

What Artists Use to Express "Reality"

ONE

PAINTING, PRINTMAKING, & PHOTOGRAPHY

WHAT ARE THEY?

Paintings, photographs, and prints differ primarily in the technique of their execution. They constitute aesthetic communication through the design of two-dimensional space. Our initial level of response to all three is to subject matter. A picture might be a landscape, seascape, portrait, or still life; or a religious picture, nonobjective (non-representational), or abstract—or something else. So this level of response is a rather simple and straightforward matter of observation, although subject matter can be a significant factor in the meaning of a work.

HOW ARE THEY PUT TOGETHER?

MEDIA

First of all, our technical level of response is more complex. Our response to how a work is put together is to the medium by which the work was executed.

Paintings and Drawings

Paintings and drawings can be executed with oils, water-colors, tempera, acrylics, fresco, gouache, ink, pastels, and pencils, to name just a few of the more obvious. An artist may combine these media, and may use some others as well. Each medium has its own characteristics, and to a great extent these dictate what the artist can or cannot achieve.

Oils are perhaps the most popular of the painting media, and have been since their development around the beginning of the fifteenth cenury. Their popularity stems principally from the fact that they offer a tremendous range of color possibilities; they can be reworked; they present many options for textural manipulation; and, above all, perhaps, they are durable. If we compare two oils, van Gogh's *The Starry Night* (Fig. **1.1**) and Giovanni Vanni's *Holy Family with St. John* (Fig. **1.2**), the importance of the medium can be seen. Vanni creates light and shade in the Baroque tradition, and his *chiaroscuro* depends upon the capacity of the medium to blend smoothly among color areas. Van Gogh, on the other hand, requires a medium that will form obvious brushstrokes. Vanni demands the paint to be flesh and cloth.

Van Gogh demands the paint to be paint, and to call attention to itself.

Watercolor is a broad category that includes any color medium that uses water as a diluent. The term has traditionally referred to a transparent paint usually applied to paper. Since watercolors are transparent, an artist must be very careful to control them. In overlapping one area of color with another, the overlap will show as a third area combining the previous hues. It is their transparency that gives watercolors a delicacy that cannot be produced in any other medium.

Tempera is an opaque, watercolor medium. It was employed by the Ancient Egyptians, and is still used today by such painters as Andrew Wyeth. Tempera refers to ground pigments and their color binders, such as gum or glue, but is best known in its egg tempera form. It is a fast-drying medium that virtually eliminates brushstroke, and gives extremely sharp detail. Colors in tempera paintings appear gemlike in their clarity and brilliance.

1.1 (*above*) Vincent van Gogh, *The Starry Night*, 1889. Oil on canvas, 29 x 36¼ ins (74 x 92 cm). Collection, The Museum of Modern Art, New York (acquired through the Lillie P. Bliss Bequest).

1.2 (*right*) Giovanni Battista Vanni, *Holy Family with St. John.* Oil on canvas, 70 x 58 ins (178 x 147 cm). Palmer Museum of Art, Pennsylvania State University.

Acrylics, in contrast with tempera, are modern, synthetic products. Most acrylics are water-soluble, and the binding agent for the pigment is an acrylic polymer. Acrylics are flexible media, offering the artist a wide range of possibilities both in color and technique. An acrylic paint can be either opaque or transparent, depending upon dilution. It is fast-drying, thin, and resistant to cracking under temperature and humidity extremes. It is perhaps less permanent than some other media but adheres to a wider variety of surfaces. It will not darken or yellow with age, as does oil, and dries more rapidly, too.

Fresco is a wall-painting technique in which pigments suspended in water are applied to fresh, wet plaster. Michelangelo's Sistine Chapel frescoes are the best-known examples of this technique. Since the end result becomes part of the plaster wall rather than being painted on it, fresco is long-lasting. However, it is an extremely difficult process, and once the pigments are applied, no changes can be made without replastering the entire section of the wall.

Gouache is watercolor medium in which gum is added to ground opaque colors mixed with water. Transparent watercolors can be made into gouache by adding Chinese white, which is a special white, opaque, water-soluble paint. The final product, in contrast to watercolor, is opaque.

Ink as a painting medium has many of the same characteristics as transparent watercolor. It is difficult to control, yet its effects are nearly impossible to achieve in any other medium. Because it must be worked quickly and freely, it has a spontaneous and appealing quality (Fig. **1.3**).

Drawing media such as pen and ink, pastels (crayon or chalk), and pencils all create an effect through build-up of line. Each has its own characteristics, but all are relatively inflexible in their handling of color and color areas (Fig. **1.4**).

Printmaking

Printmaking falls generally into three main categories, based essentially on the nature of the printing surface. First is *relief printing*, such as *woodcut*, *wood engraving*, *linoleum cut*, and *collograph*. Second is *intaglio*, which

1.3 Chu Ta (Pata-shan-jen), *Lotus*, 1705. Brush and ink, 6½ x 28 ins (17 x 71 cm). Palmer Museum of Art, Pennsylvania State University.

1.4 Hobson Pittman, *Violets No. 1*, 1971. Pastel, 9½ x 10¼ ins (24 x 26 cm). The Museum of Art, Pennsylvania State University.

include etching, aquatint, drypoint, and again, collograph. Third is the planographic process, which includes lithography, *silkscreen* (serigraphy) and other forms of stenciling. Other combinations and somewhat amorphous processes such as monoprinting are also used by printmakers. Because the printmaker's techniques are unfamiliar to most of us, we need to spend some time in further explanation.

To begin with, we need to ask, "What is a print?" A print is a hand-produced picture that has been transferred from a printing surface to a piece of paper. The artist prepares the printing surface and directs the printing process. Each step in the production of a print is accomplished by hand. In some cases a press is used, but it is always operated by hand. The unique value of a print lies in the fact that the block or surface from which the print is made is usually destroyed after the desired number of prints has been made. In contrast, a *reproduction* is not an original, but a *copy* of an original painting or other artwork, reproduced usually by a photographic process. As a copy, the reproduction does not bear the handiwork of the artist.

On every print there is a number. On some prints the number may appear as a fraction—for example, "36/100." The denominator indicates how many prints were produced from the plate or block. This number is called the *issue number*, or edition number. The numerator indicates where in the series the individual print was produced. If only a single number appears, such as "500," it simply indicates the total number of prints in the series; this is also called the issue number. The numerator is an item of curiosity only; it has nothing to do with a print's value, monetarily or qualitatively. The issue number does have some value in comparing, for example, an issue of 25 with one of 500, and is usually reflected in the price of a print. However, the edition number is not the sole factor in determining the value of a print. The quality of the print and the reputation of the artist are more important considerations.

In relief printing, the image is transferred to the paper by cutting away nonimage areas and inking the surface that remains. The image protrudes in relief from the block or plate, and produces a picture that is reversed from the image carved by the artist. This reversal is a characteristic of all printmaking media. Woodcuts and wood engravings are two popular techniques. A woodcut, one of the oldest techniques, is cut into the plank of the grain; a wood engraving is cut into the butt of the grain (Fig. **1.5**). Figure **1.6** illustrates the linearity of the woodcut, and shows the precision possible in the hands of a master.

The *collograph* is a new printmaking process in which assorted objects are glued to a board or plate. A collograph represents relief printing when the raised surfaces are inked and printed. When the recessed areas are inked and printed, the collograph becomes an intaglio work.

The intaglio process is the opposite of relief printing. The ink is transferred to the paper not from raised areas, but rather from grooves cut into a metal plate. Line engraving, etching, drypoint, and aquatint are some of the methods of intaglio.

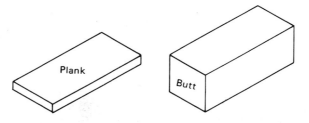

1.5 Wood plank and butt.

1.6 Albrecht Dürer, *Lamentation*, c. 1497–1500. Woodcut, 15½ x 11¼ ins (39 x 29 cm). The Museum of Art, Pennsylvania State University (gift of the Friends of the Museum of Art).

1.7 Daniel Hopfer, *Ceiling Ornament*. Etching, 10 x 8¾ ins (25 x 22 cm). The Museum of Art, Pennsylvania State University.

Line engraving involves cutting grooves into the metal plate with special sharp tools. It requires great muscular control because the pressure must be continuous and constant if the grooves are to produce the desired image. The print resulting from the line-engraving process is very precise. This form of intaglio is the most difficult and demanding.

Etchings are less demanding. Here, the artist removes the surface of the plate by exposing it to an acid bath. First the plate is covered with a thin, waxlike substance called a *ground*. The artist then scratches away the ground to produce the desired lines. The plate is immersed in the acid, which burns away the exposed areas. The longer a plate is left in the acid, the deeper the resulting etches; the deeper the etch, the darker the final image. Artists wishing to produce lines or areas of differing darkness must cover the lines they do not desire to be more deeply cut before further immersions in the acid. The desired number of repetitions of the process yields a plate that will produce a print with the desired differences in light and dark lines. Figure 1.7 consists only of individual lines, either single or in combination. The lighter lines required less time in the acid than the darker ones. Because of the precision and clarity of the lines, it would be difficult to determine whether this print is an etching or an engraving. Drypoint, on the other hand, produces lines with less sharp edges.

Drypoint is a technique in which the surface of the metal plate is scratched with a needle. Unlike line engraving, which gives a clean, sharp line, the drypoint technique leaves a ridge on either side of the groove. The resulting line is somewhat fuzzy.

Once the plate is prepared, whether by line engraving, etching, aquatint, drypoint, or a combination of methods, it is placed in a press and a special dampened paper is laid over it. Padding is placed on the paper, and then a roller is passed over it, forcing the plate and the paper together with great pressure. The ink, which has been carefully applied to the plate and left only in the grooves, is transferred as the paper is forced into the grooves by the roller of the press. Even if no ink had been applied to the plate, the paper would still receive an image. This *embossing* effect is the mark of an intaglio process; the three-dimensional *platemark* is very obvious.

The artist may wish to create large areas of subdued tonality, which cannot be produced effectively with lines. The plate is dusted with a resin substance, heated, which fixes the resin, and put into the acid bath. The result is a plate whose surface is rough in texture, like sandpaper, and a print whose tonal areas reflect that texture. This is called aquatint.

In a *planographic process*, the artist prints from a plane surface—neither relief nor intaglio. *Lithography* (the term's literal meaning is "stone writing") is based on the principle that water and grease do not mix. To create a lithograph, artists begin with a stone, usually limestone, and grind one side until it is absolutely smooth. They then draw an image on the stone with a greasy substance. The darkness of the final image can be varied by the amount of grease used: The more grease, the darker the image. After the image has been drawn, the artist treats the stone with gum arabic and nitric acid, and then rinses it with water. This bath fixes the greasy areas to the surface of the stone. When the artist rinses the stone and fans it dry, the surface is clean! However, the water, gum, and acid have impressed the grease on the stone, and when the stone is wetted it absorbs water (limestone being porous) only in those areas that were not previously greased. Finally, a grease-based ink is applied to the stone. It, in turn, will not adhere to the water-soaked areas. As a result the stone, with ink adhering only to the areas on which the artist has drawn, can be placed in a press and the image transferred to the waiting paper. In Figures **1.8** and **1.9** we see the characteristic most attributable to lithography—a crayon-drawing appearance. Since the lithographer usually draws with a greasy material on the stone, the final print has exactly that quality.

Silkscreening is the most common of the *stenciling* processes. Silkscreens are made from a wooden frame covered with a finely meshed silk fabric. The nonimage areas are blocked out with a glue mixture painted directly on the silk fabric or blocked out by a cut-paper stencil. The stencil is placed in the frame and ink is applied. By means of a rubber instrument called a squeegee, the ink is forced through the openings of the stencil, through the screen, and on to the paper below. This technique allows the printmaker to achieve large, flat, uniform areas, as in

1.8 Thomas Hart Benton, *Cradling Wheat*, 1938. Lithograph, 9½ x 12 ins (24 x 30 cm). Palmer Museum of Art, Pennsylvania State University (gift of Carolyn Wose Hull).

1.9 Charles Sheeler, *Delmonico Building*, 1925. Lithograph, 10 x 7⅛ ins (25 x 18 cm). Palmer Museum of Art, Pennsylvania State University.

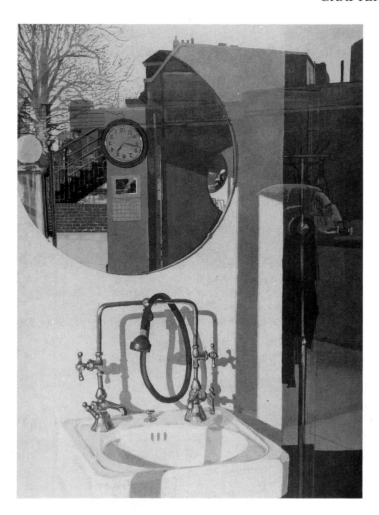

1.10 Nancy McIntyre, *Barbershop Mirror*, 1976. Silkscreen, 26½ x 19 ins (67 x 48 cm). Palmer Museum of Art, Pennsylvania State University.

Figure **1.10**. Here the artist has, through successive applications of ink, built up a complex composition, with highly lifelike detail.

Prints reflect recognizable differences in technique. It is not always possible to discern the technique used in executing a print, and some prints reflect a combination of techniques. However, in seeking the method of execution, we add another layer of potential response to a work.

Photography

In some cases, photography is merely a matter of personal record, executed with equipment of varying degrees of expense and sophistication (Fig. **1.11**). Certainly, photography as a matter of pictorial record, or even as photojournalism, may lack the qualities we believe are requisite to art. A photograph of a baseball player sliding into second base, or of Aunt Mable cooking hamburgers at the family reunion may trigger expressive responses for us, but it is doubtful that the photographers had aesthetic

1.11 The single-lens reflex (SLR) camera.

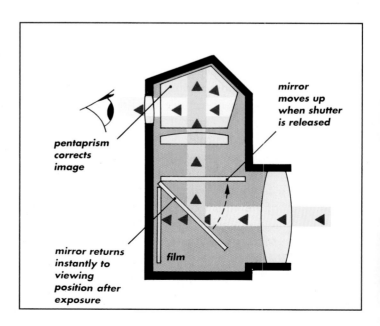

communication or design in mind when they snapped the shutter. On the other hand, a carefully composed and sensitively designed photograph can contain every attribute of human expression possible in any art form.

Ansel Adams believed the photographer to be an interpretative artist; he likened the photographic negative to the musical score, and the print to a performance. Despite all the choices the artist may make in committing an image to film, they are only the beginning of the artistic process. The photographer still has the choice of *size*, *texture* and *value contrast* or *tonality*. A photo of the grain of a piece of wood, for example, has an enormous range of aesthetic possibilities depending upon how the artist employs and combines these three elements.

Consequently, the question "Is it art?" may have a cogent application to photography. However, the quality of our aesthetic repayment from the photographic experience is higher if we view photography in the same way as we do the other arts—as a visualization of reality manifested through a technique and resulting in an aesthetic response or communication.

COMPOSITION

A discussion of how any artwork is put together eventually results in a discussion of how it is composed. What kind of considerations go through artists' minds when they prepare to capture their subjects on canvas, or on film? The goal is organic unity, that state in which line, color, mass, and texture work together to produce a coherent composition. The elements and principles of composition are basic to all the arts, and we shall return to them time and time again as we proceed.

The Elements

The basic building block of a visual design is *line*. To most of us a line is a thin mark: ——————. We find that denotation in art as well. In Figure **1.12** there are amorphous shapes. Some of these are like cartoon figures— they are identifiable from the background because of their outline. Line identifies form, and illustrates the first sentence of this paragraph. However, the other shapes also

1.12 Joan Miró, *Composition*, 1933. Oil on canvas, 51⅜ x 64 ins (130.5 x 165 cm). The Wadsworth Atheneum, Hartford, Connecticut.

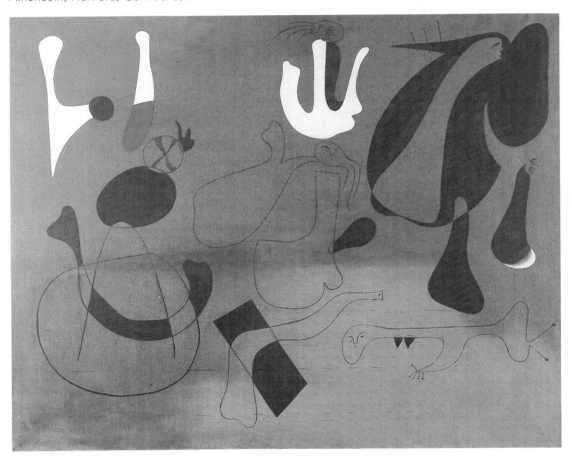

exemplify line. These shapes appear black or white against the background. If we put our finger on the edge of these shapes, we have identified a second aspect of line—the boundary between areas of color, and between shapes or forms. There is one further aspect of line, which is implied rather than physical. The three rectangles in Figure **1.13** create a horizontal "line" that extends across the design. There is no physical line between the tops of the forms, but their spatial arrangement creates one by implication. A similar use of line occurs in Figure **1.1**, where we can see a definite linear movement from the upper left border through a series of swirls to the right border. That "line" is quite clear although it is composed not of a form edge or outline but of a carefully developed relationship of numerous color areas. This treatment of line is also seen in Figure **1.14**, although here it is much more subtle and sophisticated. By dripping paint on to canvas—a task not as easily executed as it might appear—the artist was able to subordinate form, in the sense of recognizable and distinct areas, and thereby focal areas, to form a dynamic

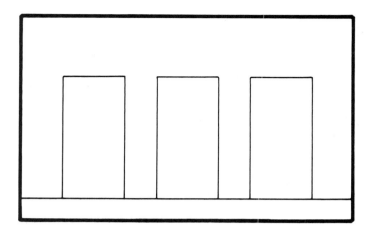

1.13 Outline and implied line.

1.14 Jackson Pollock, *Number 1, 1948*, 1948. Oil and enamel paint on unprimed canvas, 5 ft 8 ins x 8 ft 8 ins (172.7 x 264.2 cm). Collection, The Museum of Modern Art, New York. Purchase.

network of complex lines. The effect of this technique of execution has a very strong relationship to the actual force and speed with which the pigment was applied.

Line is used by an artist to control our vision, to create unity and emotional value, and ultimately to develop meaning. In pursuing those ends, and by employing the three aspects noted earlier, the artist finds that line has one of two characteristics: It is curved or it is straight. Whether it is expressed as an outline, as an area edge, or by implication, and whether it is simple or in combination, a line is some derivative of straightness or curvedness. It is interesting to speculate on whether line can also be thick or thin. Certainly, that quality is helpful in describing some works of art. Those who deny line that quality, however, have a point that is difficult to refute: "If line can be thick or thin, at what point does it cease to be a line and become a form?"

Definitions can be problematic. We are attempting to deal with the perception of artworks by noting what we can look for and what we call it. While this approach is important, all the terms it employs are highly related, and only make it more convenient for us to talk about an artwork. More important than complete agreement on definitions is the ability to apply the concepts they represent to the artwork. How has the artist used line? Does it make his composition active or passive? Are the forms sharp or fuzzy? Is the photograph in focus or not?

Form and *line* are closely related both in definition and in effect. Form is the shape of an object within the composition, and shape often is used as a synonym for form. Form is that space described by line. A building is a form. So is a tree. We perceive them as buildings or trees, and we also perceive their individual details because of the line by which they are composed; form cannot be separated from line in two-dimensional design.

Color is a complex phenomenon, and no less than three theories exist as to its nature. It is not important to understand these theories, but knowing they exist helps us to understand why some sources use different terms to describe the same color characteristics, and other sources use the same terms to describe different characteristics.

Color characteristics differ depending upon whether we are discussing color in light or color in pigment. In light, the *primary hues* (those hues that cannot be achieved by mixing other hues) are red, green, and blue; in pigment they are red, yellow, and blue. If we mix equal proportions of yellow and blue pigments we will have green. Since green can be achieved by mixing, it cannot be a primary in pigment. However, no matter how hard we try, we cannot mix any hues that will achieve green light.

Inasmuch as our response to artworks most often deals with colored pigment, the discussion that follows concerns color in pigment. We will not discuss color in light.

Hue is the spectrum notation of color; a hue is a specific pure color with a measurable wavelength. The visible range of the color spectrum extends from violet on one end to red on the other. The color spectrum consists of the three primaries—blue, yellow, and red—and three additional hues that are direct derivatives of them—green, orange, and violet. These six hues are the basic hues of the spectrum, and each has a specific, measurable wavelength (Fig. **1.15**). In all there are from ten to twenty-four perceivably different hues, including these six, depending upon which theory one follows. These perceptible hues are the composite hues of the color spectrum.

For the sake of clarity and illustration, let us assume there are twelve basic hues. Arranged in a series, they would look like Figure **1.16**. However, since combinations of these hues are possible beyond the straight-line configuration of the spectrum, it is helpful to visualize

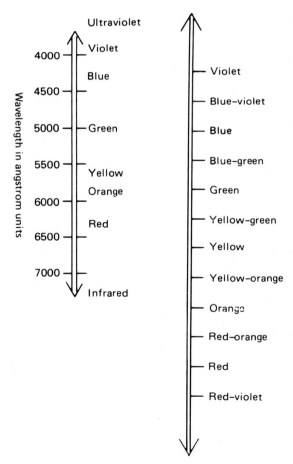

1.15 (*left*) Basic color spectrum.
1.16 (*right*) Color spectrum, including composite hues.

1.17 Color wheel.

color by turning the color spectrum into a *color wheel* (Fig. **1.17**). With this visualization we now can discuss what an artist can do to and with color. First, an artist can take the primary hues of the spectrum, mix them two at a time in varying proportions, and create the other hues of the spectrum. For example, red and yellow in equal proportions make orange, a *secondary* hue. Varying the proportions—adding more red or more yellow—makes yellow-orange or red-orange, which are *tertiary* hues. Yellow and blue make green, and also blue-green and yellow-green; red and blue give us violet, blue-violet, and red-violet. Hues directly opposite each other on the color wheel are *complementary*. When they are mixed together in equal proportions, they produce gray. First, therefore, an artist can vary hue.

In discussing photography, we noted the concept of *value contrast*—the relationship of blacks to whites and grays. The range of possibilities from black to white forms the *value scale*, which has black at one end, white at the other, and medium gray in the middle. The perceivable tones between black and white are designated light or dark (Fig. **1.18**).

It is most helpful if we approach the subject of the effects of value on color less from a theoretical point of view and more from a practical one—that is, what can painters do to color in order to create a painting that gives the effect they desire? As we indicated, they may mix

primaries to create secondary and tertiary hues, thereby changing hue. Every hue has its own value—that is, in its "pure" state each hue falls somewhere on the value scale in Figure **1.19**. An artist may change the value of a hue by raising or lowering it.

How does one change a hue to a different value? Many authorities propose that value is changed by adding white or black. White raises value; black lowers it. However, the mixing of paints to achieve different values is not quite that simple. For example, if we take primary red, whose value is medium dark, and add various amounts of pure white, the changes that occur are perceivably different from the changes that occur when medium gray, medium-light gray, light gray, and high-light gray are added to the same pure red. Identical ranges of color do not result from the two processes. Let us take it from another direction. Suppose we wish to create a gray-pink color for our painting. We take primary red and add white. The result is pink. To subdue the pink, we add just a bit of black. What we have just done is both raise and lower the value of our original red—at the same time. We have merely raised our

1.18 (*left*) Value scale.
1.19 (*right*) Color-value equivalents.

red to a lighter value by adding light-gray (black and white).

There is a broad range of color possibilities between high-light gray and pure white, or between a pure hue and white, which does not fall on the traditional value scale. That range of possibilities is described by the term *saturation*. A saturated hue is a pure hue. An unsaturated hue is a hue to which some quantity of white alone has been added. Unsaturated hues, such as pink, are known as *tints*. What is not entirely clear is whether saturation is part of or separate from value—that is, whether the two terms should be considered as separate properties of color change or whether value includes saturation. More on this in a moment.

We can easily see that some colors are brighter than others. As we noted, the perceivable difference in brightness between primary yellow and primary blue is due to their difference in value. However, it is possible to have a bright yellow and a dull yellow. The difference in brightness between the two may be a matter of value, as we just observed—a pure yellow versus a grayed yellow. It may also be a matter of surface brilliance, or reflectance, a factor of considerable importance to all visual artists. A highly reflective surface creates a brighter color, and therefore a different response from the observer, than does a surface of lesser reflection, although all other color factors may be the same. This is the difference between high-gloss, semigloss, and flat paints, for example. Probably surface reflectance is more a property of texture than of color. However, the term brilliance is often used to describe not only surface gloss, but also characteristics synonymous with value. Some sources also use brilliance as a synonym for saturation, while still others use saturation as a synonym for an additional color-change possibility, *intensity*.

Intensity is the degree of purity of a hue. It also is sometimes called *chroma*. Returning to the color wheel (Fig. 1.17), we note that movement around the wheel creates a change in hue. Movement across the wheel creates a change in intensity. If we add green to red we alter its intensity. When, as in this case, hues are directly opposite each other on the color wheel, such mixing has the practical effect of graying the original hue. Therefore, since graying a hue is a value change, one occasionally finds intensity and value used interchangeably. Some sources use the terms independently but state that changing a color's value automatically changes its intensity. There is a difference between graying a hue by using its complement, and graying a hue by adding black (or gray derived from black and white). A gray derived from com-

plementaries, because it has color, is far livelier than a gray derived from black and white, which are not colors.

One can use descriptive terminology as an aid to understanding what is happening in a work of art. Divergences are not necessarily a matter of being correct or incorrect: often they are simply attempts to describe the indescribable so as to promote a clearer interchange. The difficulties regarding color terminology essentially stem from differences in theory and the application of theory to practice. Attempts to create color wheels, three-dimensional color models, and all-inclusive terminology are often attempts to explain a complex natural phenomenon—color perception.

The overall use of color by the artist is termed *palette*. An artist's palette can be broad, restricted, or somewhere in between, depending upon whether the artist has utilized the full range of the color spectrum and/or whether he or she explores the full range of *tonalities*—brights and dulls, lights and darks.

As to *mass* (space), only three-dimensional objects take up space and have density. However, two-dimensional objects give the illusion of mass, relative only to the other objects in the picture.

Then there is the *texture* of a picture—its apparent roughness or smoothness. Texture ranges from the smoothness of a glossy photo to the three-dimensionality of *impasto*, a painting technique wherein pigment is applied thickly with a palette knife. The texture of a picture may be anywhere within these two extremes. The texture may be illusory, in that the surface of a picture may be absolutely flat but the image gives the impression of three-dimensionality, so the term can be applied to the pictorial arts either literally or figuratively.

Principles

Probably the essence of any design is repetition: how the basic elements in the picture are repeated or alternated. The three terms used are rhythm, harmony, and variation.

Rhythm is the ordered recurrence of elements in a composition. If the relationships among elements are equal, the rhythm is regular (Fig. 1.13). If not, the rhythm is irregular. However, one must examine the composition as a whole to discern patterns of relationships, and whether or not the patterns are regular, as they are in Figure 1.20.

Harmony is the logic of the repetition. Harmonious relationships are those whose components appear to join naturally and comfortably. If the artist employs forms, colors, or other elements that appear incongruous or illogical, then we would use a musical term and say the

1.21 Pablo Picasso, *Girl Before a Mirror*, Boisgeloup, March 1932. Oil on canvas, 64 x 51¼ ins (162.3 x 130.2 cm). Collection, The Museum of Modern Art, New York (gift of Mrs. Simon Guggenheim).

picture is *dissonant.* However, we need to understand that ideas and ideals often reflect cultural conditioning or arbitrary understandings.

Variation is the relationship of repeated items to each other; it is similar to theme and variation in music. How does an artist take a basic element in the composition and use it again with slight or major changes? Picasso, the artist of Figure **1.21**, has used two geometric forms, the diamond and the oval, and created a complex painting via repetition. The diamond with a circle at its center is repeated over and over to form the background. Variation occurs in the color given to these shapes. Similarly, the oval of the mirror is repeated with variations in the composition of the girl. The circular motif also is repeated throughout the painting, with variations in color and size.

The concept of *balance* is very important. It is not difficult to look at a composition and almost intuitively perceive that it does or does not appear balanced. *How artists achieve balance in their pictures is our concern.*

The most mechanical method of achieving balance is *symmetry*, specifically bilateral symmetry, the balancing of like forms, mass, and colors on opposite sides of the vertical axis (Figs. **1.22** and **1.23**). Symmetry is so precise that we can measure it. Pictures employing absolute symmetry tend to be stable, stolid, and without much sense of motion. They are also, probably for that very reason, quite rare. Many works approach symmetry, but nearly all retreat from placing mirror images on opposite sides of the centerline.

Asymmetrical balance, sometimes referred to as psychological balance, is achieved by careful placement of unlike items (Fig. **1.24**). Every painting illustrated in this chapter is asymmetrical. Comparative discussion as to how balance has been achieved is a useful exercise, especially if colors are considered. Often color is used to balance line and form. Since some hues, such as yellow, have a great attaction for the eye, they can counterbalance tremendous mass and activity.

An important characteristic in a work of art is the means by which unity is achieved. All of the elements of composition work together to provide us with a picture that "hangs together." Often, compositional elements are juxtaposed in an unusual fashion to achieve a particular effect. None the less, that effect usually entails a conscious attempt at making a unified statement. Every element we have discussed in this section may be utilized in such a manner to give us a picture that is unified. Our discussion of how an artist uses compositional devices is not complete until we understand how the composition works as a totality.

1.20 Repetition of patterns.

1.22 Closed composition (composition kept within the frame).

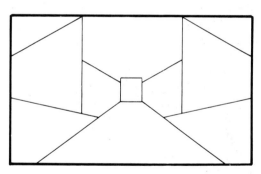

1.23 Open composition (composition allowed to escape the frame).

With regard to unity, we speak of *closed composition,* in which use of line and form always directs the eye into the painting (Fig. **1.22**) as unified, and *open composition,* in which the eye is allowed to wander off the canvas, or escape the frame (Fig. **1.23**), as disunified. Such is not the case. Keeping the artwork within the frame is a stylistic device that has an important bearing on the artwork's meaning. For example, painting in the *Classical* style is predominantly within the frame, illustrating a concern for the self-containment of the artwork and for precise structuring. *Baroque* design tends to force the eye to escape the frame, suggesting the world or universe outside, or the individual's place in an overwhelming cosmos. Unity can be achieved by keeping the composition closed, but it is not a prerequisite.

When we look at a picture for the first time, our eye moves around it, pausing briefly at those areas that seem to be of greatest visual appeal. These are focal areas. A painting may have a single focal area from which the eye will stray only with conscious effort. Or it may have an infinite number of focal points whereby the eye bounces from one point to another on the picture – in this way, the elements vie for our attention.

Focal areas are achieved in a number of ways—through confluence of line, by encirclement (Fig. **1.25**), or by color, to name just a few. To draw attention to a particular point in the picture the artist may make all lines lead to that point. The focal object or area may be placed in the center of a ring of objects, or the object may be of a color that demands our attention more than the other colors in the picture. For example, bright yellows attract our eye more readily than dark blues. The artist uses focal areas to control what we see and when we see.

1.24 St. Mark and St. Luke from the Gospel Book of Godescale, 781–3. Vellum, 12¼ x 8¼ ins (31 x 21 cm). Bibliothèque Nationale, Paris.

1.25 (*right*) St. Mark from the Gospel Book of St. Médard of Soissons, France, early 9th century. Paint on vellum, 14⅜ x 10¼ ins (37 x 26 cm). Bibliothèque Nationale, Paris.

Explain this. What this road means, where it goes

CHAPTER ONE

1.26 Jean-Baptiste-Camille Corot, *A View Near Volterra*, 1838. Oil on canvas, 27⅜ x 37½ ins (70 x 95 cm). The National Gallery of Art, Washington, D C (Chester Dale Collection).

OTHER FACTORS

Perspective

Perspective is a tool by which the artist indicates the spatial relationships of objects in a picture. It is based on the perceptual phenomenon which causes objects further away from us to appear smaller. If we examine a painting, we can identify the spatial relationships between the objects in the foreground and the objects in the background. We also can discern whether or not the relationships of the objects appear as we see them in life. For example, paintings executed prior to the Italian Renaissance, when mechanical procedures for rendering perspective were developed, look rather strange because while background objects are painted smaller than fore-

ground objects, the positioning does not appear rational. Their composition strikes us as being rather primitive.

Two types of perspective may be used. The first, *linear perspective*, is characterized by the phenomenon of standing on railroad tracks and watching the two rails apparently come together at the horizon (known as the *vanishing point*). It uses line to achieve the sense of distance. In Figure **1.26**, the road recedes from foreground to background and becomes narrower as it does so. We perceive that recession, which denotes distance, through the artist's use of line.

The second, *aerial perspective*, indicates distance through the use of light and atmosphere. For example, mountains in the background of a picture are made to appear distant by being painted in less detail. In the upper left of **1.2**, a castle appears at a great distance. We know it

1.27 Chü-jan, *Buddhist Monastery by Stream and Mountains*, c. A.D. 960–85. Ink on silk, 33⅝ x 22⅝ ins (85.5 x 57.5 cm). The Cleveland Museum of Art, Gift of Katharine Holden Thayer.

is distant because it is smaller and, more important, because it is indistinct.

Another treatment of perspective can be seen in the painting *Buddhist Monastery by Stream and Mountains* by Chü-jan (Fig. **1.27**). This hanging scroll illustrates a device fairly common in Chinese paintings with a vertical format. The artist divides the picture into two basic units—foreground and background. The foreground of the painting consists of details reaching back toward the middle ground. At that point a division occurs, so that the background and the foreground are separated by an openness in what might have been a deep middle ground. The foreground represents the nearby, and its rich detail causes us to pause and ponder on numerous elements, including the artist's use of brushstroke in creating foliage, rocks, and water. Then, there is a break, and the background appears to loom up or be suspended—almost as if it were a separate entity. Although the foreground gives us a sense of dimension—of space receding from the front plane of the painting—the background seems flat, a factor that serves to enhance further the sense of height of the mountains. Despite the conventions of composition applied to this and other vertical landscapes of the period, ultimately the artist sought to create for the viewer a believable path through the painting.

Subject Matter

We can regard treatment of subject matter as ranging from verisimilitude, or representationalism, to nonobjectivity (Fig. **1.28**). We will use this continuum again in later chapters, substituting the term *theatricality* for nonobjectivity. Between the two ends of this continuum are many of the "-isms" of the art world: Realism, Impressionism, Expressionism, Cubism, Fauvism, and so forth. Each is a particular method of treatment of subject matter.

1.28 Subject-matter continuum.

1.30 Salvador Dali, *The Persistence of Memory*, 1931. Oil on canvas, 9½ x 13 ins (24 x 33 cm). Collection, The Museum of Modern Art, New York (given anonymously).

Chiaroscuro

Chiaroscuro (sometimes called modeling), whose meaning in Italian is "light and shade," is the device used by artists to make their forms appear *plastic*—that is, three-dimensional. Making two-dimensional objects appear three-dimensional depends on the artist's ability to render highlight and shadow effectively. Without them, all forms are two-dimensional in appearance.

Chiaroscuro gives a picture much of its character. For example, the dynamic and dramatic treatment of light and shade in Figure 1.29 gives this painting a quality quite different from what would have resulted had the artist chosen to give full, flat, front light to the face. The highlights, falling as they do, create not only a dramatic effect but also a compositional triangle extending from shoulder to cheek, down to the hand, and then across the sleeve and back to the shoulder. Consider the substantial change in character had highlight and shadow been executed in a different manner. The treatment of chiaroscuro in a highly verisimilar fashion in Figure 1.30 helps give the painting its strangely real yet dreamlike appearance.

1.29 Jan Vermeer, *The Girl with the Red Hat*, c. 1665. Oil on wood, 9⅛ x 7⅛ ins (23 x 18 cm). The National Gallery of Art, Washington, D C (Andrew W. Mellon Collection, 1937).

HOW DO THEY STIMULATE THE SENSES?

We do not touch pictures, and so we cannot feel their roughness or their smoothness, their coolness or their warmth. We cannot hear pictures and we cannot smell them. When we conclude that a picture affects our senses in a particular way, we are responding in terms of visual stimuli that are transposed into mental images of our senses of touch, taste, sound, and so forth.

COLOR

The colors of an artist's palette are referred to as warm or cool depending upon which end of the color spectrum they fall. Reds, oranges, and yellows are said to be warm colors. They are the colors of the sun and therefore call to mind our primary source of heat, so they carry strong implications of warmth. Colors falling on the opposite end of the spectrum—blues and greens—are cool colors because they imply shade, or lack of light and warmth. As we will notice frequently, this is a stimulation that is mental but has a physical basis. Tonality and color contrast also affect our senses. The stark value contrasts of

1.31 Pablo Picasso, *Guernica*, 1937. Oil on canvas, 11 ft 5 ins x 25 ft 5¾ ins (3.4 x 7.76 m). Copyright ARS NY SPADEM, 1988.

Figure **1.31** contribute significantly to the harsh and dynamic qualities of the work. The colorlessness of this monochromatic black, white, and gray is a horrifying comment on the tragic bombing of Guernica. In the opposite vein, the soft, yet dramatic, tonal contrasts of Figure **1.29** and the strong warmth and soft texture of the red hat create a completely different set of stimuli.

CONTRAST

Many of the sense-affecting stimuli work in concert, and cannot be separated from each other. We already have noted some of the effects of chiaroscuro, but one of the most interesting effects is the treatment of flesh. Some flesh appears like stone, other flesh appears soft and true to life. Our response to whatever treatment has been given is very tactile—we want to touch, or we believe we know what we would feel if we did touch. Chiaroscuro is essential to achieve those effects. Harsh shadows and strong

1.32 Sir Peter Paul Rubens, *Rape of the Daughters of Leucippus*, c. 1616–17. Canvas, 87½ x 82¼ ins (222 x 209 cm). Alte Pinakothek, Munich.

contrasts create one set of responses; diffused shadows and subdued contrasts create another. Figure **1.32** presents softly modeled flesh whose warmth and softness come from color and chiaroscuro. Highlight and shadow create softness, and predominantly red hues warm the composition; our sensual response is heightened dramatically.

1.34 Grant Wood, *American Gothic*, 1930. Oil on beaver board, 30 x 25 ins (76 x 63 cm). Friends of American Art Collection. Photograph © 1990. Collection, The Art Institute of Chicago. All rights reserved.

DYNAMICS

Although pictures are static, they can stimulate a sense of movement and activity, and create a sense of stable solidity. The artist stimulates these sensations by using certain conventional devices. Composition that is principally vertical can express, for example, a sense of dignity and grandeur (Figs. **1.33** and **1.34**). A picture that is horizontal can elicit a sense of stability and placidity. The triangle is a most interesting form in engineering because of its structural qualities. It is also interesting in art because of its psychological qualities. If we place a triangle so that its base forms the bottom of a picture, we

1.33 Giorgio de Chirico, *Nostalgia of the Infinite*, c. 1913–14, dated on the painting 1911. Oil on canvas, 53¼ x 25½ ins (135 x 65 cm). Collection, The Museum of Modern Art, New York (Purchase).

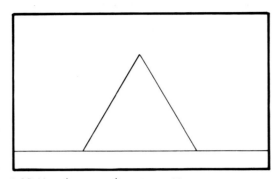

1.35 Upright-triangular composition.

create a definite sense of solidarity and immovability (Fig. **1.35**). If that triangle were a pyramid sitting on a level plane, a great deal of effort would be required to tip it over. If we invert the triangle so that it balances on its apex, a sensation of instability and action results (Figs. **1.36** and **1.37**). Although we can feel clearly the sensations stimulated by these simple geometric forms, we should not conclude that such devices are either explicit or limited in their communication. Nonverbal communication in the arts is not that simple. None the less, the basic compositional devices do influence our response, and impact on our perceptions.

1.37 Giotto, *The Lamentation*, 1305–6. Fresco. 7 ft 7 ins x 6 ft 7½ ins (2.31 x 2.02 m). Arena Chapel, Padua.

1.36 Inverted-triangular composition.

1.39 Broken line.

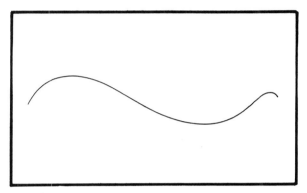

1.38 Curved line.

because it uses strong diagonal line, which tends to stimulate a sense of movement. Precision of linear execution also can create sharply defined forms or soft, fuzzy images. Figure **1.40** shows how straight lines and right angles can create the basic principles of life itself. Vertical lines signify vitality and life; horizontal lines signify tranquility and death. The intersection of vertical and horizontal lines represent life's tensions.

1.40 Piet Mondrian, *Composition in White, Black, and Red*, 1936. Oil on canvas, 40¼ x 41 ins (102 x 104 cm). Collection, The Museum of Modern Art, New York (gift of the Advisory Committee).

TROMPE L'OEIL

Trompe l'oeil, or "trick of the eye," gives the artist a varied set of stimuli by which to affect our sensory response. Occasionally this device forms the core of a painting; at other times it is used to enhance a work's appeal. For example, all objects drawn with parallel sides recede to a vanishing point. Some artists make subtle changes in the placement of the vanishing point, with the effect that the picture, while appearing verisimilar, gives the impression of rotating forward at the top and thus becoming much more dynamic.

LINE

The use of line also affects sense response. Figure **1.38** illustrates how this use of curved line can elicit a sense of relaxation. The broken line in Figure **1.39** creates a much more dynamic and violent sensation. We can also feel that the upright triangle in Figure **1.35**, although solid and stable, is more dynamic than a horizontal composition

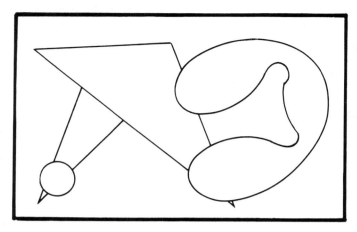

1.41 Juxtaposition.

JUXTAPOSITION

We can also receive stimuli from the results of juxtaposing curved and straight lines, which results in linear dissonance or consonance. Figure **1.41** illustrates the juxtaposing of inharmonious forms, which creates instability. Careful use of this device can stimulate some very interesting and specific sense responses.

The metaphysical fantasies of Giorgio de Chirico (1888–1978) have Surrealist associations. Works such as *Nostalgia* (Fig. **1.33**) contain no rational explanation for their juxtaposition of strange objects. They have a dreamlike quality, associating objects that are not normally grouped together. Such works are not rational, and show a world humankind does not control. In them, "there is only what I see with my eyes open, and, even better, closed."

FOCUS

The work of François Boucher (1703–70) in the Rococo tradition gives us a taste of the decorative, mundane, and slightly erotic painting popular in the early and mid-eighteenth century. As a protégé of Madame de Pompadour, mistress of King Louis XV, Boucher enjoyed great popularity. His work has a highly decorative surface, and portrays pastoral and mythological settings such as shown in Figure **1.42**. Boucher's figures almost always appear amid exquisitely detailed drapery. His rendering technique is nearly flawless, and his displays of painterly virtuosity provide fussily pretty works whose main subjects compete with their decorative backgrounds for our attention. In comparison with the power and sweep of the Baroque, Boucher appears gentle and shallow. The intricate formal design of the Baroque is lost here in intricate and delicate details, each of which takes on a separate focus of its own and leads the eye first in one direction and then another.

SUBJECT MATTER

Subject matter, which, of course, involves any or all of the characteristics we have discussed, is a powerful device for effecting both sensory responses and more intense, subjective responses. The use of verisimilitude or nonobjectivity is the most noticeable stimulant of individual response. It would seem logical for individuals to respond intellectually to nonobjective pictures, since the subject matter should be neutral, with no inherent expressive stimuli. However, nothing creates so extreme a subjective response (especially a negative one) as nonobjectivity. When asked whether they feel more comfortable with the subject matter in Figure **1.2** or that in Figure **1.14**, most individuals choose the former, even though the latter is of our age, our society, our world. Does the contemporary work tell us something about ourselves that we do not wish to hear? Our responses may depend on how directly or explicitly the subject matter is communicated.

The Spanish painter and printmaker Francisco de Goya (1746–1828) used his paintings to attack the government, both Spanish and French. His highly imaginative and

1.42 François Boucher, *Venus Consoling Love*, 1751. Oil on canvas, 42¼ x 33⅜ ins (107 x 85 cm). The National Gallery of Art, Washington, D C (Chester Dale Collection).

1.43 Francisco Goya, *Execution of the Citizens of Madrid, 3 May 1808*, 1814. Oil on canvas, 8 ft 6 ins x 11 ft 4 ins (2.59 x 3.45 m). Prado, Madrid.

nightmarish works reveal humanity and nature, often at their most malevolent. Figure **1.43** also tells a story of an actual event. On May 3, 1808 the citizens of Madrid rebelled against the invading army of Napoleon. As a result, individuals were arbitrarily arrested and executed. It is impossible to escape the focal attraction of the man in white, about to die. Goya's strong value contrasts force the eye to the victim; only the lantern behind the soldiers keeps the composition in balance. However, Goya leads us beyond the death of individuals, because these figures are not realistically depicted.

Does the more explicit appeal cause a more profound response? Or does the stimulation provided by the unfamiliar cause us to think more deeply and respond more fully, since our imagination is left free to wander? The answers to these questions are worth considering as we perceive artworks, many of whose keys to response are not immediately obvious.

TWO

SCULPTURE

WHAT IS IT?

Sculpture is aesthetic communication through the design of three-dimensional space. It may take the form of whatever it seeks to represent, from pure, or nonobjective form, to lifelike depiction of the human being or any other entity. Sometimes sculpture, because of its three dimensionality, comes very close to reality in its depiction. Duane Hanson and John DeAndrea, for example, use plastics to render the human form so realistically that the viewer must approach the artwork and examine it closely to determine that it is not a real human. Every art form employs some degree of abstraction, and so it is with sculpture.

HOW IS IT PUT TOGETHER?

DIMENSIONALITY

Sculpture may be *full round*, *relief*, or *linear*. Full round works are freestanding and fully three-dimensional (Fig. 2.1). A work that can be viewed from only one side—that is, one that projects from a background—is said to be in

2.1 Apollo playing the lyre (Roman copy of a Greek statue), from the Temple of Apollo at Cyrene, 1st century A.D. Marble, over life-size. The British Museum, London.

2.2 East frieze, Halicarnassus. The British Museum, London.

relief (Fig. **2.2**). A work utilizing materials two-dimensionally is called *linear* (*Fig.* **2.17**). A sculptor's choice of full round, relief, or linearity as a mode of expression dictates to a large extent what he or she can and cannot do, both aesthetically and practically.

Full Round

All sculpture is three-dimensional, but we can refine that characteristic further by noting the quality of three-dimensionality which adheres to a given work. Sculptural works that explore full three-dimensionality and are meant to be viewed from any angle are termed full round (Fig. **2.3**). Some subjects and styles pose certain constraints in this regard, however. Painters, printmakers, and photographers have virtually unlimited choice of subject matter and compositional arrangements. Full round sculptures dealing with such subjects as clouds, oceans, and panoramic landscapes are problematic for the sculptor. Since sculpture occupies real space, the use of perspective, for example, to increase spatial relationships poses certain obvious problems. In addition, since full round sculpture is freestanding and three-dimensional, sculptors must concern themselves with the practicalities of engineering and gravity. They cannot, for example, create a work with great mass at the top unless they can find a way (within the bounds of acceptable composition) to keep the statue from falling over. After we have viewed

numerous full round works, we begin to note the small animals, branches, tree stumps, rocks, and other devices that have been employed to give practical stability to a work.

2.3 Auguste Rodin, *The Burghers of Calais*, 1866. Bronze, height 82½ ins (209 cm). Hirshhorn Museum and Sculpture Garden, Smithsonian Institution, Washington D.C. (gift of Joseph H. Hirshhorn, 1966).

Relief

On the other hand, the sculptor who creates a work in relief does not have quite so many restrictions. Since the work is attached to a background, he or she has freer choice of subjects and need not worry about their positions or supports. Clouds, seas, and perspective landscapes are within the relief sculptor's reach, since the work needs to be viewed only from one side. Relief sculpture, then, is three dimensional. However, because it protrudes from a background, it maintains a two-dimensional quality, as compared to full round sculpture.

Linear

The third category of sculpture, linear sculpture, emphasizes construction with linear items such as wire or neon tubing. Artworks using linear materials and occupying three-dimensional space will occasionally puzzle us as we consider or try to decide whether they are really linear or full round. Here again, absolute definition is less important than the process of analysis and aesthetic experience and response.

METHODS OF EXECUTION

In general, we may say that sculpture is executed using additive, subtractive, substitute, or manipulative techniques, or any combination of these. A fifth category, that of found sculpture, may or may not be considered a "method" of execution, as we shall see later.

Subtraction — *carving*

Carved works are said to be subtractive. That is, the sculptor begins with a large block, usually wood or stone, and cuts away (subtracts) the unwanted material. In previous eras, and to some extent today, sculptors had to work with whatever materials were at hand. Wood carvings emanated from forested regions, soapstone carvings from the Inuits, and great works of marble from the regions surrounding the quarries of the Mediterranean. Anything that can yield to the carver's tools can be formed into a work of sculpture. However, stone, with its promise of immortality, has proven to be the most popular material.

Three types of rock hold potential for the carver. *Igneous* rocks, of which granite is an example, are very hard and potentially long-lasting. However, they are difficult to carve and are therefore not popular. *Sedimentary* rocks such as limestone are relatively long-lasting, easy to carve, and polishable. Beautifully smooth and lustrous surfaces are possible with sedimentary rocks. *Metamorphic*

rocks, including marble, seem to be the sculptor's ideal. They are long-lasting, are "a pleasure to carve," and exist in a broad range of colors. Whatever the artist's choice, one requirement must be met: The material to be carved, whether wood, stone, or a bar of soap, must be free of flaws.

A sculptor who sets about to carve a work does not begin simply by imagining a *Samson Slaying a Philistine* (Fig. **2.4**) and then attacking the stone. The first step would be to create a model, usually smaller than the intended sculpture. The model is made of clay, plaster, or wax and is completed in precise detail—a miniature of the final product.

2.4 Giambologna, *Samson Slaying a Philistine,* c. 1562. Courtesy of the Victoria and Albert Museum, London.

3 models
1. Round
2. Relief
3. Linear
4. Kinetic

Once the likeness of the model has been enlarged and transferred, the artist begins to rough out the actual image ("knocking away the waste material," as Michelangelo put it). In this stage of the sculpting process, the artist carves to within two or three inches of what is to be the finished area, using specific tools designed for the purpose. Then, using a different set of carving tools, the material is carefully taken down to the precise detail. Finishing work and polishing follow.

Addition

In contrast with carving from a large block of material, the sculptor using an additive process starts with raw material and adds element to element until the work is finished. The term built *sculpture* is often used to describe works executed in an additive technique. The materials employed in this process can be plastics, metals such as aluminum or steel, terracottas (clay), epoxy resins, or wood. Many times materials are combined (Fig. **2.5**). It is not uncommon for sculptors to combine methods as well. For example, built sections of metal or plastic may be combined with carved sections of stone.

2.5 (*above*) Bakota ancestor figure from Gabon, late 19th century. Wood and copper sheeting, height 26¾ ins (68 cm). The British Museum, London.

2.6 Henry Moore, *Two Large Forms*, 1969. The Serpentine, Hyde Park, London.

Substitution

Any material that can be transformed from a plastic, molten, or fluid state into a solid state can be molded or *cast* into a work of sculpture. Of course, the material must hold together permanently in its solid state. The creation of a piece of cast sculpture always involves the use of a mold. First, the artist creates an identically sized model of the intended sculpture. This is called a *positive*. The positive is then covered with a material, such as plaster of Paris, that when hardened and removed will retain the surface configurations of the positive. This form is called a *negative* and becomes the mold for the actual sculpture. The molten or fluid material is poured into the negative and allowed to solidify. When the mold is removed, the work of sculpture emerges. Surface polishing, if desired, brings the work to its final form (Figs. **2.6**, **2.7**, and **2.8**).

2.7 (*right*) Giovanni Bologna, *Mercury*, c. 1567. Bronze, height 69 ins (175 cm). Museo Nationale del Bargello, Florence.

2.8 So-called statuette of Charlemagne, c. 860–70. Bronze cast and gilt, height 9½ ins (24 cm). The Louvre, Paris.

Very often sculpture is cast so that it is hollow. This method, of course, is less expensive, since it requires less material. It also results in a work that is less prone to crack, since it is less susceptible to expansion and contraction resulting from changes in temperature. Finally, hollow sculpture is, naturally, lighter and thus more easily shipped and handled.

Manipulation *clay*

In this technique, materials such as clay are shaped by skilled use of the hands. A term of similar meaning is *modeling*. The difference between this technique and addition is clear when we watch an artist take a single lump of clay and skillfully transform it, as it turns on a potter's wheel, into a final shape (Fig. **11.1**).

Found

This category of sculpture is exactly what its name implies. Very often natural objects, whether shaped by human hands or not, are discovered that for some reason have taken on characteristics that stimulate aesthetic response. They become *objets d'art* not because an artist put them together (although an artist may combine found objects to create a work), but because an artist chose to take them from their original surroundings and hold them up to the rest of us as vehicles for aesthetic communication. In other words, an "artist" decided that such an object said something aesthetically. As a result, he or she chose to present it in that vein.

Some may have concern about such a category, however, because it removes *techne* or skill from the artistic process. As a result, objects such as driftwood and interesting rocks can assume perhaps an unwarranted

place as art products or objects. However, if a "found" object is altered in some way to produce an artwork, then the process would probably fall under one of our previously noted methods, and the product could be termed an artwork in the fullest sense of the word.

Ephemeral

Ephemeral art has many different expressions and includes the works of the conceptualists, who insist that "art is an activity of change, of disorientation and shift, of violent discontinuity and mutability." Designed to be transitory, ephemeral art makes its statement and then, eventually, ceases to exist. Undoubtedly the largest work of sculpture ever designed was based on that concept. Christo's *Running Fence* (Fig. **2.9**) was an event and a process, as well as a sculptural work. In a sense, Christo's works are conceptual in that they call attention to the experience of art in opposition to its actual form. At the end of a two-week viewing period, *Running Fence* was removed entirely and ceased to be.

2.9 Christo, *Running Fence Sonoma and Marin Counties, California*, 1972–6. Woven nylon fabric and steel cables, height 18 ft (5.49 m), length 24½ miles (39.2 km) © Christo, 1976. Photograph Wolfgang Volz.

2.10 *The Fates*, from the east pediment of the Parthenon, c. 438–432 B.C. Marble, over life-size. The British Museum, London.

COMPOSITION

Composition in sculpture comprises the same elements and principles as composition in the pictorial arts—mass, line, form, balance, repetition, color, proportion, and unity. Sculptors' uses of these elements are significantly different, however, since they work in three dimensions.

Elements

Unlike a picture, a sculpture has literal *mass*. It takes up three-dimensional *space*, and its materials have *density*. Mass in pictures is *relative* mass: The mass of forms in a picture has application principally in relation to other forms within the same picture. In sculpture, however, mass is literal and consists of actual volume and density. So, the mass of a sculpture that is 20 ft (6 m) high, 8 ft (2.5 m) wide, and 10 ft (3 m) deep, but made of balsa wood, would seem less than a sculpture 10 ft (3 m) high, 4 ft (1.25 m) wide, and 3 ft (1 m) deep, made of lead. Space and density must both be considered. What if the material of a statue is disguised to look and feel like a different material? We will discuss this later in the chapter, when we look at how a sculpture affects our senses.

As we stated in the last chapter, *line* and *form* are highly related. We can separate them (with some difficulty) when we discuss pictures, since in two dimensions an artist uses line to define form. In painting, line is a construction tool. Without using line, artists cannot reveal their forms, and when we analyze a painting, line is perhaps more important to us than the actual form it reveals. However, in sculpture the case is nearly reversed. It is the form that draws our interest, and when we discuss line in sculpture, we do so in terms of how it is revealed in form.

The east pediment of the Parthenon contains marvelous sculptural examples (Fig. **2.10**). What strikes us first is the compositional accommodation to the confines of the pediment. Originally, it formed part of the architectural decoration high on the Parthenon, and probably, through its diagonal curvilinearity, was intended to off-set the straight lines and strong verticals and horizontals of the temple. It depicts the mythological story of the birth of Athena from her father's head. Also from the east pediment is the figure of Dionysus (Fig. **0.10**). Together they illustrate Greek idealization of their suprahuman deities. To begin with, treatment of cloth is highly sophisticated. The drape and flow of fabric carefully reinforce the overall but reasonably simple line of the work, representing considerable technical achievement. However, this depiction is far from mere decoration—in Figure **2.10** the cloth is used to reveal the perfected human female form beneath it in a way which once again demonstrates the classical purpose—not naturalism but the ideal. The aim here is to raise these forms above the human or the specific to a symbolic level. Even in repose they show subtle and controlled grace and movement. The dynamic counterthrust of tensions and releases is obvious, but it is always restrained, never explosive or emotional.

When we view a sculpture its elements direct our eye from one point to another, just as focal points do, via line and color, in a picture. In some works the eye is directed through the piece and then off into space. Such sculptures have an *open* form. In Figures **2.4** and **2.7** the eye is directed outward from the work in the same fashion as composition that escapes the frame in painting. If, on the other hand, the eye is directed continually back into the form, we say the form is *closed*. If we allow our eye to follow the linear detail of Figure **2.11**, we find that we are continually led back into the work. This is similar to composition kept within the frame in painting and to closed forms in music, which we will discuss in Chapter

3. Often it is difficult to fit a work precisely into one or the other of these categories.

Obviously, not all sculptures are completely solid; they may have openings. We call any such holes in a sculpture *negative space*, and we can discuss this characteristic in terms of its role in the overall composition. In some works negative space is inconsequential; in others it is quite significant. It is up to us to decide which, and how it contributes to the overall piece. In Figure **2.6** negative space plays a significant role. It could be argued that negative space is as instrumental to the overall concept of the work as is the metal form. On the other hand, in Figure **2.1** negative space is clearly incidental.

2.11 Aristide Maillol, *The Mediterranean*, 1902–5. Bronze (cast c. 1951–53), 41 x 45 x 29¾ ins (104.1 x 114.3 x 75.6 cm), including base. Collection, The Museum of Modern Art, New York (gift of Stephen C. Clark).

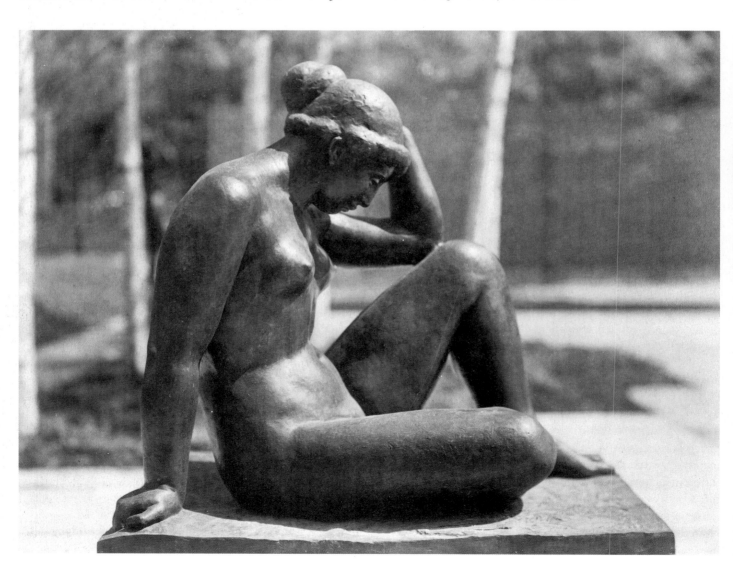

Perhaps *color* does not seem particularly important to us as we think of sculpture. We tend to see ancient sculpture as white and modern sculpture as natural wood or rusty iron. Color is as important to the sculptor as it is to the painter. In some cases the material itself may be chosen because of its color; in others, such as terracottas, the sculpture may be painted. The lifelike sculptures of Duane Hanson depend on color for their effect. They are so lifelike that one could easily confuse them with real persons. Finally, still other materials may be chosen or treated so that nature will provide the final color through oxidation or weathering.

Texture, the roughness or smoothness of a surface, is a tangible characteristic of sculpture. Sculpture is unique in that we can perceive its texture through our sense of touch. Even when we cannot touch a work of sculpture, we can perceive and respond to texture, which can be both physical and suggested. Sculptors go to great lengths to achieve the texture they desire for their works. In fact, much of a sculptor's technical mastery manifests itself in that final ability to impart a surface to the work. We will examine texture more fully in our discussion of sense responses.

Principles

Proportion is the relationship of shapes. Just as we have a seemingly innate sense of balance, so we have a feeling of proportion. That feeling tells us that each form in the sculpture is in proper relationship to the others. However, as any student of art history will tell us, proportion—or the ideal of relationships—has varied from one civilization or culture to another. For example, such a seemingly obviously proportioned entity as the human body has varied greatly in its proportions as sculptors over the centuries have depicted it. Study the differences in proportion in the human body among Maillol's *The Mediterranean* (Fig. **2.11**), the Chartres' Saints (Fig. **2.12**), an ancient Greek Kouros figure (Fig. **2.13**), and Giacometti's *Man Pointing* (Fig. **2.14**). Each depicts the human form, but each utilizes differing proportions. This difference in proportion helps transmit the message the artist wishes to communicate about his or her subject matter.

2.12 Jamb statues, west portal, Chartres Cathedral, begun 1145.

2.13 Kouros figure. The Metropolitan Museum of Art, New York (Fletcher Fund, 1932).

2.14 Alberto Giacometti, *Man Pointing*, 1947. Bronze, 70½ x 40¾ x 16⅜ ins (179 x 103.4 x 41.5 cm), at base 12 x 13¼ ins (30.5 x 33.7 cm) Collection, The Museum of Modern Art, New York (gift of Mrs. John D. Rockefeller 3rd).

Rhythm, harmony, and variation constitute *repetition* in sculpture, as they did in the pictorial arts. However, in sculpture we must look more carefully and closely to determine how the artist has employed these elements. If we reduce a sculpture to its components of line and form, we begin to see how (as in music) rhythmic patterns—regular and irregular—occur. In Figure **2.2**, for example, a regular rhythmic pattern is established in space as the eye moves from figure to figure and from leg to leg of the figures. We also can see whether the components are consonant or dissonant. For instance, again in Figure **2.2**, a sense of dynamics—that is, action or movement—is created by the dissonance that results from juxtaposing the strong triangles of the stances and groupings with the *biomorphic* lines of the human body. On the other hand, unity of the curves in Figure **2.15** provides us with a consonant series of relationships. Finally, we can see how line and form are used in theme and variation. We noted the repetition of triangles in Figure **2.2**. In contrast, the sculptor of Figure **2.16** varies his motif, the oval, as the eye moves from the child's face to the upper arm, the hand, and finally the cat's face.

2.15 (*right*) Tree Spirit, 1st century A.D. Central Indian bracket figure. The British Museum, London.

2.16 (*below*) William Zorach, *Child with Cat*, 1926. Bronze, 17½ × 10 × 7½ ins (44 × 25 × 19 cm). Palmer Museum of Art, Pennsylvania State University.

OTHER FACTORS

Articulation

Important, also, in viewing sculpture is noting the manner by which we move from one element to the next. That manner of movement is called articulation, and it applies to sculpture, painting, photography, and all the other arts. As an example, let us step outside the arts to consider human speech. Sentences, phrases, and individual words are nothing more than sound syllables (vowels) articulated (that is, joined together) by consonants. We understand what someone says to us because that individual articulates as he or she speaks. Let us put the five vowel sounds side by side: Eh–EE–Ah–O–OO. As yet we do not have a sentence. Articulate those vowels with consonants, and we have meaning: "Say, she must go too." The nature of an artwork depends on how the artist has repeated, varied, harmonized, and related its parts and how he or she has articulated the movement from one part to another—that is, how he or she indicates where one stops and the other begins.

Focal Area (Emphasis)

Sculptors, like painters or any other visual artists, must concern themselves with drawing the respondent's eye to those areas of their work that are central to what they wish to communicate. They also must provide the means by which the eye can move around the work. However, their task is much more complicated, because they deal in three dimensions and they have little control over the direction from which the viewer will first perceive the piece; the entire 360-degree view contributes to the total message communicated by the work.

The devices of convergence of line, encirclement, and color work for sculptors as they do for painters. The encircling line of the tree and body parts in Figure **2.15** causes us, however we proceed to scan the work, to focus ultimately on the torso of this sensuous fertility figure. One further device is available—movement. Sculptors have the option of placing moving objects in their work. Such an object immediately becomes a focal point of the sculpture. A mobile (Fig. **2.17**) presents many ephemeral patterns of focus as it turns at the whim of the breezes.

HOW DOES IT STIMULATE THE SENSES?

TEXTURE

Our discussion of the ways in which sculpture stimulates our senses can be presented in physical as well as mental terms. We can touch sculpture and feel its roughness or its smoothness, its coolness or perhaps its warmth. Even if we are prohibited by museum regulations from touching a sculpture, we can see the surface texture and translate the image into an imaginary tactile sensation. That is a much more direct form of sense response than the translation from sight to mind that occurs in viewing a picture. Unfortunately, museums often are forced to prohibit us from touching their sculptures. Such prohibitions are practical. Repeated touching of anything, whether it be stone, metal, or plastic, wears the surface. Even the oils from our fingers may deteriorate the surface. Certainly touching causes problems for the museum in keeping sculptures clean. Nevertheless, any work of sculpture cries out to be touched. Probably this is the first and most compelling response that any of us has to a sculpture. When we can touch, our sense responses are repaid many times over.

2.17 Alexander Calder, *Spring Blossoms*, 1965. Painted metal and heavy wire, extends 52 x 102 ins (135 x 259 cm). The Museum of Art, Pennsylvania State University (gift of the class of 1965).

COLOR

As we indicated earlier, we do not usually think of color as significant in our response to a sculpture, at least not as significant as in our response to a picture. However, color in sculpture stimulates our response by utilizing the same universal symbols as it does in paintings, photographs, and prints. Reds, oranges, and yellows stimulate sensations of warmth; blues and greens, sensations of coolness. In sculpture, color can result from the conscious choice of the artist, either in the selection of material or in the selection of the pigment with which the material is painted. Or, as we indicated earlier, color may result from the artist's choice to let nature color the work through wind, water, sun, and so forth.

This weathering effect, of course, creates very interesting patterns, but in addition it gives the sculpture the attribute not only of space but also of time, because the work obviously will change as nature works her wonders. A copper sculpture early in its existence will be a different work, a different set of stimuli, from what it will be five, ten, or twenty years hence. This is not entirely accidental; the artist chooses copper knowing what weathering will do to it. He or she obviously cannot predict the exact nature of the weathering or the exact hues of the sculpture at any given time in the future, but such predictability is irrelevant.

In this regard it is interesting to note how our response to a work of art may be shaped by the effects of age on it. There is a great deal of charm and character in ancient objects. When you see a spotlessly clean, "restored" historic monument, it seems too new and quite sterile. Even if that was how the building originally looked, grime

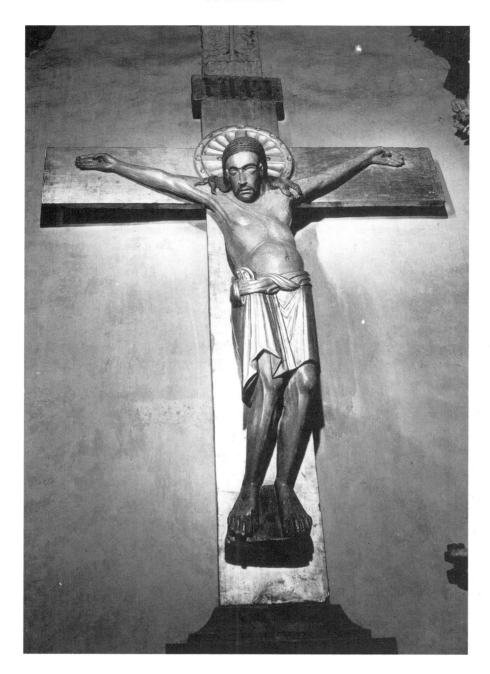

2.18 Gero Crucifix, c. 975–1000. Wood, height 6 ft 2 ins (1.87 m). Cologne Cathedral. Courtesy of Heaton-Sessions, Stone Ridge, New York.

is more appealing. It looks old—and historic. So it might be, when we view a weathered wooden icon from the Middle Ages (Fig. 2.18). Our response can be enhanced or diminished by the weathering of centuries—even though the artist may not have intended the work to appeal through the effects of nature on it.

DYNAMICS

An artist's use of line, form, and juxtaposition impart to a sculpture varying characteristics of motion or activity in the same sense that it does to a painting (see Figs. **2.2** and **2.6**). The activity of a sculpture, however, tends to be heightened because of its three-dimensionality. In addition, we experience a certain sense of dynamics as we walk around it. Although we are moving and not the sculpture, we perceive and respond to what seems to be movement in the work itself.

2.19 Egyptian statuary. The Metropolitan Museum of Art, New York (gift of Edward S. Harkness, 1914).

LINE & FORM

Line and form can, of course, work apart from dynamics. Figures **2.5** and **2.15** are both symbols of fertility. However, even though both exhibit full development of the breast, the latter is the more sensuous because each area of the body is treated with greater softness of line. (Of course, *what* one finds to be sensuous may be a result more of convention than of treatment. Certainly, convention leads to treatment. Our modern conception of glamour, illustrated in the tall, leggy, and slender fashion model, contrasts sharply with that of the High Renaissance or Baroque, in which corpulence was considered sexually appealing.)

MASS

Since sculpture has mass—that is, takes up space and has density—our senses respond to the weight or the size of a work. Egyptian sculpture, which is solid, stable, and oversized (Fig. **2.19**), has mass and proportion as well as line and form that make it appear heavier than a non-Egyptian work of basically the same size and material, such as Figure **2.7**. Moreover, the very same treatment of texture, verisimilitude, and subject elicits a completely different sense response if one work is 3 ft (1 m) and another 130 ft (39.6 m) tall.

Sculptures such as Trajan's Column are made to tell the story. Erected in the Emperor's Forum, it rose 128 ft (39 m) above the pavement on an 18 ft (5.5 m) base. Atop its 97 ft (29.6 m) column was a 13 ft (4 m) statue of Trajan. Inside the column is a circular staircase. From bottom to top a spiral band of relief sculpture (Fig. **2.20**) reveals the story of Trajan's defence of Rome and the Empire. He appears ninety times in the upward spiral of the narration, each appearance marking the start of a new episode. Its mass is overpowering.

Early in the chapter we mentioned the possibility of an artist's *disguising the material* from which the work is made. Marble polished to appear like skin or wood polished to look like fabric can change the appearance of mass of a sculpture and significantly affect our response to it.

We also must consider the purpose of disguising material. For example, does the detailing of the sculpture reflect a formal concern for design, or does it reflect a concern for the greatest verisimilitude? Examine the cloth represented in Figures **2.1** and **2.15**. In both cases the sculptor has disguised the material by making stone appear to be cloth. In Figure **2.1** the cloth is detailed to reflect reality. It drapes as real cloth would drape, and as a result its effect in the composition depends upon the subtlety of line characteristic of draped cloth. However, in Figure **2.15** the sculptor has depicted cloth in such a way that its effect in the design is not dependent upon how cloth drapes, but rather upon the decorative function of line as the sculptor wishes to use it. Real cloth cannot drape as the sculptor has depicted it. Nor, probably, did the sculptor care. The main concern here was for decoration, for using line (that looks like cloth) to emphasize the rhythm of the work.

2.20 Apollódorus of Damascus, Column of Trajan, Rome, 106–13. Marble, height of base 18 ft (5.5 m), height of column 97 ft (29.6 m).

We might also consider whether or not a sculpture appears conscious of its own weight. For example, a work that has been carved from a huge block of stone, sitting squarely on the ground, and has a natural, undisguised texture and very little definition in terms of line would give us a strong impression of being *conscious of its own weight*. In contrast, a large sculpture of a human form positioned with all the weight on one foot and possessing a skinlike texture would appear totally *unconscious of its own weight*.

Mass, mass consciousness, and the disguising of materials leads us to another term: *glyptic*. Glyptic sculpture emphasizes the material from which the work is created and usually retains the fundamental geometric qualities of that material.

LIGHTING & ENVIRONMENT

One final factor that significantly influences our sense response to a sculpture, a factor that we very often do not consider and that is outside the control of the artist unless he or she personally supervises every exhibition in which the work is displayed, is that of *lighting and environment*. As we will see in Chapter 4, light plays a seminal role in our perception of and thereby our response to three-dimensional objects. The direction and number of sources of light striking a three-dimensional work can change the entire composition of that work. Whether the work is displayed outdoors or indoors, the method of lighting affects the overall presentation. Diffuse room lighting allows us to see all aspects of a sculpture without external influence. However, if the work is placed in a darkened room and illuminated from particular directions by spotlights, it becomes much more dramatic and our response is affected accordingly.

Where and how a work is exhibited also contribute to our response. The response given to a sculpture placed in a carefully designed environment that screens our vision from distracting or competing visual stimuli will be different if the sculpture is exhibited among other works amid the bustle of a public park.

Put your self in this picture walking thru.

THREE

MUSIC

Music often has been described as the purest of the art forms because it is free from the physical restrictions of space that adhere to the other arts. However, the freedom enjoyed by the composer becomes a constraint for the respondent, because music is an art in time that places significant responsibility in the hands (or the ears) of the listener. That consideration is especially critical for the respondent trying to learn and apply musical terminology, because he or she has only a fleeting moment to capture many of the characteristics of music. A painting or a sculpture stands still for us; it does not change or disappear, despite the length of time it takes us to find or apply some new characteristic. Such is not the case with music.

We live in a society that is very aural in its perceptions, but these perceptions usually do not require any kind of active listening. An excellent example is the Muzak that we hear in many stores, restaurants, and office buildings, which is intended solely as a soothing background designed *not* to attract attention. We hear music constantly on the radio, the television, and in the movies, but nearly always in a peripheral role. Since we are not expected to pay attention to it, we do not. Therefore, we simply do not undertake the kind of practice we need to be attentive to music and to perceive it in detail. However, like any skill, the ability to hear perceptively is enhanced through repetition and training. Individuals who have had

limited experience in responding to music have some difficulty in the "live" concert hall hearing what there is to hear in a piece of music that passes in just a few seconds. Likewise, their ability to *remember* what they have heard is impaired if they have not practiced that skill. To deduce the structure of a musical work, listeners must remember at the end what they heard at the beginning. These abilities require skills that most individuals in our society have not acquired.

WHAT IS IT?

Music is aesthetic communication through the design of time in motion using sound and silence. Musical design at the formal level of response is that shape we find in the finished work. So, at this level of response, music is a sonata, symphony, concerto, suite, concert overture, opera, oratorio, cantata, mass, or requiem, or motet, to name only a few of the most familiar types.

SONATA

A sonata is a group of movements loosely related and played in succession. Unlike the movements of a suite, these are not all in the same key but are in related tonalities.

The first movement of a sonata generally has a special form, which has taken on particular importance in musical composition —hence its name, sonata form. In discussing sonatas, we must be careful not to confuse *sonata* with *sonata form*, a particular structure we will discuss later.

SYMPHONY

The symphony is a large musical composition for orchestra which reached its full maturity in the late eighteenth century. Typically the symphony has four separate sections, called "movements." The tempos of the four movements are usually fast, slow, moderate, and fast. In addition, the first movement usually is in sonata form, sometimes with a slow introduction. The second movement generally consists of binary or sonata form; the third movement comprises a minuet and trio, in ternary form; the fourth movement explores sonata, rondo, or a combination of those forms. The symphony as a musical type has been shaped by, and to a large extent cannot be separated from, the development of the instruments for and the theories and styles of the historical periods in which it was composed. "Symphony" as a musical form may also apply to works composed for string quartet and chamber orchestra, for example. A symphony such as Beethoven's Symphony No. 9, which utilizes chorus as well as orchestra is unique. Some symphonies have only three movements, some have more than four movements, and some do not adhere to the characteristics just noted in relation to their movements.

CONCERTO

This term usually refers to a composition for solo instrument with accompaniment. It originated during the Baroque era as the *concerto grosso*, which uses a solo group called the *concertino* and a full ensemble called the *ripieno*. By the end of the age the *solo concerto* emerged. The solo concerto usually has three movements, which alternate in a fast–slow–fast relationship.

SUITE

If we think of the term suite as it is frequently used outside of music, we have an insight into its musical implications. A grouping of items of furniture in the design of a living room is called a living-room *suite*. The ensemble of trousers, vest, and jacket designed in the same fabric and style and worn together is called a *suit*. The musical suite is a grouping of clichéd rhythms and meters of particular dances, usually unrelated except by key and contrast. Suites were written primarily for keyboard instruments, specifically the harpsichord, but also for a solo instrument accompanied by harpsichord, or a group of stringed or wind instruments.

CONCERT OVERTURE

An overture is customarily a single-movement introduction to, for example, an opera. However, in concert it has been popular to perform many of these introductions apart from the work they introduce. As this practice became more popular, composers began to write concert overtures with no larger work intended to follow.

OPERA

Because of its special combination of art forms, we will discuss opera in detail later (see p. 82).

ORATORIO

An oratorio is a large choral work for soloists, chorus, and orchestra which was developed in the Baroque period. It is usually presented in concert form—that is, there is no physical action, staging, setting, costumes, or properties. The soloists in the oratorio may take the role of characters, and the work may have a plot, although perhaps the most familiar example, Handel's *Messiah*, does neither.

CANTATA

The cantata is a composition for chorus and/or solo voice(s) accompanied by an instrumental ensemble. Developed in the Baroque period, it comprises several movements and uses either sacred or secular texts.

MASS

The mass as a choral type concerns itself directly with the Roman Catholic service, the Mass. As such it includes six musical parts: *Kyrie, Gloria, Credo, Sanctus, Benedictus,* and *Agnus Dei.* The Mass is the heart of the Church rite and is based on the Last Supper of Christ. Two kinds of texts accompanied the Mass, the *Ordinary,* appropriate throughout the year, and the *Proper,* which had texts appropriate to particular feast days. Masses may or may not be written for inclusion in the church service. The concert mass has been an important part of musical composition since the Middle Ages. Many masses have taken a special form—for example, the *requiem mass,* or mass for the dead.

MOTET

A motet is a choral composition of *polyphonic* texture. Motets, like symphonies, oratorios, cantatas, masses, and so on, are associated with specific historical periods. Early motets of the thirteenth century often utilized three voices and combined sacred and secular texts. By the fifteenth and sixteenth centuries the motet was a contrapuntal work for four or five voices, usually with a sacred text. In that form it is differentiated from the *madrigal*, which utilized a secular text.

HOW IS IT PUT TOGETHER?

As we examine the nature of how music is put together, we can find ourselves adrift in a sea of unusual technical vocabulary, most of it Italian. Understanding the vocabulary and being able to identify its application in a musical work help us to comprehend the communication which uses the musical language, and thereby to understand the creative communicative intent of the composer and the musicians who bring the composition to life. The ways in which musical artists shape the characteristics that follow bring us experiences which can challenge our intellects and excite our emotions. As in all communication, meaning depends upon each of the parties involved; communicators and respondents must assume responsibility for facility in the language utilized. Effort is required to communicate effectively and significantly and to understand that communication. The rewards, the unlocking of the depths of our own being, are well worth the effort.

Music is composed through the designing of sound and silence. The latter is reasonably understandable, but what of the former? What is sound? Sound is vibration that stimulates the auditory nerves. It includes sirens, speech, crying babies, jet engines, falling trees, and so forth. We might call such sources noise. However, even noise may have a part in a musical composition. Cannons and even floor polishers have found their way into serious musical works. So we must be careful about what we include or exclude from sound in music. On the other hand, musical design does depend primarily upon sound of a specific character—sound that can be controlled and shaped, sound that can be consistent in its qualities. One aspect of sound that is not limited to musical instruments but is fundamental to the designing of sound in music is tone.

TONE

Tone has four characteristics: pitch, duration, timbre, and intensity.

Pitch

Pitch is a physical phenomenon measurable in vibrations per second. So, when we describe differences in pitch we are describing recognizable and measurable differences in sound waves. A pitch has a steady, constant frequency. A faster frequency produces a higher pitch, a slower frequency, a lower pitch. If a sounding body—a vibrating string, for example—is shortened, it vibrates more rapidly. Musical instruments designed to produce high pitches, such as the piccolo, therefore tend to be small. Instruments designed to produce low pitches tend to be large—for instance, bass viols and tubas.

In Chapter 1 we discussed color. Color comprises a range of light waves within a visible spectrum. Sound also comprises a spectrum, one whose audible pitches range from 16 to 38,000 vibrations per second. We can perceive 11,000 different pitches! Obviously that is more than is practical for musical composition. Therefore, *by convention* the sound spectrum is divided into at least ninety equally spaced frequencies comprising seven and a half *octaves*. The piano keyboard, consisting of eighty-eight keys (seven octaves plus two additional notes) representing the same number of equally spaced pitches, serves as an illustration (Fig. **3.1**). The thirteen pitches represented by the adjacent keys of the piano from C to C constitute an octave. The distance in frequency from C to C♯ is the same as that from C♯ to D, and so forth. The higher C vibrates at exactly twice the frequency of the lower C. Such is the case with every note and the note one octave below it. The A one octave above the lower one shown would vibrate at twice that rate. Again by convention, each musical note is usually tuned to a specific pitch, in vibrations per second. Normally, A is tuned to 440 vibrations per second, for example, and its octaves to 110, 220, 880, 1,760, and so forth.

3.1 Part of the piano keyboard and its pitches.

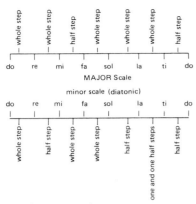

3.2 The major and minor scales.

The thirteen equally spaced pitches in an octave are called a *chromatic scale*. However, the scales that sound most familiar to us are the major and minor scales, which consist of an octave of eight pitches. The distance between any two pitches is an *interval*. Intervals between two adjacent pitches are *half steps*. Intervals of two half steps are *whole steps*. The major scale—*do re mi fa sol la ti do* (recall the song, "Doe, a deer . . ." from *The Sound of Music*)—has a specific arrangement of whole and half steps (Fig. **3.2**). Lowering the third and sixth notes of the major scale gives us the diatonic (the most common) minor scale.

To reiterate, a scale, which is an arrangement of pitches played in ascending or descending order, is a conventional organization of the frequencies of the sound spectrum. Not all music conforms to this convention. Music of Western civilization prior to approximately A.D. 1600 does not, nor does Eastern music, which makes great use of quarter tones. In addition, some contemporary Western music departs from the conventions of tonality of the major or minor scale.

Duration

A second characteristic of tone is duration, the length of time in which vibration is maintained without interruption. Duration in musical composition is relative and is designed within a set of conventions called musical notation (Fig. **3.3**). This system consists of a series of

3.3 Musical notation.

Note Values

Whole Half Quarter Eighth Sixteenth Thirty-second Sixty-fourth

Rests

Whole Half Quarter Eighth Sixteenth Thirty-second Sixty-fourth

symbols (notes) by which the composer indicates the relative duration of each pitch. The system is progressive—that is, each note is either double or half the duration of an adjacent note. Musical notation also includes a series of symbols that denote the duration of *silences* in a composition. These symbols are called *rests*, and have the same durational values as the symbols for duration of tone.

Timbre

Timbre is the characteristic of tone that allows us to distinguish a pitch played on a violin, for example, from the same pitch played on a piano. Timbre is also referred to as "voice print" and tone "color." In addition to identifying characteristic differences among sound-producing sources, timbre characterizes differences in quality of tones produced by the same source. Here the analogy of tone "color" is particularly appropriate. A tone that is produced with an excess of air—for example, by the human voice—is described as "white." Figure **3.4** illustrates some of the various sources that produce musical tone and account for its variety of timbres.

The piano could be considered either a stringed or a percussion instrument since it produces its sound by vibrating strings *struck* by hammers. The harpsichord's strings are set in motion by plucking.

Electronically produced music, extant since the development of the RCA synthesizer at the Columbia-Princeton Electronics Music Center, has become a standard source in assisting contemporary composers. Originally electronic music fell into two categories: (1) the electronic altering of acoustically produced sounds, which came to be labeled as *musique concrète* (see Glossary) and (2) electronically generated sounds. However, advances in technology have blurred those differences over the years.

Intensity

A final characteristic of tone is intensity. Any tone of any pitch, duration, or timbre can be loud, soft, or anywhere in between. Intensity is the *decibel* level of the tone, and depends upon the physical phenomenon of *amplitude* of vibration. When greater force is employed in the production of a tone, the resulting sound waves are wider and cause greater stimulation of the auditory nerves. The *size* of the sound wave, not its number of vibrations per second, is changed.

Composers indicate intensity, or *dynamic level*, with a series of specific notations:

3.4 The key sources of musical tone in an orchestra (instruments not to scale).

pp	pianissimo	very soft
p	piano	soft
mp	mezzo piano	moderately soft
mf	mezzo forte	moderately loud
f	forte	loud
ff	fortissimo	very loud

The notations of intensity that apply to an individual tone, such as *p*, *mp*, and *f*, also may apply to a section of music. *Dynamics* is the term used to refer to intensity levels throughout a composition. Changes in dynamics may be abrupt, gradual, wide, or small. A series of symbols also governs this aspect of music:

Crescendo	becoming louder
Decrescendo	becoming softer
> ∧ *sfz* Sforzando	"with force;" a strong accent immediately followed by *p*

As we listen to and compare musical compositions we can consider the use and breadth of dynamics in the same sense that we consider the use and breadth of palette in painting.

MELODY

Melody is a succession of sounds with rhythmic and tonal organization. We can visualize melody as linear and essentially horizontal. Thus, any organization of musical tones occurring *one after another* constitutes a melody. Two other terms, *tune* and *theme*, relate to melody as parts to a whole. For example, the *tune* in Figure **3.5** is a melody—that is, a succession of tones. However, a melody is not always a tune. For most people the term tune implies singability, and there are many melodies that cannot be considered singable. A *theme* is also a melody. However, in musical composition it specifically means a central musical idea, which may be restated and varied throughout a piece. Thus a melody is not necessarily a theme.

3.5 "The Star-Spangled Banner" (excerpt).

Related to theme and melody is the *motif*, or *motive*, a short melodic or rhythmic idea around which a composer may design a composition. For example, in Mozart's Symphony No. 40 the allegro movement is developed around a rhythmic motif of three notes:

In listening for how a composer develops melody, theme, and motive we can use two terms to describe what we hear: *conjunct* and *disjunct*. Conjunct melodies comprise notes close together, stepwise, on the musical scale. For example, the interval between the opening notes of the soprano line of J. S. Bach's chorale "Jesu Joy of Man's Desiring" from his Cantata 147 (Fig. **3.6**) is never more than a whole step. Such melodic development is highly conjunct. Disjunct melodies contain intervals of a third or more. However, there is no formula for determining disjunct or conjunct characteristics; there is no line at which a melody ceases to be disjunct and becomes conjunct. These are relative and comparative terms that assist us in description. For example, we would say that the opening melody of "The Star Spangled Banner" (Fig. **3.5**) is more disjunct than the opening melody of "Jesu Joy of Man's Desiring"—or that the latter is more conjunct than the former.

3.6 "Jesu Joy of Man's Desiring" (excerpt).

HARMONY

When two or more tones are sounded at the same time, we have harmony. Harmony is essentially a vertical arrangement, in contrast with the horizontal arrangement of melody.

However, as we shall see, harmony also has a horizontal property—movement forward in time. In listening for harmony we are interested in how simultaneous tones *sound together*.

Two tones played simultaneously are an interval; three or more form a *chord*. When we hear an interval or a chord our first response is to its *consonance* or *dissonance*. Consonant harmonies sound stable in their arrangement. Disonant harmonies are tense and unstable. Consonance and dissonance, however, are not absolute properties. Essentially they are conventional and, to a large extent, cultural. What is dissonant to our ears may not be so to someone else's. What is important in musical response is determining *how* the composer utilizes these two properties. Most Western music is primarily consonant. However, dissonance can be used for contrast, to draw attention to itself, or as a normal part of *harmonic progression*.

As its name implies, harmonic progression involves the movement forward in time of harmonies. In discussing pitch we noted the convention of the major and minor scales—that is, the arrangement of the chromatic scale into a system of *tonality*. When we play or sing a major or minor scale we note a particular phenomenon: Our movement from *do* to *re* to *mi* to *fa* to *sol* to *la* is smooth and seems natural. But when we reach the seventh note of the scale, *ti*, something strange happens. It seems as though we *must* continue back to *do*, the *tonic* of the scale. Try it! Sing a major scale and stop at *ti*. You feel uncomfortable. Your mind tells you that you must *resolve* that discomfort by returning to *do*. That same sense of tonality—that sense of the tonic—applies to harmony. Within any scale a series of chords may be developed on the basis of the individual tones of the scale. Each of the chords has a subtle relationship to each of the other chords and to the tonic—that is, the *do* of the scale. That relationship creates a sense of progression that leads back to the chord based on the tonic.

As I indicated, scales and harmonies are conventions. However, not all conventions are arbitrary. Harmonic progression, which is based on tonality, has a physical root. Physicists call it *sympathetic vibration*. If we take two tightly stretched strings, each of the same length, on a sounding board, we can easily set the second string in motion by plucking the first. Because both strings are the same length, their sound waves are identical and the waves from the plucked string will stir the second, setting it in motion. A little experimentation shows that by dividing the second string into various lengths we can develop a systematic chart of sympathetic vibration. Length A vibrates more easily than B, which vibrates more easily than C, and so on. The relationships we would establish in such an experiment basically govern harmonic progression. Chords based on the notes—that is, the lengths of string—most easily vibrated sympathetically are closer to, and lead to, the tonic. For example, other than the same length of string or its double (the octave), the length of string, or note, most easily vibrated sympathetically is the fifth note (*sol*) of the scale; next is the fourth note, and then the second. If we played chords based on these tones in an order from difficult to easy sympathetic vibration, our progression would move us comfortably to a resolution on the tonic chord. So, harmonic progression is both conventional and physical.

The harmonic movement toward, and either resolving or not resolving to, the tonic is called *cadence*. Three different cadences are shown in Figure **3.7**. The use of cadence is one way of articulating sections of a composition or of surprising us by upsetting our expectations. A composer using a full cadence uses a harmonic progression that resolves just as our ear tells us it should. We

3.8 *(opposite left)* Open (loose) structure.

3.9 *(opposite right)* Closed (tight) structure.

3.7 Full, half, and deceptive cadences.

Full   Half   Deceptive

have a sense of ending, of completeness. However, when a half cadence or a deceptive cadence is used, the expected progression is upset and the musical development moves in an unexpected direction.

As we listen to music of various historical periods we may note that in some compositions tonal centers are blurred because composers frequently *modulate*—that is, change from one key (see Glossary) to another. In the twentieth century many composers, some of them using purely mathematical formulas to utilize equally all tones of the chromatic scale, have removed tonality as an arranging factor and have developed *atonal* music, or music without tonality. A convention of harmonic progression is disturbed when tonality is removed. However, we still have harmonic progression, *and* we still have harmony—dissonant or consonant.

TONALITY

Utilization of pitch and tonality has taken composers in various directions over the centuries. Conventional tonality, employing the major and minor scales and keys previously mentioned, forms the basis for most pre-twentieth-century music, as well as traditionally oriented music of the twentieth century. In addition, we find *serialism* and *twelve-tone technique*, which, since World War II, have reflected a desire to exert more control and to apply a predetermined hierarchy of values to all elements of a composition. In the early twentieth century, traditional tonality was abandoned by some composers and a new *atonal* harmonic expression occurred. Exemplified in Schoenberg's "pantonality" (as he called it), atonal compositions seek the freedom to use any combination of tones without the necessity of having to resolve chordal progressions. Schoenberg referred to this as "the emancipation of dissonance."

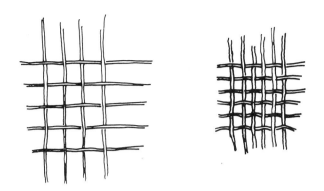

TEXTURE

The aspect of musical relationships known as texture is treated differently by different sources. The term itself has various spatial connotations, and using a spatial term to describe a nonspatial phenomenon creates part of the divergence of treatment. Texture in painting and sculpture denotes surface quality—that is, roughness or smoothness. Texture in weaving denotes the interrelationship of the warp and the woof—that is, the horizontal and vertical threads of fibers. The organization in Figure **3.8** would be described as open or loose texture; that in Figure **3.9**, closed or tight. However, there is really no single musical arrangement that corresponds to either of these spatial concepts. The characteristic called *sonority* by some comes the closest. Sonority describes the relationship of tones played at the same time. A chord with large intervals between its members would have a more open, or thinner, sonority (or texture) than a chord with small intervals between its tones; that chord would have a tight, thick, or close sonority or texture. Sonority is a term that does not have universal application; some sources do not mention it at all.

In a musical context *texture* (again, some sources do not use this term and treat the following characteristics as part of harmony) usually has two, and sometimes three, characteristics: *homophony* and *polyphony* (or *counterpoint*), and sometimes *monophony*. Monophony consists solely of one melodic line. There may be 500 voices singing a melody, but if it is the same melody it is monophonic. In homophonic music one melodic line dominates and the other voices play a subordinate or supporting role. Polyphony is the development of two or more independent melodic lines. Most music is not exclusively monophonic, homophonic, or polyphonic. Much music alternates, especially between homophonic and polyphonic textures.

RHYTHM & BEAT

In all of the arts, rhythm comprises recurring pulses and accents which create identifiable patterns. Without rhythm we have only an aimless rising and falling of tones. Earlier we noted that each tone and silence has duration. Composing music means placing each tone into a time or rhythmical relationship with every other tone. As with the dots and dashes of the Morse code we can "play" the rhythm of a musical composition without reference to its pitches. Each symbol (or note) of the musical-notation system denotes a duration relative to each other symbol in the system. The individual stresses we hear are called *beats*. Beats may be grouped into rhythmic patterns by placing accents every few beats. Rhythm and beat combine to form *meter*.

METER

Normal musical practice is to group clusters of beats into units called *measures*. When these groupings are regular and reasonably equal they comprise *simple* meters. When the number of beats in a measure equals three or two it constitutes *triple* or *duple* meter. In the musical score, measures are indicated by *bar lines*, which are simple vertical dividing lines telling the performer that a measure has just ended or begun. We, as listeners, can distinguish between duple and triple meters because of their different *accent* patterns. In triple meter we hear an accent every third beat—ONE two three, ONE two three—and in duple meter the accent is every other beat—ONE two, ONE two. If there are four beats in a measure (sometimes called quadruple meter), the second accent is weaker than the first—ONE two THREE four, ONE two THREE four.

Not all rhythm in music is regular, and not all meter is simple or consistent. Often it is difficult to hear precisely what is happening because the composer changes metrical patterns (in some cases almost every measure) throughout the piece. Changes in meter are communicated to the performers by *time signatures* noted in the score—for example, $\frac{2}{4}$ (*two* beats to the measure; *quarter note* equals one beat), $\frac{3}{2}$ (*three* beats to the measure; *half note* equals one beat); $\frac{7}{8}$ (*seven* beats to the measure; *eighth note* equals one beat), and so on. However, we, as audience members, can hear those changes only by perceiving the changes in accent patterns which accompany changes in meter. Such changes create variety in the rhythmical structure and add interest, and sometimes *chaos*, to it. Often, a composer will disturb our expectations by accenting normally unaccented beats, i.e. *syncopation*.

TEMPO

The development of meter (rhythm and beat) has an *internal* order of relationships. As we indicated, each beat is assigned a duration relative to other durations, and beats are clustered to form measures and thereby metrical arrangements. However, none of these conventions indicates the amount of *actual* time assigned to each beat. Determining the length of a beat determines the rate of speed, or the *tempo*, of the composition. A composer may notate tempo in two ways. The first is by a *metronome marking*, such as $\quarternote = 60$. This means that the piece is to be played at the rate of sixty quarter notes ($\quarternote$) per minute. Such notation is precise. The other method is less precise and involves more descriptive terminology in Italian:

Largo (broad) Grave (grave, solemn)	Very slow
Lento (slow) Adagio (leisurely)	Slow
Andante (at a walking pace) Adantino (somewhat faster 　than adante) Moderato (moderate)	Moderate
Allegretto (briskly) Allegro (cheerful, faster than 　allegretto)	Fast
Vivace (vivacious) Presto (very quick) Prestissimo (as fast as possible)	Very fast

The tempo may be quickened or slowed, and the composer indicates this by the words, *accelerando* (accelerate) and *ritardando* (retard, slow down). A performer who takes liberties with the tempo is said to use *rubato*.

STRUCTURE

Musical structure, the organization of musical elements and relationships into successive events or sections, is concerned principally with two characteristics, variety and unity. *Variety* creates interest by avoiding monotony, and composers can use variety in every musical characteristic we have discussed in order to hold our attention or pique our interest. However, since music has design, composers must also concern themselves with *coherence*. Notes and rhythms that proceed without purpose or stop arbitrarily make little sense to the listener. Therefore, just as the painter, sculptor, or any other artist must try to develop design that has focus and meaning, the musician must attempt to create a coherent composition of sounds

and silences—that is, a composition that has *unity*. The principal means by which an artist creates unity is repetition. As we noted in the *Introduction*, the 1953 Volkswagen (Fig. **0.8**) achieved unity through strong geometric repetition which varied only in size. Music achieves unity through repetition in a similar fashion. However, since in music we are dealing with time as opposed to space, repetition in music usually involves recognizable themes.

Structure can thus be seen as organization through repetition to create unity. Structure may be divided into two categories: *closed form* and *open form*. These terms are somewhat similar to the same ones as used in sculpture and to composition kept within or allowed to escape the frame in painting. Closed form directs the "musical eye" back into the composition by restating at the end of the thematic section that which formed the beginning of the piece. Open form allows the "eye" to escape the composition by utilizing repetition of thematic material only as a departure point for further development, and by ending without repetition of the opening section. A few of the more common examples of closed and open forms follow.

Closed Forms

Binary form, as the name implies, consists of two parts: the opening section of the composition and a second part which often acts as an answer to the first: AB. Each section is then repeated.

Ternary form is three-part development in which the opening section is repeated after the development of a different second section: ABA.

Ritornello, which developed in the Baroque period, and *rondo*, which developed in the classical period, employ a continuous development which returns to modified versions of the opening theme after separate treatments of additional themes. Ritornello alternates orchestral or *ripieno* passages with solo passages. Rondo alternates a main theme in the tonic key with subordinate themes in contrasting keys.

Sonata form, or *sonata-allegro form*, takes its name from the conventional treatment of the first movement of the sonata. It is also the form of development of the first movement of many symphonies. The pattern of development is ABA or AABA. The first A section is a statement of two or three main and subordinate themes, known as the *exposition*. To cement the perception of section A, the composer may repeat it: AA. The B section, the *development*, takes the original themes and develops them with several fragmentations and modulations. The movement then returns to the A section; this final section is called the *recapitulation*. Usually, the recapitulation section is not an exact repetition of the opening section; in fact, it may be difficult to hear in some pieces. In Mozart's Symphony No. 40 the opening movement (allegro) is in sonata-allegro form. However, the recapitulation section is identified only by a very brief restatement of the first theme, as it was heard in the exposition, not a repetition of the opening section. Then, after a lengthy *bridge*, the second theme from the exposition appears. Mozart closes the movement with a brief *coda*, or closing section, in the original key, based on the first phrase of the first theme.

Open Forms

The *fugue* is a polyphonic development of one, two, or sometimes three short themes. Fugal form, which takes its name from the Latin *fuga* ("flight"), has a traditional, though not a necessary, scheme of development consisting of seven elements, only some of which may be found in any given fugue. However, two characteristics are common to all fugues: (1) counterpoint and (2) a clear dominant-tonic relationship—that is, imitation of the theme at the fifth above or below the tonic. Each voice in a fugue (as many as five or more) develops the basic subject independent from the other voices, and passes through as many of the seven elements as the composer deems necessary. Unification is achieved not by return to an opening section, as in closed form, but by the varying recurrences of the subject throughout.

The *canon* is a contrapuntal form based on note-for-note imitation of one line by another. The lines are separated by a brief time interval—for example (the use of letters here does *not* indicate sectional development):

Voice 1:   a b c d e f g
Voice 2:   a b c d e f g
Voice 3:   a b c d e f g

The interval of separation is not always the same among the voices. The canon is different from the *round*, an example of which, "Row, row, row your boat," we all sang as children. A round is also an exact melodic repeat; however, the canon develops new material indefinitely, while the round repeats the same phrases over and over. The interval of separation in the round stays constant—a phrase apart.

Variation form is a compositional structure in which an initial theme is modified through melodic, rhythmic, and harmonic treatments, each more elaborate than the last. Each section usually ends with a strong cadence.

HOW DOES IT STIMULATE THE SENSES?

It should be obvious by now that when we respond to any work of art we can examine it in a cause-and-effect manner to see how the artist has used any or all of the elements of technical and formal development to stimulate a particular sensation or expressive response in us. In music one might think that all our sense responses must stem from what we hear. If our only exposure to music were the record or tape recording, that would be true. However, there is more to music than sitting in an easy chair and listening to the record player. Much of the excitement of music comes from its live performance. So much of our response can be triggered by what we see as well as by what we hear. We can observe the emotional performance of the musician. What we see does have an effect on our response. If we see no involvement by the performer, we may hear very little as well. This is not always the case, but many critics have noted the phenomenon. We miss much of the response to a work of music if we deprive ourselves of the opportunity of seeing the performance and experiencing the *event* by limiting our exposure to music to tape recordings or records.

How do the composer and the performer work on our senses through their music? The most obvious device for effecting response is the combination of rhythm and meter. We have all at one time or another heard music that caused us involuntarily to tap our toes, drum our fingers, or bounce in our seats in a purely physical response to the strongly accented beat of the music. This involuntary motor response to a "beat" is perhaps the most primitive of our sensual involvements. If the rhythm is regular and the beat strong, our body may respond as a unit. However, if the rhythm is irregular or the beat divided or syncopated, we may find one part of our body doing one thing and another part doing something else. Dynamics also have much to do with our sense response to music: The way that a composer manipulates volume and intensity in a piece can lull us to sleep or cause us to sit bolt upright in astonishment. A familiar example of manipulated dynamics is the second movement of Haydn's Symphony No. 94, in which the composer relaxes his audience with very soft passages and then inserts a sudden fortissimo. The result (and the "name" of the symphony ever since) was *surprise!*

From time to time throughout this chapter we have referred to certain historical conventions that permeate the world of music. Some of these have a potential effect on our sense response. Certain notational patterns, such as *appoggiaturas* (see Glossary), are a kind of musical shorthand, or perhaps mime, that conveys certain kinds of emotion to the listener. They, of course, have little meaning for us *unless we take the time and effort to study* music history. Some of Mozart's string quartets indulge in exactly this kind of communication. This is another illustration of how expanded knowledge can increase the depth and value of the aesthetic experience.

The timbre of a musical composition also works on our senses. A composer's use of timbre is analogous to a painter's use of palette. Only a study of an individual work will tell us how broad or narrow the composer's use of timbre is. However, the size of the musical ensemble has a nearly automatic control of our response. A large symphony orchestra can overwhelm us with diverse timbres and volumes; a string quartet cannot. Our expectations and our focus may change as we perceive the performance of one or the other. Because, for example, we know our perceptual experience with a string quartet will not involve the broad possibilities of an orchestra, we tune ourselves to seek the qualities that challenge the composer and performer within the particular medium. The difference between listening to an orchestra and listening to a quartet is similar to the difference between viewing a museum painting of huge dimension and viewing the exquisite technique of a miniature.

Texture, rhythm, meter, and timbre, in combination, have much to do with sensual response to a musical work. The combinations of these elements that a composer uses to stimulate us in many different ways are infinite. The isolation of the woodwinds, the irregular rhythms, and the melodic development of Debussy's *Prèlude à l'après-midi d'un faune* combine to call up in us images of Pan frolicking through the woodlands and cavorting with the nymphs on a sunny afternoon. Of course, much of what we see has been stimulated by the title of the composition. Our perception is heightened further if we are familiar with the poem by Mallarmé on which the symphonic poem is based. Titles and especially text in musical compositions may be the strongest devices a composer has for communicating directly with us. Images are triggered by words, and a text or title can stimulate our imaginations and senses to wander freely and fully through the musical development. Johannes Brahms called a movement in his *Ein Deutsches Requiem* "All Mortal Flesh is as the Grass;" we certainly receive a philosophical and religious communication from that title. Moreover, when the chorus ceases to sing and the orchestra plays alone, the

instrumental melodies stimulate images of fields of grass blowing in the wind. Our senses are stimulated significantly.

Harmony and tonality are both of considerable importance in stimulating our senses. Just as paintings and sculpture stimulate sensations of rest and comfort or action and discomfort, so harmonies create a feeling of repose and stability if they are consonant and a sensation of restlessness and instability if they are dissonant. Harmonic progression that leads to a full cadential resolution leaves us feeling fulfilled; unresolved cadences are puzzling and perhaps irritating. Major or minor tonalities have significantly differing effects: Major sounds positive; minor, sad or mysterious. The former seems close to home, and the latter, exotic. Atonal music sets us adrift to find the unifying thread of the composition.

Melody, rhythm, and tempo are very similar to the use of line in painting, and the term *melodic contour* could be seen as a musical analogue to this element of painting. When the tones of a melody are conjunct and undulate slowly and smoothly, they trace a pattern having the same sensual effect as their linear visual counterpart — that is, soft, comfortable, and placid.

When melodic contours are disjunct and tempos rapid, the pattern and response change:

In conclusion, it remains for us as we respond to music to analyze how each of the elements available to the composer has in fact become a part of the channel of communication, and how the composer, consciously or unconsciously, has put together a work that elicits sensory responses from us.

OPERA

We have identified opera as one of the formal divisions of music. One might ask, Why devote the time to study this particular kind of music when we do not spend an equal amount of time studying the symphony and the other types of music we have identified? Part of the answer to this question stems from the history of the opera and from its position as a major art form. However, one could say the same of the oratorio or the symphony. Another part of the answer is that opera is more than just one of the formal divisions of music. Some would argue that opera is *drama* set to music, or even a separate discipline that is not drama or music but a third and equal art form. However, a traditional description of opera is that it is not drama set to music but rather a combination of music and drama in which music is not an equal or incidental partner but is the predominant element. It also is clear that the supportive elements of opera production, such as scenery, costumes, and staging, make it (while still a form of music) something apart from its musical brethren.

Traditions of opera are strong, deep, and also, as some would argue, part of the problem that opera has had in gaining popular support in the twentieth century. There have been recent attempts to make opera more like contemporary drama, with greater focus on plot, character development, and so on. Plays such as *Of Mice and Men* have been made into operas to make the form less exag-gerated and implausible. In addition, some individuals find great distress in the traditional inability of opera singers to act and the frequent portrayal of supposedly sexually appealing heroines by obese singers. How much of this is tradition, and how much is irrelevant, and how we as audience members ought to regard it is often a source of irritation for the neophyte and the opera buff alike.

Many devotees of opera regard it as the purest integration of all the arts. It contains music, drama, poetry, and, in the *mise en scène*, visual art. Certainly one could even include architecture, because an opera house is a particular architectural entity, with its own specific requirements for stage space and machinery, orchestra pit, and audience seating space. Because of opera's integration of art forms, much of what we respond to in opera at the formal, technical, and sensual levels is discussed in other chapters of this text. But since opera tends to be the art form most

3.10 Giacomo Puccini, *Manon Lescaut.* Opera Company of Philadelphia. Photo by Trudy Cohen.

3.11 Georges Bizet, *Carmen*. Opera Company of Philadelphia. Composite photo by Trudy Cohen.

3.12 Giuseppi Galli de Bibiena, Scene design for an opera, 1719. Contemporary engraving. The Metropolitan Museum of Art, New York (the Elisha Whittelsey Fund, 1951).

removed from popular awareness, let us examine a few additional characteristics.

Opera is a live art form. Recordings and television presentations make it available to a mass audience but are not substitutes for sitting in the large auditorium that comprises an opera house and witnessing a musical and dramatic spectacle unfold on a stage perhaps 50 ft (15 m) wide and 70 ft (21 m) deep, filled with scenery rising 20 or 30 ft (6 or 9 m) in the air, and peopled by a chorus of perhaps 100 people, all fully costumed and singing over a full orchestra (Figs. **3.10**, **3.11**, and **3.12**). The scope and the spectacle of such an event is *opera*, or at least comprises the circumstances of the bulk of operatic repertoire, which emanates from the romantic tradition. Some operas of earlier and contemporary styles are much more intimate. Nonetheless, listening to the music of opera on the radio or from a record, or watching the miniscule productions brought to us through the medium of television falls short of the experience the live performance affords.

Opera can be divided more or less accurately into four varieties. *Opera* (without a qualifying adjective) is the serious or *tragic opera* that we perhaps think of immediately. This type also has been called *grand opera*, which implies to some an early operatic form consisting usually of five acts. *Opera seria* ("serious opera"), another name for tragic or grand opera, is generally highly stylized and treats heroic subjects, such as gods and heroes of ancient times.

Opéra comique, the second variety of opera, is any opera, *regardless of subject matter*, that has *spoken dialogue*.

The third type, *opera buffa*, is *comic* opera (do not confuse it with *opéra comique*), which usually does *not* have spoken dialogue. Opera buffa usually uses satire to treat a serious topic with humor—for example, Mozart's *Marriage of Figaro*.

The fourth variety, which we will mention again in the next chapter, is *operetta*. Operetta also has spoken dialogue, but it has come to refer to a light style of opera characterized by popular themes, a romantic mood, and often a humorous tone. It is frequently considered more theatrical than musical, and its story line is usually frivolous and sentimental.

Opera does have some unique characteristics. The text of an opera, which is called the *libretto*, is probably the single most important barrier to the appreciation of opera by American audiences. Since the large majority of operas in the contemporary repertoire are not of American origin, the American respondent usually has to overcome the language barrier to understand the dialogue and thereby the plot. It is not a desire for snobbery or exclusivity that causes the lack of English-translation performances; rather, opera loses much of its musical character in translation. We spoke of tone color, or timbre, earlier in this chapter. There are timbre characteristics implicit in the Russian, German, and Italian languages that are lost when they are translated into English. In addition, inasmuch as opera is in a sense the Olympic Games of the vocal-music world—that is, the demands made on the human voice by the composers of opera call for the highest degree of skill and training of any vocal medium—tone placement, and the vowels and consonants requisite to that placement, becomes very important to the singer. It is one thing for a tenor to sing the vowel "eh" on high B-flat in the original Italian. If the translated word to be sung on the same note employs an "oo" vowel, the technical demand is changed considerably. So, the translation of opera from its original tongue into English is a far more difficult and complex problem than simply providing an accurate translation for a portion of the audience that does not know the text—as important as that may seem. Translation must concern itself with tone quality, color, and the execution of tones in the *tessitura* of the human voice.

Experienced opera goers may study the score before attending a performance. However, every concert program contains a plot synopsis (even when the production is in English), so that even the neophyte can follow what is happening. Opera plots, unlike mysteries, have few surprise endings, and knowing the plot ahead of time does not diminish the experience of responding to the opera.

The first element in opera itself is the overture. This orchestral introduction may have two characteristics. First, it may set the mood or tone of the opera. Here the composer works directly with our sense responses, putting us in the proper frame of mind for what is to follow. In his overture to *I Pagliacci*, for example, Ruggiero Leoncavallo creates a tonal story that tells us what we are about to experience. Using only the orchestra, he tells us we will see comedy, tragedy, action, and romance. If we listen to this overture, we will easily identify these elements, and in doing so understand how relatively unimportant the work's being in English is to comprehension. Add to the "musical language" the language of body and mime, and we can understand even complex ideas and character relationships—*without* words. In addition to this type of introduction, an overture may provide melodic introductions—passages introducing the *arias* and *recitatives* that will follow.

The plot is unfolded musically through *recitative*, or sung dialogue. The composer uses recitative to move the plot along from one section to another; recitative has little emotional content to speak of, and the words are more important than the music. There are two kinds of recitative. The first is *recitativo secco*, for which the singer has very little musical accompaniment, or none at all. If there is accompaniment it is usually in the form of light chording under the voice. The second type is *recitativo stromento*, in which the singer is given full musical accompaniment.

The real emotion and poetry of an opera lie in its *arias*. Musically and poetically, an aria is the reflection of high dramatic feeling. The great opera songs with which we are likely to be familiar are arias.

In every opera there are duets, trios, quartets, and other small ensemble pieces. There also are chorus sections in which everyone gets into the act. In addition, ballet or dance interludes are not uncommon. These may have nothing to do with the development of the plot, but are put in to add more life and interest to the dramatic production, and in some cases to provide a *segue* from one scene into another.

Bel canto, as its name implies, is a style of singing emphasizing the beauty of sound. Its most successful composer, Gioacchino Rossini, had a great sense of melody and sought to develop the *art song* to its highest level. In bel canto singing the melody is the focus.

Richard Wagner gave opera and theatre a prototype that continues to influence theatrical production—*organic unity*. Every element of his productions was integral and was shaped so as to help create a work of total unity. Wagner was also famous for the use of *leitmotif*, a common element in contemporary film. A leitmotif is a musical theme associated with a particular person or idea. Each time that person appears or is thought of, or each time the idea surfaces, the leitmotif is played.

Late in the nineteenth century, the *verismo* movement flourished. From the same root as the word verisimilitude, with which we have dealt previously, verismo opera treated themes, characters, and events from life in a down-to-earth fashion. The composer Pietro Mascagni is reported to have said, "In my operas do not look for melody or beauty . . . look only for blood!" Certainly in the works of Mascagni, Leoncavallo, and Puccini there is plenty of blood—as well as fine drama.

Describe the situation

FOUR

THEATRE

The word "theatre" comes from the Greek *theatron*—the area of the Greek theatre building where the audience sat. Its literal meaning is "a place for seeing." The Greeks' choice of this word suggests how they may have perceived the essence of theatre, which is to a large extent a visual experience. In addition to the words of the script, provided by the playwright, and the treatment of those words by the actors, the theatre artwork, the production, also involves visual messages. These include actor movement, costume, setting, lighting, and the physical relationship of the playing space to the audience.

Like the other performing arts, theatre is an interpretive discipline. Between the playwright and the audience stand the director, the designers, and the actors. Although each functions as an individual artist, each also serves to communicate the playwright's vision to the audience. Sometimes the play becomes subordinate to the expressive work of its interpreters, sometimes the concept of director as master artist places the playwright in a subordinate position. None the less, a theatrical production always requires the interpretation of a concept through spectacle and sound by theatre artists.

What Is It?

Theatre represents an attempt to reveal a vision of human life through time, sound, and space. It gives us flesh-and-blood human beings involved in human action—we must occasionally remind ourselves that the dramatic experience is not reality: it is an imitation of reality, acting as a symbol to communicate something about the human condition. Theatre is make-believe: through gesture and movement, language, character, thought, and spectacle, it imitates action. However, if this were all theatre consisted of, we would not find it as captivating as we do, and as we have for more than 2,500 years.

At the formal level, theatre comprises *genre*—or type of play—from which the production evolves. Some of the genres of theatre are *tragedy*, *comedy*, *tragicomedy*, *melodrama*, and *musical comedy*. Some are products of specific periods of history, and illustrate trends that no longer exist; others are still developing and as yet lack definite form. Our response to genre is a bit different from our formal response or identification in music, for example, because we seldom find generic identification in the theatre program. Some plays are well-known examples of a specific genre, for example, the tragedy *Oedipus the King* by Sophocles. In these cases, as with a symphony, we can see how the production develops the conventions of genre. Other plays, however, are not well known or may be open to interpretation. As a result, we can draw our conclusions only after the performance has finished.

TRAGEDY

We commonly describe tragedy as a play with an unhappy ending. The playwright Arthur Miller describes tragedy as "the consequences of a man's total compulsion to evaluate himself justly, his destruction in the attempt posits a wrong or an evil in his environment." In the centuries since its inception, tragedy has undergone many variations as a means by which the playwright makes a statement about human frailty and failing.

Typically, tragic heroes make free choices that bring about suffering, defeat, and, sometimes, triumph as a result of defeat. The protagonist often undergoes a struggle that ends disastrously. In Greek Classical tragedy (see Chapter 11) of the fifth century B.C., the hero generally was a larger-than-life figure who gained a moral victory amid physical defeat. The Classical hero usually suffers from a tragic flaw—some defect that causes the hero to participate in his or her own downfall. In the typical structure of Classical tragedies, the climax of the play occurs as the hero or heroine recognizes his or her rôle, and accepts destiny. In the years from Ancient Greece to the present, however, writers of tragedy have employed many different approaches. Playwright Arthur Miller argues the case for tragic heroes of "common stuff," suggesting that "the tragic right is a condition of life, a condition in which the human personality is able to flower and realize itself."

COMEDY

In many respects, comedy is much more complex than tragedy, and even harder to define. Comedy embraces a wide range of theatrical approaches, ranging from the intellectual and dialogue-centered high comedy of the seventeenth century, to the slapstick, action-centered low comedy found in a variety of plays from nearly every historical period. Low comedy may include *farce*, typically a wildly active and hilarious comedy of situation, usually involving a trivial theme. It is the kind of comedy we associate with actions such as pies in the face, mistaken identities, and pratfalls. Whatever happens in a farce carries little serious consequence. It perhaps provides an opportunity for the viewer to express unconscious and socially unacceptable desires without having to take responsibility for them. Its differences from other varieties of comedy appear to lie in the method of farcical treatment of material, rather than its intent or purpose.

Between the extremes just noted exist a variety of comic forms. One of these is the popular domestic comedy, in which family situations are the focus of attention, and in which members of a family and their neighbors find themselves in various complicated and amusing situations, for example Neil Simon's plays *Brighton Beach Memoirs* and *Broadway Bound*.

Defined in its broadest terms, comedy may not involve laughter. Many employ stinging *satire*, although we probably can say with some accuracy that humor forms the root of all comedy. In many circumstances comedy treats a serious theme, but remains basically lighthearted in spirit: characters may be in jeopardy, but not *too* seriously so. Comedy deals with the world as we find it, focusing on everyday people through an examination of the incongruous aspects of behavior and relationships. The idea that comedy ends happily is probably due to our expectations that in happy endings everyone is left more or less to do what they please. However, happy endings often imply different sets of circumstances in different plays. Comedy appears to defy any such thumbnail definitions.

TRAGICOMEDY

As the name suggests, tragicomedy is a mixed form of theatre, which, like the other types, has been defined in different terms in different periods. Until the nineteenth century, the ending determined the necessary criterion for this form. Traditionally, characters reflect diverse social standings—kings (like tragedy) and common folk (like comedy), and reversals went from bad to good and good to bad. It also included language appropriate to both tragedy and comedy. Tragicomedies were serious plays that ended, if not happily, then at least by avoiding catastrophe. In the last century and a half, the term has been used to describe plays in which the mood may shift from light to heavy, or plays in which endings are neither exclusively tragic or comic.

MELODRAMA

Melodrama is another mixed form. It takes its name from the terms *melo*, Greek for music, and "drama." Melodrama first appeared in the late eighteenth century, when dialogue took place against a musical background. In the nineteenth century, it was applied to describe serious plays without music. Melodrama uses stereotypical characters involved in serious situations in which suspense, pathos, terror, and occasionally hate are all aroused. Melodrama portrays the forces of good and evil battling in exaggerated circumstances. As a rule, the issues involved are either black or white—they are simplified and uncomplicated: Good is good and evil is evil; there are no ambiguities.

Geared largely for a popular audience, the form concerns itself primarily with situation and plot. Conventional in its morality, melodrama tends toward optimism—good always triumphs in the end. Typically, the hero or heroine is placed in life-threatening situations by the acts of an evil villain, and then rescued at the last instant. The forces against which the characters struggle are external ones—caused by an unfriendly world rather than by inner conflicts. Probably because melodrama took root in the nineteenth century, at a time when scenic spectacularism was the vogue, many melodramas depend on sensation scenes for much of their effect. This penchant can be seen in the popular nineteenth-century adaptation of Harriet Beecher Stowe's novel *Uncle Tom's Cabin*, as Eliza and the baby, Little Eva, escape from the plantation and are pursued across a raging, ice-filled river. These effects taxed the technical capacities of contemporary theatres to their maximum, but gave the audience what it desired—spectacle. Not all melodramas use such extreme scenic devices, but such use was so frequent that it has become identified with the type.

MUSICALS

The musical has a variety of applications, beginning with a type of opera called *opéra comique*, which has spoken dialogue. As we think of it today, the form is probably an outgrowth of a musical form called operetta, which also has spoken dialogue but represents a lighter style of opera, characterized by popular themes, a romantic mood, and often a humorous tone (See Chapter 3). It is frequently considered more theatrical than musical. The term "operetta" has slowly evolved into "musical," with a stopover in the middle of the twentieth century in the term "musical comedy."

Musical comedy has been called the United States' unique contribution to the world of theatre. Whether or not this is true, musical comedy, or musical, is a popular form. The musical is characterized by the interspersing of dialogue and vocal solos, choruses, and dances; the ratio of dialogue to music varies greatly from one musical to another. In many musicals, scenic spectacle plays an important role, in some cases replacing the story and the music as a primary focus, for example, *Starlight Express* and *Phantom of the Opera*. The term "musical comedy" has now been replaced by the term "musical" because the form has increasingly treated serious and even tragic stories, as, for example, in *West Side Story*, *A Little Night Music*, and *Cabaret*.

HOW IS IT PUT TOGETHER?

Theatre consists of a complex combination of elements that form a single entity called a performance, or a production. Understanding the theatre production as a work of art can be enhanced if we have some tools for approaching it, which come to us from the distant past.

Writing 2,500 years ago in the *Poetics*, Aristotle argued that tragedy consisted of plot, character, diction, music, thought, and spectacle. We can use and expand upon Aristotle's terminology to describe the basic parts of a production, and to use them as a set of tools for understanding theatrical productions as these six parts—and their descriptive terminology—still cover the entire theatrical product.

In the paragraphs that follow, we will reshape Aristotle's terms into language that is more familiar to us, explain what the terms mean, and learn how we can use them to know how a theatrical production is put together—things to look and listen for in a production. We will examine first the script, and include in that discussion Aristotle's concept of diction, or *language*. Next, we will examine plot, thought—themes and ideas—character, and spectacle, which we will call the visual elements. That will be followed by a brief discussion of what Aristotle called music but which, to avoid confusion, we will call aural elements.

THE SCRIPT

A playwright creates a written document called a script, which contains the dialogue used by the actors. Aristotle called the words written by playwright diction, however, we will refer to this part of a production as its language. The playwright's language tells us at least part of what we can expect from the play. For example, if he has used everyday speech, we generally expect the action to resemble everyday truth, or reality. In the play *Fences*, playwright August Wilson uses everyday language to bring the characters to life in the context of the period, 1957:

(Act I, scene iii. Troy is talking to his son.)

Like you? I go out of here every morning . . . bust my butt . . . putting up with them crackers everyday . . . cause I like you? You about the biggest fool I ever saw.
   (Pause)
   It's my job. It's my responsibility! You understand that? A man got to take care of his family. You live in my house . . . sleep you behind on my bedclothes . . . fill you belly up with my food . . . cause you my son.[1]

Poetic language, on the other hand, usually indicates less realism and perhaps stronger symbolism. Compare the language of *Fences* with the poetry used by Jean Racine, seventeenth-century dramatist, in *Le Cid* to create a mythical hero who is larger than life:

(Act III, scene iv)

Rodrigue: I'll do your bidding, yet still do I desire
To end my wretched life, at your dear hand.
But this you must not ask, that I renounce
My worthy act in cowardly repentance.
The fatal outcome of too swift an anger
Disgraced my father, covered me with shame.[2]

In both plays, we use language and its tone to help determine the implication of the words. Language helps to reveal the overall tone and style of the play. It also can reveal character, theme, and historical context.

PLOT

Plot is the structure of the play, the skeleton that gives the play shape, and on which the other elements hang. The nature of the plot determines how a play works: how it moves from one moment to another, how conflicts are structured, and how ultimately the experience comes to an end. We can examine the workings of plot by seeing the play somewhat as a timeline, beginning as the script or production begins, and ending at the final curtain, or the end of the script. In many plays plot tends to operate like a climactic pyramid (Fig. **4.1**). In order to keep our attention, the dynamics of the play will rise in intensity until they reach the ultimate crisis—the climax—after which they will relax through a resolution called the denouement, to the end of the play.

Depending on the playwright's purpose, plot may be shaped with or without some of the features described below. Sometimes plot may be so de-emphasized that it virtually disappears. However, as we try to evaluate a play critically, the elements of plot give us things to look for—if only to note that they do not exist.

Exposition

Exposition provides necessary background information: through it the playwright introduces the characters, their personalities, relationships, backgrounds, and their present situation. Exposition is frequently a recognizable section at the beginning of a play. It can be presented through dialogue, narration, setting, lighting, costume—or any device the playwright or director chooses. The amount of exposition in a play depends on where the playwright takes up the story, called the point of attack. A play told chronologically may need little expositional material, others require a good bit of prior summary.

4.1 Hypothetical dynamic and structural development of a three-act play.

Complication

Drama is about conflict. Although not every play fits that definition, in order to interest an audience, conflict of some sort is a fundamental dramatic device. At some point in the play, the normally expected course of events is usually frustrated, giving the audience a reason to be interested in what transpires. At a specific moment, an action is taken or a decision is made that upsets the current state of affairs. This is sometimes called the inciting incident and it opens the middle part of the plot—the complication. The complication is the meat of the play, and it comprises a series of conflicts and decisions—called crises (from the Greek word *krisis*, meaning "to decide")—that rise in intensity until they reach a turning point—the climax—that constitutes the end of the complication section.

Denouement

The denouement is the final resolution of the plot. It is the period of time during which the audience is allowed to sense that the action is ending; a period of adjustment, downward in intensity, from the climax. Ideally, the denouement brings about a clear and ordered resolution.

Exposition, complication, and denouement comprise a time-frame in which the remaining parts of the play operate. The neat structural picture of plot that exposition, complication, and denouement, however, describe will not always be so neat. The fact that a play does not conform to this kind of plot structure does not make it a poorly constructed play, or one of inferior quality. Nor does it mean that these concepts cannot be used as a means for describing and analyzing how a play is put together.

Foreshadowing

Preparation for subsequent action—foreshadowing—helps to keep the audience clear about where they are at all times. Foreshadowing provides credibility for future action, keeps action logical, and avoids confusion. It builds tension and suspense: the audience is allowed to sense that something is about to happen, but because we do not know exactly what or when, anticipation builds suspense and tension. In *Jaws* a rhythmic musical theme foreshadows the presence of the shark. Just as the audience becomes comfortable with that device, the shark suddenly appears—without the music. As a result, uncertainty as to the next shark attack are heightened

immensely. Foreshadowing also moves the play forward by pointing toward events that will occur later.

Discovery

Discovery is the revelation of information about characters, their personalities, relationships, and feelings. Hamlet discovers from his father's ghost that his father was murdered by Claudius, and is urged to revenge the killing—a discovery without which the play cannot proceed. The skill of the playwright in structuring the revelation of such information in large part determines the overall impact of the play on the audience.

Reversal

Reversal is any turn of fortune; for example, Oedipus falls from power and prosperity to blindness and exile; King Lear goes from ruler to disaster. In comedy, reversal often changes the roles of social classes, as peasants jump to the upper class, and vice versa.

CHARACTER

Character is the psychological motivation of the persons in the play. In most plays, the audience will focus on why individuals do what they do, how they change, and how they interact with other individuals, as the plot unfolds.

Plays reveal a wide variety of characters—both persons and motivating psychological forces. In every play we will find characters that fulfill major functions and on which the playwright wishes us to focus. We will also find minor characters—those whose actions may interact with the major characters, and whose actions constitute subordinate plot lines. Much of the interest created by the drama lies in the exploration of how persons with specific character motivations react to circumstances. For example, when Rodrigue discovers that his father has been humiliated, what is it in his character that makes him decide to avenge the insult, even though it means killing the father of the woman he loves, thereby jeopardizing that love? Such responses, driven by character, are the choices that drive plays forward.

THE PROTAGONIST

Inside the structural pattern of a play some kind of action must take place. We must ask ourselves: How does this play work? How do we get from the beginning to the end? Most of the time, we take that journey via the actions and decisions of the *protagonist*, or central personage. Deciding the protagonist of a play is not always easy, even for directors. However, it is important to understand whom the play is about if we are to understand it. In Terence Rattigan's *Cause Célèbre* we could have three different responses depending upon whom the director decided was the protagonist. The problem is this: There are two central feminine roles. A good case could be made for either as the central personage of the play. Or they both could be equal. What we understand the play to be about depends on whom the director chooses to focus.

THOUGHT

In order to describe the intellectual content of the play, Aristotle uses "thought," a term that we will use to refer to the themes and ideas that the play communicates. In Lanford Wilson's *Burn This* (1987), for example, a young dancer, Anna, lives in a Manhattan loft with two gay roommates, Larry and Robby. As the play opens, we learn that Robby has been killed in a boating accident; Anna has just returned from the funeral, and a set of bizarre encounters with Robby's family. Larry, a sardonic

advertising executive, and Burton, Anna's boyfriend, maintain a constant animosity. Into the scene bursts Pale, Robby's brother and a threatening, violent figure. Anna is both afraid and irresistibly attracted to Pale; the conflict of their relationship drives the play forward to its climax.

The above brief description summarizes the *plot* of a play. However, what the play is about—its thought—remains for us to discover and develop. Some might say the play is about loneliness, anger, and the way not belonging is manifested in human behavior. Others might focus on abusive relationships, and others would see a thought content dealing with hetero- and homosexual conflicts and issues. The process of coming to conclusions about meaning involves several layers of interpretation. One involves the playwright's interpretation of the ideas through the characters, language, and plot. A second layer of interpretation lies in the director's decisions about what the playwright has in mind, which will be balanced by what the director wishes to communicate, because, or in spite, of the playwright. Finally, it is important that we interpret what we actually see and hear in the production, along with what we may perceive independently from the script.

4.2 Ground plan of an arena theatre.

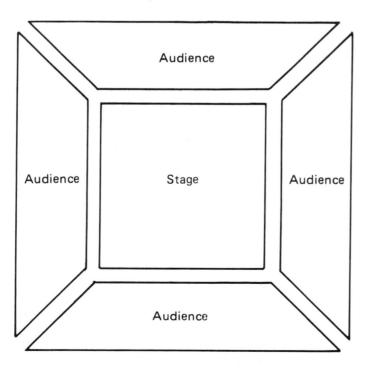

4.3 Ground plan of a thrust theatre.

VISUAL ELEMENTS

The director takes the playwright's language, plot, and characters and translates them into action by using, among other things, what Aristotle called "spectacle," but which we can simply call the visual elements. The visual elements of a production include, first of all, the physical relationship established between actors and audience. The actor/audience relationship can take any number of shapes. For example, the audience might sit surrounding, or perhaps on only one side of, the stage. The visual elements also include stage settings, lighting, costumes, and properties, as well as the actors and their movements. Whatever the audience can see contributes to this part of the theatrical production.

Part of our response to a production is shaped by the design of the space in which the play is produced. The earliest and most natural arrangement is the theatre-in-the-round, or *arena* theatre (Fig. **4.2**), in which the audience surrounds the playing area on all sides. Whether the playing area is circular, square, or rectangular is irrelevant. Some argue that the closeness of the audience to the stage space in an arena theatre provides the most intimate kind of theatrical experience. A second possibility is the *thrust*, or three-quarter, theatre (Fig. **4.3**), in which the audience surrounds the playing area on three sides. The most familiar illustration of this theatre is what we understand to be the theatre of the Shakespearean period. The third actor-audience relationship, and the one most widely used in the twentieth century, is the *proscenium* theatre, in which the audience sits on only one side and views the action through a frame (Fig. **4.4**).

There are also experimental arrangements of audience and stage space. On some occasions acting areas are placed in the middle of the audience, creating little island stages. In certain circumstances, these small stages create quite an interesting set of responses and relationships between actors and audience.

Common experience indicates that the physical relationship of the acting area to the audience has a causal effect on the depth of audience involvement. Experience has also indicated that some separation is necessary for certain kinds of emotional responses. We call this mental and physical separation aesthetic distance. The proper aesthetic distance allows us to become involved in what we know is fictitous and even unbelievable.

The visual elements may or may not have independent communication with the audience; this is one of the options of the director and designers. Before the nineteenth century, there was no coordination of the various elements of a theatre production. This, of course, had all kinds of curious, and in some cases catastrophic, consequences. However, for the last century, most theatre productions have adhered to what is called the organic theory of play production: That is, everything, visual and aural, is designed with a single purpose. Each production has a specific goal in terms of audience response, and all of the elements in the production attempt to achieve this.

4.4 Ground plan of a proscenium theatre.

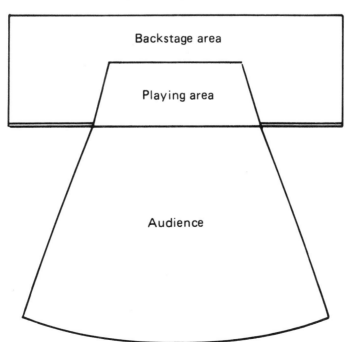

Scene Design

Simply stated, the purpose of scene design in the theatre is to create an environment conducive to the production's ends. The scene designer uses the same tools of composition—line, form, mass, color, repetition, and unity—as the painter. In addition, since a stage design occupies three-dimensional space and must allow for the movement of the actors in, on, through, and around the elements of scenery, the scene designer becomes a sculptor as well. Figures **4.5**, **4.6**, **4.7**, and **4.8** illustrate how emphasis on given elements of design highlight different characteristics in the production. C. Ricketts's design for *The Eumenides* (Fig. **4.5**) stresses formality, asymmetricality, and symbolism. Thomas Grieve's *Richard II* (Fig. **4.6**) is formal, but light and spacious. His regular rhythms and repetition of arches create a completely different feeling from the one elicited by Ricketts's design. William Telbin's *Hamlet* (Fig. **4.7**), with its strong central triangle and monumental scale, creates an overwhelming weight that, while utilizing diagonal activity in the sides of the triangles, cannot match the action of Robert Burroughs's zigzagging diagonals juxtaposed among verticals in his

4.6 (*top*) Shakespeare's *Richard II*, Act II, scene ii. Entrance into St. Stephen's Chapel. Producer: Charles Kean, London, 1857. Courtesy of the Victoria and Albert Museum, London.

4.7 Scene design (probably an alternate design) for Charles Fechter's revival of Shakespeare's *Hamlet*, Lyceum Theatre, London, 1864. Designer: William Telbin. Courtesy of the Victoria and Albert Museum, London.

4.5 Scene design for Aeschylus's *The Eumenides*, c. 1922. Designer: C. Ricketts. Courtesy of the Victoria and Albert Museum, London.

4.8 Scene design for Ibsen's *Peer Gynt*, the University of Arizona Theatre. Director: Peter R. Marroney. Scene designer: Robert C. Burroughs.

design for *Peer Gynt* (Fig. **4.8**). Unlike the painter or sculptor, however, the scene designer is limited by the stage space, the concepts of the director, the amount of time and budget available for the execution of the design, and elements of practicality, for example, can the design withstand the wear and tear of the actors? A scene designer also is limited by the talent and abilities of the staff available to execute the design. A complex setting requiring sophisticated painting and delicate carpentry may be impossible to do if the only staff available are unskilled. These are the constraints, and also the challenges, of scene design.

Lighting Design

Lighting designers are perhaps the most crucial of all the theatre artists in modern productions. Without their art nothing done by the actors, the costume designer, the property master, the director, or the scene designer would be seen by the audience. Yet lighting designers work in an ephemeral medium. They must sculpt with light and create shadows that fall where they desire them to fall; they must "paint" over the colors provided by the other designers. In doing so, they use lighting instruments with imperfect optical qualities. Lighting designers do their work in their minds, unlike scene designers, who can paint a design and then calculate it in feet and inches. Lighting designers must imagine what their light will do to an actor, to a costume, to a set. They must enhance the color of a costume, accent the physique of an actor, and reinforce the plasticity of a setting. They also try to reinforce the dramatic structure and dynamics of the play. They work within the framework of light and shade. Without shadows and highlights, the human face and body become imperceptible: A human face without shadows cannot be seen clearly more than a few feet away. In a theatre, such small movements as the raising of an eyebrow must be seen clearly as much as 100 feet away. It is the lighting designer who makes this possible.

Costume Design

One is tempted to think of the costumes of the theatre merely as clothing that has to be researched to reflect a particular historical period and constructed to fit a particular actor. But costuming goes beyond that. Costume designers work with the entire body of the actor. They design hair styles and clothing and sometimes makeup to suit a specific purpose or occasion, a character, a locale, and so forth (Figs. **4.9** and **4.10**).

The function of stage costuming is threefold. First, it accents—that is, it shows the audience which personages are the most important in a scene, and it shows the relationship between personages. Second, it reflects—a particular era, time of day, climate, season, location, or occasion. The designs in Figure **4.9** reflect a historical period. We recognize different historical periods primarily through silhouette, or outline. Costume designers may merely suggest full detail or may actually provide it, as has been done in Figure **4.9**. We see here the designer's concern not only for period, but also for character in her choice of details, color, texture, jewelry, and also hair style. Notice the length to which the designer goes to indicate detail, providing not only front but also back views of the costume, and also a head study showing the hair without a covering. Third, stage costuming reveals—the style of the performance, the characters of the personages, and the personages' social position, profession, cleanliness, age, physique, and health. In Figure **4.10** the

4.9 Costume designs for Shakespeare's *Twelfth Night*, the Old Globe Theatre, San Diego, California. Director: Craig Noel. Costume designer: Peggy J. Kellner.

KING LEAR
Act IV scene VI

4.10 Costume designs for Shakespeare's *King Lear*, the Old Globe Theatre, San Diego, California. Director: Edward Payson Call. Costume designer: Peggy J. Kellner.

concern of the designer is clearly less with historical period than with production style and character. This costume design reveals the high emotional content of the particular scene, and we see at first glance the deteriorated health and condition of King Lear as he turns mad on the heath. The contrast provided by the king in such a state heightens the effect of the scene, and details such as the bare feet, the winter furs, and the storm-ravaged cape are precise indicators of the pathos we are expected to find and respond to. Costume designers work, as do scene and lighting designers, with the same general elements as painters and sculptors: the elements of composition. A stage costume is an actor's skin: It allows her to move as she must, and occasionally it restricts her from moving as she should not.

Properties

Properties fall into two general groups: set props and hand props. Set properties are part of the scene design: furniture, pictures, rugs, fireplace accessories, and so on. Along with the larger elements of the set, they identify the mood of the play and the character of those who inhabit the world they portray. Hand properties used by the actors in stage business also help to portray characters: cigarettes, papers, glasses, and so forth. The use of properties can be significant to our understanding of a play. For example, if at the opening curtain all properties appear to be neat and in order, but as the play develops the actors disrupt the properties, so that at the end of the play the entire scene is in disarray, that simple transition can help illustrate what may have happened in the play.

AURAL ELEMENTS

What we hear also contributes to the production. Aristotle's term for the aural elements of a production is "music," which meant something quite different from today. The aural elements, whether the actors' voices, the background music, or the clashing of swords, is an important part of the theatrical production. How a production sounds—and looks, and feels, and reads—represents a series of conscious choices on the part of all the artists involved: playwright, director, actors, and designers. Just as a composer of a musical piece creates harmonies, dynamics, rhythms, and melodies, the director, working with the actors and sound designer makes the production develop in an aural sense so that the audience is put into the proper mood, drawn in the proper emotional direction, and captured by the proper attention points.

DYNAMICS

Every production has its own dynamic patterns, which we can chart (for example, as in Figure 4.1). The structural pattern of a play, about which we just spoke, is made clear to us by the dynamic patterns the director establishes. These patterns also help to hold the interest of the audience. Scientific studies indicate that attention or interest is not a constant factor; human beings are able to concentrate on specific items only for very brief periods. Therefore, to hold audience attention over the two-hour span of a production, it is essential to employ devices whereby from time to time interest or attention is allowed to peak and then relax. However, the peaks must be carefully controlled. A production should build to a high point of dramatic interest—the climax. However, each scene or act has its own peak of development—again, to maintain interest. So, the rise from the beginning of the play to the high point of dramatic interest is not a steady rise, but a series of peaks and valleys. Each successive peak is closer to the ultimate one. The director controls where and how high these peaks occur by controlling the dynamics of the actors—volume and intensity, both bodily and vocal. These are the same two qualities that make up dynamics in music.

THE ACTOR

Although it is not always easy to tell which functions in a production are the playwright's, which the director's, and which the actor's, the main channel of communication between the playwright and the audience is the actors. It is through their movements and speech that the audience perceives the play.

Our purpose is not to study acting, however, we can look for two elements in an actor's portrayal of a role that will enhance our response. The first is speech. Language is the playwright's words. Speech is the manner in which the actor delivers those words. Speech, like language, can range from high verisimilitude to high theatricality. If speech adheres to normal conversational rhythms, durations, and inflections, we respond in one way. If it utilizes extended vowel emphasis, long, sliding inflections, and dramatic pauses, we respond quite differently—even though the playwright's words are identical in both cases.

The second element of an actor's portrayal that aids our understanding is the physical reinforcement he or she gives to the character's basic motivation. Most actors try to identify a single basic motivation for their character. That motivation is called a spine, or superobjective. Everything that pertains to the decisions the person makes is kept consistent for the audience because those decisions and actions stem from this basic drive. Actors will translate that drive into something physical they can do throughout the play. For example, Blanche, in Tennessee Williams' *A Streetcar Named Desire*, is driven by the desire to clean what she encounters, because of the way she regards herself and the world around her. Ideally, the actress playing Blanche will disover that element of Blanche's personality as she reads the play and develops the role. To make that spine clear to us in the audience, the actress will translate it into physical action. Therefore, we will see Blanche constantly smoothing her hair, rearranging and straightening her dress, cleaning the furniture, brushing imaginary dust from others' shoulders, and so forth. Nearly every physical move she makes will relate somehow to the act of cleaning. Of course, these movements will be subtle, but if we are attentive, we can find them, thereby understanding the nature of the character we are perceiving.

VERISIMILITUDE

In describing the relationship of the visual elements to the play, we have noted the designers' use of compositional elements. The use of these elements relative to life can be placed on a continuum, one end of which is theatricality and the other, verisimilitude. Items high in verisimilitude are those with which we deal in everyday life: language, movements, furniture, trees, rocks, and so forth. As we progress on our continuum from verisimilitude to theat-

4.11 A proscenium setting for Jean Kerr's *Mary, Mary*, the University of Arizona Theatre. Director: H. Wynn Pearce. Scene and lighting designer: Dennis J. Sporre.

ricality, the elements of the production express less and less relationship to everyday life. They become distorted, exaggerated, and perhaps even nonobjective. Items far removed from verisimilitude are high in theatricality. Poetry, as we noted, is high in theatricality; everyday speech is high in verisimilitude. The position of the various elements of a production on this continuum suggests the style of the play, in the same sense that brushstroke, line, and palette indicate style in painting.

Figures 4.11—4.16 illustrate the range between

4.12 An arena setting for Tennessee Williams's *The Glass Menagerie*, State University of New York at Plattsburgh. Director: H. Charles Kline. Scene and lighting designer: Dennis J. Sporre.

4.13 A proscenium setting for Oscar Wilde's *The Importance of Being Earnest*, the University of Arizona Theatre. Director: William Lang. Costume designer: Helen Workman Currie. Scene and lighting designer: Dennis J. Sporre.

verisimilitude and theatricality. Figure **4.11** is a proscenium setting high in verisimilitude—including a full ceiling over the setting. Figure **4.12** is an arena setting high in verisimilitude; it reflects the basically lifelike overall style of the presentation. However, the requirement of the arena configuration that there be no walls can cause problems in some productions. Note that some theat-

ricality—specifically, the empty picture frame—is present in the decoration of this set. This is not an inconsistency since the play develops as a flashback in the mind of its main personage. In Figure **4.13** the designer has attempted to heighten the theatrical nature of the production by using set props high in verisimilitude and a setting that is representational, but pushed toward theatricality

4.14 Scene design for Jerry Devine and Bruce Montgomery's *The Amorous Flea*, the University of Iowa Theatre. Director: David Knauf. Scene and lighting designer: Dennis J. Sporre.

4.15 A proscenium setting for Stephen Sondheim's *Company* (musical), the University of Arizona Theatre. Director: Peter R. Marroney. Scene and lighting designer: Dennis J. Sporre.

4.16 Scene design for Euripides's *The Bacchae*, University of Illinois at Chicago Circle. Director: William Raffeld. Scene and lighting designer: Dennis J. Sporre.

by the use of open space where one might expect solid walls in this proscenium production. The setting in Figure **4.14** moves further toward theatricality, and indicates clearly through exaggerated detail and two-dimensionality the whimsical and fun nature of the production. The design in Figure **4.15** creates a purely formal and theatrical environment. No locale is specifically depicted, but the use of representational detail (various areas of the set served as locations and had realistic furniture) keeps the setting tied to the overall approach of the actors. Finally, in Figure **4.16**, neither time nor place is indicated nor remotely suggested. Here the emphasis is on reinforcement of the high action of the production. The steep ramps throughout the set make it impossible for the actors to walk from one level to the next; the setting forces them to run.

In most arts the artist's style is unique—a recognizable mark on his or her artwork. Some artists change their style, but they do so by their own choice. Interpretive artists such as costume, scene, and lighting designers, and to a degree conductors as well, must submerge their personal style to that of the work with which they are involved. The playwright or the director sets the style, and the scene designer adapts to it and makes his or her design reflect that style.

HOW DOES IT STIMULATE THE SENSES?

In each of the elements we have just discussed, our senses are stimulated in a particular manner. We respond to the play's structure and how it works; we respond to dynamics. We are stimulated by the theatricality or verisimilitude of the language of the playwright and the movements and speech of the actors. We find our response shaped by the relationship of the stage space to the audience, and by the sets, lights, properties, and costumes. All of these elements bombard us simultaneously with complex visual and aural stimuli. How we respond, and how much we are able to respond, will determine our ultimate reaction to a production.

The theatre is unique in its ability to stimulate our senses, because only in the theatre is there a direct appeal to our emotions through the live portrayal of other individuals involved directly in the human condition. Being in the presence of live actors gives us more of life in two hours than we could experience outside the theatre in that same time span. That phenomenon is difficult to equal. The term we use to describe our reaction to and involvement with what we experience in a theatrical production is *empathy*. Empathy causes us to cry when individuals whom we know are only actors become involved in tragic or emotional situations. Empathy makes us wince when an actor slaps the face of another actor, or when two football players collide at full speed. Empathy is our mental and physical involvement in situations in which we are not direct participants.

Now let us examine a few of the more obvious ways a production can appeal to our senses. In plays that deal in conventions, the language may act as virtually the entire stimulant of our senses. Through the language the playwright sets the time, the place, the atmosphere, and even the small details of decoration. We become our own

scene, lighting, and even costume designer, imagining what the playwright tells us ought to be there. In the opening scene of *Hamlet* we find Bernardo and Francisco, two guards. The hour is midnight; it is bitter cold; a ghost appears, in "warlike form." How do we know all of this? In a modern production we might see it all through the work of the costume and set designers. But this need not be the case, because the playwright gives us all of this information in the dialogue. Shakespeare wrote for a theatre that had no lighting save for the sun. His theatre (such as we know of it) probably used no scenery. The costumes were the street clothes of the day. The theatrical environment was the same whether the company was playing *Hamlet*, *Richard III*, or *The Tempest*. So what needed to be seen needed to be imagined. The language provided the stimuli for the audience.

We also respond to what we see. A sword fight performed with flashing action, swift movements, and great intensity sets us on the edge of our chair. Although we know the action is staged and the incident fictitious, we are caught in the excitement of the moment. We also can be gripped and manipulated by events of a quite different dynamic quality. In many plays we witness character assassination, as one life after another is laid bare before us. The intense but subtle movements of the actors—both bodily and vocal—can pull us here and push us there emotionally, and perhaps cause us to leave the theatre feeling emotionally drained. Part of our response is caused by subject matter, part by language—but much of it is the result of careful manipulation of dynamics.

Mood is an important factor in communication. Before the curtain is up, our senses are tickled by stimuli designed to put us in the mood for what follows. The houselights in the theatre may be very low, or we may see a cool or warm light on the front curtain. Music fills the theatre. We may recognize the raucous tones of a 1930s jazz piece, or a melancholy ballad. Whatever the stimuli, they are all carefully designed to cause us to begin to react the way the director wishes us to react. Once the curtain is up, the assault on our senses continues. The palette utilized by the scene, lighting, and costume designers helps communicate the mood of the play and other messages about it. The rhythm and variation in the visual elements capture our interest and reinforce the rhythmic structure of the play. In Figure **4.8**, the use of line and form as well as color provides a formal and infinite atmosphere reflecting the epic grandeur of Ibsen's *Peer Gynt*.

The degree of plasticity or three-dimensionality created by the lighting designer's illumination of the actors and the set causes us to respond in many ways. If the lighting designer has placed the primary lighting instruments directly in front of the stage, plasticity will be diminished and the actors will appear washed out or two-dimensional. We respond quite differently to that visual stimulant than to the maximum plasticity and shadow resulting from lighting coming nearly from the side.

We also react to the mass of a setting. Scenery that towers over the actors and appears massive in weight is different in effect from scenery that seems minuscule in comparison with the human form. The settings in Figures 4.5, 4.6, 4.7, and 4.13 are different from one another in scale, and each places the actors in a different relationship with their surroundings. In Figure 4.13, the personages are at the center of their environment; in Figure 4.7 they are clearly subservient to it.

Finally, focus and line act on our senses. Careful composition can create movement, outlines and shadows that are crisp and sharp. Or it can create images that are soft, fuzzy, or blurred. Each of these devices is a stimulant; each has the potential to elicit a relatively predictable response. Perhaps in no other art are such devices so available and full of potential for the artist. We, as respondents, benefit through nearly total involvement in the life situation that comes to us over the footlights.

FIVE

FILM*

It is only within the last two decades that film has become accepted as a legitimate form of art and that serious and responsible critics and scholars have begun to examine the component parts of films and how they interact with the general form of the film to create both form and style. Of the forms of art considered in this volume, the film is the most familiar and the most easily accessible; it is usually accepted almost without conscious thought, at least in terms of the story line or the star image presented or the basic entertainment value of the product. Yet all these elements are carefully crafted out of editing techniques, camera usage, juxtaposition of image, and structural rhythms—among others. It is these details of cinematic construction that can enhance the viewing of a film and can raise the film from mere entertainment into the realm of serious art. Bernard Shaw once observed that "details are important; they make comments." The perception of the details of the film is not as easy as it might seem, since at the same time serious students are searching them out the entertainment elements of the film are drawing their attention away from the search. Because of these entertainment elements and the inundation of our society with film, the serious perception of the art of the film is not an easy one, but time and a conscious effort can reward the student with insights that are not those of the casual film viewer.

WHAT IS IT?

Film is aesthetic communication through the design of time and of three-dimensional space compressed into a two-dimensional image. Of all the arts discussed in this volume, film is the only one that also is an invention. Once the principles of photography had evolved and the mechanics of recording and projecting cinematic images were understood, society was ready for the production of pictures that could move, be presented in color, and eventually talk.

If you examine a strip of film, you will notice that it is only a series of pictures arranged in order the length of the strip. Each of these pictures, or *frames*, is about 4/5 in (22 mm) wide and 3/5 in (16 mm) high. If you study the frames in relation to one another, you will see that even though each frame may seem to show exactly the same scene, the position of the objects in the separate frames is slightly different. When this film, which contains sixteen frames per foot (30 cm) of film, is run on a projecting device and passed before a light source at the rate of

*The text for this chapter was prepared by M. Ellis Grove. I have edited and expanded where necessary to conform to the rest of the text.

105

twenty-four frames per second (sixteen to eighteen frames per second for silent films), the frames printed on it are enlarged through the use of a magnifying lens, are projected on a screen, and appear to show movement. However, the motion picture, as film is popularly called, does not really move but only seems to. This is due to an optical phenomenon called *persistence of vision*, which according to legend was discovered by the astronomer Ptolemy sometime around the second century A.D. The theory behind persistence of vision is that the eyes take a fraction of a second to record an impression of an image and send it to the brain. Once the impression is received, the eye retains it on the retina for about one-tenth of a second after the actual image has disappeared. The film projector has built into it a device that pulls the film between the light source and a lens in a stop-and-go fashion, the film pausing long enough at each frame to let the eye take in the picture. Then a shutter on the projector closes, the retina retains the image, and the projection mechanism pulls the film ahead to the next frame. Holes, or *perforations*, along the right-hand side of the filmstrip enable the teeth on the gear of the driving mechanism to grasp the film and not only move it along frame by frame but also hold it steady in the gate or slot between the light source and the magnifying lens. It is this stop-and-go motion that gives the impression of continuous movement; if the film did not pause at each frame, the eye would receive only a blurred image.

The motion picture was originally invented as a device for recording and depicting motion. But once this goal was realized, it was quickly discovered that this machine could also record and present stories—in particular, stories that made use of the unique qualities of the medium of film.

Our formal response to film recognizes three basic techniques of presentation. These are narrative film, documentary film, and absolute film.

NARRATIVE FILM

The narrative film is one that tells a story; in many ways it uses the technique of theatre. The narrative film follows the rules of literary construction in that it begins with expository material, adds levels of complications, builds to a climax, and ends with a resolution of all the plot elements. As in theatre, the personages in the story are portrayed by professional actors under the guidance of a director; the action of the plot takes place within a *mise en scène* that is designed and constructed primarily for the action of the story but that also allows the camera to move

freely in photographing the action. Many narrative films are genre films, constructed out of familiar literary styles—the western, the detective story, and the horror story, among others. In these films the story elements are so familiar to the audience that it usually knows the outcome of the plot before it begins. The final showdown between the "good guy" and the "bad guy," the destruction of a city by an unstoppable monster, and the identification of the murderer by the detective are all familiar plot elements that have become clichés or stereotypes within the genre; their use fulfills audience expectations. Film versions of popular novels and stories written especially for the screen are also part of the narrative-film form, but since film is a major part of the mass-entertainment industry the narrative presented is usually material that will attract a large audience and thus assure a profit.

DOCUMENTARY FILM

Documentary film is an attempt to record actuality using primarily either a sociological or a journalistic approach. It is normally not reenacted by professional actors and often is shot as the event is occurring, at the time and place of its occurrence. The film may use a narrative structure, and some of the events may be ordered or compressed for dramatic reasons, but its presentation gives the illusion of reality. The footage shown on the evening television news, programming concerned with current events or problems, and full coverage either by television or film companies of a worldwide event, such as the Olympics, are all kinds of documentary film. All convey a sense of reality as well as a recording of time and place.

ABSOLUTE FILM

Absolute film is to narrative film as absolute music is to program music (see Glossary). It is simply film that exists for its own sake, for its record of movement or form. It does not use narrative techniques—although documentary techniques can be used in some instances. Created neither in the camera nor on location, absolute film is built carefully, piece by piece, on the editing table or through special effects and multiple-printing techniques. It tells no story but exists solely as movement or form. Absolute film is rarely longer than twelve minutes (one reel) in length, and it usually is not created for commercial intent but is meant only as an artistic experience. Narrative or documentary films may contain sections that can be labeled absolute, and these sections can be studied either in or out of the context of the whole film.

HOW IS IT PUT TOGETHER?

MAGNITUDE & CONVENTION

In addition to considering whether a film is narrative, documentary, or absolute, the student of film must also realize both the magnitude of the film and the film's use of certain conventions. In considering the magnitude of a film, one must be aware of the means by which the film is to be communicated. In other words, was the film made for a television showing or for projection in a large film theatre? Due to the size of the television receiver, large panoramas or full-scale action sequences are not entirely effective on the TV—they become too condensed. TV films, to be truly effective, should be built around the close-up and around concentrated action and movement, since the TV audience is closer to the image than are the viewers in a large theatre. Scenes of multiple images with complex patterns of movement or scenes of great violence will become confusing because of the intimacy of television, and will seem more explicit than they really are. On the other hand, when close shots of intimate details are enlarged through projection in a theatre they may appear ridiculous. The nuance of a slightly raised eyebrow that is so effective in the living room will appear either silly or overly dramatic when magnified on a 60 ft (18 m) screen. Today's filmmakers, when creating a film, must be aware of how it will appear if translated to the home screen or enlarged in a theatre; their work ought to be designed to accommodate the size of either medium.

The film, as with theatre, has certain conventions or customs that the viewer accepts without hesitation. When an exciting chase scene takes place, no one asks where the orchestra is that is playing the music that enhances the sequence; they merely accept the background music as part of the totality of the film. A film photographed in black and white is accepted as a recording of reality, even though the viewers know that the real world has color while this particular reel world does not. When a performer sings and dances in the rain in the middle of a city street, no member of the audience worries if the orchestra is getting wet or wonders if the performer will be arrested for creating a public spectacle. The conventions of the musical film are equally acceptable to an audience conditioned to accept them.

This consideration of conventions is especially important to the acceptance of the silent film as a form of art. The silent film should not be thought of as a sound film without sound but as a separate entity with its own special conventions. These conventions revolve around the methods used to indicate sound and dialogue without actually using them. The exaggerated pantomime and acting styles, the use of titles, character stereotyping, and visual metaphors are all conventions that were accepted during the silent era but appear ludicrous today, because of changes in style and taste and improvements in the devices used for recording and projecting film. The action in the silent film was recorded and presented at a speed of sixteen to eighteen frames per second; when that action is presented today on a projector that operates at twenty-four frames per second, the movement becomes too fast and appears to be jerky and disconnected. However, once you learn to accept these antiquated conventions, you may find that the silent film is an equally effective form of cinematic art.

EDITING

Film is rarely recorded in the order of its final presentation; it is filmed in bits and pieces and put together, after all the photography is finished, as one puts together a jigsaw puzzle or builds a house. The force or strength of the final product depends upon the editing process used, the manner in which the camera and the lighting are handled, and the movement of the actors before the camera. Naturally, the success of a film depends equally on the strength of the story presented and the ability of the writers, actors, directors, and technicians who have worked on the film. However, this level of success is based on the personal taste of the audience and the depth of perception of the individual, and therefore does not lie within the boundaries of this discussion.

Perhaps the greatest difference between film and the other arts discussed within this volume is the use of *plasticity*, the quality of film that enables it to be cut, spliced, and ordered according to the needs of the film and the desires of the filmmaker. If twenty people were presented with all the footage shot of a presidential inauguration and asked to make a film commemorating the event, you would probably see twenty completely different films; each filmmaker would order the event according to his or her own views and artistic ideas. The filmmaker must be able to synthesize a product out of many diverse elements. This concept of plasticity is, then, one of the major advantages of the use of the machine in consort with an art form.

It is the editing process, then, that creates or builds the

film, and within that process are many ways of meaningfully joining shots and scenes to make a whole. Let's examine some of these basic techniques. The *cut* is simply the joining together of shots during the editing process. A *jump cut* is a cut that breaks the continuity of time by jumping forward from one part of the action to another part that obviously is separated from the first by an interval of time, location, or camera position. It is often used for shock effect or to call attention to a detail, as in commercial advertising on television. The *form cut* cuts from an image in a shot to a different object that has a similar shape or contour; it is used primarily to make a smoother transition from one shot to another. For example, in D. W. Griffith's silent film *Intolerance*, attackers are using a battering ram to smash in the gates of Babylon. The camera shows the circular frontal area of the ram as it is advanced towards the gate. The scene cuts to a view of a circular shield, which in the framing of the shot is placed in exactly the same position as the front view of the ram.

Montage can be considered the most aesthetic use of the cut in film. It is handled in two basic ways: first, as an indication of compression or elongation of time, and, second, as a rapid succession of images to illustrate an association of ideas. A series of stills from Leger's *Ballet mécanique* (Fig. **5.1**) illustrates how images are juxtaposed to create comparisons. For example, a couple goes out to spend an evening on the town, dining, and dancing. The film then presents a rapid series of cuts of the pair—in a restaurant, then dancing, then driving to another spot, then drinking, and then more dancing. In this way the audience sees the couple's activities in an abridged manner. Elongation of time can be achieved in the same way. The second use of montage allows the filmmaker to depict complex ideas or draw a metaphor visually. Sergei Eisenstein, the Russian film director, presented a shot in one of his early films of a Russian army officer walking out of the room, his back to the camera and his hands crossed behind him. Eisenstein cuts immediately to a peacock strutting away from the camera and spreading its tail. These two images are juxtaposed, and the audience is allowed to make the association that the officer is as proud as a peacock.

CAMERA VIEWPOINT

Camera position and viewpoint are as important to the structure of film as is the editing process. How the camera is placed and moved can be of great value to filmmakers as an aid in explaining and elaborating upon their cinematic ideas. In the earliest days of the silent film the camera was

5.1 *Ballet mécanique*, 1924. A film by Fernand Léger.

merely set up in one basic position; the actors moved before it as if they were performing before an audience on a stage in a theatre. However, watching an action from one position became dull, and the early filmmakers were forced to move the camera in order to add variety.

The Shot

The *shot* is what is recorded by the camera over a particular period of time and is the basic unit of filmmaking. Several varieties are used. The *master shot* is a single shot of an entire piece of action, taken to facilitate the assembly of the component shots of which the scene will finally be composed. The *establishing shot* is a long shot introduced at the beginning of a scene to establish the interrelationship of details, a time, or a place, which will be elaborated upon in subsequent shots. The *long shot* is a shot taken with the camera a considerable distance from the subject. The *medium shot* is taken nearer to the subject. The *close-up* is a shot taken with the camera quite near the subject. A *two-shot* is a close-up of two persons with the camera as near as possible while keeping both subjects within the frame. A *bridging shot* is a shot inserted in the editing of a scene to cover a brief break in the continuity of the scene.

Objectivity

An equally important variable of camera viewpoint is whether the scene is shot from an objective or subjective viewpoint. The *objective viewpoint* is that of an omnipotent viewer, roughly analogous to the technique of third-person narrative in literature. In this way filmmakers allow their audience to watch the action through the eyes of a universal spectator. However, filmmakers who wish to involve their audience more deeply in a scene may use the *subjective viewpoint*: The scene is presented as if the audience were actually participating in it, and the action is viewed from the filmmaker's perspective. This is analogous to the first-person narrative technique, and is usually found in the films of the more talented directors.

CUTTING WITHIN THE FRAME

Cutting within the frame is a method used to avoid the editing process. It can be created by actor movement, camera movement, or a combination of the two. It allows the scene to progress more smoothly and is used most often on television. In a scene in John Ford's *Stagecoach*, the coach and its passengers have just passed through hostile territory without being attacked; the driver and his passengers all express relief. Ford cuts to a long shot of the coach moving across the desert and *pans*, or follows, it as it moves from right to left on the screen. This movement of the camera suddenly reveals in the foreground, and in close-up, the face of a hostile person watching the passage of the coach. In other words, the filmmaker has moved from a long shot to a close-up without needing the editing process. He has also established a spatial relationship. The movement of the camera and the film is smooth and does not need a cut to complete the sequence. In a scene from *Jaws* (Fig. **5.2**) the camera moves from the distant objects to the face in the foreground, finally including them both in the frame; the pan across the scene in so doing is accomplished without editing of the film.

DISSOLVES

During the printing of the film negative transitional devices can be worked into a scene. They are usually used to indicate the end of the scene and the beginning of another. The camera can cut or jump to the next scene, but the transition can be smoother if the scene fades out into black and the next scene fades in. This is called a *dissolve*. A *lap dissolve* occurs when the fade-out and the fade-in are done simultaneously and the scene momentarily overlaps. A *wipe* is a form of optical transition in which a line moves across the screen, eliminating one shot and revealing the next, much in the way a windshield wiper moves across the windshield of a car. In silent film the transition could also be created by closing or opening the aperture of the lens; this process is called an *iris-out* or an *iris-in*.

MOVEMENT

Camera movement also plays a part in film construction. The movement of the camera as well as its position can add variety or impact to a shot or a scene. Even the manner in which the lens is focused can add to the meaning of the scene. If the lens clearly shows both near and distant objects at the same time, the camera is using *depth of focus*. In Figure **5.2** foreground and background are equally in focus. In this way actors can move in the scene without necessitating a change of camera position. Many TV shows photographed before an audience usually use this kind of focus. If the main object of interest is photographed clearly while the remainder of the scene is blurred or out of focus, the camera is using *rack* or *differential focus*. With this technique the filmmaker can focus the audience's attention on one element within a shot.

5.2 *Jaws*, 1975. Universal Pictures. Director: Steven Spielberg. Copyright © by Universal Pictures, a Division of Universal City Studios, Inc. All Rights Reserved.

5.3 *The Birth of a Nation*, 1915. Director: D.W. Griffith.

There are many kinds of physical (as opposed to apparent) camera movement that can have a bearing upon a scene. The *track* is a shot taken as the camera is moving in the same direction, at the same speed, and in the same place as the object being photographed. A *pan* is taken by rotating the camera horizontally while keeping it fixed vertically. The pan is usually used in enclosed areas, particularly TV studios. The *tilt* is a shot taken while moving the camera vertically or diagonally; it is used to add variety to a sequence. A *dolly shot* is taken by moving the camera toward or away from the subject. Modern sophisticated lenses can accomplish the same movement by changing the focal length. This negates the need for camera movement and is known as a *zoom shot*.

Of course, the camera cannot photograph a scene without light, either natural or artificial. Most television productions photographed before a live audience require a flat, general illumination pattern. For close-ups, stronger and more definitely focused lights are required to highlight the features, eliminate shadows, and add a feeling of depth to the shot. Cast shadows or atmospheric lighting (in art, *chiaroscuro*) is often used to create a mood, particularly in films made without the use of color (Fig. 5.3). Lighting at a particular angle can heighten the feeling of texture, just as an extremely close shot can. These techniques add more visual variety to a sequence.

If natural or outdoor lighting is used and the camera is hand-held, an unsteadiness in movement is found in the resulting film; this technique and effect is called *cinéma verité*. This kind of camera work, along with natural lighting, is found more often in documentary films or in sequences photographed for newsreels or television news programming. It is one of the conventions of current-events reporting and adds to the sense of reality necessary for this kind of film recording.

These techniques and many others are all used by filmmakers to ease some of the technical problems in making a film. They can be used to make the film smoother or more static, depending upon the needs of the story line, or to add an element of commentary to the film. One school of cinematic thought believes that camera technique is best when it is not noticeable; another, more recent way of thinking believes that the obviousness of all the technical aspects of film adds meaning to the concept of cinema. In any case, camera technique is present in every kind of film made and is used to add variety and commentary, meaning and method, to the shot, the scene, and the film.

HOW DOES IT STIMULATE THE SENSES?

The basic aim of film, as with any art, is to involve the audience in its product, either emotionally or intellectually. Of course, there is nothing like a good plot with well-written dialogue delivered by trained actors to create audience interest. But there are other ways in which filmmakers may enhance their final product, techniques that manipulate the audience toward a deeper involvement or a heightened intellectual response. Figure 5.4 illustrates how angles and shadows within a frame help create a feeling of excitement and variety. An in-depth study of the films of Fellini, Hitchcock, or Bergman may indicate how directors can use some of the technical aspects of film to underline emotions or strengthen a mood or an idea.

5.4 Still from an unidentified silent film.

It is in the area of technical detail that perception is most important for students of film. They should begin to cultivate the habit of noticing even the tiniest details in a scene, for often these details may add a commentary that the average member of an audience may miss. For example, in Hitchcock's *Psycho*, when the caretaker of the motel (Tony Perkins) wishes to spy upon the guests in cabin 1, he pushes aside a picture that hides a peephole. The picture is a reproduction of *The Rape of the Sabine Women*. Hitchcock's irony is obvious. Thus, perception becomes the method through which viewers of film may find its deeper meanings as well as its basic styles.

CROSSCUTTING

There are many techniques that filmmakers can use to heighten the feeling they desire their film to convey. The most familiar and most easily identified is that of crosscutting. This is an alternation between two separate actions that are related by theme, mood, or plot but are usually occurring within the same period of time. Its most common function is to create suspense. Consider this familiar cliché. Pioneers going west in a wagon train are besieged by Indians. The settlers have been able to hold them off, but ammunition is running low. The hero has been able to find a cavalry troop, and they are riding to the rescue. The film alternates between views of the pioneers fighting for their lives and shots of the soldiers galloping to the rescue. The film continues to cut back and forth, the pace of cutting increasing until the sequence builds to a climax— the cavalry arriving in time to save the wagon train. The famous chase scene in *The French Connection*, the final sequences in *Wait Until Dark*, and the sequences of the girl entering the fruit cellar in *Psycho* are built for suspense through techniques of crosscutting.

In fact, the crosscut is so effective in creating rhythm and tension in film that we can find it everywhere. This device gives the film its unique ability to create for the audience a perfectly believable representation of multiple actions occuring within the exact same timeframe.

A more subtle case of crosscutting, *parallel development* occurs in *The Godfather, Part I*. At the close of that film Michael Corleone is acting as godfather for his sister's son; at the same time his men are destroying all his enemies. The film alternates between views of Michael at the religious service and sequences showing violent death. This parallel construction is used to draw an ironic comparison; actions are juxtaposed. By developing the two separate actions, the filmmaker allowed the audience to draw their own inferences and added meaning.

TENSION BUILD-UP AND RELEASE

If the plot of a film is believable, the actors competent, and the director and film editor talented and knowledgeable, a feeling of tension will be built up. If this tension becomes too great, the audience will seek some sort of release, and an odd-sounding laugh, a sudden noise, or a loud comment from a member of the audience may cause the rest of the viewers to laugh, thus breaking the tension and in a sense destroying the atmosphere so carefully created. Wise filmmakers therefore build into their film a *tension release* that deliberately draws laughter from the audience, but at a place in the film where they wish them to laugh. This tension release can be a comical way of moving, a gurgle as a car sinks into a swamp, or merely a comic line. It does not have to be too obvious, but it should be present in some manner. After a suspenseful sequence the audience needs to be relaxed; once the tension release does its job, the audience can be drawn into another suspenseful or exciting situation.

Sometimes, to shock the audience or maintain their attention, a filmmaker may break a deliberately created pattern or a convention of film. In *Jaws*, for example, each time the shark is about to appear, a four-note musical *motif* is played. The audience thereby grows to believe that it will hear this warning before each appearance, and so it relaxes. However, toward the end of the film the shark suddenly appears without benefit of the motif, shocking the audience. From that point until the end of the film it can no longer relax, and its full attention is directed to it.

DIRECT ADDRESS

Another method used to draw attention is that of *direct address*. It is a convention in most films that the actors rarely look at or talk directly to the audience. However, in *Tom Jones*, while Tom and his landlady are arguing over money, Tom suddenly turns directly to the audience and says, "You saw her take the money." The audience's attention is focused on the screen more strongly than ever after that. This technique has been effectively adapted by television for use in commercial messages. For example, a congenial man looks at the camera (and you) with evident interest and asks if you are feeling tired, rundown, and sluggish. He assumes you are and proceeds to suggest a remedy. In a sense, the aside of nineteenth-century melodrama and the soliloquy of Shakespeare were also ways of directly addressing an audience and drawing them into the performance.

112

5.5 *Your Darn Tootin'*, 1928. A Hal Roach Production for Pathé Films. Director: Edgar Kennedy.

Of course, silent films could not use this type of direct address to the audience; they had only the device of titles. However, some of the silent comedians felt that they should have direct contact with their audience, and so they developed a *camera look* as a form of direct address. After an especially destructive moment in his films, Buster Keaton would look directly at the camera, his face immobile, and stare at the audience. When Charlie Chaplin achieved an adroit escape from catastrophe he might turn toward the camera and wink. Stan Laurel would look at the camera and gesture helplessly (Fig. 5.5), as if to say, "How did all this happen?" Oliver Hardy, after falling into an open manhole, would register disgust directly to the camera and the audience. These were all ways of commenting to the audience and letting them know that the comedians knew they were there. Some sound comedies adapted this technique. In the "road" pictures of Bob Hope and Bing Crosby both stars, as well as camels, bears, fish, and anyone else who happened to be around, would comment on the film or the action directly to the audience. However, this style may have been equally based on the audience's familiarity with radio programs, in which the performer usually spoke directly to the home audience.

STRUCTURAL RHYTHM

Much of the effectiveness of a film relies on its success as a form as well as a style. By that I mean that filmmakers create rhythms and patterns that are based on the way they choose to tell their stories or that indicate deeper meanings and relationships. The *structural rhythm* of a film is the manner in which the various shots are joined together and juxtaposed with other cinematic images, both visual and aural.

Symbolic images in film range from the very obvious to the extremely subtle, but they are all useful to filmmakers in directing the attention of the audience to the ideas inherent in the philosophical approach underlying the film. This use of symbolic elements can be found in such clichés as the hero dressed in white and the villain dressed in black, in the more subtle use of water images in Fellini's *La Dolce Vita*, or even in the presence of an X whenever someone is about to be killed in *Scarface*.

Sometimes, symbolic references can be enhanced by form cutting—for example, cutting directly from the hero's gun to the villain's gun. Or the filmmaker may choose to repeat a familiar image in varying forms, using it as a composer would use a motif in music. Hitchcock's shower sequence in *Psycho* is built around circular images: the shower head, the circular drain in the tub, the mouth open and screaming, and the iris of the unseeing eye. In *Fort Apache* John Ford uses clouds of dust as a curtain to cover major events; the dust is also used to indicate the ultimate fate of the cavalry troop. Grass, cloud shapes, windblown trees, and patches of color have all been used symbolically and as motifs. Once such elements are perceived, serious students of film will find the deeper meanings of a film more evident and their appreciation heightened.

Another part of structural rhythm is the repetition of certain visual patterns throughout a film. A circular image positioned against a rectangular one, a movement from right to left, an action repeated regularly throughout a sequence—all can become observable patterns or even thematic statements. The silent film made extreme use of thematic repetition. In *Intolerance*, D.W. Griffith develops four similar stories simultaneously and continually cross-cuts between them. This particular use of form enabled him to develop the idea of the similarity of intolerance throughout the ages. In their silent films Laurel and Hardy often built up a pattern of "you do this to me and I'll do that to you;" they called it "tit for tat." Their audience would be lulled into expecting this pattern, but at that point the film would present a variation on the familiar theme (a process quite similar to the use of *theme* and *variation* in musical composition). The unexpected breaking of the pattern would surprise the audience into laughter.

Parallel development, discussed earlier, can also be used to create form and pattern throughout a film. For example, Edwin S. Porter's *The Kleptomaniac* alternates between two stories: a wealthy woman caught shoplifting a piece of jewelry, and a poor woman who steals a loaf of bread. Each sequence alternately shows crime, arrest, and punishment; the wealthy woman's husband bribes the judge to let her off, while the poor woman is sent to jail. Porter's final shot shows the statue of justice holding her scales, one weighted down with a bag of gold. Her blindfold is raised over one eye, which is looking at the money. In this case, as in others, the form is the film.

When sound films became practicable, filmmakers found many ways of using the audio track, in addition to just recording dialogue. This track could be used as symbolism, as a motif that reinforced the emotional quality of a scene, or for stronger emphasis or structural rhythm.

Some filmmakers believe that a more realistic feeling can be created if the film is cut rather than dissolved. They feel that cutting abruptly from scene to scene gives the film a staccato rhythm that in turn augments the reality they hope to achieve. A dissolve, they think, creates a slower pace and tends to make the film *legato* and thus more romantic. If the abrupt cutting style is done to the beat of the sound track, a pulsating rhythm is created for the film sequence; this in turn is communicated to the audience and adds a sense of urgency to the scene. In Fred Zinnemann's *High Noon* the sheriff is waiting for the noon train to arrive. The sequence is presented in *montage*, showing the townspeople, as well as the sheriff, waiting. The shot is changed every eight beats of the musical track. As the time approaches noon, the shot is changed every four beats. Tension mounts. The feeling of rhythm is enhanced by shots of a clock's pendulum swinging to the beat of the sound track. Tension continues to build. The train's whistle sounds. There is a series of rapid cuts of faces turning and looking, but there is only silence on the sound track, which serves as a tension release. This last moment of the sequence is also used as transition between the music and silence. In other films the track may shift from music to natural sounds and back to the music again. Or a pattern may be created of natural sound, silence, and a musical track. All depends on the mood and attitude the filmmaker is trying to create. In Hitchcock's films music is often used as a tension release or an afterthought, as Hitchcock usually relies on the force of his visual elements to create structural rhythm.

Earlier in this chapter I mentioned the use of motif in *Jaws*. Many films make use of an audio motif to introduce visual elements or convey meaning symbolically. Walt Disney, particularly in his pre-1940 cartoons, often uses his sound track in this manner. For example, Donald Duck is trying to catch a pesky fly, but the fly always manages to elude him. In desperation Donald sprays the fly with an insecticide. The fly coughs and falls to the ground. But on the sound track we hear an airplane motor coughing and sputtering and finally diving to the ground and crashing. In juxtaposing these different visual and audio elements, Disney is using his track symbolically.

John Ford often underlines sentimental moments in his films by accompanying the dialogue of a sequence with traditional melodies; as the sequence comes to a close the music swells and then fades away to match the fading out of the scene. In *The Grapes of Wrath*, when Tom Joad says goodbye to his mother, "Red River Valley" is played on a concertina; as Tom walks over the hill the music becomes louder, and when he disappears from view it fades out. Throughout this film, this familiar folk song serves as a thematic reference to the Joads' home in Oklahoma and also boosts the audience's feelings of nostalgia. In *She*

Wore a Yellow Ribbon the title of the film is underlined by the song of the same name, but through the use of different tempos and timbres the mood of the song is changed each time it is used. As the cavalry troop rides out of the fort the song is played in a strong ¾ meter with a heavy emphasis on the brass; the sequence is also cut to the beat of the track. In the graveyard sequences the same tune is played by strings and reeds in ¾ time and in a much slower tempo, which makes the song melancholy and sentimental. In the climactic fight sequence in *The Quiet Man* John Ford cuts to the beat of a sprightly Irish jig, which enriches the comic elements of the scene and plays down the violence.

Our discussion in these last few paragraphs touches only the surface of the techniques and uses of sound in film; of course, there are other ways of using sound and the other elements discussed thus far. But part of the challenge of the film as an art form is the discovery by the viewer of the varying uses to which film technique can be put, and this in turn enhances further perceptions.

Film is basically a visual art; the pictures tell the story. How these pictures are recorded, arranged, and enhanced can raise the mechanical, commercial movie form into a work of art. Full response to that art demands an informed and knowledgeable audience. Perception, or visual literacy, is the key.

SIX

DANCE

Dance is one of the most natural and universal of human activities. In virtually every culture, regardless of location or level of development, we find some form of dance. Dance appears to have sprung from humans' religious needs. For example, scholars are relatively sure that the theatre of Ancient Greece developed out of that society's religious, tribal dance rituals. So, there can be no doubt that dance is part of human communication at its most fundamental level. We can see this expression even in little children, who, before they begin to paint, sing, or imitate, begin to dance.

Most of us at one time or another have participated in some form of dancing. Doubtless, we hardly believe that participation approximates art. However, we do have some understanding of what the term *dance* means.

WHAT IS IT?

Dance is aesthetic communication through the design of time, sound, and two- and three-dimensional space focusing on the human form. In general it follows one of three traditions: ballet, modern dance, and folk dance. Other forms or traditions of dance exist. These include jazz dance, tap, and musical comedy. Their properties or qualities as concert dance are often debated. The reader is encouraged to explore these in detail elsewhere. We will note jazz dance in passing later in the chapter and will focus our brief discussion on ballet, modern dance, and folk dance.

BALLET

Ballet comprises what can be called "classical" or formal dance; it is rich in tradition and rests heavily upon a set of prescribed movements and actions, as we shall see. In general, ballet is a highly theatrical dance presentation consisting of solo dancers, duets, and choruses, or the *corps de ballets*. According to Anatole Chujoy in the *Dance Encyclopedia*, the basic principle in ballet is "the reduction of human gesture to bare essentials, heightened and developed into meaningful patterns." George Balanchine saw the single steps of a ballet as analogous to a single frame in a motion picture. Ballet, then, became a fluid succession of images, all existing within specialized codes of movement. As with all dance and all the arts, ballet expresses basic human experiences and desires.

MODERN DANCE

Modern dance is a label given to a broad variety of highly individualized dance works limited to the twentieth century, essentially American in derivation, and antiballetic in philosophy. It began as a revolt against the stylized and tradition-bound elements of ballet. The basic principle of modern dance could probably be stated as an emphasis on natural and spontaneous or uninhibited movement, in strong contrast with the conventionalized and specified movement of ballet. The earliest modern dancers found stylized ballet movement incompatible with their need to communicate in twentieth-century terms. As Martha Graham characterized it, "There are no general rules. Each work of art creates its own code." Nonetheless, in its attempts to be nonballetic, certain conventions and characteristics have accrued to modern dance. While there are narrative elements in many modern dances, there may be less emphasis on them than in traditional ballet. There also are differences in the use of the body, the use of the dance floor, and the interaction with the visual elements.

FOLK DANCE

Folk dance, somewhat like folk music, is a body of group dances performed to traditional music. It is similar to folk music in that we do not know the artist who developed it; there is no choreographer of record for folk dances. They began as a necessary or informative part of certain cultures, and their characteristics are stylistically identifiable with a given culture. They developed over a period of years, without benefit of authorship, passing from one generation to another. They have their prescribed movements, their prescribed rhythms, and their prescribed music and costume. At one time or another they may have become formalized—that is, committed to some form of record. But they are part of a heritage, and usually not the creative result of an artist or a group of interpretative artists, as is the case with the other forms of dance. Likewise, they exist more to involve participants than to entertain an audience.

Folk dancing establishes an individual sense of participation in society, the tribe, or a mass movement. "The group becomes one in conscious strength and purpose, and each individual experiences a heightened power as part of it . . . [a] feeling of oneness with one's fellows which is established by collective dancing."[1]

6.1 First position.

HOW IS IT PUT TOGETHER?

Dance is an art of time and space that utilizes many of the elements of the other arts. In the visual elements and in the line and form of the human body it involves many of the compositional elements of pictures, sculpture, and theatre. Dance also relies heavily on the elements of music—whether or not music accompanies the dance presentation. However, the essential ingredient of dance is the human body and its varieties of expression. So, it is with the human body that we will begin our examination of how a dance work is put together.

FORMALIZED MOVEMENT

The most obvious repository of formalized movement in dance is ballet. All movement in ballet is based upon five basic leg, foot, and arm positions. In the *first position* (Fig. 6.1) the dancer stands with weight equally distributed between the feet, heels together, and toes open and out to the side. In ballet all movements evolve from this basic *open* position; the feet are never parallel to each other and both pointing straight forward. The *second position* (Fig. **6.2**) is achieved by opening the first position the length of one's foot, again with the weight placed evenly on both feet. In the *third position* (Fig. **6.3**) the heel of the front foot touches the instep of the back foot; the legs and feet must be well turned out. In the *fourth position* (Fig. **6.4**) the heel of the front foot is opposite the toe of the back foot. The feet are parallel and separated by the length of the dancer's foot; again, the weight is placed evenly on both feet. The *fifth position* (Fig. **6.5**) is the most frequently used of the basic ballet positions. The feet are close together with the front heel touching the toe of the back foot. The legs and the feet must be well turned out to achieve this position correctly, and the weight is placed

6.2 (*above*) Second position.

6.3 (*left*) Third position.

6.4 (*right*) Fourth position.

evenly on both feet. As is clear from Figures **6.1–6.5**, each position changes the attitude of the arms as well as that of the legs and feet. From these five basic positions a series of fundamental movements and poses is developed; these are the core of every movement of the human body in formal ballet.

Some of the fundamental ballet poses and movements can be recognized throughout a dance work, including modern dance; a few lend themselves to photographic illustration. Figure **6.6** shows a *demi-plié* in first position. This half-bend of the knees can be executed in any position. The *grand plié* shown in Figure **6.7**, also in first position, carries the bend to its maximum degree. The *arabesque* is a pose executed on one foot with arms and foot extended. It can appear in a variety of positions; it is

6.5 (*below*) Fifth position.

6.6 (*above right*) *Demi-plié* in first position.

6.7 (*below right*) *Grand plié* in first position.

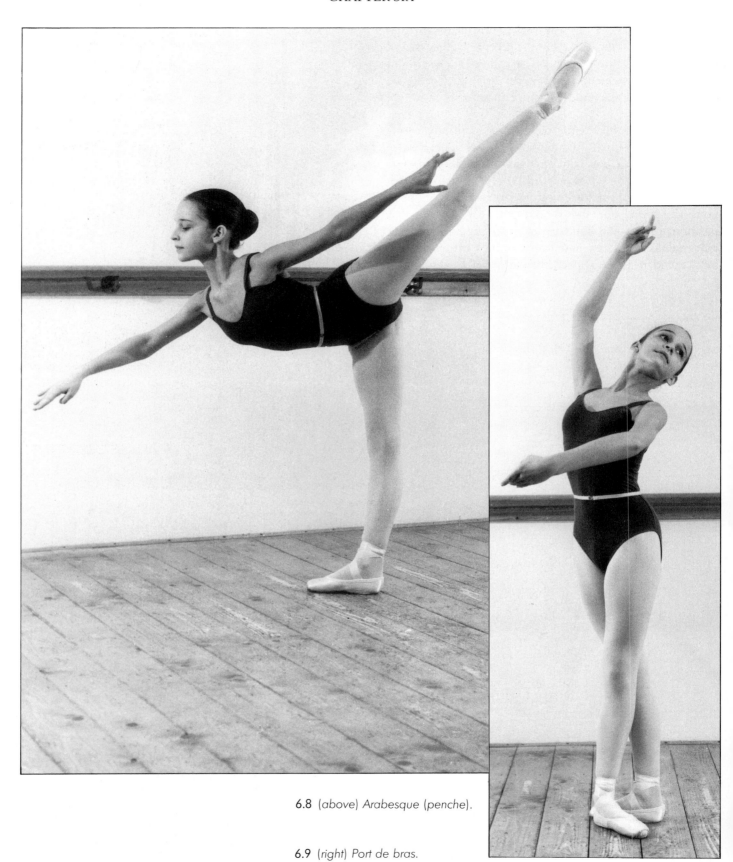

6.8 (above) *Arabesque (penche)*.

6.9 (right) *Port de bras.*

shown in Figure **6.8** in the *penche*, or leaning position. The *port de bras* (Fig. **6.9**) is simply the technique of moving the arms correctly. As might be imagined, many variations can be made upon the five basic positions. For example, the *grande seconde* (Fig. **6.10**) is a variation upon second position in which the leg is elevated to full height. The leg also is elevated in the *demi-hauteur*, or "half height" (Fig. **6.11**). Full height requires extension of the leg at a 90-degree angle to the ground; half height requires a 45-degree extension. Movements carry the same potential for variety. For example, in the *ronds de jambe à terre* (Fig. **6.12**) the leg from the knee to and including the foot is rotated in a semicircle. Other basic movements (defined in the Glossary) include the *assemblé, changement de pied, jeté, pirouette*, and *relevé*. As we develop expertise in perceiving dance it will become obvious to us in watching formal ballet (and to a lesser degree, modern dance) that we see a limited number of movements and poses, turns and leaps, done over and over again. In this sense these bodily compositions form a kind of theme and variation, and they are interesting in that right alone.

6.10 *Grande seconde.*

6.11 *Demi-hauteur.*

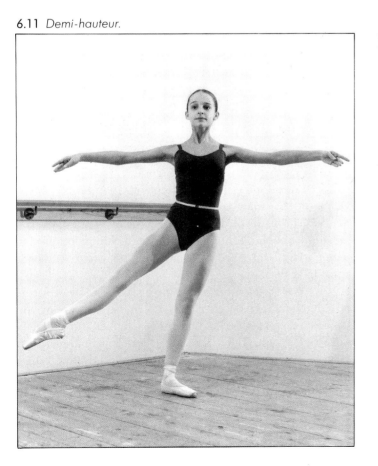

6.12 *Ronds de jambe à terre.*

6.13 On point. (above) *Detail.*

In addition, it is possible for us to find a great deal of excitement in the bodily movements of formal ballet if for no other reason than the physical skills required for their execution. The standards of quality that are applied to a ballet dancer are based on the ability of the dancer to execute these movements properly. Just as in gymnastics or figure skating, the strength and grace of the individual in large part determine his or her qualitative achievement. It goes without saying, however, that ballet is far more than just a series of gymnastic exercises.

Perhaps the most familiar element of ballet is the female dancer's toe work or dancing *on point* (Fig. **6.13**). A special kind of footgear is required for toe work (see p. 116). Dancing on point is a fundamental part of the female dancer's development. It usually takes a minimum of two years of thorough training and development before a dancer can begin to do toe work. Certain kinds of turns are not possible without toeshoes and the technique for using them—for example, spinning on point or being spun by a partner.

We have focused on ballet in this discussion of formalized movement because it is the most familiar of the traditional, formalized dance forms. Ballet, however, is not alone in adhering to formalized patterns of movement. It is, in part, formalized movement that allows us to distinguish among folk and other dances, such as the *pavane*, the *galliard*, the *waltz*, and the *mambo*. All have formal or conventional patterns of movement. Perhaps only modern dance resists formal movement, and even then not completely.

LINE, FORM, & REPETITION

The compositional elements of line, form, and repetition apply to the use of the human body in exactly the same sense that they apply to those elements in painting and sculpture—the latter especially. The body of the dancer can be analyzed as a sculptural, three-dimensional form that reflects the use of line, even though the dancer is continually in motion. The body as a sculptural form moves from one pose to another, and if we were to take a stop-action movie of a dance, we could analyze, frame by frame or second by second, the compositional qualities of the human body. The human form in every illustration in this chapter, including those that show groupings of dancers, can be analyzed as a composition of line and shape. Dance, therefore, can be seen at two levels: first, as a type of pictorial communication employing symbols that occur only for a moment, and, second, as the design of transition with movement between those moments.

Because the dancer moves through time, the concept of repetition becomes an important consideration in analyzing how a dance work is put together. The relationship of the movements to each other as the dance progresses shows us a repetitional pattern that is very similar to theme and variation in music. So, *choreographers* concern themselves with the use of the individual dancer's body as well as combinations of dancers' bodies in duets, trios, or the entire corps de ballet (Figs. **6.14** and **6.15**).

6.14 *Nameless Hour,* Jazz Dance Theatre at Penn State, Pennsylvania State University. Choreographer: Jean Sabatine. Photo by Roger Greenawalt.

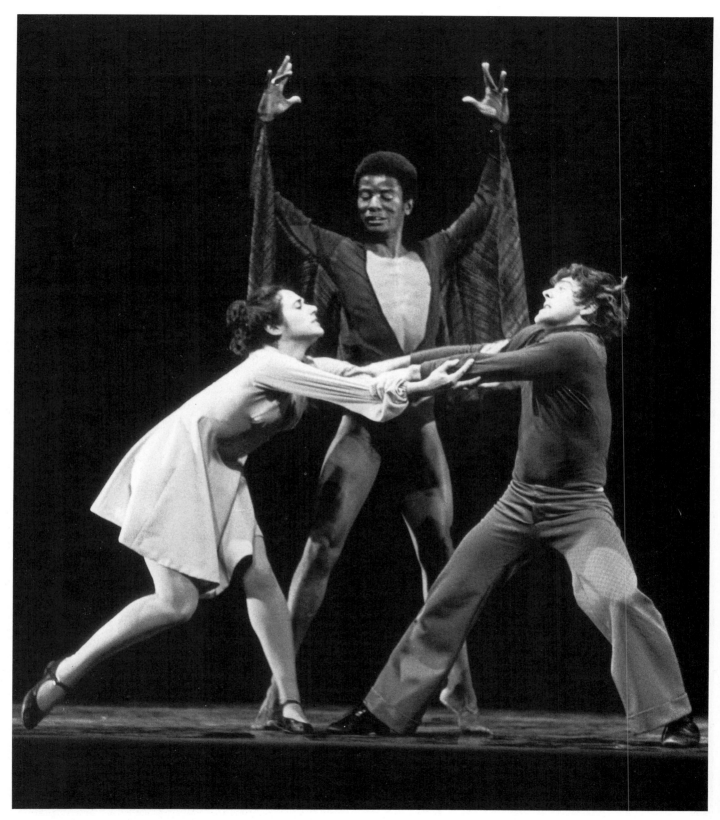

6.15 *Family Tree*, Jazz Dance Theatre at Penn State, Pennsylvania State University. Choreographer: Jean Sabatine. Photo by Roger Greenawalt.

RHYTHM

As we watch a dance we can see that the steps are related and coherent. Dance phrases are held together by their rhythm, in the same sense as in musical rhythm. Sequences of long and short motions occur which are highlighted by accents. In a visual sense dance rhythms occur in spatial arrangements, up and down, back and forth, curved and linear, large and small. We also can perceive rhythmic relationships in the ebb and flow of dancers' energy levels. Energy, of course, calls to mind dynamics in the sense that we discussed the term in music and theatre.

MIME & PANTOMIME

Within any dance form, modern dance included, there may be elements of bodily movement that we call *mime* and *pantomime*. Bodily movement is *mimetic* whenever it suggests the kinds of movements we associate with people or animals. It is also mimetic if it employs any of the forms of conventional sign language, such as the Delsarte system. Of course, if there are narrative elements in the dance and the dancer actually portrays a character in the theatrical sense, there also may be pantomimetic action. Pantomime is the "acting out" of dramatic action without words. In the romantic style of ballet from the nineteenth century, for example, pantomime helps to carry forward the story line. We sense the emotions, the feelings, and the character relationships in the dancers' steps, gestures, movements, and facial expressions. Only when the movement of the dance is purely an emotional expression of the dancer can we say that it is free of mime.

IDEA CONTENT

Our consideration of the presence or absence of mime leads us to a consideration of how dance communicates its idea content. There are three general possibilities. First, the dance may contain *narrative* elements—that is, it may tell a story. Second, the dance may communicate through *abstract* ideas. There is a specific theme to be communicated in this case, but no story line. The ideas are abstract and general and relate to some aspect of human emotion or the human condition. Modern dance, especially, tends to deal with human psychology and behavior. Social themes occur frequently, as do impressions or expressions from plays, poems, and novels. Religious themes as well as folk themes can be found in the wide treatments and explorations of subject ideas in modern dance. The third possibility is the absence of narrative or abstract com-

munication. The work may be a *divertissement*, or diversion. Romantic ballet usually has strong narrative elements. However, some ballets are divertissements. Modern ballet—that is, twentieth-century ballet—has dealt increasingly with abstract ideas. Modern dance often concerns itself with abstract ideas; it may have narrative elements as well.

A final variable of idea content in dance is the presence or absence of *ethnic influence*. It is interesting to note how elements of dance reflect sociocultural background. Jazz dance, for example, may stimulate us to consider the black heritage in the United States. Jazz dance has emerged strongly in the twentieth century, and many would include it as a form equal to ballet, modern, and folk. Jazz dance has its own history, which is linked closely with the black experience in the United States, show business, and jazz as a musical idiom.

MUSIC

We associate music with dance as a matter of course. Most of the time music serves as a basis for the bodily movement of the work we are perceiving, although it is not necessary for dance to be accompanied by music. However, it is impossible to have dance without one element of music—rhythm, as we noted previously. Every action of the dancer's body has some relationship in time to every other movement, and those relationships establish rhythmic patterns that are musical regardless of the presence or absence of auditory stimuli.

When we hear music accompanying a dance we can respond to the relationship of the dance to the musical score. The most obvious relationship we will see and hear is the one between the gestures and footfalls of the dancer and the beat of the music. In some cases the two are in strict accord; the *beat-for-beat* relationship is one to one. In other cases there may be virtually no perceivable beat-for-beat relationship between the dancer's movements and the accent or rhythmic patterns of the musical score.

Another relationship is that of the *dynamics* of the dance to those of the music. Of prime importance in this relationship is the intensity, or *force*, of the dance movement. Moments of great intensity in a dance can manifest themselves in rapid movement and forceful leaps. Or they may be reflected in other qualities. We must discern how the actual performance employs dynamics.

We can use the same kind of analysis in dance as we did in theatre in plotting dynamic levels and overall structure. For maximum interest there must be variety of intensity. So, if we chart the relationship of the peaks and valleys of dynamic levels, we are likely to conclude that the dynamic structure of a dance is quite similar to the dynamic structure of a play in that it tends to be pyramidal: It builds to a high point and then relaxes to a conclusion. This kind of analysis applies whether or not narrative elements are present.

MISE EN SCÈNE

Because dance is essentially a visual and theatrical experience, part of our response must be to those theatrical elements of dance that are manifested in the environment of the presentation. In other words, we can respond to the *mise en scène* of the dance (Fig. **6.15**). We can note the elements of verisimilitude in the *mise en scène* and how those elements reflect or otherwise relate to the aural and visual elements of the dance. A principal consideration here is the interrelationship of the dance with properties, settings, and the floor of the theatrical environment. The dance may use *properties* in significant or insignificant ways. As for *settings*, some dances employ massive stage designs. Others have no setting at all; they are performed in a neutral environment. Again, part of our response is to the relationship of the elements of the setting to the rest of the dance.

A principal difference between formal ballet and modern dance lies in the use of the *dance floor*. In formal ballet the floor acts principally as an agent from which the dancer springs and to which the dancer returns. But in modern dance the floor assumes an integral role in the dance, and we are likely to see the dancers sitting on the floor, rolling on it—in short, *interacting with* the floor. So, consideration of the use of the floor in dance concerns not only whether or not it is employed as an integral part of a dance, but also how the use of the floor relates to the idea content of the dance.

In discussing the relationship of *costume* to dance, we would do well to return to the section on costume design in Chapter 4 to note the purposes of costume, because those purposes apply to dance in the same manner that they apply to a theatre production. In some dances costume will be traditional, conventional, and neutral. There would be little representation of story line or character in the tights and *tutu* of the female dancer shown in Figure **6.16**. However, in many dances we are likely to see costumes high in verisimilitude. Costumes may help portray character, locality, and other aspects of the dance (Figs. **6.14** and **6.15**).

6.16 Traditional tights and tutu.

In addition, it is especially important that the costume should allow the dancer to do whatever it is that the choreographer expects him or her to do. In fact, costume may become an integral part of the dance itself. An extreme example of this is Martha Graham's *Lamentation*, in which a single dancer is costumed in what could be best described as a tube of fabric—no arms, no legs, just a large envelope of cloth. Every movement of the dancer stretches that cloth so that the line and form of the dancer is not the line and form of a human body but rather the line and form of a human body enveloped in a moving fabric.

The final element of the dance costume to be considered, and one of great significance, is footgear. Dancers' footgear ranges from the simple, soft, and supple ballet slipper to the very specialized toeshoe of formal ballet, with street shoes, character Oxfords, and a variety of representational or symbolic footwear in between. In addition, modern dance often is done in bare feet. Of course, the fundamental requirements of footgear are comfort and enough flexibility to allow the dancer to do whatever he or she must do. Footgear, whether it be toeshoe, ballet slipper, character Oxford, or bare feet, must be appropriate to the surface of the stage floor. Great care must be taken to ensure that the dance floor is not too hard, too soft, too rough, too slippery, or too sticky. The floor is so important that many touring companies take their own floor with them to insure that they will be able to execute their movements properly.

LIGHTING

Inasmuch as the entire perception of a dance relies on perception of the human body as a three-dimensional form, the work of the lighting designer is of critical importance in the art of dance. How we perceive the human form in space depends on how that body is lit. Certainly our emotional and sense response is highly shaped by the nature of the lighting that plays on the dancer and the dance floor.

Lighting designers can work with the human body in dance as though the body were pure sculptural form. When narrative qualities are present, lighting tends to be much like theatre lighting, with emphasis, first, on visibility of faces. However, careful selection of instrumentation, for harsh or soft light, angles, for degrees of plasticity, and color, for mood, turns the human body into meaningful, three-dimensional form in motion. How we see these bodily forms in motion depends entirely on the lighting designer.

HOW DOES IT STIMULATE THE SENSES?

The complex properties of the dance make possible perhaps the most diverse and intense communicative stimuli of any of the arts. We noted earlier that opera is a synthesis of all of the arts. The dance, as well, integrates elements of all of the arts, and it does so in such a way as to communicate in a highly effective symbolic and nonverbal manner.

We noted previously that it is possible to respond at different levels to an artwork. To some extent we can respond even at a level of total ignorance. In many ways artworks are like onions. If they lack quality we can call them rotten. But more important, and more seriously, an artwork, like an onion, has a series of skins. As we peel away one that is obvious to us, we reveal another and another and another, until we have gotten to the core of the thing. There will be levels of understanding, levels of meaning, levels of potential response for the uninitiated as well as the thoroughly sophisticated viewer. The more sophisticated a *balletomane* one becomes, the fuller one's understanding and response.

LINE & FORM

Like every other artwork that exists in space, the dance appeals to our senses through the compositional qualities of line and form. These qualities exist not only in the human body but in the visual elements of the *mise en scène*. Essentially, horizontal line stimulates a sense of calm and repose. Vertical lines suggest grandeur and elegance. Diagonal lines stimulate a feeling of action and movement (Fig. **6.16**), and curved lines, grace. As we respond to a dance work we respond to how the human body expresses line and form, not only when it is standing still but also when it moves through space. If we are alert and perceptive we will recognize not only how lines and forms are created but also how they are repeated from dancer to dancer and from dancer to *mise en scène*.

Often, the kind of line created by the body or body characteristics of a dancer is the key to understanding the work of the choreographer. George Balanchine, for example, insisted that his dancers be almost skin and bone; you would not see a corpulent or overly developed physique in his company. So, bodies themselves appeal to our senses, and choreographers capitalize on that appeal in their dance conceptions.

DYNAMICS

We noted in Chapter 3 that the beat of music is a fundamental appeal to our senses. Beat is the aspect of music that sets our toes tapping and our fingers drumming. Probably our basic response to a dance is to the dynamics expressed by the dancers and in the music. A dancer's use of vigorous and forceful action, high leaps, graceful turns, or extended pirouettes, appeals directly to us, as does the tempo of the dance. Variety in dynamics—the louds and softs and the highs and lows of bodily intensity as well as musical sound—is the dancer's and choreographer's means of providing interest, just as it is the actor's, the director's, and the painter's.

SIGN LANGUAGE

The dancer, like the actor, can stimulate us directly because he or she is another human being and can employ many symbols of communication (Fig. **6.15**). Most human communication requires us to learn a set of symbols, and, therefore, we can respond to the dance at this level only when we have mastered the language. There are systems of sign language, such as the Delsarte, in which the positions of the arms, the hands, and the head have meanings. Likewise, in our response to the hula dance, experts tell us, we ought not to concentrate on the vigorous hip movements of the dancer but rather on the hand movements, each of which communicates an idea. But until we learn what each of these movements means, we cannot respond in any significant way. However, there is a set of universal body symbols to which all of us respond (so psychologists tell us), regardless of our level of familiarity or understanding. For example, the gesture of acceptance in which the arms are held outward with the palms up has the same universal meaning. The universal symbol of rejection is the hands held in front of the body with the palms out as if to push away. When dancers employ universal symbols we respond to their appeal to our senses just as we would to the nonverbals or body language in everyday conversation.

COLOR

Although the dancer uses facial and bodily expressions to communicate some aspect of the human condition, we do not receive as direct a message from them as we do from the words of the actor. So, to enhance the dancer's communication the costume, lighting, and set designers must strongly reinforce the mood of the dance through the *mise en scène* they create. The principal means of expression of mood is color. In dance, lighting designers are free to work in much more obvious ways with color because they do not have to create patterns of light and shadow as high in verisimilitude as those of their counterparts in the theatre. As a result, they do not have to worry if the face of a dancer is red or blue or green, an attribute that would be disastrous in a play. So, we are apt to see much stronger, more colorful, and more suggestive lighting in dance than in theatre. Colors will be more saturated, intensity will be much higher, and the qualities of the human body, as form, will be explored much more strongly by light from various directions. The same is true of costumes and settings. Because dancers obviously do not portray a role in a highly verisimilar way, their costume can be very communicative in an abstract way. On the other hand, scene designers must be careful to utilize color in such a way that the dancer receives the focus in the stage environment. In any but the smallest of stage spaces it is very easy for the human body to be overpowered by the elements of the *mise en scène* since it occupies much more space. So, scene designers, in contrast with lighting designers, must be careful to provide a background against which the dancer will stand out in contrast unless a synthesis of the dancer with the environment is intended, as in the case, for example, of some works by choreographer Merce Cunningham. Nevertheless, scene designers use color as forcefully as they can to help reinforce the overall mood of the dance.

The examples of how dance affects our senses that we have just noted are rudimentary ones. Perhaps more than any other art, dance causes us to ascend beyond our three cognitive questions—What is it? How is it put together? How does it affect the senses?—and dwell in that fourth level of meaningful response—What does it mean?

SEVEN

ARCHITECTURE

In approaching architecture as an art, it is virtually impossible for us to separate aesthetic properties from practical or functional properties. In other words, architects first have a particular function to achieve in their building. That function is their principal concern. The aesthetics of the building are important, but they must be tailored to overall practical considerations. For example, when architects set about to design a 110-story skyscraper, they are locked into an aesthetic form that will be vertical rather than horizontal in emphasis. They may attempt to counter verticality with strong horizontal elements, but the physical fact that the building will be taller than it is wide is the basis from which the architects must work. Their structural design must take into account all the practical needs implicit in the building's use. Nonetheless, considerable room for aesthetics remains. Treatment of space, texture, line, and proportion can give us buildings of unique style and character or buildings of unimaginative sameness.

Architecture is often described as the art of *sheltering*. To consider it as such we must use the term *sheltering* very broadly. Obviously there are types of architecture within which people do not dwell and under which they cannot escape the rain. Architecture encompasses more than buildings. So, we can consider architecture as the art of sheltering people both physically and spiritually from the raw elements of the unaltered world.

WHAT IS IT?

As we noted, architecture can be considered the art of sheltering. In another large sense, it is the design of three-dimensional space to create practical enclosure. Its basic forms are residences, churches, and commercial buildings. Each of these forms can take innumerable shapes, from single-family residences to the ornate palaces of kings to high-rise condominiums and apartments. We also could expand our categorization of architectural forms to include bridges, walls, monuments, and so forth.

HOW IS IT PUT TOGETHER?

In examining how a work of architecture is put together we will limit ourselves to ten fundamental elements: structure, building materials, line, repetition, balance, scale, proportion, context, space, and climate.

7.1 Stonehenge, Salisbury Plain, England, c. 1800–1400 B.C. British Information Services Photo.

STRUCTURE

There are many systems of construction or systems of structural support. We will deal with only a few of the more prominent. *Post-and-lintel*, *arch*, and *cantilever* systems can be viewed, essentially, as historical systems. Contemporary architecture, however, can better be described by two additional terms, which to some extent overlap the others. These "contemporary" systems are *bearing-wall* and *skeleton frame*.

Post-and-Lintel

Post-and-lintel structures consist of horizontal beams (lintels) laid across the open spaces between vertical supports (posts). In this architectural system the traditional material is stone. Post-and-lintel structures are similar to *post-and-beam* structures, in which series of vertical posts are joined by horizontal members, traditionally of wood. The wooden members of post-and-beam structures are held together by nails, pegs, or lap joints.

7.2 The Parthenon, Acropolis, Athens, 448–432 B.C. AC & R Photo.

Because of the lack of tensile strength in its fundamental material, stone, post-and-lintel structures are limited in their ability to define space. *Tensile strength* is the ability of a material to withstand bending. If we lay a slab of stone across an open space and support it at each end, we can span only a narrow space before it cracks in the middle and falls to the ground. On the other hand, stone has great *compressive strength*—the ability to withstand compression or crushing.

A primitive example of a post-and-lintel structure is Stonehenge, that ancient and mysterious religious configuration of giant stones in Great Britain (Fig. 7.1). The Ancient Greeks refined this system to high elegance; the most familiar of their post-and-lintel creations is the Parthenon (Fig. 7.2).

The Greek refinement of post-and-lintel structure is a *prototype* for buildings throughout the world and across the centuries. One of the more interesting aspects of the style is its treatment of columns and *capitals*. Figure 7.3 shows the three basic Greek orders —Ionic, Doric, and Corinthian. These are not the only styles of post-and-lintel structure. Column capitals can be as varied as the imagination of the architect who designed them. Their primary purpose is to act as a transition for the eye as it moves from post to lintel. Columns also may express a variety of detail. A final element, present in some columns, is *fluting*—vertical ridges cut into the column.

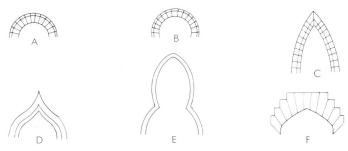

7.4 The arch: (A) Round (Roman) arch, (B) Horseshoe (Moorish) arch, (C) Lancet (pointed, gothic) arch, (D) Ogee arch, (E) Trefoil arch, (F) Tudor arch.

Arch

A second type of architectural structure is the arch. As we indicated earlier, post-and-lintel structure is limited in the amount of unencumbered space it can achieve. The arch, on the other hand, can define large spaces, since its stresses are transferred outward from its center (the *keystone*) to its legs. So it does not depend on the tensile strength of its material.

There are many different styles of arches, some of which are illustrated in Figure 7.4. The characteristics of different arches may have structural as well as decorative functions. As an example, examine St. Alban's Cathedral (Fig. 7.5), built in the English Norman style. This style of building, with its accent on rounded arches, was loosely based on the classical architecture of Roman times.

7.3 Greek columns and capitals (*left*) Doric, (*center*) Ionic, (*right*) Corinthian.

7.5 St. Alban's Cathedral, the nave, facing east.

A	Entablature	D	Frieze	G	Shaft	1	Guttae	4	Abacus	7	Fluting
B	Column	E	Architrave	H	Base	2	Metope	5	Echinus	8	Dentils
C	Cornice	F	Capital	I	Plinth	3	Triglyph	6	Volute	9	Fascia

7.6 The buttress is any projecting structure, generally of stone, built against a wall to support it.

7.7 (*above right*) Flying buttresses. (*right*) The flying buttresses on the side of Notre Dame, Paris.

The transfer of stress from the center of an arch outward to its legs dictates the need for a strong support to keep the legs from caving outward. Such a reinforcement is called a *buttress* (Fig. **7.6**). The designers of Gothic cathedrals sought to achieve a sense of lightness. Since stone was their basic building material, they recognized that some system had to be developed that would overcome the bulk of a stone buttress. Therefore, they developed a system of buttresses that accomplished structural ends but were light in appearance. These are called *flying buttresses* (Fig. **7.7**).

Several arches placed side by side form an *arcade* (Fig. **7.8**). Arches placed back to back to enclose space form a *tunnel vault* (Fig. **7.9**). When two tunnel vaults intercept at right angles, as in the floor plan of the traditional Christian cathedral, they form a *groin vault* (Fig. **7.10**). The protruding masonry indicating diagonal juncture of arches in a tunnel vault is *rib vaulting* (Fig. **7.11**).

7.8 Arcade.

7.9 (*left*) Tunnel vault.

7.10 (*middle*) Groin vault.

7.11 (*far right*) Ribbed vault. (*below*) The choir in Canterbury Cathedral, England, showing ribbed vaulting.

7.12 Dome, St. Paul's Cathedral, London, 1675–1710.

7.14 Dome with pendentives (P).

When arches are joined at the top with their legs forming a circle, the result is a *dome* (Fig. **7.12**). The dome, through its intersecting arches, allows for more expansive, freer space within the structure. However, if the structures supporting the dome form a circle, the result is a circular building such as the Pantheon in Rome (Fig. **7.13**). To permit squared space beneath a dome, the architect can transfer weight and stress through the use of *pendentives* (Fig. **7.14**).

7.13 Giovanni Paolo Panini, *The Interior of the Pantheon, Rome*, c. 1734/35. Oil on canvas, 50½ x 39 ins (128 x 99 cm). The National Gallery of Art, Washington, DC (Samuel H. Kress Collection).

CROSS SECTION LOOKING EAST

The problems architects face in utilizing one form or another for structural support are illustrated by the story of St. Paul's Cathedral, London. Its dome measures 112 ft (34 m) in diameter and stands 365 ft (110 m) tall at the top of the cross. The lantern and cross alone weigh 700 tons (711 tonnes), while the dome and its superstructure weigh in at 64,000 tons (65,000 tonnes). In designing this cathedral Wren was faced with seemingly endless problems of supporting such a tremendous load. His solution was ingenious—the dome comprises nothing more than a timber shell covered in lead, the actual weight of the dome was only a fraction of what it would have been. This allowed Wren to create a wonderful silhouette on the outside and to have the high ceiling in the interior (Fig. 7.15). It was a solution never used before.

Cantilever

A cantilever is an overhanging beam or floor supported only at one end (Fig. 7.16). Although not a twentieth-century innovation—many nineteenth-century barns in the central and eastern parts of the United States employed it—the most dramatic uses of cantilevers have emerged with the introduction of modern materials such as steel beams and prestressed concrete (Fig. 7.17).

7.16 Cantilever.

7.15 (left) Christopher Wren, St. Paul's Cathedral, London, 1675–1710. Cross-section of dome.

7.17 Eduardo Torroja, Grandstand, Zarzuela Race Track, Madrid, 1935.

7.18 Aqueduct, Pont du Gard, near Nîmes, France, 1st century B.C.

Bearing-Wall

In this system, the wall supports itself, the floors, and the roof. Log cabins are examples of bearing-wall construction; so are solid masonry buildings, in which the walls are the structure. In variations of bearing-wall construction, such as Figure **7.34**, the wall material is continuous—that is, not jointed or pieced together. This variation is called *monolithic* construction.

Skeleton Frame

Here a framework supports the building; the walls are attached to the frame, thus forming an exterior skin. When skeleton framing utilizes wood, as in house construction, the technique is called *balloon construction*. When metal forms the frame, as in skyscrapers, the technique is known as *steel-cage construction*.

BUILDING MATERIALS

Historic and contemporary architectural practices and traditions often center on specific materials, and to understand architecture further, we need to note a few.

Stone

The use of stone as a material turns us back to post-and-lintel systems and Figures **7.1** and **7.2**. When stone is used together with mortar, for example, in arch construction, that combination is called *masonry* construction. The most obvious example of masonry, however, is the brick wall, and masonry construction is based on that principle. Stones, bricks, or blocks are joined together with mortar, one on top of the other, to provide basic, structural, weight-bearing walls of a building, a bridge, and so forth (Fig. **7.18**). There is a limit to what can be accomplished with masonry because of the pressures that play on the joints between blocks and mortar and the foundation on which they rest. However, when one considers that office buildings such as Chicago's Monadnock Building (Fig. **7.19**) are skyscrapers and that their walls are built solely of masonry—that is, there are no hidden steel reinforcements in the walls—it becomes obvious that much is possible with this elemental combination of stone and mortar.

7.19 Monadnock Building, Chicago, 1889–91. Daniel Hudson Burnham and John Wellborn Root.

7.20 Richard Buckminster Fuller, Geodesic dome, Climatron, St. Louis, Missouri, 1959.

Build house material /pick material - Y?

Concrete

The use of concrete is central to much contemporary architectural practice, but it was also significant as far back in the past as Ancient Rome. The Pantheon (Fig. **7.13**) comprises a masterful structure of concrete with a massive concrete dome, 142 ft (43 m) in diameter, resting on concrete walls 20 ft (6 m) thick. In contemporary architecture, we find *precast* concrete, which is concrete cast in place using wooden forms around a steel framework. We also find *ferroconcrete* or *reinforced concrete*, which utilizes metal reinforcing embedded in the concrete. Such a technique combines the tensile strength of the metal with the compressive strength of the concrete. *Prestressed* and *post-tensioned* concrete use metal rods and wires under stress or tension to cause structural forces to flow in predetermined directions. Both comprise extremely versatile building materials.

Wood

Whether in balloon framing for houses or in laminated beaming for modern churches, wood has played a pivotal role, especially in the United States, where its supply seems endless.

Steel

The use of steel has nearly endless variation and gives almost limitless possibilities for construction. Its introduction into the nineteenth-century industrial age forever changed style and scale in architecture. *Steel cage* construction and cantilever construction were noted earlier. *Suspension* construction in bridges, superdomes, aerial walkways, and so on has carried architects to the safe limits of space spansion and, sometimes, beyond those limits. The *geodesic dome* (Fig. **7.20**) is a unique use of materials invented by an American architect, R. Buckminster Fuller. Consisting of a network of metal rods and hexagonal plates, the dome is a light, inexpensive, yet strong and easily assembled building. Although it has no apparent size limit (Mr. Fuller claims he could roof New York City, given the funds), its potential for variation and aesthetic expressiveness seems somewhat limited.

LINE, REPETITION, & BALANCE

Line and repetition perform the same compositional functions in architecture as in painting and sculpture. In his Marin County Courthouse (Fig. **7.21**), Frank Lloyd Wright takes a single motif, the arc, varies only its size, and repeats it almost endlessly. The result, rather than being monotonous, is dynamic and fascinating.

7.21 Frank Lloyd Wright, Marin County Courthouse, California, 1957–63.

Let's look at three other buildings. The main gate of Hampton Court Palace (Fig. **7.22**), built in the English Tudor style around 1515 by Thomas Wolsey, at first appears haphazard to us because we seem to see virtually no repetition. Actually, this section of the palace is quite symmetrical, working its way left and right of the central gatehouse in mirror images. However, the myriad of chimneys, the imposition of the main palace, which is not centered on the main gate, and our own vantage point cause an apparent clutter of line and form that prompts our initial reaction. Line and its resultant form give Hampton Court Palace the appearance of a substantial castle.

Although it seems impossible, Figure **7.23** is the same Hampton Court Palace. Figure **7.22** reflects the style and taste of England during the reign of Henry VIII (who appropriated the palace from its original owner, Cardinal

Wolsey). Later monarchs found the cumbersome and primitive appearance unsuited to their tastes, and Christopher Wren was commissioned to plan a ''new'' palace. So, in 1689, in the reign of William and Mary, renovation of the palace proper began. The result was a new and classically oriented façade in the style of the English Baroque.

As we can see in Figure **7.23**, Wren has designed a sophisticated and overlapping system of repetition and balance. Note first that the façade is symmetrical. The outward wing at the far left of the photograph is duplicated at the right (but not shown in the photo). In the center of the building are four attached columns surrounding three windows. The middle window forms the exact center of the design, with mirror-image repetition on each side. Now note that above the main windows is a series of relief sculptures, pediments (triangular casings), and circular windows. Now return to the main row of

7.22 Hampton Court Palace, England. Tudor entry, c. 1515.

7.23 Hampton Court Palace, England. Wren façade, 1689.

windows at the left border of the photo and count toward the center. The outer wing contains three windows; then seven windows, then the central three; then seven; and finally the three of the unseen outer wing. Patterns of threes and sevens are very popular in architecture and carry religious and mythological symbolism. Wren has established a pattern of three in the outer wing, repeated it at the center, and then repeated it within each of the seven-window groups to create yet three additional patterns of three! How is it possible to create three patterns of three with only seven windows? First, locate the center window of the seven. It has a pediment and a relief sculpture above it. On each side of this window are three windows (a total of six) without pediments. So, we have *two* groupings of three windows each. Above each of the outside four windows is a circular window. The window on each side of the center window does not have a circular window above it. Rather, it has a relief sculpture, the presence of which joins these two windows with the center window to give us our third grouping of three. Line, repetition, and balance in this façade form a marvelous perceptual exercise and experience.

Buckingham Palace, London (Fig. **7.24**), and the Palace of Versailles (Fig. **7.25**) illustrate different treatments of line and repetition. Buckingham Palace uses straight line exclusively, with repetition of rectilinear and triangular form. Like Hampton Court Palace, it exhibits *fenestration* groupings of threes and sevens, and the building itself is symmetrically balanced and divided by three pedimented, porticolike protrusions. Notice how the predominantly horizontal line of the building is broken by the three major pediments and given interest and contrast across its full length by the window pediments and the verticality of the attached columns.

Contrast Buckingham Palace with the Palace of Versailles, in which repetition occurs in groupings of threes and fives. Contrast is provided by juxtaposition and repetition of curvilinear line in the arched windows and baroque statuary. Notice how the horizontal line of the building, despite three porticoes, remains virtually undisturbed, in contrast with Buckingham Palace.

SCALE & PROPORTION

The mass, or *scale*, and proportion of a building and its component elements are very important compositional qualities. Scale refers to the building's size and the relationship of the building and its decorative elements to the human form.

Proportion, or the relationship of individual elements in a composition to each other, also plays a role in the overall analysis and appearance of a design. Let's step outside architecture for a familiar example. The Concorde supersonic airliner appears to be a rather large plane when we view it on the movie screen or on television. Yet if we were to see the plane in actuality, we would be surprised to find that it is not particularly large—in comparison with a DC10, a Boeing 747, or even a Boeing 707. The proportion of the Concorde's window area to its overall size is misleading when we see the plane out of context with the human body. The Concorde's windows are very small, much smaller than in other airliners. So when we see the Concorde in a newsreel we immediately equate the window size with which we are familiar with the windows in the Concorde. We assume that the relationship or *proportion* of window size to overall fuselage is conventional, and that assumption gives us a larger-than-actual image of the size of the plane. In terms of architecture, proportion

7.24 Buckingham Palace, London, c. 1825.

7.25 Palace of Versailles, France, 1669–85. Architects: Louis LeVau and Jules Hardouin-Mansart. Pan American World Airways Photo.

and scale are tools by which the architect can create relationships that may be straightforward or deceptive. We must decide how these elements are used and to what effect. In addition, proportion in many buildings is mathematical: The relationship of one part to another often is based on ratios of three to two, one to two, one to three, and so on, as were the parts of the highboy (Fig. 0.1) discussed in the Introduction. Discovering such relationships in the buildings we see is one of the fascinating ways in which we can respond to architecture.

CONTEXT

An architectural design must take into account its context, or environment. In many cases context is essential to the statement made by the design. For example, Chartres Cathedral (Fig. 7.26) sits at the center of and on the highest point in the village of Chartres. Its placement at that particular location had a purpose for the medieval artisans and clerics responsible for its design. The centrality of the cathedral to the community was an essential statement of the centrality of the church to the life of the medieval community. Context also has a psychological bearing on scale. A skyscraper in the midst of skyscrapers has great mass but does not appear as massive in scale when overshadowed by another, taller skyscraper. A cathedral, when compared with a skyscraper, is relatively small in scale. However, when standing at the center of a community of small houses, it appears quite the opposite.

Two additional aspects of context concern the design of line, form, and texture relative to the physical environment of the building. On one hand, the environment can be shaped according to the compositional qualities of the building. Perhaps the best illustration of that principle is Louis XIV's palace at Versailles, whose formal symmetry is reflected in the design of thousands of acres around it.

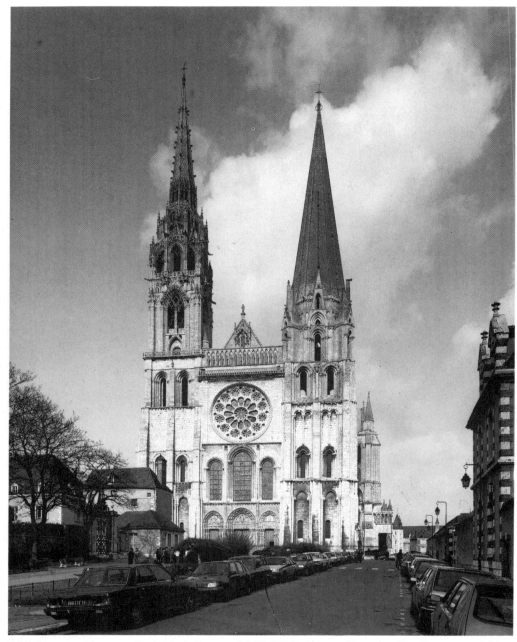

7.26 Exterior, Chartres Cathedral, France, 1145–1220. Photo: Giraudon/Art Resources, NY.

On a more modest scale, the formal gardens of Hampton Court (Fig. **7.27**) reflect the line and form of the palace.

On the other hand, a building may be designed so as to reflect the natural characteristics of its environment. Such an idea has been advanced by many architects and can be seen especially in residences in which large expanses of glass allow us to feel a part of the outside while we are inside. The interior decoration of such houses often takes as its theme the colors, textures, lines, and forms of the environment surrounding the home. Natural fibers, earth tones, delicate wooden furniture, pictures that reflect the surroundings, large open spaces—together they form the core of the design, selection, and placement of nearly every item in the home, from walls to furniture to silverware.

Frank Lloyd Wright was a great exponent of this style of work. His buildings seem to grow out of, and never violate, their environments. Perhaps his most inventive design is the Kaufmann House, "Falling Water," at Bear Run, Pennsylvania (Fig. **7.28**). Cantilevered over a waterfall, its dramatic imagery is most exciting. The inspiration was probably the French Renaissance chateau of Chenonceaux, which is built on a bridge across the River Cher. However, "Falling Water" is no mere house built on a bridge. It seems to erupt out of the natural rock, and its beige concrete terraces blend smoothly with the colors of

7.27 View of formal landscaping, Hampton Court Palace, England.

7.28 Frank Lloyd Wright, Kaufmann House, ''Falling Water,'' Bear Run, Pennsylvania, 1936–37.

the natural surrounding stone. Wright has successfully blended two seemingly dissimilar styles—the house is at one with its content, and yet is built in the rectilinear lines of the international style, to which Wright was opposed. He has taken that spare sterility of boxes and made them harmonize with the natural surroundings.

SPACE

It seems almost absurdly logical to state that architecture must concern space—for what else, by definition, is architecture? However, the world is overwhelmed with examples of architectural design that have not met that need. Design of space essentially means the design and flow of contiguous *spaces* relative to function. Take, for example, a sports arena. Of primary concern is the space necessary for the sports intended to occupy the building. Will it play host to basketball, hockey, track, football, or baseball? Each of these sports places a design restriction on the architect, and there may be curious results when functions not intended by the design are forced into its

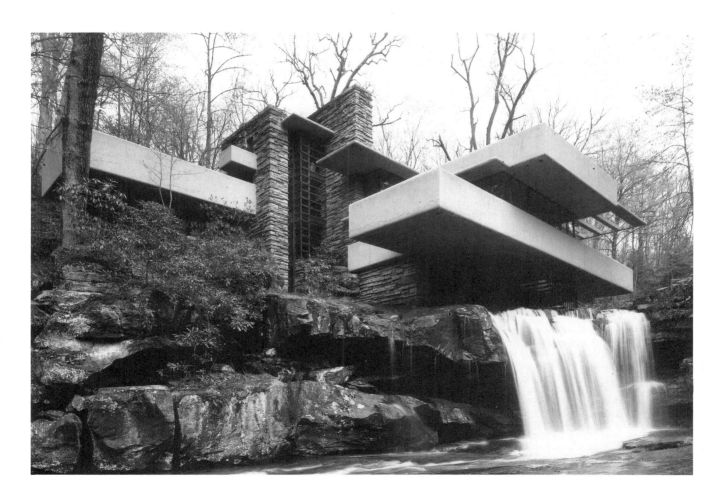

parameters. In addition to the requirements of the game, a sports arena must also accommodate the requirements of the spectators. Pillars that obstruct the spectator's view do not create good will and the purchase of tickets.

Finally, the design of space must concern the relationship of various needs peripheral to the primary functions of the building, such as rest rooms and concession stands.

Eero Saarinen's Trans-World Airline Terminal takes the dramatic shape of flight in curved lines and carefully designed spaces, which accommodate large masses of people and channel them to and from waiting aircraft. (Such shapes could be executed only by modern construction techniques and materials such as reinforced concrete.) Flight has also been suggested by Le Corbusier's dynamic church Notre-Dame-du-Haut (Fig. **7.29**). However, this pilgrimage church appears more like a work of sculpture than a building. Here function cannot be surmised from form. Rather, the juxtaposed rectilinear windows and curvilinear walls and the overwhelming roof nestled lightly on thin pillars above the walls all appear as a "pure creation of the spirit."

CLIMATE

Climate has always been a factor in architectural design in zones of severe temperature, either hot or cold. As the world's energy supplies diminish, this factor will grow in importance. In the temperate climate of much of the United States, solar systems and designs that make use of the moderating influence of the earth are common. These are passive systems—that is, their design accommodates natural phenomena rather than adding technological devices such as solar collectors. For example, in the colder sections of the United States a building can be made energy-efficient by being designed with no glass, or minimal glass, on its north-facing side. Windows facing south can be covered or uncovered to catch existing sunlight, which even in midwinter provides considerable warmth. Also, since temperatures at the shallow depth of

7.29 Le Corbusier, Notre-Dame-du-Haut, France, 1950–54. From the southeast.

148

3 ft (1 m) below the earth's surface rarely exceed or go below 50° F (10° C) regardless of season, the earth presents a gold mine of potential for design. Houses built into the sides of hills or recessed below the earth's surface require much less heating or cooling than those standing fully exposed—regardless of climate extremes. Even in zones of uniform and moderate temperature, climate is a design factor. The "California lifestyle," as it often is known, is responsible for design that accommodates easy access to the out-of-doors, and large, open spaces with free-flowing traffic patterns.

HOW DOES IT STIMULATE THE SENSES?

As should be clear at this point, our sensual response to a form of aesthetic design is a composite experience. To be sure, the individual characteristics we have discussed previously are the stimuli for our response. However, response is a product of the moment and happens because stimuli working in concert affect us in a particular manner. So, since in other chapters we have already considered how particular design considerations might affect us, I wish to make this chapter's analysis a bit more like our actual experience—that is a spontaneous response to the artwork. My remarks will be brief; much more could be said of each example. However, in the following progression of comparisons, I wish not to be impeded by excessive detail concerning each work.

GOTHIC CATHEDRALS

The upward, striving line of the Gothic arch makes a simple yet powerful appeal to the senses. The simplicity and grace of the design have an effect on most who view a Gothic cathedral (Fig. 7.30).

The cathedral at Amiens (Fig. 7.31) is similar in basic composition to Notre Dame, but rather than creating a sense of four-square power, it gives a feeling of delicacy. Amiens Cathedral illustrates a late development of Gothic style. The differences between Amiens and Notre Dame provide an important lesson in the ways design can be used to elicit a response. Amiens is more delicate than Notre Dame, and this feeling is encouraged by the greater detail that focuses our attention on space as opposed to flat stone. Both churches are divided into three very obvious horizontal and vertical sections of roughly the

same proportion. Notre Dame appears to rest heavily on its lowest section, whose proportions are diminished by the horizontal band of sculptures above the portals. Amiens, on the other hand, carries its portals upward to the full height of the lower section. In fact, the central portal, much larger than the central portal of Notre Dame, reinforces the line of the side portals to form a pyramid whose apex penetrates into the section above. The roughly similar size of the portals of Notre Dame reinforces its horizontal sense, thereby giving it stability. Similarly each use of line, form, and proportion in Amiens reinforces lightness and action, as compared with stability and strength in Notre Dame. This discussion does not imply that one design is better than the other. Each is different and displays a different approach.

Together with the grandeur of simple vertical line in Gothic cathedrals is an ethereal lightness that defies the material from which they were constructed. The medieval architect has created in stone not the heavy yet elegant composition of the early Greeks, which focused upon treatment of stone, but rather a treatment of stone that focuses on space—the ultimate mystery. Inside the

7.30 Notre Dame, Paris, west front, 1163–1250.

7.31 Amiens Cathedral, west front, c. 1220–59.

cathedrals the design of stained glass kept high above the worshippers' heads so controls the light entering that the overwhelming effect is, again, one of mystery. Line, form, scale, color, structure, balance, proportion, context, and space all combine to form unified compositions that have stood for hundreds of years as prototypes and symbols of the Christian experience.

A totally different appeal to the emotions emerges from the ornate German Baroque style Kaisersaal Residenz (Fig. **7.34**), wherein ornateness and opulence form the object of line and form.

HOLY FAMILY CHURCH

The Christian experience is also the denominator of the design of the Holy Family Church (Fig. **7.32**). However, despite the clarity of line and the upward striving power of its composition, this church has a modern sophistication, perhaps speaking more of our own conception of space, which to us is less unknowable and more conquerable, than did the churches of our medieval predecessors. The juxtaposing of rectilinear and curvilinear lines creates an active and dynamic response, one that prompts in us abruptness rather than mystery. The composition is cool, and its material calls attention to itself—to its starkness and to its lack of decoration. The Church of the Holy Family achieves its balance psychologically, by intent rather than by accident, as was the case with Chartres Cathedral.

Each part of the church is distinct and is not quite subordinate to the totality of the design. This building perhaps represents a philosophy intermediate between the philosophy underlying the Chartres Cathedral, whose entire design can be reduced to a single motif—the Gothic arch—and the philosophy such as the Baroque, as seen in the Hall of Mirrors of the Palace of Versailles (Fig. **7.35**). No single part of the design of this hall epitomizes the whole, yet each part is subordinate to the whole. Our response to the hall is shaped by its ornate complexity, which calls for detachment and investigation and intends to overwhelm us with its opulence. Here, as in most art, the expression and the stimuli reflect the patron. Chartres Cathedral reflects the medieval church, the Church of the Holy Family, the contemporary church, and Versailles, King Louis XIV. Versailles is complex, highly active, and yet warm. The richness of its textures, the warmth of its colors, and its curvilinear softness create a certain kind of comfort despite its scale and formality.

UNITED STATES CAPITOL BUILDING

In this neoclassic house of government (Fig. **7.33**), formality creates a foursquare, solid response. The symmetry of its design, the weight of its material, and its coldness give us a sense of impersonal power, which is heightened by the crushing weight of the dome. Rather than the upward-striving spiritual release of the Gothic arch, or even the powerful elegance of the Greek post-and-lintel, the Capitol Building, based on a Roman prototype, elicits a sense of struggle. This effect is achieved through upward

7.32 Holy Family Church, Parma, Ohio, 1965. Architects: Conrad and Fleishman.

7.33 United States Capitol Building, 1792–1856. Washington Area Convention and Visitors Association Photo.

7.34 (*opposite*) Balthasar Neumann, Kaisersaal, Residenz, Würzburg, Germany, 1719–44.

7.35 (*opposite, below*) Hall of Mirrors, Palace of Versailles, France, 1680. Architects: Jules Hardouin-Mansart and Charles LeBrun.

columnar thrust (heightened by the context provided by Capitol Hill) and downward thrust (of the dome) focused toward the interior of the building.

GUGGENHEIM MUSEUM

The architect Louis Sullivan (who employed Frank Lloyd Wright as an engineering student to work with him on the concept of a Tall Building, which led to the principle of the skyscraper) is credited with the concept that form follows function. To a degree we have seen that concept in the previous examples, even though, with the exception of the Church of the Holy Family, they all precede Sullivan in time. A worthy question concerning the Guggenheim Museum (Fig. 7.36) might be how well Wright followed Sullivan's philosophy. There is a story that Wright hated New York City because of unpleasant experiences he had had with the city fathers during previous projects. As a result, the Guggenheim, done late in his life, became his final gesture of derision to the city. This center of contemporary culture and art, with its single, circular ramp from street level to roof, was built (so the story goes) from the plans for a parking garage! Be that as it may, the line and form of this building create a simple, smoothly flowing, leisurely, upward movement juxtaposed against a stark and dynamic rectilinear form. The building's line and color and the feeling they produce are contemporary statements appropriate to the contemporary art the museum houses. The modern design of the Guggenheim is quite in contrast with the classical proportions of the Metropolitan Museum of Art, just down the street, which houses great works of ancient and modern art. The interior design is outwardly expressed in the ramp, and one can speculate that the slowly curving, unbroken line of the ramp is highly appropriate to the leisurely pace that one should follow when going through a museum.

7.36 Frank Lloyd Wright, Guggenheim Museum, New York City, 1942–59.

7.37 Skidmore, Owings, and Merrill, Sears Tower, Chicago, 1971.

ZARZUELA RACE TRACK

Leisurely progress through the Guggenheim is opposite to the sensation stimulated by the cantilevered roof of the grandstand at Zarzuela Race Track in Spain (Fig. **7.17**). Speed, power, and flight are its preeminent concerns. The sense of dynamic instability inherent in the structural form—cantilever—and this particular application of that form, mirror the dynamic instability and forward power of the race horse at full speed. However, despite the form and the strong diagonals of this design, it is not out of control; the architect has unified the design through repetition of the track-level arcade in the arched line of the cantilevered roof. The design is dynamic and yet humanized in the softness of its curves and the control of its scale.

SEARS TOWER

Nothing symbolizes the technological achievement of modern humans more than the skyscraper. Also, nothing symbolizes the subordination of humans to their technology more than the scale of this monumental building (Fig. **7.37**). Designed of rectangular components placed side by side, the Sears Tower is a glass and steel monolith overwhelming in its scale and proportions and cold in its materials. As a point of departure, its appeal to our senses raises the question of what comes next, the conquest of space or a return to respect for its natural mysteries?

EIGHT

LITERATURE

WHAT IS IT?

Literature is language whose purpose is to communicate. In the same sense that all artworks communicate through a particular medium someone's perception of reality or truth, so literature communicates using the forms we shall examine momentarily. There is a difference between literature that some call utilitarian and literature that may be called creative. Creative literature has a different approach than utilitarian literature. The approach determines the category in the same sense that a picture composed of line, form, and color is termed "art," whereas another picture, composed of those same characteristics but whose purpose is merely to provide a visual copy, is termed "illustration."

As with any work of art, creative literature has many layers which make it a symbolic rather than a literal presentation. Nonetheless, there is a difference between literature and the other arts. Perhaps the difference is academic, but I believe it is important if we are to understand how art and literature work to create responses in us. Literature operates in an explicit fashion. (Poetry, in which the visual format of the poem contributes to its meaning, is, of course, an exception.) That is, literature

operates through a system of language in which the words themselves are the triggers for our symbolic understandings. The traditional arts, which we have previously examined, trigger our responses through nonverbal, that is to say, nonexplicit means. Even in the theatre, artistic communication goes far beyond the explicit language of the playwright. That is why the Greeks called it "theatre," from their word *theatron*, "a place of *seeing*". However, in its written form, which we call drama, the play script is a part of literature. When it is performed, with the addition of actors and *mise en scène*, it becomes theatre. So, what are the formal divisions of literature? They are fiction, poetry, biography, essay, and drama.

FICTION

Fiction is a work created from the author's imagination rather than from fact. Normally it takes one of two approaches to its subject matter: *realistic*—that is, the appearance of observable, true-to-life details; or *nonrealistic*—that is, fantasy. Other literary forms such as narrative poetry and drama can also be fiction, and fictional elements can be introduced into forms such as biography and epic poetry. Fiction traditionally is divided into *novels* and *short stories*.

Novels

The novel is a prose narrative of considerable length which has a plot that unfolds from the actions, speech, and thoughts of the characters. Normally the novel treats events within the range of ordinary experience and draws upon original subject matter rather than traditional or mythic subjects. Novels typically have numerous characters and employ normal, daily speech. The subject matter of novels can be divided into two general categories, *sociological-panoramic*, covering a wide-ranging story of many years and various settings, and *dramatic-intimate*, which is restricted in time and setting.

Often, novels are formally classified by their subject matter. A few of these categories are:

picaresque   the adventures of a rogue
manners   problems of personal relations
sentimental   the development of emotionality, especially a sentimental appreciation of simplicity
Gothic   the trials of a pure, sensitive, and noble heroine who undergoes terrifying experiences, emerging undamaged— usually this type of novel is stilted, melodramatic, and exploitive of the darker side of emotional psychology
historical   intertwines historical events and fictional characters
realistic   focuses on familiar situations and ordinary people
lyrical   a short work with a metaphoric structure and a limited number of characters.

Short Stories

As the name implies, short stories are short prose fictional works focusing on unity of characterization, theme, and effect.

POETRY

Poetry is a type of work designed to convey a vivid and imaginative sense of experience. Poetry uses condensed language selected for its sound, suggestive power, and meaning, and employs specific technical devices such as meter, rhyme, and metaphor. Poetry can be divided into three major types: *narrative*, *dramatic*, and *lyric*.

Narrative

Narrative poetry tells a story. *Epic* poetry is narrative poetry of substantial length and elevated style. It uses strong symbolism, and has a central figure of heroic proportions. A *ballad* is a sung or recited narrative. A *metrical romance* is a long narrative, romantic tale in verse.

Dramatic

Dramatic poetry utilizes dramatic form or dramatic technique. Its major form is the dramatic monologue.

Lyric

Lyric poetry was originally intended to be sung and accompanied by a lyre. It is a brief, subjective work employing strong imagination, melody, and feeling to create a single, unified, and intense impression of the personal emotion of the poet.

BIOGRAPHY

Over the centuries, biography has taken many forms and witnessed many techniques and intentions, including literary narratives, catalogues of achievement, and psychological portraits. Biography is a written account of a person's life. Accounts of the lives of the saints and other religious figures are called *hagiographies*.

ESSAYS

Traditionally, the essay is a short literary composition on a single subject, usually presenting the personal views of the author. The word comes from the French, meaning "to try" and the vulgar Latin, meaning "to weigh." Essays include many subforms and a variety of styles, but they uniformly present a personal point of view with a conscious attempt to achieve grace of expression. Essays characteristically are marked by clarity, grace, good humor, wit, urbanity, and tolerance.

An essay is a work of nonfiction reflecting the author's attitudes toward a specific subject. In so doing, it may reveal the author's personality or speculations. For the most part, essays are brief, but occasionally much longer works, such as John Locke's treatise, *Essay Concerning Human Understanding*, 1690, have appeared. Traditionally, essays fall into two categories: *informal*, or *formal*.

Informal

Informal essays tend to be brief and very personal. They are conversational in tone and loose in structure. This type of essay can be further divided into categories called *familiar* or *personal* and *character*. The personal essay presents an aspect of the author's personality as he or she reacts to an event. Character essays describe persons, isolating their dominant traits, for example.

Formal

Formal essays are longer and more tightly structured than informal essays. Formal essays tend to focus on impersonal subjects and place less emphasis on the personality of the author.

DRAMA

Drama is the written script, or play, upon which a theatre performance may be based. We examined this genre in Chapter 4.

HOW IS IT PUT TOGETHER?

FICTION

Point of View

Fiction is a story told by someone at a particular time and place to a particular audience. So it has a definite perspective, and, therefore, certain limitations of objectivity. It raises questions about the right way of seeing things. For the story to achieve credibility as fiction, the author must appear to distance himself or herself from the representative truth of the story and the reader. The "point of view" is a device to objectify the circumstances. Four types of narrative point of view are *first person; epistolary*—that is, told through the use of letters written by the characters; *omniscient narration* or "third person;" and *stream of consciousness* or "interior monologue," wherein a flow of thoughts, feelings, and memories come from a specific character's psyche. These arbitrary definitions regarding point of view may vary, or be combined by authors to suit their own purposes. Point of view, as we have discussed it here, means merely that one of the means by which fiction is put together is usable by an author in several ways, at several levels, to communicate meaning.

Appearance and Reality

Fiction claims to be true to actuality, but it is built on invented sequences of events. It refers back on itself, layering the fictional and the factual.

Tone

Tone may also be called the atmosphere of the story. In essence, it is the author's attitude toward the story's literal facts. Reading is much like listening to conversation. That is, the words carry meaning, but the way in which they are said—their tone—shapes meaning much more effectively. In addition, the atmosphere of the story sometimes includes the setting or the physical environment. In many stories, atmosphere is psychological as well as physical, and when all of these characteristics of tone are taken together, they provide subtle and powerful suggestions leading to our fuller understanding of the work.

Character

What gives literature its appeal is people, but not just people alone. Our interest is drawn because we see a human character involved in some kind of conflict—that is, a struggle with some important human problem. Authors write to that potential interest and usually strive to focus our attention, and to achieve unity, by drawing a central character with whose actions, decisions, growth, and development we can identify, and in whom we can find an indication of some broader aspect of the human condition. As we noted in Chapter 4, the term character goes beyond the mere identification of a "person." Character means the psychological spine of the individual, the driving force which makes that individual respond the way he or she does when faced with a given set of circumstances. Character is what we are interested in: Given a set of troubling or challenging circumstances, what does the character of the individual lead him or her to do?

In developing character, an author has numerous choices, depending, again, on his or her purposes. Character may be fully three-dimensional and highly individualistic—that is, as complex as the restrictions of the medium allow. Novels, because of their length and the fact that the reader can go back to double-check a fact or description, allow much more complex character development or individuality than do plays, whose important points must be found by the audience the moment they are presented. Also, a change of narrative viewpoint, appropriate to the novel but not a play (unless a narrator is used, as in *Our Town*), can give the reader aspects of character in a more efficient manner than can revelation through action or dialogue. On the other hand, the author's purpose may be served by presenting character not as a fully developed individual but as a type. Whatever the author's choice, the nature of character development tells us much about the meaning we are to find in the work.

Plot

Plot is the structure of the work. It is more than the story line or the facts of the piece. In literature, as in the theatre, we find our interest dependent upon action. We are here to witness character in action. Plot is the structure of that action. It creates unity in the work and thereby helps us to find meaning. Plot is the skeleton which determines the ultimate shape of the piece, once the elements of flesh have been added to it. The action of a literary work is designed to dramatize a fully realized theme, situation, or character.

Plot may be the major or subordinate focus in a work, and it can be open or closed. Closed plots rely on the Aristotelian model of pyramidal action with exposition, complication, and resolution or denouement. An open plot has little or no resolution. We merely leave the characters at a convenient point and imagine them continuing on as their characters will dictate.

Theme

Most good stories have an overriding idea or theme by which the other elements are shaped. Quality in works of art may rest on the artist's ability to utilize the tools of his or her medium and on whether the artist has something worthwhile to say. Some critics argue that the quality of a theme is less important than what the author does with it. Yet, the conclusion is inescapable: The best artworks are those in which the author has taken a meaningful theme and developed it exceptionally. So the theme or idea of a work is what the author has to say. The other devices of the piece will help us to understand the ultimate idea. Theme may mean a definite intellectual concept, or it may indicate a highly complex situation such as occurs in "A Rose for Emily," which is reprinted in this chapter. Clues to understanding the idea can come as early as our exposure to the title. Beyond that, the theme is usually revealed in small pieces as we move from beginning to conclusion.

Symbolism

Every work of literature is symbolic to one degree or another. It stands for something greater than its literal reality. Words are symbols, as is language. So any story is symbolic inasmuch as it symbolizes human experience. Often the symbols that occur in a story are cultural in derivation. That is why we often have difficulty understanding the levels of meaning in works from other cultures. We also find it difficult to grasp the symbols in works from our own Western tradition. The more we

know about our culture and its various points of view through history, the more we are able to grasp the symbolism, and thereby the meaning, of the great thinkers, writers, and artists whose insights into the human condition can help us cope with the significant questions of our time and our personal condition.

Sometimes symbols are treated as if they are private or esoteric. In other words, sometimes writers will purposely try to hide some levels of meaning from all but the thoroughly initiated or truly sophisticated. Sometimes authors will try to create new symbol systems. Whatever the case, symbolism gives the story its richness and much of its appeal. When we realize that a character, for example, is a symbol, regardless of how much of an individual he or she may be, the story takes on new meaning for us. We often discover that every character in the story symbolizes us—that is, some aspect of *our* complex and often contradictory characters. Symbols can be hidden, profound, or simple. When we discover them and unlock their revelations, we have made a significant stride toward understanding meaning.

POETRY

Language

Rhythm can be broken into four types: quantitative, accentual, syllabic, and accentual-syllabic. Quantitative rhythm has a regular succession of long and short syllables. Accentual rhythm creates rhythm through stress—that is, accented syllables. Syllabic rhythm has a fixed number of syllables in a line that set the rhythm. Accentual-syllabic rhythm combines accents with a relatively fixed number of syllables to create rhythm.

Imagery comprises a verbal representation of a sensory experience. It can be literal or figurative. In the former, there is no change or extension in meaning; for example, "green eyes" are simply eyes that are a green color. In the latter, there is a change in literal meaning; for example, green eyes might become "green orbs."

Figures, like images, take words beyond their literal meaning. Much of poetic meaning comes in comparing objects in ways that go beyond the literal. For example, in Robert Frost's "Stopping by Woods on a Snowy Evening," snowflakes are described as *downy*, which endows them with the figurative quality of soft, fluffy feathers on a young bird. In the same sense, Frost uses "sweep" and "easy" to describe the wind.

Metaphors are figures of speech by which new implications are given to words. For example, the expression "the twilight of life" takes the word *twilight* and applies it to the concept of life to create an entirely new image and meaning.

Symbols also are often associated with figures of speech, but not all figures are symbols, and not all symbols are figures. Symbolism is critical to poetry, which uses compressed language to express, and carry us into, its meanings. In poetry "the whole poem helps to determine the meaning of its parts, and in turn, each part helps to determine the meaning of the whole poem."[1]

Structure

Form or structure in poetry derives from fitting together lines of similar structure and length tied to other lines by end rhyme. For example, the sonnet has fourteen lines of iambic pentameters rhymed 1–3, 2–4, 5–7, 6–8, 9–11, 10–12, 13–14.

Stanzas, which are any recurring groupings of two or more lines in terms of length, meter, and rhyme, are part of structure. A stanza usually presents a unit of poetic experience, and if the poem has more than one stanza, the pattern is usually repeated.

Sound Structures

Rhyme is the most common sound structure. Rhyme is, of course, the coupling of words that sound alike. Its function in poetry is to tie the sense together with the sound. Rhyme can be masculine, feminine, or triple. Masculine rhyme is based on single-syllable vowels such as "hate" and "mate." Feminine rhyme is based on sounds between accented and unaccented syllables, for example, "hating" and "mating." Triple rhyme comprises a correspondence among three syllables such as "despondent" and "respondent."

Alliteration is a second type of sound structure in which an initial sound is repeated for effect; for example, *fancy free*.

Assonance is a similarity among vowels but not consonants.

Meter

Meter comprises the type and number of rhythmic units in a line. Rhythmic units are called *feet*. Four common kinds of feet are *iambic, trochaic, anapestic,* and *dactyllic*. Iambic meter alternates one unstressed and one stressed syllable; trochaic meter alternates one stressed and one unstressed syllable; anapestic meter alternates two unstressed and one stressed syllable; and dactyllic meter alternates one stressed and two unstressed syllables.

Line, also called verse, determines the basic rhythmic pattern of the poem. Lines are named by the number of feet they contain. One foot is monometer; two, dimeter; three, trimeter; four, tetrameter; five, pentameter; six, hexameter; seven, heptameter; and eight, octameter.

BIOGRAPHY

Facts

Facts are the verifiable details around which a biography is shaped. However, facts, other than matters such as birth, death, marriage, and other date-related occurrences, often have a way of becoming elusive. "Facts" often turn out to be observations filtered through the personality of the observer. Incontrovertible facts may comprise a chronological or skeletal framework for a biography, but often they do not create much interest. Often they do not provide much of a skeleton either. Many individuals about whose lives we would like to learn more have few facts recorded about them. On the other hand, the lives of other important individuals have been chronicled in such great detail that too many facts exist. Artistry entails selection and composition, and in the latter case, interest may require leaving many facts out of the narrative. Of course, another issue related to facts and biography is the question of what the author should do with the facts. If the facts are injurious, should they be used? In what context should they be used? Whatever the situation, facts alone do not comprise a sufficient quality for an artistic or interesting biography.

Anecdotes

Anecdotes are stories or observations about moments in a biography. Anecdotes take the basic facts and expand them for illustrative purposes, thereby creating interest. Anecdotes may be true or untrue. Their purpose, often, is to create a memorable generalization. They may also generate debate or controversy.

Quotations form part of anecdotal experience. Their purpose is to create interest by changing the presentational format to that of dialogue. In one sense, dialogue brings us closer to subjects of the biography by helping to create the impression that we are part of the scene, as opposed to being third parties listening to someone else describe a situation.

HOW DOES IT APPEAL TO THE SENSES?

The following seven selections serve as illustrations of literature. Literature appeals to our senses by the way in which the writer uses the tools of the medium. We have applied the formal and technical elements of the arts enough times now that to do so again would be to restate the obvious. Read the following examples and decide for yourself how your response is manipulated by the author's use of the devices we have discussed. Discuss each example with a friend to see if your reactions were similar or different. Where differences arise, try to determine why.

FICTION

"A Rose for Emily"
William Faulkner
1897–1962

1

When Miss Emily Grierson died, our whole town went to her funeral; the men through a sort of respectful affection for a fallen monument, the women mostly out of curiosity to see the inside of her house, which no one save an old manservant—a combined gardener and cook—had seen in at least ten years.

It was a big, squarish frame house that had once been white, decorated with cupolas and spires and scrolled balconies in the heavily lightsome style of the seventies, set on what had once been our most select street. But garages and cotton gins had encroached and obliterated even the august names of that neighborhood; only Miss Emily's house was left, lifting its stubborn and coquettish decay above the cotton wagons and the gasoline pumps—an eyesore among eyesores. And now Miss Emily had gone to join the representatives of those august names where they lay in the cedar-bemused cemetery among the ranked and anonymous graves of Union and Confederate soldiers who fell at the battle of Jefferson.

Alive, Miss Emily had been a tradition, a duty, and a care; a sort of hereditary obligation upon the town, dating from that day in 1894 when Colonel Sartoris, the mayor—he who fathered the edict that no Negro woman should appear on the streets without an apron—remitted her taxes, the dispensation dating from the death of her father on into perpetuity. Not that Miss Emily would have accepted charity. Colonel Sartoris invented an involved tale to the effect that Miss Emily's father had loaned money to the town, which the town, as a matter of business, preferred this way of repaying. Only a man of Colonel Sartoris' generation and thought could have invented it, and only a woman could have believed it.

When the next generation, with its more modern ideas, became mayors and aldermen, this arrangement created some little dissatisfaction. On the first of the year they mailed her a tax notice. February came, and there was no reply. They wrote her a formal letter, asking her to call at the sheriff's office at her convenience. A week later the mayor wrote her himself, offering to call or send his car for her, and received in reply a note on paper of an archaic shape, in a thin flowing calligraphy in faded ink, to the effect that she no longer went out at all. The tax notice was also enclosed, without comment.

They called a special meeting of the Board of Aldermen. A deputation waited upon her, knocked at the door through which no visitor had passed since she ceased giving china-painting lessons eight or ten years earlier. They were admitted by the old Negro into a dim hall from which a stairway mounted into still more shadow. It smelled of dust and disuse—a close, dank smell. The Negro led them into the parlor. It was furnished in heavy, leather-covered furniture. When the Negro opened the blinds of one window, they could see that the leather was cracked; and when they sat down, a faint dust rose sluggishly about their thighs, spinning with slow motes in the single sun-ray. On a tarnished gilt easel before the fireplace stood a crayon portrait of Miss Emily's father.

They rose when she entered—a small, fat woman in black, with a thin gold chain descending to her waist and vanishing into her belt, leaning on an ebony cane with a tarnished gold head. Her skeleton was small and spare; perhaps that was why what would have been merely plumpness in another was obesity in her. She looked bloated, like a body long submerged in motionless water, and of that pallid hue. Her eyes, lost in the fatty ridges of her face, looked like two small pieces of coal pressed into a lump of dough as they moved from one face to another while the visitors stated their errand.

She did not ask them to sit. She just stood in the door and listened quietly until the spokesman came to a stumbling halt. Then they could hear the invisible watch ticking at the end of the gold chain.

Her voice was dry and cold. "I have no taxes in Jefferson. Colonel Sartoris explained it to me. Perhaps one of you can gain access to the city records and satisfy yourselves."

"But we have. We are the city authorities, Miss Emily. Didn't you get a notice from the sheriff, signed by him?"

"I received a paper, yes," Miss Emily said. "Perhaps he considers himself the sheriff . . . I have no taxes in Jefferson."

"But there is nothing on the books to show that, you see. We must go by the—"

"See Colonel Sartoris. I have no taxes in Jefferson."

"But, Miss Emily—"

"See Colonel Sartoris." (Colonel Sartoris had been dead almost ten years.) "I have no taxes in Jefferson. Tobe!" The Negro appeared. "Show these gentlemen out."

2

So she vanquished them, horse and foot, just as she had vanquished their fathers thirty years before about the smell. That was two years after her father's death and a short time after her sweetheart—the one we believed would marry her—had deserted her. After her father's death she went out very little; after her sweetheart went away, people hardly saw her at all. A few of the ladies had the temerity to call, but were not received, and the only sign of life about the place was the Negro man—a young man then—going in and out with a market basket.

"Just as if a man—any man—could keep a kitchen properly," the ladies said; so they were not surprised when the smell developed. It was another link between the gross, teeming world and the high and mighty Griersons.

A neighbor, a woman, complained to the mayor, Judge Stevens, eighty years old.

"But what will you have me do about it, madam?" he said.

"Why, send her word to stop it," the woman said. "Isn't there a law?"

"I'm sure that won't be necessary," Judge Stevens said. "It's probably just a snake or a rat that nigger of hers killed in the yard. I'll speak to him about it."

The next day he received two more complaints, one from a man who came in diffident deprecation. "We really must do something about it, Judge. I'd be the last one in the world to bother Miss Emily, but we've got to do something." That night the Board of Aldermen met—three graybeards and one younger man, a member of the rising generation.

"It's simple enough," he said. "Send her word to have her place cleaned up. Give her a certain time to do it in, and if she don't . . ."

"Dammit, sir," Judge Stevens said, "will you accuse a lady to her face of smelling bad?"

So the next night, after midnight, four men crossed Miss Emily's lawn and slunk about the house like burglars, sniffing along the base of the brickwork and at the cellar openings while one of them performed a regular sowing motion with his hand out of a sack slung from his shoulder. They broke open the cellar door and sprinkled lime there, and in all the outbuildings. As they recrossed the lawn, a window that had been dark was lighted and Miss Emily sat in it, the light behind her, and her upright torso motionless as that of an idol. They crept quietly across the lawn and into the shadow of the locusts that lined the street. After a week or two the smell went away.

That was when people had begun to feel really sorry for her. People in our town, remembering how old lady Wyatt, her great aunt, had gone completely crazy at last, believed that the Griersons held themselves a little too high for what they really were. None of the young men were quite good enough for Miss Emily and such. We had long thought of them as a tableau. Miss Emily a slender figure in white in the background, her father a spraddled silhouette in the foreground, his back to her and clutching a horsewhip, the two of them framed by the backflung front door. So when she got to be thirty and was still single, we were not pleased exactly, but vindicated; even with insanity in the family she wouldn't have turned down all of her chances if they had really materialized.

When her father died, it got about that the house was all that was left to her; and in a way, people were glad. At last they could pity Miss Emily. Being left alone, and a pauper, she had become humanized. Now she too would know the old thrill and the old despair of a penny more or less.

The day after his death all the ladies prepared to call at the house and offer condolence and aid, as is our custom. Miss Emily met them at the door, dressed as usual and with no trace of grief on her face. She told them that her father was not dead. She did that for three days, with the ministers calling on her, and the doctors, trying to persuade her to let them dispose of the body. Just as they were about to resort to law and force, she broke down, and they buried her father quickly.

We did not say she was crazy then. We believed she had to do that. We remembered all the young men her father had driven away, and we knew that with nothing left, she would have to cling to that which had robbed her, as people will.

3

She was sick for a long time. When we saw her again, her hair was cut short, making her look like a girl, with a vague resemblance to those angels in colored church windows—sort of tragic and serene.

The town had just let the contracts for paving the sidewalks, and in the summer after her father's death they began the work. The construction company came with niggers and mules and machinery, and a foreman named Homer Barron, a Yankee—a big, dark, ready man, with a big voice and eyes lighter than his face. The little boys would follow in groups to hear him cuss the niggers, and the niggers singing in time to the rise and fall of picks. Pretty soon he knew everybody in town. Whenever you heard a lot of laughing anywhere about the square, Homer Barron would be in the center of the group. Presently we began to see him and Miss Emily on Sunday afternoons driving in the yellow-wheeled buggy and the matched team of bays from the livery stable.

At first we were glad that Miss Emily would have an interest, because the ladies all said, "Of course a Grierson would not think seriously of a Northerner, a day laborer." But there were still others, older people, who said that even grief could not cause a real lady to forget *noblesse oblige*—without calling it *noblesse oblige*. They just said, "Poor Emily. Her kinsfolk should come to her." She had some kin in Alabama; but years ago her father had fallen out with them over the estate of old lady Wyatt, the crazy woman, and there was no communication between the two families. They had not even been represented at the funeral.

And as soon as the old people said, "Poor Emily," the whispering began. "Do you suppose it's really so?" they said to one another. "Of course it is. What else could . . ." This behind their hands; rustling of craned silk and satin behind jalousies closed upon the sun of Sunday afternoon as the thin, swift clop-clop-clop of the matched team passed: "Poor Emily."

She carried her head high enough—even when we believed that she was fallen. It was as if she demanded more than ever the recognition of her dignity as the last Grierson; as if it had wanted that touch of earthiness to reaffirm her imperviousness. Like when she bought the rat poison, the arsenic. That was over a year after they had begun to say, "Poor Emily," and while the two female cousins were visiting her.

"I want some poison," she said to the druggist. She was over thirty then, still a slight woman, though thinner than usual, with cold, haughty black eyes in a face the flesh of which was strained across the temples and about the eyesockets as you imagine a lighthouse-keeper's face ought to look. "I want some poison," she said.

"Yes, Miss Emily. What kind? For rats and such? I'd recom—"

"I want the best you have. I don't care what kind."

The druggist named several. "They'll kill anything up to an elephant. But what you want is—"

"Arsenic," Miss Emily said. "Is that a good one?"

"Is . . . arsenic? Yes, ma'am. But what you want—"

"I want arsenic."

The druggist looked down at her. She looked back at him, erect, her face like a strained flag. "Why, of course," the druggist said. "If that's what you want. But the law requires you to tell what you are going to use it for."

Miss Emily just stared at him, her head tilted back in order to look him eye for eye, until he looked away and went and got the arsenic and wrapped it up. The Negro delivery boy brought her the package; the druggist didn't come back. When she opened the package at home there was written on the box, under the skull and bones: "For rats."

4

So the next day we all said, "She will kill herself"; and we said it would be the best thing. When she had first begun to be seen with Homer Barron, we had said, "She will marry him." Then we said, "She will persuade him yet," because Homer himself had remarked—he liked men, and it was known that he drank with the younger men in the Elks' Club—that he was not a marrying man. Later we said, "Poor Emily" behind the jalousies as they passed on Sunday afternoon in the glittering buggy. Miss Emily with her head high and Homer Barron with his hat cocked and a cigar in his teeth, reins and whip in a yellow glove.

Then some of the ladies began to say that it was a disgrace to the town, and a bad example to the young people. The men did not want to interfere, but at last the ladies forced the Baptist minister—Miss Emily's people were Episcopal—to call upon her. He would never divulge what happened during that inter-

view, but he refused to go back again. The next Sunday they again drove about the streets, and the following day the minister's wife wrote to Miss Emily's relations in Alabama.

So she had blood-kin under her roof again and we sat back to watch developments. At first nothing happened. Then we were sure that they were to be married. We learned that Miss Emily had been to the jeweler's and ordered a man's toilet set in silver, with the letters H. B. on each piece. Two days later we learned that she had bought a complete outfit of men's clothing, including a nightshirt, and we said, "They are married." We were really glad. We were glad because the two female cousins were even more Grierson that Miss Emily had ever been.

So we were not surprised when Homer Barron—the streets had been finished some time since—was gone. We were a little disappointed that there was not a public blowing-off, but we believed that he had gone on to prepare for Miss Emily's coming, or to give her a chance to get rid of the cousins. (By that time it was a cabal, and we were all Miss Emily's allies to help circumvent the cousins.) Sure enough, after another week they departed. And, as we had expected all along, within three days Homer Barron was back in town. A neighbor saw the Negro man admit him at the kitchen door at dusk one evening.

And that was the last we saw of Homer Barron. And of Miss Emily for some time. The Negro man went in and out with the market basket, but the front door remained closed. Now and then we would see her at a window for a moment, as the men did that night when they sprinkled the lime, but for almost six months she did not appear on the streets. Then we knew that this was to be expected too; as if that quality of her father had thwarted her woman's life so many times had been too virulent and too furious to die.

When we next saw Miss Emily, she had grown fat and her hair was turning gray. During the next few years it grew grayer and grayer until it attained an even pepper-and-salt iron-gray, when it ceased turning. Up to the day of her death at seventy-four it was still that vigorous iron-gray, like the hair of an active man.

From that time on her front door remained closed, save for a period of six or seven years, when she was about forty, during which she gave lessons in china-painting. She fitted up a studio in one of the downstairs rooms; where the daughters and grand-daughters of Colonel Sartoris' contemporaries were sent to her with the same regularity and in the same spirit that they were sent to church on Sundays with a twenty-five cent piece for the collection plate. Meanwhile her taxes had been remitted.

The newer generation became the backbone and the spirit of the town, and the painting pupils grew up and fell away and did not send their children to her with boxes of color and tedious brushes and pictures cut from the ladies' magazines. The front door closed upon the last one and remained closed for good. When the town got free postal delivery, Miss Emily alone refused to let them fasten the metal numbers above her door and attach a mailbox to it. She would not listen to them.

Daily, monthly, yearly we watched the Negro grow grayer and more stooped, going in and out with the market basket. Each December we sent her a tax notice, which would be returned by the post office a week later, unclaimed. Now and then we would see her in one of the downstairs windows—she had evidently shut up the top floor of the house—like the carven torso of an idol in a niche, looking or not looking at us, we could never tell which. Thus she passed from generation to generation—dear, inescapable, impervious, tranquil, and perverse.

And so she died. Fell ill in the house filled with dust and shadows, with only a doddering Negro man to wait on her. We did not even know she was sick; we had long since given up trying to get any information from the Negro. He talked to no one, probably not even to her, for his voice had grown harsh and rusty, as if from disuse.

She died in one of the downstairs rooms, in a heavy walnut bed with a curtain, her gray head propped on a pillow yellow and moldy with age and lack of sunlight.

5

The Negro met the first of the ladies at the front door and let them in, with their hushed, sibilant voices and their quick, curious glances, and then he disappeared. He walked right through the house and out the back and was not seen again.

The two female cousins came at once. They held the funeral on the second day, with the town coming to look at Miss Emily beneath a mass of bought flowers, with the crayon face of her father musing profoundly above the bier and the ladies sibilant and macabre; and the very old men—some in their brushed Confederate uniforms—on the porch and the lawn, talking of Miss Emily as if she had been a contemporary of theirs, believing that they had danced with her and courted her perhaps,

confusing time with its mathematical progression, as the old do, to whom all the past is not a diminishing road but, instead, a huge meadow which no winter ever quite touches, divided from them now by the narrow bottleneck of the most recent decade of years.

Already we knew that there was one room in that region above the stairs which no one had seen in forty years, and which would have to be forced. They waited until Miss Emily was decently in the ground before they opened it.

The violence of breaking down the door seemed to fill this room with pervading dust. A thin, acrid pall as of the tomb seemed to lie everywhere upon this room decked and furnished as for a bridal: upon the valance curtains of faded rose color, upon the rose-shaded lights, upon the dressing table, upon the delicate array of crystal and the man's toilet things backed with tarnished silver, silver so tarnished that the monogram was obscured. Among them lay a collar and tie, as if they had just been removed, which, lifted, left upon the surface a pale crescent in the dust. Upon a chair hung the suit, carefully folded; beneath it the two mute shoes and the discarded socks.

The man himself lay in the bed.

For a long while we just stood there, looking down at the profound and fleshless grin. The body had apparently once lain in the attitude of an embrace, but now the long sleep that outlasts love, that conquers even the grimace of love, had cuckolded him. What was left of him, rotted beneath what was left of the nightshirt, had become inextricable from the bed in which he lay; and upon him and upon the pillow beside him lay that even coating of the patient and biding dust.

Then we noticed that in the second pillow was the indentation of a head. One of us lifted something from it, and leaning forward, that faint and invisible dust dry and acrid in the nostrils, we saw a long strand of iron-gray hair.[2]

POETRY

The Seven Ages of Man
William Shakespeare
1564–1616

All the world's a stage,
And all the men and women merely
  players.
They have their exits and their entrances,
And one man in his time plays many parts,
His acts being seven ages. At first the
  infant,
Mewling[1] and puking in the nurse's arms.
Then the whining schoolboy, with his
  satchel
And shining morning face, creeping like
  snail
Unwillingly to school. And then the lover,
Sighing like furnace, with a woeful
  ballad[2]
Made to his mistress' eyebrow. Then a soldier,
Full of strange oaths and bearded like the
  pard,[3]
Jealous in honor,[4] sudden and quick in quarrel,
Seeking the bubble reputation[5]
Even in the cannon's mouth. And then the
  justice,
In fair round belly with good capon lined,[6]
With eyes severe and beard of formal cut,
Full of wise saws[7] and modern instances;[8]
And so he plays his part. The sixth age
  shifts
Into the lean and slippered Pantaloon,[9]
With spectacles on nose and pouch on side;
His youthful hose, well saved, a world too
  wide
For his shrunk shank, and his big manly
  voice,
Turning again toward childish treble, pipes
And whistles in his sound. Last scene of all,
That ends this strange eventful history,
Is second childishness and mere oblivion,
Sans[10] teeth, sans eyes, sans taste, sans everything.
                —*As You Like It*, Act II, scene vii, 139–66.

[1]Whimpering. [2]Poem. [3]Leopard. [4]Sensitive about honor. [5]As quickly burst as a bubble. [6]Magistrate bribed with a chicken. [7]Sayings. [8]Commonplace illustrations. [9]The foolish old man of Italian comedy. [10]Without.

The Canterbury Tales
Geoffrey Chaucer
c. 1340–1400

THE COOK'S PROLOGUE

The cook from London, while the reeve yet spoke,
Patted his back with pleasure at the joke.
"Ha, ha!" laughed he, "by Christ's great suffering,
This miller had a mighty sharp ending
Upon his argument of harbourage!
For well says Solomon, in his language,
'Bring thou not every man into thine house;'
For harbouring by night is dangerous.
Well ought a man to know the man that he
Has brought into his own security.
I pray God give me sorrow and much care
If ever, since I have been Hodge of Ware,
Heard I of miller better brought to mark.
A wicked jest was played him in the dark.
But God forbid that we should leave off here;
And therefore, if you'll lend me now an ear,
From what I know, who am but a poor man,
I will relate, as well as ever I can,
A little trick was played in our city."
  Our host replied: "I grant it readily.
Now tell on, Roger; see that it be good;
For many a pasty have you robbed of blood,
And many a Jack of Dover have you sold
That has been heated twice and twice grown cold.
From many a pilgrim have you had Christ's curse,
For of your parsley they yet fare the worse,
Which they have eaten with your stubble goose;
For in your shop full many a fly is loose.
Now tell on, gentle Roger, by your name.
But yet, I pray, don't mind if I make game,
A man may tell the truth when it's in play."
  "You say the truth," quoth Roger, "by my fay!
But 'true jest, bad jest' as the Fleming saith.
  And therefore, Harry Bailey, on your faith,
Be you not angry ere we finish here,
If my tale should concern an inn-keeper.
Nevertheless, I'll tell not that one yet.
But ere we part your jokes will I upset."
  And thereon did he laugh, in great good cheer,
And told his tale, as you shall straightway hear.

Thus ends the prologue of the cook's tale

THE COOK'S TALE

There lived a 'prentice, once, in our city,
And of the craft of victuallers was he;
Happy he was as goldfinch in the glade,
Brown as a berry, short, and thickly made,
With black hair that he combed right prettily.
He could dance well, and that so jollily,
That he was nicknamed Perkin Reveller.
He was as full of love, I may aver,
As is a beehive full of honey sweet;
Well for the wench that with him chanced to meet
At every bridal would he sing and hop,
Loving the tavern better than the shop.

    When there was any festival in Cheap,
Out of the shop and thither would he leap,
And, till the whole procession he had seen,
And danced his fill, he'd not return again.
He gathered many fellows of his sort
To dance and sing and make all kinds of sport.
And they would have appointments for to meet
And play at dice in such, or such, a street.
For in the whole town was no apprentice
Who better knew the way to throw the dice
Than Perkin; and therefore he was right free
With money, when in chosen company.
His master found this out in business there;
For often-times he found the till was bare.
For certainly a revelling bond-boy
Who loves dice, wine, dancing, and girls of joy —
His master, in his shop, shall feel the effect,
Though no part have he in this said respect;
For theft and riot always comrades are,
And each alike he played on gay guitar.
Revels and truth, in one of low degree,
Do battle always, as all men may see.

    This 'prentice shared his master's fair abode
Till he was nigh out of his 'prenticehood,
Though he was checked and scolded early and late
And sometimes led, for drinking, to Newgate;
But at the last his master did take thought,
Upon a day, when he his ledger sought,
On an old proverb wherein is found this word:
"Better take rotten apple from the hoard
Than let it lie to spoil the good ones there."
So with a drunken servant should it fare;
It is less ill to let him go, apace,
Than ruin all the others in the place.
Therefore he freed and cast him loose to go
His own road unto future care and woe;
And thus this jolly 'prentice had his leave.
Now let him riot all night long, or thieve.

But since there's never thief without a buck
To help him waste his money and to suck
All he can steal or borrow by the way,
Anon he sent his bed and his array
To one he knew, a fellow of his sort,
Who loved the dice and revels and all sport,
And had a wife that kept, for countenance,
A shop, and whored to gain her sustenance.

Of this cook's tale Chaucer made no more.[3]

"Stopping by Woods on a Snowy Evening"
Robert Frost
1874–1963

Whose woods these are I think I know.
His house is in the village though;
He will not see me stopping here
To watch his woods fill up with snow.

My little horse must think it queer
To stop without a farmhouse near
Between the woods and frozen lake
The darkest evening of the year.

He gives his harness bells a shake
To ask if there is some mistake.
The only other sound's the sweep
Of easy wind and downy flake.

The woods are lovely, dark and deep.
But I have promises to keep,
And miles to go before I sleep.
And miles to go before I sleep.[4]

"Musée Des Beaux Arts"
W. H. Auden
1907–73

About suffering they were never wrong,
The Old Masters; how well they
    understood
Its human position; how it takes place
While someone else is eating or opening
    a window or just walking dully along;
How, when the aged are reverently,
    passionately waiting
For the miraculous birth, there always must
    be
Children who did not specially want it to
    happen, skating
On a pond at the edge of the wood:
They never forgot
That even the dreadful martyrdom must
    run its course
Anyhow in a corner, some untidy spot
Where the dogs go on with their doggy life
    and the torturer's horse
Scratches its innocent behind on a tree.
In Brueghel's *Icarus*, for instance:
    how –   everything turns away
Quite leisurely from the disaster; the
    ploughman may
Have heard the splash, the forsaken cry;
But for him it was not an important failure;
    the sun shone
As it had to on the white legs disappearing
    into the green
Water; and the expensive delicate ship that
    must have seen
Something amazing, a boy falling out of the
    sky,
Had somewhere to get to and sailed calmly
    on.[5]

BIOGRAPHY

God Brought Me Safe
John Wesley
1703–91

[Oct. 1743.]

Thur. 20.—After preaching to a small, attentive congregation, I rode to Wednesbury. At twelve I preached in a ground near the middle of the town to a far larger congregation than was expected, on "Jesus Christ, the same yesterday, and to-day, and for ever." I believe every one present felt the power of God; and no creature offered to molest us, either going or coming; but the Lord fought for us, and we held our peace.

I was writing at Francis Ward's in the afternoon when the cry arose that the mob had beset the house. We prayed that God would disperse them, and it was so. One went this way, and another that; so that, in half an hour, not a man was left. I told our brethren, "Now is the time for us to go;" but they pressed me exceedingly to stay; so, that I might not offend them, I sat down, though I foresaw what would follow. Before five the mob surrounded the house again in greater numbers than ever. The cry of one and all was, "Bring out the minister; we will have the minister." I desired one to take their captain by the hand and bring him into the house. After a few sentences interchanged between us the lion became a lamb. I desired him to go and bring one or two more of the most angry of his companions. He brought in two, who were ready to swallow the ground with rage; but in two minutes they were as calm as he. I then bade them make way, that I might go out among the people. As soon as I was in the midst of them I called for a chair, and, standing up, asked, "What do any of you want with me?" Some said, "We want you to go with us to the Justice." I replied, "That I will, with all my heart." I then spoke a few words, which God applied; so that they cried out with might and main, "The gentleman is an honest gentleman, and we will spill our blood in his defence." I asked, "Shall, we go to the Justice to-night, or in the morning?" Most of them cried, "To-night, to-night;" on which I went before, and two or three hundred followed, the rest returning whence they came.

The night came on before we had walked a mile, together with heavy rain. However, on we went to Bentley Hall, two miles from Wednesbury. One or two ran before to tell Mr. Lane they had brought Mr. Wesley before his Worship. Mr. Lane replied, "What have I to do with Mr. Wesley? Go and carry him back again." By this time the main body came up, and began knocking at the door. A servant told them Mr. Lane was in bed. His son followed, and asked what was the matter. One replied, "Why an't please you, they sing psalms all day; nay, and make folks rise at five in the morning. And what would your Worship advise us to do?" "To go home," said Mr. Lane, "and be quiet."

Here they were at a full stop, til one advised to go to Justice

Persehouse at Walsall. All agreed to this; so we hastened on, and about seven came to his house. But Mr. P. likewise sent word that he was in bed. Now they were at a stand again; but at last they all thought it the wisest course to make the best of their way home. About fifty of them undertook to convoy me. But we had not gone a hundred yards when the mob of Walsall came, pouring in like a flood, and bore down all before them. The Darlaston mob made what defense they could; but they were weary, as well as outnumbered; so that in a short time, many being knocked down, the rest ran away, and left me in their hands.

To attempt speaking was vain, for the noise on every side was like the roaring of the sea. So they dragged me along till we came to the town, where, seeing the door of a large house open, I attempted to go in; but a man, catching me by the hair, pulled me back into the middle of the mob. They made no more stop till they had carried me through the main street, from one end of the town to the other. I continued speaking all the time to those within hearing, feeling no pain or weariness. At the west end of the town, seeing a door half open, I made toward it, and would have gone in, but a gentleman in the shop would not suffer me, saying they would pull the house down to the ground. However, I stood at the door and asked, "Are you willing to hear me speak?" Many cried out, "No, no! knock his brains out; down with him; kill him at once." Others said, "Nay, but we will hear him first." I began asking, "What evil have I done? Which of you all have I wronged in word or deed?" and continued speaking for above a quarter of an hour, till my voice suddenly failed. Then the floods began to lift up their voice again, many crying out, "Bring him away! Bring him away!"

In the meantime my strength and my voice returned, and I broke out aloud into prayer. And now the man who had just before headed the mob turned and said, "Sir, I will spend my life for you: follow me, and not one soul here shall touch a hair of your head." Two or three of his fellows confirmed his words, and got close to me immediately. At the same time, the gentleman in the shop cried out, "For shame, for shame! Let him go." An honest butcher, who was a little farther off, said it was a shame they should do thus; and pulled back four or five, one after another, who were running on the most fiercely. The people then, as if it had been by common consent, fell to the right and left; while those three or four men took me between them, and carried me through them all. But on the bridge the mob rallied again: we therefore went on one side over the mill-dam, and thence through the meadows, till, a little before ten, God brought me safe to Wednesbury, having lost only one flap of my waistcoat and a little skin from one of my hands.[6]

ESSAY

The Benefits of Luxury, in Making a People More Wise and Happy
Oliver Goldsmith
1730?–74

From such a picture of nature in primeval simplicity, tell me, my much respected friend, are you in love with fatigue and solitude? Do you sigh for the severe frugality of the wandering Tartar, or regret being born amidst the luxury and dissimulation of the polite? Rather tell me, has not every kind of life vices peculiarly its own? Is it not a truth, that refined countries have more vices, but those not so terrible; barbarous nations few, and they of the most hideous complexion? Perfidy and fraud are the vices of civilized nations, credulity and violence those of the inhabitants of the desert. Does the luxury of the one produce half the evils of the inhumanity of the other? Certainly those philosophers who declaim against luxury have but little understood its benefits; they seem insensible, that to luxury we owe not only the greatest part of our knowledge, but even of our virtues.

It may sound fine in the mouth of a declaimer, when he talks of subduing our appetites, of teaching every sense to be content with a bare sufficiency, and of supplying only the wants of nature; but is there not more satisfaction in indulging those appetites, if with innocence and safety, than in restraining them? Am not I better pleased in enjoyment than in the sullen satisfaction of thinking that I can live without enjoyment? The more various our artificial necessities, the wider is our circle of pleasure; for all pleasure consists in obviating necessities as they rise; luxury, therefore as it increases our wants, increases our capacity for happiness.

Examine the history of any country remarkable for opulence and wisdom, you will find they would never have been wise had they not been first luxurious; you will find poets, philosophers, and even patriots, marching in luxury's train. The reason is obvious: we then only are curious after knowledge, when we find it connected with sensual happiness. The senses ever point out the way, and reflection comments upon the discovery. Inform a native of the desert of Kobi, of the exact measure of the parallax of the moon, he finds no satisfaction at all in the information; he wonders how any could take such pains, and lay out such treasures, in order to solve so useless a difficulty: but connect it with his happiness, by showing that it improves navigation, that by such an investigation he may have a warmer coat, a better gun, or a finer knife, and he is instantly in raptures at so great an improvement. In short, we only desire to know what we desire to possess; and whatever we may talk against it, luxury adds the spur to curiosity, and gives us a desire to becoming more wise.

But not our knowledge only, but our virtues are improved by luxury. Observe the brown savage of Thibet, to whom the fruits of the spreading pomegranate supply food, and its branches are habitation. Such a character has few vices, I grant, but those he has are of the most hideous nature; rapine and cruelty are scarcely crimes in his eye; neither pity nor tenderness, which ennoble every virtue, have any place in his heart; he hates his enemies, and kills those he subdues. On the other hand, the polite Chinese and civilized European seem even to love their enemies. I have just now seen an instance where the English have succoured those enemies, whom their own countrymen actually refused to relieve.

The greater the luxuries of every country, the more closely, politically speaking, is that country united. Luxury is the child of society alone; the luxurious man stands in need of a thousand different artists to furnish out his happiness; it is more likely, therefore, that he should be a good citizen who is connected by motives of self-interest with so many, than the abstemious man who is united to none.

In whatsoever light, therefore, we consider luxury, whether as employing a number of hands naturally too feeble for more laborious employment; as finding a variety of occupation for others who might be totally idle; or as furnishing out new inlets to happiness, without encroaching on mutual property; in whatever light we regard it, we shall have reason to stand up in its defence, and the sentiment of Confucius still remains unshaken: *that we should enjoy as many of the luxuries of life as are consistent with our own safety, and the prosperity of others; and that he who finds out a new pleasure is one of the most useful members of society.*[7]

PART TWO

THE STYLES OF THE ARTS

How Artists Portray "Reality"

NINE

WHAT IS STYLE?

A work of art or an art form is a way of looking at the universe that is manifested in a particular medium and shared with others. That summation indicates briefly what the aesthetic experience is about. The manner in which artists express themselves constitutes their style. *Style*, then, is the composite use of the devices and characteristics applicable to their medium of expression. Style is tantamount to the personality of an artwork.

However, applying its connotations to a body of artworks calls for breadth and depth of knowledge. Style is that body of characteristics that identifies an artwork with an individual, a historical period, a "school" of artists, or a nation. Applying the term means assimilating materials and, inductively, drawing conclusions.

Therefore, determining the style of any artwork requires analysis of how the artist has utilized the characteristics applicable to his or her medium. If the usage is similar to others', we might conclude that they exemplify the same style. For example, Bach and Handel typify the *Baroque* style in music; Haydn and Mozart, the *Classical*. Listening to works by these composers quickly leads to the conclusion that the ornate melodic developments of

Bach are like those of Handel, and quite different from the precise concern for structure and clearly articulated motifs of Mozart and Haydn. The precision and symmetry of the Parthenon compared with the ornate opulence of the Palace of Versailles suggest that in line and form the architects of these buildings treated their medium differently. Yet the design of the Parthenon is very much a visual companion, stylistically, of Mozart and Haydn; Versailles reflects an approach to design similar to that of Bach and Handel.

We can take our examination one step further and play a game of stylistic analysis with four paintings. The first three of these paintings were done by three different artists; the fourth, by one of those three. By stylistic analysis we will determine the painter of the fourth painting.

The first painting (Fig. **9.1**) is Corot's *A View Near Volterra*. We can see that Corot has used curvilinear line primarily, and that line (which creates the edges of the forms or shapes in the painting) is somewhat softened. That is, many of the forms—the rocks, trees, clouds, and so on—do not have crisp, clear edges. Color areas tend to blend with each other, giving the painting a softened,

9.1 Jean-Baptiste-Camille Corot, *A View Near Volterra*, 1838. Oil on canvas, 27⅜ x 37½ ins (70 x 95 cm). The National Gallery of Art, Washington, DC (Chester Dale Collection).

somewhat fuzzy or out-of-focus appearance. That comfortable effect is heightened by Corot's use of palette. Palette, as we noted, encompasses the total use of color and contrast, and since our illustrations are black and white we can deal with only one aspect of palette, and that is value contrast. As with his use of line, Corot maintains a subtle value contrast—that is, a subtle relationship of blacks to whites. His movement from light to dark is gradual, and he avoids stark contrasts. He employs a full range of black, grays, and whites, but does so without calling attention to their positioning. His brushstroke is somewhat apparent. That is, if we look carefully we can see brush marks, individual strokes where paint has been applied. Even though the objects in the painting are life-like, Corot has not made any pretensions about the fact that his picture has been painted. We can tell that the foliage was executed by *stippling*—that is, by dabbing the brush to the canvas as one would dot an "i" with a pencil. Likewise, we can see throughout the painting marks made by the brush. The overall effect of the painting is one of realism, but we can see in every area the spontaneity with which it was executed.

The second painting (Fig. **9.2**) is Picasso's *Guernica*. We hardly need be an expert to tell that this painting is by a different painter—or certainly in a different style than the previous one. Picasso has joined curved lines and straight lines, placing them in such relationships that they create a great sense of movement and discomfort. The edges of color areas and forms are sharp and distinct; nothing here is soft or fuzzy. Likewise, the value contrasts are stark and extreme. Areas of the highest value—that is, white—are forced against areas of the lowest value—black. In fact, the range of tonalities is far less broad than in the previous work. The mid or medium (gray) tones are there, but they play a very minor role in the effect of the palette. Our examination of palette does not suffer here, because the work is executed only in blacks, whites, and grays. The starkness of the work is also reinforced by brushstroke, which is noteworthy in its near absence. Tonal areas are flat, and few traces of brush exist.

The third painting (Fig. **9.3**) is van Gogh's *The Starry Night*. Use of line is highly active although uniformly curvilinear. Forms and color areas have both hard and soft edges, and van Gogh, as does Picasso, uses outlining to

9.2 Pablo Picasso, *Guernica*, 1937. Oil on canvas, 11 ft 5 ins x 25 ft 5¾ ins (3.4 x 7.76 m). Copyright ARS NY SPADEM, 1988.

9.3 Vincent van Gogh, *The Starry Night*, 1889. Oil on canvas, 29 x 36¼ ins (74 x 92 cm). Collection, The Museum of Modern Art, New York (acquired through the Lillie P. Bliss Bequest).

9.4 Exercise painting. See page 42 for identification.

broadly. However, the principal utilization is of strong contrast—the darkest darks against the whitest whites. This is not like Corot, a bit like van Gogh, and most like Picasso. Finally, brushstroke is generally unobtrusive. Tonal areas mostly are flat. This is definitely not a van Gogh and probably not a Corot. Three votes out of three go to Picasso, and the style is so distinctive that you probably had no difficulty deciding, even without my analysis. However, could you have been so certain if asked whether Picasso painted Figure 1.12? A work by another Cubist painter would pose even greater difficulty. So some differences in style are obvious; some are unclear. Distinguishing the work of one artist from another who designs in a similar fashion becomes even more difficult. However, the analytical process we just completed is indicative of how we can approach artworks in order to determine *how* they exemplify a given style.

We recognize differences in style sometimes without thinking much about it. Our experience or formal training need not be extensive to recognize that the buildings in Figures **9.5** and **9.7** reflect different cultural circumstances, even though they each can be found in the same nation. The Russian Orthodox Church in Figure **9.5** is distinguishable by its characteristic domes and by the icons which decorate its walls (Fig. **9.6**). In the same

strengthen his images and reduce their reality. The overall effect of line is a sweeping and undulating movement, highly dynamic and yet far removed from the starkness of the Picasso. On the other hand, van Gogh's curvilinearity and softened edges are quite different in effect from the relaxed quality of the Corot. Van Gogh's value contrasts are very broad, but moderate. He ranges from darks through medium grays to white, all virtually equal in importance. Even when movement from one area to another is across a hard edge to a highly contrasting value, the result is moderate: not soft, not stark. It is, however, brushstroke that gives the painting its unique personality. We can see thousands of individual brush marks where the artist applied paint to canvas. The nervous, almost frenetic use of brushstroke makes the painting come alive.

Now that we have examined three paintings in different styles and by different artists, can you determine which of the three painted Figure 9.4? First, examine the use of line. Form and color edges are hard. Outlining is used. Curved and straight lines are juxtaposed. The effect is active and stark. By comparison, use of line is not like Corot, a bit like van Gogh, and very much like Picasso. Next, examine palette. Darks, grays, and whites are used

9.5 (*right*) The Church of Nikolai Khamovnik, 1679–82. Moscow, Russia.

9.6 (*below*) Detail, front portal, The Church of Nikolai Khamovnik, 1679–82. Moscow, Russia.

9.7 Tomb of the Shirvanshah, 15th century. Baku, Azerbaijan.

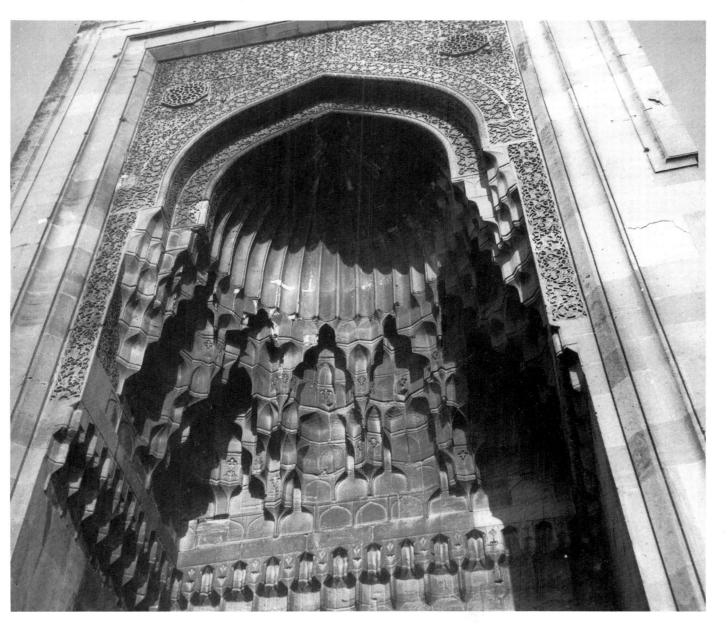

9.8 Detail, entrance portal, tomb of the Shirvanshah, 15th century. Baku, Azerbaijan.

sense, the tomb in Figure **9.7** is typically Muslim, identifiable by its arch. The decorative embellishment (Fig. **9.8**), in contrast to the icons of the Orthodox Church, reflect the prohibition of the Islamic faith of depicting human form in architectural decoration.

Finally, how does a style get its name? Why is some art called Classical, some Pop, some Baroque, and some Impressionist? Some styles were named hundreds of years after they occurred, with the definition accruing from extended, common usage or an historical viewpoint. The Athenian Greeks, whose works we know as Classical, were centuries removed from the naming of the style they

shared. Some labels were coined by artists themselves. Many stylistic labels are attributed to individual critics who, having experienced the emerging works of several artists and noting a common or different approach, invented a term (sometimes a derogatory one) to describe that approach. Because of the influence of the critic or the catchiness of the term, the name was adopted by others, and commonly used. Thus, a style was born.

We must be careful, however, when we use the labels by which we commonly refer to artworks. Occasionally such labels imply stylistic characteristics; occasionally they identify broad attitudes or tendencies which are not really stylistic. Often debate exists as to which is which. For example, Romanticism has stylistic characteristics in some art disciplines, but the term connotes a broad philosophy toward life in general. Often a style label is really a composite of several styles whose characteristics may be dissimilar, but whose objectives are the same. Terminology is convenient but not always agreed upon in fine detail. Occasionally experts disagree as to whether certain artworks fall within the descriptive parameters of one style or another, even while agreeing on the definition of the style itself.

In addition, we can ask how the same label might identify stylistic characteristics of two or more unrelated art disciplines, such as painting and music. Is there an aural equivalent to visual characteristics, or vice versa? These are difficult questions, and potential answers can be troublesome as well as debatable. More often than not, similarity of objectives and data, as opposed to directly transferable technical characteristics, result in the same stylistic label being used for works in quite different disciplines. Nevertheless, some transference is possible, especially in a perceptual sense. For example, undulating line in painting is similar in its sense-stimuli to undulating melodic contours in music. However, the implications of such similarities have many hidden difficulties, and we must be careful in our usage, regardless of how attractive similarities in vocabulary may seem.

Styles do not start and stop on specific dates, nor do they recognize national boundaries. Some styles reflect deeply held convictions or creative insights; some styles are imitations of previous styles. Some styles are profound; others are superficial. Some styles are intensely individual. However, merely dissecting artistic or stylistic characteristics can be a dull experience. What makes the experience come alive is the actual experience of artworks themselves, describing to ourselves and to others such things about our reactions as can be described, and attempting to find the deepest level of meaning possible. Within every artwork there is the reflection of another human being attempting to express some view of the human condition. We can try to place that viewpoint in the context of the time or the specific biography that produced it and speculate upon why its style is as it is. We can attempt to compare those contexts with our own. We may never know the precise stimuli that caused a particular artistic reflection, but our attempts at understanding make our responses more informed and exciting, and our understanding of our own existence more profound.

TEN

ANCIENT APPROACHES

30,000 B.C. TO 600 B.C.

PALEOLITHIC EUROPE

OUR EARLIEST ART

Humankind's first-known sculpture apparently predates drawings and occurs during the period from approximately 30,000 to 15,000 B.C. The head and body of a man carved from mammoth ivory were found in a burial site at Brno, Czechoslovakia (Fig. **10.1**). Although many body parts are missing, we can see that the head, in contrast to the body, shows a remarkable degree of verisimilitude. The hair is closely cropped, the brow is low, and the eyes are deeply set.

Western European art probably began approximately 25,000 to 30,000 years before the Christian era, and at its earliest, consisted of simple lines scratched in damp clay. The people making these line scratchings lived in caves and seem, eventually, to have elaborated their simple line "drawings" into the outlines of animals. This development from what appears to be idle doodling into sophisticated art seems to have come in three phases. The first comprises black outline drawings of animals with a single

10.1 Man from Brno, c. 27,000–20,000 B.C. Ivory, height 8 ins (20 cm). Moravian Museum, Brno, the Czech Republic.

colored filler. Next came the addition of a second color within the outline, so as to create a sense of light and shade, or modeling. As we shall see, these depictions often incorporated projecting portions of the cave walls to add a sense of three-dimensionality. In many cases it appears as though the artist picked an actual rock protrusion or configuration specifically for his or her animal drawing. The third step in the development of Ice Age art brought forth exciting multicolored paintings which show an impressive naturalistic style. In this category are the well-known paintings of Altamira (Fig. **10.2**). Here the artists have captured detail, essence, mass, and a remarkable sense of movement, using only earth colors and charcoal.

Early in the twentieth century Henri Breuil traced the development of Paleolithic art over 20,000 years. According to Breuil, art began with simple animal outlines and progressed to the multicolored animals just noted, changing stylistically from naturalistic depiction toward greater abstraction until, in the Mesolithic period, an animal was represented by only a few characteristic strokes.

Paleolithic artists seem to have shied away from the difficulties of suggesting three-dimensionality, keeping their subjects in profile (as, much later, the Egyptians were to do). Only an occasional turning of head or antlers tests the artist's skill at dimensional portrayal.

10.3 The Woman from Willendorf, Lower Austria, c. 30,000–25,000 B.C. Limestone, height 4⅓ ins (11 cm). Naturhistorisches Museum, Vienna.

10.2 Bison, c. 14,000–10,000 B.C. Paint, length 8 ft 3 ins (2.51 m). Altamira, Spain.

VENUS FIGURES

Venus figures have been found on burial sites in a band stretching approximately 1,100 miles (1,833 km) from western France to the central Russian plain. Many scholars believe that these figures are the first works in the representational style. The figures share certain stylistic features and are remarkably similar in overall design. They may be symbolic fertility figures or they may be no more than objects for exchange or recognition. Whatever the case, each figure has the same tapering legs, wide hips, and tapering shoulders and head, forming a diamond-shaped silhouette.

The Woman from Willendorf

The Woman from Willendorf (Fig. **10.3**) is the best-known example of the Venus figures. Like the others, she is a unique and naturalistic portrayal, within the stylistic framework. The emphasis is on swollen thighs and breasts and prominent genitals. The image is without doubt a fertility symbol, and some have gone so far as to suggest that these works reveal an obsession of their makers. Carved from limestone, the figure was originally colored red,

the color of blood, perhaps symbolizing life itself. Corpses were painted red by many primitive peoples.

Although faceless, these figures usually have hair, often wear bracelets, beads, aprons, or a waist band, and often show markings that may represent tattoos. Although the culture was dominated by the male hunting ethos, women alone are represented by the extant statuary, which emphasizes their sexuality. The mystery and apparent miracle of birth and the uniquely female role therein must clearly have influenced the carvers' perception of reality.

THE CAVE OF LASCAUX

The cave of Lascaux lies slightly over a mile from the little French town of Montignac, in the valley of the Vézère River. It was discovered by a group of children who, investigating a tree uprooted by a storm, scrambled down a fissure into a world undisturbed for thousands of years.

Here, underground, we find ourselves in the undeniable presence of our early ancestors. The hundreds of paintings here add to those found elsewhere in France, Spain, and other parts of Europe. The significance of the Lascaux works lies in the quantity and the quality of an intact group.

An overwhelming sense of the power and sweep of Lascaux emerges from the main hall or "Hall of Bulls" (Fig. **10.4**). The thundering herd moves below a sky of

10.4 Main hall, or "Hall of Bulls," Lascaux, France.

rolling contours formed in the stone ceiling of the cave, sweeping our eyes forward as we travel into the cave itself. At the entrance of the hall an 8-ft (2.5-m) unicorn begins a monumental montage of bulls, horses, and deer, whose shapes intermingle one with another and whose colors radiate warmth and power. With heights ranging to 12 ft (3.5 m), these magnificent creatures overwhelm us and remind us that the artists were fully capable technicians who captured the essences beyond the photographic surface of their world. Although the paintings in the main hall were created over a long period of time and by a succession of artists, the cumulative effect of this 30- by 100-ft (9- x 30-m) domed gallery strikes us as that of a single work, carefully composed for maximum dramatic and communicative impact. We must remember, however, that our experience of the work, illuminated by electric floodlighting, may be very different from that of people who could only ever see small areas at a time, lit by flickering stone lamps of oil or animal fat.

MESOPOTAMIA

The mythological Tower of Babel rose to connect heaven and earth. In much the same way the arts of the Mesopotamians symbolized humankind's relationship to its kings and, through them, its gods. Here, for the first time, agriculture, metal technology, literacy, the specialization of labor, and a hierarchically organized urban community were combined. Kingdoms rose and fell as one power plundered its enemies, obliterated their cities, and was, in turn itself plundered and obliterated, until,

spilling out of the Crescent north into Asia Minor and south as far as Egypt, the vast empires of Mesopotamia clashed with and influenced the Greeks.

EARLY SUMERIAN ART

Bridging prehistory and history, the cities of the Fertile Crescent, the land between the Tigris and the Euphrates, were the prototypes for civilization.

The majority of surviving artworks from Mesopotamia prior to 3000 B.C. consist of painted pottery and stamp seals. The decoration of pottery served to satisfy the creative urge of providing the functional with an aesthetic appeal. Decoration was abstract. Stamp seals, whether round or rectangular, went beyond tool status and clearly came to be regarded as surfaces ideally suited to exercise the artist's creative ingenuity. Later, for reasons unknown to us, the cylindrical seal came into being. A carved wooden roller was applied to wet clay to produce a ribbon-like design of indefinite length. The creative possibilities for individuality in design in the cylinder seal, a stamp of sorts, were far greater than those of the stamp seal. What must have fascinated the Sumerians is the intricate design capable of infinite repetition. Scenes of sacrifice, hunting, and battle all appear in the examples of cylinder seal art which have survived. Throughout the early periods of Sumerian art there seems to be a conflict, or at least an alternation, between symbolism and naturalism in the depictions in cylinder art.

Figure 10.5 combines two aspects of fertility: the lioness and the intertwined snake. This fertility-based design and the cycle it presents exemplifies the cyclical Sumerian religious philosophy, and it appears again and again in Sumerian art.

10.5 Mesopotamian cylinder seal and impression, showing snake-necked lions, c. 3300 B.C. Green jasper, height 1¾ ins (4 cm). The Louvre, Paris.

Low-relief art of the early Sumerians provides further insights into everyday life. In works such as Figure **10.6** we find a preoccupation with ritual and the gods. This alabaster vase, which stands 3 feet tall, celebrates the cult of E-anna, goddess of fertility and love. The vase is divided into four bands, commemorating the marriage of the goddess, which was reenacted to insure fertility. The bottom band has alternate stalks of barley and date palms; above it, rams and ewes. In the third band we see naked worshippers carrying baskets of fruit and other offerings. At the top the goddess herself stands before her shrine, two coiled bundles of reeds, to receive a worshipper or priest, also nude, whose tribute basket brims with fruit.

The composition exhibits an alternating flow of movement from left to right in the rams and ewes, and right to left in the worshippers. Conventions of figure portrayal are similar to but not as rigid as those in Egyptian art. Here bodies are depicted in profile, as are heads. However, the representation of the torso seems more naturalistic. On the other hand, anatomical proportions, especially in the torso, display varying degrees of adherence to reality. Yet the muscular little men seem to show the strain of the weight of their burden far more realistically than the always upright, relaxed figures of Egyptian art. Finally, the faces are clearly not portrayals of individuals.

THE ARCHAIC PERIOD

In the years from 3000 to 2340 B.C. persons and events become less anonymous. Here we find kings portrayed in devotional acts rather than as warlords. We also grasp a sense of the cylindrical mass of Sumerian sculpture, so different from the heavy, block-like style of the Egyptian. The famous statues from Tell Asmar and the Temple of Abu illustrate this (Fig. **10.7**).

10.6 Vase with ritual scene in relief, from the E-anna precinct, Uruk (Warka), Iraq, c. 3500–3100 B.C. Alabaster, height 36 ins (91 cm). Iraq Museum, Baghdad.

10.7 Statues of worshippers and deities from the Square Temple at Tell Asmar, Iraq, c. 2750 B.C. Gypsum, height of tallest figure 30 ins (76 cm). Iraq Museum, Baghdad, and The Oriental Institute, University of Chicago.

10.8 (*above right*) Soundbox panel of the royal harp from the tomb of Queen Puabi at Ur, Iraq, 2650–2550 B.C. Shell inlay set in bitumen, height 13 ins (33 cm). The University Museum, University of Pennsylvania.

10.9 (*left*) Royal harp from the tomb of Queen Puabi at Ur. Wood with gold, lapis lazuli, and shell inlay. The University Museum, University of Pennsylvania.

10.10 (*opposite*) He-goat from Ur, c. 2600 B.C. Wood with gold and lapis lazuli overlay, height 20 ins (51 cm). The University Museum, University of Pennsylvania.

If crudity marks the depiction of the human figure in the votive statues, grace and delicacy mark two other works from this period (Figs. **10.8** and **10.9**). These works illustrate the golden splendor of the Sumerian court. Inlaid in gold, the bearded bull symbolizes the royal personage of Ancient Mesopotamia. Also laden with the symbolism of masculine fertility is the equally dazzling golden goat from the royal graves at Ur (Fig. **10.10**). Here we see what was basic to the Sumerians—that is, the divine revelation and incorporation of animal power, wisdom, and perfection. The goat clearly manifests on Earth the character of Tammuz, one of the gods of vegetation. He is crisp and elegant in portrayal and undoubtedly superhuman.

The Tell Asmar Statues

The most striking features of these figures (Fig. **10.7**) are the enormous, staring eyes, with their dramatic composition, in a blend of shell, lapis lazuli, and black limestone. Representing Abu, a god of vegetation (the large figure), a goddess assumed to be his spouse, and a crowd of worshippers, the statues occupied places around the inner walls of an early temple, as though they were at prayer, awaiting the divine presence.

Certain geometric and expressive qualities are clearly exhibited by these statues. Each form is based on the cone or cylinder—in typical Sumerian style, in contrast to the cubic mass of Egyptian statues. The arms and legs are stylized and pipe-like, rather than realistic depictions of the subtle curves of human limbs. Abu and the mother goddess can be distinguished from the rest by their size and by the large diameter of their eyes.

The meaning in these statues clearly bears out what we know of Mesopotamian religious thought: The gods were believed to be present in their images. The statues of the worshippers were substitutes for the real worshippers, although no attempt appears to have been made to make them look like any particular individual. Every detail is simplified, focusing attention on the remarkable eyes.

Sargon II at Dur Sharrukin

Under Sargon II, who came to power in 722 B.C., the high priests of the country regained many of the privileges they had lost under previous kings, and the Assyrian Empire reached the peak of its power. Early in his reign he founded the new city of Dur Sharrukin (on the site of the modern city of Khorsabad), about 9 miles (15 km) northeast of Nineveh. His vast royal citadel, occupying an area of some quarter of a million square feet, was built as an image not only of his empire but of the cosmos itself. A reconstruction of the citadel shown in Figure **10.11** synthesizes the style of architecture and the priorities of Assyrian civilization at this time. It is quite clear that in Sargon's new city secular architecture took precedence over temple architecture. The rulers of Assyria seem to have been far more preoccupied with building fortifications and pretentious palaces than with erecting religious shrines. Dur Sharrukin represents a city built, occupied and abandoned within a single generation.

10.11 Reconstruction of Sargon II's citadel at Khorsabad.

10.12 Gate of Sargon II's citadel at Khorsabad (during excavation), with pair of winged and human-headed bulls. Limestone.

The citadel, representing the ordered world, rises like the hierarchy of Assyrian gods, from the lowest levels of the city through a transitional level, to the king's palace, which stands on its own elevated terrace. Two gates connect the walled citadel to the outside world. The first was undecorated; the second was adorned with and guarded by winged bulls and genii (Fig. **10.12**).

Remarkably, excavations at the site have shown building methods to be fairly inadequate. Buildings are arranged haphazardly and within the inner walls, five minor palaces were crowded with obvious difficulty into the available space.

The main palace comprises an arrangement of ceremonial apartments around a central courtyard. Entrances to the throne room were guarded by winged bulls and other figures. The walls of the room itself stood approximately 40 ft (12 m) high and were decorated with floor-to-ceiling murals. Three small temples adjoined the palace and beside these rose a *ziggurat* with successive stages painted in different colors, connected by a spiral staircase. Construction was of mud brick, laid without mortar while still damp and pliable, and of dressed and undressed stone. Some roof structures utilized brick barrel vaulting, although the majority appear to have had flat ceilings with painted beams.

Corresponding to the vast scale and attitude of the buildings are the great guardian figures of which Figure **10.12** is representative. Undoubtedly symbolizing the supernatural powers of the king, these colossal hybrids are majestically powerful in stature and scale. Carved partly in relief and partly in the round, they are rationalized to be seen from front or side: the sculptor has provided the figure with a fifth leg, with the result that the viewer can always see four legs. Each of these monoliths was carved from a single block of stone upwards of 15 ft (4.5 m) square.

Subject matter in murals and relief sculpture consisted primarily of tributes to the victorious campaigns of the king. Since warfare tended to be a seasonal activity, the intervening time was, apparently, spent in hunting; and so we find alternating scenes of the slaughter of men and beasts, as well as some cult ceremonies. These represent narratives, and while probably more symbolic than actual, the historicizing of these events appears to have yielded a greater naturalism in style than we have seen previously.

As we examine reliefs such as Figure **10.13** we recognize a composition of pictorial space more like that of the medieval period. Here is an artist's attempt to portray deep space—that is, to remove the image from the surface plane of the work and to suggest perspective. Of course,

10.13 Mural relief from the palace of Sargon II at Khorsabad. Basalt, length 5 ft 10 ins (1.7 m). The British Museum, London.

the understanding of vanishing points and horizon lines, which was to revolutionize visual art in the Renaissance, is absent. Nonetheless, the attempt to portray distance through diminution stands out clearly. A hurried roughness haunts the works, and the stylization of the figures counteracts spatial naturalism.

JERUSALEM

THE TEMPLE OF SOLOMON

The Temple of Jerusalem was the symbol of Israel's faith as early as its third King, Solomon, son of David (c. 1000 B.C.). Described in the Old Testament in I Kings, 5–9, the Temple of Solomon was primarily the house of the Lord God, as opposed to a place for common people to come to worship.

The temple itself, as reconstructed in Figure 10.14, stood on a platform with a dominating entrance of huge wooden doors flanked by two bronze pillars about 18 ft (5.5 m) tall. The doors were decorated with carved palms, flowers, and cherubim (guardian winged beasts sometimes shown with human or animal faces). The entrance hall, or vestibule, measured approximately 15 ft

by 30 ft (4.5 x 9 m). Inside the temple proper was a Holy Place or *Hekal*, about 45 ft (13.5 m) high, 60 ft (18 m) long, and 30 ft (9 m) wide. The cedarwood paneled walls were *fenestrated* at the top by small rectangular windows, allowing light to enter. The walls themselves were made from cedars of Lebanon and exhibited rich floral carvings. In the room itself were various sacred furnishings: ten large lampstands, an inlaid table for priestly offerings, and a cedarwood altar covered with gold.

From a staircase behind the altar one entered the Holy of Holies, the most sacred part of the Temple. This comprised a windowless cubicle 30 ft (9 m) square and contained the Ark of the Covenant, the symbol of God's presence, which the Jews had carried with them from the wilderness. The Ark was flanked by two large cherubim.

10.14 Reconstruction drawing of Solomon's Temple. The significance of the two bronze pillars is uncertain, but some scholars suggest that they may have represented the twin pillars of fire and smoke that guided the Israelites during their wanderings in the desert after the Exodus from Egypt.

THE BIBLE

The Bible, meaning "books," is a collection of works held sacred by Jews and Christians. The Old Testament comprises, with a few exceptions, the same contents (that is, the Law, Prophets, and Writings) as do the Jewish scriptures. The Old Testament presents a sweeping history, detailed laws, ethics, poetry, psalms, and literature. The New Testament is the story of the life and teachings of Jesus and the establishment of the Christian Church.

The Psalter is the hymnal of ancient Israel. Most of the Psalms were probably composed to accompany worship in the temple. They can be divided into various categories such as hymns, enthronement hymns, songs of Zion, laments, songs of trust, thanksgiving, sacred history, royal psalms, wisdom psalms, and liturgies. Here we include Psalm 22 (a psalm of David), and Psalms 130 and 133 (Songs of Ascent).[1]

PSALM 22

My God, my God, why has thou forsaken me?
Why art thou so far from helping me,
from the words of my groaning?
  2 O my God, I cry by day, but thou dost not
    answer;
  3 Yet thou art holy, enthroned on the praises of
    Israel.
  4 In thee our fathers trusted;
    they trusted, and thou didst deliver them.
  5 To thee they cried, and were saved;
    in thee they trusted, and were not disappointed.

  6 But I am a worm, and no man;
    scorned by men, and despised by the people.
  7 All who see me mock at me,
    they make mouths at me, they wag their heads;
  8 He committed his cause to the LORD; let
    him deliver him,
    let him rescue him, for he delights in him!

  9 Yet thou art he who took me from the womb;
    thou didst keep me safe upon my mother's
    breasts.
  10 Upon thee was I cast from my birth,
    and since my mother bore me thou hast been my
    God.
  11 Be not far from me,
    for trouble is near
    and there is none to help.

  12 Many bulls encompass me
    strong bulls of Bashan surround me;
  13 they open wide their mouths at me,
    like a ravening and roaring lion.

  14 I am poured out like water,
    and all my bones are out of joint;
    my heart is like wax,
    it is melted within my breast;
  15 my strength is dried up like a potsherd,
    and my tongue cleaves to my jaws;
    thou dost lay me in the dust of death.

  16 Yea, dogs are round about me;
    a company of evildoers encircle me;
    they have pierced my hands and feet—

  17 I can count all my bones—
    they stare and gloat over me;
  18 They divide my garments among them,
    and for my raiment they cast lots.

  19 But thou, O LORD, be not far off!
    O thou my help, hasten to my aid!
  20 Deliver my soul from the sword,
    my life from the power of the dog!
  21 Save me from the mouth of the lion,
    my afflicted soul from the horns of the wild
    oxen!

  22 I will tell of thy name to my brethren;
    in the midst of the congregation I will praise
    thee:
  23 You who fear the LORD, praise him!
    all you sons of Jacob, glorify him,
    and stand in awe of him, all you sons of Israel!
  24 For he has not despised or abhorred
    the affliction of the afflicted;
    and he has not hid his face from him,
    but has heard, when he cried to him.

  25 From thee comes my praise in the great
    congregation;
    my vows I will pay before those who fear him.
  26 The afflicted shall eat and be satisfied;
    those who seek him shall praise the LORD!
    May your hearts live for ever!

  27 All the ends of the earth shall remember
    and turn to the LORD;
    and all the families of the nations shall
    worship before him.
  28 For dominion belongs to the LORD,
    and he rules over the nations.

  29 Yea, to him shall all the proud of the earth
    bow down;
    before him shall bow all who go down to the
    dust,
    and he who cannot keep himself alive.
  30 Posterity shall serve him;
    men shall tell of the Lord to the coming
    generation,

  31 And proclaim his deliverance to a people yet
    unborn,
    that he has wrought it.

PSALM 130

Out of the depths I cry to thee, O LORD!
   Lord, hear my voice!
 2 Let thy ears be attentive
    to the voice of my supplications!

 3 If thou, O LORD, shouldst mark iniquities,
    Lord, who could stand?
 4 But there is forgiveness with thee,
    that thou mayest be feared.

 5 I wait for the LORD, my soul waits,
    and in his word I hope;
 6 My soul waits for the LORD
    more than watchmen for the morning,
    more than watchmen for the morning.

 7 O Israel, hope in the LORD!
    For with the LORD there is steadfast love,
    and with him is plenteous redemption.
 8 And he will redeem Israel
    from all his iniquities.

PSALM 133

Behold, how good and pleasant it is
   when brothers dwell in unity!
2 It is like the precious oil upon the head,
   running down upon the beard,
   upon the beard of Aaron,
   running down on the collar of his robes!
3 It is like the dew of Hermon,
   which falls on the mountains of Zion!
   For there the LORD has commanded the blessing,
   life for evermore.

ANCIENT EGYPT

Protected by deserts and confined to a narrow river valley, Ancient Egypt experienced a relatively isolated cultural history, virtually unbroken for thousands of years. It was a unified civilization, rural in nature, under the control of an absolute monarch, and uniquely dependent upon the regular annual flooding of a single river, the Nile. Death—or, rather, everlasting life in the hereafter—was the focus of much of the art of the Egyptians. Appearing mostly in the service of the cult of a god or to glorify the power and wealth of a pharoah, art and architecture centered on the provision of an eternal dwelling-place for the dead.

OLD KINGDOM

Sculpture was the major art form of the Egyptians. It not only provided the "other self" for the deceased in his or her tomb, to provide an immortalizing function, but also stood in temples. By the time of the Old Kingdom sculptors had overcome many of the technical difficulties that plagued their predecessors of the pre-dynastic period. It may also be the case that religious tenets confounded sculptors during those archaic times. Many primitive peoples throughout history have regarded the naturalistic portrayal of the human figure as inviting danger. Making a likeness of an individual may be thought to capture the soul. Concerning technical problems, pre-dynastic sculpture left detailing rough and simple. Convention rather than naturalism prevailed. It seems certain that sculptors relied on memory to portray the human form rather than working from live models. Since pre-dynastic sculpture is also pre-written history, we really cannot do more than speculate as to how much convention reflected technical mastery, or philosophy, or both. As we examine Classical Greek sculpture, we are certain that the idealized form of its sculpture was philosophical because the technical skill was obviously there. In pre-dynastic Egypt the reverse appears more logical.

Old Kingdom sculpture shows technical mastery and is well crafted. Life-size sculpture which captured the human form in exquisite natural detail came to the fore. At the same time conventional portrayal of certain ideals of pharaonic demeanor also prevailed. The divine characteristics of the pharaoh dictated a dignified and majestic portrayal. Although such rigidity of treatment lessened as time went on, the softening and human-centered qualities such softening connotes never completely divested the pharaonic statue of its divine repose.

The dual sculpture of Prince Rahotep and his wife Nofret (Fig. **10.17**) comes from the tomb of Prince Rahotep, one of Snofru's sons. The stylized posture is the trademark of Egyptian art, with its intellectual or conceptual, as opposed to naturalistic or visual, nature. The striking colors of the statues exemplify the Egyptian tendency to use painting to provide a decorative surface for sculpture, but the work is in no way commonplace. The eyes of both figures are dull and light-colored quartz. The eyelids are painted black. Both figures wear the costume of the time. In a somewhat conventionalized treatment, the skin tones of the woman are several shades lighter than those of the man. A woman's skin traditionally exhibited a creamy yellow hue, whereas a man's ranged from light to dark brown. In Dynasty IV the kings rose from peasant stock, an ancestry which is apparent in the sturdy, broad-shouldered, well-muscled physique of the king. At the same time his facial characteristics, particularly the eyes and expression, exhibit alertness, wisdom, strength, and capacity. The portrayal of Nofret expresses similar individuality. Probably for the first time in Egyptian art we find in this work the full development of the naturalistic, three-dimensional female body. She is wearing the typical gown of the period, cut to reveal well-formed and voluptuous breasts. Here, as is the case with all the details of the upper portion of both statues, the artist has been meticulous in observation and depiction.

Egyptian admiration for the human body reveals itself clearly in both statues. Precise modeling and attention to detail are seen in the smallest items. In the statue of Nofret the gown at once covers and reveals the graceful contours of the body beneath. Comparison of facial features reveals in Nofret an individual of less distinct character than her husband. She has a sensual and pampered face. Her hair is obviously a wig shaped in the style of the day. Beneath the constricting head band we can see Nofret's own hair, of much finer character, parted in the middle and swept back beneath the wig. A precise and delicate treatment of the hand held open against the body reveals both the artist's skill and perception and also the care and attention Nofret has given to herself. The hand is, indeed, delicate and feminine. Small dimples decorate the fingers and the nails exhibit extraordinary care. The unpainted nails are correctly observed as being lighter than normal skin tone.

Dynasty IV gave us the most remarkable edifices of Egyptian civilization—the pyramid area of Giza. In addition to the three most obvious pyramids, the area comprises burial places for almost all of the important individuals of Dynasties IV and V. Each pyramid complex has four buildings. The largest pyramid, that of Cheops (Fig. 10.15) measures approximately 750 ft (228 m) square (440 cubits) and rises at an angle of approximately 51° to a height of 481 ft (146 m). The burial chamber of the pharaoh lay hidden in the middle of the pyramid (Fig. 10.16). Construction consisted of irregularly placed, rough-hewn stone blocks covered by a carefully dressed limestone facing approximately 17 ft (5 m) thick. The famous Sphinx

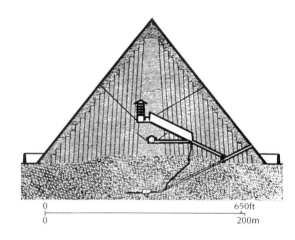

0   650ft

0   200m

10.15 The Great Pyramid of Cheops, 2680–2565 B.C.

10.16 Longitudinal section, direction south–north, of the Great Pyramid of Cheops.

10.18 The Sphinx, c. 2650 B.C.

(Fig. 10.18) is a colossal figure carved from natural rock, lying at the head of the causeway leading from the funerary temple adjoining the pyramid of Cheops' son Chephren, whose pyramid originally measured 707 ft (215 m) square, and rose at an angle of 52° to a height of 471 ft (143 m).

10.17 Prince Rahotep and his wife Nofret from Medum, c. 2580 B.C. Painted limestone, height 47½ ins (120 cm). The Egyptian Museum, Cairo.

PAINTING

Painting for the most part was a decorative medium which provided a surface finish to a work of sculpture. Sculptures in relief and in the round were painted. Flat surfaces were also painted, although such painting appears to be a substitute for relief sculpture. In the period of the Middle Kingdom (c. 2130–c. 1700 B.C.) painting largely replaced relief sculpture and the scenes presented vividly portrayed a genuine human interest and original insight. The same may be said of painting in the New Kingdom (c. 1575–1100 B.C.). Here we often find humor in portrayals of daily life and, again, a high level of technical craftsmanship. Nonetheless, it may be that the only time painting was regarded as a true art was in the New Kingdom during the reign of Akhenaton. Painting appears to have died out as even a subsidiary art after the New Kingdom.

NEW KINGDOM

Leaving the pyramids behind, we move to Dynasty XVIII and a building of great luxury and splendor—the temple at Luxor (Fig. **10.20**). It approaches more nearly our conception of architecture as a useful place for mankind to spend the present rather than eternity. Built by Amenhotep III the temple is dedicated to Amun, Mut, and Chons. Amenhotep III was a great builder and his taste for splendid buildings drew sustenance from a number of architects, who appear to have been the best Egypt had produced since the time of Sesostris. Notable among these was Athribis, whose likeness at age eighty is preserved in a magnificent statue which shows that he had retained his intellectual and physical abilities and that he expected to reach the age of 110, which the Egyptians considered to be the natural human life span.

Amenhotep III removed all traces of the Middle Kingdom at Luxor, erecting in their place the magnificent temple. The pylon, obelisk, and first courtyard were added by Rameses II. In the time of Dynasty XVIII we would have entered the temple through a vestibule comprising giant pillars with palmiform capitals (Fig. **10.19**). From the vestibule we would have progressed to a huge courtyard surrounded by bunched columns, followed by the *hypostyle* room, and the Holy of Holies. The temple served two purposes. First, it was the place of worship for the Theban Triad of Amun, Mut, and Chons. Second, during the great feast of the middle of the flood, the barques of Amun, Mut, and Chons were anchored there for several days. We cannot escape the loveliness of the columns. The balance between the open spaces and the mass of the columns creates a beautiful play of light and shade. We can get a feel for the proportions of the great temple of Luxor when we realize that the seven pairs of central pillars in the Hall of Pillars stand nearly 52 ft (15.8 m) tall. Surviving the centuries, the temple grew by the addition of a forecourt by Rameses II. The inner sanctuary served as a sanctuary for Alexander the Great, and in the early Christian period it was used as a Christian church.

N

10.19 Plan of the temple at Luxor, 1417–1397 B.C.
10.20 The temple at Luxor.

10.22 Queen Nefertari guided by Isis, from the tomb of Queen Nefertari at Thebes, Egypt, 1290–1224 B.C.

Theban Rock Tombs

The functions of tomb paintings and low-relief carvings were to furnish the dead with an "eternal castle" with durable effects and to establish the status, attained on earth, which they would have in the hereafter. The painted tombs of Thebes provide most of our knowledge of Egyptian painting of this period. Representations of gods are found for the first time here. Ceiling decorations are common and elaborate. The paintings portray the vivacity and humor of daily life. Theban tombs portray workmen and peasants differently from the tombs of the Old Kingdom, particularly in the shape of the heads and in the garments worn.

The Tomb of Nefertari

Queen Nefertari-mi-en-Mat, of Dynasty XIX, was one of the four principal wives of King Rameses II, and her tomb lies in the Valley of Queens in western Thebes (now the west bank at Luxor) (Fig. 10.21). Nefertari was Rameses's favorite. Her tomb rests under the precipitous cliff walls at the end of the gloomy valley of Biban el Harin. Exemplifying a style of painting done in low relief, the paintings adorning the walls of Nefertari's tomb exhibit great elegance, charm, and vivacious color. The tomb is entered

through the First Room, shown in Figure 10.21. Off this room and to the south lies the Main Room or offering chamber. Connected to these chambers is the major part of the tomb, in which the Hall of Pillars or Sarcophogus Chamber provides the central focus. Off and surrounding the Hall of Pillars lie three side rooms.

The northeast wall of the First Room houses a vibrant painting showing, on the extreme left, the goddess Selkis with a scorpion on her head (Fig. 10.22). On the extreme right appears the goddess Maat. On her head rests her hieroglyph, the feather. The rear wall of the recess depicts Queen Nefertari led by Isis toward the beetle-headed Khepri, a form assumed by the sun god which implies his everlasting resurrection (Fig. 10.22). Over the door to the

10.21 The ground plan of the tomb of Queen Nefertari-mi-en-Mat, 1290–1224 B.C.

main room, on the extreme right of the illustration, we see the vulture goddess Nekhbet of El-Kab. Her claws hold the shen-sign, which symbolizes eternity and sovereignty. The goddess Isis wears on her crown the horns of a cow, surrounded by the sun-disc from which hangs a cobra. In her left hand she carries the divine scepter. Queen Nefertari is dressed according to the fashion of the time, and over the vulture hood she wears the tall, feathered crown of the Divine Consort.

The painting itself is rich and warm, elegant, and highly stylized. The limited palette uses four hues, which never change in value throughout the work. Yet, the overall effect of this wall decoration is one of great variety. The composition maintains the conventionalized style established since Dynasty I, which treats the human form in flat profile. Eyes, hands, head, and feet show no attempt at verisimilitude. Quite the contrary, the fingers become extenuated designs, elongating the arms to balance the elegant and sweeping lines of legs and feet. The matching figures of Selkis and Maat, extreme left and right, exhibit arms of unequal length and proportion. Although the basic style remains consistent, we can observe a significant change in body proportions from those of the Old and Middle Kingdom.

Akhenaton & Monotheism: The Tell el Amarna Period

The reign of Akhenaton marked a break in the continuity of artistic style in Egypt. The stiff poses disappear and a more natural form of representation replaces them. The pharaoh, moreover, is depicted in intimate scenes of domestic life rather than in the formal ritual or military acts which were traditional and expected. He is no longer seen associating with the traditional gods of Egypt. Rather, he and his queen are depicted worshipping the disc of the sun, whose rays end in hands that either bless the royal pair or hold to their nostrils the *ankh*, the symbol of life.

What accounts for this revolution is not certain, but evidence suggests that the priesthood of Heliopolis, the ancient seat of the sun cult, had reestablished the primacy of their god. Amenhotep IV, as Akhenaton was called before changing his name to reflect his god, possessed a "strange genius" for religious experience and its expression. Depictions of him show that he apparently suffered from physical deformity. The realistic trends of the period and Akhenaton's desire for truth seem to have resulted in his graphic representation as a man with a misshapen

10.23 Nofretete (Nefertiti), c. 1360 BC. Painted limestone, height 19 ins (48 cm). The Egyptian Museum, Berlin.

body, an elongated head, and drooping jaw. Yet, the eyes are deep and penetrative. The effect is one of a brooding genius.

In the fifth or sixth year of his reign, the king moved his court to a sandy desert ground on the east side of the Nile to the newly constructed city of Tell el Amarna. It was a new city for a new king intent on establishing a new order based on a new religion. Because the movement failed and the city was abandoned, we are left with an encapsulated artistic synthesis, including the city itself. Tell el Amarna lay away from cultivated land, and once abandoned was never built over.

The town itself is dominated by the large estates of the wealthy, who chose the best sites and laid them out in the style of the Egyptian country house, with large gardens and numerous outbuildings, enclosed within a wall. In between these large estates lay the smaller dwellings of the less wealthy. There was even a slum area outside the northern suburb. Nearby was the grand North Palace.

In many ways Amarna reflects the regular features of New Kingdom domestic architecture, but seems much less sumptuous. Its lines and style are relatively simple. Structures are open, in contrast to the dark and secret character of the temple of Luxor, for example. At Amarna numerous unroofed areas lead to the altar of the god, Aton, left open to provide access to the rays of his sun.

Sculpture at Amarna departed from tradition. It became more a form of secular art, with less emphasis, apparently, on sculpture for tombs and temples. Perhaps as a result of the king's religious fervor, the Amarna sculptor seems to have sought to represent the uniqueness and individuality of humankind through the human face. In one sense Amarna sculpture is highly naturalistic, and yet, in another, departs from the merely natural into the realm of the spiritual. The bust of Queen Nofretete illustrates these characteristics (Fig. **10.23**). Of course, we have no way of knowing how Queen Nofretete actually looked, but the figure is so anatomically correct that it could be a natural-istic representation. Nonetheless, the line and proportions of the neck and head are almost certainly elongated, to increase her spiritual appearance. This technique is not unlike the Mannerist style of the sixteenth century.

Isolated by geographical and religious circumstance, Tell el Amarna brings us a complete and vivid encapsulation of artistic interrelationships centered on a philosophical and religious concept. Although his religious reforms failed, Akhenaton's experiment in monotheism has, nonetheless, left us with a clear portrait of an integrated scheme of life and culture.

10.24 Funerary mask of King Tutankhamun, c. 1340 B.C. Gold inlaid with enamel and semiprecious stones, height 21¼ ins (54 cm). The Egyptian Museum, Cairo.

Tutankhamun

One of the most popular artifacts from the succeeding period must be the exquisite sculpture from the tomb of Tutankhamun, son of Akhenaton (Fig. **10.24**). The tomb was discovered in the Valley of Kings near Thebes. The funerary mask is of solid beaten gold inlaid with semiprecious stones and colored glass. Designed to cover the face of the king's mummy, the mask is highly naturalistic in style, and apparently a true likeness of the young king. The mask wears the royal *nemes* headdress with two lappets hanging down at the sides. A ribbon holds the king's queue at the back. The hood formed by the headdress exhibits two symbolic creatures, the uraeus serpent and the vulture goddess Nekhbet of El-Kab, divinities who protected Lower and Upper Egypt.

CHINA

East Asians are consciously aware of their historical traditions and heritage. They see themselves in their historical context, and from that cultural context come the primary requisites for their art. East Asian art and culture to a large degree derives from Ancient China, which was, along with Ancient India, Mesopotamia and Egypt, an important center of ancient civilization. That being the case, the social heritage of China plays a fundamental role in all East Asian culture. It focuses on concepts of family, which subordinate the individual and result in particular political and ethical systems.

From the earliest times, China witnessed the crowding of populations into tight-walled villages. That packing-in of people governed social and family relationships. The family, as opposed to the individual, state, or church, formed the most significant social unit. This was reinforced by the religious practice of ancestor worship. The family also formed the basic political unit. A system of mutual responsibility called the Pao-chia system made individuals in the same household responsible for each other's actions. Within the family, a hierarchical system existed. The position of each individual was dictated by birth and marriage. The individual was subordinate to the family, and the greatest virtue was filial piety. Marriages were arranged more as a union of families than of individuals, and women in general were subordinate to men. As a result, pluralism, such as became the cornerstone of Western culture, could not exist as a social base. The norms for social conduct, such as loyalty, sincerity, and benevolence, were inculcated in the family system. Later, the precepts of Confucianism, an ethical system, fulfilled the role played by law and religion in the West. The Chinese social model was authoritarian and class-conscious.

THE SHANG DYNASTY

At a time slightly prior to the Israelites' enslavement in Egypt, verifiable Chinese history was beginning. From approximately 1400–1100 B.C., the Shang Dynasty emerged. As in Egypt, the dynasty was the basic organizational unit of history, conforming to the period of a particular family of rulers. In the third or Zhou (Chou) Dynasty, from c. 1100 to c. 256 B.C., an accurate documentation of Chinese history begins.

The earliest Chinese books date to the early centuries of the first millennium B.C. Mostly mythological, these early histories wove a pattern of ethics, philosophy, and mythology. From this strong sense of history came also an ideal of political unity and a belief in the uniqueness of the Central Country, or Chung-kuo (Middle Kingdom, or China).

At a time parallel to the time of the Old Testament prophets and the great philosophers of Greece, China entered into its great period of philosophy and classicism. This was called the Eastern Zhou period and lasted from approximately 770 to 250 B.C. This period of time is remarkable for its cultural accomplishments. During the Eastern Zhou period, China drew abreast of other cultures in technology.

Shang Bronzes

Shang bronzes from approximately 1400 B.C. in China comprise two types: weapons and ceremonial vessels. Both are frequently covered with elaborate designs, either incised or in high-relief. The craftmanship of the design is

10.25 Ritual wine vessel or *hu* c. 1300–1100 B.C. Bronze, 16 ins (40.6 cm) high, 11 ins (27.9 cm) wide. Nelson Gallery, Atkins Museum, Kansas City.

exquisite and surpasses the quality of virtually every era, including the Western Renaissance. Each line has perfectly perpendicular sides and a flat bottom, meeting at a precise 90-degree angle, in contrast, for example, with incising which forms a groove. The approach to design seen in animal representation illustrates a vision unlike Western culture's and similar to later East Asian and Pacific Northwest Indian design, in which the animal appears as if it had been skinned and laid out with the pelt divided on either side of the nose. A rigid bilateral balance occurs. The grace and symmetry of the bronze ritual vessel of the shape known as *hu* (Fig. **10.25**) exhibits subtle patterns carefully balanced and delicately crafted. The graceful curves of the vessel are broken by deftly placed ridges and gaps, and while the designs are delicate, the overall impression exhibits solidity and stability.

Stone Sculpture

Another innovation of the Shang culture is stone sculpture in high-relief or in the round. Most numerous are small-scale images in jade. They represent a broad

10.26 Elephant feline head, Chinese, Shang Dynasty c. 1200 B.C. Jade, length 1⅝ ins (4 cm). The Cleveland Museum of Art, Anonymous Gift, 52.573.

vocabulary, from fish, owls, and tigers, for example, as single units to combinations and metamorphoses such as the elephant head of Figure **10.26**. This design expresses a simplicity of form with incised, subtle detail. We can easily see the metamorphic intention of the piece as we note the feline head with large, sharp teeth, elephant's trunk, and bovine horns.

Native American Culture

When we speak of American Indian art and culture, we speak of a variety of cultures and styles. In North America alone, no less than ten general cultural areas exist. Mexico and Central America add additional numbers. The history of native American peoples in Mexico and Central America emerges on either side of a dividing line created by the European invasions of the late fifteenth and early-to-mid-sixteenth centuries. Art is thus labeled as either *pre-Columbian*—before Columbus—or not pre-Columbian. South America was home to a wide variety of tribes, and the artistry of these diverse peoples encompassed weaving, metalsmithing, and pottery as major arts. Probably the focal point of South American Indian art is Peru, because it was the territory of the Incas.

Indian artists, like all artists, developed their own set of conventions or ground rules, and these are quite different from the artistic conventions of Western culture. Many of the subtleties of Indian art emerge from the culture itself. Indian art portrays not only visual qualities, but emotional and psychological qualities as well. All works of art are not of equal qualitative value; however, judging the quality of works of art from different cultural traditions often requires the imposition of different criteria. Those who do not come from an Indian cultural heritage may

never, probably cannot ever, fully engage a work of art from this tradition. In fact, it may be difficult for a non-Indian to approach Indian art—to comprehend what art in Indian terms comprises.

In many respects, Indian art is the same as Western art, Chinese art, or any other art: It is an expression of a human perception of reality manifested in a particular medium and shared with others. In a very real sense art is human reflection. Our separation of it into various categories stems from a need to organize our examination, not as a suggestion that art is more or less advanced in one culture than it is in another.

Within the Native American culture exists a wide variety of expressions, approaches to materials, and general styles. Among many tribes there is no specific word that is equivalent to the word "art." In Native American culture in general, however, art is anything "that was well done in the technical sense, or in the end result. This effect might be magical, or it might be power . . . the concept of an artist was simply a person who was better at the job than another." Only a few Indian tribes, for example the Northwest Coast, Mayan, and Inca, had a group of professionals who earned a living by producing art.

The earliest identifiable art in Mexico comes from the Olmec people—called the "rubber people"—and can be dated to approximately 1000 B.C. These people carved a number of subjects, for example, the delicate, baby-faced figure shown in Figure **10.27**. This finely carved figurine has a characteristic turned-down mouth. That facial feature is a common characteristic of Olmec sculpture of this period. Even though much of the body is missing, we can see that the carefully carved details on this green-gray stone effigy make a powerful statement.

10.27 Fragment of carved stone figurine; Olmec-style head with trace of red paint inlay. Xochipala, Guerrero, Mexico, 1250–750 B.C., 3 x 1 ins (7.6 x 2.5 cm). The National Museum of the American Indian, Smithsonian Institution.

ELEVEN

ARTISTIC REFLECTIONS IN THE PRE-MODERN WORLD

600 B.C. TO A.D. 1650

CLASSICAL GREECE

Under the ruler Pericles, Classical Greek culture reached its miraculous zenith. In the brief span of time between approximately 600 and 200 B.C. Greek influence and civilization spread throughout the Mediterranean world until, under Alexander the Great, it stretched—for the span of a single lifetime—from Spain to the Indus. All this was achieved by a people whose culture, at its height, took as its measure the human intellect. In society as in the arts, rationality, clarity, and beauty of form were the aim, although as the style we call Hellenistic developed in the fourth century B.C., artists increasingly sought to imbue their works with the expression of feeling.

CLASSICAL STYLE

Fifth-century Athenian painting of the Classical style reflected some characteristics of earlier work, including the principally geometric nature of the design. This indicated a concern for form and order in the organization of space and time. What separated the Classical style in vase painting (our only extant evidence of Greek two-dimensional art of this period) from earlier styles was a new sense of idealized reality in figure depiction.

Such realism reflected a technical advance as well as a change in attitude. Many of the problems of foreshortening (the perceivable diminution of size as the object recedes in space) had been solved, and, as a result, figures

11.1 Achilles Painter, white ground lekythos from Eretria, showing woman and her maid, 440 B.C. 15 ins (38 cm). Courtesy, Francis Bartlett Fund, The Museum of Fine Arts, Boston.

had a new sense of depth. Depth and reality were also heightened in some cases by the use of light and shadow. Some records imply that mural painters of this period were highly skillful in representation, but we have no surviving examples to study. The restrictions inherent in vase painting do not allow us to assess the true level of skill and development of the two-dimensional art of this period. Vase painting does demonstrate, however, the artists' concern for formal design—that is, logical, evident, and perfectly balanced organization of space.

The fifth century also saw many of the most talented artists turn to sculpture, mural painting, and architecture. The idealism and dignity of the Classical style is none the less aptly portrayed by such artists as the Achilles Painter, whose work is seen in Figure **11.1**. Here a quiet grandeur infuses the elegant and stately figures, which are reminiscent of those on carved grave reliefs. The portrayal of feet in the frontal position is a significant development, reflecting the new skill in depicting space.

By the end of the fifth century the convention we have seen in Egyptian and Mesopotamian art of putting all the figures along the baseline on the front plane of the design gave way to suggestions of depth, as some figures are occasionally placed higher than others. By the end of the fourth century the problems of depth and foreshortening were fully overcome.

We generally relate style to treatment of form rather than content or subject matter, but often form and content cannot be separated. When Classicism was modified by a more individualized and naturalistic treatment of form, its subject matter broadened to include the mundane, as opposed to the heroic.

Appeal to the intellect was the cornerstone of Classical style in all the arts. In painting, as well as in other disciplines, four characteristics reflected that appeal. First and foremost is an emphasis on form, on the formal organization of the whole into logical and structured parts. A second characteristic is idealization, an underlying purpose to portray things as better than they are, as according to Aristotle in his *Poetics*, or to raise them above the level of common humanity. For example, the human figure is treated as a type rather than as an individual. A third characteristic is the use of convention. A fourth characteristic is simplicity. Simplicity does not mean lack of sophistication. Rather, it means freedom from unnecessary ornamentation and complexity.

The age of Greek Classical style in sculpture probably began with the sculptors Myron and Polyklitus in the middle of the fifth century B.C. Both contributed to the development of cast sculpture. Polyklitus is reported to have achieved in Figure **11.2** the ideal proportions of the male athlete. It is important to note, again, in our pursuit of the elements of Greek Classical style, that the *Lance Bearer* represents *the* male athlete, and not *a* male athlete. In this work the body's weight is thrown onto one leg in the *contrapposto* stance. The resulting sense of relaxation and controlled dynamics in the realistically treated human body and the subtle play of curves made possible by this simple but important change in posture are also characteristic of Greek Classical style.

Myron—Discus Thrower

Myron's best-known work displays both concern for restraint, for subtle control of movement coupled with balance, and concern for flesh and the idealized human form. Figure **11.3** is a much later marble copy; Myron worked in bronzes and so was freed from many of the constraints of marble. A work of statuary, as opposed to relief sculpture, must stand on its own, and supporting the weight of a marble statue on the small area of one ankle poses significant structural problems. Metal, having greater tensile strength, provides a solution to many of these problems.

Greek statuary may be portraiture, but the features are idealized. Man may be the measure of all things, but in art

11.2 *Doryphoros (Lance Bearer)*, Roman copy after an original of *c.* 450–440 B.C., by Polyklitus. Marble, height 6 ft 6 ins (1.98 m). Museo Archeologico Nazionale, Naples.

11.3 *Diskobolus (Discus Thrower)*, Roman copy after a bronze original of *c.* 450 B.C., by Myron. Marble, life size. Museo Nazionale Romano, Rome.

he is raised above human reality to the state of perfection found only in the gods.

This representation of an athlete in an Olympic event brought a new sense of dynamics to Greek sculpture. It captures a dramatic moment, freezing the figure in the split second before the explosive release of the discus, and Myron achieves, thereby, a conflict of opposing forces. His composition draws its tension not only from the expectation of the impending explosive force, but also in the dramatic intersection of two opposing arcs: One in the downward thrust of the arms and shoulders; the other, in the forward thrusting of the thighs, torso, and head.

Typical of Greek freestanding statues, the *Discus Thrower* is designed to be seen from one direction only. As such it comprises a sort of freestanding, three-dimensional "super-relief." The beginnings of Classical style represented by this celebration of the powerful nude male figure or *kouros* type are an outgrowth of what is called the severe style, a transitional style between archaic and Classical. From this style, in which Myron was trained, come suggestions of moral idealism, dignity, and self-control, qualities inherent in Classicism. However, the *Discus Thrower* steps forward in a chain of increasing vitality of figure movement.

For Myron, the geometrical composition remains the focus of the work. Form takes precedence over feeling.

CLASSICAL THEATRE

The theatre of Periclean Athens was a theatre of convention, and the term convention, as it applies here, takes on another dimension. Every era and every style have their conventions, those underlying, accepted expectations and/or rules which influence the artist subtly or otherwise. In some styles conventions are fundamental; in others the conventions are unconventional. Theatre of convention implies a style of production lacking in illusion or stage realism. So in contrast to sculpture and painting, which pursued the noble and the ideal with fair dependence upon a verisimilar but idealized treatment of subject matter, the Greek Classical theatre pursued the same ends through a slightly different means.

Theatre of convention is to a large extent freer to explore the ideal than theatre of illusion, in which scenic details are realistically portrayed, because dependence upon stage mechanics does not hamper the playwright. An audience will accept a description in poetic dialogue, but by convention does not demand to see it. Imagination is the key to theatre of convention. The Greek dramatist found that with freedom from the restraints imposed by

dependence on illusion or depiction, he was much better able to pursue the lofty moral themes fundamental to his perception of the universe. Although we have some extant plays from the era indicating what and how the playwright wrote, we are at a loss to know specifically how that work became theatre—that is, a production. Nevertheless, we can try to build a picture of production from descriptions in the plays themselves, other literary evidence, and from a few extant archeological examples.

Theatre productions in Ancient Greece were part of religious festivals held three times a year: the City Dionysia, Rustic Dionysia, and Lenaea. The first of these was a festival of tragic plays and the last, of comic. The City Dionysia was held in the Theatre of Dionysus in Athens. The contests were begun in 534 B.C., before the Classical era. Our knowledge of Greek theatre is enhanced somewhat by the fact that although we do not have most of the plays, we do know the titles and the authors who won these contests from the earliest to the last. From the records (inscriptions in stone) we know that three playwrights figured prominently and repeatedly as winners in the contests of the era.[1] They were Aeschylus, Sophocles, and Euripides. Our entire collection of complete tragedies is from these three playwrights—seven from Aeschylus, seven from Sophocles, and eighteen from Euripides.

A playwright entering the contests for tragedy or comedy was required to submit his plays to a panel of presiding officers, who selected three playwrights for actual production. The early plays of the Classical style had only one actor plus a chorus, and at the time of play selection the playwright was assigned the chief actor plus a *choregus*, a patron who paid all the expenses for the production. The playwright was author, director, choreographer, and musical composer. He often also played the leading role.

Aeschylus

Aeschylus was the most famous poet of Ancient Greece. Clearly fitting the classic mold, he wrote magnificent tragedies of high poetic nature and lofty moral theme. In *Agamemnon*, the first play in the *Oresteia* trilogy, Aeschylus's chorus warns us that success and wealth are insufficient without goodness.

Justice shines in sooty dwellings
Loving the righteous way of life,
But passes by with averted eyes
The house whose lord has hands unclean.

Be it built throughout of gold.
Caring naught for the weight of praise
Heaped upon wealth by the vain, but turning
All alike to its proper end.[2]

Aeschylus probed questions that we still ask: How responsible are we for our own actions? How much are we controlled by the will of heaven? His characters were larger than life; they were types rather than individuals, in accordance with the idealism of the time. Yet his characters were also human, as evidenced by his portrayal of Clytemnestra in *Agamemnon*. Aeschylus's early plays consisted of the traditional single actor, plus a chorus of fifty, but he is credited with the addition of a second actor. By the time Aeschylus ended his career a third actor had been added and the chorus reduced to twelve.

In Aeschylus's plays we find a strong appeal to the intellect. Aristophanes, the master of Greek comedy, has Aeschylus, a character in *The Frogs*, defend his writing as an inspiration to patriotism, to make men proud of their achievements. This is inspiration in an intellectual, not a rabble-rousing, sense. Aeschylus lived through the Persian invasion, witnessed the great Athenian victories, and fought at the battle of Marathon. His plays reflect this experience and spirit.

Sophocles

Overlapping with Aeschylus was Sophocles, who reached the peak of his personal career during the zenith of the Greek Classical style with works like *Oedipus tyrannus*. Sophocles's plots and characterizations illustrate a trend toward increasing realism, similar to that in Classical sculpture. The movement toward realism was not a movement into theatre of illusion and even Euripides's plays, the most realistic of the Greek tragedies, are not realistic in our sense of the word. However, Sophocles was a less formal poet than Aeschylus. His themes are more humane and his characters more subtle, although his exploration of the themes of human responsibility, dignity, and fate is of the same intensity and seriousness as we see in Aeschylus. His plots show increasing complexity, but with the formal restraints of the Classical spirit. Sophocles lived and wrote beyond the death of Pericles in 429 B.C. and so he experienced the shame of Athenian defeat. Even so, his later plays show nothing of the "action" noted in sculpture. Classical Greek theatre was mostly discussion and narration. Themes often dealt with bloodshed, but, though the play led up to violence, blood was never shed on stage.

Euripides

Euripides was younger than Sophocles, although both men died in 406 B.C. They did, however, compete with each other. They do not share the same style. Euripides's plays carry realism to the furthest extent we see in Greek tragedy. They deal with individual emotions rather than great events, and his language, though still basically poetic, is higher in verisimilitude and much less formal than that of his predecessors. Euripides also experimented with, and ignored, many of the conventions of his theatre. He explored the mechanics of scenography and questioned in his plays the religion of his day. His tragedies are more tragicomedies than pure tragedies. Some critics have described many of his plays as melodramas. He was also less dependent on the chorus.[3]

Plays such as *The Bacchae* reflect the changing Athenian spirit and dissatisfaction with contemporary events. Euripides was not particularly popular in his time, perhaps because of his less idealistic, less formal, and less conventional treatment of dramatic themes and characters. Was he perhaps too close to the reality of his age? His plays were received with enthusiasm in later years and are unquestionably the most popular of the Greek tragedies today.

Aristophanes

Tragedies and satyr plays (Euripides's *Cyclops* is the only example we have of that *genre*) were not the only works produced in the theatre of the Classical era in Athens. The Athenians were extremely fond of comedy, although no examples survive from the Periclean period. Aristophanes (*c.* 450–*c.*380 B.C.), of whose plays we have eleven, was the most gifted of the comic poets, and his comedies of the post-Classical period, such as the *Acharnians*, are highly satirical, topical, sophisticated, and often obscene. Translated productions of his comedies are still staged, but the personal and political targets of his invective are unknown to us, and so these modern productions are mere shadows of what took the stage at the turn of the fourth century B.C.

Theatre Design

The form of the Greek theatre owes much to the choral dances associated with the worship of Dionysus from which it originated. In 534 B.C. Thespis is reported to have introduced a single actor to these choric dances or dithyrambs. In 472, Aeschylus added a second actor, and in 458, Sophocles added a third. So throughout its history

11.4 Reconstruction of the Hellenistic theatre at Ephesus, Turkey, c. 280 B.C., rebuilt c. 150 B.C.

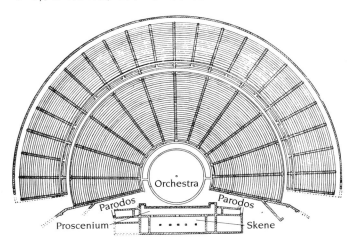

11.5 Plan of the theatre at Epidaurus.

11.6 Polykleitus the Younger, theatre at Epidaurus, c. 350 B.C. Diameter 373 ft (114 m), orchestra 80 ft (24 m) across.

the Greek theatre comprised a large circular orchestra—acting and dancing area—with an altar at its center, and a semicircular *theatron*—auditorium or viewing place—usually cut into or occupying the slope of a hill. Since the actors played more than one role, they needed somewhere to change costume, and so a *skene*—scene building or retiring place—was added. The gradual development of the *skene* into a raised stage is somewhat obscure and problematical, but later, by Hellenistic times, it had become a rather elaborate, two-storied affair (Fig. **11.4**) with projecting wings at each end and a raised stage.

The earliest extant theatre is the theatre of Dionysus, on the south slope of the Acropolis, dating from the fifth century B.C., where the plays of Aeschylus, Sophocles, Euripides, and Aristophanes were staged. Its current form dates back to a period of reconstruction work around 338–326 B.C. The theatre at Epidaurus (Figs. **11.5** and **11.6**) is the best preserved, and was built by Polykleitus the Younger about 350 B.C. Its sheer size demonstrates the monumental character the theatre had assumed by that time. The orchestra measures 80 ft (24 m) in diameter, with an altar to Dionysus in the center. The auditorium, comprising slightly more than a semicircle, is divided by an ambulatory about two-thirds of the way up, and by radiating stairways. All the seats were of stone, and around the first or lowest row were seats for the dignitaries of Athens. These seats had backs and arms, and some were decorated with relief sculptures.

There was undoubtedly variation in the design of theatres in different locations, but, again, time has removed most examples from our grasp. The many theories of how Greek theatre productions worked, how scenery was or was not used, and whether or not and when a raised stage was present make fascinating reading, and the reader is encouraged to explore this area in detail elsewhere.

CLASSICAL ARCHITECTURE

Existing examples of Greek architecture, to which the arts of the Western world have returned over the past 2,300 years, offer a clear and consistent picture of basic Classical style. Nothing brings that picture so clearly to mind as the term Greek temple. We all have an amazingly accurate concept of the structure and proportions of a Greek temple. H. W. Janson suggests that the crystallization of the characteristics of a Greek temple is so complete that when we think of one Greek temple, we basically think of all Greek temples. Even so obvious a structure as a Gothic cathedral does not have this capacity, for despite the explicit symbol of the Gothic arch, its employment is so diverse that no one work typifies the many.

The Classical Greek temple, as seen in Figure **11.7**, has a structure of horizontal blocks of stone laid across vertical columns. This is the post-and-lintel structure we have seen earlier (Chapter 7). It is not unique to Greece, but certainly the Greeks refined it to its highest aesthetic level. As we have seen, this type of structure creates some very basic problems. Stone is not high in tensile strength—the ability to withstand bending and twisting—although it is high in compressive strength—the ability to withstand crushing. Downward thrust works against tensile qualities in horizontal slabs (lintels) and works for compressive qualities in vertical columns (posts). As a result, columns can be relatively delicate, whereas lintels must be massive.

Only limited open space can be created using this structural system. Such a limitation was not of great concern to the Greeks because a Greek temple was to be seen and used from the outside. The Greek climate does not dictate that worshippers crowd inside a building. Exterior structure and aesthetics were of primary concern.

Greek temples were of three orders—Ionic, Doric, and Corinthian (Fig. **7.3**). The first two of these are Classical, the third, though of classical derivation, is of the later, Hellenistic style. The contrasts between these types make an important, if subtle, stylistic point. Simplicity was an important characteristic of the Greek Classical style, and the Ionic and Doric orders maintain clean and simple lines in their capitals. The Corinthian order has more ornate and complex capitals. When taken in the context of an entire building, this small detail does not appear to be of great consequence, but it is significant in understanding the rudiments underlying this style. Columns and capitals are convenient tags for identifying the order of a Greek temple. Differences are apparent in column bases and the configuration of the lintel, as well as in the columns and capitals.

The earlier of the two types, the Doric, has a massive appearance compared to the Ionic. The Ionic, with a round base, has a curved profile which raises the column above the baseline of the building. The flutings of the Ionic order, usually twenty-two per column, are deeper and separated by wider edges than are those of the Doric, giving it a more delicate appearance. The Ionic capital is surrounded by a crown of hanging leaves or a *kymation*. The architrave shows a three-part division, each section of which diminishes downward, creating a much lighter impression than the more massive architrave of the Doric.

The Parthenon

Perched on the top of the Acropolis at Athens, the Parthenon (Fig. **11.7**) stands as the greatest temple built by the Greeks and the prototype for all Classical buildings

11.7 Iktinos and Kallikrates, the Parthenon, Acropolis, Athens, from the northwest, 447–438 B.C.

thereafter. When the Persians sacked Athens in 480 B.C. they destroyed the then existing temple and its sculpture. When Pericles rebuilt the Acropolis in the late fifth century, Athens was at her zenith, and the Parthenon was her crowning glory.

In plan the Parthenon is a peripteral temple—that is, columns surround the interior room or *cella*, and the number of columns on the sides is two times the number across the front, plus one. Its interior, divided into two parts, housed the 40-ft (12-m) high ivory and gold statue of Athena Parthenos.

The Parthenon typifies every aspect of Greek Classical style in architecture. It is Doric in character and geometric in configuration. Balance is achieved through symmetry, and the clean, simple line and plan hold the composition together perfectly. For the Greeks, deities were just slightly more than mortals, and this human-centered philosophy is reflected by the human scale of the temple.

The number of columns across the front and down the sides of the temple represents a specific convention. The internal harmony of the design rests in the regular repetition of virtually unvaried form. To the casual glance each column appears alike and seems to be equidistant from its neighbor, except at the corners, where the spacing is clearly lessened in subtle, aesthetic adjustment. Each element is carefully adjusted. A great deal has been written about the so-called "refinements" of the Parthenon, those elements which form intentional departures from strict geometric regularity. According to some, the slight outward curvature of horizontal elements compensates for the tendency of the eye to perceive a downward sagging if all elements are actually parallel. Each column has about a 7-ins (17 cm) gradual dilation, supposedly to compensate for the tendency of vertical parallel lines to appear to curve inward. The columns also tilt inward at the top so as to appear perpendicular. The *stylobate* is raised toward the center so as not to appear to sag under the immense weight of the stone columns and roof. Even the white marble color, which in other circumstances might appear stark, may have been chosen to harmonize with and reflect the intense Athenian sunlight, although parts of the temple and its statuary were brightly painted.

So here we have the perfect embodiment of Classical characteristics: *convention, order, balance, idealization, simplicity, grace,* and *restrained vitality*—of this earth but mingled with the divine.

LATE CLASSICAL STYLE

Sculpture of the fourth century B.C. illustrates clearly the change in attitudes reflected in late Classical styles. Praxiteles is famous for *individualism* and delicacy of themes such as the *Cnidian Aphrodite* (Fig. **11.8**). There is a looking inward in this work which is different from the formal detachment of earlier sculpture. Female nudity also appears for the first time. Originally, Aphrodite rested her weight on one foot. Her body sways to the left in the famous Praxitelean s-curve. Strain on the ankle of the sculpture was minimized by the arm's attachment to drapery and a vase.

11.8 *Cnidian Aphrodite*, probably Hellenistic copy of 4th century B.C. bronze original by Praxiteles. Marble, height 60½ ins (154 cm). The Metropolitan Museum of Art, New York (Fletcher Fund, 1952).

HELLENISTIC STYLE

As the age of Pericles gave way to the Hellenistic period, the dominant characteristics of Classicism were gradually modified to a less formal, more naturalistic, and more emotional style.

Like other media and art forms, vase painting around the year 400 B.C. had a highly ornate style. Thick lines, dark patterns on garments, and a generous use of white and yellow characterized compositions of crowded figures represented mainly in three-quarter views. Illustrative of this change in style is the combat scene from an *amphora* painted by the Suessula Painter (Fig. **11.10**). Here we also see the illusion of spatial depth, as the figures leave the baseline of the frontal plane.

In the Hellenistic era, everyday scenes, sometimes comic and vulgar, were common in wall painting. These scenes are remarkable for the use of aerial and linear perspective to indicate three-dimensional space. Unfortunately for us, the few extant examples of Classical

11.10 Attributed to the Suessula Painter, amphora showing combat of Greeks and Amazons, 5th–6th century B.C. Height 14 ins (36 cm). The Metropolitan Museum of Art, New York (Fletcher Fund, 1944).

11.9 *Apoxyomenos (Scraper)*, Roman copy, probably after a bronze original of c. 330 B.C. by Lysippos. Marble, height 6 ft 9 ins (2.05 m). The Vatican Museums, Rome.

The late fourth century found in the sculpture of Lysippos (a favorite of Alexander the Great) a dignified naturalness and a new concept of space. His *Scraper* (Fig. **11.9**) illustrates an attempt to put the figure into motion, in contrast to the posed figures at rest we have seen previously. The theme of the *Scraper* is mundane—an athlete scraping dirt and oil from his body. The proportions of the figure are even more naturalistic than those of Polyklitus, but the naturalism is still far from perfect. Style had moved dramatically from earliest Classical reflections, but Classical influence remained.

11.11 *The Dying Gaul*, Roman copy of a bronze original of c. 230–220 B.C. Marble, life-size. Museo Capitolino, Rome.

11.12 *(left) Nike of Samothrace*, c. 190 B.C. Marble, height 8 ft (2.43 m). The Louvre, Paris.

and Hellenistic two-dimensional art furnish us with only a glimpse of these two important styles, so closely linked, but reflecting such different attitudes.

Hellenistic style in sculpture continued to dominate the Mediterranean world until the first century B.C., and as time progressed, style changed to reflect an increasing interest in individual human differences. Rather than idealization, the Hellenistic sculptor often turned to pathos, banality, trivia, and flights of individual virtuosity in technical exploration. *The Dying Gaul* (Fig. 11.11) is a powerful expression of emotion and of pathos as it depicts a noble warrior on the verge of death. This Roman copy of a statue from Pergamon places the figure on a stage, as if to act out a drama. Representing a Gallic casualty in the wars between Pergamon and barbarian invaders, the warrior is slowly bleeding to death from a chest wound. In the same sense, the *Nike of Samothrace* (Fig. 11.12), or *Winged Victory*, displays a dramatic, dynamic technical

11.13 *Laocoön and his Sons*, 1st century. Marble, height 5 ft (1.52 m). The Vatican Museums, Rome.

The temple of the Olympian Zeus (Fig. **11.14**), illustrates Hellenistic modification of Classical style in architecture, similar to that in painting, sculpture, and theatre. Scale and complexity are considerably different from the Parthenon, and the philosophy of emotionalism is clearly evident. Order, balance, moderation, and consonant harmony are still present, but in these huge ruins we can see the change in proportions from the Parthenon in the slender and ornate *Corinthian* columns. Temple architecture in this style was designed to produce an overpowering emotional experience. This temple, begun by the architect Cossutius for King Antiochus IV of Syria, is the first major Corinthian temple. Its elaborate detail pushed its completion date into the second century A.D. under the Roman emperor Hadrian. The remaining ruins only vaguely suggest the scale and richness of the original building, which was surrounded by an immense, walled precinct.

virtuosity. Symbolizing a triumph of one of the successors to Alexander, she "brings strength, weight, and airy grace into an equipoise one would not expect to be achieved in the hard mass of sculptured marble." The sculptor has treated stone almost as if the work were a painting. We sense, as a result, the full, awesome reality of wind and sea.

The common Hellenistic theme of suffering is taken up explosively in the Laocoön group (Fig. **11.13**). The Trojan priest Laocoön and his sons are depicted being strangled by sea serpents. Based on Greek myth, the subject is Laocoön's punishment for defying Poseidon, god of the sea, and warning the Trojans of the Greek strategy of the Trojan horse. Emotion and movement are freed from all restraint, and straining muscles and bulging veins are portrayed with stark realism.

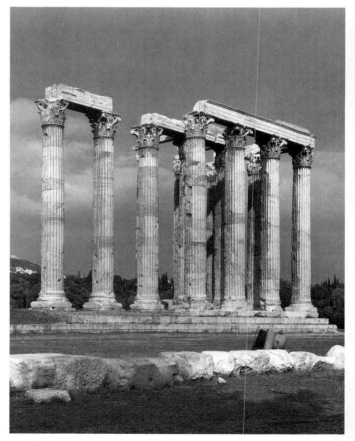

11.14 (*above*) The Temple of Olympian Zeus, Athens, 174 B.C.–A.D. 130.

AFRICA

For thousands of years, African artists and craftsmen have created objects of sophisticated vision and masterful technique. The modern banalities of so-called primitive "airport art" sold to tourists belie the rich cultural history of the African continent, which witnessed trade with the Middle East and Asia as early as A.D. 600, as documented by Chinese T'ang Dynasty coins found on the maritime coast of East Africa. Climate, materials, and the nature of tribal culture doomed much of African art to extinction; only a small fraction remains. None the less, what has survived traces a rich vision which varies from culture to culture, and whose style runs from abstract to naturalistic. Its purposes range from magical to utilitarian, portraying visions of human reality that individuals from other cultural traditions may be ill-equipped to understand. Works from African traditions—as from any other tradition—are nevertheless capable of rewarding the viewer with great satisfaction.

Approximately 10,000 years ago, Africa, as well as other regions of the world, entered the Neolithic or New Stone Age epoch. This era marked a tremendously important change for humankind because it witnessed the appearance of animal breeding, agriculture, and pottery, and the first farming communities. Settlement in villages became widespread. In Africa, pottery was introduced very early and numerous indigenous plants were progressively brought into cultivation—for example, sorghum, millet, African rice, and yams. Much later, in the time of the Roman Empire (third to first centuries B.C.), records indicate the advance of the Bantu tribes of the Cameroon and Congo forests into the savannahs of the south and east of Africa, taking with them agricultural skills and iron. By the Middle Ages, both Islam and Christianity had made significant inroads into Africa, and the continent witnessed a variety of major cultures and political centers—for example, in Zimbabwe, Ethiopia, Benin, Ghana, and Mali.

Nok Style

During the first millennium B.C., on the Jos plateau of northern Nigeria, the Noks, a nonliterate culture of farmers, entered the Iron Age and developed an accomplished artistic style. Working in terracotta, and apparently nearly as sophisticated in its firing as were the makers of the Qin Dynasty terracotta warriors of China, these artists produced boldly designed sculptures (Fig. **11.15**). Some works represent animals in naturalistic

11.15 Head from Jemaa, c. 400 B.C. Terracotta, height 10 ins (25 cm). The National Museum, Lagos.

form and others portray life-sized human heads. Although stylized, with flattened noses and segmented lower eyelids, for example, each work reveals individualized character. Facial expressions and hairstyles differ and "it is this unusual combination of human individuality and artistic stylization which gives them their peculiar power."[4] Probably these heads are portraits of ancestors of the ruling class. The technique and medium of execution seem to have been chosen to insure permanence and for magical rather than artistic reasons. The Nok style appears seminal to several West African styles.

Igbo-Ukwu Roped Pot on a Stand

The level of skill achieved by the ninth and tenth centuries A.D. can be seen in a ritual water pot from the village of Igbo-Ukwu in eastern Nigeria (Fig. **11.16**). Cast using the *cire-perdu* or lost-wax process, this leaded bronze artifact is amazing in its virtuosity. The graceful

11.16 Roped pot on a stand, from Igbo-Ukwu, 9th–10th century. Leaded bronze, height 12½ ins (32 cm). The National Museum, Lagos.

design of its recurved lines and flaring base by themselves are exquisite, but the addition of the delicate and detailed rope overlay reflects sophistication of both technique and vision.

Head of a Queen

A link between the Nok culture and that of Ife, also in Nigeria, may have existed to draw these two cultures together in their art across the centuries. Ife was an important cultural and religious center in the southwest. The accomplishments of its artists, in their mastery of the terracotta medium, their rendering skills, and the depth of their vision, suggest to some scholars a long developmental period, culminating in twelfth- to thirteenth-century works such as Figure 11.17. There can be little question that this represents a mature artistic style. We cannot escape the temperament of this young woman: The

anatomical detail is remarkable and even today the textures are so exquisite that the figure seems ready to come to life. The full mouth and expressive eyes suggest extreme sensitivity. The high brow and minutely detailed headdress complete this naturalistic portrait, which captures more than photographic reality as it brings to its surface detail the innermost essences of the individual.

Djenne Style

The styles of African art range widely from the naturalistic to the highly expressive and abstract. Up the Niger River at Djenne, in Mali, we find an expression of the latter in a small, fourteenth-century terracotta figure of a bearded male (Fig. 11.18). The most striking aspect is its thrusting chin, which flies in the face of anatomical realism. The lower and upper jaws protrude grotesquely from a plate-like appendage, probably a stylized beard, where the jaw would normally be. The eyes are lightly incised on the conical surface of the head. The proportions of the torso pinch inward, as if compressed by the undetached arms. The details of what could be armor show exquisite workmanship, and the sophisticated rendering of the entire form suggests an intentional style whose purpose again is to reflect inner essence.

11.17 Head of a queen, 12th–13th century. Terracotta, height 10 ins (25 cm). Museum of Ife Antiquities, Ife.

11.18 Bearded male figure from Djenne, Mali, 14th century. Terracotta, height 15 ins (38 cm). Detroit Institute of Arts (Eleanor Clay Ford Fund for African Art).

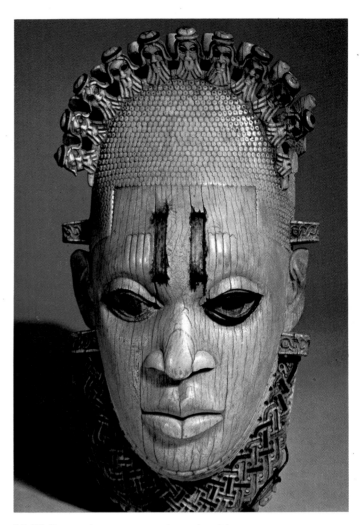

11.19 Pectoral or waist mask, early 16th century. Ivory, height 9¼ ins (25 cm). The British Museum, London.

Benin Style

Superb craftsmanship also dominates an early-sixteenth-century ivory mask of the Benin school. The origins of this style are ascribed by local tradition to either a master from Ife or the Portuguese. Whatever the root, the result is an exquisite portrayal made for the Oba, or King of Benin (Fig. 11.19), reigning when the Portuguese arrived in Africa. Again, we find expressive qualities reflected in the elongated head and stylized features, yet the carver's mastery of the medium leaves no doubt about his or her sophistication of vision or technique. The details of the mask reflect precision and delicacy, and the heads of Portuguese men with beards, woven skillfully into the head-dress, hold some symbolic, if unclear, meaning.

Benin Head

In the sixteenth century, bronze-casting in Benin reached great levels of technical accomplishment. In Figure 11.20

11.20 Benin Head, Nigeria, 16th century. Bronze casting, height 9¼ ins (23 cm). The Metropolitan Museum of Art, New York (the Michael C. Rockefeller Memorial Collection of Primitive Art).

a freestanding likeness of the head of a royal personage shows realistic detail and an apparent understanding of compositional principles. The rendering of facial detail is anatomically correct and individual enough to suggest that the head represents a particular individual. At the same time, facial features seem simplified, suggesting idealization to reveal the subject's character. In addition, the elaborate details of the headgear and neck ornamentation (which doubles as a base), juxtaposed with the simplicity of the facial treatment, make the face the focus of attention. Focus is created subtly through contrast coupled with radial balance—that is, the detailed rectilinear elements of the cap, side flaps, and neck ornamentation surround the face and, because the details are unvaried, force us to focus on the facial features.

CHINA

At a time roughly parallel to the rise of the Greek philosophers, the Hebrew prophets, and the Buddha in India, China produced its classical philosophy and thought. Chinese philosophy focused on humankind as a social and political animal and was distinctly humanistic in tone, in contrast to the divine philosophies of India and parts of the Mediterranean world. Philosophers further strengthened the historical-mindedness of China by using the past as a model for the present. Amid this drift came the establishment of a classic canon of Chinese literature— a set of books associated with the Confucian tradition called *The Five Classics*.

CONFUCIANISM

Confucius (551–479 B.C.), probably the first professional teacher and philosopher in China, also was recognized as the greatest of all teachers and philosophers. His work, the Analects, comprises his answers to questions prefaced by "The Master said." However, his thought tends to be on a far more pragmatic plane than the intellectual pursuits of Plato or Socrates. His primary interest seemed to lie in politics. He proposed a return to the ancient way, in which persons must play their proper, assigned roles subject to authority. None the less, his ingenuity came in his perception of government as fundamentally an ethical problem. A ruler's virtue, rather than power, yielded contentment in the people. His aim was to convince rulers to pursue ethical principles; he thereby became China's first moralist, and founder of a great ethical tradition.

TAOISM

In contrast to Confucianism, Taoism, or "the Way," taught the independence of the individual. Taoism was a philosophy of protest of the common individual against despotic rulers, and of the sensitive intellectual against the rigidity of the Confucian moralists. If Confucianism was pragmatic, Taoism was mystical. China witnessed reunification under a Qin (Ch'in) king in 246 B.C. However, by 206 B.C. the Qin had disappeared, and a new dynasty arose, which consolidated the imperial system started by the Qin. The Han Dynasty brought prosperity and relative internal peace to a land previously torn by war. War, however, continued externally, and China set about occupying Korea and Central Asia. Often compared to the rise and fall of the Roman Empire, the Han Dynasty disintegrated economically and administratively. By the late second century A.D., the great local families had grown too rich and powerful to be curbed by any central authority, and a centralized government became impossible. By the early third century, China had been broken into three separate kingdoms and was unable to resist invasions by Turks, Mongols, and Tibetans. With foreign pressures came other foreign influences, especially Buddhism. An unprecedented upturn in religious fervor occurred.

BUDDHISM

Closely related to another Indian religion, Brahmanism, Buddhism was a system of philosophy and ethics founded by the Buddha (563–483 B.C.). With less formalism, and a greater emphasis on self-denial than Brahmanism, the "four noble truths" of Buddha are: existence is suffering; the origin of suffering is desire; suffering ceases when desire ceases; the way to reach the end of desire is to follow the "noble eightfold path," which comprises right belief, right resolve (to renounce carnal pleasure, harm no living creature, and so on), right speech, right conduct, right occupation or living, right effort, right contemplation or right-mindedness, and right ecstasy. The final goal of the religious man is to escape from existence into blissful nonexistence—*nirvana*. Individuals are made up of elements that existed before they were born, which separate at death and may be recombined in a somewhat similar fashion after death. It is from this chain of being that humans seek to escape by religious living.

Qin Dynasty Realism: Terracotta Warriors

Although the Qin Dynasty lasted less than fifty years, during the third century B.C., the emperor spent that entire time preparing his palace and mausoleum. Over the years minor pilfering and excavation have occurred, since the location of the underground vaults was well known. In March 1974, however, during the digging of a well near the vaults, some life-size and lifelike pottery figures were unearthed. The vaults containing the terracotta warriors, horses and bronze chariots had been located. In one vault (measuring 760 ft by 238 ft [231 × 72 m]) alone, 6,000 terracotta warriors and horses were found. A total of three vaults contain over 8,000 figures (Fig. **11.21**).

The warriors have different expressions. Some are dignified; others, vigorous; some are cheerful; others, debonair. Some appear lost in brooding, while still others look witty and handsome. Each figure displays an almost knowable character as if some living form had been miraculously frozen in time. The realistic style and the consummate skill of the artists who created these figures are breathtaking. Detailing is so precise that in addition to temperament, we can determine the rank and provenance of these warriors. Common soldiers, for example, appear in short battle tunics or laceless armored suits; their heads are covered by small round caps, and they wear square-toed sandals on their feet.

The horses appear well bred, and all look muscular and vigorous. Their proportions are exquisite (Fig. **11.22**) and even their expressions reflect the strong insight, understanding, and skill of the artists. The eyes stare ahead

11.22 A clay rider with saddled horse, Qin Dynasty, China, 3rd century B.C. Life-size. Courtesy, People's Republic of China.

intensely and the necks stretch in magnificent curvature, reflecting energy and power.

The quality of these works indicates clearly that Chinese technical mastery had reached a high level. To create such masterpieces, the artists needed to master scientific manufacturing processes and to know how to control firing temperatures. The hardness of the figures and their almost flaw-free condition testify to the superior clay-making technology of the Qin Dynasty.

11.21 Terracotta warriors, Qin Dynasty, China, 3rd century B.C. Life-size. Courtesy People's Republic of China.

11.23 Lintel and Pediment of Tomb, Han Dynasty, 50 B.C.– A.D. 50. Earthenware, hollow tiles painted in ink and colors on a whitewashed ground, 29 x 80½ ins (73.8 x 204.7 cm). Denman Waldo Ross Collection. Courtesy, Museum of Fine Arts, Boston.

Han Dynasty Style

Three styles of painting existed in the Han period of the first century A.D. The first was a rather formal and stiff style, very geometric and hieratic, which stressed silhouette. The second contrasted greatly, depicting lively action and deep space. The third was in between these two, being more painterly and exhibiting movement and lively depictions of, for example, mythical beings, dragons, and rabbits. In Figure **11.23** we can see in a painted tile masterfully rendered figures whose brushstroke suggests liveliness and movement. The figures appear in three-quarter poses, which gives the painting a sense of depth and action. The active line, with its diagonal sweeps, adds to the sense of action. The poses of the personages suggest character—that is, the psychology of the figure portrayed. Although the use of pose and direction reflects a sophisticated approach and technique, the figures remain on the same baseline, with no sense of placement in deeper space.

BUDDHIST INFLUENCE

Buddhist influence in sculpture and the demand for religious images in the sixth century made the period one of significant sculptural output. It was probably the one great age of Chinese sculpture. Chinese sculpture showed deeply religious spiritualism, and, in contrast to the

realism of the past, exhibited a stiff, austere abstraction while limiting realism to the details of clothing (Fig. **11.24**). In this depiction of the Bodhisattva Kuan-yin, carved in stone, we find the Bodhisattva in its later, feminine, state as the "Goddess of Mercy" (Japanese, Kannon). The flow of line from all points in the image uses gentle curves to direct the eye upward to the serene visage of the face. Repetition of the deep curve unifies the composition, giving it grace, harmony, and softness. In this feminine form the Bodhisattva or "Enlightened Existence," although having attained the enlightenment of a Buddha, stays in this world to help others achieve salvation before passing onto nirvana herself, and becomes a gentle and compassionate protectress. Later, when Chinese interests turned in a more humanistic direction, sculpture reflected a more intimate and human depiction. Images became rounder and more lifelike, approximating Chinese concepts of human beauty. Throughout this period both religious and secular sculpture occurred side by side. Monumental sculpture for the tombs of emperors and other great men seemed especially popular.

11.24 *Kuan-yin, The Bodhisattva of Compassion*, China, Northern Chou-sui Dynasty, about 580. From the Ku Shihfo Ssu monastery, Sion, Shensi Province, Limestone 6⅜ ins (2.49 cm).

216

The Monastery of the Buddha's Halo

Very little has survived of early Chinese architecture, because it was mostly constructed of wood. We can capture a sense of its style, however, by examining a reconstruction drawing of the main hall of the ninth-century Fo-kuang-ssu (Monastery of the Buddha's Halo) on Mount Wu-t'ai (Fig. **11.25**). This is China's oldest wooden building and is located in northern Shansi. We can see here the indicators that have come to represent Asian style in the curved roof lines with their deep overhangs and ornate decoration.

11.25 Front elevation and cross section of the main hall of the Fo-kuang-ssu, Mount Wu-t'ai.

Liurong Temple

Also typical and common is the Liurong Temple or "Six Banyan Pagoda" of Guangzhou (Fig. **11.26**). Built in its final form in approximately 989, the pagoda rises 188 ft (57 m) in nine stories from the outside. From the inside it contains seventeen stories. The pagoda is richly painted in red, green, gold, and white, so colorfully that it was at one

11.26 Liurong Temple, Guangzhou, China, c. 989.

time called the Flowery Pagoda. The current name comes from the famous writer and calligrapher Su Dong-po, who visited it in 1100 and was attracted to the six banyan trees surrounding it. Again, we can see in the upward curving line of the eaves and the colorful glazed roof tiles the characteristics of Chinese architecture which become typical from this time onward.

Sung Dynasty Style

In China's Sung Dynasty of the eleventh to thirteenth centuries, we find extant paintings of impressive quality, and it is from this time on that the Chinese have seen painting as their greatest art. The basic canons were established then and reached a zenith that has probably never been surpassed. Buddhist influence remained strong in painting, although secular art saw greater prominence than before. In secular painting the emphasis was placed on landscapes, as opposed to human events and images. Figure **11.27** reflects a soft and atmospheric style. It is part of a larger scroll entitled *Twelve Views from a Thatched Cottage* by Hsia Kuei (c. 1180–1230). In it we see a mountain range and a lake with boats on the water. Each of the sections of the scroll carries an inscription, for example, "Distant Mountains and Wild Geese." Taken as a whole, the scroll reveals time as well as space as it moves from daylight to dusk. Subtle technique merges soft washes with firm brushstrokes, and images move from sharp focus to indistinct suggestion. Certainly the detail-

11.27 Hsia Kuei, *Twelve Views from a Thatched Cottage* (detail), c. 1200–1230. Hand scroll, ink on silk, 11 ins (28 cm) high. Nelson Gallery, Atkins Museum, Kansas City.

ing gives the subject a degree of realism, but we are taken beyond realism to a "sense" of nature. The images are impressions rather than verisimilar depictions. Details are highly selective and the artist's concentration focuses on essences. In the eleventh century, color took little importance, and most Chinese painting was monochromatic. Landscapes, for the Chinese, represent nature as a whole. Each small detail symbolizes the larger universe. In this painting an overriding sense of mysticism emerges and probably reflects the Taoist belief system.

CHINESE THEATRICAL STYLES

Just as the dogmas of Confucianism shaped Chinese culture, Confucianism also gave shape to early Chinese drama. Tradition holds that Confucius put to death an entire troupe of actors who took part in a play that violated his teaching. Taoism also provided important building blocks for the theatre in China. As a result, we can find in some Chinese drama the mystical leanings of Taoism, in which the exploration of reality—in this case, the relationship between individuals and society—reflects an intuitive and emotional drift, with great imagination and flights into fantasy. One significant characteristic of Chinese drama that emerged from its socioreligious roots concerned women on the stage. Women in China were subjected to severe restrictions, and were forbidden to act in the theatre. Therefore, women in the theatre until the twentieth century were portrayed by men. These portrayals mimicked the teetering style of walking which resulted from the practice of footbinding among the upper classes, and utilized a device called *tsai jiao* to keep the actor "on point" throughout the performance.

Legend documents the presence of actors and clowns and a dramatic form known as the Peking (now Beijing) play as early as the nineteenth century B.C. By the Han Dynasty of the third century A.D., the court was entertained by dramatic presentations performed with masks, song, and dance. However, the traditional founding of Chinese theatre came in the seventh to tenth centuries during the Dang Dynasty, when the Emperor Minghuang established the Pear Garden Conservatory for the training of professional actors. During this time theatre performances explored a number of themes, including satire of government officials.

The period of time roughly equivalent to the Gothic period in Western history witnessed the Chinese golden age of literature in which popular theatre and literature flourished. At this time the Mongols were in control of China, and the subject of drama and literature often dealt with various aspects of injustice and despotism. Written in the vernacular, as opposed to the classical written form, Mongol period drama sought to reach a broader and less-highly-educated audience than literature had in the past. The use of the vernacular reflected a general trend in Chinese society wherein all written materials sought to reach out to those who had not been classically educated.

As the Western world entered its Renaissance, China entered the Ming Dynasty (1368–1644). The Mongols had been deposed; however, in pursuit of social stability, the new rulers severely limited popular entertainment. Nothing could be produced which in any way criticized or offended the emperor, the establishment, or Confucius. The theatre which developed during this period was aristocratic, or court, theatre, and had little to do with the common people.

The major form of Chinese drama was the Peking opera. This form had two major types, civil and military. In Peking opera of the civil type, themes dealt with domestic and social issues. The military type explored the exploits of warriors and/or robbers. The Peking opera plays often were based on history, legend, or popular novels. In these plays the action always ends happily. Chinese dramas concentrate on high points, and relegate the development of the story to narrative passages. Thus, interest is focused on climactic moments rather than on a fully dramatized story.

"On stage" in Chinese theatre means "center stage." When an actor exits, he merely moves to an area away from center. Although he remains in full view of the audience, by convention he is not there, and so he can do whatever tasks need to be done, from drinking tea to adjusting his costume. All entrances occur from stage left, and all exits from stage right.

Costume and makeup play a significant and symbolic role in Chinese theatre. Color, especially, portrays emotion and social standing. Red connotes individuals of high social standing; yellow means royalty. Dark crimson is reserved for military personages, as well as barbarians. Red also connotes loyalty. Black symbolizes the poor and the fierce. Green stands for virtue; white represents the old, the very young, and the bereaved. Color also distinguishes character types, for example, the *sheng* utilize five primary colors; secondary colors appear in other character types. We can get an impression of the sublety, complexity, and depth of Chinese drama and its audience relationships when we realize that costume is used to make very specific and detailed statements about character, with perhaps as many as three hundred combinations of headdresses, shoes, and other costume items per character—all of which would be understood by the audience.

Chinese theatrical costume, like its scenery, does not attempt to depict historical accuracy. Styles and periods mix freely so as to create dramatic effect and reinforce subtle nuances. Nuance and subtle inflection form important parts of Chinese philosophy and language, and the same is true for the theatre. Both color and design motifs indicate meaning for an audience: For example, animal and insect designs connote specific information for the Chinese audience—the emperor was symbolized by a dragon; butterflies mean long life and happiness; tigers symbolize power; and the phoenix, good fortune. Flowers also have meaning: spring and beauty are represented by the peony while wisdom and charm are represented by the plum blossom.

Often flags appear appended to the shoulders of a character. Such characters represent generals and the higher the general's rank, the more flags stick out of his shoulders. Chinese costume is similar to Classical Greek costume in that rank and station are indicated through the use of padding and *kothurnoi* or thick-soled boots. The melodramatic American movie form, the Western, was not unlike Chinese drama in its use of costume. In the former case, the "good guys" wore white hats, and the "bad guys," black ones. In Chinese theatre, the good guys wear square hats, and the bad guys, round ones.

IMPERIAL ROMAN CLASSICISM

By A.D. 70 the Romans had destroyed the Temple of Jerusalem and colonized Britain, spreading their pragmatic and pluralistic version of Hellenistic Mediterranean civilization to peoples of the Iron Age in north and west Europe. Under Augustus, Roman culture turned again to Greek Classicism and in that spirit glorified Rome, the Emperor and the Empire. Inventive and utilitarian, Roman culture left us roads, fortifications, viaducts, planned administration, and a sophisticated yet robust legal system.

ROMAN STYLE

We should beware of classifying all Roman art as an imitative and sterile reconstruction of Greek prototypes. Although some Roman statues fit that description, others display vigorous creativity that is uniquely Roman and uniquely expressive of Roman circumstances. All the same, scholars are divided not only on what various works of Roman sculpture reveal but also on what motivated them. The *Portrait of an Unknown Roman* (Fig. **11.28**) dates from a time when Hellenistic influence was becoming well established in Rome. It is tempting to attribute the highly naturalistic representation of this work to the same artistic viewpoint which governed Hellenistic style, and conclude that it is a copy of Hellenistic work. Such a conclusion, however, neglects an important Etruscan–Roman religious practice, undoubtedly of stronger influence. Portraits were an integral part of household and ancestor worship, and the image of a departed ancestor was maintained in a wax death mask. Wax is not a substance ideally suited for immortality, and there is a possibility that the naturalism of portraiture of this bust stems from the fact that it was made from a death mask. However, there may be more than mere portrait accuracy in this work, and some scholars point to an apparent selectivity of features and a reinforcement of an idea or ideal of ruggedness and character.

The straightforward naturalism of the Republican era changed during the Augustan period. Hellenistic influence had grown by the late first century B.C. In

11.28 *Portrait of an Unknown Roman*, 1st century B.C. Marble, height 14⅜ ins (36 cm). The Metropolitan Museum of Art, New York (Rogers Fund, 1912 [12.233]).

11.29 Augustus in armor, Villa of Livia, Prima Porta, c. 20 B.C. Marble, 6 ft 8 ins (2.03 m). The Vatican Museums, Rome.

11.30 (*opposite*) Head of Constantine the Great (part of an original colossal seated statue), 313. Marble, height 8 ft 6¾ ins (2.61 m). Palazzo dei Conservatori, Rome.

certain quarters Greek Classical influence dominated, but always with a Roman—that is, a more practical and individual—character. By the time of the Empire, Classical influence had returned sculpture to the idealized characteristics of Periclean Athens.

Augustus boasted that when he took Rome over it was a city of sun-dried bricks, and that when he left it it had become a metropolis in marble. Greek Classical form in sculpture was duplicated, recast, and translated into vital forms of the present. The Greek concept of the "perfect body" predominated. It was also a common practice to copy the idealized body of a well-known Greek statue and add to it a highly realistic portrait head of a contemporary Roman. Other figures were similarly Romanized. One statue portrayed a male figure draped in a toga, while another showed Augustus in armor (Fig. **11.29**). The aesthetics of sculptural depiction thus remained Greek with Roman clothing added. The pose, rhythm, and movement of the body originated in the past. The purpose of much sculpture at this time was the portrayal of the emperor. Emperors were raised to the status of gods, perhaps because a far-flung empire required assurances of stability and suprahuman characteristics in its leaders.

The reality that men are men and not gods was not long in returning to Roman consciousness, however, and third-century sculpture exhibited a stark and expressive reality. In the fourth century a new and powerful emperor had taken the throne, and his likeness (Fig. **11.30**), part of a gigantic sculpture (the head is over 8 ft [2.5 m] tall), shows an exaggerated, ill-proportioned intensity that we can compare with expressionist works of the early twentieth century. This work is not an actual likeness of Constantine. Instead, it is the artist's view of Constantine's perception of himself as emperor and of the office of emperor itself.

Virgil—The Aeneid

At such time when literature became reasonably acceptable to the practical Romans, it was chiefly through the contributions of Greek slaves that it was nurtured. At first literary works were imitations of Greek works and written in Greek. Latin was initially seen as a peasant language with few words capable of expressing abstract notions. The credit for developing a Latin prose style and vocabulary for the expression of philosophical ideas probably belongs to Cicero.

During the reign of Augustus, the poets Horace and Virgil wrote verses glorifying the emperor, the origins of Rome, the simple honesty of rural Roman life, patriotism, and the glory of dying for one's country. Livy set about retelling Roman history in sweeping style. Virgil's *Aeneid* tells the story of Rome, in an epic account of the journey of Aeneas from the ruins of Troy to the shores of Italy, far surpassing any mere propagandistic brief. Here we include the main section of Book 1.

ARMS and the man I sing, who first made way
Predestined exile, from the Trojan shore
To Italy, the blest Lavinian strand.
Smitten of storms he was on land and sea
By violence of Heaven, to satisfy
Stern Juno's sleepless wrath; and much in war.
He suffered, seeking at the last to found
The city, and bring o'er his fathers' gods
To safe abode in Latium; whence arose
The Latin race, old Alba's reverend lords,
And from her hills wide-walled, imperial Rome.

O Muse, the causes tell! What sacrilege,
Or vengeful sorrow, moved the heavenly Queen
To thrust on dangers dark and endless toil
A man whose largest honor in men's eyes
Was serving Heaven? Can gods such anger feel?

In ages gone an ancient city stood—
Carthage, a Tyrian seat, which from afar
Made front on Italy and on the mouths
Of Tiber's stream; its wealth and revenues
Were vast, and ruthless was its quest of war.

'T is said that Juno, of all lands she loved,
Most cherished this—not Samos' self so dear.
Here were her arms, her chariot; even then
A throne of power o'er nations near and far,
If Fate opposed not, 't was her darling hope
To 'stablish here; but anxiously she heard
That of the Trojan blood there was a breed
Then rising, which upon the destined day
Should utterly o'erwhelm her Tyrian towers;
A people of wide sway and conquest proud
Should compass Libya's doom;—such was the web
The Fatal Sisters spun.
                              Such was the fear
of Saturn's daughter, who remembered well
What long and unavailing strife she waged
For her loved Greeks at Troy. Nor did she fail
To meditate th' occasions of her rage,
And cherish deep within her bosom proud
Its griefs and wrongs: the choice by Paris made;
Her scorned and slighted beauty; a whole race
Rebellious to her godhead; and Jove's smile
That beamed on eagle-ravished Ganymede.
With all these thoughts infuriate, her power
Pursued with tempests o'er the boundless main
The Trojans, though by Grecian victor spared
And fierce Achilles; so she thrust them far
From Latium; and they drifted, Heaven-impelled
Year after year, o'er many an unknown sea—
O labor vast, to found the Roman line!

Below th' horizon the Sicilian isle
Just sank from view, as for the open sea
With heart of hope they sailed, and every ship
Clove with its brazen beak the salt, white waves.
But Juno of her everlasting wound
Knew no surcease, but from her heart of pain
Thus darkly mused: "Must I, defeated, fail
Of what I will, not turn the Teucrian King
From Italy away? Can Fate oppose?
Had Pallas power to lay waste in flame
The Argive fleet and sink its mariners,
Revenging but the sacrilege obscene
By Ajax wrought, Oileus' desperate son?
She, from the clouds, herself Jove's lightning threw,
Scattered the ships, and ploughed the sea with storms.
Her foe, from his pierced breast out-breathing fire,
In whirlwind on a deadly rock she flung.
But I, who move among the gods a queen,
Jove's sister and his spouse, with one weak tribe
Make war so long! Who now on Juno calls?
What suppliant gifts henceforth her altars crown?"

So, in her fevered heart complaining still,
Unto the storm-cloud land the goddess came,
A region with wild whirlwinds in its womb,
Æolia named, where royal Æolus
In a high-vaulted cavern keeps control
O'er warring winds and loud concourse of storms.
There closely pent in chains and bastions strong,
They, scornful, make the vacant mountain roar,
Chafing against their bonds. But from a throne
Of lofty crag, their king with sceptred hand
Allays their fury and their rage confines.
Did he not so, our ocean, earth, and sky
Were whirled before them through the vast inane
But over-ruling Jove, of this in fear,
Hid them in dungeon dark: then o'er them piled
Huge mountains, and ordained a lawful king
To hold them in firm sway, or know what time,
With Jove's consent, to loose them o'er the world.

To him proud Juno thus made lowly plea:
"Thou in whose hands the Father of all gods
And Sovereign of mankind confides the power
To calm the waters or with winds upturn,
Great Æolus! a race with me at war
Now sails the Tuscan main towards Italy,
Bringing their Ilium and its vanquished powers.
Uprouse thy gales! Strike that proud navy down!
Hurl far and wide, and strew the waves with dead!
Twice seven nymphs are mine, of rarest mould,
Of whom Deiopea, the most fair,
I give thee in true wedlock for thine own,
To mate thy noble worth; she at thy side

Shall pass long, happy years, and fruitful bring
Her beauteous offspring unto thee their sire."
Then Æolus: " 'T is thy sole task, O Queen,
To weigh thy wish and will. My fealty
Thy high behest obeys. This humble throne
Is of thy gift. Thy smiles for me obtain
Authority from Jove. Thy grace concedes
My station at your bright Olympian board,
And gives me lordship of the darkening storm."
Replying thus, he smote with spear reversed
The hollow mountain's wall; then rush the winds
Through that wide breach in long embattled line,
And sweep tumultuous from land to land:
With brooding pinions o'er the waters spread,
East wind and south, and boisterous Afric gale
Upturn the sea; vast billows shoreward roll;
The shout of mariners, the creak of cordage,
Follow the shock; low-hanging clouds conceal
From Trojan eyes all sight of heaven and day;
Night o'er the ocean broods; from sky to sky
The thunders roll, the ceaseless lightnings glare;
And all things mean swift death for mortal man.

Straightway Æneas, shuddering with amaze,
Groaned loud, upraised both holy hands to Heaven,
And thus did plead: "O thrice and four times blest,
Ye whom your sires and whom the walls of Troy
Looked on in your last hour! O bravest son
Greece ever bore, Tydides! O that I
Had fallen on Ilian fields, and given this life
Struck down by thy strong hand! where by the spear
Of great Achilles, fiery Hector fell,
And huge Sarpedon; where the Simois
In furious flood engulfed and whirled away
So many helms and shields and heroes slain!"
While thus he cried to Heaven, a shrieking blast
Smote full upon the sail. Up surged the waves
To strike the very stars; in fragments flew
The shattered oars; the helpless vessel veered
And gave her broadside to the roaring flood,
Where watery mountains rose and burst and fell.
Now high in air she hangs, then yawning gulfs
Lay bare the shoals and sands o'er which she drives.
Three ships a whirling south wind snatched and flung
On hidden rocks,—altars of sacrifice
Italians call them, which lie far from shore
A vast ridge in the sea; three ships beside
An east wind, blowing landward from the deep,
Drove on the shallows,—pitiable sight,—
And girdled them in walls of drifting sand.

That ship, which, with his friend Orontes, bore
The Lycian mariners, a great, plunging wave
Struck straight astern, before Æneas' eyes.

Forward the steersman rolled and o'er the side
Fell headlong, while three times the circling flood
Spun the light bark through swift engulfing seas.
Look, how the lonely swimmers breast the wave!
And on the waste of waters wide are seen
Weapons of war, spars, planks, and treasures rare,
Once Ilium's boast, all mingled with the storm.
Now o'er Achates and Ilioneus.
Now o'er the ship of Abas or Aletes,
Burst the tempestuous shock; their loosened seams
Yawn wide and yield the angry wave its will.

Meanwhile, how all his smitten ocean moaned,
And how the tempest's turbulent assault
Had vexed the stillness of his deepest cave,
Great Neptune knew; and with indignant mien
Uplifted o'er the sea his sovereign brow.
He saw the Teucrian navy scattered far
Along the waters; and Æneas' men
O'erwhelmed in mingling shock of wave and sky.
Saturnian Juno's vengeful stratagem
Her brother's royal glance failed not to see;
And loud to eastward and to westward calling,
He voiced this word: "What pride of birth of power
Is yours, ye winds, that, reckless of my will,
Audacious thus, ye ride through earth and heaven,
And stir these mountainous waves? Such rebels!—
Nay, first I calm this tumult! But yourselves
By heavier chastisement shall expiate
Hereafter your bold trespass. Haste away
And bear your king this word! Not unto him
Dominion o'er the seas and trident dread,
But unto me, Fate gives. Let him possess
Wild mountain crags, thy favored haunt and home,
O Eurus! In his barbarous mansion there,
Let Æolus look proud, and play the king
In yon close-bounded prison-house of storms!"

He spoke, and swiftlier than his word subdued
The swelling of the floods, dispersed afar
Th' assembled clouds, and brought back light to heaven.
Cymothoë then and Triton, with huge toil,
Thrust down the vessels from the sharp-edged reef
While, with the trident, the great god's own hand
Assists the task; then, from the sand-strewn shore
Out-ebbing far, he calms the whole wide sea,
And glides light-wheeled along the crested foam.
As when, with not unwonted tumult, roars
In some vast city a rebellious mob,
And base-born passions in its bosom burn,
Till rocks and blazing torches fill the air
(Rage never lacks for arms)—if haply then
Some wise man comes, whose reverend looks attest
A life to duty given, swift silence falls;

All ears are turned attentive; and he sways
With clear and soothing speech the people's will.
So ceased the sea's uproar, when its grave Sire
Lookd o'er th' expanse, and, riding on in light,
Flung free rein to his winged obedient car.

Æneas' wave-worn crew now landward made,
And took the nearest passage, whither lay
The coast of Libya. A haven there
Walled in by bold sides of a rocky isle,
Offers a spacious and secure retreat,
Where every billow from the distant main
Breaks, and in many a rippling curve retires.
Huge crags and two confronted promontories
Frown heaven-high, beneath whose brows outspread
The silent, sheltered waters; on the heights
The bright and glimmering foliage seems to show
A woodland amphitheatre; and yet higher
Rises a straight-stemmed grove of dense, dark shade.
Fronting on these a grotto may be seen,
O'erhung by steep cliffs; from its inmost wall
Clear springs gush out; and shelving seats it has
Of unhewn stone, a place the wood-nymphs love.
In such a port, a weary ship rides free
Of weight of firm-fluked anchor or strong chain.
Hither Æneas, of his scattered fleet
Saving but seven, into harbor sailed;
With passionate longing for the touch of land,
Forth leap the Trojans to the welcome shore,
And fling their dripping limbs along the ground.[5]

The influence of Horace, Virgil, and Livy on Western culture is difficult to overestimate; "they are so much a part of us that we take their values for granted and their epigrams for truisms."[6] As far as the Emperor Augustus was concerned, they fully expressed the Roman tradition and Roman language. Horace, Virgil, and Livy created a literature which distracted the upper classes from Greek "free thought" and which the emperor could exploit to rally them to the Ancient Roman order as represented in his person.

Throughout the literature of the Augustan period runs a moralizing stoicism. The most remarkable product of stoicism in poetry was satire, which allowed writers to combine morality with popular appeal. Martial and Juvenal utilized poetry to attack vice, and were thereby able to describe it in graphic detail. Petronius produced satirical picaresque novels of verse and prose, whose details were as readable as Martial's and Juvenal's but void of their morality. Finally, Apuleius and Lucan followed in the same literary tradition. Apuleius's *Golden Ass* is among

the earliest novels ever written. The author creates a fictional biography describing how he was tried and condemned for the murder of three wineskins. He was brought back to life by a sorceress, and in the process of trying to follow her in the form of a bird, he was changed instead into an ass. The only cure for his affliction appeared to be the procurement of rose leaves, and in his search for these, he fell into some bizarre and fantastic adventures.

ARCHITECTURAL CLASSICISM

Given the practicality of the Roman viewpoint, we should not be surprised to find that it is in architecture that an immediately distinctive Roman style is most evident. The clear crystallization of form we found in the post-and-lintel structure of the Classical Greek temple is also apparent in the Roman arch. However, here the whole is suggested, and to a certain degree summarized, by the part, whereas the Greek composition finds the part subordinate to the whole.

Very little remains of the architecture of the Republican period, but what there is suggests a strong Hellenistic influence with Corinthian orders and fairly graceful lines. There were notable differences, however. Hellenistic temples were on an impressive scale. Roman temples were even smaller than the Classical Greek ones, principally because Roman worship was mostly a private rather than public matter. Roman temple architecture also employed engaged columns—that is, columns partly embedded in the wall. As a result, on three sides Roman temples lacked the open colonnade of the Greek temple. The Temple of Fortuna Virilis (Fig. **11.31**) is the oldest and best preserved example of its kind, dating from the second century B.C. The influence of Greek style can be seen in the delicate Ionic columns and entablature, and yet

11.31 Temple of Fortuna Virilis, Rome, late 2nd century B.C.

11.33 Colosseum, interior.

11.32 Colosseum, Rome, c. 70–82.

Etruscan elements are present in the deep porch and engaged columns, necessitated by the wide cella (main enclosed space). The cella, containing only one room, is a departure from the Etruscan convention of three rooms. Roman temples needed more spacious interiors as they were used to display trophies from military campaigns, as well as to house the image of the deity.

In the Augustan age a refashioning of Roman architecture according to Greek style, as we saw in the case of sculpture, took place. This accounts for the dearth of surviving buildings from previous eras. Temples were built on Greek plans, but the proportions were significantly different.

The first through fourth centuries brought us what we typically identify as the Roman style, the most significant characteristic of which is the use of the arch as a structural system in arcades and tunnel and groin vaults. The Colosseum (Figs. 11.32 and 11.33), the best known of Roman buildings and one of the most stylistically typical, could seat 50,000 spectators. Combining an arcaded exterior with vaulted corridors, it was a marvel of engineering. Its aesthetics are reminiscent of Greek Classicism, but fully Roman in style. The circular sweep of each level is carefully countered by the vertical line of engaged columns flanking each arch. Doric, Ionic, and Corinthian columns mark each level and progress upward from heavy to lighter orders.

Placed in the center of the city of Rome, the Colosseum was the site of gladiatorial games, including the martyrdom of Christians by turning lions loose on them as a gruesome "spectator sport." Emperors competed with each other to produce the most lavish spectacles here. The Colosseum was a new type of building called an "amphitheatre," in which two "theatres," facing each other, are combined to form an arena surrounding an oval space. Originally a series of poles and ropes supported awnings to provide shade for the spectators. The space below the arena contained animal enclosures, barracks for gladiators, and machines for raising and lowering scenery.

Roman triumphal arches were also impressive architectural monuments. In the second Arch of Titus (Fig. 11.34), the Roman classical style survives in a memorial

11.34 Arch of Titus, Forum Romanum, Rome, 81. Marble.

11.35 Pantheon, Rome, c. 118–28.

to Titus raised by his younger brother, Domitian. It memorializes the accomplishments which Titus shared with his father, Vespasian, in the conquest of Jerusalem. The sculptural reliefs on the arch show Titus alone as *Triumphator*. The reliefs represent allegories of political reverence rather than illustrations of an historical event. Accompanying Titus in these reliefs are figures such as the *Genius Senatus* and the *Genius Populi Romani*, embodiments of the spirit of the Senate and general populace. What is important to recognize in this work is the contrast of external appearance—that is, the richly and delicately ornamented façade, with the massive internal structure of the arch, a characteristic which will reappear in Renaissance architecture.

The Pantheon

The Pantheon (Figs. 7.13, 11.35, and 11.36) fuses Roman engineering, practicality, and style in a domed temple of unprecedented scale, dedicated, as its name suggests, to all the gods.

Around the circular interior, niches carved out of the massive walls are occupied by statues of the gods. Corin-

11.36 Plan and section of the Pantheon.

thian columns add grace and lightness to the lower level. Heavy horizontal moldings accentuate the feeling of open space made possible by the huge dome, which is 143 ft (43 m) in both diameter and height (from the floor to the *oculus* (eye), the round opening at the top of the dome). The circular walls supporting the dome are 20 ft (6 m) thick and 70 ft (21 m) high. Recessed square coffers on the underside of the dome give an added sense of lightness and reflect the framework into which concrete was poured. Originally the dome was gilded to suggest "the golden dome of heaven."

In both plan and section the Pantheon is a round temple. From the exterior we glimpse a cella comprising a simple, unadorned cylinder capped by a gently curving dome. The entrance is a Hellenistic porch with graceful Corinthian columns. Originally the porch was approached by a series of steps and attached to a rectangular forecourt, so we see only part of a more complex design. Inside, the scale and detail overwhelm us. Support piers for the dome alternate rectangular and rounded niches, each of which supports a vault designed to transfer the weight of the dome onto solid footings.

How could the Romans build such a colossal structure? Historians argued that the key lay with a novel form of concrete containing a specific kind of cement developed near Naples. The secret, however, may lie in the mysterious rings around the dome, as suggested by a recent study at Princeton University: "Probably they perform a function similar to the buttresses of a Gothic cathedral ... The extra weight of the rings ... helps stabilize the lower portion of the dome: Rather than functioning like a conventional dome, the Pantheon behaves like a circular array of arches, with the weight of the rings holding the end of each arch in place."[7]

JAPAN

Chinese chronicles mention Japan for the first time in the first century A.D. Japan by that time had entered the Metals Age, and had developed a major rice-growing economy. The first development of any major political center, however, appears to have occurred in the fourth century. The country was controlled by a strongly entrenched aristocracy, the Yamato, whose dominance continued throughout the fifth and sixth centuries. At this time Japan experienced a strong Korean cultural influence.

Between the sixth and eighth centuries Japan passed from what historians call "protohistory" into that of civilization. The Yamato created a state centered on the Chinese model. Buddhism was introduced and adopted by the court sometime in the sixth century—although Shinto, Japan's ancient animistic religion appears to have been maintained. A constitution modeled on Confucian ethics, land reform which transformed the aristocracy into a bureaucracy paid by the state, the introduction of legal and penal codes, and the development of historical chronicles occurred over the next two hundred years. An official break with China in 894 testified to the progress of Japanese culture.

Japanese aesthetics had matured as well. By the fifteenth century, Japanese culture and society reached one of its highest points. Homogeneity among local economies, technological advances, and a burgeoning sea trade each contributed their part. As in the Western world, a new middle class, or bourgeoisie, made a significant impact on Japanese culture. Zen gardens proliferated and the tea ceremony was invented. Architectural masterpieces emerged, and Noh theatre was founded. Nevertheless, Japan politically could not maintain a level course of centralized government. Civil strife continued, and centralized authority all but disappeared. The shogunate became incapable of controlling the vassals, and became so weak that the opposite condition adhered. Despite its prosperity and cultural accomplishment, Japan was a sorely divided state when the Portuguese arrived in 1543 bringing Christianity and firearms.

The Kondo of Muro-ji

Buddhism also made a significant impact on Japan during the Jogan or Early Heian period, between 794 and 897. The Mikkyo, also called Esoteric Buddhism, emphasized secrecy and mystery, and its precepts can be found in the kondo of Muro-ji (Fig. 11.37), which stands in the remote area of Nara. The secluded location removes the temple from "distractions and corruptions." The design is asymmetrical, with a close relationship to the natural site. The shingled roof sets the kondo of Muro-ji apart from the tiled-roof structures of Chinese influence and argues for a native Japanese style in temple architecture.

11.37 Kondo of Muro-ji. Nara prefecture, Japan. Early Heian period, ninth century.

JAPANESE STYLE: PAINTING AND SCULPTURE

In the thirteenth century in Japan, sculpture reached a new maturity, turning to simple works that stressed strength and virility. A series of civil wars had led to the military dictatorship of the shoguns and their samurai (warriors) and to a wider based feudal regime. This was reflected in the works of sculptors, such as Unkei, whose demonic and colossal wooden Buddhist deities (Fig. 11.38) guard the entrance to the Todaiji temple at Nara.

11.38 Unkei, *Nio*, 1203. Wood, height 26 ft 6 ins (8 m). Todaiji temple, Nara.

We are drawn by both the statue's power, expressed in the fierce facial expression and forbidding hand, and by its simplicity, through the clean lines of the swirling fabrics.

Kumano Mandala

In the period just prior to the Ashikaga shogunate in Japan—that is, in the late thirteenth century—painting expanded its subject matter from individual portraiture to landscape (Fig. 11.39). The Kumano Mandala draws into close proximity three Shinto shrines which are geographically many miles apart. Above the shrines appear circular *mandorlas* or *mandaras* (Chinese: *mandala*) with Buddhist deities inside. The presence of the Buddhist deities in portrayals of Shinto shrines attests to the dominance of

Buddhism at the time. The mandala itself comprises a ceremonial incantation or magic formula represented in a schematic, cosmological drawing. Around and between the depiction of the shrines there is delicately rendered landscape. The presentational style creates both a shorthand of essences and also a beautiful design device of delicate and active line, which holds the entire work together and leads the eye from section to section.

Heiji Monogatori Scroll

In contrast to the contemplative esotericism of the Kumano Mandala, the Japanese Heiji Monogatori scroll (Fig. 11.40) depicts a dramatically active fire scene replete with crowds and emotion. As the Sanjo Palace burns, figures and flames explode from the right border to the left. In a stylized fashion, the artist creates a masterful scene which is so tightly controlled compositionally that it could be a study for any painter of any age. The forceful diagonals and the powerful, horizontal, dark thrust of the palace roof meet to form an arrow shooting across the paper. In a design as intricate and powerful as any Baroque painting, this work builds detailed individual pieces, stimulating in their own right, into a large and complicated unity of contrasting colors, values, and textures. Straight and curved lines are juxtaposed to create further conflict and dramatic tension.

11.39 Kumano Mandala, Japanese, Kamakura Period, c. 1300. Color on silk. The Cleveland Museum of Art, John L. Severance Fund, 53.16.

11.40 Scroll with depictions of the Night Attack on the Sanjo Palace from the Heiji Monogatori Emaki, Japan, Kamakura period, second half of the 13th century. Handscroll, ink and colors on paper, 16¼ ins x 23 ft (41.3 cm x 6.99 m). Fenolloso-Wel Collection. Courtesy, Museum of Fine Arts, Boston.

JAPANESE STYLE IN THEATRE

Japan's two great dramatic forms, Noh and Kabuki, both originated from religious rituals dating to the late eighth and early ninth century, when dramatic devices were used as teaching tools by Buddhist monks. In a fashion very similar to medieval miracle, mystery, and morality plays, the dramatizing of religious ritual in Buddhism slowly became more and more secularized, found its way out of the sanctuary, and gained in popularity. The results emerged as dramatic forms that were performed in markets as well as temples.

Japanese Noh drama emerged from the fourteenth century. It represented the most significant and original literary and performing art development of the Ashikaga period. A highly conventionalized art form, Noh drama grew out of two sources: simple dramas based on symbolic dances performed to music at the imperial court, and similar mimetic performances popular with the common people. Its final form is credited to a Shinto priest named Kan'ami and his son Seami. They also founded one of the hereditary lines of Noh performers, the Kanze, which still perform today.

Noh drama is performed on a simple, almost bare stage and, like Classical Greek tragedy, uses only two actors. Also, as in Classical Greek drama, actors wear elaborate masks and costumes, and a chorus functions as a narrator. Actors chant the highly poetic dialogue to orchestral, musical accompaniment. All actions suggest rather than depict, which gives the drama its sense of stylization and conventionality; symbolism and restraint characterize both acting and staging.

Noh drama's subjects range from Shinto gods to Buddhist secular history, and usually center on the more popular Buddhist sects. The tone of Noh plays tends to be serious—appealing to the intellect—with a focus on the spirit of some historical person who wishes salvation but is tied to this earth by worldly desires. The plays tend to be short, and an evening's performance encompasses several plays interspersed with comic burlesques called Kyogen ("Crazy Words"). Although Noh drama is performed today and is extremely popular, it remains primarily a fourteenth-century form. Almost all of its canon of scripts (approximately 240) come from that period, with more than 100 written by Seami, alone: for example, Atsumori.

Noh plays can be classified, in general, into five types: these are plays about the gods; warriors; women; spirits or mad persons; and about demons. Traditionally, an evening's performance included all five types, performed in the order noted. Contemporary practice, however, has shortened the program to two or three.

BYZANTIUM

Astride the main land route from Europe to Asia and its riches, Byzantium possessed tremendous potential as a major metropolis. In addition, the city was a defensible deep-water port, which controlled the passage between the Mediterranean and the Black Sea. Blessed with fertile agricultural surroundings, it formed the ideal "New Rome." For this was the objective of the Emperor Constantine when he dedicated his new capital in 330 and changed its name to Constantinople. The city prospered, and became the center of Christian Orthodoxy and mother to a unique and intense style in the visual arts and architecture. When Rome fell to the Goths in 476 it had long since handed the torch of civilization to Constantinople. Here it was that the arts and learning of the Classical world were preserved and nurtured, along with an Eastern orientation, while Western Europe underwent the turmoil and destruction of barbarian invasion.

BYZANTINE STYLE

A fundamental characteristic of Byzantine visual art is the concept that in art exists the potential to interpret as well as to represent perceived phenomena. Byzantine art, like its literature, was conservative and mainly anonymous and impersonal. Much of Byzantine art remains undated, and questions concerning derivation of styles, if not the styles themselves, lie unresolved. The physical expansion of artistic form from the constrained style of the late Roman and Roman Christian churches to the vast wall surfaces of new Byzantine churches posed problems of style which took time to resolve. The development of narrative Christian art with its relatively new approach dates back to the mid-fifth century. Early attempts at iconography can be traced to the third and fourth centuries.

The content and purpose of Byzantine art was always religious, although the style of representation underwent numerous changes. Classical standards subsided with a decline in enlightened patronage and skilled craftsmanship. The period of Justinian marks an apparently deliberate break with the past. What we describe as the distinctly Byzantine style, with its characteristic abstraction and focus on feeling rather than form, began to take shape in the fifth and sixth centuries, although the classical Hellenistic tradition seems to have survived as an undercurrent. High realism in some works has led to occasional confusion among scholars over dating, where the style of a work appears to predate the work itself. Throughout the seventh century Classicism and decorative abstraction intermingled in Byzantine art.

Certainly by the eleventh century Byzantine style had adopted a hierarchical formula in wall painting and mosaics, coupled with a reduced emphasis on narrative. The Church represented the kingdom of God, and as one moved up the hierarchy, one encountered figures changing in form from human to divine. Placement in the composition depended upon religious, not spatial, relationships. Depiction is not illusionistic, but flat and antique. Here again, the Byzantine style is penetrated from time to time by several renaissance movements, mostly in the minor arts. By the eleventh century a strictly two-dimensional style appears which is elegant and decorative. Stylization and dramatic intensity characterize twelfth-century art, a style further intensified in the thirteenth century with turbulent movement, architectural backdrops, and elongated figures. The fourteenth century produced small-scale, crowded works of narrative content. Use of space is confused and perspective is irrational. Figures are distorted, with small heads and feet. A more intense spiritualism is obvious.

Stretching as it did over 1,000 years, and influenced by turbulent history, Byzantine art represents a complex repertoire of styles.

11.41 San Vitale, Ravenna, Italy, 526–47.

11.42 San Vitale, interior.

11.43 Plan and transverse section of San Vitale.

San Vitale in Ravenna

San Vitale in Ravenna (Figs. **11.41** and **11.42**) is the major Justinian monument in the West, and was probably built as a testament to orthodoxy in the declining kingdom of the Ostrogoths.

The prismatic geometry and warm brick texture of the exterior envelop an exhilarating, expanding well of strongly verticalized interior space. The key to the design is in the ingenious reciprocal manner in which volumenic parts are interlocked. For example, the eastern apse and its flanking spaces are composed of cylinders, prisms, and blocks which pile up dramatically against the outer octagonal shell, carrying the eye continuously across a concatenated play of surfaces. Each unit, delimited by the shadow lines of a sketchy terracotta cornice, can be read as an entity but is simultaneously joined and subordinated to the whole effect.[8]

The structure consists of two concentric octagons (Fig. **11.43**). The hemispherical dome rises 100 ft (30.5 m) above the inner octagon, and floods the interior with light.

Eight large piers alternate with columned niches to define precisely the central space and to create an intricate, *multifoliate* design. An inexplicable feature is the placement of the *narthex* at an odd angle. Two possible explanations encompass both the practical and the spiritual. One suggests that the narthex paralleled a then-existing street; the other, that it was designed in order to make worshippers reorient themselves on entering the complex arrangement of spaces, and thereby experience a transition from the outside world to the spiritual one.

On the second level of the *ambulatory* was a special gallery reserved for women—a standard feature of Byzantine churches. The design is one of intricate complexity, as the visitor experiences an ever-changing panoply of arches within arches, and flat and curved spaces. The aisles and gallery spaces contrast strikingly with the calm area under the dome. The clerestory light reflects off the mosaic tiles with a greater richness than in any Western churches. In fact, new construction techniques in the vaulting allow for windows on every level and open the sanctuary to much more light than previously possible, or than was found in the West until the end of the Romanesque style and the advent of the Gothic.

The sanctuary itself is alive with mosaics of the imperial court and sacred events. Figure **11.44** provides a vivid picture of the emperor. Particularly fascinating here is the stylistic contrast of two mosaics in the same church. *Abraham's Hospitality and the Sacrifice of Isaac* (Fig. **11.45**) demonstrates a relaxed naturalism whereas the mosaic depicting Justinian and his court demonstrates the orientalized style, more typically Byzantine, with the figures posed rigidly and frontally rather than naturalistically. The mosaics clearly link the church to the Byzantine court, reflecting, again, the connection of Emperor to the Faith, of Christianity to the State, and, indeed, the concept of the "Divine Emperor." Justinian and Theodora are portrayed as analogous to Christ and the Virgin. The emperor has a golden halo with a red border, is robed in regal purple, and presents a golden bowl to Christ, pictured in the semidome above.

11.44 (*right*) Emperor Justinian and his court, *c.* 547. Wall mosaic, San Vitale, Ravenna.

11.45 (*below*) *Abraham's Hospitality and the Sacrifice of Isaac.* Wall mosaic, San Vitale, Ravenna.

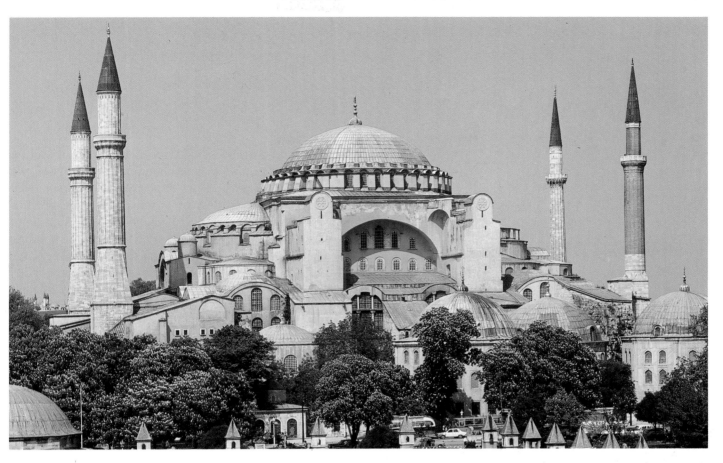

11.46 Anthemius of Tralles and Isidorus of Miletus, Hagia Sophia, 532–7.

If San Vitale praises the emperor and orthodoxy in the West, Hagia Sophia in Istanbul (Constantinople) represents a crowning memorial in the East (Figs. **11.46–49**). Characteristic of Justinian Byzantine style, called *arcuate domicile*, Hagia Sophia uses well-rehearsed vaulting techniques of Roman economy plus Hellenistic design and geometry. The result is a richly colored building in a style of orientalized antiquity. Basic to the conception is the elevated central pavilion with its domical image of heaven and large, open, and functional spaces. The magnificent Hagia Sophia provides us with a rare experience of Byzantine artistry. We know a little of its architect, Anthemius, who was a natural scientist and geometer from Tralles in Asia Minor. The church was built to replace an earlier basilica. This monument, which for a long time was the largest church in the world, was completed in only five years and ten months. The speed of the work, together with Byzantine masonry techniques, in which courses of brick alternate with courses of mortar as thick or thicker than the bricks, caused great weight to be placed on insufficiently dry mortar. As a result arches

11.47 Plan of Hagia Sophia.

11.48 Hagia Sophia, interior.

11.49 (*below*) Axonometric section (bird's eye view) of Hagia Sophia.

buckled and buttresses had to be erected almost at once. Because of the rapid construction and the effects of two earthquakes, the eastern arch and part of the dome itself fell in 557. The flatness of a dome that large remains unique. Also remarkable is the delicate proportioning of the vaults which support such great weight. The building is intensely spiritual and yet capable of holding large numbers of worshippers; it creates a transcendental environment, where thoughts and emotions are at once wafted to a spiritual rather than a mundane sphere. "It seemed as if the vault of heaven were suspended above one," wrote Procopius.

Justinian's reign thus inaugurated the style called Byzantine, blending all traces of previous styles, Eastern or Western, together in a new style. Forms and relationships were imbued with a spiritual essence built on Classical models but shaped in its own unique way. The wide range of works from the reign of Justinian synthesizes the relationships between God, the state, philosophy, and art. The emperor was the absolute monarch and also defender of the faith, governing by and for the will of God. Reality thus became spiritualized and was reflected in works of art which depicted earthly habitation in a hieratic style.

HIERATIC STYLE

By the middle centuries a style known as "hieratic"—holy or sacred—presented a formalized, almost rigid depiction intended not so much to represent people as to inspire reverence and meditation. One formula of the hieratic style ordained that an individual should measure nine heads (seven heads would be our modern measurement). The hairline was a nose's length above the forehead. "If the man is naked, four nose's lengths are needed for half his width." By the thirteenth century mosaics display a return to more naturalistic depictions, but with a clear sense of spiritualism; for example, the Ravenna mosaic shown in Figure **11.44**. Illustrations of this style also occur in other media; for example, the ivory, Figure **11.50**. It exhibits the frontal pose, formality, solemnity, and slight elongation of form which typify the Byzantine hieratic style.

11.50 *The Harbaville Triptych*, interior, late 10th century. Ivory, height 9½ ins (24 cm); central panel width 5⅜ ins (14 cm). The Louvre, Paris.

Byzantine Ivories

Ivory, traditionally a luxury material, was always popular in Byzantium. A number of carved works of different styles provide evidence of the varying influences and degrees of technical ability in the Eastern Empire. Many of the ivories are consular *diptychs* and others are imperial diptychs, although not all ivories were in diptych form.

Later ivories of the tenth century show delicate elegance and a highly finished style. The Harbaville Triptych has been described as the most beautiful of all the Byzantine ivories (Fig. **11.50**). It represents the hieratic style in sculpture, here producing a sense of detachment from the world and evoking a deep spirituality.

The Harbaville Triptych

Called a *triptych* because of its three sections (*tri-*), it was probably intended as a portable altar or shrine. Each of the two wings folded shut across the center panel. In the top center we see Christ enthroned and flanked by John the Baptist and the Virgin Mary, an arrangement called a *Deesis*. They plead for mercy on behalf of all humanity. Five of the apostles appear below. An ornament, repeated with the addition of rosettes at the bottom border and three heads in the top border, divides the two registers of the central panel. On either side of Christ's head appear medallions depicting angels holding the symbols of the sun and the moon. The figures reflect a hieratic formality and solemnity, and yet the depiction here exhibits a softness which counters the hard formality of other hieratic works. Perhaps this may result from a stronger Classical influence at the time.

ISLAM

The Islamic tradition springs from the religion of Islam (meaning submission), of which Mohammed was the prophet. Adherents are called Moslems or Muslims. Muslims are those who submit to the will of God ("Allah" in Arabic). The latest of the three great monotheistic religions, it drew upon the other two—Judaism and Christianity; Abraham and Jesus are in the list of prophets preceding Mohammed. Muslims generally believe that Jesus will return as the Mahdi—Messiah—at the end of the world. Islam is based on the sacred book the Koran, which Muslims believe was revealed by God to Mohammed. Muslim concepts of God, heaven, and hell are akin to those in Judaism and Christianity. Five duties are prescribed for every Muslim, the last being that he must, if he can, once in his life make the pilgrimage (Hajj) to Mecca. This last provision has made the pilgrimage the greatest in the world and a great unifying force in Islam. In addition to the Koran, Islam accepts the Sunna—collections of moral sayings and anecdotes of Mohammed. These were collected as early as the ninth century. There are contradictions in the Sunna, but they are resolved by the doctrine of Ijma: every Muslim holds that a belief of the greater part of Islam is infallibly true—a principle that has made the religion flexible.

Early in its history, a great split occurred in Islam between Sunnites and Shiites, and this split has persisted. The original split was over the caliphate, which was the crowning institution of the theocratic structure of Islam—the placement of both religious and political leadership in the hands of a single ruler. The caliphs were the successors—deputies—of Mohammed, and their claim to authority rested on their descent from the families of the Prophet or his early associates. Though secularism has modified the unity somewhat, in theory the civil law in Muslim countries is not separate from religious law; religion governs all aspects of life. There have developed some four different systems of interpretation of the law in Sunnite Islam, all regarded as orthodox. Islamic philosophy is in effect part theology; rationalism and mysticism both grew up in Islam, but were equally absorbed.

The spread of the religion after its founding by Mohammed was tremendously rapid in the seventh and eighth centuries, and it soon was dominant from Spain to India. Today, it spreads across Asia to the South Pacific, prevails in North Africa, and is still gaining converts in the rest of Africa. Originally spread "by the sword," Islam held an appeal in its openness to everyone: it stresses the brotherhood of the faithful before God, regardless of race or culture. Interestingly, the Arab warriors who started out to conquer the world for Allah, did not expect to make converts of conquered peoples—they merely expected the unbelievers to be obedient to them—the servants of the One True God. Converts were expected to become Arabs: the Koran was not translated into any languages because it was dictated by God to Mohammad in Arabic. Converts also had to submit to the social and legal precepts of the Muslim community. As a result, the conquering Arabs resisted the usual fate of conquerors—to be absorbed into the culture of the conquered.

ISLAMIC STYLE IN VISUAL ART

Theoretically, all human and animal figures are prohibited from Islamic art. In reality, images are widespread: the only prohibition seems to have been on those objects intended for public display. In the courts of the caliphs, images of living things were commonplace. They were considered harmless if they did not cast a shadow, were small in scale, or appeared on everyday objects.

A continuity of visual art seems to have occurred during the early years of Islam through the illustration of scientific texts. The Arabs obtained manuscripts from Byzantium, and were tremendously interested in Greek science. The result was a plethora of texts translated into Arabic. Illustrations from original Greek works also were copied. Typical of the illustration drawn in Arab manuscripts is a pen-and-ink sketch perhaps from a Mesopotamian manuscript of the fourteenth century (Fig.

11.51 Al-Qasim ibn 'Ali al-Hariri, *Maqamat al-Hariri* (a book of stories), 1323. Mesopotamian manuscript. Oriental Collection, The British Library, London.

11.51). The drawing has a clear presentation, with many of the strokes seeming to act as accents. The lines flow freely in subtle curvilinear movements to establish a comfortable rhythm across the page. In very simple line, the artist is able to capture human character, thus showing a strong observational ability. The witty flavor of the drawing goes far beyond mere illustration.

Even before Islam, Arab traders had penetrated the Far East, and as a result Chinese influence can be seen throughout the Middle East. This is particularly true in the emergence of religious subjects for visual art. The Mongol rulers were very familiar with the Buddhist tradition in Chinese art, and brought that interest to Islamic art—ignoring their predecessors' reluctance to pictorialize Mohammed. Thus, in the fourteenth century painting that depicted narratives about Mohammed became quite common. Chinese influences are strongly at work in an Islamic manuscript illustration from sixteenth-century Persia. *The Ascension of Mohammed* (Fig. **11.52**) tells the story from the Koran, in which Mohammed ascends into paradise after "a journey by night . . . to the remote place of worship." The reference in the Koran was later expanded upon: Mohammed ascended from Jerusalem under the guidance of the Angel Gabriel, rising through seven heavens and meeting Adam, Abraham, Moses, and Jesus before coming into the presence of God.

The images in the painting are fascinating. Mohammed rides a curiously oriental centaur—a mythological beast with a horse's body and the head of a man. The surrounding angels have oriental faces, and the composition seems to divide along the diagonal axis—also similar to some oriental works. The crescent-shaped figures appear to swirl in an elliptical path around Mohammed, and the artist shows a sophisticated color composition by carrying the predominant colors of one section into another section—for example, the white of the clouds carries into the upper parts of the painting in small details of trim and in the lighter flesh tones; reds that provide an encircling motif in the upper portion are carried into the lower section where they accent rather than dominate.

11.52 Unknown illustrator, *The Ascension of Mohammed*, 1539–43. Persian manuscript. Oriental Collection, The British Library, London.

ISLAMIC STYLE IN LITERATURE

Probably the most familiar Islamic literature, aside from the Koran, is a collection of tales called *The Arabian Nights* or *The Thousand and One Nights*. These tales accumulated during the Middle Ages, and as early as the tenth century they were part of the oral traditions of Islam in the Near East. Over the years more tales were added, including a unifying device called a frame-tale, which placed all of the separate stories within a larger framework. By around 1450 the work had assumed its final form.

The frame-tale recounts the story of a jealous Sultan who, convinced that all women were unfaithful, married a new wife each evening and put her to death the following morning. A new bride, Shaharazad, gained a reprieve by beginning a story on her wedding night and artfully maintaining the Sultan's curiosity about the stories. She was able to gain a reprieve for one thousand and one nights—during which she produced three male heirs—after which the Sultan abandoned his original practice. The tales capture the spirit of Islamic life, its exotic setting, and sensuality. Although no particular moral purpose underlies the stories, there is a moral code within the fantasies. The tales cover a variety of subjects and range from fact to fiction. They include stories of camel trains, desert riders, and insistent calls to prayers. They are supernatural, aristocratic, romantic, bawdy, and satiric.

ISLAMIC STYLE IN ARCHITECTURE

The first major example of Islamic architecture did not begin until A.D. 685, when work started on the Dome of the Rock in Jerusalem (Fig. **11.53**). Built near the site of the Temple of Solomon, it was begun by Islamic emperors who were direct descendants of the Prophet's companions. Shaped as an octagon, it was designed as a special holy place—not an ordinary mosque. Inside, it contains two concentric ambulatories (walkways) surrounding a central space capped by the dome. The mosque sits on a site revered by Jews as the tomb of Adam and the place where Abraham prepared to sacrifice Isaac. According to Muslim tradition, it also is the place from which Mohammed ascended into heaven. Written accounts suggest that it was built to overshadow a sacred temple of similar construction on the other side of Jerusalem—the Holy Sepulchre. Calif Abd al-Malik wanted a monument that would outshine the Christian churches of the area, and, perhaps, the Ka'ba in Mecca. The exterior was later decorated with the glazed blue tiles that give the façade its dazzling appearance; the inside glitters with gold, glass, and mother-of-pearl, multi-

11.53 Dome of the Rock, Jerusalem, late 7th century.

colored mosaics. A detail of the richly intricate mosaics of the Dome of the Rock in Jerusalem can be seen in Fig. **11.54**. This symmetrical pattern in deep red and gold, highlighted with accents of white and purple, illustrates the skill and delicacy which Muslim artists brought to this form. Undoubtedly, the Dome of the Rock was intended to speak to Christians as well as Muslims, distracting the latter from the splendor of Christian churches. Inside the mosque is an inscription: ''The Messiah Jesus Son of Mary

11.54 *(left)* Details of mosaic decoration, Dome of the Rock, Jerusalem, A.D. 691–2.

11.55 *(below)* Great Mosque, Damascus. Courtyard looking west, c. 715.

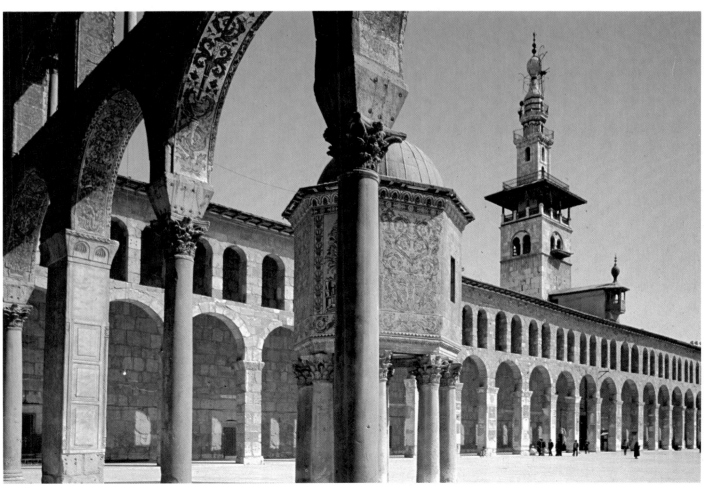

11.56 and **11.57** *(below and right)* Details of mosaic decoration, Great Mosque, Damascus, c. 715.

is only an apostle of God, and His Word which he conveyed into Mary, and a Spirit proceeding from Him. Believe therefore in God and his apostles and say not 'Three.' It will be better for you. God is only one God. Far be it from his glory that He should have a son.''

Another excellent example of Islamic architecture is the Great Mosque of Damascus (Fig. **11.55**). When the Muslims captured Damascus in 635, they adapted the precinct of a pagan temple, which had been converted into a Christian church, into an open-air mosque. Seventy years later, al-Walid demolished the church and set about building the largest mosque to Islam. The only feature of the original buildings left standing was the Roman wall, though the four original towers were metamorphosed into the first minarets, from which the faithful were called to prayer. Unfortunately, the centuries have not been kind to the Great Mosque. Sacked a number of times, much of the splendor of its lavish decorations has been lost. However, some of its grandeur can be seen in the arcaded courtyard, with fine, gold-inlaid detailing visible in the returns of the arches (Fig. **11.55**). Inside, colorful mosaics (Figs. **11.56** and **11.57**) express great subtlety of detail and texture. These works rank among the most accomplished of mosaics and were probably produced by Byzantine craftsmen.

NATIVE AMERICAN ART

Native American art tends to be portable and functional. Indians were primarily nomadic, and practicality demanded that possessions be kept to a minimum and provide maximum utilization. If works of art—objects of beauty—were necessary, then they should fulfill their aesthetic function *and* some domestic function as well. There were, however, works of art designed for their own sake—for example, Figure **11.58**, an openwork vessel with a design representing a bird. This ceramic object, with its cut-out areas, which could not be used as a container, appears to be only aesthetic in function. In cultures such as the plains Indians, Aztecs, and Incas that were strongly militaristic, artistic expression found its way into ceremonial objects, as well as costumes and weaponry.

The Inca culture came late to South America, beginning around A.D. 1200 and reaching empire status around 1438. When the Spaniards arrived in 1532, the Inca Empire was at its zenith, and extended from Argentina and Chile to Ecuador. Characteristic of Inca art is a pottery shape called the aryballus shown in Figure **11.59**. Delicate in design, this polychrome ceramic urn reflects carefully painted geometric figures arranged in symmetrical patterns. The insect appended to the bowl creates an intriguing focal point, and provides a visual counterpoint to the smooth and lustrous surface of the urn. A clear aesthetic sensitivity, intent, and sophistication can be seen

11.59 Arybal-shaped Inca vessel, Bolivar, Ecuador, 10½ × 8¾ ins (26.7 × 22.2 cm). National Museum of the American Indian, Smithsonian Institution.

11.58 Openwork bird jar, Ocklockonee Bay, Florida. Redware, with pre-fired "kill" hole in base, height 10½ ins (26.7 cm). National Museum of the American Indian, Smithsonian Institution.

in the treatment of the lip. The neck of the urn rises in a graceful curve, and then splays outward into a disk-like lip, divided symmetrically by underhung droplets. The asymmetrical handles placed below the center-line of the bowl give it a dynamic force and create additional interest for the viewer.

MEDIEVAL EUROPE

At its broadest, the Middle Ages is the name we have come to use for the 1,000 years from the fall of Rome to the Renaissance in Italy. The so-called Dark Ages, when humankind seemed to withdraw into a barricaded world of mental and physical isolation, comprise the early part of this period. In monasteries and convents throughout Europe, literacy, learning, and artistic creativity were nurtured. It was widely believed that the year 1000 would see the end of the world.

The later Middle Ages saw a spiritual and intellectual revival, perfectly expressed in the Gothic cathedral—the mystery of faith embodied in the mystery of space. The austere and fortresslike massiveness of the Romanesque style was transformed, as emphasis shifted from the wrath of God to the sweetness and mercy of the loving Savior and the Virgin Mary. The growth of towns and cities accelerated the pace of life, turning the focus of wealth and power away from the feudal countryside, and the new universities replaced monasteries as centers of learning.

ROMANESQUE STYLE

As Charlemagne's empire and the ninth and tenth centuries passed, a new and radical style in architecture emerged. Unlike its stylistic counterparts in painting and sculpture, Romanesque architecture was a fairly identifiable style, despite its diversity. The Romanesque style took hold throughout Europe in a relatively short period of time. It took its name from the Roman-like arches of its doorways and windows. To Renaissance persons, who saw these examples throughout Europe, the characteristics were clearly pre-Gothic and post-Roman (but Roman-like) and, therefore, they called them Romanesque. In addition to arched doorways and windows, characteristic of this style was a massive, static, and lightless quality in which we perceive a further reflection of the barricaded mentality and lifestyle generally associated with the Middle Ages.

The Romanesque style none the less exemplified the power and wealth of the Church Militant and Triumphant. If the style mirrored the social and intellectual system that produced it, it also reflected a new religious fervor and a turning of the Church toward its growing flock. Romanesque churches were larger than their predecessors and we can appreciate their scale in Figures 11.60

11.61 St. Sernin, interior.

11.60 St. Sernin, Toulouse, France, c. 1080–1120.

and 11.61. St. Sernin is an example of southern French Romanesque, and it reflects a heavy elegance and complexity we have not seen previously. The plan of the church describes a Roman cross, and the side aisles are extended beyond the crossing to create an ambulatory or walking space so that pilgrims, who were mostly on their way to Spain, could walk around the altar without disturbing the service. One additional change is worth noting. The roof of this church is stone, whereas earlier buildings had wooden roofs. As we view the magnificent vaulted interior we wonder how or whether the architect reconciled the conflicting forces of engineering, material, and aesthetics. Given the properties of stone and the increased force of added height, did he try to push his skills to the edge of practicality in order to create an interior of breathtaking scale? Were his efforts reflective of the glory of God or the abilities of Man?

Returning to the exterior view, we can see how some of the stress of the high tunnel vaulting was diffused. In a complex series of vaults, transverse arches, and bays, the tremendous weight and outward thrust of the central

11.62 Gislebertus, Last Judgement tympanum c. 1130–35. Autun Cathedral, France.

vault was transferred to the ground, leaving a high and unencumbered central space. If we compare this structural system with that of post-and-lintel and consider the compressive and tensile properties of stone, we can easily see the superiority of the arch as a structural device for creating open space. Because of the stresses and weight in this style, only very small windows were possible. So, although the fortresslike and lightless characteristics of Romanesque architecture reflect the historical context of the era, they also had a practical explanation.

In the case of sculpture Romanesque refers more to an era than to a style. Examples are so diverse that if most sculptural works were not decorations attached to Romanesque architecture, we probably could not group them under a stylistic label. However, we can draw some general conclusions about Romanesque sculpture. First, it is associated with Romanesque architecture. Second, it is heavy and solid. Third, it is stone. Fourth, it is monumental. These last two characteristics represent a distinct departure from previous sculptural style. Monumental stone sculpture had all but disappeared in the fifth century. Its reemergence across Europe in such a short time was remarkable. As we shall see, Church architecture was prolific during the Christian era, but the emergence of sculptural decoration indicated at least a beginning of an outward dissemination of knowledge from the cloistered world of the monastery to the general populace. Romanesque sculpture was applied to the exterior of the building, from where it could appeal to the lay worshipper. The relationship of this artistic development to the increase in religious zeal among the laity is not without significance. In such works as the Last Judgement tympanum (Fig. 11.62), the illiterate masses could now read the message of the Church, an opportunity previously the prerogative only of the clergy. The message here is quite clear. In the center of the composition, framed by a Roman-style arch, is an awe-inspiring figure of Christ. Around him are a series of malproportioned figures in various degrees of torment. The inscription of the artist, Gislebertus, tells us that their purpose was "to let this horror appal those bound by earthly sin." Death was still central to medieval thought, and devils share the stage, gleefully pushing the damned into the flaming pit.

The Bronze Doors of Hildesheim Cathedral

Of the Ottonian rulers, Henry II was the greatest patron of the arts, and in the Church the honor belongs to Bernward of Hildesheim, tutor of Otto III. During his years as Bishop (993–1022), Hildesheim became a center for manuscript painting and other arts. His patronage, however, was largely confined to the decoration of metal

The scenes portrayed on Bernward's doors display carefully arranged biblical stories. For example, The Temptation of Adam and Eve (third from the top, left) depicts the fall of humankind, and that panel is purposely aligned with the Crucifixion (third from the top, right), which illustrates the redemption of humankind. What is striking about all the scenes is the strong sense of bodily composition and physical movement. Every set of images, set against a plain background of open space, speaks forcefully in pantomime. The doors tell their story in medieval fashion, as a vivid drama of silent action, effectively communicating the message of the Christian faith to a largely illiterate public.

The Song of Roland

In the early Middle Ages, with the notable exception of the Carolingian court, the politically powerful cared little for culture, and for the most part could neither read nor write. Thanks to the efforts of the monastic community, and particularly the Benedictine monks, important books and manuscripts were carefully preserved and copied. St. Benedict (c. 480–c. 550) was one of the few great scholars of the Middle Ages. Literature flourished in Spain, where Muslim contact with Greek scholarship, established when they invaded Egypt, led to the setting up of schools in Cordoba. Aristotle, Plato, and Euclid were on the curriculum alongside the Koran. Toledo and Seville were also centers of learning. It was biblical literature, however, which became the central focus of the period.

However, there were also the poems of the troubadours, *Minnesänger*, and *trouvères* or court poets, who were popular throughout Europe. These professional storytellers produced fantastic legends and romances, such as the *Song of Roland*. In the *Song of Roland*, an unknown poet tells, with fine but simple dramatic skills, the story of a great battle between Charlemagne and the Saracens of Saragossa in the Pyrenees. Charlemagne is deceived by the Saracens, draws his main army back into France, and leaves Roland with a rearguard to hold the pass. The Saracens are aided by recreant Christian knights, and after a furious struggle, Roland and his entire army are killed. Our extract describes the battle between Roland's army and the Saracens.

11.63 Doors of Hildesheim Cathedral, 1015. Bronze, height 16 ft 6 ins (5.03 m). Hildesheim, Germany.

objects, and in particular the bronze doors of the Hildesheim Cathedral (Fig. **11.63**) which employed the *cire-perdue* technique, a lost-wax process that had been used for the casting of the bronze doors at Aachen 200 years earlier.

King Marsilion comes along a valley
with all his men, the great host he assembled:
twenty divisions, formed and numbered by the King,
helmets ablaze with gems beset in gold,

and those bright shields, those hauberks sewn with brass.
Seven thousand clarions sound the pursuit,
and the great noise resounds across that country.
Said Roland then: "Oliver, Companion, Brother,
that traitor Ganelon has sworn our deaths:
it is treason, it cannot stay hidden,
the Emperor will take his terrible revenge.
We have this battle now, it will be bitter,
no man has ever seen the like of it.
I will fight here with Durendal, this sword,
and you, my companion, with Halteclere—
we've fought with them before, in many lands!
how many battles have we won with these two!
Let no one sing a bad song of our swords." AOI.[9]

When the French see the pagans so numerous,
the fields swarming with them on every side,
they call the names of Oliver, and Roland,
and the Twelve Peers: protect them, be their warranter.
The Archbishop told them how he saw things:
"Barons, my lords, do not think shameful thoughts,
do not, I beg you all in God's name, run.
Let no brave man sing shameful songs of us:
let us all die here fighting: that is far better.
We are promised: we shall soon find our deaths,
after today we won't be living here.
But here's one thing, and I am your witness:
Holy Paradise lies open to you,
you will take seats among the Innocents."
And with these words the Franks are filled with joy,
there is no man who does not shout Munjoie! AOI.

A Saracen was there of Saragossa,
half that city was in this pagan's keeping,
this Climborin, who fled before no man,
who took the word of Ganelon the Count,
kissed in friendship the mouth that spoke that word,
gave him a gift: his helmet and its carbuncle.
Now he will shame, says he, the Land of Fathers,
he will tear off the crown of the Emperor;
sits on the horse that he calls Barbamusche,
swifter than the sparrowhawk, than the swallow;
digs in his spurs, gives that war horse its head,
comes on to strike Engeler of Gascony,
whose shield and fine hauberk cannot save him;
gets the head of his spear into his body,
drives it in deep, gets all the iron through,
throws him back, dead, lance straight out, on the field.
And then he cries: "It's good to kill these swine!
At them, Pagans! At them and break their ranks!"
"God!" say the French, "the loss of that good man!" AOI.

Roland the Count calls out to Oliver:
"Lord, Companion, there is Engeler dead,

we never had a braver man on horse."
The Count replies: "God let me avenge him";
and digs with golden spurs into his horse,
grips—the steel running with blood—Halteclere,
comes on to strike with all his mighty power:
the blow comes flashing down; the pagan falls.
Devils take away the soul of Climborin.
And then he killed Alphaïen the duke,
cut off the head of Escababi,
struck from their horses seven great Arrabites:
they'll be no use for fighting any more!
And Roland said: "My companion is enraged!
Why, he compares with me! he earns his praise!
Fighting like that makes us dearer to Charles";
lifts up his voice and shouts: "Strike! you are warriors!"
AOI.

And now again: a pagan, Valdabrun,
the man who raised Marsilion from the font,
lord of four hundred dromonds that sail the sea:
there is no sailor who does not call him lord;
the man who took Jerusalem by treason:
he violated the temple of Solomon,
he killed the Patriarch before the fonts;
took the sworn word of Ganelon the Count,
gave him his sword and a thousand gold coins.
He rides the horse that he calls Gramimund,
swifter by far than the falcon that flies;
digs hard into its flanks with his sharp spurs,
comes on to strike Sansun, our mighty duke:
smashes his shield, bursts the rings of his hauberk,
drives in the streamers of his bright gonfanon,
knocks him down, dead, lance straight out, from the saddle:
"Saracens, strike! Strike and we will beat them."
"God!" say the French, "the loss of that great man!" AOI.

Roland the Count, when he sees Sansun dead—
now, lords, you know the rage, the pain he felt;
digs in his spurs, runs at that man in fury,
grips Durendal, more precious than fine gold,
comes on, brave man, to strike with all his power,
on his helmet, beset with gems in gold,
cuts through the head, the hauberk, the strong body,
the good saddle beset with gems in gold,
into the back, profoundly, of the horse,
and kills them both, praise him or damn him who will.
Say the pagans: "A terrible blow for us!"
Roland replies: "I cannot love your men,
all the wrong and presumption are on your side." AOI.

An African, come there from Africa,
is Malquidant, the son of King Malcud,
his battle gear studded with beaten gold:

245

he shines to heaven, aflame among the others
rides the war horse that he calls Salt Perdut—
no beast on earth could ever run with him;
comes on to strike Anseïs, strikes on his shield
straight down, and cut away the red and blue,
burst into shreds the panels of his hauberk,
thrust into him the iron and the shaft.
The Count is dead, his days are at an end.
And the French say: "Lord, you fought well and died!"

Across the field rides Archbishop Turpin.
Tonsured singer of masses! Where is the priest
who drove his body to do such mighty deeds?
said to the pagan: "God send you every plague,
you killed a man it pains my heart to remember";
and sent his good war horse charging ahead,
struck on that pagan shield of Toledo;
and he casts him down, dead, on the green grass.

And now again: a pagan, Grandonie,
son of Capuel, the king of Cappadocia;
he is mounted on the horse he calls Marmorie,
swifter by far than the bird on the wing;
loosens the reins, digs in sharp with his spurs,
comes on to strike with his great strength Gerin,
shatters the dark red shield, drags it from his neck,
and driving bursts the meshes of his hauberk,
thrusts into him the blue length of his banner
and casts him down, dead, upon a high rock;
and goes on, kills Gerer, his dear companion,
and Berenger, and guion of Saint Antonie;
goes on still, strikes Austorie, a mighty duke
who held Valence and Envers on the Rhone;
knocks him down, dead, puts joy into the pagans.
The French cry out: "Our men are losing strength!"

Count Roland holds his sword running with blood;
he has heard them: men of France losing heart;
filled with such pain, he feels he will break apart;
said to the pagan: "God send you every plague,
the man you killed, I swear, will cost you dear";
his war horse, spurred, runs straining every nerve.
One must pay, they have come face to face.

Grandonie was a great and valiant man,
and very strong, a fighter; and in his path
he came on Roland, had never seen him before;
but knew him now, knew him now, knew him now,
that fury on his face, that lordly body,
that look, and that look, the tremendous sight of him;
does not know how to keep down his panic,
and wants to run, but that will not save him;
the blow comes down, Roland's strength is in it,
splits his helmet through the nosepiece in two,

cuts through the nose, through the mouth, through the teeth,
down through the trunk, the Algerian mail,
the silver bows of that golden saddle,
into the back, profoundly, of the horse;
and killed them both, they never rode again.
The men of Spain cry out their rage and grief.
And the French say: "Our defender has struck!"

The battle is fearful, there is no rest,
and the French strike with all their rage and strength,
cut through their fists and their sides and their spines,
cut through their garments into the living flesh,
the bright blood flows in streams on the green grass.
The pagans cry: "We can't stand up to this!
Land of Fathers, Mahummet's curse on you!
Your men are hard, we never saw such men!"
There is not one who does not cry: "Marsilion!
Come to us, King! Ride! We are in need! Help!"

The battle is fearful, and vast,
the men of France strike hard with burnished lances.
There you would have seen the great pain of warriors,
so many men dead and wounded and bleeding,
one lies face up, face down, on another.
The Saracens cannot endure it longer.
Willing and unwilling they quit the field.
The French pursue, with all their heart and strength. AOI.

Marsilion sees his people's martyrdom.
He commands them: sound his horns and trumpets;
and he rides now with the great host he has gathered.
At their head rides the Saracen Abisme:
no worse criminal rides in that company,
stained with the marks of his crimes and great treasons,
lacking the faith in God, Saint Mary's son.
And he is black, as black as melted pitch,
a man who loves murder and treason more
than all the gold of rich Galicia,
no living man ever saw him play or laugh;
a great fighter, a wild man, mad with pride,
and therefore dear to that criminal king;
holds high his dragon, where all his people gather.
The Archbishop will never love that man,
no sooner saw than wanted to strike him;
considered quietly, said to himself:
"That Saracen—a heretic, I'll wager.
Now let me die if I do not kill him—
I never loved cowards or cowards' ways." AOI.

Turpin the Archbishop begins the battle.
He rides the horse that he took from Grossaille,
who was a king this priest once killed in Denmark.
Now this war horse is quick and spirited,

his hooves high-arched, the quick legs long and flat,
short in the thigh, wide in the rump, long in the flanks,
and the backbone so high, a battle horse!
and that white tail, the yellow mane on him,
the little ears on him, the tawny head!
No beast on earth could ever run with him.
The Archbishop—that valiant man—spurs hard,
he will attack Abisme, he will not falter,
strikes on his shield, a miraculous blow:
a shield of stones, of amethysts, topazes,
esterminals, carbuncles all on fire—
a gift from a devil, in Val Metas,
sent on to him by the Amiral Galafre.
There Turpin strikes, he does not treat it gently—
after that blow, I'd not give one cent for it;
cut through his body, from one side to the other,
and casts him down dead in a barren place.
And the French say: "A fighter, that Archbishop!
Look at him there, saving souls with that crozier!"

Roland the Count calls out to Oliver:
"Lord, Companion, now you have to agree
the Archbishop is a good man on horse,
there's none better on earth or under heaven,
he knows his way with a lance and a spear."
The Count replies: "Right! Let us help him then."
And with these words the Franks began anew,
the blows strike hard, and the fighting is bitter;
there is a painful loss of Christian men.
To have seen them, Roland and Oliver,
these fighting men, striking down with their swords,
the Archbishop with them, striking with his lance!
One can recount the number these three killed:
it is written—in charters, in documents;
the Geste tells it: it was more than four thousand.
Through four assaults all went well with our men;
then comes the fifth, and that one crushes them.
They are all killed, all these warriors of France,
all but sixty, whom the Lord God has spared:
they will die too, but first sell themselves dear. AOI.

Count Roland sees the great loss of his men,
calls on his companion, on Oliver:
"Lord, Companion, in God's name, what would you do?
All these good men you see stretched on the ground
We can mourn for sweet France, fair land of France!
a desert now, stripped of such great vassals.
Oh King, and friend, if only you were here!
Oliver, Brother, how shall we manage it?
What shall we do to get word to the King?"
Said Oliver: "I don't see any way.
I would rather die now than hear us shamed." AOI.[10]

GOTHIC STYLE

In the twelfth to the fifteenth centuries traditional paintings in the form of frescoes and altar panels returned to prominence while manuscript illumination continued. Two-dimensional art continued to illustrate the gradual flow of one style into another without the emergence of a clearly dominant identity. Because this period is so closely identified with Gothic architecture, and because painting found its primary outlet within the Gothic cathedral, we need to ask what qualities reflect a Gothic style. The answer is not as readily apparent as it is in architecture and sculpture, but several characteristics can be identified. One is the beginnings of three-dimensionality in

11.64 *David Harping*, from the Oscott Psalter, c. A.D. 1270. 7½ x 4¾ ins (20 x 11.1 cm). The British Library, London.

figure representation. Another is a striving to give these figures mobility and life within three-dimensional space. Space is the essence of Gothic style. The Gothic painter and illuminator had not mastered perspective, and his compositions do not exhibit the spatial rationality of later works, but if we compare him with his predecessors of the earlier medieval eras, we discover that he has more or less broken free from the static, frozen, two-dimensionality of earlier styles. Gothic style also exhibits spirituality, lyricism, and a new humanism (mercy versus irrevocable judgement). Gothic style is less crowded and frantic—it was a changing style with many variations.

The Gothic style of two-dimensional art found magnificent expression in manuscript illumination. The court style of France and England produced some truly exquisite works. In *David Harping* (Fig. **11.64**) the curious proportions of the face and hands of David, and the awkward linear draping of fabric juxtaposed against the curvilinear forms of the harp and chair create a sense of unease and nervous tension. There is almost a carelessness about the layout of the background screen. The upward curving arcs at the top are intended to be symmetrical, but their departure from symmetry is reinforced by the lack of precision in the repetition of diamond shapes. A touch of realism appears in the curved harp string which David is plucking. Rudimentary use of highlight and shadow give basic three-dimensionality to cloth and skin, and while unbalanced in the interior space, the figure, none the less, does not appear to crowd the borders.

THE GOTHIC CATHEDRAL

Gothic style in architecture took many forms, but it is best exemplified in the Gothic cathedral. The cathedral, in its synthesis of intellect, spirituality, and engineering, perfectly expresses the medieval mind. Gothic style was widespread in Europe. Like the other arts it was not uniform in application, nor was it uniform in date. It developed initially as a very local style on the Ile de France in the late twelfth century, and spread outward to the rest of Europe. It had died as a style in some places before it was adopted in others. The "slipping, sliding, and overlapping" circumstances of artistic development were fully applicable to Gothic architecture.

The cathedral was, of course, a church building whose purpose was the service of God. However, civic pride as well as spirituality inspired cathedral building. Various local guilds contributed their services in financing or in the actual building of the churches, and guilds were often

memorialized in special chapels and stained-glass windows. The Gothic church occupied the central, often elevated, area of the town or city. Its physical centrality and context symbolized the dominance of the universal Church over all affairs of humankind, both spiritual and secular. Probably no other style has exercised such an influence across the centuries or played such a central role, even in twentieth-century Christian architecture. The Gothic church spins an intricate and fascinating story, only a few details of which we can highlight here.

The beginnings of Gothic architecture can be pinpointed between 1137 and 1144 in the rebuilding of the royal Abbey Church of St. Denis near Paris. There is ample evidence that Gothic was a physical extension of philosophy, rather than a practical response to the structural limitations of the Romanesque style—that is, Gothic theory preceded its application. The philosophy of the Abbot Suger, who was advisor to Louis VI and a driving force in the construction of St. Denis, held that harmony, the perfect relationship of parts, is the source of beauty, that Light Divine is a mystic revelation of God, and that space is symbolic of God's mystery. The composition of St. Denis and subsequent Gothic churches perfectly expressed that philosophy. As a result, Gothic architecture is more unified that Romanesque. Gothic cathedrals use refined, upward-striving line to symbolize, both in exterior spires and the pointed arch, humanity's upward striving to escape (at the tip) from earth into the mystery of space (the Kingdom of Heaven).

The pointed arch is the most easily identifiable characteristic of this style, and it represents not only a symbol of Gothic spirituality but also an engineering practicality. The pointed arch completely changes the thrust of downward force into more equal and controllable directions, whereas the round arch places tremendous pressure on its keystone, which then transfers thrust outward to the sides. The pointed arch controls thrust into a downward path through its legs. It also adds design flexibility. Dimensions of space encompassed by a round arch are limited to the radii of specific semicircles. Since the proportions of a pointed arch are flexible, dimensions may be adjusted to whatever practical and aesthetic parameters are desired. The Gothic arch also increased the sense of height in its vaults. Some sources suggest that this structure actually made increased heights possible. That implication is not quite correct. Some Romanesque churches had vaults as high as any Gothic churches, but the possibility for change in proportion of height to width did increase the apparent height of the Gothic church.

Engineering advances implicit in the new form made

possible larger clerestory windows (hence more light) and more slender ribbing (hence a greater emphasis on space as opposed to mass). Outside, practical and aesthetic flying buttresses carry the outward thrust of the vaults through a delicate balance of ribs, vaults, and buttresses gracefully and comfortably to the ground. Every detail is carefully integrated into a tracery of decoration emphasizing mysterious space.

The importance of stained-glass windows in Gothic cathedrals cannot be overemphasized. They carefully controlled light entering the sanctuary, reinforcing a marvelous sense of mystery. They also took the place of wall paintings in telling the story of the gospels and the saints, the walls of the Romanesque style having been replaced by space and light in the Gothic.

Salisbury Cathedral

With the exception of St. Paul's Cathedral in London, Salisbury (Fig. **11.65**) is the only English cathedral

11.65 Salisbury Cathedral from the southwest, begun 1220.

11.67 Salisbury Cathedral, nave and choir.

11.66 Plan of Salisbury Cathedral.

whose entire interior structure was built to the design of a single architect and completed without a break, in 1265. However, what is perhaps the most perfect part of the cathedral took another fifty-five years to complete. The famous spire, built between 1285 and 1310, added an additional 404 ft (123 m) to a very squat tower which rose only a few feet above the nave. The spire thus became the highest in England and the second highest in Europe. Unfortunately, the piers and foundations were not designed to carry the additional 6,400 tons, and the masons were forced to add a strong stone vault at the crossing of the nave below the tower, one of the few stylistic modifications in the building.

Compared to the soaring vertical cathedrals of France, Salisbury seems long, low, and sprawling. The west front functions more as a screen wall, wider than the nave, whose horizontal bands of decoration further emphasize the horizontal thrust of the building. The plan of the cathedral (Fig. 11.66), with its double transept, retains the features of the Romanesque style. The same emphasis on the horizontal appears in the interior, where the nave wall looks more like a succession of arches and supports (Fig. 11.67). Typical of Early English Gothic, the nave vaults curve steeply with the ribs extending down to the *triforium* level and thereby tucking the clerestory windows into the vaults. Also characteristic of the Early English style is the use of dark Purbeck marble for the colonnettes and capitals, establishing an almost Romanesque color contrast. The building is free of tracery and the lancet windows are grouped in threes and fives.

GOTHIC SCULPTURE

Gothic sculpture again reveals the changes in attitude of the period. It portrays serenity, idealism, and simple naturalism. Gothic sculpture, like painting, has a human quality, and takes a kindlier view of life. The vale of tears, death, and damnation are replaced with conceptions of Christ as a benevolent teacher and of God as beautiful. This style has a new order, symmetry, and clarity. Its visual images carry with greater distinctness over a distance. The figures of Gothic sculpture are less entrapped in their material and stand away from their backgrounds (Fig. 11.68).

11.68 Jamb statues, west portal, Chartres Cathedral, France. c. 1145–70.

Schools of sculpture developed throughout France, and although individual stone carvers worked alone, their common links with a school gave their works a unified character. Reims, for example, had an almost classical quality, while Paris was dogmatic and intellectual (perhaps a reflection of its role as a university city). As the period progressed, sculpture became more naturalistic. Spiritualism was sacrificed to everyday appeal, and sculp-

ture reflected the increasing influence of secular interests, both middle class and aristocratic.

Compositional unity also changed from early to late Gothic. Early architectural sculpture was subordinate to the overall design of the building. Later work lost much of that integration as it gained in emotionalism (Fig. **11.69**).

The Sculptures of Chartres Cathedral

The sculptures of Chartres Cathedral, which bracket nearly a century, illustrate clearly the transition from early to late Gothic. The attenuated figures of Figure **11.68** display a relaxed serenity, idealism, and simple naturalism. Although an integral part of the portal columns, they also emerge from them, each in its own space. Detail is somewhat formalized and shallow, but we now see the human figure beneath the fabric—in contrast to the previous use of fabric as mere compositional decoration. Naturalistic qualities are even more pronounced in the figures of 100 years later (Fig. **11.69**). Here we can see the characteristics of the High Gothic style.

Proportion is more lifelike, and the figures have only the most tenuous connection to the building. Figures are carved in subtle s-curves rather than as rigid perpendicular columns. Fabric drapes are much more naturally depicted, with deeper and softer folds. In contrast to the idealized older saints, these figures have the features of specific individuals expressing qualities of spirituality and determination.

The content of Gothic sculpture is also noteworthy. Gothic sculpture, like most church art, was didactic, or designed to teach. Many of its lessons are fairly straightforward, and can be appreciated by anyone with a basic knowledge of the Bible. Christ appears as a ruler and judge of the universe above the main doorway of Chartres Cathedral, with a host of symbols of the apostles and others (Fig. **11.70**). Also decorating the portals are the prophets and kings of the Old Testament, whose purpose is to proclaim the harmony of secular and spiritual rule by making the kings of France the spiritual descendants of biblical rulers—in much the same sense as we note in the art of Justinian at Ravenna.

Other lessons of Gothic cathedral sculpture are more complex and hidden. According to some scholars specific conventions, codes, and sacred mathematics are involved. These factors relate to positioning, grouping, numbers, symmetry, and recognition of subjects. For example, the numbers three, four, and seven (which we often see in compositions of post-Gothic periods) symbolize the Trinity, the Gospels, the sacraments, and the deadly sins.

11.69 Jamb statues, south transept portal, Chartres Cathedral, c. 1215–20.

11.70 Central tympanum, west portal, Chartres Cathedral, c. 1145–70.

The positioning of the figures around Christ show their relative importance, with the position on the right being the most important. Amplifications of these codes and symbols are carried to highly complex levels. All of this is consistent with the mysticism of the period, which held to strong beliefs in allegorical and hidden meanings in holy sources.

THE RENAISSANCE

The Renaissance was explicitly seen by its leading exponents as a rebirth of our understanding of ourselves as social and creative beings. "Out of the sick Gothic night our eyes are opened to the glorious touch of the sun," was how Rabelais expressed what most of his educated contemporaries felt. At the center of Renaissance concerns were the visual arts, whose new ways of looking at the world soon had their counterparts in the performing arts as well. For the first time, it seemed possible not merely to emulate the works of the Classical world but to surpass them.

However, there was nervousness and unease in many leading minds in the decades following the close of the High Renaissance. The Reformation had challenged institutional Christian faith and its authority. The proposal of a heliocentric universe knocked humankind from its previously assured place at the center of all things. Harmony seemed once more to be an unattainable ideal as Europe was riven by wars and as philosophers cast doubt on the certainties of the Renaissance. The modern age was in the making.

FLEMISH PAINTING

In the north of Europe lies a small area known as the Low Countries. In the fifteenth century the Low Countries included Flanders, and amid a dominant atmosphere of late Gothic architecture and sculpture, Flemish painters and musicians forged new approaches, which departed significantly from the International Gothic style, formed a link with their contemporaries in northern Italy, and influenced European painters and musicians for the next century. Many scholars believe that early-fifteenth-century Flemish arts remained totally a part of the late Gothic style, but clearly the painters of this locale had significant contact with Italy, the heart of the Early Renaissance in art. Clearly, also, the Italians of this new Renaissance spirit admired Flemish painting.

Flemish painting of this period was revolutionary. In Gothic art painters attempted to create realistic sensations of deep space. For all their ingenuity, they essentially retained a two-dimensional feeling and a lack of continuity or rationality in their perspective. Gothic work contains a certain childish or fairy-tale quality. Flemish painters, however, achieved pictorial reality and rational perspective, and the sense of completeness and continuity found in Flemish works marked a new and clearly different style. Line, form, and color were painstakingly controlled to compose subtle, varied, three-dimensional, clear, and logically unified statements.

Part of the drastic change in Flemish painting stemmed from a new development in painting media—oil paint. Oil's versatile characteristics gave the Flemish painter new opportunities to vary surface texture and brilliance, and to create far greater subtlety of form. Oils allowed blending of color areas, because oil could be worked wet on the canvas, whereas egg tempera, the previous painting medium, dried almost immediately upon application. Gradual transitions between color areas made possible by oil paints allowed fifteenth-century Flemish painters to enhance use of atmospheric perspective—that is, the increasingly hazy appearance of objects furthest from the viewer—and thereby to control this most effective indicator of deep space. Blending between color areas also enhanced chiaroscuro, by which all objects assume three-dimensionality—without highlight and shadow perceptible plasticity is lost. Early-fifteenth-century Flemish painters used sophisticated exploration of light and shade not only to heighten three-dimensionality of form but also to achieve rational unity in their compositions. Pictures which do not exhibit consistent light sources or which omit natural shadows on surrounding objects create very strange effects, even if their individual form depiction is high in verisimilitude. This new rational unity and realistic three-dimensionality separated fifteenth-century Flemish style from the Gothic style and tied it to the Renaissance.

Van Eyck—The Arnolfini Marriage

Jan van Eyck's *Arnolfini Marriage*, or *Giovanni Arnolfini and His Bride* (Fig. 11.71), illustrates the qualities of Flemish painting, and also provides a marvelous range of aesthetic responses. Van Eyck used the full range of values from darkest darks to lightest lights and blended them with extreme subtlety to achieve a soft and realistic appearance. His colors are rich, varied, and predominantly warm in feeling. All forms achieve three-dimensionality through subtle color blending and softened shadow edges. Natural highlights and shadows emanate from obvious sources, such as the window, and tie the figures and objects together.

The painting depicts a young couple taking a marriage vow in the sanctity of the bridal chamber and the painting is thus both a portrait and a marriage certificate. The artist has signed the painting in legal script above the mirror "Johannes de Eyck fuit hic. 1434" (Jan van Eyck was here. 1434). In fact, we can see the artist and another witness reflected in the mirror.

RENAISSANCE PAINTING IN FLORENCE

It was in Italy, and more precisely in Florence, that the Renaissance, whatever connotations we attach to it, found its early spark and heart in about 1400. Florence was a wealthy port and commercial center and, like Athens, leapt into a golden age on a soaring spirit of victory as the city successfully resisted the attempts of the Duke of Milan to subjugate it. Under the patronage of the Medici family the outpouring of art made Florence the focal point of the early Italian Renaissance.

Two general trends in Florentine painting can be identified in this period. The first was lyrical and decorative. Its adherents were the painters Fra Angelico, Fra Lippo Lippi, Benozzo Gozzoli, and Sandro Botticelli. This tradition is best expressed in the paintings of Botticelli.

11.71 Jan van Eyck, *The Arnolfini Marriage (Giovanni Arnolfini and His Bride)*, 1434. Oil on panel, 33 x 22½ ins (84 x 57 cm). The National Gallery, London.

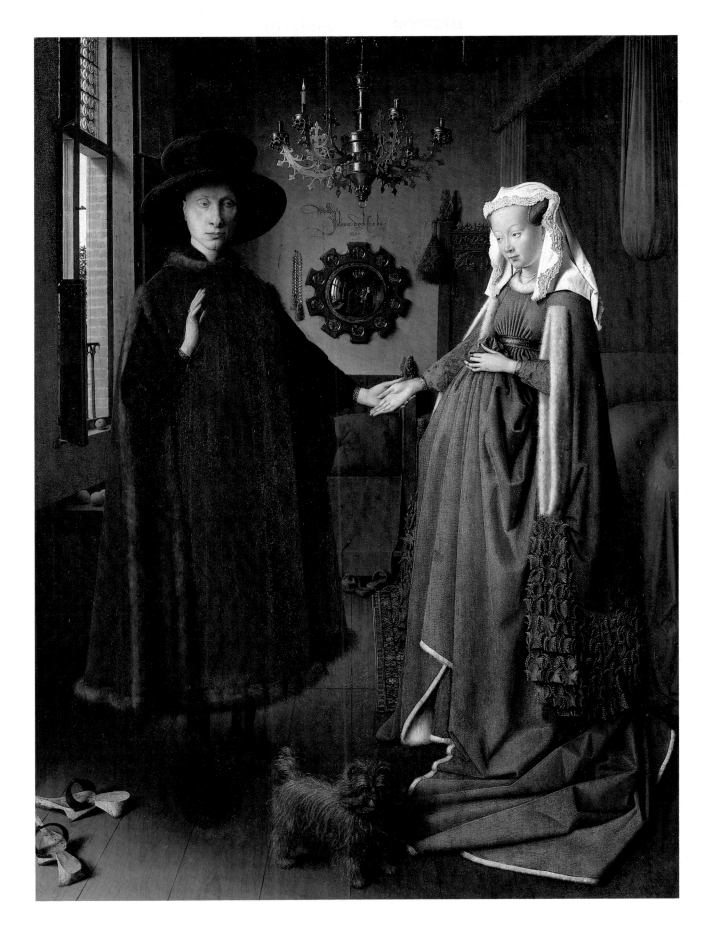

The linear quality of *Spring* (Fig. **11.72**) suggests an artist apparently unconcerned with deep space or subtle plasticity in light and shade. Rather, forms emerge through outline. Botticelli's use of line brings the form to life, as opposed to the medieval practice of denying the body. The composition moves gently from side to side through a lyrical combination of undulating, curved lines, with focal areas in each grouping. Mercury, the Three Graces, Venus, Flora, Spring, and Zephyrus—each part of this human, mythical (notice the non-Christian subject matter) composition carries its own emotions, from contemplation to sadness to happiness. Beyond the immediate qualities there is deeper symbolism and emotion relating not only to the mythological figures, but also to the Medici family, the patron rulers of Florence.

Botticelli's figures further exhibit anatomical simplicity quite unlike the detailed muscular concerns we will find elsewhere in Florentine Renaissance painting. Although figures are rendered three-dimensionally and shaded subtly, they appear almost like balloons, floating in space without anatomical definition.

The second tradition in Florentine and other Italian painting of this period is much more clearly Renaissance in approach. The works of Masaccio (1401–28) and others have a unifying monumentality, so they are, or seem to be, larger than lifesize. The use of deep space, plasticity, and chiaroscuro to create dramatic contrasts, gives figures solidity and unifies the composition. Atmospheric and linear perspective—that is, a new and significant scientific mechanization of single and multiple vanishing-point perspective (an invention that allowed the artist to plot foreshortened objects with photographic accuracy)—enhanced deep, spatial realism. Figures are warm, strong, detailed, and very human. At the same time composition carefully subordinated parts to the whole.

This tradition was initiated by Masaccio in the early 1420s, and in the space of two years Florence had progressed from the International Gothic style to this radically different approach.

Masaccio—The Tribute Money

The most famous of Masaccio's frescoes in the Brancacci family chapel in the Church of Santa Maria del Carmine is *The Tribute Money* (Fig. **11.73**). Its setting makes full use of the new discovery of linear perspective, as the rounded figures move freely in unencumbered deep space. It employs a technique called "continuous narration," unfolding a series of events across a single canvas—here the New Testament story from Matthew (17:24–27).

The figures in this fresco are remarkably accomplished. In the first place, they are "clothed nudes," dressed in fabric which falls like real cloth. Next, weight and volume are depicted in an entirely new way. Each figure stands in classical contrapposto stance; the sense of motion is not particularly remarkable, but the accurate rendering of the feet makes these the first painted figures to seem to stand on real ground. Comparing the figures with Botticelli, we see that whereas Botticelli reveals form and volume through line, Masaccio uses chiaroscuro. The key to chiaroscuro is to establish a source for the light which strikes the figures and then to render the objects in the painting so that all highlights and shadows occur as if caused by that single light source.

In addition, the figures form a circular and three-dimensional grouping rather than a flat line across the surface of the work as in the Botticelli. Even the haloes of the apostles appear in the new perspective and overlap at odd angles. Compositionally, the single vanishing point, by which the linear perspective is controlled, sits at the head of Christ, a device for achieving focus which we will see again in Leonardo da Vinci's *Last Supper* (Fig. **11.78**). In addition, Masaccio has rediscovered atmospheric perspective, in which distance is indicated through diminution of light and blurring of outlines.

RENAISSANCE SCULPTURE IN FLORENCE

An attempt to capture the essence of European sculpture in the early Renaissance can, again, best be served by looking to fifteenth-century Florence, where sculpture also enjoyed the patronage of the Medicis. The early Renaissance sculptors developed the skills to create images of high verisimilitude. The goal, however, was not the same as that of the Greeks, with their idealized reality of human form. Rather, the Renaissance sculptor found his ideal in individualism. The ideal was the glorious individual—even if not quite perfect. Sculpture of this style presented an uncompromising and stark view of humankind—complex, balanced, and full of action. Relief sculpture, like painting, revealed a new means of representing deep space through systematic, scientific perspective. Freestanding statuary works, long out of favor, returned to dominance. Scientific inquiry and interest in anatomy were reflected in sculpture as well as painting. The nude, full of character and charged with energy, made its first reappearance since ancient times. The human form was built up layer by layer upon its skeletal

11.72 Sandro Botticelli, *La Primavera (Spring)*, c. 1478. Tempera on panel, 6 ft 8 ins x 10 ft 4 ins (2.03 x 3.15 m). Galleria degli Uffizi, Florence.

11.73 Masaccio, *The Tribute Money*, c. 1427. Fresco, Santa Maria del Carmine, Florence.

11.74 Lorenzo Ghiberti, *The Story of Jacob and Esau*, panel of the *Gates of Paradise*, c. 1435. Gilt bronze, 31¼ ins (79 cm) square. The Baptistery, Florence.

and muscular framework. Even when clothed, fifteenth-century sculpture revealed the body under the outer sculpture, quite unlike the decorative shell which often clothed medieval works.

Notable and typical among fifteenth-century Italian sculptors were Ghiberti and Donatello. In Ghiberti's *Gates of Paradise*, we see the same concern for rich detail, humanity, and feats of perspective that we saw in Florentine painting. In these doors of the Baptistery in Florence, Ghiberti, trained as a goldsmith and painter, creates beautiful surfaces with delicate and careful detail. He also conveys a tremendous sense of space in each of the ten panels. In The Story of Jacob and Esau (Fig. **11.74**), for example, he uses receding arcades to create depth and perspective. Every detail is exact, and the bold relief of these scenes took Ghiberti twenty-one years to complete.

However, the greatest masterpieces of fifteenth-century Italian Renaissance sculpture came from the unsurpassed master of the age, Donatello (1386–1466). He had a passion for antiquity, and began his career as an assistant on the Florentine Baptistry doors of Ghiberti. His early statues were similar to medieval works in that they were architectural. However, even though his statues occupied niches, in his *St. George*, the niche is so shallow that the work actually emerges as free-standing, almost separated from the building. His magnificent *David* (Fig. **11.75**) was

11.75 Donatello, *David*, dated variously 1430–40. Bronze, height, 5 ft 2¼ ins (1.58 m). Museo Nationale del Bargello, Florence.

the first freestanding nude since Classical times. However, unlike Classical nudes, David is partially clothed. His armor and helmet, along with bony elbows and adolescent character, invest him with rich detail of a highly individualized nature. *David* exhibits a return to classical contrapposto stance, but its carefully executed form expresses a new humanity whose individual parts seem almost capable of movement. The work symbolizes Christ's triumph over Satan. The laurel crown on the helmet and laurel wreath on which the work stands allude to the Medici family, in whose palace the statue was displayed in 1469.

RENAISSANCE LITERATURE

Boccaccio

The work of Giovanni Boccaccio (1313–75) culminated in the writing of the *Decameron*, which tells the story of ten young people fleeing from the plague in Florence in 1348. *Decameron* means "Ten Days' Work," and consists of 100 stories told over a fourteen-day period.

Here we include the first tale from day one, a lively day spent in witty conversation. Days two and three are focused on tales of adventure. Day four presents unhappy love, and five treats the same subject in a somewhat lighter vein. Day six returns to the happiness of day one, and days seven, eight and nine comprise laughter, trickery, and license. Day ten ties the previous themes together into a conclusion. In total, the *Decameron* extols the virtue of humankind, proposing that in order to be noble one must accept life as one finds it, without bitterness, and above all, accept the responsibility for and consequences of one's own actions. The *Decameron* is an early reflection of the Renaissance spirit.

Master Ciappelletto dupeth a holy friar with a false confession and dieth; and having been in his lifetime the worst of men, he is, after his death, reputed a saint and called Saint Ciappelletto.

"It is a seemly thing, dearest ladies, that whatsoever a man doth, he give it beginning from the holy and admirable name of Him who is the maker of all things. Wherefore, it behoving me, as the first, to give commencement to our story-telling, I purpose to begin with one of His marvels, to the end, that, this being heard, our hope in Him, as in a thing immutable, may be confirmed and His name be ever praised of us. It is a manifest that, like as things temporal are all transitory and mortal, even so both within and without are they full of annoy and anguish and travail and subject to infinite perils, against which it is indubitable that we, who live enmingled therein and who are indeed part and parcel thereof, might avail neither to endure nor to defend ourselves, except God's especial grace lent us strength and foresight; which latter, it is not to be believed, descendeth unto us and upon us by any merit of our own, but of the proper motion of His own benignity and the efficacy of the prayers of those who were mortals even as we are and having diligently ensued His commandments, what while they were on life, are now with Him become eternal and blessed and unto whom we,—belike not daring to address ourselves unto the proper presence of so august a judge,—proffer our petitions of the things which we deem needful unto ourselves, as unto advocates informed by experience of our frailty. And this more we discern in Him, full as He is of compassionate liberality towards us, that, whereas it chanceth whiles (the keeness of mortal eyes availing not in any wise to penetrate the secrets of the Divine intent), that we peradventure, beguiled by report, make such an one our advocate unto His majesty, who is outcast from His presence with an eternal banishment,—nevertheless He, from whom nothing is hidden, having regard rather to the purity of the suppliant's intent than to his ignorance or to the reprobate estate of him whose intercession he invoketh, givether ear unto those who pray unto the latter, as if he were in very deed blessed in His aspect. The which will manifestly appear from the story which I purpose to relate; I say manifestly, ensuing, not the judgment of God, but that of men.

It is told, then, that Musciatto Franzesi, being from a very rich and considerable merchant in France become a knight and it behoving him thereupon go into Tuscany with Messire Charles Sansterre, brother to the King of France, who had been required and bidden thither by Pope Boniface, found his affairs in one part and another sore embroiled (as those of merchants most times are), and was unable lightly or promptly to disentangle them; wherefore he bethought himself to commit them unto diverse persons and made shift for all, save only he abode in doubt whom he might leave sufficient to the recovery of the credits he had given to certain Burgundians. The cause of his doubt was that he knew the Burgundians to be litigious, quarrelsome fellows, ill-conditioned and disloyal, and could not call one to mind, in whom he might put any trust, curst enough to cope with their perversity. After long consideration of the matter, there came to his memory a certain Master Ciapperello da Prato, who came often to his house in Paris and whom, for that he was little of person and mighty nice in his dress, the French, knowing not what Cepparello meant and thinking it be the same with Cappello, to wit, in their vernacular, Chaplet, called him, not Capello, but Ciappelletto, and accordingly as Ciappelletto he was known every where, whilst few knew him for Master Ciapperello.

Now this said Ciappelletto was of this manner life, that, being a scrivener, he thought very great shame whenas any of his instruments was found (and indeed he drew few such) other than false; whilst of the latter he would have drawn as many as might be required of him and these with a better will by way of gift than any other for a great wage. False witness he bore with especial delight, required or not required, and the greatest regard being in those times paid to oaths in France, as he recked nothing of forswearing himself, he knavishly gained all the suits concerning which he was called upon to tell the truth upon his faith. He took inordinate pleasure and was mighty diligent in stirring up troubles and enmities and scandals between friends and kinsfolk and whomsoever else, and the greater the mischiefs he saw ensue thereof, the more he rejoiced. If bidden to manslaughter or whatsoever other naughty deed, he went about it with a will, without ever saying nay thereto; and many a time of his proper choice he had been known to wound men and do them to death with his own hand. He was a terrible blasphemer of God and the saints, and that for every trifle, being the most choleric man alive. To church he went never and all the sacraments thereof he flouted in abominable terms, as things of no account; whilst, on the other hand, he was still fain to haunt and use taverns and other lewd places. Of women he was as fond as dogs of the stick; but in the contrary he delighted more than any filthy fellow alive. He robbed and pillaged with as much conscience as a godly man would make oblation to God; he was a very glutton and a great wine bibber, insomuch that bytimes it wrought him shameful mischief, and to boot, he was a notorious gamester and a caster of cogged dice. But why should I enlarge in so many words? He was belike the worst man that ever was born. His wickedness had long been upheld by the power and interest of Messer Musciatto, who had many a time safeguarded him as well from private persons, to whom he often did a mischief, as from the law, against which he was a perpetual offender.

This Master Ciappelletto, then, coming to Musciatto's mind, the latter, who was very well acquainted with his way of life, bethought himself that he should be such an one as the perversity of the Burgundians required and accordingly, sending for him, he bespoke him thus: 'Master Ciapelletto, I am, as thou knowest, about altogether to withdraw hence, and having to do, amongst others, with certain Burgundians, men full of guile, I know none whom I may leave to recover my due from them more fitting than myself, more by token that thou dost nothing at this present; wherefore, an thou wilt undertake this, I will e'en procure thee the favor of the Court and give thee such part as shall be meet of that which thou shalt recover.'

Dan Ciappelletto, who was then out of employ and ill provided with the goods of the world, seeing him who had long been his stay and his refuge about to depart thence, lost no time in deliberation, but, as of necessity constrained, replied that he would well. They being come to an accord, Musciatto departed and Ciappelletto, having gotten his patron's procuration and letters commendatory from the king, betook himself into Burgundy, where well nigh none knew him, and there, contrary to his nature, began courteously and blandly to seek to get in his payments and do that wherefor he was come thither, as if reserving choler and violence for a last resort. Dealing thus and lodging in the house of two Florentines, brothers, who there lent at usance and who entertained him with great honor for the love of Messer Musciatto, it chanced that he fell sick, whereupon the two brothers promptly fetched physicians and servants to tend him and furnished him with all that behoved unto the recovery of his health.

But every succor was in vain, for that, by the physicians' report, the good man, who was now old and had lived disorderly, grew daily worse, as one who had a mortal sickness; wherefore the two brothers were sore concerned and one day, being pretty near the chamber where he lay sick, they began to take counsel together, saying one to the other, 'How shall we do with yonder fellow? We have a sorry bargain on our hands of his

affair, for that to send him forth of our house, thus sick, were a sore reproach to us and a manifest sign of little wit on our part, if the folk, who have seen us first receive him and after let tend and medicine him with such solitude, should now see him suddenly put out of our house, sick unto death as he is, without it being possible for him to have done aught that should displease us. On the other hand, he hath been so wicked a man that he will never consent to confess or take any sacrament of the church; and he dying without confession, no church will receive his body; nay, he will be cast into a ditch, like a dog. Again, even if he do confess, his sins are so many and so horrible that the like will come of it, for that there is nor priest nor friar who can or will absolve him thereof; wherefore, being unshriven, he will still be cast into the ditches. Should it happen thus, the people of the city, as well on account of our trade, which appeareth to them most iniquitous and of which they missay all day, as of their itch to plunder us, seeing this, will rise up in riot and cry out, "These Lombard dogs, whom the church refuseth to receive, are to be suffered here no longer";—and they will run to our houses and despoil us not only of our good, but may be of our lives, to boot; wherefore in any case it will go ill with us, if yonder fellow die.'

Master Ciappelletto, who as we have said lay near the place where the two brothers were in discourse, being quick of hearing, as is most times the case with the sick, heard what they said of him and calling them to him, bespoke them thus: 'I will not have you unwise misdoubt of me nor fear to take any hurt by me. I have heard what you say of me and am well assured that it would happen even as you say, should matters pass as you expect; but it shall go otherwise. I have in my lifetime done God the Lord so many an affront that it will make neither more nor less, an I do Him yet another at the point of death; wherefore do you make shift to bring me the holiest and worthiest friar you may avail to have, if any such there be, and leave the rest to me, for that I will assuredly order your affairs and mine own on such wise that all shall go well and you shall have good cause to be satisfied.'

The two brothers, albeit they conceived no great hope of this, nevertheless betook themselves to a brotherhood of monks and demanded some holy and learned man to hear the confession of a Lombard who lay sick in their house. There was given them a venerable brother of holy and good life and a past master in Holy Writ, a very reverend man, for whom all the townsfolk had a very great and special regard, and they carried him to their house; where, coming to the chamber where Master Ciappelletto lay and seating himself by his side, he began first tenderly to comfort him and after asked him how long it was since he confessed last; whereto Master Ciappelletto, who had never confessed in his life, answered, 'Father, it hath been my usance to confess every week once at the least and often more; it is true that, since I fell sick, to wit, these eighty days past, I have not confessed, such is the annoy that my sickness hath given me.' Quoth the friar, 'My son, thou hast done well and so must thou do henceforward. I see, since thou confessest so often, that I shall be at little pains either of hearing or questioning.' 'Sir,' answered Master Ciappelletto, 'say not so; I have never confessed so much nor so often, but I would still fain make a general confession of all my sins that I could call to mind from the day of my birth to that of my confession; wherefore I pray you, good my father, question me as punctually of everything, nay, everything, as if I had never confessed; and consider me not because I am sick, for that I had far liefer displease this my flesh than, in consulting its ease, do aught that might be the perdition of my soul, which my Savior redeemed with His precious blood.'

These words much pleased the holy man and seemed to him to argue a well-disposed mind; wherefore, after he had much commended Master Ciappelletto for that his usance, he asked him if he had ever sinned by way of lust with any woman. 'Father,' replied Master Ciappelletto, sighing, 'on this point I am ashamed to tell you the truth, fearing to sin by way of vainglory.' Quoth the friar, 'Speak in all security, for never did one sin by telling the truth, whether in confession or otherwise.' 'Then,' said Master Ciappelletto, 'since you certify me of this, I will tell you; I am yet a virgin, even as I came forth of my mother's body.' 'O blessed be thou of God!' cried the monk. 'How well hast thou done! And doing thus, thou hast the more deserved, inasmuch as, an thou wouldst, thou hadst more leisure to do the contrary than we and whatsoever others are limited by any rule.'

After this he asked him if he had ever offended against God in the sin of gluttony; whereto Master Ciappelletto answered, sighing, 'Ay had he, and that many a time; for that, albeit, over and above the Lenten fasts that are yearly observed of the devout, he had been wont to fast on bread and water three days at the least in every week,—he had oftentimes (and especially whenas he had endured any fatigue, either praying or going a-pilgrimage) drunken the water with as much appetite and as keen a relish as great drinkers do wine. And many a time he had longed to have such homely salads of potherbs as women make when they go into the country; and whiles eating had given him more pleasure than him seemed it should do to one who fasteth for devotion, as did he. 'My son,' said the friar, 'these sins are natural and very slight and I would not therefore have thee burden thy conscience withal more than behoveth. It happeneth to every man, how devout soever he be, that, after long fasting, meat seemeth good to him, and after travail, drink.'

'Alack, father mine,' rejoined Ciappelletto, 'tell me not this to comfort me; you must know I know that things done for the service of God should be done sincerely and with an ungrudging mind; and whoso doth otherwise sinneth.' Quoth the friar, exceeding well pleased, 'I am content that thou shouldst thus apprehend it and thy pure and good conscience therein pleaseth me exceedingly. But, tell me, hast thou sinned by way of avarice, desiring more than befitted or withholding that which it behoved thee not to withhold?' 'Father mine,' replied Ciappelletto, 'I would not have you look to my being in the house of these userers; I have naught to do here; nay, I came hither to

admonish and chasten them and turn them from this their abominable way of gain; and methinketh I should have made shift to do so, had not God thus visited me. But you must know that I was left a rich man by my father, of whose good, when he was dead, I bestowed the most part in alms, and after, to sustain my life and that I might be able to succor Christ's poor, I have done my little traffickings, and in these I have desired to gain; but still with God's poor have I shared that which I gained, converting my own half to my occasions and giving them the other, and in this so well hath my Creator prospered me that my affairs have still gone from good to better.'

'Well hast thou done,' said the friar, 'but hast thou often been angered?' 'Oh,' cried Master Ciappelletto, 'that I must tell you I have very often been! And who could keep himself therefrom, seeing men do unseemly things all day long, keeping not the commandments of God neither fearing His judgments? Many times a day I had liefer been dead than alive, seeing young men follow after vanities and hearing them curse and forswear themselves, haunting the taverns, visiting not the churches and ensuing rather the ways of the world than that of God.' 'My son,' said the friar, 'this is a righteous anger, nor for my part might I enjoin thee any penance therefor. But hath anger at any time availed to move thee to do any manslaughter or to bespeak any one unseemly or do any other unright?' 'Alack, sir,' answered the sick man, 'you, who seem to me a man of God, how can you say such words? Had I ever had the least thought of doing any one of the things whereof you speak, think you I believe that God would so long have forborne me? These be the doings of outlaws and men of nought, whereof I never saw any but I said still, "Go, may God amend thee!"'

Then said the friar, 'Now tell me, my son (blessed be thou of God!), hast thou never borne false witness against any or missaid of another or taken others' good, without leave of him to whom it pertained?' 'Ay, indeed, sir,' replied Master Ciappelletto; 'I have missaid of others; for that I had a neighbor aforetime, who, with the greatest unright in the world, did nought but beat his wife, insomuch that I once spoke ill of him to her kinsfolk, so great was the compassion that overcame me for the poor woman, whom he used as God alone can tell, whenassoever he had drunken overmuch.' Quoth the friar, 'Thou tellest me thou hast been a merchant. Hast thou never cheated any one, as merchants do whiles?' 'I' faith, yes, sir,' answered Master Ciappelletto; 'but I know not whom, except it were a certain man, who once brought me monie which he owed me for cloth I had sold him and which I threw into a chest, without counting. A good month after, I found that they were four farthings more than they should have been; wherefore, not seeing him again and having kept them by me a full year, that I might restore them to him, I gave them away in alms.' Quoth the friar, 'this was a small matter, and thou didst well to deal with it as thou didst.'

Then he questioned him of many other things, all of which he answered after the same fashion, and the holy father offering to proceed to absolution, Master Ciappelletto said, 'Sir, I have yet sundry sins that I have not told you.' The friar asked him what they were, and he answered, 'I mind me that one Saturday, afternone, I caused my servant sweep out the house and had not that reverence for the Lord's holy day which it behoved me have.' 'Oh,' said the friar, 'that is a light matter, my son.' 'Nay,' rejoined Master Ciappelletto, 'call it not a light matter, for that the Lord's Day is greatly to be honored, seeing that on such a day our Lord rose from the dead.' Then said the friar, 'Well, hast thou done aught else?' 'Ay, sir,' answered Master Ciappelletto; 'once, unthinking what I did, I spat in the church of God.' Thereupon the friar fell a-smiling and said, 'My son, that is no thing to be reckoned of; we who are of the clergy, we spit there all day long.' 'And you do very ill,' rejoined Master Ciappelletto; 'for that there is nought which it so straitly behoveth to keep clean as the holy temple wherein is rendered sacrifice to God.'

Brief, he told him great plenty of such like things and presently fell a-sighing and after weeping sore, as he knew full well to do, whenas he would. Quoth the holy friar, 'What aileth thee, my son?' 'Alas, sir,' replied Master Ciappelletto, 'I have only one sin left, whereof I never yet confessed me, such shame have I to tell it; and every time I call it to mind, I weep, even as you see, and meseemeth very certain that God will never pardon it me.' 'Go to, son,' rejoined the friar; 'what is thou sayest? If all the sins that were ever wrought or are yet to be wrought of all mankind, what while the world endureth, were all in one man and he repented him thereof and were contrite therefor, as I see thee, such is the mercy and loving-kindness of God that, upon confession He would freely pardon them to him. Wherefore do thou tell it in all assurance.' Quoth Master Ciappelletto, still weeping sore, 'Alack, father mine, mine is too great a sin, and I can scarce believe that it will ever be forgiven me of God, except your prayers strive for me.' Then said the friar, 'Tell it me in all assurance, for I promise thee to pray God for thee.'

Master Ciappelletto, however, still wept and said nought; but, after he had thus held the friar a great while in suspense, he heaved a deep sigh and said, 'Father mine, since you promise me to pray God for me, I will e'en tell it you. Know, then, that, when I was little, I once cursed my mother.' So saying, he fell again to weeping sore. 'O my son,' quoth the friar, 'seemeth this to thee so heinous a sin? Why, men blaspheme God all day long and He freely pardoneth whoso repenteth him of having blasphemed Him; and deemest thou not He will pardon thee this? Weep not, but comfort thyself: for, certes, wert thou one of those who set Him on the cross, He would pardon thee, in favor of such contrition as I see in thee.' 'Alack, father mine, what say you?' replied Ciappelletto. 'My kind mother, who bore me nine months in her body, day and night, and carried me on her neck an hundred times and more, I did passing ill to curse her and it was an exceeding great sin; and except you pray God for me, it will not be forgiven me.'

The friar, then, seeing that Master Ciappelletto had no more to say, gave him absolution and bestowed on him his benison, holding him a very holy man and devoutly believing all that he had told him to be true. And who would not have believed it, hearing a man at the point of death speak thus? Then, after all this, he said to him, 'Master Ciappelletto, with God's help you will speedily be whole; but, should it come to pass that God call your blessed and well-disposed soul to himself, would it please you that your body be buried in our convent?' 'Ay, would it, sir,' replied Master Ciappelletto. 'Nay, I would fain not be buried otherwhere, since you have promised to pray God for me; more by token that I have ever had a special regard for your order. Wherefore I pray you that, whenas you return to your lodging, you cause bring me that most veritable body of Christ, which you consecrate a-mornings upon the altar, for that, with your leave, I purpose (all unworthy as I am) to take it and after, holy and extreme unction, to the intent that if I have lived as a sinner, I may at the least die like a Christian.' The good friar replied that it pleased him much and that he said well and promised to see it presently brought him; and so it was done.

Meanwhile, the two brothers, misdoubting them sore lest Master Ciappelletto should play them false, had posted themselves behind a wainscot, that divided the chamber where he lay from another, and listening, easily heard and apprehended that which he said to the friar and had whiles so great a mind to laugh, hearing the things which he confessed to having done, that they were like to burst and said, one to another, 'What manner of man is this, whom neither old age nor sickness nor fear of death, whereunto he seeth himself near, nor yet of God, before whose judgment-seat he looketh to be ere long, have availed to turn from his wickedness nor hinder him from choosing to die as he hath lived?' However, seeing that he had so spoken that he should be admitted to burial in a church, they recked nought of the rest.

Master Ciappelletto presently took the sacrament and growing rapidly worse, received extreme unction, and a little after evensong of the day he had made his fine confession, he died; whereupon the two brothers, having, of his proper monies, taken order for his honorable burial, sent to the convent to acquaint the friars therewith, bidding them come hither that night to hold vigil, according to usance, and fetch away the body in the morning, and meanwhile made ready all that was needful thereunto.

The holy friar, who had shriven him, hearing that he had departed this life, betook himself to the prior of the convent and letting ring to chapter, gave out to the brethren therein assembled that Master Ciappelletto had been a holy man, according to that which he had gathered from his confession, and persuaded them to receive his body with the utmost reverence and devotion, in the hope that God should show forth many miracles through him. To this the prior and brethren credulously consented and that same evening, coming all whereas Master Ciappelletto lay dead, they held high and solemn vigil over him and on the morrow, clad all in albs and copes, book in hand and crosses before them, they went, chanting the while, for his body and brought it with the utmost pomp and solemnity to their church, followed by well nigh all the people of the city, men and women.

As soon as they had set the body down in the church, the holy friar, who had confessed him, mounted the pulpit and fell a-preaching marvellous things of the dead man and of his life, his fasts, his virginity, his simplicity and innocence and sanctity, recounting, amongst other things, that which he had confessed to him as his greatest sin and how he had hardly availed to persuade him that God would forgive it him; thence passing on to reprove the folk who hearkened, 'And you, accursed that you are,' quoth he, 'for every waif of straw that stirreth between your feet, you blaspheme God and the Virgin and all the host of heaven.' Moreover, he told them many other things of his loyalty and purity of heart; brief, with his speech, whereto entire faith was yielded of the people of the city, he so established the dead man in the reverent consideration of all who were present that, no sooner was the service at an end, than they all with the utmost eagerness flocked to kiss his hands and feet and the clothes were torn off his back, he holding himself blessed who might avail to have never so little thereof; and needs must they leave him thus all that day, so he might be seen and visited of all.

The following night he was honorably buried in a marble tomb in one of the chapels of the church and on the morrow the folk began incontinent to come and burn candles and offer up prayers and make vows to him and hang images of wax at his shrine, according to the promise made. Nay, on such wise waxed the fame of his sanctity and men's devotion to him that there was scarce any who, being in adversity, would vow himself to another saint than him; and they styled and yet style him Saint Ciappelletto and avouch that God through him hath wrought many miracles and yet worketh them every day for whoso devoutly commendeth himself unto him.

Thus, then, lived and died Master Ciappelletto da Prato and became a saint, as you have heard; nor would I deny it to be possible that he is beatified in God's presence, for that, albeit his life was wicked and perverse, he may at his last extremity have shown such contrition that peradventure God had mercy on him and received him into His kingdom; but, for that this is hidden from us, I reason according to that which is apparent and say that he should rather be in the hands of the devil in perdition than in Paradise. And if so it be, we may know from this how great is God's loving-kindness towards us, which, having regard not to our error, but to the purity of our faith, whenas we thus make an enemy (deeming him a friend) of Him our intermediary, giveth ear unto us, even as if we had recourse unto one truly holy, as intercessor for His favor. Wherefore, to the end that by His grace we may be preserved safe and sound in this present adversity and in this so joyous company, let us, magnifying His name, in which we have begun our diversion, and holding Him in reverence, commend ourselves to Him in our necessities, well assured of being heard." And with this he was silent.[11]

ARCHITECTURE

Brunelleschi

Early Renaissance architecture was centered in Florence and departed from medieval architecture in three significant ways. First was its concern with the revival of Classical models along very mechanical lines. Ruins of Roman buildings were measured carefully and their proportions became those of the Renaissance buildings. Rather than seeing Roman arches as limiting factors, Renaissance architects saw them as geometric devices by which a formally derived design could be composed. The second departure from the medieval was the application of decorative detail—that is, nonstructural ornamentation—to the façade of the building. Third, and a manifestation of the second difference, was a radical change in the outer expression of structure. The outward form of a building was previously closely related to its actual structural systems—that is, the structural support of the building, for example, post-and-lintel, masonry, and the arch. In the Renaissance, these supporting elements were hidden from view and the external appearance was no longer sacrificed to structural concerns.

11.76 Filippo Brunelleschi, Pazzi Chapel, c. 1440–61. Santa Croce, Florence.

Early architecture of the period, such as the dome on the Cathedral of Florence (Fig. **11.77**) designed by Brunelleschi (1377–1446), was an imitation of a Classical form appended to a medieval structure. In this curious design, added in the fifteenth century to a fourteenth-century building, the soaring dome rises 180 ft (55 m) into the air, and its height is apparent from both outside and within. If we compare it with the Pantheon (Figs. **11.36** and **11.37**), Brunelleschi's departure from traditional practice becomes clearer. The dome of the Pantheon is impressive only from the inside of the building, because its exterior supporting structure is so massive that it clutters the visual experience. That Brunelleschi's dome rises to a phenomenal height is apparent on the inside because the architect has hidden from view the supporting elements such as stone and timber girdles and lightweight ribbings. The result is an aesthetic statement, where visual appearance is foremost and structural considerations are subordinate.

The use of Classical ornamentation can be seen in Brunelleschi's Pazzi Chapel (Fig. **11.76**). Small in scale, its walls serve as a plain background for a wealth of surface decoration. Concern for proportion and geometric design is very clear, but the overall composition is not a slave to pure arithmetical considerations. Rather, the Pazzi Chapel reflects Brunelleschi's sense of Classical aesthetics. Brunelleschi's influence was profound in the first half of the fifteenth century, and he served as a model and inspiration for later Renaissance architects.

The second half of the fifteenth century was dominated by the Florentine scholar, writer, architect, and composer Leon Battista Alberti. His treatise *Concerning Architecture* was based on Vitruvius and provided a scholarly approach to architecture that influenced Western building for centuries. His scientific approach to sculpture and painting, as well as architecture, encompassed theories on Roman antiquity that typified the reduction of aesthetics to rules.

However, the problems of Renaissance architects were different from those of their predecessors. Faced with an expanding range of types of building, such as townhouses, hospitals, and business establishments, for which Classical forms had to be adapted, the architect had to meet specific practical needs, which, apparently, the ancients did not. As a result, Classical detail was applied to a wide range of forms and structures, many of which, like the cathedral of Florence, were nonclassical in origin.

11.77 Filippo Brunelleschi, dome of Florence Cathedral, 1420–36.

THE HIGH RENAISSANCE IN ROME

As important and revolutionary as the fifteenth century was, both in Flanders and Italy, the high point of the Renaissance came in the early sixteenth century, as papal authority was reestablished and artists were called to Rome. Its importance as the apex of Renaissance art has led scholars to call this period in the visual arts the High Renaissance. Painters of the High Renaissance included the titans and giants of Western visual art: Leonardo da Vinci, Michelangelo, Raphael, Giorgione, and Titian.

Implicit in humanistic exploration of the individual's earthly potential and fulfillment is a concept of particular importance to our overview of visual art in the High Renaissance style—the concept of genius. In Italy between 1495 and 1520 everything in visual art was subordinate to the overwhelming genius of two men, Leonardo da Vinci and Michelangelo Buonarroti. Their great genius and impact have led many to debate whether the High Renaissance of visual art was a culmination of earlier Renaissance style or a new departure.

By 1500 the courts of the Italian princes had become important sources of patronage and cultural activity. In pursuit of their world of beauty, the Italian nobility needed artists, writers, and musicians. The arts of the early Renaissance now seemed vulgar and naïve. A more aristocratic, elegant, dignified, and exalted art was demanded. This new style is lofty. The wealth of the popes and their desire to rebuild and transform Rome on a grand scale also contributed significantly to the shift in style and the emergence of Rome as the center of High Renaissance patronage. Music came of age as a major art, finding a great patron in Pope Leo X. There was a revival of Ancient Roman sculptural and architectural style. Important discoveries of ancient sculptures such as the *Apollo Belvedere* and the *Laocoön* (Fig. **11.13**) were made. Because the artists of the High Renaissance had such a rich immediate inheritance of art and literature from the early Renaissance period, and felt they had developed even further, they considered themselves on an equal footing with the artists of the antique period. Their approach to the antique in arts and letters was therefore different from that of their early Renaissance predecessors.

High Renaissance painting sought a universal ideal achieved through impressive art, as opposed to overemphasis on tricks of perspective or on anatomy. Figures became types again, rather than naturalistic individuals—Godlike human beings in the Greek Classical tradition. Artists and writers of the High Renaissance sought to

11.78 Leonardo da Vinci, *The Last Supper*, c. 1495–8. Mural painting. Santa Maria della Grazie, Milan.

capture the essence of Classical art and literature without resorting to copying, which would have captured only the externals. They tried to emulate, and not to imitate. As a result, High Renaissance art idealizes all forms and delights in composition. Its impact is one of stability without being static, variety without confusion, and clear definition without dullness. High Renaissance artists carefully observed how the ancients borrowed motifs from nature, and they then set out to develop a system of mathematically defined proportion and compositional beauty emanating from a total harmonization of parts. Such faith in harmonious proportions reflected a belief among artists, writers, and composers that a harmonious universe and nature also possessed perfect order. In addition, High Renaissance style departed from previous styles in its meticulously arranged composition, based almost exclusively on geometric devices. Composition was closed—line, color, and form or shape kept the viewer's eye continually redirected into the work, as opposed to leading the eye off the canvas. Organization centered upon a geometric shape, such as a central triangle or an oval.

Leonardo da Vinci

The work of Leonardo da Vinci (1452–1519) contains an ethereal quality which he achieved by blending light and shadow (called *sfumato*). His figures hover between reality and illusion as one form disappears into another, and only

highlighted portions emerge. It is difficult to say which of Leonardo's paintings is the most popular or admired, but certainly *The Last Supper* (Fig. **11.78**) ranks among the greatest. It captures the drama of Christ's prophecy, "One of you shall betray me," at the moment that the apostles are responding with disbelief. Leonardo's choice of medium proved most unfortunate because his own mixtures of oil, varnish, and pigments, as opposed to fresco, were not suited to the damp wall. The painting began to flake and was reported to be perishing as early as 1517. Since then it has been clouded by retouching, defaced by a door cut through the wall at Christ's feet, and bombed during World War II. Miraculously, it survives. Recent attempts at restoration have created great controversy in the art world.

In *The Last Supper* human figures and not architecture are the focus. The figure of Christ dominates the center of the painting, forming a stable, yet active, central triangle. All line, actual and implied, leads outward from the face of Christ, pauses at various subordinate focal areas, is directed back into the work, and returns to the central figure. Various postures, hand positions, and groupings of the disciples direct the eye from point to point. Figures emerge from the gloomy architectural background in strongly accented relief; nothing anchors these objects to the floor of the room of which they are a part. Although this is not the greatest example of Leonardo's use of sfumato, the technique is there. This typically geometric

11.79 Michelangelo, Sistine Chapel ceiling, 1508–12, The Vatican, Rome.

composition is amazing in that so much drama can be expressed within such a mathematical format. Yet, despite the drama, the mood in this work and others is calm, belying the conflict of Leonardo's own life and times.

Michelangelo

Perhaps the most dominant figure of the High Renaissance, however, was Michelangelo Buonarroti (1475–1564), who was entirely different in character from Leonardo. Leonardo was a skeptic, while Michelangelo was a man of great faith. Leonardo was fascinated by science and natural objects; Michelangelo showed little interest in anything other than the human form.

Michelangelo's Sistine Chapel ceiling (Fig. **11.79**) is a shining example of the ambition and genius of this era and its philosophies. Some scholars see in this monumental work a blending of Christian tradition and a Neoplatonist view of the soul's progressive ascent through contemplation and desire. In each of the triangles along the sides of the chapel the ancestors of Christ await the Redeemer. Between them, amidst painted pillars, are the sages of antiquity. In the corners Michelangelo depicts various biblical stories, and across the center of the ceiling he unfolds the episodes of Genesis. The center of the ceiling captures, at the moment of fulfillment, the Creation of Adam (Fig. **11.80**) and does so in sculpturesque human form and beautifully modeled anatomical detail.

God, in human form, stretches outward from his matrix of angels to a reclining, but dynamic, Adam, awaiting the divine infusion, the spark of the soul. The figures do not touch, and we are left with a supreme feeling of anticipation of what we imagine will be the power and electricity of God's physical contact with mortal man.

The Sistine Chapel ceiling creates a visual panoply of awesome proportions. It is not possible to get a comprehensive view of the entire ceiling, standing at any point in the Chapel. If we look upward and read the scenes back toward the altar, the prophets and sibyls appear on their sides. If we view one side as upright, then the other appears upside down. These opposing directions are held together by the structure of simulated architecture, whose transverse arches and diagonal bands separate vault compartments. Twenty nudes appear at intersections and harmonize the composition because they can be read either with the prophets and sibyls below them or with the Genesis scenes, at whose corners they appear. We thus see the basic High Renaissance principle of composition created by the interaction of the component elements.

Michelangelo believed, as did Plato, that the image from the artist's hand must spring from the idea in his mind. The idea is the reality, and it is revealed by the genius of the artist. The artist does not create the ideas, but finds them in the natural world, which reflects the absolute idea: beauty. So, to the Neoplatonist, imitation of nature in art reveals hidden truths within nature.

11.80 Michelangelo, *The Creation of Adam*, Sistine Chapel ceiling (detail), 1508–12. The Vatican, Rome.

11.81 Michelangelo, *David*, 1501–4. Marble, height 13 ft 5 ins (4.08 m) high. The Academy, Florence.

Michelangelo broke with earlier Renaissance artists in his insistence that measurement was subordinate to judgement. He believed that measurement and proportion should be kept "in the eyes," and so established a rationale for the release of genius to do what it would, free from any preestablished "rules." This enabled him to produce works such as *David* (Fig. **11.81**), a colossal figure and the earliest monumental sculpture of the High Renaissance. Towering some 18 ft (5.5 m) above the floor, this nude champion exudes a Neoplatonic pent-up energy as the body seems to act as an earthly prison of the soul. The upper body moves in opposition to the lower. The eye is led downward by the right arm and leg of the figure, and then upward along the left arm. The entire composition seeks to break free from its confinement through thrust and counterthrust.

Inspired by the Hellenistic sculptures he had seen in Rome, Michelangelo set out in pursuit of an emotion-charged, heroic ideal. The heroic scale, musculature, emotion, superhuman beauty, and power of the earlier works became a part of his style. However, in contrast with the Hellenistic approach to realism, in which the "body 'acts out' the spirit's agony," "David, at once calm and tense, shows the action-in-repose so characteristic of Michelangelo."[12]

Papal Splendor: The Vatican

Here for almost 2,000 years has been the center of a spiritual communion; in countries all over the world, Christians aspire to achieve a community of spirit with the successor to St. Peter. By comprehending this significance of the Vatican, one can also understand what it was that led Roman Catholicism to embellish the center of its spiritual power with the diversity of human knowledge, including the arts.[13]

The Renaissance—and particularly the High Renaissance, when the papacy called all great artists to Rome—contributed most of the splendor of Vatican art and architecture. The papacy as a force and the Vatican as the symbol of that force represent a synthesis of Renaissance ideas and reflections. Rome was the city of the arts in the fifteenth and sixteenth centuries. The artists of the age rediscovered Classical antiquity and emulated what they found. Imitation was frowned upon, and the Classical nature of Renaissance art lies in its expressiveness, which is indeed comparable to that of Greece and Rome. St. Peter's and the Vatican have earthly and heavenly qualities which reflect the reality of the Church on earth and the mystery of the spiritual church of Christ (Fig. **11.83**).

11.83 Michelangelo, St. Peter's, Rome, from the west, 1546–64 (dome completed by Giacomo della Porta, 1590).

Plans for replacement of the original basilica of Old St. Peter's were made in the fifteenth century, but it was Pope Julius II (1503–13) who decided to put into effect the plans of Nicholas V (1447–55). Julius commissioned Bramante to construct the new basilica. Bramante's design called for a building in the form of a Greek cross (Fig.

11.82 Bramante's design for St. Peter's, 1506.

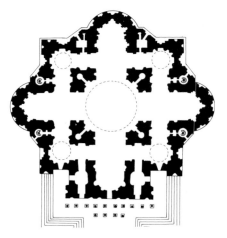

11.84 Michelangelo's design for St. Peter's, 1547.

11.85 Plan of St. Peter's as built to Michelangelo's design with alterations by Carlo Maderno, 1606–15.

11.82). The work was planned as "an harmonious arrangement of architectural forms" in an "image of bright amplitude and picturesque liveliness."

Bramante died in 1514 and was succeeded by two of his assistants and Raphael. Liturgical considerations required an elongated structure. Subsequent changes were made by additional architects, and these designs were severely criticized by Michelangelo. Following the death of the last of these architects, Pope Paul III (1534–49) convinced Michelangelo to become chief architect. Michelangelo set aside liturgical considerations and returned to Bramante's original conceptions, which he described as "clear and pure, full of light ... whoever distances himself from Bramante, also distances himself from the truth" (Fig. 11.84). Michelangelo's project was completed in May of 1590 as the last stone was added to the dome and a High Mass was celebrated. Work on the thirty-six columns continued, however, and was completed by Della Porta and Fontana after Michelangelo's death. Full completion of the basilica as it stands today was under the direction of yet more architects, including Maderno. Maderno was forced to yield to the wishes of the cardinals and change the original form of the Greek cross to a Latin cross (Fig. 11.85). As a result, the Renaissance design of Michelangelo and Bramante, with its central altar, was rejected. It was replaced by Maderno's design of a travertine façade of gigantic proportions and sober elegance. His extension of the basilica was influential in the development of Baroque architecture. The project was completed in 1614.

THE LATE RENAISSANCE IN ENGLAND

Shakespeare and Marlowe

While late Renaissance Italy prepared the way for our modern theatre building and certain acting techniques, sixteenth-century England produced a new theatre of convention, and history's foremost playwright.

We must always be careful when we try to draw conclusions about why the arts developed as they did within a particular historical context. While Italy and France saw the arts prosper under varying forms of extravagant patronage, England saw a theatre of great literary consequence and conventional nature prosper under a monarch who loved the theatre only as long as it did not impose upon her financially. In other words, Elizabeth I encouraged the arts not by patronage of the kind provided by the Medicis, the Church, or Kings Francis I or Louis XIV, but, rather, by benign neglect.

England's drama in the mid- to late sixteenth century was national in character, influenced undoubtedly by the severance of Church and state under Henry VIII. Nevertheless, literary influences in England in the sixteenth century were strongly Italian, and the theatre reflected these influences.

The Elizabethans loved drama, and the theatres of London saw prince and commoner together among its audiences. They sought and found, usually in the same play, action, spectacle, comedy, character, and intellectual stimulation so deeply reflective of the human condition that Elizabethan plays have found universal appeal through the centuries since their first production.

Shakespeare (1564–1616) was the preeminent Elizabethan playwright, and his and English sensitivity to and appreciation of the Italian Renaissance can be seen in the Renaissance Italian settings of many of his plays. In true Renaissance expansiveness, Shakespeare took his audiences back into history, both British and Classical, and far beyond, to the fantasy world of Caliban in *The Tempest*. We gain perspective on the Renaissance world's perception of their own or their fellows' condition when we compare the placid, composed reflections of Italian painting with Shakespeare's tragic portraits of Renaissance Italian intrigue.

Like most playwrights of his age, Shakespeare wrote for a specific professional company (of which he became a partial owner). The need for new plays to keep the company alive from season to season provided much of the impetus for his prolific writing, in the same sense that a required weekly cantata stimulated Bach and Scarlatti. A robust quality exists in Shakespeare's plays. His ideas have universal appeal because of his understanding of human motivation and character and his ability to probe deeply into emotion. He provided insights dramatically equivalent to Rembrandt's visual probings. Shakespeare's plays reflect life and love, action and nationalism; and they present those qualities in a magnificent poetry that explores the English language in unrivaled fashion. Shakespeare's use of tone, color, and complex or new word meanings give his plays a musical as well as dramatic quality, which appeals to every generation.

11.86 Interior of the Swan Theatre, Bankside, London (opened 1598). Contemporary pen drawing.

We know more about the theatres that Shakespeare played in than we do about his life, but that information is far from complete. Most authorities believe that the Elizabethan theatre took a unique form. The only previous theatres that approach it are the Spanish corrales, although the Elizabethan theatres may have some distant connections with the Dutch and the Italian. Our sources of information about the Elizabethan playhouse are: first, the great halls and inn yards, where plays were given before the theatres were built; second, the buildings used for bearbaiting and bullbaiting; third, four sketches ranging in date from about 1596 to 1640, one of which is shown in Figure 11.86; fourth, the wording of the contract for the building of the Fortune Theatre; and fifth, evidence from the stage directions of Elizabethan plays.

When we examine the Elizabethan play, we soon realize how flexible the stage must have been. *Antony and Cleopatra*, for example, has forty-three scenes.

Shakespeare was not the only significant playwright of the English Renaissance stage, however, and the plays of Christopher Marlowe (1564–93) and Ben Jonson (1573–1637) still captivate theatre audiences. Marlowe's love of sound permeates his works, and if his character development is weak, his heroic grandeur has the Classical qualities of Aeschylus and Sophocles. His most famous play is *Doctor Faustus (The Tragical History of the Life and Death of Doctor Faustus)*, first published in 1604. The story resembles the plot of a morality play, narrating a man's temptation, fall, and damnation, in richly poetic language. His language was a breakthrough in drama of the time. His flexible use of blank verse and the brilliance of his imagery combine to stimulate emotion and rivet his audience's attention. The imagery of terror in the final scene is among the most powerful in all of drama. In addition, Marlowe's language and imagery unify the play: the patterns in Faust's references to Heaven provide a subtle implication of the force from which Faust cannot escape and yet which he must, at the beginning, deny. "He cannot escape from a world order and from responsibility; nor can he escape from a dream of unfettered domination. That is his tragedy."[14]

TWELVE

ARTISTIC STYLES IN THE EMERGING MODERN WORLD

1650 TO 1900

THE MING DYNASTY IN CHINA

In 1368, the Ming Dynasty was proclaimed by a former peasant who led a revolt against the Mongolians. By the end of the century, all of China had been liberated, and a major policy of public works had been introduced. By the end of the sixteenth century, capitalism existed throughout China, emerging in small pockets, which the bureaucracy of the central government tried to restrict. At the same time, an official policy of population control was established. As China rediscovered its former prosperity, it spread its influence again throughout southeast Asia from Mongolia to Vietnam. Major sea expeditions exported culture as well as goods; however, the emperor's lack of interest in seafaring and Japanese pirate adventur-

ism soon took their toll on China's outward expansion. European incursion occurred at the same time, from first the Portuguese and then the Dutch. Industrial development and prosperity tended to undermine China's agrarian foundations and the privileges of the aristocracy and its bureaucracy. Dissatisfaction spread among the peasants of the countryside and among city-dwellers; this led to internal conflicts, which, when exacerbated by a new threat from Mongolia, brought down the Ming Dynasty in 1644.

MING DYNASTY STYLES

During the lengthy Ming Dynasty (fourteenth to seventeenth centuries), the style of Chinese art—and painting in particular—changed dramatically. Although subject matter remained unchanged, ostentation, detail, and dramatic presentation increased tremendously. In order to reflect on that change, let us begin by examining a work from the period examined in the last chapter. Ch'ien Hsuan's *Doves and Pear Blossoms* (Fig. **12.1**) represents the thirteenth-century style. It takes much of the same feeling of the previous landscapes and applies it to a more detailed subject. The pigeons and the branch have a sense of formality, and, although the composition captures a mood of peace and tranquility, it remains dynamic

12.1 *(left)* Ch'ien Hsuan, *Doves and Pear Blossoms*, c. 1235. Painting on paper, 38½×12 ins (97.8×30.5 cm). Cincinnati Art Museum, Museum Purchase: J.J. Emery Endowment.

12.3 *(below)* Lu Chi, *Winter*, c. 1500. Hanging scroll, ink and color on silk, height 69 ins (175 cm). National Museum, Tokyo.

12.2 Wen Cheng-ming, *Seven Juniper Trees*, 1532. Detail of handscroll, ink on paper, height 11⅛ ins (28.3 cm). Honolulu Academy of Arts, Hawaii.

through its asymmetrical balance. The strength of the darker tones holds the viewer's eye within the frame, and deftly leads it from one edge to the other. The strong attraction of the central figures is balanced by the delicate lightness of the pear blossoms. Thus, although there is movement on a slight diagonal, with deviations up and down, the contours remain comparatively gentle, and the overall sense of the painting stays horizontal and restful. Again, we find careful attention to detail. The bark is delicately shaded to give the limbs volume. The painter's technique also creates a textured effect in the bark that skillfully suggests realism and yet remains stylized. The flowers provide contrast, not only in their tonality, but also in their delicacy. They are soft and precise and reinforce the painting's sensitive mood.

When we compare Wen Cheng-ming's handscroll *Seven Juniper Trees* (Fig. **12.2**)—a work from the mid-sixteenth century—with *Doves and Pear Blossoms* we discover that, although the horizontal composition of the two works is similar, the tone, mood, and details are not. *Seven Juniper Trees* seems, by contrast, unrestrained in its dynamics: the diagonals carry greater distances and conflict with each other. Their abrupt changes of direction create intense motion and a mood of disquiet. The treatment of bark and foliage exhibits strong contrast between light and dark tonalities: hard color edges juxtapose light and dark and give the painting a forcefulness that demands our attention, and motion rather than rest.

A similar feeling and treatment exists in Lu Chi's *Winter* (Fig. **12.3**)—also from the Ming period. Here again strong contrasts, copious detail, hard, color edges, and conflicting diagonals create strong action, exaggeration, and intensity. Although the curvilinear treatment of line makes the dynamics of this painting broader, more sweeping, and perhaps somewhat softer than *Seven Juniper Trees*, the open spaces and hardedged outlining give the work more power and substance. At the same time, an immense amount of delicate detail—in the pheasant, the blossoms, and some of the smaller branches—is captured within the broad openness of this painting. Thus, the contrasts—lights and darks, hard edges and curved lines, broad spaces and delicate detail—create a curious mystery and opulence that is quite different from the classical restraint we witnessed in Sung Dynasty works.

SCULPTURE & CERAMICS

The Ming Dynasty brought about a centralization of power and money in the court of the emperor. As a result, the demand for decorative arts caused a tremendous increase in the number and quality of ceramic works. The celebrated Ming vases have become a symbol for the wide variety of ceramicware produced during this period. Strong traditions in ceramic style and technique had been established as early as the Sung Dynasty. The Ming Dynasty capitalized on these earlier accomplishments, and took ceramic art to even higher levels, especially in porcelains. By the fifteenth century an underglaze decoration of cobalt blue was applied, and artisans achieved remarkable skill in color control. Familiar blue-and-white porcelains had their classic period between the years 1426 and 1435. Clarity of detail and variety of shapes marked this approach, and over the next one hundred years works were enriched by adding multicolored enamels to the basic blue. The result can be seen in a five-color enamel jar from the reign of Wan Li (1573–1620). The complex process of adding layers of color called for refined designs and repeated firings. The white ground and blue designs came first and were glazed and fired. Then, over this fired glaze, the decoration was completed in red, green, yellow, and brown; the work was then refired. The entire process required several firings and resulted in a rich and delicate ceramic such as the covered jar pictured in Figure **12.4**. The resulting, freely painted narrative scenes and floral compositions have charm, grace, and appeal. Their shapes tend to be slightly irregular: thus they have a uniqueness and human quality that adds warmth to their otherwise perfect execution.

12.4 Covered jar, mark of Wan Li, c. 1600. Porcelain, height 4 ins (10.2 cm). The Cleveland Museum of Art, John L. Severance Fund, 57.62.

1 Gate of Divine Pride
2 Pavilion of Imperial Peace
3 Imperial Garden
4 Palace of Earthly Tranquility
5 Hall of Union
6 Palace of Heavenly Purity
7 Gate of Heavenly Purity
8 Hall of the Preservation of Harmony
9 Hall of Perfect Harmony
10 Hall of Supreme Harmony
11 Gate of Supreme Harmony
12 Meridian Gate
13 Kitchens
14 Gardens
15 Former Imperial Printing House
16 Flower Gate
17 Palace of the Culture of the Mind
18 Hall of the Worship of the Ancestors
19 Pavilion of Arrows
20 Imperial Library
21 Palace of Culture
22 Palace of Peace and Longevity
23 Nine Dragon Screen

12.5 Plan of the Imperial Palace, Peking.

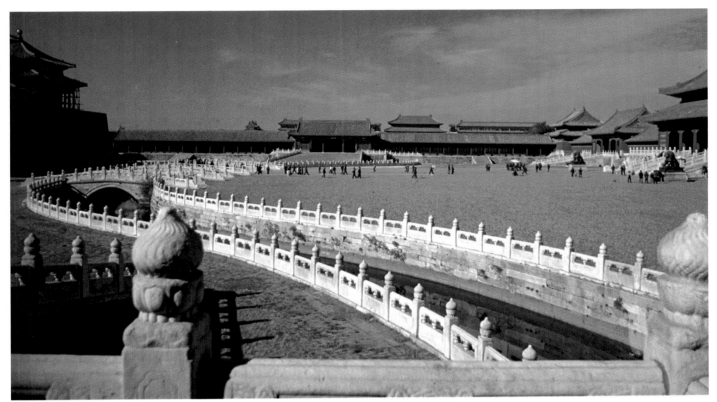

12.6 The first courtyard of the Imperial Palace, Peking, with the outer gate on the left, 1420, later restored.

IMPERIAL ARCHITECTURE

The third Ming emperor, Yongle, moved his capital from Nanjing to Peking in 1417. In a lust for ostentatious display, he laid out his new palace according to Zhou Dynasty ritual, which indicated that the "Son of Heaven should rule from three courts." Consequently, a fifteen-mile wall was constructed to surround the courts separating the three great halls of state, which were built with wooden columns and beams and wide roofs of glazed yellow tiles—a color reserved for imperial buildings (Fig. **12.5**) The outer gate to the capital enters into the first courtyard across a bridge over the "Golden Water River" (Fig. **12.6**) The white bridge and river railings blend harmoniously with the pavement of the courtyard and stand in charming contrast to the red columns and golden roof tiles of the buildings. An even larger courtyard stands beyond the "Gate of Supreme Harmony." The scale and detail of these spaces and buildings more than met the emperor's desire to "outshine the splendor of buildings which Marco Polo had thought 'so vast, so rich and beautiful that no man on earth could design anything superior.' "[1]

INDIA

THE ARYA

Indian history can be seen to consist of two periods: the first occupies the unrecorded period up to the conquest of Alexander the Great in the late fourth century B.C., the second occurs from that time to the present. Accounts of events prior to the invasion of the Hellenes and Alexander comprise largely myths and legends. No written records exist.

Around 1400 B.C. the Arya clans moved into the Punjab, and during the following centuries spread throughout the East and South. By 600 B.C. they apparently ruled the entire Ganges Valley. These clans were the dominant force in India for nearly a thousand years, occupying an area from the Persian Gulf and the Bay of Bengal, the Himalayas and the Vindhya mountains, and the Decan north of the Godavari. The language spoken by the Arya and assimilated by the native peoples was an Indo-European language called Sanskrit. Sanskrit began as a religious language, but eventually it became a secular and literary language as well. Even today, India divides in half by language: Sanskrit in the north, and Dravidian languages, specifically Tamil, in the south.

The religious rites of the Arya came from the Veda, a form of polytheism which emphasized sacrificial ceremonies. As it came into contact with native religions, Vedism adopted images, included other gods and balanced a more personal relationship between the believer and the divinity with its original ritual. The result became Hinduism. In the sixth century B.C., two new religions came into being: Jainism, founded by the Jina Mahavira, and Buddhism. Both advocated nonviolence, detachment, and monasticism.

The social order of the Arya divided the people into four classes: Brahmans or religious personnel; Ksatriya or warriors and political leaders; Vaisya or wealth producers such as farmers, craftsmen, and merchants; and the Sudra or servants of the first three. The real groups of society, the castes, were arranged hierarchically within these theoretical divisions. Essentially the Arya were shepherds, and when they expanded into new areas, they destroyed any town with which they came in contact. However, by the sixth century B.C., new urban areas had emerged and later were to become the centers of intellectual and economic life. By 518 B.C., parts of India were Satraps of the Persian Empire.

ALEXANDER & BEYOND

From 327 to 325 B.C. Alexander the Great took his expedition into India. After his defeat of King Puru, Alexander sought to move onward, but his troops refused, and so he retreated toward the mouth of the Indus River. Three years later in the north of the continent, Candragupta the Maurya came to power. After his death the country divided into several states and small kingdoms. However, in 272 B.C. his grandson, India's most famous ruler—Ashoka, the perfect emperor—took political power and unified the continent. Eschewing war, he sought to bring about the Buddhist ideal of universal goodwill. His political and religious principles are recorded on pillars and rocks throughout the Empire. After he died, the Empire disintegrated. The next four hundred years witnessed a series of invasions, rulers, and divisions. From A.D. 270 to 500 India unified under the Gupta Empire. By the end of the sixth century, the Pallava of Kanci gained a control over the southeastern part of the India peninsula, which lasted until the ninth century.

The Muslims

The eighth century saw the invasions of Islam. Coming as it did toward the ebb of the Muslim expansion, a strong enough base to conquer the entire peninsula could not be established. Further, the Muslims showed relative tolerance for the Hindus, whose religious practices continued uninterrupted. Thus, Islam remained essentially only a peripheral influence in Indian culture. Such conditions did not recur from 1000 to 1200, when Turkish invasions brought massacres and repression. The end result was a Muslim state, which brought about profound changes in Indian society. By the end of the thirteenth century, a fourth of India's population was Muslim. Buddhism was the hardest hit of India's religions when the local populations converted to Islam. Hinduism, however, proved resistant, although the appeal of the casteless Islam to the lower castes of Hindus proved quite strong. As a result, Islam became an integral part of Indian culture.

12.7 *Alam Shah Closing the Dam at Shishan Pass* (leaf from *The Romance of Amir Hamza*), Mughal, c. 1570. Color and gold on cotton, 27⅛ × 20½ ins (69 × 52.2 cm). The Cleveland Museum of Art, Gift of George P. Bickford, 76.74.

12.8 *Madhu Madhavi Ragini*, Malwa, India, c. 1630–40. Color on paper, $7\frac{9}{16} \times 5\frac{13}{16}$ ins (19.2 × 14.8 cm). The Cleveland Museum of Art, Gift of J.H. Wade, 25.1336.

Akbar and the Mughals

The period of the sixteenth to eighteenth centuries focused on the significant accomplishments of a kingdom centered in Delhi. This sultanate was founded by Babur, a descendant of Tamerlane and Genghis Khan. By the end of the reign of Akbar in the late sixteenth century, a large number of India's 100 million people were among the subjects of the sultanate. Land reform gave land rights to the peasants, and a new class of civil servants had arisen. Akbar tried to create a synthesis of Hinduism and Islam.

INDIAN PAINTING STYLES

Mughal Style

Although mural painting and frescos can be found dating to early in India's history, a sampling of painting from the Mughal Dynasty can give us a good sense of India's two-dimensional art. Our first example comes from a manuscript, the *Amir Hamza*, a major manuscript produced during the reign of Akbar. These paintings, done on fine linen, unify Persian and Indian images into a Mughal style. Typical of Indian art, they depict their subjects in fairly realistic detail with bold colors and dynamic composition. *Alam Shah Closing the Dam at Shishan Pass* (Fig.

12.7) tells its narrative with its hero taking the predominate position at the top of the work. Although the details are naturalistic in portrayal, Indian painting makes little use of natural perspective—the painting exists solely on the surface plane. Although the images are fragmented, the composition achieves its balance psychologically. A strong diagonal moves from upper left to lower right and is countered by an opposite diagonal from lower left to upper right. Each segment of the painting carries its own narrative content, and the pieces of the composition fit together like multicolored tiles of a mosaic. The work is unified by its underlying and framing use of gold. The "frame" is part of the painting itself.

Rajput Style

A second style of Indian painting, called the Rajput style, has a folk art quality and takes much of its subject matter from Hindu literature. The treatment of subject matter in Rajput style ranges widely—from abstract to intellectual to concrete and emotional. Figure **12.8**, *Madhu Madhavi Ragini*, is a typical example of a particular series—called

12.9 *Shiva and Devi on Gajasura Hide (Gajahamurti)*, Basohli, India, c. 1657–80. Color on paper, $9\frac{1}{4} \times 6\frac{1}{4}$ ins (23.5 × 15.8 cm). The Cleveland Museum of Art, Edward L. Whittemore Fund, 52.287.

the Coomsway series—in Rajput painting. Its primary characteristic is its distinctive dark-blue background. The title of the painting refers both to a musical mode and to a representation of a heroine who goes into the night to meet her lover, peacocks flying around her, and lightning flashing. However, there seems little here that is ominous. Space is limited to the surface plane. Crossing diagonals give the work a sense of movement, and strong colors and contrasts make the painting forceful and appealing. The conventions of figure portrayal are similar to Egyptian styles (see Chapter 10).

Punjab Style

A third major school of Indian painting, the Punjab hills style, emphasized linear drawing expressed in a gentle, lyrical mode. For example, *Gajahamurti*, which means "after the death of the elephant-demon" (Fig. **12.9**), presents deities posed very formally in a perfectly balanced composition of gently curvilinear forms and careful coloring. The deities Siva and Pavrati are presented in rigid formality. Siva, the slayer of the demon, takes focus and the two deities float in the sky on the elephant's

hide. The swirling clouds seem to suggest a storm, especially in their strong contrast to the dark blue background. The sky takes predominance over a rather conventionally and sparsely illustrated earth. The flowers, none the less, show fine detailing and individuality. The ducks also are delicate and graceful both in the water and in flight. Overall, the tone is subdued rather than violent.

MUSLIM VS. HINDU ARCHITECTURE

The Islamic Mughal emperors of India were patrons of architecture, and the most famous of all Indian architectural accomplishments also qualifies as an example of Islamic work—the Taj Mahal at Agra (Fig. **12.10**). However, the Taj Mahal blends Islamic and indigenous Indian styles. It was built by Shah Jahan as a mausoleum for his favorite wife Mumtaz Mahal (1593–1631). Such a tomb for a wife was entirely without precedent in Islam, and it is possible that the building also was intended as an allegory of the day of Resurrection: the building is a symbolic replica of the throne of God. Four intersecting waterways in the garden by which one approaches the Taj

12.10 Ustad Ahmad Lahori (architect), the Taj Mahal, Agra, 1632–48.

BAROQUE STYLE

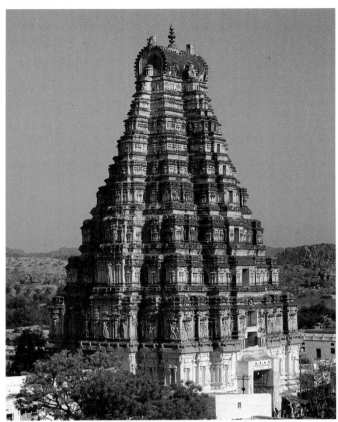

12.11 *Gopura* (gateway tower) of the Pampapati temple, Vijayanagar, India, 16th century (renovated in the 17th century).

The Baroque meant opulence, intricacy, ornateness, and appeal to the emotions, and outdid its predecessors in reflecting the grandiose expectations of its patrons. Diverse and widespread, Baroque art took Renaissance clarity of form and recast it into intricate patterns of geometry and fluid movement. The idea of proving one's position to one's peers by overwhelming art infected the aristocracy, the bourgeoisie, and the Roman Catholic Church, whose strategy for coping with the Reformation and the spread of Protestantism included attracting worshippers back into the Church with magnificent art, architecture, and music. Systematic rationalism sprang forth as an organizational concept for works of art and as a means of explaining the universe in more secular and scientific terms as well. The world became more and more secularized as power shifted from the Church to more worldly institutions, above all of whom reigned the absolute monarch.

With the seventeenth century came an age of intellectual, spiritual, and physical action. Along with the new age came a new style, the *Baroque*, which reflected the characteristics and concerns of its age, and did so in forms that acknowledged the presence of middle-class patronage in addition to that of the Church and the nobility. Painting appealed to the emotions and to a desire for magnificence through opulent ornamentation, but it also adopted a systematized and rational composition in which ornamentation was unified through variation on a single theme. Realism replaced beauty as an objective for painting. Color and grandeur were emphasized, as was dramatic use of lights and darks which carry the viewer's eye off the page. In all Baroque art a sophisticated organizational scheme subordinated a multitude of single parts to the whole and carefully merged one part into the next to create an exceedingly complex but highly unified design. Open composition was used to symbolize the notion of an expansive universe. The viewer's eye traveled off the canvas to a wider reality. The human figure, as an object or focus in painting, could be monumental in full Renaissance fashion, but could also now be a minuscule figure in a landscape, part of, but subordinate to, an overwhelming universe. Above all, Baroque style was characterized by intensely active compositions that emphasized feeling rather than form, emotion rather than the intellect.

Baroque painting was diverse in application, although fairly easily identifiable as a general style. It was used to glorify the Church and religious sentiment—both Catholic and Protestant. It portrayed the magnificence of

symbolized the four flowing rivers of Paradise as described in the Koran. The scale of the building is immense, and yet the details are exquisitely refined. Proportions are well-balanced and symmetrical. The effect of this huge, white octagonal structure, with its impressive dome and flanking minarets, is nothing short of breathtaking.

The Hindu architectural tradition was almost defiantly anti-Islamic, by contrast, with its abundance of figurative sculpture celebrating a plurality of deities. Good examples of this countervailing trend can be seen in the south of India, especially in the ten-square-mile city of Vijayanagar. Here, huge and exquisite temples came alive with brilliantly colored sculpture depicting the Hindu pantheon (Fig. **12.11**). Upward-striving terraces with ornate detail reach toward a vaulted pinnacle. In Vijayanagar the concept of the temple went beyond a single shrine and encompassed an entire complex of buildings within concentric enclosures. These were entered through tall gate towers called *gopuras*, which were packed with friezes of the Hindu gods, and which increased in size as one moved from inner to outer walls.

secular wealth, both noble and common, and it spread throughout Europe, with examples in every corner.

The idea of absolutism dominated individual as well as collective psychology in the baroque age, each man governing his life like an absolute monarch. Balthasar Gracian advises the courtier: "Let all your actions be those of a king, or at least worthy of a king in due proportion to your estate." Every man was inwardly a king. The ego, or the superego, became an entity which recognized no limits beyond itself . . . The baroque artist exercised this sovereignty "in due proportion to his estate" as Balthasar Gracian would have any man do; that is, his art. The seventeenth century produced artists who, if not solitaries, were at least independent men . . . who considered their art, even if it depended upon commissions, as a personal activity, allowing no limits to be placed on their creative power.[2]

Individual paintings exhibit clear individuality. Virtuosity emerged as each artist sought to establish a style that was distinctly his own. Baroque style was nearly universal in the period between 1600 and 1725.

COUNTER-REFORMATION BAROQUE

Counter-Reformation Baroque art was art in the Baroque style which pursued the objectives and visions of the Roman Catholic Church after the Council of Trent.

12.12 Caravaggio, *The Calling of St. Matthew*, c. 1596–98. Oil on canvas, 11 ft 1 in x 11 ft 5 ins (3.38 x 3.48 m). Contarelli Chapel, Santo Luigi dei Francesi, Rome.

Caravaggio

In Rome—the center of early Baroque—papal patronage and the Counter-Reformation spirit brought artists together to make Rome the "most beautiful city of the entire Christian world." Caravaggio (1569–1609) was probably the most significant of the Roman Baroque painters, and in his works we can see his extraordinary style, in which verisimilitude is carried to new heights. In *The Calling of St. Matthew* (Fig. **12.12**) highlight and shadow create a dynamic portrayal of the moment when the future apostle is touched by divine grace. However, we find here a religious subject depicted in contemporary terms. Realistic imagery turns away from idealized and rhetorical form, and presents itself, rather, in a mundane form. The call from Christ streams, with dramatic chiaroscuro, across the two groups of figures via the powerful gesture of Christ to Matthew. Focus occurs through counterthrust of implied line. As Matthew looks down, the others' eyes lead us to Christ, whose gesture, and that of the figure in the center of the grouping, point to Matthew. This great painting expresses one of the central themes of Counter-Reformation belief: that faith and grace are open to all who have the courage and simplicity to transcend intellectual pride, and that the spiritual understanding is a personal, mysterious and overpowering emotional experience.

The splendor of the Baroque was particularly noticeable in sculpture. Form and space were charged with energy, which carried beyond the limits of actual physical confines in the same sense as did Bologna's work. As with painting, sculpture appealed to the emotions through an inwardly directed vision that invited participation rather than neutral observation. Feeling was the focus. Baroque sculpture also treated space pictorially, almost like a painting, to describe action scenes rather than single sculptural forms. The best examples we can draw upon are those of the sculptor Gianlorenzo Bernini (1598–1680).

Bernini

David (Fig. **12.13**) exudes dynamic power, action, and emotion as he curls to unleash his stone at a Goliath standing somewhere outside the statue's frame. Our eyes sweep upward along a diagonally curved line and are propelled outward by the concentrated emotion of David's expression. A wealth of detail occupies the composition. Detail is part of the work, elegant in nature but ornamental in character. Repetition of the curvilinear theme carries throughout the work in deep, rich, and fully contoured form. Again the viewer participates emotionally, feels the

12.13 Bernini, *David*, 1623. Marble, height 67 ins (170 cm). Galleria Borghese, Rome.

drama, and responds to the sensuous contours of dramatically articulated muscles. Bernini's *David* flexes and contracts in action, rather than repressing pent-up energy as did Michelangelo's giant-slayer (Fig. **11.81**).

ARISTOCRATIC BAROQUE

Aristocratic Baroque was art in the general Baroque style which reflected the visions and purposes of the aristocracy. At this time, the power of the aristocracy had become increasingly threatened by the growing bourgeoisie, or middle class.

12.14 Peter Paul Rubens, *The Assumption of the Virgin*, c. 1626. Oil on wood, 49⅜ x 37⅛ ins (125 x 94 cm). The National Gallery of Art, Washington DC (Samuel H. Kress Collection).

Rubens

Peter Paul Rubens (1577–1640) painted in the Baroque style with vast, overwhelming canvases and fleshy female nudes. His work also illustrates the use of art as religious propaganda. In *The Assumption of the Virgin* (Fig. **12.14**) he presents a swirling and complex composition full of lively action, color, and curvilinear repetition. Typical of Rubens are corpulent cupids and women whose flesh has a sense of softness and warmth we find in few other artists. Rubens's colors here are warm and predominantly limited to the red end of the spectrum. A diagonal sweep of green pulls through the figures in the upper left, but like all the low-value colors in this painting, it is subdued in brilliance. As a result the composition shows a strong contrast in light and dark and in lively and subdued tones.

This work swirls comfortably through its uniformly curvilinear line. Detail is richly naturalistic, but each finely rendered part is subordinate to the whole. Rubens leads the eye around the painting, upward, downward, inward, and outward, occasionally escaping the frame entirely. Nevertheless, he maintains a High Renaissance central triangle beneath the complexity, thus holding the broad base of the painting solidly in place and leading the eye upward to the lovely face of the Virgin at the apex. The overall feeling inspired by this painting is one of richness, glamor, decorativeness, and emotional optimism. Religious and artistic appeal is to worldly emotion and not to intellectualism or mystical asceticism.

Rubens produced works at a prolific rate, primarily because he ran what was virtually a painting factory, where he employed numerous artists and apprentices to assist in his work. He priced his paintings on the basis of their size and on the basis of how much actual work he, personally, did on them. We should not be overly disturbed by this fact, especially when we consider the individual qualities and concepts expressed in his work. His unique Baroque style emerges from every painting, and even an untutored observer can recognize a Rubens with relative ease. Clearly artistic value here lies in the conception, not merly in the handiwork.

BOURGEOIS BAROQUE

Bourgeois Baroque was art in the Baroque style which reflected the visions and objectives of the new and wealthy middle class, the bourgeoisie. The wealth of this class in some cases was greater than that of the aristocracy, and, as a result, a power struggle was at hand.

Rembrandt

Rembrandt van Rijn (1606–69), in contrast to Rubens, could be called a middle-class artist. Born in Leiden, he trained under local artists and then moved to Amsterdam. His early and rapid success gained him many commissions and students. Rembrandt became what can only be called the first capitalist artist. He believed that the quality of art was represented not only in itself but also in its market value. He reportedly spent huge sums of money in buying his own works to increase their value.

Rembrandt's genius lay in depicting human emotions and characters. He suggests rather than depicts great detail, a characteristic we can find in *The Night Watch*, one of his greatest works (Fig. **12.15**). He concentrates here on atmosphere and shadow, implication and emotion. As in most Baroque art, the viewer is invited to share in an emotion, to enter into an experience rather than to observe as an impartial witness.

12.15 Rembrandt van Rijn, *The Night Watch* (*The Company of Captain Frans Burnign Cocq*), 1642. Oil on canvas, 12 ft 2 ins x 14 ft 6 ins (3.7 x 4.44 m). Rijksmuseum, Amsterdam.

The huge canvas now in the Rijksmuseum in Amsterdam is only a portion of the original, which was cut down in the eighteenth century to fit into a space in the Town Hall of Amsterdam and no longer shows the bridge over which the members of the watch were about to cross. Group portraits, especially of military units, were popular at the time. They usually showed the company in a social setting such as a gathering around a banquet table. Rembrandt chose to break with the norm and portrayed the company, led by Captain Cocq, as if on duty. The result was a scene of greater vigor and dramatic intensity true to the Baroque spirit, but it displeased his patrons.

A recent cleaning has revealed the vivid color of the original; however, its dramatic highlights and shadows reflect no natural light whatsoever. Although the painting is now a good deal brighter than in its previous state, no analysis of light can solve the problem of how these figures are illuminated. Another problem lies in the very title of the work. It has been suggested that this is, in fact, a "Day Watch," so that the intense light at the center of the work is explained as morning sunlight. However, an examination of the highlights and shadows in the painting shows that Rembrandt has based his choice of light for dramatic purposes only. While the figures are rendered with a fair degree of verisimilitude, no such claim can be made for the light sources.

BAROQUE MUSIC

The adjectives generally used to describe Baroque painting and sculpture—ornate, complex and emotionally appealing—are applicable in a non-visual sense to music. Reflective of the systematic rationalism of the era, Baroque music stressed a refined systematizing of harmonic progression around tonal centers and led to tonal concepts of harmonic progression and major and minor keys that were basic to Western music for the next 300 years.

Baroque composers also began to write for specific instruments, in contrast to previous practices of writing music that might be either sung or played. They also brought to their music implicit forces of action and tension—for example, strong and immediate contrasts in tonal color or volume, and rhythmic strictness played against improvisatory freedom. The Baroque era produced great geniuses in music and many new ideas, new instruments, and, most significantly, an entirely new form, opera.

Handel—The Messiah

Another major development in the same vein was the *oratorio*. Broad in scale like an opera, it combined a sacred subject with a poetic text, and, like the cantata, was designed for concert performances, without scenery or costume. Many oratorios could be staged and have highly developed dramatic content with soloists portraying specific characters. Oratorio began in Italy in the early seventeenth century, but all other oratorio accomplishments pale in comparison with the works of its greatest master, George Frederick Handel (1685–1759). Although Handel was German by birth he lived in England and wrote his oratorios in English. His works continue to enjoy wide popularity, and each year his *Messiah* has thousands of performances around the world. Most of Handel's oratorios are highly dramatic in structure and contain exposition, conflict or complication and *denouement* or resolution sections. Many could be staged in full operatic tradition (except for two outstanding examples, *Israel in Egypt* and the *Messiah*). Woven carefully into the complex structure of Handel's oratorios was a strong reliance on the chorus. His choral sections (as well as his arias and recitatives) are carefully developed and often juxtapose complex polyphonic sections and homophonic sections. Each choral movement has its own internal structure, which, like the oratorio itself, rises to a climax and resolves to a conclusion. Most of the solo and choral sections of Handel's oratorios can stand on their own as performance pieces. They also fit magnificently together in a systematic development, losing their separate importance to the overall composition.

The most popular of all oratorios, Handel's *Messiah*, was written in 1741 in twenty-four days. The work is divided into three parts: the birth of Jesus; Jesus's death and resurrection; and the redemption of humanity. The music comprises an overture, choruses, recitatives, and arias, and is written for small orchestra, chorus, and soloists. The choruses provide some of the world's best-loved music, including the famous *Hallelujah Chorus*.

The chorus *For Unto Us a Child is Born* is the climax of the first part. First, the orchestra presents the opening theme and then the voices restate it (Fig. **12.16**).

12.16 (*right*) Handel, *For Unto Us a Child is Born*, opening theme of chorus.

Later the texture will alternate between polyphonic (contrapuntal) and homophonic (chordal). The opening key is G major, which then modulates to D major and C major, returning to G major. The meter is quadruple, and the tempo lively; the chorus quickly moves into long melismatic passages—that is, single words sustained over many notes. These melismas are characteristic of Handel's works. The climax of the chorus comes with the words "and his name shall be called Wonderful! Counselor!" Over the course of the piece that text is repeated three times. A second theme appears before the climax and consists of a rising and falling melodic contour with a new phrase of text (Fig. **12.17**).

The structure of the piece works around an alternation of the first and second themes. The chorus ends with a repeat of the opening theme in the orchestra.

12.17 Handel, *For Unto Us a Child is Born*, second theme of chorus.

Bach—Fugue in G Minor

Bach's organ compositions are famous for their drama, bold pedal solos, and virtuoso techniques. The *Fugue in G Minor*, or "Little Fugue," is a characteristic example.

The *fugue* is a polyphonic development of one, two, or sometimes three short themes. Fugal form, which takes its name from the Latin *fuga* ("flight"), has a traditional scheme of seven elements, only some of which may be found in any given fugue. However, two characteristics are common to all fugues: first, counterpoint and, second, a clear dominant-tonic relationship—that is, imitation of the theme or subject at the fifth above or below the tonic. Each voice in a fugue develops the basic subject independently from the other voices, and passes through as many of the seven elements as the composer deems necessary. Unification is achieved not by return to an opening section, as in closed form, but by the varying recurrences of the subject throughout.

The *Fugue in G Minor* is typical of Bach's fugues in that the texture begins as a monophonic phrase that is followed with polyphony. This fugue has four voices, and the subject is stated in the top voice and then answered by the alto voice (Fig. **12.18**).

12.18 Bach, *Fugue in G Minor*, statement of subject.

The meter is duple and the texture monophonic, moving to polyphony or counterpoint. The exposition of the piece closes after the subject has been stated in each of the four voices. Immediately following the exposition Bach inserts a brief episode based on the first three notes of the subject. The work then modulates to the dominant key of D minor and returns to a restatement of the subject in this new key. Below the restatement of the subject and counter-subject, all of which is somewhat hidden in a complex texture, Bach sustains a bass pedal tone, called a pedal point, a characteristic element of the fugue.

Once he has restated the subject and counter-subject in the dominant key, he makes a brief statement on the subject in a third key, B-flat major, the relative major to G minor. In this episode Bach presents the subject and counter-subject once each. A third episode follows and remains in B flat, stating the subject and counter-subject once more. In a fourth episode, based on the first, the fugue not only restates the subject but changes its rhythmic pattern as well. The ending episode of the piece moves into a complex harmonic development in several keys and homophonic texture, climaxing in a rising chromatic scale and ending in a strong cadence. The final statement of the subject comes in the bass line.

COURT BAROQUE

Absolutism at Versailles

Probably no monarch better represents the absolutism of the Baroque era than Louis XIV, and no artwork better represents the magnificence and grandeur of the Baroque style than does the Palace of Versailles and its sculpture and grounds—a grand design of buildings and nature to reflect man's systematic rationalism. The great Versailles complex grew from the modest hunting lodge of Louis XIII into the grand palace of the Sun King over a number of years, involving several architects and amid curious political and religious circumstances.

The Versailles château was rebuilt in 1631 by Philibert Le Roy. The façade was decorated by Louis Le Vau with bricks and stone, sculpture, wrought iron and gilt lead. In

12.19 The Queen's Staircase, Palace of Versailles.

12.20 Louis de Vau and Jules Hardouin-Mansart, garden façade, Palace of Versailles, 1669–85.

1668 Louis XIV ordered Le Vau to enlarge the château by enclosing it in a stone envelope containing the king's and queen's apartments (Fig. 12.19). The city side of the château retains the spirit of Louis XIII, but the park side reflects classical French influence (Fig. 12.20). François d'Orbay and, later, Jules Hardouin-Mansart expanded the château into a palace whose west façade extends over 2,000 ft (609 m). The palace became Louis XIV's permanent residence in 1682. French royalty was at the height of its power and Versailles was the symbol of the Divine Right of Kings—the absolute authority of the monarch.

As much care, elegance, and precision was employed on the interior as on the exterior. With the aim of developing French commerce, Louis XIV had his court live in unparalleled luxury. He also decided to furnish his château permanently, something which was unheard of. The result was a fantastically rich and beautiful set of furnishings. Royal manufactories produced mirrors, tapestries, and brocades. The highest quality was required, and these furnishings became highly sought after in Europe. Le Brun kept a meticulous eye on anything for the State Apartments, such as the creation of statues the design of ceilings. The grounds are adorned throughout with fountains and statues. The Fountain of Apollo (Fig. 12.21) emphasizes the symbolism of the gardens and sits astride the east–west axis of the grounds. This magnificent composition by Tuby was originally covered with gold. The sculpture was executed from a drawing by Le Brun and inspired by a painting by Albani. It continues the theme of allegorical glorification of *Le Roi Soleil* by representing the break of day, as the sun god rises in his chariot from the waters. Apollo was the perfect symbol for Louis XIV, whose absolutism shone in glorious Baroque splendor.

12.21 The Fountain of Apollo, Palace of Versailles.

JAPAN

In the middle of the sixteenth century, civil war was a constant feature of the Japanese landscape. In 1603, Tokugawa Ieyasu became shogun and established his capital at Edo (Tokyo), Christianity was outlawed, and all ports were closed to outside trade; the only exception was the port of Nagasaki, where the Dutch trading post of the East India Company was established in 1641. The seventeenth century witnessed impressive economic growth and a tripling of the population to more than thirty million. Samurai were forced to live in towns near their masters. They became an administrative class responsible for managing the revenue of the shogun. The samurai attended special schools in which, among other subjects, they were taught Neo-Confucianism. Japanese society became increasingly urban through the eighteenth century, and a strong middle class of merchants and artisans developed. The arts flourished; the puppet theatre and the Kabuki theatre emerged. The reign of the Tokugawa shoguns was at its peak.

In the nineteenth century, although the emperor tried to close the country to foreign influences, some Japanese intellectuals became interested in Western ideas that filtered throughout the country from the port of Nagasaki. From the beginning of the century revolts became more frequent, and in the Southwest, where vassals were more prosperous, the control of the shoguns dissolved. At the same time, there was increasing Western pressure on Japan to establish free trade, and in 1844 King William II of the Netherlands demanded that she open her ports. The shogun refused, but in 1853 Commodore Perry of the American navy brought his fleet into Edo harbor. Under threat of military intervention the shogunate agreed in the following year to a treaty with the United States which brought about an end to Japanese isolationism. The reign of the Tokugawas collapsed as a result.

A series of particularly unfavorable trade agreements forced on Japan by the more powerful West caused the samurai to grow increasingly xenophobic and led to numerous provincial revolts and violent protests. As a result, certain reforms were put in place to ensure that the growth of a Western-style industry was leavened by the benefits of "Japanese spirit." "Enrich the country, strengthen the army" was the slogan. The effort was successful, and Japan emerged as a prosperous, stable, and efficient member of the industrialized world.

JAPANESE STYLE IN PAINTING

Nonomura Sotatsu was a highly creative painter of the late sixteenth and early seventeenth centuries. In contrast with other Japanese painters, who tended to use Chinese motifs and patterns, Sosatsu painted in a style that emphasized boldness, severity, and asymmetry. His silhouettes are simplified and he deftly broadened his use of colors and ink. He developed a notable skill in fading the edges of color areas, and in creating blurred and pooled effects in wet colors by allowing ink and color to run together. He also looked to sources in Japanese traditions for his subject matter. His hanging paper scroll *Zen Priest Choka* (Fig. **12.22**) shows the priest sitting in a tree. The remarkable aspect of this painting is its use of space. The subject occupies only a small portion of the work. The tree in which Choka sits is only faintly suggested at the left border: Its trunk and limbs ebb and flow up the boundary and give us a glimpse here and there of their presence, but mostly leave a full configuration to our imaginations. The priest himself is curiously de-emphasized: Sotatsu portrays him with pale color and soft lines of medium tonality. Although most of the painting is void of images, it is fully in balance. Sotatsu has cleverly divided the universe of this work into halves divided on the lower left/upper right diagonals. This is a fascinating example of how philosophically and visually something can be balanced by nothing.

12.22 Nonomura Sotatsu, *The Zen Priest Choka*, Japanese, late 16th century. Ink on paper, 37¾ × 15¼ ins (95.9 × 38.7 cm). The Cleveland Museum of Art, Norman O. Stone and Ella A. Stone Memorial Fund.

12.23 Vase, Japanese, late 17th century, Imari ware. Porcelain, 22 ins (55.9 cm) high. The Cleveland Museum of Art, Gift of Ralph King, 19.837.

IMARI PORCELAIN

Chinese influence also can be found in the development of ceramics as an art form in Japan. The discovery of porcelain clay in Japan in the early seventeenth century, and the importation of Chinese techniques led to some remarkable accomplishments in ceramic art. Typical of Japanese mastery of this medium is an Imari porcelain from the late seventeenth century (Fig. **12.23**). The exquisite recurved silhouette of this piece has a relaxing flow. The proportions call attention to themselves as the design divides in half at the top of the lower bowl, is balanced by a gracefully slim neck that enlarges into an asymmetrical bulb, and ends in a delicate lip at the top. The ornate flowers have elegance and fine detail that give the vase delicacy and refinement. Typical of this style of ceramics is the inclusion of Europeans: Dutch and Portuguese men, as well as Western ships, often appear.

KABUKI THEATRE

Kabuki theatre has changed significantly since the mid sixteenth century because of its abilities to shift with the tides and to incorporate aspects of other theatre traditions. It has borrowed freely from Noh drama and from the popular Japanese puppet theatre whose plays and stage machinery it also has incorporated. This form of drama began as "middle-class theatre," and, as such, was the object of contempt by the samurai and the court. The earliest Kabuki plays were simple sketches; two-act plays did not appear until the middle of the seventeenth century. By the middle of the eighteenth century, the plays of the popular writer Takeda Izumo (1691–1756) reached eleven acts in length, and required a day to perform. However, the most important Kabuki playwright was the legendary seventeenth-century writer Chikamatsu.

The focus of a Kabuki play tends to be a climactic moment, as opposed to plot. Connections between scenes in Kabuki plays tend to be very vague, in contrast with much of Western theatre, whose plot development follows a causal scheme. Productions continue to be lengthy, although the day-long practice of the eighteenth century has been pared back to two five-hour performances per day. A narrator and chorus play predominant roles in Kabuki productions, because actors do not sing. The narrator describes the scene, comments on the action, and even speaks portions of the dialogue. The overall style of Kabuki drama tends to be somewhere between convention and depiction. Every location is portrayed scenically, and scenery is changed in full view of the audience.

12.24 Katsushika Hokusai, page from *Manga*, vol. 8, 1817. Woodcut, 9×5¾ ins (22.8×14.6 cm). British Museum, London.

JAPANESE STYLE IN PRINTMAKING

In the nineteenth century as Japan began to look westward, the style of the country's two-dimensional art began to evolve as well, and we can see some of these changes in the works of two printmakers, Katsushika Hokusai and Ando Hiroshige. Hokusai broadened his subject matter to include all aspects of Japanese life. In particular, his prints document in detail the streetlife in and around Edo. When he was finished, his works filled fifteen volumes, entitled *Manga*, which he began to publish in 1814. His treatment of the human condition is full of vibrancy, virility, and humor, and his works show humankind in all its contrasting nobility and gracelessness. In a woodcut from *Manga* he portrays acrobats in various attitudes (Fig. **12.24**). They seem oblivious of any observer, and their antics reveal an earthy forthrightness that seems totally at odds

12.25 Katsushika Hokusai, *The Great Wave off Kanazawa*, 1823–9. Polychrome woodblock print, 10 × 14¾ ins (25.5 × 37.5 cm). Victoria and Albert Museum, London.

12.26 (opposite) Ando Hiroshige, *Maple Leaves at the Tekona Shrine, Mamma*, 1857. Polychrome woodblock print, 13¾ × 9¾ ins (35 × 24 cm). British Museum, London.

with the graceful power one would normally associate with them. They seem cartoonish caricatures, and yet there is vitality, energy, and suppleness within the unflattering representation.

In his landscapes, Hokusai forged new directions in Japanese art. In *The Great Wave off Kanazawa*, for example (Fig. **12.25**), he gives us a boldly colored rendering that is neither realistic nor idealized. While Mount Fuji reposes calmly in the background, the great wave breaks over the boats with raging fury, and the foam reaches out like grasping fingers to crash down on the fragile craft. There is a new sense of directness here, and yet his response to natural forms and his decorative patterning lies firmly within the traditions of Japanese art. A similar freshness can be seen in the strongly colored landscape, *Maple Leaves at the Tekona Shrine, Mamma*, by Ando Hiroshige (Fig. **12.26**). Unlike the perspective treatment of artists we have previously seen, he generates deep space in a novel fashion, by using the foreground to "frame" the distance. He uses neither linear nor atmospheric perspective to achieve the illusion of deep space, and, yet, the portrayal appears rational. The distance seems logical even if the colors and details are the same in foreground and background. Only the trees exhibit any degree of foreshortening. Our vision is pulled back and forth in space as the red maple leaves—placed directly in our line of sight to the distance—constantly compete with middle

ground and background for our attention. Thus, we are invited to focus on the series of huts staggered across a line, which divides the print into fourths. Downward deflecting leaves and a strong, dark border redirect us into the painting at the top, while the framing diagonals of the tree trunks carry us back into the lower fourth of the work. There is clever manipulation of hue, value, and contrast to keep us interested and controlled. The red leaves and complementary gray-green limbs and mountains strike a completely harmonious visual chord, and the ocher grass, thatched roofs, and lightened sky stand in contrast—both in tone and value—to create a counterpoint and to hold our vision stable in the center of the work.

THE ENLIGHTENMENT

The eighteenth century in Europe was an age of change and revolution in some areas and prosperous stability in others. The idea of the absolute monarch was challenged—though with varying success. The middle class rose to demand its place in society, and the human condition—social philosophy in action—attempted to make a place for all classes in the scheme of things. Knowledge, for the *philosophes*, was a transcendent and universal goal. The *philosophes* were writers and scholars who undertook the challenge of making the great ideas and texts of human intellect accessible to the general public. In short, they were popularizers. The aristocracy found itself in decline, and the Rococo style reflected their increasingly superficial and delicate condition. The pendulum then swung back from exquisite refinement and artifice to intellectual seriousness, at least for a while. The structural clarity of Classicism returned in painting, sculpture, and architecture, and above all in music, which found the culmination of a remarkable century in works of emotional depth and formal inventiveness. The cult of "sensibility" with which the century closed presaged the upheavals of *Sturm und Drang* and the Romantics.

ROCOCO

The change from grand Baroque courtly life to that of the small salon and intimate townhouse was reflected in a new style of painting called Rococo. This was a product of its time. Rococo art satirized the mores of the age, criticizing with humor the behavior of the times. Its intimate grace, charm, and delicate superficiality tend to reflect the social ideals and manners of the age. Informality replaced formality in life and painting. The logic and academic character of the Baroque of Louis XIV was found lacking in feeling and sensitivity. Its overwhelming scale and grandeur were too ponderous. Deeply dramatic action faded into lively effervescence and melodrama. Love, sentiment, pleasure, and sincerity became predominant themes. None of these characteristics conflicts significantly with the overall tone of the Enlightenment, whose major goal was the refinement of man. The arts of the period dignified the human spirit through social consciousness and bourgeois social morality, as well as through the graceful gamesmanship of love. Delicacy, informality, lack of grandeur, and lack of action did not always imply superficiality or limp sentimentality.

The transitional quandary of the aristocracy can be seen in the Rococo paintings of Antoine Watteau (1683–1721). Although largely sentimental, much of Watteau's work refrains from gaiety or frivolousness. *Embarkation for Cythera* (Fig. **12.27**) illustrates idealized concepts of aristocratic social graces. Cythera is a mythological land

of enchantment, the island of Venus, and Watteau portrays aristocrats as they await departure for that faraway place idling away their time in amorous pursuits. Fantasy qualities in the landscape are created by fuzzy color areas and hazy atmosphere. A soft, undulating line underscores the human figures, all posed in slightly affected attitudes. Watteau's fussy details and decorative treatment of clothing stand in contrast to the diffused quality of the background. Each grouping of couples engages in graceful conversation and love games typical of the age. Delicacy pervades the scene, over which an armless bust of Venus presides. Underlying this dreamlike fantasy there is a deep, poetic melancholy. These doll-like figurines, which are only symbols, engage in sophisticated and elegant pleasure, but the softness and affectation of the work counterbalance gaiety with languid sorrow.

Sculpture struggled in the eighteenth century. The Academy of Sculpture and the French Academy in Rome encouraged the copying of antique sculpture, and resisted changes in style. Sculpture continued in the Baroque style

12.27 Antoine Watteau, *Embarkation for Cythera*, 1717. Oil on canvas, 51 x 76½ ins (129.5 x 194.3 cm). The Louvre, Paris.

12.28 Étienne-Maurice Falconet, *Madame de Pompadour as the Venus of the Doves*, 1782. Marble, height 29½ ins (75 cm). The National Gallery of Art, Washington DC (Samuel H. Kress Collection).

Claude Michel, best known as Clodion, reinforces the delicate themes of the time in dynamic miniatures such as the *Satyr and Bacchante* (Fig. **12.29**). "His groups of accurately modeled figures in erotic abandon are made all the fresher and more alluring by his knowing use of pinkish terracotta as if it were actually pulsating flesh, rendering each incipient embrace 'forever warm and still to be enjoyed'."[3]

Rococo also exhibited itself in interior design. Its refinement and decorativeness applied nicely to furniture and décor. The difference between opulence and delicacy

12.29 Clodion (Claude Michel), *Satyr and Bacchante*, c. 1775. Terracotta, height 23¼ ins (59 cm). The Metropolitan Museum of Art, New York (Bequest of Benjamin Altman, 1913 [14.40.687]).

and lacked originality. Rococo style did find expression in the work of Falconet (1716–91) and Clodion (1738–1814), with their myriad decorative cupids, nymphs, and so on, recurring motifs in painting of this style. Venus appears frequently, often depicted in the thinly disguised form of a prominent lady of the day. Madame de Pompadour, who epitomized love, charm, grace, and delicacy for the French, appears often as a subject in sculpture as well as in painting. Rococo sculpture was not on the monumental scale of its predecessors. Rather, in the spirit of decoration that marked the era, sculpture often took the form of delicate and graceful porcelain and metal figurines. Falconet's *Madame de Pompadour as the Venus of the Doves* (Fig. **12.28**) fully captures the erotic sensuality, delicacy, lively intelligence, and charm of the Rococo heritage. The unpretentious nudity indicates the complete comfort and naturalness the eighteenth century found in love and affairs of the flesh.

Rococo sculpture exhibits masterful technique. Its surface textures, detail, and line all display superb delicacy and control of the medium. If this style and the society it exemplifies is found wanting in profundity, it must be admired for its technical achievement.

12.30 G.H. Krohne, The Music Room, 1742–51. Thuringer Museum, Eisenach, Germany.

was apparent. Figure **12.30** shows a polygonal music room characteristic of German Rococo. Broken wall surfaces made possible stucco decoration of floral branches in a pseudo-naturalistic effect. In Venice curved leg furniture, cornices, and gilded carvings were *à la mode*. French designer François de Cuvilliés (1695–1768) combined refinement, lightness, and reduced scale to produce a pleasant atmosphere of grace and propriety (Fig. **12.31**).

12.31 Francois de Cuvilliés, The Pagondenburg, c. 1722. Schloss Nymphenburg, Munich, Germany.

Jonathan Swift—A Modest Proposal

Jonathan Swift (1667–1745) was an Anglo-Irish satirist and churchman. His *Gulliver's Travels* mocked pomposity and woolly-headed idealism equally, while his other famous work in prose, *A Modest Proposal* (included here), took satire to the very edge of horror with its chillingly deadpan suggestion that the English should solve the "Irish Problem" by eating the babies of the poor. He represents enlightened Rococo spirit in literature.

For Preventing the Children of Poor People in Ireland from Being a Burden to Their Parents or Country, and for Making Them Beneficial to the Public

It is a melancholy object to those who walk through this great town or travel in the country, when they see the streets, the roads and cabin doors, crowded with beggars of the female sex, followed by three, four, or six children, all in rags and importuning every passenger for an alms. These mothers, instead of being able to work for their honest livelihood, are forced to employ all their time in strolling to beg sustenance for their helpless infants, who, as they grow up, either turn thieves for want of work, or leave their dear native country to fight for the Pretender in Spain, or sell themselves to the Barbadoes.

I think it is agreed by all parties that this prodigious number of children in the arms, or on the backs, or at the heels of their mothers, and frequently of their fathers, is in the present deplorable state of the kingdom a very great additional grievance; and therefore whoever could find out a fair, cheap, and easy method of making these children sound, useful members of the commonwealth would deserve so well of the public as to have his statue set up for a preserver of the nation.

But my intention is very far from being confined to provide only for the children of professed beggars; it is of a much greater extent, and shall take in the whole number of infants at a certain age who are born of parents in effect as little able to support them as those who demand our charity in the streets.

As to my own part, having turned my thoughts for many years upon this important subject, and maturely weighed the several schemes of other projectors, I have always found them grossly mistaken in their computation. It is true, a child just dropped from its dam may be supported by her milk for a solar year, with little other nourishment; at most not above the value of two shillings which the mother may certainly get, or the value in scraps, by her lawful occupation of begging; and it is exactly at one year old that I propose to provide for them in such a manner as instead of being a charge upon their parents or the parish, or wanting food and raiment for the rest of their lives, they shall on the contrary contribute to the feeding, and partly to the clothing, of many thousands.

There is likewise another great advantage in my scheme, that it will prevent those voluntary abortions, and that horrid practice of women murdering their bastard children, alas, too frequent among us, sacrificing the poor innocent babes, I doubt, more to avoid the expense than the shame, which would move tears and pity in the most savage and inhuman breast.

The number of souls in this kingdom being usually reckoned one million and a half, of these I calculate there may be about two hundred thousand couples whose wives are breeders; from which number I subtract thirty thousand couples who are able to maintain their own children, although I apprehend there cannot be so many under the present distresses of the kingdom; but this being granted, there will remain an hundred and seventy thousand breeders. I again subtract fifty thousand for those women who miscarry, or whose children die by accident or disease within the year. There only remain an hundred and twenty thousand children of poor parents annually born. The question therefore is, how this number shall be reared and provided for, which, as I have already said, under the present situation of affairs, is utterly impossible by all the methods hitherto proposed. For we can neither employ them in handicraft or agriculture; we neither build houses (I mean in the country) nor cultivate land. They can very seldom pick up a livelihood by stealing till they arrive at six years old, except where they are of towardly parts; although I confess they learn the rudiments much earlier, during which time they can however be looked upon only as probationers, as I have been informed by a principal gentleman in the county of Cavan, who protested to me that he never knew above one or two instances under the age of six, even in a part of the kingdom so renowned for the quickest proficiency in that art.

I am assured by our merchants that a boy or a girl before twelve years old is no salable commodity; and even when they come to this age they will not yield above three pounds, or three pounds and half a crown at most on the Exchange; which cannot turn to account either to the parents or the kingdom, the charge of nutriment and rags having been at least four times that value.

I shall now therefore humbly propose my own thoughts, which I hope will not be liable to the least objection.

I have been assured by a very knowing American of my acquaintance in London, that a young healthy child well nursed is at a year old a most delicious, nourishing, and wholesome food, whether stewed, roasted, baked, or boiled; and I make no doubt that it will equally serve in a fricassee or a ragout.

I do therefore humbly offer it to public consideration that of the hundred and twenty thousand children, already computed, twenty thousand may be reserved for breed, whereof only one fourth part to be males, which is more than we allow to sheep, black cattle, or swine; and my reason is that those children are seldom the fruits of marriage, a circumstance not much regarded by our savages, therefore one male will be sufficient to serve four females. That the remaining hundred thousand may at a year old be offered in sale to the persons of quality and fortune through the kingdom, always advising the mother to let them suck plentifully in the last month, so as to render them plump and fat for a good table. A child will make two dishes at an entertainment for friends; and when the family dines alone, the fore or hind quarter will make a reasonable, dish, and seasoned with a little pepper or salt will be very good boiled on the fourth day, especially in winter.

I have reckoned upon a medium that a child just born will weigh twelve pounds, and in a solar year if tolerably nursed increaseth to twenty-eight pounds.

I grant this food will be somewhat dear, and therefore very proper for landlords, who, as they have already devoured most of the parents, seem to have the best title to the children.

Infant's flesh will be in season throughout the year, but more plentiful in March, and a little before and after. For we are told by a grave author, an eminent French physician, that fish being a prolific diet, there are more children born in Roman Catholic countries about nine months after Lent than at any other season; therefore, reckoning a year after Lent, the markets will be more glutted than usual, because the number of popish infants is at least three to one in this kingdom; and therefore it will have one other collateral advantage, by lessening the number of Papists among us.

I have already computed the charge of nursing a beggar's child (in which list I reckon all cottagers, laborers, and four fifths of the farmers) to be about two shillings per annum, rags included; and I believe no gentleman would repine to give ten shillings for the carcass of a good fat child, which, as I have said, will make four dishes of excellent nutritive meat, when he hath only some particular friend or his own family to dine with him. Thus the squire will learn to be a good landlord, and grow popular among the tenants; the mother will have eight shillings net profit, and be fit for work till she produces another child.

Those who are more thrifty (as I must confess the times require) may flay the carcass; the skin of which artificially dressed will make admirable gloves for ladies, and summer boots for fine gentlemen.

As to our city of Dublin, shambles may be appointed for this purpose in the most convenient parts of it, and butchers we may be assured will not be wanting; although I rather recommend buying the children alive, and dressing them hot from the knife as we do roasting pigs.

A very worthy person, a true lover of his country, and whose virtues I highly esteem, was lately pleased in discoursing on this matter to offer a refinement upon my scheme. He said that many gentlemen of this kingdom, having of late destroyed their deer, be conceived that the want of venison might be well supplied by the bodies of young lads and maidens, not exceeding fourteen years of age nor under twelve, so great a number of both sexes in every county being now ready to starve for want of work and service; and these to be disposed of by their parents, if alive, or otherwise by their nearest relations. But with due deference to so excellent a friend and so deserving a patriot, I cannot be altogether in his sentiments, for as to the males, my American acquaintance assured me from frequent experience that their flesh was generally tough and lean, like that of our schoolboys, by continual exercise, and their taste disagreeable; and to fatten them would not answer the charge. Then as to the females, it would, I think with humble submission, be a loss to the public, because they soon would become breeders themselves; and besides, it is not improbable that some scrupulous people might be apt to censure such a practice (although indeed very unjustly) as a little bordering upon cruelty; which I confess, hath always been with me the strongest objection against any project, how well soever intended.

But in order to justify my friend, he confessed that this expedient was put into his head by the famous Psalmanazar, a native of the island Formosa, who came from thence to London above twenty years ago, and in conversation told my friend that in his country when any young person happened to be put to death, the executioner sold the carcass to persons of quality as a prime dainty; and that in his time the body of a plump girl of fifteen, who was crucified for an attempt to poison the emperor, was sold to his Imperial Majesty's prime minister of state, and other great mandarins of the court, in joints from the gibbet, at four hundred crowns. Neither indeed can I deny that if the same use were made of several plump young girls in this town, who without one single groat to the fortunes cannot stir abroad without a chair, and appear at the playhouse and assemblies in foreign fineries which they never will pay for, the kingdom would not be the worse.

Some persons of a desponding spirit are in great concern about that vast number of poor people who are aged, diseased, or maimed, and I have been desired to employ my thoughts what course may be taken to ease the nation of so grievous an encumbrance. But I am not in the least pain upon that matter, because it is very well known that they are every day dying and rotting by cold and famine, and filth and vermin, as fast as can be reasonably expected. And as to the younger laborers, they are now in almost as hopeful a condition. They cannot get work and consequently pine away for want of nourishment to a degree that if at any time they are accidentally hired to common labor, they have not strength to perform it; and thus the country and themselves are happily delivered from the evils to come.

I have too long digressed, and therefore shall return to my subject. I think the advantages by the proposal which I have made are obvious and many, as well as of the highest importance.

For first, as I have already observed, it would greatly lessen the number of Papists, with whom we are yearly overrun, being the principal breeders of the nation as well as our most dangerous enemies; and who stay at home on purpose to deliver the kingdom to the Pretender, hoping to take their advantage by the absence of so many good Protestants, who have chosen rather to leave their country than stay at home and pay tithes against their conscience to an Episcopal curate.

Secondly, the poorer tenants will have something valuable of their own, which by law be made liable to distress, and help to pay their landlord's rent, their corn and cattle being already seized and money a thing unknown.

Thirdly, whereas the maintenance of an hundred thousand children, from two years old and upwards, cannot be computed at less than ten shillings a piece per annum, the nation's stock will be thereby increased fifty thousand pounds per annum, besides the profit of a new dish introduced to the tables of all gentlemen of fortune in the kingdom who have any refinement in taste. And the money will circulate among ourselves, the goods being entirely of our own growth and manufacture.

Fourthly, the constant breeders, besides the gain of eight shillings sterling per annum by the sale of their children, will be rid of the charge of maintaining them after the first year.

Fifthly, this food would likewise bring great custom to taverns, where the vintners will certainly be so prudent as to procure the best receipts for dressing it to perfection, and consequently have their houses frequented by all the fine gentlemen, who justly value themselves upon their knowledge in good eating; and a skillful cook, who understands how to oblige his guests, will contrive to make it as expensive as they please.

Sixthly, this would be a great inducement to marriage, which all wise nations have either encouraged by rewards or enforced by laws and penalties. It would increase the care and tenderness of mothers toward their children, when they were sure of a settlement for life to the poor babes, provided in some sort by the public, to their annual profit instead of expense. We should see an honest emulation among the married women, which of them could bring the fattest child to the market. Men would become as fond of their wives during the time of their pregnancy as they are now of their mares in foal, their cows in calf, or sows when they are ready to farrow; nor offer to beat or kick them (as is too frequent a practice) for fear of a miscarriage.

Many other advantages might be enumerated. For instance, the addition of some thousand carcasses in our exportation of barreled beef, the propagation of swine's flesh, and improvement in the art of making good bacon, so much wanted among us by the great destruction of pigs, too frequent at our tables, which are no way comparable in taste or magnificence to a well-grown, fat, yearling child, which roasted whole will make a considerable figure at a lord mayor's feast or any other public entertainment. But this and many others I omit, being studious of brevity.

Supposing that one thousand families in this city would be constant customers for infants' flesh, besides others who might have it at merry meetings, particularly weddings and christenings, I compute that Dublin would take off annually about twenty thousand carcasses, and the rest of the kingdom (where probably they will be sold somewhat cheaper) the remaining eighty thousand.

I can think of no one objection that will possibly be raised against this proposal, unless it should be urged that the number of people will be thereby much lessened in the kingdom. This I freely own, and it was indeed one principal design in offering it to the world. I desire the reader will observe, that I calculate my remedy for this one individual kingdom of Ireland and for no other that ever was, is, or I think even can be upon earth. Therefore let no man talk to me of other expedients: of taxing our absentees at five shillings a pound: of using neither clothes nor household furniture except what is of our own growth and manufacture: of utterly rejecting the materials and instruments that promote foreign luxury: of curing the expensiveness of pride, vanity, idleness, and gaming in our women: of introducing a vein of parsimony, prudence, and temperance: of learning to love our country, in the want of which we differ even from Laplanders and the inhabitants of Topinamboo: of quitting our animosities and factions, nor acting any longer like the Jews, who were murdering one another at the very moment their city was taken: of being a little cautious not to sell our country and conscience for nothing: of teaching landlords to have at least one degree of mercy toward their tenants: lastly, of putting a spirit of honesty, industry, and skill into our shopkeepers; who, if a resolution could now be taken to buy only our native goods, would immediately unite to cheat and exact upon us in the price, the measure, and the goodness, nor could ever yet be brought to make one fair proposal of just dealing, though often and earnestly invited to it.

Therefore I repeat, let no man talk to me of these and the like expedients, till he hath at least some glimpse of hope that there will ever be some hearty and sincere attempt to put them in practice.

But as to myself, having been wearied out for many years with offering vain, idle, visionary thoughts, and at length utterly despairing of success, I fortunately fell upon this proposal, which, as it is wholly new, so it hath something solid and real, and no expense and little trouble, full in our own power, and whereby we can incur no danger in disobliging England. For this kind of commodity will not bear exportation, the flesh being of too tender a consistence to admit a long continuance, in salt, although perhaps I could name a country which would be glad to eat up our whole nation without it.

After all, I am not so violently bent upon my own opinion as to reject any offer proposed by wise men, which shall be found equally innocent, cheap, easy, and effectual. But before something of that kind shall be advanced in contradiction to my scheme, and offering a better, I desire the author or authors will be pleased maturely to consider two points. First, as things now stand, how they will be able to find food and raiment for an hundred thousand useless mouths and backs. And secondly, there being a round million of creatures in human figure throughout this kingdom, whose sole subsistence put into a common stock would leave them in debt two millions of pounds sterling, adding those who are beggars by profession to the bulk of farmers, cottagers, and laborers, and their wives and children who are beggars in effect; I desire those politicians who dislike my overture, and may perhaps be so bold to attempt an answer, that they will first ask the parents of these mortals whether they would not at this day think it a great happiness to have been sold for food at a year old in the manner I prescribe, and thereby

have avoided such a perpetual scene of misfortunes as they have since gone through by the oppression of landlords, the impossibility of paying rent without money or trade, the want of common sustenance, with neither house nor clothes to cover them from the inclemencies of the weather, and the most inevitable prospect of entailing the like or greater miseries upon their breed forever.

I profess, in the sincerity of my heart, that I have not the least personal interest in endeavoring to promote this necessary work, having no other motive than the public good of my country, by advancing our trade, providing for infants, relieving the poor, and giving some pleasure to the rich. I have no children by which I can propose to get a single penny; the youngest being nine years old, and my wife past childbearing.[4]

THE HUMAN CONDITION

In strong contrast to the aristocratic frivolity of Rococo style was the biting satire and social comment of enlightened individuals such as William Hogarth (1697–1764) in England in the 1730s. Hogarth portrayed dramatic scenes on moral subjects, and his *Rake's Progress* and *Harlot's Progress* series are an attempt to instil solid middle-class values. He attacked the foppery of the aristocracy, drunkenness, and social cruelty. In the *Harlot's Progress* series the harlot is a victim of circumstances. She arrives in London, is seduced by her employer, and ends up in Bridewell Prison. Hogarth portrays her final fate less as a punishment for her sins than as a comment on humankind's general cruelty. The same may be said of the *Rake's Progress*, which portrays the unfortunate downfall of a foolish young man from comfortable circumstances. This series moves through several unusual and exciting incidents (Fig. **12.32**) to a final fate in Bedlam insane asylum. Hogarth's concern for and criticism of social conditions are expressed in his paintings and represent incitement to action characteristic of eighteenth-century humanitarianism. The fact that his paintings were made into engravings and widely sold as prints to the public illustrates the popularity of attacks on social institutions of the day.

12.32 William Hogarth, *The Rake's Progress: The Orgy*, 1733–34. Oil on canvas, 24½ x 29½ ins (62 x 75 cm). By Courtesy of the Trustees of Sir John Soane's Museum, London.

LANDSCAPE & PORTRAITURE

The popularity of portraiture and landscape also increased in the eighteenth century. One of the most influential English painters of the time was Thomas Gainsborough (1727–88), whose landscapes bridge the gap between the styles of Baroque and Romantic and whose portraits range from Rococo to sensitive elegance.

Although the elegant attenuation of his lords and ladies is indebted to his study of Van Dyck, Gainsborough achieved in his full-length portraits a freshness and lyric grace all his own. Occasional objections to the lack of structure in his weightless figures are swept away by the beauty of his color and the delicacy of his touch, closer to the deft brushwork of Watteau than to Boucher's enameled surface ... His landscapes ... exhale a typically English freshness.[5]

In *The Market Cart* (Fig. **12.33**) we find a delicate use of wash reminiscent of Watteau and other Rococo painters in mainland Europe. We are caught up in an exploration of tonalities and shapes which express a deep and almost mystical response to nature. Although a pastoral, the composition has energy from its diagonal character. The tree forms on the right border are twisted and gnarled. The foremost tree leads the viewer's eye up and to the left, to be caught by the downward circling line of the trees and clouds in the background and returned on the diagonal. Gainsborough does not wish us to become too interested in the humans in the picture; they are warmly rendered, but not as specific individuals, their forms remain, in many respects, indistinct. Rather, we see them as a subordinate to the forces of nature, which ebb and flow around and through them.

12.33 Thomas Gainsborough, *The Market Cart*, 1786–7. Oil on canvas, 72½ x 60¼ ins (184 x 153 cm). The Tate Gallery, London.

12.34 Jean-Baptiste Siméon Chardin, *Menu de Gras*, 1731. Oil on canvas, 13 x 16⅛ ins (33 x 41 cm). The Louvre, Paris.

GENRE & SOCIAL COMMENT

A new bourgeois flavor could be found in the mundane (genre) subjects of France's Jean-Baptiste Siméon Chardin (1699–1779). He was the finest still-life and genre painter of his time, and a rival to the Dutch masters of the previous century. His early works are almost exclusively still lifes, and *Menu de Gras* (Fig. **12.34**) illustrates how the everyday could be raised to exquisite levels. With gentle insight and sympathy, the artist invests cooking pot, ladle, pitcher, bottles, cork, a slab of meat, and other small items with significance. Richness of texture and color combined with sensitive composition and the use of chiaroscuro make these humble items somehow noble. The eye moves slowly from point to point, carefully directed by shapes and angles, color and highlight. The work controls the speed of our viewing; each new focus demands that we pause and savor its richness. There is pure poetry in Chardin's brush. We are subtly urged to go beyond the surface impression of the objects themselves into a deeper reality.

Goldsmith

Contemporary literature also reflected the eighteenth-century focus on the commonplace which we see in the paintings of Chardin. Day-to-day occurrences are frequently used as symbols of a higher reality—for example, in the work of Oliver Goldsmith (1730–74), a prominent English eighteenth-century poet and playwright. He grew up in the village of Lissoy, where his father was vicar. The *Deserted Village*, written in 1770, describes the sights and personalities of his village.

Sweet Auburn! Loveliest village of the plain
Where health and plenty cheered the laboring swain;
Where smiling spring its earliest visit paid,
And parting summer's lingering blooms delayed,
Dear lovely bowers of innocence and ease,
Seats of my youth, where every sport could please;
How often have I loitered o'er thy green,
Where humble happiness endeared each scene!

His portrait of the old village parson includes a lovely simile:

To them his heart, his love, his griefs were given,
But all his serious thoughts had rest in heaven.
As some tall cliff that lifts its awful form,
Swells from the vale, and midway leaves the storm,
External sunshine settles on its head.

Finally, we find great tenderness in his description of his unfulfilled dream of ending his life amid the scenes in which it had begun.

In all my wanderings round this world of care,
In all my griefs—and God has given my share—
I still had hopes, my latest hours to crown,
Amid these humble bowers to lay me down,
To husband out life's taper at the close,
And keep the flame from wasting by repose.

And as an hare whom hounds and horns pursue,
Pants to the place from which at first she flew,
I still had hopes my long vexations past,
Here to return—and die at home at last.[6]

Johnson

The mid-eighteenth century is often called the Age of Johnson. Samuel Johnson (1709–84) began his literary career as a sort of miscellaneous journalist, writing for a newspaper. His principal achievement was as an essayist and the 208 *Rambler* essays covered a huge variety of topics including "Folly of Anger: Misery of a Peevish Old Age" and "Advantages of Mediocrity: An Eastern Fable." His purpose in the essays was to promote the glory of God and the salvation of himself and others.

In 1758, Johnson began the *Idler Essays*, a weekly contribution to the *Universal Chronicle*. In these we find the moralist and social reformer still present, together with an increasingly comic element.

The Idler
No. 22. Saturday, September 9, 1758

Many naturalists are of opinion, that the animals which we commonly consider as mute, have the power of imparting their thoughts to one another. That they can express general sensations is very certain; every being that can utter sounds, has a different voice for pleasure and for pain. The hound informs his fellows when he scents his game; the hen calls her chickens to their food by her cluck, and drives them from danger by her scream.

Birds have the greatest variety of notes; they have indeed a variety, which seems almost sufficient to make a speech adequate to the purposes of a life, which is regulated by instinct, and can admit little change or improvement. To the crisis of birds, curiosity or superstition has been always attentive, many have studied the language of the feathered tribes, and some have boasted that they understood it.

The most skillful or most confident interpreters of the silvan dialogues have been commonly found among the philosophers of the East, in a country where the calmness of the air, and the mildness of the seasons, allow the student to pass a great part of the year in groves and bowers. But what may be done in one place by peculiar opportunities, may be performed in another by peculiar diligence. A shepherd of Bohemia has, by long abode in the forests, enabled himself to understand the voice of birds, at least he relates with great confidence a story of which the credibility may be considered by the learned.

"As I was sitting (said he) within a hollow rock, and watching my sheep that fed in the valley, I heard two vultures interchangeably crying on the summit of the cliff. Both voices were earnest and deliberate. My curiosity prevailed over my care of the flock; I climbed slowly and silently from crag to crag, concealed among the shrub, till I found a cavity where I might sit and listen without suffering, or giving disturbance.

"I soon perceived, that my labour would be well repaid; for an old vulture was sitting on a naked prominence, with her young about her, whom she was instructing in the arts of a vulture's life, and preparing, by the last lecture, for their final dismission to the mountains and the skies.

" 'My children,' said the old vulture, 'you will the less want my instructions because you have had my practice before your eyes; you have seen me snatch from the farm the household fowl, you have seen me seize the leveret in the bush, and the kid in the pasture, you know how to fix your talons, and how to balance your flight when you are laden with your prey. But you remember the taste of more delicious food; I have often regaled you with the flesh of man.' 'Tell us,' said the young vultures, 'where man may be found, and how he may be known; his flesh is surely the natural food of a vulture. Why have you never brought a man in your talons to the nest?' 'He is too bulky,' said the mother; 'when we find a man, we can only tear away his flesh and leave his bones upon the ground.' 'Since man is so big,' said the young ones, 'how do you kill him? You are afraid of the wolf and of the bear, by what power are vultures superior to man, is man more defenseless than a sheep?' 'We have not the strength of man,' returned the mother, 'and I am sometimes in doubt whether we have the subtilty; and the vultures would seldom feast upon his flesh, had not nature, that devoted him to our uses, infused into him a strange ferocity, which I have never observed in any other being that feeds upon the earth. Two herds of men will often meet and shake the earth with noise, and fill the air with fire. When you hear noise and see fire which flashes along the ground, hasten to the place with your swiftest wing, for men are surely destroying one another; you will then find the ground smoking with blood and covered with carcasses, of which many are dismembered and mangled for the convenience of the vulture.' 'But when men have killed their prey,' said the pupils, 'why do they not eat it? When the wolf has killed a sheep he suffers not the vulture to touch it till he has satisfied himself. Is not man another kind of wolf?' 'Man,' said the mother, 'is the only beast who kills that which he does not devour, and this quality makes him so much a benefactor to our species.' 'If men kill our prey and lay it in our way,' said the young one, 'what need shall we have of labouring for ourselves.' 'Because man will, sometimes,' replied the mother, 'remain for a long time quiet in his den. The old vultures will tell you when you are to watch his motions. When you see men in great numbers moving close together, like a flight of storks, you may conclude that they are hunting, and that you will soon revel in human blood.' 'But still,' said the young one, 'I would gladly know the reason of this mutual slaughter. I could never kill what I could not eat.' 'My child,' said the mother, 'this is a question which I cannot answer, tho' I am reckoned the most subtle bird of the mountain. When I was young I used

12.35 Jacques-Louis David, *The Oath of the Horatii*, 1784–5. Oil on canvas, c. 14 x 11 ft (4.27 x 3.35 m). The Louvre, Paris.

frequently to visit the ayry of an old vulture who dwelt upon the Carpathian rocks; he had made many observations; he knew the places that afforded prey round his habitation, as far in every direction as the strongest wing can fly between the rising and setting of the summer sun; he had fed year after year on the entrails of men. His opinion was, that men had only the appearance of animal life, being really vegetables with a power of motion; and that as the boughs of an oak are dashed together by the storm, that swine may fatten upon the falling acorns, so men are by some unaccountable power driven one against another, till they lose their motion, that vultures may be fed. Others think they have observed something of contrivance and policy among these mischievous beings, and those that hover more closely round them, pretend, that there is, in every herd, one that gives directions to the rest, and seems to be more eminently delighted with a wide carnage. What it is that intitles him to such pre-eminence we know not; he is seldom the biggest or the swiftest, but he shews by his eagerness and diligence that he is, more than any of the others, a friend to vultures.' "[7]

NEOCLASSICISM

Discovery of the ruins of Pompeii, Winckelmann's interpretation of Greek Classicism, Rousseau's Noble Savage, and Baumgarten's aesthetics sent the late eighteenth century whirling back to antiquity and in particular to nature. Rather than seeing the past as a single, continuous cultural stream broken by a medieval collapse of Classical values, theoreticians of the eighteenth century saw history as a series of compartments—for example, Antiquity, Middle Ages, Renaissance, and so on. A principal proponent of Neoclassicism in painting was Jacques-Louis David (1748–1825). His works illustrate the newly perceived grandeur of antiquity and its reflection in subject matter, composition, depiction, and historical accuracy. Although propagandist in tone (he sought to inspire patriotism and democracy), his Neoclassical works show a Roman two-dimensionality and a strong, simple compositional unity. Accurate historical detail and antiquarian subject matter complete the works. In *The Oath of the Horatii* (Fig. **12.35**), David exploits his political ideas amidst Greek and Roman themes. He implies a devotion to ideals so strong that one should be prepared to die in their defense. David's belief in a rational and ordered existence is reinforced by his sparse and classically simple composition. We must recognize, however, that the Neoclassicism of David and others is not confined to copying ancient works. Classical detail and principles are treated selectively and adapted.

David—The Oath of the Horatii

The painting was inspired by Corneille's play *Horace*, whose subject is the conflict between love and patriotism. In legend, the leaders of the Roman and Alban armies, on the verge of battle, decide to resolve their conflicts by means of an organized combat between three representatives from each side. The three Horatius brothers represented Rome; the Curatius sons represented the Albans. A sister of the Horatii was the fiancée of one of the Curatius brothers. David's painting depicts the Horatii as they swear on their swords to win or die for Rome, disregarding the anguish of their sister. The work captures a directness and an intensity of expression that were to play an important role in Romanticism, but the starkness of outline, strong geometric composition (which juxtaposes straight line in the men and curved line in the women), and the smooth color areas and gradations hold it to the more formal, Classical tradition.

The form is academic Neoclassicism. The scene takes place in "a shallow picture box, defined by a severely simple architectural framework" and the people reflect historical reality. The musculature, even the arms and legs of the women, has a surface devoid of warmth or softness as does the drapery.

Curiously David's work was admired and purchased by King Louis XVI, against whom David's revolutionary cries were directed and whom he, as a member of the French Revolutionary Convention, would sentence to death. David's career flourished; Neoclassicism in painting increased in popularity and continued beyond the Revolution to the era of Napoleon and beyond.

ARCHITECTURAL NEOCLASSICISM

In the mid-eighteenth century architecture's viewpoints changed entirely and embraced the complex philosophical concerns of the Enlightenment. Three important concepts emerged as a result of this change in viewpoint. First was the archeological concept, which viewed the present as continually enriched by persistent inquiry into the past (progress). Second was the *eclectic*, which allowed the artist to choose among styles, or, more importantly, to combine elements of various styles. The third was the modernist concept, which viewed the present as unique and, therefore, possible of expression in its own terms. These three concepts profoundly influenced eighteenth-century architecture, had important bearing on the other arts and fundamentally changed the basic premises of art from that time forward.

Neoclassicism as applied to architecture encompasses these three concepts and reflects a variety of treatment and terminology. Basic to it, of course, are the identifiable forms of Greece and Rome. Neoclassicism in architecture took considerable impetus from the *Essai sur l'architecture* (Paris, 1753) by the Abbé Laugier. Laugier's work was strictly rationalistic and expressed Neoclassicism in a nutshell. He discarded the architectural language developed since the Renaissance. Rather, he urged the architect to seek truth in principles demonstrated in the architecture of the ancient world and to use those principles to design modern buildings that expressed the same logical limitations as the Classical temple. Laugier's Classicism descended directly from the Ancient Greeks, with only passing reference to the Romans.

In Italy, the architect Giambattista Piranesi (1720–78) was incensed by Laugier's arguments, which placed Greece above Rome, and he retaliated with an overwhelmingly detailed work that professed to prove (perhaps by sheer weight of evidence) the superiority of Rome over Greece. Both Piranesi (*Della Magnificenza ed Architettura dei Romani*) and Laugier were instigators of the Neoclassical tradition. The revival of Classicism in architecture was seen in many quarters as a revolt against the frivolity of the Rococo with an art that was serious and moral.

In America Neoclassicism had special meaning as the colonies struggled to rid themselves of the monarchical rule of England's George III. For revolutionary Americans Classicism meant Greek and Greece meant democracy. The designs of colonial architects like Thomas Jefferson (Fig. **12.36**) reflect the complex interrelationships of this period. Jefferson was highly influenced by Palladio, who enjoyed popularity in a significant revival in English villa architecture between 1710 and 1750. Jefferson, in a uniquely eighteenth-century way, considered architecture objectively within the framework of contemporary thought. His philosophy of architecture, of which Monticello is illustrative, was founded on a belief that the architecture of antiquity embodied indisputable natural principles. He considered Palladian reconstruction of the Roman temple a foundation on which a theory of architecture could be built. Monticello contains a center with superimposed Doric and Ionic porticos (porches) with short, low wings attached to the center by continuing Doric entablatures. The simplicity and refinement of Jefferson's statement here goes beyond reconstruction of Classical prototypes and appeals directly to the intellect.

12.36 Thomas Jefferson, Monticello, Charlottesville, Virginia, 1770–84; (rebuilt 1796–1800).

MUSICAL CLASSICISM

In 1785 Michel Paul de Chabanon wrote, "Today there is but one music in all of Europe." The basis of this statement was music composed to appeal not only to the aristocracy but to the broad middle classes as well. Egalitarian tendencies and popularizing of ideals typical of the *philosophes* had also influenced artists, turning them toward a larger audience. Pleasure became a legitimate artistic purpose. Eighteenth-century rationalism regarded excessive ornamentation and excessive complexity (both Baroque characteristics) as contrary to meeting a wide audience on its own terms. Those sentiments, against the background of Neoclassicism, prompted a move to order, simplicity, and careful attention to form. We call this style in music Classical (the term was not applied until the nineteenth century) rather than Neoclassical or Classical revival because although the other arts returned (more or less) to Greek and Roman prototypes, music had no known Classical antecedents to revive, despite a fairly detailed understanding of Greek music theory. Music thus turned to Classical *ideals*, though not to Classical models.

One very clear characteristic of Classical style was a definitely articulated structure. Each piece was organized into short statements called phrases, which recurred regularly and clearly. The most frequently cited example of this practice is Mozart's *Symphony No. 40 in G Minor*, whose opening movement is based on a three-note rhythmic pattern or motif, organized into two contrasting phrases. These phrases are then grouped into themes which comprise sections in the movement. Classical music also avoided the Baroque style of polyphony, introducing instead its own, which relied upon a melodic line that could be shaped into clear and expressive contours and brought to a definite cadence (conclusion).

A third change from the Baroque lay in rhythmic patterns. Baroque's numerous ornamented parts flowing together in complex design fostered essentially unchanging rhythmic patterns. Classical phrase structure and melodic linearity allowed far more opportunity for rhythmic variety and also for rhythmic contrasts among or between lines. For example, the featured upper melodic line could carry one rhythmic impulse while the chordal supporting lines could carry another. Usually the chordal voices had more regular rhythms than the independent voice. Classical style also changed harmonic relationships, including the invention of a true modulation.

Major musical forms such as the opera, oratorio, and concerto changed according to Classical priorities. For example, Mozart's the *Marriage of Figaro* (1786), a comic opera on the theme of love and marriage, with a fast-paced plot, subplot, and dramatic conflicts, shows concern for simplicity and clarity. Haydn's oratorio, *The Creation*, reflects the Enlightenment's concepts of God and nature, reason and benevolence. *The Creation* also exhibits concern for simplicity and clear form. Operas and oratorios continued in popularity, but for the most part instrumental music became the dominant force. The concerto adapted smoothly from its Baroque configurations into Classical form and style. Chamber music also increased in popular appeal. Its small ensemble format was perfect for performance *en chambre*, in the small rooms of the eighteenth-century salon.

The most important forms in this period, however, were the symphony and the sonata. Sonatas were composed for virtually every instrument, and composers varied in their approach. Haydn, for example employed a sonata-rondo form (*rondo* was a Classical variation of *ritornello*). The Classical sonata, sometimes called sonata cycle, is a work of three or four movements, each of which consists of a specific structure. The most important structural configuration of the sonata is the typical configuration of the first movement. This structure is so important and specific that it is called sonata or sonata-allegro form.

The symphony, which used sonata-allegro form in its opening movement, also played an important part in the Classical music tradition. By the last quarter of the eighteenth century the symphony, as well as other forms of instrumental ensemble music, had largely eliminated use of *basso continuo*, and, thereby, the harpsichord. Primary focus, then, fell on the violin section, and Classical symphonic compositions reflect that new focus. By the turn of the nineteenth century other sections, such as the woodwind, were given more, independent material.

The timbre of an orchestra was fairly close to what we know today. The size, and therefore the overall volume of sound was not. The largest orchestra of the mid-eighteenth century, the Mannheim Orchestra, consisted of forty-five players, mostly strings, with six woodwinds, five brasses, and two timpani. Haydn's orchestra between 1760 and 1785 rarely exceeded twenty-five players, and the Vienna orchestras of the 1790s averaged thirty-five.

The most illustrative symphonic literature of the Classical style came from the minds and pens of Haydn, Mozart, and Beethoven (in his early years).

Haydn

Austrian-born Franz Joseph Haydn (1732–1809) pioneered the development of the symphony from a short, simple work into a longer, more sophisticated one. Haydn's symphonies are diverse and numerous (some sources indicate that he wrote more than 104). Some are light and simple, others are serious and sophisticated. Many of his early symphonies use the pre-Classical, three-movement form. His middle symphonies from the early 1770s exhibit imaginative emotion and a larger scale than the earlier works. Exposition sections explore broadly expressed themes, followed by contrasting ideas and restatement. The development sections are dramatic and employ sudden and unexpected changes of dynamics. The slow movements contain great warmth and emotion, Haydn frequently drew on Austrian folk songs and Baroque dance music, and his modulations and changes of tonality contain great dramatic power. Among his late works the most famous is *Symphony No. 94 in G Minor* (1792), commonly known as the "Surprise Symphony."

12.37 Haydn, *Symphony No. 94 in G Major*, first theme.

The development section opens with a variation on the first theme and then goes through a series of variations built around modulations and dynamic changes. The recapitulation section starts with a return to the first theme in the original key.

Mozart

Wolfgang Amadeus Mozart (1756–91), also an Austrian, had performed at the court of Empress Maria Theresa at the age of six. As was the case throughout the Classical period, aristocratic patronage was essential for musicians to earn a living, although the middle classes provided a progressively larger portion of commissions, pupil fees, and concert attendance. Mozart's short career (he died at the age of thirty-five) was dogged by financial insecurity.

His early symphonies were simple and relatively short, like those of Haydn, while his later works were longer and more complex. His last three symphonies are generally regarded as his greatest masterpieces, and *Symphony No. 40 in G Minor* is often referred to as the typical Classical symphony. This work and Nos. 39 and 41 have clear order and yet exhibit tremendous emotional urgency, which many scholars cite as the beginning of the Romantic style.

12.38 Mozart, *Symphony No. 40 in G Minor*, first movement.

Mozart is also well known for his operas, and was especially skilled in *opera buffa*. *The Marriage of Figaro* is fast and humorous, with slapstick action in the manner of farce, but has great melodic beauty.

12.39 Mozart, *The Marriage of Figaro*, first theme of *Cinque . . . dieci duet.*

Beethoven

Ludwig van Beethoven (1770–1827) is often considered apart from the Classical period and treated as a singular transitional figure between Classicism and Romanticism. Beethoven wanted to expand the Classical symphonic form in order for it to accommodate greater emotional character. The typical Classical symphony moves through contrasting movements; Beethoven changed that to accommodate a single thematic development throughout, and thereby achieved a unified, emotional work.

Beethoven's works are significantly different from those of Haydn and Mozart. They are more dramatic and use changing dynamics for emotional effects. Silence is used as a device in pursuit of dramatic and structural ends.

His works are also longer. He lengthened the development section of sonata-allegro form and did the same to his codas, many of which take on characteristics of a second development section. He also changed traditional thematic relationships among movements especially in the *Symphony No. 6*, which has no break between the fourth and fifth movements.

Although Classical style had a simpler character and used a more symmetrical structure than Baroque, it did not sacrifice dynamic qualities in that pursuit. In the same sense that the simple qualities of Greek architecture, for example, did not lose their sophistication and interest in a slavish pursuit of apparently mathematical form and symmetry, so Classical music maintained its dynamic and sophisticated character in its pursuit of form and reason.

12.40 Beethoven, *Piano Sonata in C Minor*, third movement, first theme.

As Classical style was shaped by its advocates it moved as comfortably toward Romanticism as it had moved away from Baroque.

AFRICA AND EARLY BLACK AMERICA

ART AND ANCESTOR WORSHIP

One of the most widespread features of societies such as those in tribal Africa is ancestor worship. It takes a variety of forms, depending on the tribe, and its artistic manifestations also reflect a wide variety of forms. One of the forms taken is called a *guardian figure*, which was used to protect the remains of the dead. In Gabon in Equatorial Africa, the Kota tribe produced polished metal figures that guarded large containers of skulls of ancestors, apparently communal dwellings of ancestor spirits. The guardian figure shown in Figure **12.41** employs geometric abstrac-

12.42 Mask, from the Bamenda area, Cameroon, late 19th century. Wood, height 26½ ins (67.3 cm). Rietberg Museum, Zurich, Heydt Collection.

12.41 Guardian figure of the Kota tribe, Gabon, late 19th century. Wood, brass, ivory (?) eyes, height 16⅝ ins (42.2 cm). The Metropolitan Museum of Art, New York, the Michael C. Rockefeller Memorial Collection, Bequest of Nelson A. Rockefeller, 1979.

tion that seems fairly typical of the art of primitive societies (compare this with the geometric vase painting designs from archaic Greece). The entire design has been flattened into a single plane, and although the design is abstract, the anatomical parts of the body are clearly defined. The work is perfectly symmetrical in balance and yields a calming effect: this guardian was clearly not intended to cause fright in the viewer.

Underlying this people's preference for viewing their ancestors collectively is the basic animism of their religion. The Kota people did not think of their ancestors as individuals but in group form: the term "animism" is the belief that a spirit exists in every living thing—for example, trees have spirits that must be appeased before the tree can be cut down, and the individual tree spirit merges with a general "tree spirit," which in turn merges with a larger "life spirit." Spirits dwell in rivers, lakes, forests, the sun, the moon, wind, and rain. In dealing with the spirit world, tribal peoples such as those in Cameroon acted out relationships with the spirit world in dances and other dramatic ceremonies, disguising themselves so as temporarily to assume the role of the spirit. These people wore costumes in which a mask figured prominently. The mask shown in Figure **12.42** is typical, and it, like the guardian figure, has a symmetrical composition and distinct detailing. Again the design is abstract while leaving anatomical details recognizable. The elevated eyebrows and the delicate arching lines that represent them give the mask a sophisticated and striking appearance. It exhibits dignity and strength owing to its straightforward character and the solidity of its detailing.

TRANSPORTATION TO AMERICA

The European colonization of Africa had a significant impact on African art. More important, perhaps, was the transportation of African culture to the Americas as a result of the slave trade that serviced the plantation lifestyle of the American South. The mixture of a new American culture and the Euro- and African-centered cultures created in the colonies (that were to become the United States) a significant Black cultural heritage. It emerged publicly during and immediately after the Civil War (1861–5), and has been felt most strongly in music.

THE MUSIC OF BLACK AMERICA

African-American music consists of three basic types: folk music, art music, and popular music. Each one contains its own idiom and place in the sociology of Black culture in America. Each type of music also has its own function. Folk music—for example, spirituals—is anonymous in origin, orally transmitted, and shows the "expressive melodic and racial feeling, character, and expression of the people."[8] Art music has a technical tradition in the hands of a group of highly trained specialists involved in both creation and performance. Popular music, for example blues, ragtime, jazz, and soul, combines the art and folk traditions: it concerns itself with the contemporary world, seeks novelty, and tends to be faddish. We will examine briefly some of the folk music of the African-American tradition that is appropriate to the time-frame of this chapter.

Folk Music and the Civil War Years

As northern soldiers, journalists, and missionaries arrived in the South toward the end of the Civil War, their reports created a new interest and documentation of the culture of Black Americans, especially their music. Numerous chronicles of Black music can be found in newspaper and journal articles, letters, and other documents from the mid-1860s. In these lies the record of a musical heritage that expresses the joys and sorrows, thoughts and reactions of a people immersed in a struggle for freedom.

Black Americans played numerous roles in the war: they were, for example, body servants for Southern officers, soldiers, cooks, hospital attendants, and railroad workers. Out of one unsuccessful attempt to organize freed men for military service came a plaintive song of regret:

Oh Lord, I want some valiant soldier,
I want some valiant soldier,
I want some valiant soldier,
To help me bear de cross.
For I weep, I weep,
For I weep, I weep,
I can't hold out;
If any mercy, Lord,
O pity poor me.[9]

On the eve of the expected Emancipation Proclamation, December 31, 1862, a prayer meeting and song service vigil held in the District of Columbia produced a spontaneous musical outpouring:

"*Go Down Moses* was sung several times . . . in [the] contraband camp. Afterwards, a woman on her knees loudly sang:

> If de Debble do not ketch
> Jeff Davis, dat infernal retch,
> An roast and frigazee dat rebble,
> Wat is de use ob any Debble?

Then one contraband began the following strain:

> The first of January next, eighteen sixty-three,—
> So says the Proclamation,—the slaves will all be free!
> To every kindly heart 'twill be the day of jubillee;
> For the bond shall all go free!

Next a small black man, "with a cracking voice, appearing by his gestures to be inwardly on fire," began jumping and singing:

> Massa gone, missy too;
> Cry! niggers, cry!
> Tink I'll see de bressed Norf,
> Fore de day I die.
> Hi! hi! Yankee shot 'im.

The whole company then proclaimed:

> Oh! we all longed for freedom,
> Ah, we prayed to be free;
> Though the day was long in coming,
> That we longed to see.
> We'll strive to learn our duty,
> That all our friends may see,
> Though so long oppressed in bondage,
> We were worthy to be free.[10]

By the end of the war, nearly 200,000 Black men had served as soldiers in 166 regiments. Nearly 20,000 had served as sailors—nearly one quarter of the entire United States Navy. Casualties numbered nearly 70,000, with approximately 30,000 killed. Black Americans fought well and sang well. They linked their military struggle with their belief in a kind and liberating God. They wanted to be free, and one chronicle recorded this Black soldier's prayer:

I hab lef' my wife in de land o' bondage; my little ones dey say eb'ry night, War is my fader? But when I die, when de bressed mornin' rises, when I shall stan' in de glory, wid one foot on de water an' one foot on de land, den O Lord, I shall see my wife an' my little chil'en once more.[11]

Imprisoned slaves in Richmond echoed in song their hopes of imminent freedom:

Slavery's chain done broke at las'!
Broke at las'! Broke at las'!
Most done waiting for de mornin' star!
Gonna praise God till I die![12]

The songs of slavery and the American South fill volumes. Clearly, music formed the core of the African-American's life and culture during the two centuries of bondage. The influence of the songs of this culture permeate contemporary culture, white and Black. This musical heritage consisted of a variety of songs: there were slave songs, religious folk songs, camp meeting songs, and spirituals. Most had strong religious themes, for example, the slave song "The Old Ship of Zion" (Fig. **12.43**).

1. Oh,— what ship is that you are sail-ing a-board?
Oh glo-ry, hal-le-loo! 'Tis the old ship o' Zi-on,
hal-le-loo! 'Tis the old_ ship o' Zi-on, hal-le-loo!

2. Oh, what are the timbers for buildin' of the ship?
   Oh glory, halleloo!
   She is made o' gospel timbers, halleloo!
   She is made o' gospel timbers, halleloo!

3. Oh, what is the compass you've got aboard the ship?
   Oh glory, halleloo!
   The Bible is our compass, halleloo!
   Oh, the Bible is our compass, halleloo!

12.43 "The Old Ship of Zion"

The spiritual remains the most popular of the Black musical genres. A common misconception is that most Black music was in the minor key—it is not. However, it did express common sentiments: it was a commentary on the awful state of the African-American's daily life, but it was full of patience for that life coupled with triumph in the life to come. Some songs focused on the present and some on the future, but inexorably the two were tied together—at least by implication. For example, in the spiritual "This World Almost Done" we hear the patient reminder,

Brudder, keep your lamp trimmin' and a-burnin',
Keep your lamp trimmin' and a-burnin',
Keep your lamp trimmin' and a-burnin',
    For dis world most done.
So keep your lamp trimmin' [etc.]
    For dis world most done.[13]

In "I Want to Go Home" the patience remains, but the final reward is proclaimed:

Dere's no rain to wet you,
    O, yes, I want to go home.
Dere's no sun to burn you,
    O, yes, I want to go home.
O' push along, believers,
    O' yes, I want to go home.
Dere's no hard trials,
    O, yes, I want to go home.
Dere's no whips a crackin',
    O, yes, I want to go home.
My brudder on de wayside,
    O, yes, I want to go home.
O, push along, my brudder,
    O, yes, I want to go home.
Where dere's no stormy weather,
    O, yes, I want to go home.
Dere's no tribulation,
    O, yes, I want to go home.[14]

The influence of this outpouring of musical expression in the folk idiom has been pervasive, and it has become a significant part not only of African-American culture, but of American culture as a whole. In 1914 Henry Edward Krehbiel asserted, "Is it not the merest quibble to say that these songs are not American? They were created in America under American influences and by people who are Americans in the same sense that any other element of our population is American—every element except the aboriginal."[15]

The culture of the African-American during the first 250 years of history in America reflects a diversity of reactions—sometimes they howled in alarm; sometimes they fought back and learned the advantages of resistance. They certainly did not "accept" slavery and oppression. The music of the time reflected the mind of the people and their circumstances.

NATIVE AMERICAN ART

Native American artists pursue much the same goals as artists from any culture—they try to evoke emotional responses in the viewer: In the case of a Native American artist, the viewer might be another person or even a supernatural being. Much of such art deals with religious matters: the purpose of the art is like that of prayer—to entreat a benign God or to placate a hostile God. The manner or form in which Native American artists pursue such goals is to a large degree set by tradition. In fact, in Native American culture a major criterion for "art" is how well an artist recognizes the force of tradition. Little room for experimentation in art exists within the established tribal organization. However, exceptions do exist, and artists such as Nampeyo, the Hopi potter, have been able to introduce new elements to the cultural tradition, perhaps solely by the force of their individual talent.

Influences

Naturally, many different factors influenced Native American works of art. Function, of course, was one factor. Environment was another: the accessibility of materials played an important role in the nature of Native American art. For example, among Inuits access to soapstone and lack of access to clay made their works of art carved rather than ceramic. In addition, as one people conquered another or as intertribal marriage occurred, traditions often mixed, thereby creating new traditions. Often, however, tradition and tribal integrity was a sufficient motivation. Hopi and Navajo nations shared a common environment and lifestyle: the function of their works of art was similar. Their traditions, however, kept their styles separate, and the works of both cultures remain separate and distinguishable.

Symbolism

The meaning of works of art from the Native American cultures can prove baffling to someone raised in a Euro-centered culture. Native American artists do not draw merely to recreate a picture of something: they understand they could not draw a tree as perfectly as it could be made by the Creator. In addition, because much Native American art was religious or spiritual, those aspects often found their way into works of art. "Therefore, it can be said that Indian art is not so much drawings, carvings or reproductions *of* an object, but more the representation of the spirit *within* it. In short, it embodies the essence of the subject as well as its appearance."[16] Thus, Native American art has a magical character that does not actually "mean" anything in the sense that Western art often does.

THE INUITS

In a wide band of the Arctic, stretching across all of North America, hundreds of tribes comprise the Inuit culture. All of these tribes have a cultural and/or language interrelationship. Out of the bleak and inhospitable environment of the north—where the quest for survival would seemingly leave little room for artistry—comes a tremendously imaginative and humorous artistic tradition. The long Arctic winter nights gave individuals ample time to carve ivory obtained from walrus and killer whales and, more recently, stone. As a result of available materials, Inuit art tends to be small in scale, and, in the case of tusk ivory, larger at one end than at the other. Characteristic of Inuit art is humor: caricatures found in the form of driftwood masks are common (Fig. **12.44**). This particular example is typical of the elaborate or

12.44 Carved dance masks of the Inuit tribe, Mamtrek, Alaska, late 19th century. Wood (originally decorated with snow goose feathers), 8½ × 4½ ins (21.6 × 11.4 cm). National Museum of the American Indian, Smithsonian Institution.

grotesque dance masks that form a widespread art form among the Inuit people. They depict a variety of personations, for example humorous, sacred, or secular, of the humans and animals of the region. This mask originally was decorated with snow goose feathers.

THE NORTHWEST COAST TRIBES

The Pacific Northwest of North America produced stable Native American cultures. This is in great measure due to the abundance of resources and temperate climate, which figured prominently in the social and cultural fabric of the tribes. Fishing, hunting, and foraging produced ample means of sustenance; therefore, the Native Americans of this region had no reason to cultivate crops or domesticate animals. Their cultures tended to share certain features— probably because they traded and warred with one another. In addition, artistic motifs were alike and they shared a common religion—shamanism: an ancient form of magic, centered on wise, all-seeing men (shamans), also shared with the hunting tribes of Siberia. Although their pantheons and myths may have differed, the Northwest tribes all acknowledged the power of shamans to contact the spirits of the forests and waters, to heal the sick, and to predict the future.

The rich forests of the area provided Native American artists with a wealth of materials for sculpting. Huge spruce and cedar trees abounded, and when steel knives were obtained from fur traders and used as tools, Northwest coast artists excelled in magnificent totem poles, carved posts for wooden dwellings, masks, rattles, and other objects. Figure **12.45** shows a carved housepost that was used inside a wooden dwelling to support the roof and to give additional decoration to the interior. This example depicts the sea bear, and has a frog carved in each ear. It was presented as a token of respect to Chief Frog Ears of Sukkwan by the people of a neighboring village. Proximity to the sea also provided abalone shells that were used as inlays to give luster to sculpted works.

Although many art objects from the area concern themselves with shamanistic religious rituals—for example, masks and other objects—a fair amount of art was secular and, like some African art, concerned with maintaining the social fabric and bolstering a ruler's power. In the Tlingit tribe, for example, communities were made up of a number of families, each of which had its own chief who inherited his rank from his mother. Carefully devised social mores obliged both men and women to marry outside their own clan. In this way a balance was established in which no one family achieved dominance.

12.45 Housepost, Haida, Alaska, 19th century. Wood, height 11 ft 6½ ins (3.52 m) high. National Museum of the American Indian, Smithsonian Institution.

Nonetheless, chiefs competed fiercely with each other in displays of riches. The totem poles of the Tlingit formed a part of this ostentation, proclaiming prestige and family pride through genealogy—much like the coats of arms of the European aristocracy. Totem poles were carved from single tree trunks and often reached 90 ft (27.4 m) in height. Probably originating as funerary monuments, by the nineteenth century they had become fixtures adorning the exteriors of chiefs' houses.

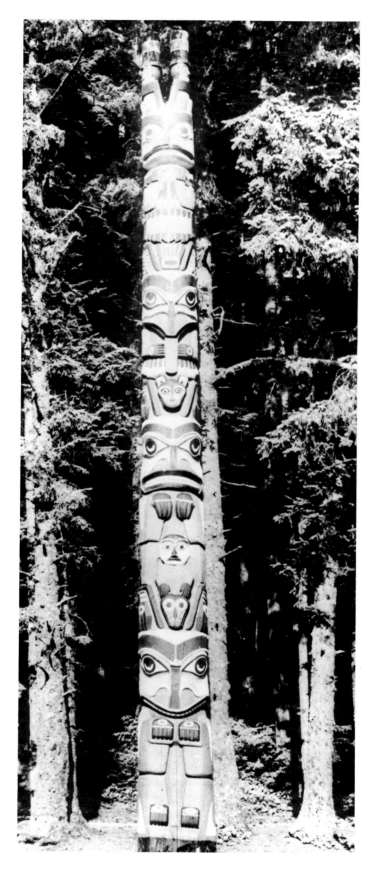

On the totem poles, we find eagles, beavers, whales, and so on (see Fig. **12.46**), which, in essence, were crests that a chief inherited from his ancestors. The Tlingit did not worship these figures or have any supernatural relationship with them; they are secular art objects with a socially ostentatious purpose and were governed by traditional artistic principles. One of these principles is that of bilateral symmetry—that is, the designs on either side of a central axis are identical. Another principle determines the transition from one motif to another: each design must appear to grow from the one below. Thus, not only the overall vertical form of the totem pole, but also the design of its interior parts, leads the eye upward along its axis. In our example, the patchwork of contrasting colors and upward striving line carry us with rhythmic precision from one motif to another until we, finally, reach the top. At the top, a darkly colored, triangular form and a strong horizontal capping band redirect the eye downward.

Totem poles, then, were designed as historical documents that recorded the wealth, social position, and relative importance of the person who paid for the pole. In this respect they are quite similar to sculptural records from other cultures—for example Trajan's column (Fig. **2.20**). The ultimate function of such art probably was to act as a gift: "The life goal of many of these tribes involved the belief that the greatest value was to give away all of one's possessions."[17] The actual working out of such a philosophy created some interesting scenarios. The more one gave away, the greater was one's prestige. In turn, one's rival was more or less obliged to give back the same or more material wealth in order to prove greater disdain for material possessions. As a result, totems and other goods often were burned, thrown into the sea, or otherwise destroyed. In fact, slaves occasionally were killed, and entire families sold into slavery.

A number of other art forms flourished among the Northwest coast peoples, and these included, for example, metalwork, carved wooden masks used in religious and social ceremonials, woven basketry, and ivory carving. Creation of ceremonial masks reached tremendous heights of achievement. Some were portraits or representations of religious deities; some were spirits. In all cases, the masks bore careful attention to design and execution. They were painted, inlaid with shell, and elaborately decorated. The human face mask shown in Figure **12.47** is an example of a mask that probably depicted a specific individual. It has a remarkable vitality and sculptural quality.

12.46 Tlingit totem pole at Sitka, Alaska, late 19th century. Carved and painted wood.

NATIVE AMERICAN LITERATURE

Literacy among Native Americans began to take hold in the late eighteenth century as a result of missionary activity—particularly that of the Methodists and Presbyterians—and a century later, increased interest in America's heritage gave rise to the publication of tribal histories written by Native Americans. Fiction writing among Native Americans appeared as early as 1823.

Between 1870 and 1920, Native American culture underwent tremendous change: tribal autonomy decreased, and all tribes within the territory of the United States were confined to reservations. By the end of 1870, the federal government had become actively involved in Native American education, and a subsequent increase in literacy produced what can be called a tribal intellectual elite. As a result, numerous authors emerged, one of whom was Susette La Flesche. Her story, "Nedawi," was first published in 1881 in a popular magazine for children. It represents, arguably, the first short story written by a Native American that is not a reworking of a legend. The author's gender testifies to the prominence of women in Native American (as well as American) literature. Subtitled "An Indian Story from Real Life," "Nedawi" is representative of much of Native American fiction prior to 1920. Describing a past way of life, in nostalgic terms, the story emphasizes ethnocentric detail, has a strong moralistic tone, and appeals to young readers.

12.47 Mask, Nass River, British Columbia. Wood, 9½×7 ins (24.1×17.8 cm). National Museum of the American Indian, Smithsonian Institution.

Nedawi
"Bright Eyes" [Susette La Flesche]

"Nedawi!" called her mother, "take your little brother while I go with your sister for some wood." Nedawi ran into the tent, bringing back her little red blanket, but the brown-faced, roly-poly baby, who had been having a comfortable nap in spite of being all the while tied straight to his board, woke with a merry crow just as the mother was about to attach him, board and all, to Nedawi's neck. So he was taken from the board instead, and, after he had kicked in happy freedom for a moment, Nedawi stood in front of her mother, who placed Habazhu on the little girl's back, and drew the blanket over him, leaving his arms free. She next put into his hand a little hollow gourd, filled with seeds, which served as a rattle; Nedawi held both ends of the blanket tightly in front of her, and was then ready to walk around with the little man.

Where should she go? Yonder was a group of young girls playing a game of *konci*, or dice. The dice were five plum-seeds, scorched black, and had little stars and quarter-moons instead of numbers. She went over and stood by the group, gently rocking herself from side to side, pretty much as white children do when reciting the multiplication table. The girls would toss up the wooden bowl, letting it drop with a gentle thud on the pillow beneath, the falling dice making a pleasant clatter which the baby liked to hear. The stakes were a little heap of beads, rings, and bracelets. The laughter and exclamations of the girls, as some successful toss brought down the dice three stars and two quarter-moons (the highest throw), made Nedawi wish that she, too, were a young girl, and could win and wear all those pretty things. How gay she would look! Just then, the little glittering heap caught baby's eye. He tried to wriggle out of the blanket to get to it, but Nedawi held tight. Then he set up a yell. Nedawi walked away very reluctantly, because she wanted to stay and see who would win. She went to her mother's tent, but found it deserted. Her father and brothers had gone to the chase. A herd of buffalo had been seen that morning, and all the men in the tribe had gone, and would not be back till night. Her mother, her sister, and the women of the household had gone to the river for wood and water. The tent looked enticingly cool, with the sides turned up to let the breeze sweep through, and the straw mats and soft robes seemed to invite her to lie down on them and dream the afternoon away, as she was too apt to do. She did not yield to the temptation, however, for she knew Mother would not like it, but walked over to her cousin Metai's tent. She found her cousin "keeping house" with a number of little girls, and stood to watch them while they put up little tents, just large enough to hold one or two girls.

"Nedawi, come and play," said Metai. "You can make the fire and cook. I'll ask Mother for something to cook."

"But what shall I do with Habazhu?" said Nedawi.

"I'll tell you. Put him in my tent, and make believe he's our little old grandfather."

Forthwith he was transferred from Nedawi's back to the little tent. But Habazhu had a decided objection to staying in the dark little place, where he could not see anything, and crept out of the door on his hands and knees. Nedawi collected a little heap of sticks, all ready for the fire, and went off to get a fire-brand to light it with. While she was gone, Habazhu crawled up to a bowl of water which stood by the intended fire-place, and began dabbling in it with his chubby little hands, splashing the water all over the sticks prepared for the fire. Then he thought he would like a drink. He tried to lift the bowl in both hands, but only succeeded in spilling the water over himself and the fire-place.

When Nedawi returned, she stood aghast; then, throwing down the brand, she took her little brother by the shoulders and, I am sorry to say, shook him violently, jerked him up, and dumped him down by the door of the little tent from which he had crawled. "You bad little boy!" she said. "It's too bad that I have to take care of you when I want to play."

You see, she was no more perfect than any little white girl who gets into a temper now and then. The baby's lip quivered, and he began to cry. Metai said to Nedawi: "I think it's real mean for you to shake him, when he doesn't know any better."

Metai picked up Baby and tried to comfort him. She kissed him over and over, and talked to him in baby language. Nedawi's conscience, if the little savage could be said to have any, was troubling her. She loved her baby brother dearly, even though she did get out of patience with him now and then.

"I'll put a clean little shirt on him and pack him again," said she, suddenly. Then she took off his little wet shirt, wrung it out, and spread it on the tall grass to dry in the sun. Then she went home, and, going to a pretty painted skin in which her mother kept his clothes, she selected the red shirt, which she thought was the prettiest. She was in such a hurry, however, that she forgot to close and tie up the skin again, and she carelessly left his clean shirts lying around as she had laid them out. When Baby was on her back again, she walked around with him, giving directions and overseeing the other girls at their play, determined to do that rather than nothing.

The other children were good-natured, and took her ordering as gracefully as they could. Metai made the fire in a new place, and then went to ask her mother to give her something to cook. Her mother gave her a piece of dried buffalo meat, as hard as a chip and as brittle as glass. Metai broke it up into small pieces, and put the pieces into a little tin pail of water, which she hung over the fire. "Now," she said, "when the meat is cooked and the soup is made, I will call you all to a feast, and Habazhu shall be the chief."

They all laughed. But alas for human calculations! During the last few minutes, a shy little girl, with soft, wistful black eyes, had been watching them from a little distance. She had on a faded, shabby blanket and a ragged dress.

"Metai," said Nedawi, "let's ask that girl to play with us; she looks so lonesome."

"Well," said Metai, doubtfully, "I don't care; but my mother said she didn't want me to play with ragged little girls."

"My father says we must be kind to poor little girls, and help them all we can; so I'm going to play with her if you don't," said Nedawi, loftily.

Although Metai was the hostess, Nedawi was the leading spirit, and had her own way, as usual. She walked up to the little creature and said, "Come and play with us, if you want to." The little girl's eyes brightened, and she laughed. Then she suddenly drew from under her blanket a pretty bark basket, filled with the most delicious red and yellow plums. "My brother picked them in the woods, and I give them to you," was all she said. Nedawi managed to free one hand, and took the offering with an exclamation of delight, which drew the other girls quickly around. Instead of saying "Oh! Oh!" as you would have said, they cried "Hin! Hin!" which expressed their feeling quite as well, perhaps.

"Let us have them for our feast," said Metai, taking them.

Little Indian children are taught to share everything with one another, so it did not seem strange to Nedawi to have her gift looked on as common property. But, while the attention of the little group had been concentrated on the matter in hand, a party of mischievous boys, passing by, caught sight of the little tents and the tin pail hanging over the fire. Simultaneously, they set up a war-whoop and, dashing into the deserted camp, they sent the tent-poles scattering right and left, and snatching up whatever they could lay hands on, including the tin pail and its contents, they retreated. The little girls, startled by the sudden raid on their property, looked up. Rage possessed their little souls. Giving shrieks of anger, they started in pursuit. What did Nedawi do? She forgot plums, baby, and everything. The ends of the blanket slipped from her grasp, and she darted forward like an arrow after her companions.

Finding the chase hopeless, the little girls came to a standstill, and some of them began to cry. The boys had stopped, too; and seeing the tears flow, being good-hearted boys in spite of their mischief, they surrendered at discretion. They threw back the articles they had taken, not daring to come near. They did not consider it manly for big boys like themselves to strike or hurt little girls, even though they delighted in teasing them, and they knew from experience that they would be at the mercy of the offended party if they went near enough to be touched. The boy who had the dinner brought the little pail which had contained it as near as he dared, and setting it down ran away.

"You have spilt all our soup. There's hardly any of it left. You bad boys!" said one of the girls.

They crowded around with lamentations over their lost dinner. The boys began to feel remorseful.

"Let's go into the woods and get them some plums to make up for it."

"Say, girls, hand us your pail, and we'll fill it up with plums for you."

So the affair was settled.

But, meanwhile, what became of the baby left so unceremoniously in the tall grass? First he opened his black eyes wide at this style of treatment. He was not used to it. Before he had time, however, to make up his mind whether to laugh or cry, his mother came to the rescue. She had just come home and thrown the wood off her back, when she caught sight of Nedawi dropping him. She ran to pick him up, and finding him unhurt, kissed him over and over. Some of the neighbors had run up to see what was the matter. She said to them:

"I never did see such a thoughtless, heedless child as my Nedawi. She really has 'no ears.' I don't know what in the world will ever become of her. When something new interests her, she forgets everything else. It was just like her to act in this way."

Then they all laughed, and one of them said:

"Never mind—she will grow wiser as she grows older," after which consoling remark they went away to their own tents.

It was of no use to call Nedawi back. She was too far off.

Habazhu was given over to the care of the nurse, who had just returned from her visit. An hour or two after, Nedawi came home.

"Mother!" she exclaimed, as she saw her mother frying bread for supper, "I am so hungry. Can I have some of that bread?"

"Where is your little brother?" was the unexpected reply.

Nedawi started. Where *had* she left him? She tried to think.

"Why, Mother, the last I remember I was packing him, and—and oh, Mother! you *know* where he is. Please tell me."

"When you find him and bring him back to me, perhaps I shall forgive you," was the cold reply.

This was dreadful. Her mother had never treated her in that way before. She burst into tears, and started out to find Habazhu, crying all the way. She knew that her mother knew where baby was, or she would not have taken it so coolly; and she knew also that her mother expected her to bring him home. As she went stumbling along through the grass, she felt herself seized and held in somebody's strong arms, and a great, round, hearty voice said:

"What's the matter with my little niece? Have all her friends deserted her that she is wailing like this? Or has her little dog died? I thought Nedawi was a brave little women."

It was her uncle Two Crows. She managed to tell him, through her sobs, the whole story. She knew, if she told him herself, he would not laugh at her about it, for he would sympathize in her troubles, though he was a great tease. When she ceased, he said to her: "Well, your mother wants you to be more careful next time, I suppose; and, by the way, I think I saw a little boy who looked very much like Habazhu, in my tent."

Sure enough, she found him there with his nurse. When she got home with them, she found mother,—her own dear self,—and, after giving her a big hug, she sat quietly down by the fire, resolved to be very good in the future. She did not sit long, however, for soon a neighing of horses, and the running of girls and children through the camp to meet the hunters, proclaimed their return. All was bustle and gladness throughout the camp. There had been a successful chase, and the led horses were laden with buffalo meat. These horses were led by the young girls to the tents to be unpacked, while the boys took the hunt-ing-horses to water and tether in the grass. Fathers, as they dismounted, took their little children in their arms, tired as they were. Nedawi was as happy as any in the camp, for her seven-teen-year-old brother, White Hawk, had killed his first buffalo, and had declared that the skin should become Nedawi's robe, as soon as it was tanned and painted.

What a pleasant evening that was to Nedawi, when the whole family sat around a great fire, roasting the huge buffalo ribs, and she played with her little brother Habazhu, stopping now and then to listen to the adventures of the day, which her father and brothers were relating! The scene was truly a delightful one, the camp-fires lighting up the pleasant family groups here and there, as the flames rose and fell. The bit of prairie where the tribe had camped had a clear little stream running through it, with shadowy hills around, while over all hung the clear, star-lit sky. It seemed as if nature were trying to protect the poor waifs of humanity clustered in that spot. Nedawi felt the beauty of the scene, and was just thinking of nestling down by her father to enjoy it dreamily, when her brothers called for a dance. The little drum was brought forth, and Nedawi danced to its accompaniment and her brothers' singing. She danced gravely, as became a little maiden whose duty it was to entertain the family circle. While she was dancing, a little boy, about her own age, was seen hovering near. He would appear, and, when spoken to, would disappear in the tall, thick grass.

It was Mischief, a playmate of Nedawi's. Everybody called him "Mischief," because mischief appeared in every action of his. It shone from his eyes and played all over his face.

"You little plague," said White Hawk; "what do you want?"

For answer, the "little plague" turned a somersault just out of White Hawk's reach. When the singing was resumed, Mischief crept quietly up behind White Hawk, and, keeping just within the shadow, mimicked Nedawi's grave dancing, and he looked so funny that Nedawi suddenly laughed, which was precisely Mischief's object. But before he could get out of reach, as he intended, Thunder, Nedawi's other brother, who had been hav-ing an eye on him, clutched tight hold of him, and Mischief was landed in front of the fire-place, in full view of the whole family. "Now," said Thunder, "you are my prisoner. You stay there and dance with Nedawi." Mischief knew there was no escape, so he submitted with a good grace. He went through all sorts of antics, shaking his fists in the air, twirling suddenly around and putting his head close to the ground, keeping time with the accompani-ment through it all.

Nedawi danced staidly on, now and then frowning at him; but she knew of old that he was irrepressible. When Nedawi sat down, he threw into her lap a little dark something and was off like a shot, yelling at the top of his voice, either in triumph at his recent achievements or as a practice for future war-whoops.

"Nedawi, what is it?" said her mother.

Nedawi took it to the fire, when the something proved to be a poor little bird.

"I thought he had something in his hand when he was shak-ing his fist in the air," said Nedawi's sister, Nazainza, laughing.

"Poor little thing!" said Nedawi; "it is almost dead."

She put its bill into the water, and tenderly tried to make it drink. The water seemed to revive it somewhat.

"I'll wrap it up in something warm," said Nedawi, "and maybe it will sing in the morning."

"Let me see it," said Nedawi's father.

Nedawi carried it to him.

"Don't you feel sorry for it, daughter?"

"Yes, Father," she answered.

"Then take it to the tall grass, yonder, and put it down where no one will step on it, and, as you put it down, say: 'God, I give you back your little bird. As I pity it, pity me.'"

"And will God take care of it?" said Nedawi, reverently, and opening her black eyes wide at the thought.

"Yes," said her father.

"Well, I will do as you say," said Nedawi, and she walked slowly out of the tent.

Then she took it over to the tall, thick grass, and making a nice, cozy little nest for it, left it there, saying just what her father had told her to say. When she came back, she said:

"Father, I said it."

"That was right, little daughter," and Nedawi was happy at her father's commendation.

Nedawi always slept with her grandmother and sister, exactly in the middle of the circle formed by the wigwam, with her feet to the fire-place. That place in the tent was always her grandmother's place, just as the right-hand side of the tent was her father's and mother's and the left-hand her brothers'. There never was any confusion. The tribe was divided into bands, and every band was composed of several families. Each band had its chief, and the whole tribe was ruled by the head-chief, who was Nedawi's father. He had his own particular band besides. Every tent had its own place in the band, and every band had its own particular place in the great circle forming the camp. Each chief was a representative, in council, of the men composing his band, while over all was the head-chief. The executive power was vested in the "soldiers' lodge," and when decisions were arrived at in council, it was the duty of its soldiers to execute all its orders, and punish all violations of the tribal laws. The office of "town-crier" was held by several old men, whose duty it was "to cry out" through the camp the announcements of councils, invitations to feasts, and to give notice of anything in which the whole tribe were called on to take part.

Well, before Nedawi went to sleep this evening, she hugged her grandmother, and said to her:

"Please tell me a story."

Her grandmother said:

"I cannot, because it is summer. In the winter I will tell you stories."

"Why not in summer?" said Nedawi.

"Because, when people tell stories and legends in summer, the snakes come around to listen. You don't want any snakes to come near us to-night, do you?"

"But," said Nedawi, "I have not seen any snakes for the longest time, and if you tell it right softly they won't hear you."

"Nedawi," said her mother, "don't bother your grandmother. She is tired and wants to sleep."

Thereupon Grandmother's heart felt sorry for her pet, and she said to Nedawi:

"Well, if you will keep still and go right to sleep when I am through, I will tell you how the turkeys came to have red eyelids.

"Once upon a time, there was an old woman living all alone with her grandson, Rabbit. He was noted for his cunning and for his tricks, which he played on everyone. One day, the old woman said to him, 'Grandson, I am hungry for some meat.' Then the boy took his bow and arrows, and in the evening he came home with a deer on his shoulders, which he threw at her feet, and said, 'Will that satisfy you?' She said, 'Yes, grandson.' They lived on that meat several days, and, when it was gone, she said to him again, 'Grandson, I am hungry for some meat.' This time he went without his bow and arrows, but he took a bag with him. When he got into the woods, he called all the turkeys together. They gathered around him, and he said to them: 'I am going to sing to you, while you shut your eyes and dance. If one of you opens his eyes while I am singing, his eyelids shall turn red.' Then they all stood in a row, shut their eyes, as he had told them, and began to dance, and this is the song he sang to them while they danced:

> Ha! wadamba thike
> Inshta zhida, inshta zhida,
> Imba theonda,
> Imba theonda.

[The literal translation is:

> Ho! he who peeps
> Red eyes, red eyes,
> Flap your wings,
> Flap your wings.]

"Now, while they were dancing away, with their eyes shut, the boy took them, one by one, and put them into his bag. But the last one in the row began to think it very strange that his companions made no noise, so he gave one peep, screamed in his fright, 'They are making 'way with us!' and flew away. The boy took his bag of turkeys home to his grandmother, but ever after that the turkeys had red eyelids."

Nedawi gave a sigh of satisfaction when the story was finished, and would have asked for more, but just then her brothers came in from a dance which they had been attending in some neighbor's tent. She knew her lullaby time had come. Her brothers always sang before they slept either love or dancing songs, beating time on their breasts, the regular beats making a sort of accompaniment for the singing. Nedawi loved best of all to hear her father's war-songs, for he had a musical voice, and few were the evenings when she had gone to sleep without hearing a lullaby from her father or brothers. Among the

Indians, it is the fathers who sing, instead of the mothers. Women sing only on state occasions, when the tribe have a great dance, or at something of the sort. Mothers "croon" their babies to sleep, instead of singing.

Gradually the singing ceased, and the brothers slept as well as Nedawi, and quiet reigned over the whole camp.[18]

THE INDUSTRIAL WEST

With its roots in the eighteenth century, the Romantic movement entered the nineteenth with a force that matched the new engines of industrial progress. Again, in the arts, the pendulum had swung. Classical formality and restraint gave way to a relentless questioning and self-questioning, and in some cases an escapism, as the artist, a moral hero now liberated from patronage, was on his or her own, to rise or fall, to experiment, and to protest. Caught between the institutionalized expectations of the Academy, the tastes of the public, and the artist's own vision of individual expression, each generation reacted more and more strongly against the style of its predecessor. The pace of change—social, technological, artistic—was quickening, and artists began to feel themselves increasingly marginalized within a materialistic society. The Impressionists and their successors tried to redefine their role and their art.

CLASSICISM

The Neoclassical traditions of the eighteenth century continued into the nineteenth, particularly in France, and the pursuit of physical and intellectual perfection initiated by David was taken up by Jean-Auguste-Dominique Ingres (1780–1867). The work of Ingres, and perhaps David as well, illustrates the confusing relationships and conflicts that surrounded the Neoclassical and Romantic traditions in painting. Ingres's *Grande Odalisque*, or *Harem Girl* (Fig. **12.48**), has been called both Neoclassical and Romantic, and in many ways represents both. Ingres professed to despise Romanticism, and yet his proportions and subject exude Romantic individualism and escape to the far away and long ago. His sensuous textures appear emotional, not intellectual. At the same time, his line is simple, his palette is cool, and his spatial effects are geometric. The linear rhythms of his painting are very precise and calculated and, therefore, Classically intellectual in appeal.

12.48 Jean-Auguste-Dominique Ingres, *Grande Odalisque*, 1814. Oil on canvas, 36¼ x 63¼ ins (92 x 161 cm). The Louvre, Paris.

Neoclassical sculpture prevailed during the early years of the nineteenth century and consisted predominantly of a reproduction of Classical works rather than a revising of them, as was the case in architecture. In France, Neoclassicism served its commemorative and idealizing functions as the political tool of Napoleon, who was glorified in various Greek and Roman settings, sometimes garbed in a toga and sometimes in the nude, as if granting him the status of a Greek god. No style is free from outside influences, and nineteenth century Neoclassical sculpture often reveals aspects of Rococo, Baroque, and Romantic style.

Antonio Canova (1757–1822) is recognized as the ablest of the Neoclassical sculptors, and his works illustrate not only this style, but also influences of the Rococo tradition. *Venus Victrix* (Fig. **12.49**), for which Pauline Borghese, Napoleon's sister, was the model, presents Classical pose and proportions, similar in many ways to Ingres's *Grande Odalisque*. Line, costume, and hairstyle reflect the ancients, but sensuous texture, individualized expression, and realistic and fussy detail suggest other approaches. At the same time, this work is almost two-dimensional. Canova appears unconcerned with the work when see from any angle other than the front.

The nineteenth century was an age of increased individualism and subjective viewpoints. However, what is possible by way of experimentation for the painter, sculptor, musician, choreographer, and to some degree, the playwright, is not always possible for the architect. An architect's work involves a client who must be satisfied, and the results are public and permanent.

The use of Greek and Roman forms after 1750 has been called Classical revival or Neoclassicism. Basically this revival can be broken into two general periods—Roman prior to 1815 and Greek from then on. Often the plethora of terms describing this period can be confusing, including Federal style, which, essentially is a specific substyle of the resurrection of ancient prototypes in the Romantic era.

12.49 Antonio Canova, *Pauline Borghese as Venus Victrix*, 1808. Marble, life-size. Galleria Borghese, Rome.

12.50 Benjamin H. Latrobe, interior, Basilica of the Assumption, Baltimore, Maryland, 1805–18.

Benjamin H. Latrobe's Catholic cathedral in Baltimore (Fig. **12.50**) illustrates many of the principles at issue here. In this view the Ionic orders of Athens are visible in the alcove behind the altar, while a Roman dome, like that of the Pantheon, dominates the nave. These basically "Classical" forms are significantly modified and added to with numerous individualized details. Traditional Roman semicircular arches flank the central opening above the altar, yet that arch and its complements are flattened and also broken by cantilevered balconies. Whimsical, starlike decoration marks the dome, and a misty panorama of painted scenes winds over and through the modified pendentives.

Classical revival found numerous examples in domestic architecture in the United States. The Belamy Mansion in Wilmington, North Carolina, is one of the most exquisite examples of this style (Fig. **12.51**). Designed by Connecticut architect Rufus H. Bunnell, the house was built by skilled, free Blacks and completed in 1859. The stately house is situated on a major thoroughfare a few blocks from the downtown business district, central to the city now as it was a century ago. The beautifully proportioned main body of the house is offset by a massive portico, whose Corinthian columns uphold a monumental cornice and pediment. The entire structure is raised some 5 ft (1.5 m) off the ground on brick pillars, hiding a basement, and crowned by a rectangular cupola.

12.51 Rufus H. Bunnell, Belamy Mansion, Wilmington, North Carolina, 1859.

12.52 Théodore Géricault, *The Raft of the Medusa*, 1819. Oil on canvas, 16 ft x 23 ft 6 ins (4.91 x 7.16 m). The Louvre, Paris.

ROMANTICISM

If Ingres believed himself to be a Neoclassicist and not a Romantic, there were those who willingly championed the banner of Romanticism. The Romantic style was diverse. It had an emotional appeal and tended toward the picturesque, nature, the Gothic, and, often, the macabre. Romanticism sought to break the geometric compositional principles of Classicism. Compositions moved toward fragmentation of images. The intent was to dramatize, to personalize, and to escape into imagination. Romantic painting reflected a striving for freedom from social and artistic rules, a subordination of formal content to expressive intent, and an intense introversion. As the writer Zola said of Romantic naturalism, "A work of art is part of the universe as seen through a temperament." Closely associated with the critic and writer Baudelaire, Romanticism dwelt upon the capacity of color and line to affect the viewer independently of subject matter.

Many Romantic painters are worthy of note, but a detailed look at Géricault and Bonheur will suffice for our overview.

Géricault

Théodore Géricault (1791–1824), pillar of the beginnings of French Romanticism, was a champion of the downtrodden and rejected. A prodigy who died young, he offers us a full conception of the Romantic hero, both in his art and in his life. Although a direct descendant of David, Géricault departed from his master in his use of brushwork. David insisted that the brushwork should not show, whereas Géricault uses the visual impact of the strokes themselves brilliantly. He accepted the heroic Napoleonic view of this period in France's history, and his paintings frequently treat the struggle between humankind and nature. The influence of the grandeur and violence of Michelangelo, is particularly clear in the famous *Raft of the Medusa* (Fig. **12.52**). The painting is in the Romantic style, tempered by Classical and even High Renaissance influences. Géricault, like David, achieved firmly modeled flesh, realistic figures, and a precise play of light and shade. His treatment of the physical form is reminiscent of Michelangelo. In contrast to David's ordered, two-dimensional paintings, however, Géricault's work had complex and fragmented compositional structures. He preferred to base the design on two triangles rather than a strong central triangle. In the *Medusa*, which tells a story of governmental incompetence resulting in tragedy, the left triangle's apex is the makeshift mast, signifying death and despair. The other triangle moves up to the right to the figure waving the fabric, signifying hope as a rescue ship appears in the distance. The dramatic composition is charged with unbridled emotion which extols the individual heroism of the survivors. Seeking maximum fidelity to truth, Géricault interviewed the survivors, read newspaper accounts, and went so far as to paint corpses and the heads of guillotined criminals. His result captures the dramatic climax at the precise moment the rescue ship is sighted. The composition builds upward from the bodies of the dead and dying in the foreground to the dynamic group whose final energies are summoned to support the figure waving to the ship. The play of light and shade heightens the dramatic effect.

Bonheur

Rosa Bonheur (1822–99), certainly the most popular woman painter of her time, has been labeled both a Realist and a Romantic in style. Her subjects were mostly animals, and their raw energy. "Wading in pools of blood," as she put it, she studied animal anatomy even in slaughter houses and was particularly interested in animal psychology. Her work *Plowing in the Nivernais* (Fig. **12.53**) expresses the tremendous power of the oxen on which European agriculture depended before the Industrial Revolution. The beasts appear almost monumental, and each detail is precisely executed. *Plowing in the Nivernais* clearly reveals Bonheur's reverence for the dignity of labor and humankind's harmony with nature.

Romantic Sculpture

Romantic sculpture never developed into a uniform style. Those works not clearly of the traditions we have just mentioned show a generally eclectic spirit and a uniformly undistinguished character. There may be a reasonable explanation for such a phenomenon in that Romantic idealism, whose strivings after nature and the far away and the long ago cannot be easily translated into sculptural expression. Certainly, nineteenth-century devotion to landscapes does not. Of course, the term Romantic is often applied to almost anything of the nineteenth century, as is the case with the most remarkable sculptor of this era, Auguste Rodin (1840–1917).

Rodin's textures, more than anything else, reflect

12.53 Rosa Bonheur, *Plowing in the Nivernais*, 1849. Oil on canvas, 5 ft 9 ins x 8 ft 8 ins (1.75 x 2.64 m). Musée Nationale du Château de Fontainebleau.

12.54 Auguste Rodin, *The Thinker*, first modeled c. 1880, executed c. 1910. Bronze, height 27½ ins (70 cm). The Metropolitan Museum of Art, New York (Gift of Thomas F. Ryan, 1910 [11.173.9]).

Impressionism; his surfaces appear to shimmer as light plays on their irregular features. The *Thinker* (Fig. **12.54**) provides a familiar example and shows the difficulty inherent in attempting to put into sculptural form what painters like Monet were trying to do with color and texture. Rodin's textures, however, are more than reflective surfaces—they give his works dynamic and dramatic qualities. Although he used a fair degree of verisimilitude, he nevertheless presented a reality beyond the surface.

Romantic Literature

The beginning of the main phase of Romantic literature can probably be dated to around 1790. One characteristic was the tendency of writers to form groups or partnerships, an example of which was the close relationship between Goethe and Schiller. Britain again produced major literary figures such as Wordsworth, Coleridge, Scott, Byron, Shelley, and Keats.

Wordsworth

William Wordsworth (1770–1850) charged the commonplace and everyday with transcendental and often indefinable significance. He created a new world of beauty through his closeness to nature and in the harmony he felt existed between man and nature.

In 1795, he met Samuel Taylor Coleridge (1772–1834), an English poet, and his relationship with Coleridge opened his life and writing. Out of this relationship came the *Lyrical Ballads*, which Wordsworth published anonymously along with four poems by Coleridge. Among these ballads, *Tintern Abbey* exhibits Wordsworth's love of nature. That love is first seen as a sensuous animal passion, then as a moral influence, and finally as a mystical communion.

**Lines Composed a Few Miles
Above Tintern Abbey, on Revisiting
the Banks of the Wye
During a Tour. July 13, 1798**

Five years have past; five summers, with the length
Of five long winters! and again I hear
These waters, rolling from their mountain-springs
With a soft inland murmur.—Once again
Do I behold these steep and lofty cliffs,
That on a wild secluded scene impress
Thoughts of more deep seclusion; and connect
The landscape with the quiet of the sky.
The day is come when I again repose
Here, under this dark sycamore, and view
These plots of cottage-ground, these orchard-tufts,
Which at this season, with their unripe fruits,
Are clad in one green hue, and lose themselves
'Mid groves and copses. Once again I see
These hedge-rows, hardly hedge-rows, little lines
Of sportive wood run wild: these pastoral farms,
Green to the very door; and wreaths of smoke
Sent up, in silence, from among the trees!
With some uncertain notice, as might seem
Of vagrant dwellers in the houseless woods,
Or of some Hermit's cave, where by his fire
The Hermit sits alone.

These beauteous forms,
Through a long absence, have not been to me
As is a landscape to a blind man's eye:
But oft, in lonely rooms, and 'mid the din
Of towns and cities, I have owed to them

In hours of weariness, sensations sweet,
Felt in the blood, and felt along the heart;
And passing even into my purer mind,
With tranquil restoration:—feelings too
Of unremembered pleasure: such, perhaps,
As have no slight or trivial influence
On that best portion of a good man's life,
His little, nameless, unremembered, acts
Of kindness and of love. Nor less, I trust,
To them I may have owed another gift,
Of aspect more sublime; that blessed mood,
In which the burthen of the mystery,
In which the heavy and the weary weight
Of all this unintelligible world,
Is lightened:—that serene and blessed mood,
In which the affections gently lead us on,—
Until, the breath of this corporeal frame
And even the motion of our human blood
Almost suspended, we are laid asleep
In body, and become a living soul:
While with an eye made quiet by the power
Of harmony, and the deep power of joy,
We see into the life of things.

If this
Be but a vain belief, yet, oh! how oft—
In darkness and amid the many shapes
Of joyless daylight; when the fretful stir
Unprofitable, and the fever of the world,
Have hung upon the beatings of my heart—
How oft, in spirit, have I turned to thee,
O sylvan Wye! thou wanderer thro' the woods,
How often has my spirit turned to thee!
And now, with gleams of half-extinguished thought,
With many recognitions dim and faint,
And somewhat of a sad perplexity,
The picture of the mind revives again:
While here I stand, not only with the sense
Of present pleasure, but with pleasing thoughts
That in this moment there is life and food
For future years. And so I dare to hope,
Though changed, no doubt, from what I was when first
I came among these hills; when like a roe
I bounded o'er the mountains, by the sides
Of the deep rivers, and the lonely streams,
Wherever nature led: more like a man
Flying from something that he dreads, than one
Who sought the thing he loved. For nature then
(The coarser pleasures of my boyish days,
And their glad animal movements all gone by)
To me was all in all.—I cannot paint
What then I was. The sounding cataract
Haunted me like a passion: the tall rock,
The mountain, and the deep and gloomy wood,

Their colours and their forms, were then to me
An appetite; a feeling and a love,
That had no need of a remoter charm,
By thought supplied, nor any interest
Unborrowed from the eye.—That time is past,
And all its aching joys are now no more,
And all its dizzy raptures. Not for this
Faint I, nor mourn nor murmur; other gifts
Have followed; for such loss, I would believe,
Abundant recompense. For I have learned
To look on nature, not as in the hour
Of thoughtless youth; but hearing often-times
The still, sad music of humanity,
Nor harsh nor grating, though of ample power
To chasten and subdue. And I have felt
A presence that disturbs me with the joy
Of elevated thoughts; a sense sublime
Of something far more deeply interfused,
Whose dwelling is the light of setting suns,
And the round ocean and the living air,
And the blue sky, and in the mind of man;
A motion and a spirit, that impels
All thinking things, all objects of all thought,
And rolls through all things. Therefore am I still
A lover of the meadows and the woods,
And mountains; and of all that we behold
From this green earth; of all the mighty world
Of eye, and ear,—both what they half create,
And what perceive; well pleased to recognise
In nature and the language of the sense,
The anchor of my purest thoughts, the nurse,
The guide, the guardian of my heart, and soul
Of all my moral being.
    Nor perchance,
If I were not thus taught, should I the more
Suffer my genial spirits to decay:
For thou art with me here upon the banks
Of this fair river; thou my dearest Friend,
My dear, dear Friend; and in thy voice I catch
The language of my former heart, and read
My former pleasures in the shooting lights
Of thy wild eyes. Oh! yet a little while
May I behold in thee what I was once,
My dear, dear Sister! and this prayer I make,
Knowing that Nature never did betray
The heart that loved her; 'tis her privilege,
Through all the years of this our life, to lead
From joy to joy: for she can so inform
The mind that is within us, so impress
With quietness and beauty, and so feed
With lofty thoughts, that neither evil tongues,
Rash judgments, nor the sneers of selfish men,
Nor greetings where no kindness is, nor all
The dreary intercourse of daily life,

Shall e'er prevail against us, or disturb
Our cheerful faith, that all which we behold
Is full of blessings. Therefore let the moon
Shine on thee in thy solitary walk;
And let the misty mountain-winds be free
To blow against thee; and, in after years,
When these wild ecstasies shall be matured
Into a sober pleasure; when thy mind
Shall be a mansion for all lovely forms,
Thy memory be as a dwelling-place
For all sweet sounds and harmonies; oh! then,
If solitude, or fear, or pain, or grief,
Should be thy portion, with what healing thoughts
Of tender joy wilt thou remember me,
And these my exhortations! Nor, perchance—
If I should be where I no more can hear
Thy voice, nor catch from thy wild eyes these gleams
Of past existence—wilt thou then forget
That on the banks of this delightful stream
We stood together; and that I, so long
A worshipper of Nature, hither came
Unwearied in that service: rather say
With warmer love—oh! with far deeper zeal
Of holier love. Nor wilt thou then forget,
That after many wanderings, many years
Of absence, these steep woods and lofty cliffs,
And this green pastoral landscape, were to me
More dear, both for themselves and for thy sake![19]

Romantic Style in Music

In pursuit of the expression of human emotion, Romantic music made stylistic changes to Classical music. The Classical-Romantic antithesis—the form versus feeling or the intellect versus emotional conflict—simply cannot be applied neatly to music of the eighteenth and nineteenth centuries. Subjectivity and emotion played a more important role in Romanticism, and even if Classicism sought sustenance in nature and antiquity, Romanticism imbued nature with a strangeness that went beyond Classical inspirations. Utopia, whether in the past or the future, and nature, whether malevolent or benevolent, were as obvious and influential in nineteenth-century music as in any other art discipline.

As in painting, spontaneity replaced control, but the primary emphasis of music in this era was on beautiful, lyrical, and expressive melody. Phrases became longer, more irregular, and more complex than in Classical music. Melodic development nearly always had individual performance virtuosity as its object.

Rhythm varied from simple to complex. Much of the Romantic rhythm was strictly traditional, but experiments produced new meters and patterns. Emotional conflict was often suggested by juxtaposing duple and triple meters, and rhythmic irregularity became increasingly common as the century progressed.

Harmony and tone color changed significantly. Harmony was seen as a means of expression, and any logic or restriction regarding key relationships was submerged by the need to achieve striking emotional effects. Form was clearly subordinate to feeling. Harmonic procedures became increasingly complex, and traditional outlines of major and minor keys were blurred in chromatic harmonies, complicated chords, and modulations to distant keys. In fact, key changes became so frequent in some composers' works that their compositions comprised virtually nothing but tonal whirls of continuous modulation. Chromaticism—the altering of normal whole- and half-tone relationships in a scale—gained increasing importance as composers sought to disrupt previously logical expectations. The result was a sense of uncertainty and of the bizarre. More and more dissonance occurred, changing in its role from that of a passing dissettlement leading to resolution to that of a principal focus. That is, dissonance was explored for its own sake, as a stimulant of emotional response, as opposed to its use merely as a device in traditional harmonic progression to resolution on the tonic. By the end of the Romantic period, exploration (and exhaustion) of chromatics and dissonance led to a search for a wholly different tonal system.

Exploration of color as a response stimulant was as important to the Romantic musician as it was to the painter. Interest in tonal color or timbre led to great diversity in vocal and instrumental performance. The technical and emotional limbs of every aspect of music were probed with enthusiasm, and music literature of this period abounds with solo works and a tremendous increase in the size and diversity of the orchestra.

Chopin

Frederic Chopin (1810–49) wrote almost exclusively for the piano. Each of his *études*, or technical studies, explored a single technical problem, usually around a single motive. More than simple exercises, these works explored the possibilities of the instrument and became short tone poems in their own right. A second group of compositions included short intimate works such as preludes, nocturnes, and impromptus and dances such as waltzes, polonaises, and mazurkas. Polish folk dance tunes were particularly influential. A final class of compositions included larger works such as scherzos, ballades, and fantasies. Chopin's compositions were highly individualized, and many were without precedent. His style was completely opposed to Classicism, almost totally without standard form and having little sense of balance of structure. His melodies were lyrical, and his moods varied from melancholy to exaltation.

Brahms

At the same time as these relatively innovative directions were being pursued by Romantic composers, a traditional direction continued in the Romantic symphony and concerto, personified by Johannes Brahms (1833–97). His direction, while employing the lyrical melodic tendencies of the period, retained Classical form, and he produced symphonic works based solely on musical information. That is, these symphonic works are built upon musical ideas such as motifs, themes and phrases, and maintain their unity through structure as opposed to nonmusical ideas or texts. These works are known as abstract or absolute music. Their melodies, rhythms, and timbres reflect the characteristics noted at the beginning of the chapter, and include an increasingly dense texture and greatly expanded dynamic range. Although their form maintains tradition, their effect is emotional—the listener is bathed in an overwhelmingly sensual experience. Contrasts in dynamics and timbre are stressed, and, as in painting, form, although maintained, is subordinated to expressive intent.

An outstanding example of the romantic symphony is Brahms' *Symphony No. 3 in F Major* (1883). Composed in four movements, the work calls for pairs of flutes, oboes, clarinets, bassoon, a contrabassoon, four horns, two trumpets, three trombones, two timpani, and strings.

12.55 Brahms, *Symphony No. 3 in F Major*, opening theme.

Tchaikovsky

We can also identify a new nationalistic trend in music of the Romantic period. The roots of such movements went deep into the past, but the political circumstances of the century prompted composers. Folk tunes and themes dominated this tendency, and localized experimentation with rhythms and harmonics created qualities which, while still within Romantic parameters, are easily associated with national identities. This was true in Russia, Bohemia (Czechoslovakia), Spain, England, Scandinavia, and in Germany and Austria.

Of all the nationalistic composers of the Romantic period, the Russian Peter Ilyich Tchaikovsky (1840–93) has enjoyed the greatest popularity. His *Violin Concerto in D Major* (1878) remains one of the best-known nineteenth-century concertos for violin.

Romantic Opera

Early Romantic opera in Italy featured the *bel canto* style, which emphasizes beauty of sound. Illustrative of this substyle of Romanticism were the works of Rossini (1792–1868). Rossini's *Barber of Seville* takes melodic singing to tremendous heights and quality. His songs are light, ornamented, and very appealing, and his drama is exciting.

Great artists often stand apart from or astride general stylistic trends, exploring on their own a unique or dominant theme. Such is the case with the Italian composer Giuseppe Verdi (1813–1901). Verdi combined earthy emotions and clear expression within a nationalistic philosophy. He refined opera into a human drama consisting of simple, beautiful melody.

His long career experienced different phases. The early phase saw works such as *La Traviata* (1853). In these works Verdi focused upon logic and structure, using recurring themes to provide unity.

Out of this second phase came *Aida* (1871), a grand opera of spectacular proportion built upon a tightly woven dramatic structure. Finally, a third phase produced operas based on Shakespearean plays. *Otello* (1887) contrasts tragedy and *opera buffa*, and explores subtle balance among voices and orchestra, in concert with strong melodic development.

Wagner

Richard Wagner (1813–83) was perhaps the master of Romantic opera. At the heart of Wagner's prolific artistry lay a philosophy which was to affect the world of the musical and legitimate stage from the mid-nineteenth century to the present day. His ideas were laid out principally in two books—*Art and Revolution* (1849) and *Opera and Drama* (1851). Wagner's philosophy centered on the *Gesamtkunstwerk*, a comprehensive work of art in which music, poetry and scenery are all subservient to the central generating idea. For Wagner the total unity of all elements reigned supreme. Fully expressive of German Romantic philosophy, which confers upon music supremacy over all other arts, Wagner's operas placed music in the predominant role. Dramatic meaning unfolded through the use of *leitmotif*, for which Wagner is famous, although he did not invent it. A leitmotif ties a musical theme to ideas, persons, or objects. Whenever those ideas, persons, or objects appear or occupy thought, the theme is played. Juxtaposing leitmotifs can suggest relationships between their subjects to the audience. These themes also provide the composer with building blocks, which can be used for development, recapitulation, and unification.

Wagner's operas are legendary. Each work deserves detailed attention. However, whatever we might say by way of description or analysis would be insignificant compared to the dramatic power these works exhibit in full production. Even a recording cannot approach the tremendous effect of these works in full production in an opera house.

Romantic Ballet

Choreographers of Romantic ballet sought magic and escape in fantasies and legends. Ballets about elves and nymphs enjoyed great popularity, as did ballets about madness, sleepwalking, and opium dreams. Fascinating subject matter came to the fore, for example, harem wives revolting against their oppressors with the help of the "Spirit of Womankind," in Filippo Taglioni's the *Revolt in the Harem* (possibly the first ballet about the emancipation of women). Not only did women come to prominence as ballerinas and in subject matter, but also as choreographers.

Giselle (1841) marked the height of Romantic achievement. It contains many fine dancing roles for women and men and has been a favorite of ballet companies since its first production. Adolphe Adam, known for his piece *O Holy Night*, composed the score. The prima ballerina was Carlotta Grisi. The choreography was created by Jean Coralli, ballet master at the Paris Opéra, although, apparently, Jules Perrot, Carlotta's teacher, choreographed all of her dances and in them lies the essence of the ballet.

Romantic Architecture

Romanticism also borrowed styles from other eras and produced a vast array of buildings reviving Gothic motifs and reflecting fantasy, a style which has come to be known as Picturesque. Eastern influence and whimsy abounded in John Nash's Royal Pavilion in Brighton, England (Fig. **12.56**). Picturesque also describes the most famous example of Romantic architecture, the Houses of

12.56 John Nash, Royal Pavilion, Brighton, England, remodeled 1815–23.

Parliament (Fig. **12.57**). The Houses of Parliament demonstrates a significant concept which can be described as a modern tendency in architectural design. The exterior walls function as a screen, and suggest nothing of structure, interior design or function. What we find inside has absolutely no spatial relationship to the outside. The strong contrast of forms and totally asymmetrical balance is also significant.

The nineteenth century was an age of industry, of experimentation and new materials. In architecture steel and glass came to the fore. At first it took courage for an architect actually to display structural honesty by allowing support materials to be seen as part of the design itself. England's Crystal Palace (Fig. **12.58**) exemplified the

12.57 (*left*) Sir Charles Barry and Augustus Welby Northmore Pugin, Houses of Parliament, London, 1839–52.

12.58 Sir Joseph Paxton, Crystal Palace, London, 1851.

nineteenth-century fascination with new materials and concepts. Built for the Great Exhibition of 1851, this mammoth structure was completed in the space of nine months. Space was defined by a three-dimensional grid of iron stanchions and girders, designed specifically for mass production and rapid assembly (in this case, disassembly as well—the entire structure was disassembled and rebuilt in 1852–4 at Sydenham). Like the Houses of Parliament, the Crystal Palace was the product of the growing dichotomy between the function of a building as reflected in the arrangement of the interior spaces, it surface decoration, and its structure.

REALISM

A new painting style called Realism arose in the mid-nineteenth century. The term occurs in varying contexts in various sources. Some refer to social Realism, which describes various styles that emphasize the contemporary scene, usually from a left-wing point of view and always with a strong thematic emphasis on the pressure of society on human beings. Others extend Realism to include painters like Manet. For others, the term appears to apply only to Courbet. Whatever the case, the term "reality" in the

nineteenth century came to have special significance because the camera, a machine to record events, people, and locations, thrust itself into what previously had been considered the painter's realm.

Courbet

The central figure of Realism was Gustave Courbet (1819–77), whose aim was to make an objective and unprejudiced record of the customs, ideas, and appearances of contemporary French society. He depicted everyday life and was influenced by the innovations of Corot in terms of the play of light on surfaces (Fig. 12.59). This painting was the first to display his philosophy to the full. Courbet painted two men as he had seen them, working beside a road. The painting is lifesize, and the treatment seems objective, and yet it makes a sharp comment on the tedium and laborious nature of the task. Also a social Realist, Courbet was more intent on social message than on meditative reaction and was therefore less dramatic and nostalgic than others.

12.59 Gustave Courbet, *The Stone Breakers*, 1849. Oil on canvas, 5 ft 3 ins x 8 ft 6 ins (1.6 x 2.59 m). Formerly Gemalde Galerie, Dresden (destroyed 1945).

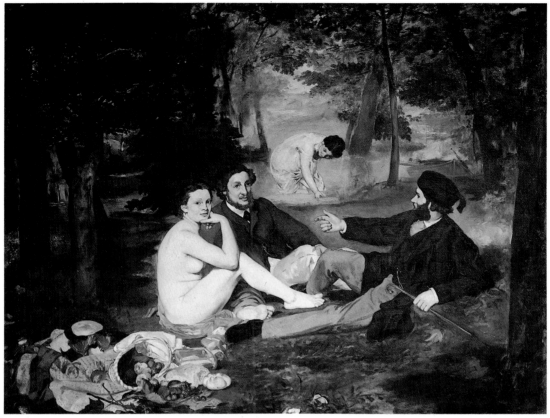

12.60 Edouard Manet, *Le Déjeuner sur l'herbe (The Picnic)*, 1863. Oil on canvas, 7 ft x 8 ft 10 ins (2.13 x 2.69 m). The Louvre, Paris.

Manet

Edouard Manet (1832–83) followed in the Realist tradition, although often he is regarded as an Impressionist (an association he denied). He strove to paint "only what the eye can see." Yet his works go beyond a mere reflection of reality to encompass an artistic reality, telling us that a painting has an internal logic different from the logic of familiar reality. Manet liberated the canvas from competition with the camera. As indicated in the catalogue for an exhibition he produced when he was excluded from the International Exhibition in Paris in 1867, Manet believed that he presented in his art, not a faultless perception, but, rather a sincere perception. In his sincerity came a form of protest—his impressions. To a certain extent Manet was both a conformist and a protester; he came from a comfortable bourgeois background and yet maintained a conviction in socialism. His work leans heavily on the masters of the past, for example, Raphael and Watteau, and at the same time explores completely new ground. He sought acceptance in the salon circles while seeking to shock those same individuals. He sought to be a man of his own time and to reject the superficiality he found in

Romantic themes. He gives the reality of the world around him a different and more straightforward interpretation. He "merely tried to be himself and not someone else." As a result, he often is hailed as the "first modern painter." *Le Déjeuner sur l'herbe* (Fig. **12.60**) shocked the public when it first appeared, at the Salon des Refusés in 1863. Manet sought specifically to "speak in a new voice." The setting is pastoral, as we might find in Watteau, for example, but the people are real and identifiable: Manet's model, his brother, and the sculptor Leenhof. The apparent immorality of a naked frolic in a Paris park outraged the public and the critics. Had his figures been nymphs and satyrs or men and women in Classical dress, all would have been well; but Manet wanted both to be accepted by the Salon, and to shock its organizers and visitors. The painting is both a modern version and a comment upon similar themes of the past. But the intrusion of reality into the sacred confines of the mythical proved more than the public could handle.

Manet's search for spontaneity, harmonious colors, subjects from everyday life, and faithfulness to observed lighting and atmospheric effects led to the development of a style by a small group of painters in the 1860s described in 1874 by a hostile critic as Impressionists.

Tanner

The first important Black painter, the American Henry O. Tanner (1859–1937), studied with the American Realist painter Thomas Eakins (1844–1916). *The Banjo Lesson* (Fig. **12.61**) presents its images in a strictly realistic manner, without sentimentality. The painting's focus is achieved through the contrast of clarity in the central objects and less detail in the surrounding areas. In many respects this technique follows Corot's experiments with the perceptual experience—that is, the natural phenomenon wherein only those objects immediately in the center of our vision are in sharp focus; the rest remain slightly out of focus. Tanner's skill is in capturing the atmosphere of concentration and the warm relationship of teacher and pupil.

IMPRESSIONISM

The Impressionists created a new way of seeing reality and sought to capture "the psychological perception of reality in color and motion." Undoubtedly Manet should be credited with the original concepts of the style. It emerged in competition with the newly invented technology of the camera, and the Impressionists tried to beat photography at its own game by portraying the essentials of perception which the camera cannot capture. The style lasted only fifteen years in its purest form, but it profoundly influenced all art that followed. Working out of doors, the Impressionists concentrated on the effects of natural light on objects and atmosphere. They discovered that color, for example, is not inherent in an object but in the perception of that object as modified by the quality of existing light. Their experiments resulted in a profoundly different vision of the world around them and way of rendering that vision. This "revolution of the color patch," as it has been called, taught that the painted canvas was, first of all "a material surface covered with pigments—that we must look *at* it, not *through* it." As we look at the paintings, we observe that the canvas is filled with small "color patches," and that our impression of the reality depicted comes as through the totality of those "flickering" patches. The result is a lively and vibrant image.

Impressionism was as collective a style as any we have seen thus far. In an age as individualistic as the nineteenth century this style reflected the common concerns of a relatively small group of artists who met together

12.61 Henry O. Tanner, *The Banjo Lesson*, c. 1893. Oil on canvas, 48 x 35 ins (122 x 89 cm). Hampton University Museum, Hampton, Virginia.

frequently and held joint exhibitions. As a result, this painting style had marked characteristics, which applied to all its exponents. Paintings of the style are impressions of landscapes, rivers, streets, cafés, theatres, and so on. *On the Seine at Bennecourt* (Fig. **12.62**) by Claude Monet (1840–1926) illustrates the concerns of the Impressionists. It portrays a pleasant picture of the times, an optimistic view, in contrast to the often pessimistic viewpoint of the Romantics. It also suggests a fragmentary and fleeting image—a new tone in a new era. The tempo increases, and life's pace is more rapid. Monet, along with Degas, Renoir, and Mary Cassatt, among others, were central figures in the development of Impressionism.

12.62 Claude Monet, *On the Seine at Bennecourt* (Au Bord de l'eau, Bennecourt), 1868. Oil on canvas, 31⅞ x 39½ ins (81.5 x 100.7 cm). Potter Palmer Collection. Photograph © 1990. Art Institute of Chicago. All rights reserved.

Renoir

Pierre Auguste Renoir (1841–1919) specialized in the human figure and sought out what was beautiful in the body. His paintings sparkle with the joy of life. In *Moulin de la Galette* (Fig. **12.63**) he depicts the bright gaiety of a Sunday crowd in a popular Parisian dance hall. The artist celebrates the liveliness and charm of these everyday folk as they talk, crowd the tables, flirt, and dance. Sunlight and shade dapple the scene and create a sort of floating sensation in light. There is a casualness here, a sense of life captured in a fleeting and spontaneous moment, and of a much wider scene extending beyond the canvas. This is not a formally composed scene like David's *Oath of the Horatii* (Fig. **12.35**). Rather, we are invited to become a part of the action. People are going about their everyday routine with no reaction to the painter's presence. As opposed to the Classicist who seeks the universal and the typical, the *realism* of the Impressionist seeks "the incidental, the momentary and the passing."

12.63 Pierre-Auguste Renoir, *Moulin de la Galette*, 1876. Oil on canvas, 51½ x 69 ins (131 x 175 cm). The Louvre, Paris.

Morisot

The original group of Impressionists included a woman, Berthe Morisot (1841–95), on equal terms. Her works have a gentle introspection, often focusing on family members. Her view of contemporary life is edged with pathos and sentimentality. In *In the Dining Room* (Fig. **12.64**) she uses Impressionist techniques to give a penetrating glimpse of psychological reality. The servant girl has a personality, and she stares back at the viewer with complete self-assurance. The painting captures a moment of disorder: the cabinet door stands ajar with what appears to be a used table cloth merely flung over it. The little dog playfully demands attention. Morisot's brushstroke is delicate, and her scenes are full of insight.

Debussy

In music the anti-Romantic spirit produced a style analogous to that of the Impressionist painters. Even among the Romantics a free use of chromatics marked later nineteenth-century style. However, a parting of the ways occurred, the effects of which still permeate contemporary music. On the one hand free use of chromatics and key shifts stayed within the parameters of traditional major/minor tonality. By the end of the century traditional tonality was rejected completely, and a new atonal harmonic expression occurred. Rejection of traditional tonality led to Impressionism in music, a movement international in scope but limited in quantity and quality. There was some influence from the Impressionist painters, but mostly Impressionism in music turned to the Symbolist poets for inspiration.

12.64 Berthe Morisot, *In the Dining Room*, 1886. Oil on canvas, 24⅛ x 19¾ ins (61 x 50 cm). National Gallery of Art, Washington DC.

Even though Impressionist music was international, it is difficult, principally for want of significance or quality, to go beyond its primary champion, Claude Debussy (1862–1918), to find its substance. However, Debussy did not like to be called an Impressionist, which is not surprising because the label was coined by a severe critic of the painters and was intended to be derogatory. He maintained that he was "an old romantic who has thrown the worries of success out the window," and he sought no association with the painters. However, similar motifs can be seen. His use of tone color has been described as "wedges of color" applied in a similar way to painters' individual brushstrokes. Oriental influence is also apparent, especially in Debussy's use of the Asian five-tone scale. He wished above all to return French music to fundamental sources in nature and move it away from the heaviness of the German tradition. He delighted in natural scenes, as did the Impressionist painters, and sought to capture the effects of shimmering light.

In contrast to his predecessors, Debussy reduced melodic development to short motifs of limited range and removed chordal harmony from traditional progression, perhaps his greatest break with tradition. For Debussy a chord was considered strictly on the merits of its expressive capabilities and apart from any context of tonal progression. As a result, gliding chords (repetition of a chord up and down the scale) have become a hallmark of musical Impressionism. Dissonance and irregular rhythm and meter further distinguish Debussy's works. Here, again, form and content are subordinate to expressive intent. His works tend to suggest, rather than to state, and to leave the listener with ambiguity, with an impression. Freedom, flexibility, and nontraditional timbres mark his compositions, the most famous of which is *Prélude à l'après-midi d'un faune*, based on a poem by Mallarmé. The piece uses a large orchestra, with emphasis on the woodwinds, most notably in the haunting theme running throughout. Although freely ranging in an irregular $\frac{9}{8}$ meter and having virtually no tonal centers, *Prélude* has a basically traditional ABA structure.

12.65 Georges Seurat, *Sunday Afternoon on the Island of La Grande Jatte*, 1884–86. Oil on canvas, 6 ft 9½ ins x 10 ft ⅜ ins (2.07 x 3.06 m). Helen Birch Bartlett Memorial Collection, 1926.224. Photograph © 1990. Art Institute of Chicago. All rights reserved.

POST-IMPRESSIONISM

In the last two decades of the nineteenth century Impressionism evolved gently into a collection of rather disparate styles called, simply, Post-Impressionism. In subject matter Post-Impressionist paintings were similar to Impressionist paintings—landscapes, familiar portraits, groups, and café and nightclub scenes. The Post-Impressionists, however, gave their subject matter a complex and profoundly personal significance. Georges Seurat (1859–91), often described as a Neo-impressionist (he called his approach and technique *divisionism*), departed radically from existing painting technique with experiments in optics and color theory. His patient and systematic application of specks of paint is called *pointillism*, because paint is applied with the point of the brush, one small dot at a time. He applied paint in accordance with his theory of color perception, and *Sunday Afternoon on the Island of Grande Jatte* (Fig. **12.65**) illustrates his concern for the accurate depiction of light and colorations of objects. The composition of this work shows attention to perspective, and yet it willfully avoids three-dimensionality. As was the case in much of Post-Impressionism, Japanese influence is apparent—color areas are fairly uniform, figures are flattened, and outlining is continuous. Throughout the work we find conscious systematizing. The painting is broken into proportions of three-eighths and halves, which Seurat believed represented true harmony. He also selected his colors by formula. Physical reality for Seurat was a pretext for the artist's search for a superior harmony, for an abstract perfection.

Post-Impressionism in painting called for a return to form and structure, characteristics the Post-Impressionists believed were essential to art and were lacking in the works of the Impressionists. Taking the evanescent light qualities of the Impressionists, Gauguin, Seurat, Van Gogh, and Cézanne brought formal patterning to their canvases, used clean color areas, and casually applied color in a systematic and almost scientific manner. The Post-Impressionists sought to return painting to traditional goals while, at the same time, retaining the clean palette of the Impressionists.

Paul Cézanne (1839–1906), considered by many as the father of modern art, illustrates concern for formal design, and his *Mont Sainte-Victoire* (Fig. **12.66**) shows a nearly geometric configuration and balance. Foreground and background are tied together in a systematic manner so that both join in the foreground to create two-dimensional patterns. Shapes are simplified and outlining is used throughout. Cézanne employed geometric shapes—the cone, the sphere, and the cylinder—to reveal the permanent reality that lay beneath surface appearance.

A highly imaginative approach to Post-Impressionist goals came from Paul Gauguin (1848–1903). An artist without training, and a nomad who believed that all European society and its works were sick, Gauguin devoted his life to art and wandering, spending many years in rural Brittany and the end of his life in Tahiti and the Marquesas Islands. His work shows his insistence on form and his resistance to naturalistic effects. The *Vision after the Sermon* (Fig. **12.67**) has Gauguin's typically flat, outlined figures, simple forms, and the symbolism for which he and his followers were known—Symbolists or Nabis (from the Hebrew word for prophet). In the background of this painting Jacob wrestles with the Angel while, in the foreground, a priest, nuns, and women in Breton costume pray. The intense reds of this work are typical of Gauguin's symbolic and unnatural use of color, used here to portray the powerful sensations of a Breton folk festival.

A final approach to Post-Impressionism was that of Vincent van Gogh (1853–90), whose emotionalism in the pursuit of form was absolutely unique. Van Gogh's turbulent life included numerous short-lived careers, impossible love affairs, a tempestuous friendship with Gauguin, and, finally, serious mental illness. Biography here is essential because van Gogh gives us one of the most personal and subjective artistic viewpoints in the history of Western art. Works such as *The Starry Night* (Fig. **1.1**) explode with frenetic energy manifested in van Gogh's brushwork. Flattened forms and outlining reflect Japanese influence. Tremendous power and controlled focal areas exist, and we can sense the dynamic, personal energy and mental turmoil present in van Gogh's art.

EXPERIMENTATION IN ARCHITECTURE

A new age of experimentation also took nineteenth-century architects in a different direction—upward. Late in the period the skyscraper was designed in response to the need to create commercial space on limited property in burgeoning urban areas. Burnham and Root's Monadnock Building in Chicago (Fig. **7.19**) was an early example. Although this prototypical "skyscraper" is all masonry—built completely of brick and requiring increasingly thick walls toward its base—it was part of the trend to combine design, materials, and new concepts of architectural space. When all these elements were finally combined, the

12.66 Paul Cézanne, *Mont Sainte-Victoire seen from Les Lauves*, 1902–4. Oil on canvas, 27½ x 35¼ ins (70 x 90 cm). The Philadelphia Museum of Art (George W. Elkins Collection).

12.68 Louis Henry Sullivan, Carson, Pirie and Scott Department Store, Chicago, 1899–1904.

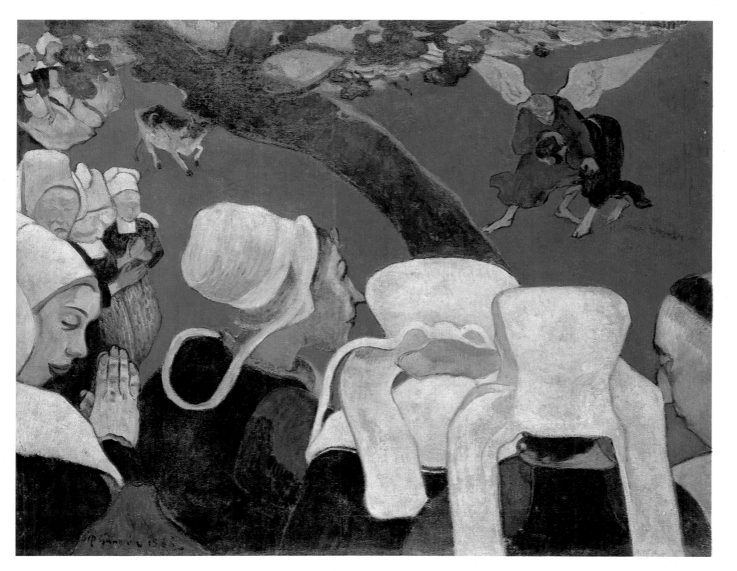

12.67 Paul Gauguin, *The Vision after the Sermon,* 1888. Oil on canvas, 28¾ x 36¼ ins (73 x 92 cm). The National Gallery of Scotland, Edinburgh.

skyscraper emerged—almost exclusively in America. Architects were able to erect buildings of unprecedented height without increasing the thickness of lower walls by erecting structural frameworks (first of iron, later of steel) and by treating walls as independent partitions. Each story was supported on horizontal girders. The concept of the skyscraper could not be realized, however, until a man named Otis had invented a safe elevator.

A very influential figure in the development of the skyscraper and the philosophy of modern architecture was Louis Sullivan, the first truly modern architect. Working in the last decade of the nineteenth century in Chicago, then the most rapidly developing metropolis in the world, Sullivan designed buildings characterized by dignity, simplicity, and strength. Most importantly, he created a rubric for modern architecture by combining form and function into a theory in which the former flowed from the latter. As Sullivan said to an observer of the Carson, Pirie, and Scott building (Fig. **12.68**), "It is evident that we are looking at a department store. Its purpose is clearly set forth in its general aspect, and the form follows the function in a simple, straightforward way."[20]

THIRTEEN

PLURALISM IN THE TWENTIETH CENTURY

The one constant in the arts of this turbulent and phenomenal century has been a seemingly inexhaustible quest for originality and freshness. Among the awesome contradictions of an age that has witnessed the worst and the best that humanity is capable of, our vision of ourselves and where we are going is as troublesome for us as it was for our Paleolithic ancestors.

In contrast to the atmosphere of flurried change in the West, many cultures still make use of the traditional practices and techniques of their forefathers. The so-called "primitive" art of Africans and Native Americans in fact masks a web of complicated rituals, myths, and beliefs in which art plays a crucial role. Despite enormous differences between the function and style of tribal and Western art, the two-way flow of influence has been significant, particularly in the modern era.

NATIVE AMERICAN STYLES

NATIVE AMERICAN FICTION

As we discussed in the last chapter, the period from 1870 to 1920 produced a profound change in Native American culture and circumstances. Confinement to reservations and an increase in formal education changed both the Indian way of life and, in particular, its tradition of oral transmission of culture. The perception of Indian and white cultures as being incompatible was a frequent issue for both cultures, and, in fact, these conflicts were a common preoccupation and central theme for Indian writers—many of whom were "half-breeds" and the products of the white man's education. "Half-breeds" were popular subjects in the nineteenth and early twentieth centuries, and writers who focused on transculturation give us a profound insight into the Native American mind.

340

Gertrude Bonnin, a South Dakota Yankton Sioux, who had a full-blooded mother and an Anglo-American father, wrote under the pen name of Red Bird (Zitkala-Sa). The mixed-blood protagonist of "The Soft-Hearted Sioux" (published in 1901), and which we include here, reflects the conflicts of the Native American caught between cultures. Unable to function in either world, he is given no alternative but to face a violent death.

The Soft-Hearted Sioux
Zitkala-Sa [Gertrude Bonnin]

1

Beside the open fire I sat within our tepee. With my red blanket wrapped tightly about my crossed legs, I was thinking of the coming season, my sixteenth winter. On either side of the wigwam were my parents. My father was whistling a tune between his teeth while polishing with his bare hand a red stone pipe he had recently carved. Almost in front of me, beyond the center fire, my old grandmother sat near the entranceway.

She turned her face toward her right and addressed most of her words to my mother. Now and then she spoke to me, but never did she allow her eyes to rest upon her daughter's husband, my father. It was only upon rare occasions that my grandmother said anything to him. Thus his ears were open and ready to catch the smallest wish she might express. Sometimes when my grandmother had been saying things which pleased him, my father used to comment upon them. At other times, when he could not approve of what was spoken, he used to work or smoke silently.

On this night my old grandmother began her talk about me. Filling the bowl of her red stone pipe with dry willow bark, she looked across at me.

"My grandchild, you are tall and are no longer a little boy." Narrowing her old eyes, she asked, "My grandchild, when are you going to bring here a handsome young woman?" I stared into the fire rather than meet her gaze. Waiting for my answer, she stooped forward and through the long stem drew a flame into the red stone pipe.

I smiled while my eyes were still fixed upon the bright fire, but I said nothing in reply. Turning to my mother, she offered her the pipe. I glanced at my grandmother. The loose buckskin sleeve fell off at her elbow and showed a wrist covered with silver bracelets. Holding up the fingers of her left hand, she named off the desirable young women of our village.

"Which one, my grandchild, which one?" she questioned.

"Hoh!" I said, pulling at my blanket in confusion. "Not yet!" Here my mother passed the pipe over the fire to my father. Then she too began speaking of what I should do.

"My son, be always active. Do not dislike a long hunt. Learn to provide much buffalo meat and many buckskins before you bring home a wife." Presently my father gave the pipe to my grandmother, and he took his turn in the exhortations.

"Ho, my son, I have been counting in my heart the bravest warriors of our people. There is not one of them who won his title in his sixteenth winter. My son, it is a great thing for some brave of sixteen winters to do."

Not a word had I to give in answer. I knew well the fame of my warrior father. He had earned the right of speaking such words, though even he himself was a brave only at my age. Refusing to smoke my grandmother's pipe because my heart was too much stirred by their words, and sorely troubled with a fear lest I should disappoint them, I arose to go. Drawing my blanket over my shoulders, I said, as I stepped toward the entranceway: "I go to hobble my pony. It is now late in the night."

2

Nine winters' snows had buried deep that night when my old grandmother, together with my father and mother, designed my future with the glow of a camp fire upon it.

Yet I did not grow up the warrior, huntsman, and husband I was to have been. At the mission school I learned it was wrong to kill. Nine winters I hunted for the soft heart of Christ, and prayed for the huntsmen who chased the buffalo on the plains.

In the autumn of the tenth year I was sent back to my tribe to preach Christianity to them. With the white man's Bible in my hand, and the white man's tender heart in my breast, I returned to my own people.

Wearing a foreigner's dress, I walked, a stranger, into my father's village.

Asking my way, for I had not forgotten my native tongue, an old man led me toward the tepee where my father lay. From my old companion I learned that my father had been sick many moons. As we drew near the tepee, I heard the chanting of a medicine-man within it. At once I wished to enter in and drive from my home the sorcerer of the plains, but the old warrior checked me. "Ho, wait outside until the medicine-man leaves your father," he said. While talking he scanned me from head to feet. Then he retraced his steps toward the heart of the camping-ground.

My father's dwelling was on the outer limits of the round-faced village. With every heart-throb I grew more impatient to enter the wigwam.

While I turned the leaves of my Bible with nervous fingers, the medicine-man came forth from the dwelling and walked hurriedly away. His head and face were closely covered with the loose robe which draped his entire figure.

He was tall and large. His long strides I have never forgot. They seemed to me then as the uncanny gait of eternal death. Quickly pocketing my Bible, I went into the tepee.

Upon a mat lay my father, with furrowed face and gray hair. His eyes and cheeks were sunken far into his head. His sallow skin lay thin upon his pinched nose and high cheek-bones.

Stooping over him, I took his fevered hand. "How, Ate?" I greeted him. A light flashed from his listless eyes and his dried lips parted. "My son!" he murmured, in a feeble voice. Then again the wave of joy and recognition receded. He closed his eyes, and his hand dropped from my open palm to the ground.

Looking about, I saw an old woman sitting with bowed head. Shaking hands with her, I recognized my mother. I sat down between my father and mother as I used to do, but I did not feel at home. The place where my old grandmother used to sit was now unoccupied. With my mother I bowed my head. Alike our throats were choked and tears were streaming from our eyes; but far apart in spirit our ideas and faiths separated us. My grief was for the soul unsaved; and I thought my mother wept to see a brave man's body broken by sickness.

Useless was my attempt to change the faith in the medicine-man to that abstract power named God. Then one day I became righteously mad with anger that the medicine-man should thus ensnare my father's soul. And when he came to chant his sacred songs I pointed toward the door and bade him go! The man's eyes glared upon me for an instant. Slowly gathering his robe about him, he turned his back upon the sick man and stepped out of our wigwam. "Hā, hā, hā! my son, I cannot live without the medicine-man!" I heard my father cry when the sacred man was gone.

3

On a bright day, when the winged seeds of the prairie-grass were flying hither and thither, I walked solemnly toward the center of the camping-ground. My heart beat hard and irregularly at my side. Tighter I grasped the sacred book I carried under my arm. Now was the beginning of life's work.

Though I knew it would be hard, I did not once feel that failure was to be my reward. As I stepped unevenly on the rolling ground, I thought of the warriors soon to wash off their war-paints and follow me.

At length I reached the place where the people had assembled to hear me preach. In a large circle men and women sat upon the dry red grass. Within the ring I stood, with the white man's Bible in my hand. I tried to tell them of the soft heart of Christ.

In silence the vast circle of bareheaded warriors sat under an afternoon sun. At last, wiping the wet from my brow, I took my place in the ring. The hush of the assembly filled me with great hope.

I was turning my thoughts upward to the sky in gratitude, when a star called me to earth again.

A tall, strong man arose. His loose robe hung in folds over his right shoulder. A pair of snapping black eyes fastened themselves like the poisonous fangs of a serpent upon me. He was the medicine-man. A tremor played about my heart and a chill cooled the fire in my veins.

Scornfully he pointed a long forefinger in my direction and asked, "What loyal son is he who, returning to his father's people, wears a foreigner's dress?" He paused a moment, and then continued: "The dress of that foreigner of whom a story says he bound a native of our land, and heaping dry sticks around him, kindled a fire at his feet!" Waving his hand toward me, he exclaimed, "Here is the traitor to his people!"

I was helpless. Before the eyes of the crowd the cunning magician turned my honest heart into a vile nest of treachery. Alas! the people frowned as they looked upon me.

"Listen!" he went on. "Which one of you who have eyed the young man can see through his bosom and warn the people of the nest of young snakes hatching there? Whose ear was so acute that he caught the hissing of snakes whenever the young man opened his mouth? This one has not only proven false to you, but even to the Great Spirit who made him. He is a fool! Why do you sit here giving ear to a foolish man who could not defend his people because he fears to kill, who could not bring venison to renew the life of his sick father? With his prayers, let him drive away the enemy! With his soft heart, let him keep off starvation! We shall go elsewhere to dwell upon an untainted ground."

With this he disbanded the people. When the sun lowered in the west and the winds were quiet, the village of cone-shaped tepees was gone. The medicine-man had won the hearts of the people.

Only my father's dwelling was left to mark the fighting-ground.

4

From a long night at my father's bedside I came out to look upon the morning. The yellow sun hung equally between the snow-covered land and the cloudless blue sky. The light of the new day was cold. The strong breath of winter crusted the snow and fitted crystal shells over the rivers and lakes. As I stood in front of the tepee, thinking of the vast prairies which separated us from our tribe, and wondering if the high sky likewise separated the soft-hearted Son of God from us, the icy blast from the north blew through my hair and skull. My neglected hair had grown long and fell upon my neck.

My father had not risen from his bed since the day the medicine-man led the people away. Though I read from the Bible and prayed beside him upon my knees, my father would not listen. Yet I believed my prayers were not unheeded in heaven.

"Hā, hā, hā! my son," my father groaned upon the first snow-fall. "My son, our food is gone. There is no one to bring me meat! My son, your soft heart has unfitted you for everything!" Then covering his face with the buffalo-robe, he said no more. Now while I stood out in that cold winter morning, I was starving. For two days I had not seen any food. But my own cold and hunger did not harass my soul as did the whining cry of the sick old man.

Stepping again into the tepee, I untied my snow-shoes, which were fastened to the tent-poles.

My poor mother, watching by the sick one, and faithfully heaping wood upon the centre fire, spoke to me:

"My son, do not fail again to bring your father meat, or he will starve to death."

"How, Ina," I answered, sorrowfully. From the tepee I started forth again to hunt food for my aged parents. All day I tracked the white levels lands in vain. Nowhere, nowhere were there any other footprints but my own! In the evening of this third fast-day I came back without meat. Only a bundle of sticks for the fire I brought on my back. Dropping the wood outside, I lifted the door-flap and set one foot within the tepee.

There I grew dizzy and numb. My eyes swam in tears. Before me lay my old gray-haired father sobbing like a child. In his horny hands he clutched the buffalo-robe, and with his teeth he was gnawing off the edges. Chewing the dry stiff hair and buffalo-skin, my father's eyes sought my hands. Upon seeing them empty, he cried out:

"My son, your soft heart will let me starve before you bring me meat! Two hills eastward stand a herd of cattle. Yet you will see me die before you bring me food!"

Leaving my mother lying with covered head upon her mat, I rushed out into the night.

With a strange warmth in my heart and swiftness in my feet, I climbed over the first hill, and soon the second one. The moonlight upon the white country showed me a clear path to the white's man's cattle. With my hand upon the knife in my belt, I leaned heavily against the fence while counting the herd.

Twenty in all I numbered. From among them I chose the best-fattened creature. Leaping over the fence, I plunged my knife into it.

My long knife was sharp, and my hands, no more fearful and slow, slashed off choice chunks of warm flesh. Bending under the meat I had taken for my starving father, I hurried across the prairie.

Toward home I fairly ran with the life-giving food I carried upon my back. Hardly had I climbed the second hill when I heard sounds coming after me. Faster and faster I ran with my load for my father, but the sounds were gaining upon me. I heard the clicking of snow-shoes and the squeaking of the leather straps at my heels; yet I did not turn to see what pursued me, for I was intent upon reaching my father. Suddenly like thunder an angry voice shouted curses and threats into my ear! A rough hand wrenched my shoulder and took the meat from me! I stopped struggling to run. A deafening whir filled my head. The moon and stars began to move. Now the white prairie was sky, and the stars lay under my feet. Now again they were turning. At last the starry blue rose up into place. The noise in my ears was still. A great quiet filled the air. In my hand I found my long knife dripping with blood. At my feet a man's figure lay prone in blood-red snow. The horrible scene about me seemed a trick of my senses, for I could not understand it was real. Looking long upon the blood-stained snow, the load of meat for my starving father reached my recognition at last. Quickly I tossed it over my shoulder and started again homeward.

Tired and haunted I reached the door of the wigwam. Carrying the food before me, I entered with it into the tepee.

"Father, here is food!" I cried, as I dropped the meat near my mother. No answer came. Turning about, I beheld my gray-haired father dead! I saw by the unsteady firelight an old gray-haired skeleton lying rigid and stiff.

Out into the open I started, but the snow at my feet became bloody.

5

On the day after my father's death, having led my mother to the camp of the medicine-man, I gave myself up to those who were searching for the murderer of the paleface.

They bound me hand and foot. Here in this cell I was placed four days ago.

The shrieking winter winds have followed me hither. Rattling the bars, they howl unceasingly: "Your soft heart! your soft heart will see me die before you bring me food!" Hark! something is clanking the chain on the door. It is being opened. From the dark night without a black figure crosses the threshold. . . . It is the guard. He tells me that tomorrow I must die. In his stern face I laugh aloud. I do not fear death.

Yet I wonder who shall come to welcome me in the realm of strange sight. Will the loving Jesus grant me pardon and give my soul a soothing sleep? or will my warrior father greet me and receive me as his son? Will my spirit fly upward to a happy heaven? or shall I sink into the bottomless pit, an outcast from a God of infinite love?

Soon, soon I shall know, for now I see the east is growing red. My heart is strong. My face is calm. My eyes are dry and eager for new scenes. My hands hang quietly at my side. Serene and brave, my soul awaits the men to perch me on the gallows for another flight. I go.[1]

NATIVE AMERICAN POETRY

In the last twenty years, Native Americans have struggled to avoid succumbing to a sense of despair about their culture's demise—a seeping assimilation into the general American "melting pot." Writers, in particular, have made the assault on such feelings a major focus of their works. In 1969, Scott Momaday's novel *House Made of Dawn* won a Pulitzer Prize and made a new generation of Native American writers aware of a powerful message: people caught between cultures can, despite a variety of problems, find ways to survive.

Paula Gunn Allen, perhaps representative of many Native American writers, believes that Momaday's book created a new future for her: it "brought my land back to me." She believes that she and many Native Americans suffer from "land sickness"—a deep sense of exile caused by the loss of her land and birthright. In the passages of *House Made of Dawn* she found that she shared a familiarity with the places Momaday described: "I knew every inch of what he was saying." It gave her the strength and inspiration—the will—to continue. In her poem, "Recuerdo," she creates images of movement, loss, and of searching. She looks for a sense of "being securely planted."

"Recuerdo"
Paula Gunn Allen

I have climbed into silence trying for clear air
and seen the peaks rising above me like the gods.
That is where they live, the old people say.
I used to hear them speak when I was a child
and we went to the mountain on a picnic
or to get wood. Shivering in the cold air then
I listened and I heard.

Lately I write, trying to combine sound and memory,
searching for that significance once heard and nearly lost.
It was within the tall pines, speaking.
There was one voice under the wind—something in it
that brought me to terror and to tears. I wanted
to cling to my mother so she could comfort me,
explain the sound and my fear, but I simply sat,
frozen, trying to feel as warm as the campfire,
the family voices around me suggested I should.

Now I climb the mesas in my dreams.
The mountain gods are still, and still I seek.
I finger peyote buttons and count the stalks of sweetsage
given me by a friend—obsessed with a memory
that will not die.

I stir wild honey into my carefully prepared cedar tea
and wait for meaning to arise,
to greet and comfort me.

Maybe this time I will not away.
Maybe I will ask instead what that sounding means.
Maybe I will find that exact hollow
where terror and comfort meet.
Tomorrow I will go back and climb the endless mesas
of my home. I will seek thistles drying in the wind,
pocket bright bits of obsidian and fragments
old potters left behind.[2]

NATIVE AMERICAN CERAMICS AND PAINTING

Pottery was the greatest of the prehistoric arts, and it continues today—even though it is now almost completely an aesthetic activity. Early pottery vessels, however, were designed for everyday use, and technique gave way to practical concerns—time taken for exquisite finishing techniques was sacrificed in favor of getting the object into use. Today, clay bowls such as that pictured in Fig. **13.1** reflect the time-honored traditions of southwest art, but have risen in quality of finish and design to the status of high art. Thus, the culture has been sustained. Other artistic forms found among these peoples include silversmithing of which the popular silver and turquoise jewelry making continues today, and sand painting. Sand paintings incorporate important religious meanings, so that many rituals cannot be performed without them.

In addition to the traditional materials of Native American art—indigenous, easily accessible materials—twentieth-century Native American artists also work in the media of traditional artists, for example, watercolor. In Figure **13.2** one of the foremost Navajo painters, Harrison Begay, documents typical Native American life—in this case, women picking corn. One aspect of Native American watercolor painting of the middle of the century that

13.1 Lucy Lewis, ceramic bowl, from the Pueblo area (Acoma, New Mexico), 1969. National Museum of the American Indian, Smithsonian Institution.

Northwest coast Native American music has a number of unique qualities. The first of these is the concept of ownership of a song. In this culture, only the owner of a song can perform it. However, it is possible to buy a song, to inherit it, or even to obtain it by murdering the owner—provided, of course, that the murderer could justify the claim. Additionally, songs were owned by secret societies within the tribes. In musical terms, northwest Native American music requires part singing. Similar to some African music, music of these tribes uses parallel harmonies and drone notes. The rhythms of this music tend toward strongly percussive and intricate patterns.

Songs among the southwestern Native Americans, especially the Pueblos, reveal complexity of tonal arrangements. Songs are based on six- or seven-note scales and appear to keep within a rather low register—that is, the pitches stay among the low notes of the range. This is in contrast to the music of the Plains Indians, who tend to use high pitches for their music. Nearly every social occasion, holy day, and ceremony has its own special music.

13.2 Harrison Begay, *Women Picking Corn*, mid 20th century. Watercolor, 15 × 11½ ins (38.1 × 29.2 cm). National Museum of the American Indian, Smithsonian Institution.

seems fairly typical is Begay's use of space: The painting stays on the surface plane and only the important subjects are depicted; no background appears. We are concerned only with the women and the corn, and no spatial environment is added. The subjects are rendered in two dimensions. The only hint of space beyond the frontal plane—three-dimensional space or perspective—is the diminutive size of the women on the left. The horizon line, or viewer's eye level, is at the bottom of the painting.

NATIVE AMERICAN MUSIC

As in the case of African tribal music, Native American music continues as an important part of their cultural reality. For example, the music of the Inuit peoples has developed into a highly complex art form. It exhibits complex rhythms that use contrasting accents and meters. Melodies tend to create limited conjunct contours in which changes of pitch occupy only limited distances, thus creating a gentle and undulating quality. The style of Inuit music often is declamatory—similar to the operatic technique of recitative in Western music.

AFRICAN STYLES

African tribal art has maintained its traditions into the twentieth century. As we examine some final examples, let us review a few characteristics of African art. First of all, and perhaps unlike much of Western art, African art was made to be used—for example, it is frequently covered with magic substances and worn as costume in a dance. Masks and carved figures play an important part in a wide variety of rituals, whose functions are to ensure the continuity of the tribe. These rituals enact complex dramas of birth, succession of power, and initiation to adulthood. Like much art from all traditions—including much from Western culture—African art frequently serves a religious function; indeed, its use permeates all facets of African life and death. It is created to represent local deities and/or personal spirits, who will grant favors to the worshiper in return for offerings and ceremonials. African art can also symbolize concepts like family unity and character traits like aggression, as well as functioning as a device for divining the future and for worshiping ancestors. For example, ancestor shrines often have figurative sculptures carved in honor of the dead.

Additionally, African art maintains a political function. Traditionally, African tribal power was held by a king *and* a governing body of tribal elders who balanced royal authority. In many regions, a queen mother (some female relative of the king) also held a powerful position within the community. Art objects frequently were created to symbolize and sustain the ruling authority. Like Native American art—and Western art from such periods as the Baroque—African art often proclaims the wealth and power of the king. Often made from the richest of materials, the works become proof positive of the king's majesty and his ability to commission works from the greatest artists.

Finally, although we have maintained that African artworks carry primarily a practical function, this does not mean that they have been made without a clear love of beauty in mind. Rarely does African art copy nature. Rather, we can think of it as conceptual—that is, the artist emphasizes the physical and symbolic characteristics of the essences, rather than the visible nature, of the subject.

AFRICAN SCULPTURE

Two carved figures of a dancing royal couple (Fig. **13.3**) from the Bangwa Kingdom of Cameroon exemplify for us some typically dynamic combinations of line, form, and texture. These cult images undoubtedly have a ritualistic purpose, encompassing, for example, the appeasing of the spirit of the tree from which they are carved. The sculptor has captured well the movement of two figures seemingly caught in a moment in the dance, complete with flexing legs and tightening muscles. The neck and chin of the female figure strain upward, and, again, provide us with a tension filled with dynamic energy. Open mouths indicate that the dance is being accompanied by a song. Both figures—the female form, especially—though carved from one piece of wood, seem to be built up out of ovoid sections. The smooth, sweeping curves create a dynamic rhythm, while the slender points of articulation between body parts heighten the intensity of motion.

Although these depictions suggest reality, they reflect a modified naturalism and stylization. Like the figures of the ancient and Classical Greeks, these statues represent types rather than individuals. However, they are very human. Facial expressions, although some proportions have been exaggerated—for example, the eyes in the male figure—communicate individual human emotion and expression. The surfaces of the works have been polished to a degree of smoothness that suggests the play of light on real skin. Clothing and accoutrements represent the costume of the tribe.

Both of these figures exude youth and health. They seem powerful and alive, and in the prime of life. Despite their less-than-accurate proportions, they communicate

grace and flexibility—characteristics particularly admired by Africans in dancers.

The lengthy European presence in Africa has had a subtle influence, in some cases, on the construction of traditional tribal artifacts, as we can see in our second example. This early twentieth-century figure, an animal from Loango (Fig. **13.4**), displays an older, symbolic significance mingling with European materials. The animal depicted is known as a "power figure" or magical effigy, whose hair or spines are iron nails and blades which have been driven into a wooden core. The act of driving the nails and blades into the figure is intended to activate its magic—which can be used either to cure or to kill. The nails are of European manufacture, and more than one expert has suggested that the concept of giving them supernatural power stemmed from the story of Christ's

13.3 Dancing royal couple from Bangwa, Cameroon, early 20th century. Wood, height 34½ and 34¼ ins (87.6 and 87 cm). Harry A. Franklin family, on loan to the Los Angeles County Museum of Art.

13.4 Magic animal from Loango, Congo Brazzaville, early 20th century. Wood, with iron nails and blades, 35 ins (88 cm) long. Musée de l'Homme, Paris.

crucifiction, told by missionaries, who first came to Africa after the great age of discovery in the sixteenth century. In fact, from the early sixteenth to the late seventeenth century, Christianity was the state religion in the Congo kingdom where these figures were found.

Although the nails are European, iron did have an older significance as a symbol in Africa. The metal had been smelted from early times in northern Nigeria, but the rituals associated with its working probably inhibited any widespread production. However, it was used widely in agriculture and warfare long before Christianity reached Africa, and it is therefore likely that iron as a magical symbol predates Christian influence. Whatever may be the case, this feisty animal bristles with life. He seems, like a worried porcupine, to be set in an aggressive posture, with quills poised at the optimum angle for attacking an enemy. A sense of imminent action is conveyed by the open mouth, extended tongue, and bulging eyes. Because the front legs slant backward, we sense that the animal is poised to spring forward.

Power figures like this one apparently had only a short life-span. Unlike some magical figures, these effigies were discarded once their original purpose had been achieved or after they had proven ineffective. Whatever their original intention, these works transcend anthropological speculation, maintaining a life and interest purely as works of sculpture. Their textures, line, and form communicate far more than their maker intended.

13.5 Helmet mask of the Mende or Bulom people, Sierra Leone and Liberia, c. 1950–70. Wood, height 14 ins (35.5 cm). Ball State University Museum of Art, Muncie, Indiana. Gift of David T. Owsley, 82.018.19.

WEST AFRICAN MASKS

We can examine the crucial role of ritual in African tribal art if we look at the part played by one artifact—the mask—in four different West African tribes.

The first example is a "helmet mask" from southern Sierre Leone and northwestern Liberia (Fig. 13.5) Following tradition, it was made some time during the twentieth century by the Mende, Bulom, or neighboring peoples, and represents "Sowei" or a water spirit. This mask is worn by women of the tribe most commonly during the initiation of girls, who are instructed in the rituals and sacred roles of wives and mothers. The women also perform with their faces masked at important funerals and some political functions. The glossy black patina and elaborate hairstyle of the mask underline the symbolic resonances of female beauty, wealth, and power. The cylindrical folds around the bottom of the mask represent "neck cuts" (not fat) that are worn as decoration by both the men and women of the Bulom. The same applies to

13.6 Elephant helmet mask of the Bamileke people, southwest Cameroon, c. 1950–70. Cloth and beads, height 25¼ ins (64.1 cm). Ball State University museum of Art, Muncie, Indiana. Gift of David T. Owsley, 82.018.16.

the rectangular scarification on the forehead. Worn over the entire head, the wooden mask has slits just below the painted eyes. When taking part in a ritual, the tribe member would wear black raffia stockings and gloves.

A second example from the southwest area of Cameroon (Fig. **13.6**) illustrates how masks can serve the function of social regulation. This beaded elephant helmet mask is part of the regalia worn by members of the Aka society, which is an elite group of the Bamileke tribe. The members of this society assisted the Fon (ruler) as warriors or administrators and, by intimidation, maintained moral standards with the community. Worn at important funerals and public performances, the mask denotes strength and wealth, through its use of the royal elephant symbol and beads, respectively. Only the vaguest formal devices suggest an elephant—that is, the long, rectangular

centerpiece, representing a trunk, and the circular side pieces, representing eyes or ears. The geometric symbols remain totally abstract, but probably have some esoteric significance. A suggestion of the creases on an elephant's trunk can be found in the horizontal lines of beadwork.

An entertainer's disguise from the Dan, Mano, Kono, or Kpelle people of eastern Liberia and western Ivory Coast provides us with our third example (Fig. **13.7**). Made recently, this "gegon" or male face mask represents a bush spirit. It is worn by an entertainer who pecks the ground as he dances, imitating the hornbill, which is the bird featured in the Senufo creation myth. Accompanied by drummers, a gong player, and singers, the entertainer wears a cylindrical hat with leather appliqué and feathers, a raffia skirt, and a blue-and-white striped wrap. As well as appearing at recreational functions he also officiates at boys' circumcision rites and at the concluding festival. The northern Dan tribe probably borrowed this design from nearby tribes to the west, because the name of "gegon" does not relate to the birdlike dance and the mask's appearance. Moreover, these neighbors use the masks to fulfill different functions—for example, as symbols of membership in men's secret societies.

13.7 Entertainer's disguise from the Dan, Mano, Kono, or Kpelle people of eastern Liberia and western Ivory Coast. Wood, c. 1950–70. Ball State University Museum of Art, Muncie, Indiana. Gift of David T. Owsley, 82.018.20.

AFRICAN INFLUENCE ON WESTERN ART

The direct influence of African art can be seen in the early sculptures of Picasso, who was searching for a way to create form that was both representational but also anti-naturalistic. Constantin Brancusi (1876–1957) went further down the road of abstraction. While his sculpture borrows freely from African tribal motifs, the smooth, precise surfaces of much of his work seem to have an abstract, mechanistic quality. His search for essential form led to very economical presentations, often ovoid and simple, yet animate. Certainly, great psychological complexity exists in *Bird in Space*. Its highly polished surface and upward striving line has a modern sleekness, and yet the primitive essence remains, reminding us of the work of African or Aboriginal tribes. *Mlle. Pogany* (Fig. **13.9**), despite the superbly polished surface and accomplished curves which lead the eye inwards, has the enigmatic character of an African mask.

13.8 Male antelope mask from the Bamana people, western Mali, c. 1950–70. Wood, height 41 ins (104 cm). Ball State University, Muncie, Indiana. Gift of David T. Owsley, 82.018.20.

Our last example, among the myriad possibilities presented by African tribal culture, is a male antelope mask, called "chi-wara" (Fig. **13.8**) Indigenous to the Bamana people of the upper region of the Niger River in western Mali, the "chi-wara" represents a half-man, half-antelope deity who taught men how to farm. In an agricultural society concerned with fertility of crops, the masks naturally have an important spiritual function.

At annual spring planting festivals, they are worn by men during dances which honor farmers. While the women sing, the men imitate the leaps of antelopes. The mask is attached to a basket-type cap worn on the head.

13.9 Constantine Brancusi, *Mlle. Pogany*, 1931. Marble on limestone base, height 19 ins (48 cm). The Philadelphia Museum of Art (Louise and Walter Arensberg Collection).

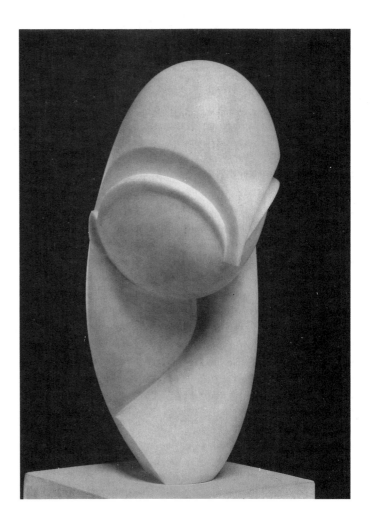

AFRICAN TRIBAL MUSIC

Although African tribal music could be introduced at any point, we place it here so that we can understand its continuing presence in Black African life. Music forms an important part of African tribal life, every aspect of which has special music—for example, there is music for communicating news, for entertainment, for legal dealings, and for working in the fields. Special ceremonies like marriage, birth, death, hunting, the new year, and the new moon have their own songs and dances. The heritage of the tribe often is communicated from generation to generation by means of song and dance. Thus, music plays a vital role in keeping alive the spirit and cohesiveness of society. Nearly every one of Africa's hundreds of tribes carries its own individual and unique musical characteristics. Because African music tends to be sung, even the language of the tribe adds its unique sounds and textures to music. This is especially true of the inflected languages—the languages in which pitch helps to denote meaning. Thus, a particular word, when sung, must stay in a specific pitch range because to move into another pitch range would change the meaning of the word.

Music in Africa is truly universal: its importance crosses all societal levels, from royalty to the common person. Typically, the music of tribal Africa consists of short melodic phrases that are repeated, alternated, and varied in order to create longer melodies. Very often African music has a responsorial quality—a phrase is sung by a leader and then repeated by a chorus. Harmony, in which voices move in parallel chords—always consistent in their separation—gives African music its characteristic and recognizable quality. The use of a *drone note* adds another interesting aspect to some African music: one voice holds a single (drone) tone while a second voice sings a phrase; the drone note then passes to the second voice while the first sings a phrase, and so on. Also typical is the use of complicated rhythms and rhythmic patterns. Quite often one voice or drum will maintain a duple meter while another voice or drum maintains a triple meter against the first. Juxtaposing contrasting rhythmic patterns is a particularly popular musical characteristic. Harmonically, melodically, and rhythmically, African music exhibits great complexity not only among tribes but also within the music of specific tribes as well.

AFRICAN-AMERICAN STYLES

HARLEM RENAISSANCE

From 1919 to 1925 Harlem, a small enclave in New York City, became the international capital of Black culture. "Harlem was in vogue" wrote the Black poet Langston Hughes (see pp. 353). Black painters, sculptors, musicians, poets, and novelists joined in a remarkable artistic outpouring. The period became an intensely controversial one, its artistic merits attacked by some critics of the time as isolationist and conventional; the qualities of the Harlem Renaissance can still provoke debate. Nonetheless, this period of intense creative activity by Black Americans "gave the artists an identifiable artistic context for their work, propelled them to the forefront of the New Negro Movement, and inspired their art for the remainder of their careers."[3]

The artistic works emanating from this period reached a national audience through exhibitions sponsored by the Harlem Foundation. The spirit of the movement, expressed through its artists, took several themes: glorification of the Black American's African heritage; the tradition of Black folklore; and general interest in the daily life of Black people. In every case Harlem Renaissance artists broke with previous Black artistic traditions. They celebrated Black history and culture and "defined a visual vocabulary for Black Americans."[4]

Black intellectuals such as W. E. B. Du Bois, Alain Locke, and Charles Spurgeon spearheaded the movement. Among the notable artists were social documentarian and photographer James Van Der Zee (1886–1983), painter William Henry Johnson (1901–1970), painter Palmer Hayden (1890–1973), painter Aaron Douglas (1899–1979), painter Jacob Lawrence (b. 1917), and sculptor Meta Vaux Warrick Fuller (1877–1968).

Jacob Lawrence is a fine example of an artist acutely aware of his privileged position and, at the same time, his membership of a dispossessed and disadvantaged section of society. In his works, Modernist effects—such as the flattening of space and the use of undifferentiated planes of color—are secondary to the need to convey an intelligible narrative to the viewer (Fig. **13.10**)

Palmer Hayden (Peyton Cole Hedgeman) trained at the Cooper Union in New York in 1919 and later at the Boothbay Art Colony. In 1927 he traveled to Europe and

13.10 Jacob Lawrence, *One of the Largest Race Riots Occurred in East St. Louis*, 1940–41, from the series *The Migration of the Negro*. Tempera on gesso on composition board, 12×18 ins (30.5×45.7 cm). Collection, The Museum of Modern Art, New York. Gift of Mrs. David M. Levy.

studied at the École des Beaux Arts. His work was exhibited widely in New York and drew heavy criticism from those who believed that his depictions mocked Black people and sustained negative stereotypes. Later in life he created the John Henry series, twelve oil paintings portraying the life and death of the Black folk hero John Henry. Hayden focused on Black American legends and folk themes, expressing visually the wealth of material from the Black oral culture of the rural South and of Africa. His main approach was to make use of folk themes to illustrate industrial America's dependence on the Black labor force. Hayden's works employ the symbols of ethnic heroism.

Aaron Douglas, perhaps the foremost painter of the Harlem Renaissance, earned a bachelor of fine arts degree

from the University of Nebraska and a master's degree from Columbia University. His training encouraged him to explore the rich vocabulary of Black American myth and culture. His work is highly stylized, explores a palette of muted tones, and is well known through its appearance as illustrations and cover designs for many books by Black writers. His mural *Aspects of Negro Life*, at the New York Public Library's Cullen Branch, documents in four panels the emergence of a Black American identity. The first panel portrays the African cultural background in images of music, dance, and sculpture. The next two panels bring to life slavery and emancipation in the American South and the flight of Blacks to the cities of the North. The third panel returns to the theme of music. Among Douglas's wide variety of stylistic approaches, his realistic

13.11 Aaron Douglas, *Aalta*, 1936. Oil on canvas, 18 x 23 ins (45.7 x 58.4 cm). Afro-American Collection of Art, The Carl Van Vechten Gallery of Fine Arts, Fisk University.

portrait of Aalta (Fig. **13.11**) provides a warm and relaxed composition, whose palette and expression express dignity, elegance, and stability.

Meta Vaux Warrick Fuller "was the first Black American artist to draw heavily on African themes and folklore for her subjects".[5] Years before the Harlem Renaissance, she began to express the pan-African ideals which later permeated the movement. After finishing graduate work at the Pennsylvania Museum and School for Industrial Arts, she studied in Paris at the École des Beaux Arts and the Academie Colarossi. One of her mentors was the sculptor Auguste Rodin, and his influence can be seen in her impressionistic surface treatment of romantic realist subjects. Fuller built her own studio in Framingham, Massachusetts, and focused on themes dealing with anti-slavery and protests against injustice to Black Americans. In one of the earliest works by a Black American focusing on the African heritage, her sculpture *Ethiopia Awakening* shows an Egyptian women emerging from her embalming wrappings. "The work symbolically represents the emergence of Black cultural awareness from the 'wrappings' of ignorance and oppression, and the beginnings of the end of colonial rule in Africa."[6] Works such as *The Talking Skull* are based on African models and illustrate the confrontation of humans with death, a prevalent theme in her career.

William Henry Johnson studied at the National Academy of Design in New York, followed by a three-year fellowship in 1926 to study in Europe. Under the influence of the European Impressionists and Realists, his style became much more personally expressive. His many works focus on the Black experience in America, with Harlem, where he spent his childhood, being the central theme. Just prior to World War II his style changed again, moving from fully rounded to flat figures.

Langston Hughes

Langston Hughes (1902–67) is often referred to as the "poet laureate of Harlem." An Afro-American poet, Hughes's poetry portrayed the life of the ordinary Black individual in the United States. He caught with sharp immediacy and intensity the humor, pathos, irony, and humiliation of being Black in America. His poetry is particularly meaningful to young people. He speaks of the basic qualities of life, that is, love, hate, aspirations, and despair. Yet, he writes with a faith in humanity in general. He interprets all life as it is experienced in the real world as well as in idealism. At the same time, some of his work comprises militant pieces which carry broad sociopolitical implications. He struggled within himself between what he wanted to write and what his audience expected him to write.

Hughes received considerable attention as a poet as early as 1921 with his poem "The Negro Speaks of Rivers." His poetry and his involvement in social causes are often intertwined. In his novel *Not Without Laughter*, Hughes created a brilliant portrayal of a Black youth's passage into manhood. In the selections that follow, readers can sense the Black experience and perception of the universe.

Theme for English B

The instructor said,
    Go home and write
    a page tonight.
    And let that page come out of you—
    Then, it will be true.
I wonder if it's that simple?

I am twenty-two, colored, born in Winston-Salem.
I went to school there, then Durham, then here
to this college on the hill above Harlem.
I am the only colored student in my class.
The steps from the hill lead down into Harlem
through a park, then I cross St. Nicholas.
Eighth Avenue. Seventh, and I come to the Y,
the Harlem Branch Y, where I take the elevator
up to my room, sit down, and write this page:
It's not easy to know what is true for you or me
at twenty-two, my age. But I guess I'm what
I feel and see and hear, Harlem, I hear you:
hear you, here me—we two—you, me, talk on this page.
(I hear New York, too) Me—who?

Well, I like to eat, sleep, drink, and be in love.
I like to work, read, learn, and understand life.
I like a pipe for a Christmas present,
or records—Bessie, bop, or Bach.
I guess being colored doesn't make me not like
the same things other folks like who are other races.
So will my page be colored that I write?
Being me, it will not be white.
But it will be
a part of you, instructor.
You are white—
yet a part of me, as I am a part of you.
that's American.
Sometimes perhaps you don't want to be a part of me,
Nor do I often want to be apart of you.
But we are, that's true!

As I learn from you
I guess you learn from me—
although you're older—and white—
and somewhat more free.

This is my page for English B.

Harlem

What happens to a dream deferred?

Does it dry up
like a raisin in the sun?
Or fester like a sore—
And then run?
Does it stink like rotten meat?
Or crust and sugar over—
like a syrupy sweet?

Maybe it just sags
like a heavy load.

Or does it explode?[7]

AFRICAN-AMERICAN POPULAR MUSIC—JAZZ

Probably the most significant African-American contribution to American music, jazz began near the turn of the century and went through many changes and forms. Jazz comprises sophisticated and complicated styles focusing on improvised variations on a theme. The earliest form—blues—went back to the music of the slaves, and consisted of two rhythmic lines and repeat of the first line (A-A-B). Performers at the end of the nineteenth century, such as Bessie Smith, gave the blues an emotional quality,

13.12 Saxophonist Charlie Parker in performance with Tommy Potter. Parker died prematurely in 1955, aged 35, but by that time he was already a legendary figure. David Redfern Photography.

which the accompanying instruments tried to imitate. At approximately the same time came ragtime, a piano style with a strict, two-part form. Syncopation—the displacement of accent from the normally accented beat to the offbeat—played an important role in this style, whose most famous exponent was Scott Joplin. New Orleans, the cradle of jazz, also produced traditional jazz, which featured improvisational development from a basic, memorized chordal sequence. All this was followed in the 1930s and 1940s by Swing, Be-bop, and Cool Jazz.

Styles stemming from traditional jazz proliferated after World War II. There was gradual move away from the big bands to smaller groups and a desire for much more improvisation within the context of the compositions. The term "*Be-bop*" was coined as a result of the characteristic long-short triplet rhythm that ended many phrases. The prime developers of this style were alto saxophonist Charlie "Bird" Parker (Fig. **13.12**), and trumpeter Dizzie Gillespie. The Cool Jazz style developed in the early 1950s with artists like Miles Davis. Although the technical virtuosity of Be-bop continued, a certain lyric quality, particularly in the slow ballads, was emphasized and, more importantly, the actual tone quality, particularly of the wind instruments, was a major distinction.

Were our space unlimited, we could look further into this African-American form and include such gifted performers as Thelonius Monk, John Coltrane, and Cecil Taylor. John Coltrane, for example, has had a tremendous influence on Black society in the United States. Coltrane's personality and charisma projected to Black Americans in his albums *A Love Supreme, Ascension Meditations*, and the albums that followed. These works acted as a tremendous spiritual reservoir for Black people and have cast a hugely influential shadow over jazz ever since.

AFRICAN-AMERICAN DANCE

The American dance scene has benefitted from a number of exceptional choreographers of African-American heritage who draw upon the African-American culture. Among this group stands Alvin Ailey, a versatile dancer whose company is known for its unusual repertoire and energetically free movements. Another form of dance that has its roots in the Black musical heritage, but which draws upon the broad experiments of modern dance is *jazz dance*. Its forms are not universally agreed upon, and like modern dance in general, its directions are still in flux. Nevertheless, stemming from sources as diverse and yet as allied as "primitive" Africa and the urban ghetto, this discipline has seen significant activity and experimentation throughout the United States (Fig. **6.14–6.15**). Choreographers such as Asadata Dafora Horton in the 1930s and Katherine Dunham and Pearl Primus in the 1940s were the pioneers in this approach, which has seen contemporary works from choreographers such as Talley Beatty and Derglas MacKayle.

BLACK LIBERATION IN THE THEATRE

The theatrical Black liberation began in the 1960s, and continues to the present. One manifestation of the civil rights movement of the 1950s and 1960s was led by angry, militant Blacks who espoused Black consciousness. Many converted to the Black Muslim version of Islam, and many longed for a completely separate Black nation. Radical groups talked about destroying Western society. A number of African-Americans turned toward Africa and sought a new identity in the Third World. In the 1980s, there was a change in self-description from Black to African-American.

Many of these ideas were expressed in the dramatic works of playwrights such as LeRoi Jones, who became Imamu Amiri Baraka. His plays dramatized the dangers of Blacks allowing Whites into their private lives and called for racial separation. Charles Gordonne's *No Place to Be Somebody* renews Baraka's cause, and espouses violence as legitimate action in the penetrating story of a fair-skinned Black searching for his own racial identity.

Many new Black theatre companies also emerged in the 1960s. The Negro Ensemble Company, for example, founded by Douglas Turner Ward, is one enduring example. From the company came the moving production of Samm-Art Williams's *Home. Home* traces the ups and downs in the life of a Southern Black named Cephus.

Raised on a farm, he leaves it for the big city. Convicted of draft evasion and sent to jail, he progresses to joblessness and welfare, disease and despair. Finally, he returns to the honest labor and creative values on the farm. The poetic language and the conventions of its production format give *Home* a unique and endearing quality. Cephus is played by a single actor, but all the other roles–old, young, male, female, Black, White–are played by two women who take on whatever role they wish by changing costumes. Sometimes they are characters in Cephus's journey and other times they act as a chorus, helping the audience to follow leaps in time and space. The chorus format helps the audience to see Cephus from the point of view of American Black history and culture. Although Cephus is constantly on the move, the stage setting never changes, and although the actors play several different roles, they never change. Through these devices, the playwright suggests that "home" is at hand all the time–waiting to be grasped. The forces that stand in the way are one's unwillingness to acknowledge one's inner yearnings, the willingness of others to help and to extend themselves by choosing a path of peace instead of confrontation.

The son of a White father and a Black mother, August Wilson (b. 1945) writes with an ear tuned to the rhythms and patterns of the blues and the speech of the Black neighborhoods. Founder of the Playwrights Center in Minneapolis, his plays range from *Jitney* (1982) to a planned series of ten plays beginning with *Ma Rainey's Black Bottom* (1984). Wilson believes that the American Black has the most dramatic story of all humankind to tell. His concern lies with the stripping away of important African traditions and religious rituals from Blacks by Whites. In plays such as *The Piano Lesson* (1987), he portrays the complexity of African-American attitudes towards themselves and their past. Indeed, the blatant and more subtle conflicts between Black and White cultures and attitudes form the central core of Wilson's work and can be seen in plays such as *Fences*.

Fences treats the lives of Black tenement-dwellers in Pittsburgh in the 1950s. Troy Maxson, a garbage collector, takes great pride in his ability to hold his family together and to take care of them. As the play opens, Troy discusses his challenge to the union concerning Blacks' access to doing the same "easy" work as Whites. He is frustrated and believes that he has been deprived of the opportunities to get what he deserves—and this becomes a central motif. He describes his wrestling match with death in 1941 when he had pneumonia. He also tells of his days in the Negro baseball leagues because he was not allowed to play in the majors—because of his race.

AMERICAN AND EUROPEAN STYLES

EXPRESSIONISM

Expressionism traditionally refers to a movement in Germany between 1905 and 1930, but its broad applications include a variety of specific approaches, essentially in Europe, that focused on a joint artist/respondent reaction to composition elements. Any element (line, form, color, and so on) could be emphasized to elicit a specific response in the viewer. The artist would consciously try to stimulate a response that had a specific relationship to his or her feelings about or commitment to the subject matter. Subject matter itself mattered little; what counted was the artist's attempt to evoke in the viewer a similar response to his or her own. In Max Beckmann's *Christ and the Woman Taken in Adultery* (Fig. **13.13**), the artist's revulsion against physical cruelty and suffering is transmitted through distorted figures crushed into shallow space. Linear distortion, changes of scale and perspective, and a nearly Gothic spiritualism communicate Beckmann's reactions to the horrors of World War I. In this approach, meaning relies on very specific nonverbal communication.

The 1970s saw a continuation of Expressionism in the lyrical work of artists such as William T. Williams (b. 1942). In *Batman* (Fig. **13.14**) we see a methodology which has been compared to jazz improvisation. In the carefully defined two-part structure, continuing verticals subtly play across the dividing line to pull the work together. At the same time delicate traceries reinforce the basic structure and provide endless variations. The resulting texture is evocative, like cracking or peeling paint on a series of old boards, perhaps. True to its Expressionist heritage, the work links the artist's memory with the experience of the viewer.

Expressionism brought to the theatre ideas which reflected disillusionment more than they did realism. But here we must tread carefully, because the theatre is both visual and oral. The painter's revolt against naturalism came to the theatre in visual form in scenic design. Settings which followed Expressionism in painting occurred often. For the playwright, Expressionism was merely an extension of realism and naturalism and allowed the playwright a more adequate means to express his own reaction to specific items in the universe around him.

13.13 Max Beckmann, *Christ and the Woman Taken in Adultery*, 1917. Oil on canvas, 58¾ x 49⅞ ins (149 x 127 cm). The Saint Louis Art Museum (Bequest of Curt Valentin).

13.14 (*opposite*) William T. Williams, *Batman*, 1979. Acrylic on canvas, 80 x 60 ins (203 x 152 cm). Collection of the artist.

August Strindberg, for example, had turned inward to the subconscious in Expressionistic plays such as the *Ghost Sonata*. In so doing, he created a presentational rather than representational style.

Expressionism also found its way to America. Elmer Rice's play *Adding Machine* (1923) depicts Mr. Zero, a cog in the great industrial machinery of twentieth-century life, who stumbles through a pointless existence. Finding himself replaced by an adding machine he goes berserk, kills his employer, and is executed. Then, adrift in the hereafter, he is too narrow-minded to understand the happiness offered to him there. He becomes an adding machine operator in Heaven and finally returns to earth to begin his tortured existence all over again.

German Expressionism made its mark in film as well as in the visual and other performing arts, and in 1919 its most masterful example, Robert Wiene's *Cabinet of Dr. Caligari*, shook the world. Macabre sets, surrealistic lighting effects, and distorted properties, all combined to portray a menacing post-war German world.

13.15 Pablo Picasso, *Les Demoiselles d'Avignon*, begun May, reworked July 1907. Oil on canvas, 8 ft x 7 ft 8 ins (2.44 x 2.34 m). Collection, The Museum of Modern Art, New York (acquired through the Lillie P. Bliss Bequest).

CUBISM

Between 1901 and 1912 an entirely new approach to pictorial space emerged to which the term Cubism was applied. Cubist space violates all concepts of two- or three-dimensional perspective. In the past the space within a composition had been thought of as separate from the main object of the work. That is, if the subject were removed, the space would remain, unaffected. Pablo Picasso (1881–1973) and Georges Braque (1882–1963) changed that relationship to one in which the artist tried to paint "not objects, but the space they engender." The area around an object became an extension of the object itself. If the object were removed, the space around it would collapse. Cubist space is typically quite shallow and gives the impression of reaching forward toward the

viewer, thereby intruding into space outside of the frame. Essentially the style developed as the result of independent experiments of Braque and Picasso with various ways of describing form. Newly evolving notions of time–space continuity were being proposed by Albert Einstein at this time. We cannot be sure whether the Theory of Relativity influenced Picasso and Braque, but it certainly helped to make their works more acceptable.

Picasso influenced the arts of the twentieth century more than any other individual. Born in Spain, in 1900 he moved to France, where he resided for most of his life. In Paris he was influenced by Toulouse-Lautrec and the late works of Cézanne, particularly in terms of their organization, analysis of forms, and assumption of different viewpoints. Very early on Picasso began to identify deeply with society's misfits and cast-offs. He was able to express that identification strongly in his art, which focused on form kept within the frame. Mass was "built up within [the frame] like a box within a box."[8]

Depression characterized his works from 1901 until around 1904 or 1905. This is known as his Blue Period, and was followed by his Rose Period (1904–6), "in which he was less concerned with the tragic aspects of poverty than with the nostalgic charm of itinerant circus performers and the school of make-believe."

In 1907, the creative revelation of *Les Demoiselles d'Avignon* (Fig. **13.15**) was released upon the art world and Cubism was born. Simplified forms and restricted color followed, as Cubism uniformly reduced its palette range to allow emphasis to fall on spatial exploration alone. This landmark painting was a deliberate break with the traditions of Western illusionistic art, stemming from Picasso's discovery of primitive African art and sculpture, and its use of flat forms and exaggeration of certain features. Three of the heads in this painting are adaptations of African masks. He used primitive art as a "battering ram against the Classical conception of beauty." Classical proportions, as well as the organic integrity and continuity of the human body are denied. The *Demoiselles* is aggressive and harsh: Forms are simplified and angular, and colors are restricted to blues, pinks, and terracottas. Cubism uniformly reduced its palette range, thereby emphasizing the exploration of space. Subjects are broken into angular wedges which are given a sense of three-dimensionality. The *trompe l'oeil* leaves us unsure whether the forms protrude out or recess in. Picasso rejects the single viewpoint, so the "reality" of nature is no longer the mirror of what we see in the world, but has been interpreted by a new set of principles. Understanding depends on knowing rather than seeing in the literal sense.

FAUVISM

Closely associated with the development of the Expressionist movement were the *Fauves* (wild beasts). The label was applied by a critic in response to a sculpture (exhibited in 1905) which seemed to him "a Donatello in a cage of wild beasts." Violent distortion and outrageous coloring mark the subjective expression of the Fauves. Their two-dimensional surfaces and flat color areas were new to European painting. The best-known artist of this short-lived movement was Henri Matisse (1869–1954). Matisse tried to paint pictures that would "unravel the tensions of modern existence." In his old age he made a series of very joyful designs for the Chapel of the Rosary at Venice, not as exercises in religious art but, rather, to express the joy and nearly religious feeling he had for life.

The Blue Nude (Fig. **13.16**) illustrates the wild coloring and distortion of Matisse and Fauvism. The painting takes its name from the energetically applied blues, which occur throughout the figure as darkened accents. For Matisse color and line were indivisible, and the bold strokes of the color in his work comprise coloristic and linear stimulants, as well as revelations of form. Matisse literally "drew with color." Underlying this work, and illustrative of the Fauves' relationship to Expressionism, is Matisse's desire, not to draw a nude as he saw it in life, but rather to try to express his feelings about the nude as an object of

13.16 Henri Matisse, *Blue Nude* ("*Souvenir de Biskra*"), 1907. Oil on canvas, 36¼ x 55¼ ins (91 x 104 cm). The Baltimore Museum of Art (the Cone Collection, formed by Dr. Claribel Cone and Miss Etta Cone of Baltimore, Maryland).

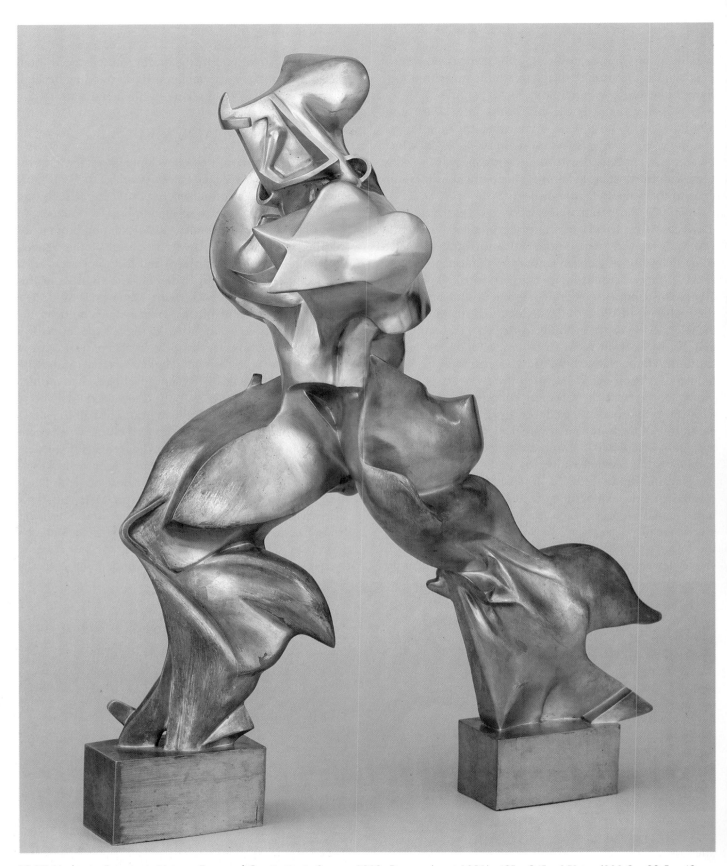

13.17 Umberto Boccioni, *Unique Forms of Continuity in Space*, 1913. Bronze (cast 1931), 43⅞ x 34⅞ x 15¾ ins (111.2 x 88.5 x 40 cm). Collection, The Museum of Modern Art, New York (acquired through the Lillie P. Bliss Bequest).

aesthetic interest. Expressionism was associated with a number of other trends, including the Bridge and Blue Rider groups and artists such as Kandinsky, Rouault, and Kokoschka.

FUTURISM

New concerns for space turned, logically, to three-dimensional space and the potential relationships it presented. Technological developments and new materials also encouraged the search for new forms characteristic of the age. Futurists in the visual arts searched for dynamic qualities representative of the times and believed that many of the new machines of the era had sculptural form. Some sculptures followed mechanistic lines and also included motion.

Boccioni's *Unique Forms of Continuity in Space* (Fig. 13.17) takes the mythological subject of Mercury, messenger of the gods, and turns him into a futuristic machine. The overall form is recognizable and the connotations of the myth move the viewer's thoughts in a particular direction. Nonetheless, this is primarily an exercise in composition of forms. The intense sense of energy and movement is created by the variety of surfaces and curves which flow into one another, in a seemingly random yet highly controlled pattern. The overall impression is of a figure in motion, rather than of the figure itself.

ABSTRACTION

Abstract or nonrepresentational art contains minimal reference to natural objects—that is, objects in the phenomenal or natural world. In many ways abstract art contrasts with Impressionism and Expressionism in that the observer can read little or nothing in the painting of the artist's feelings about the universe. Abstract art seeks to explore the expressive qualities of formal design elements in their own right. These elements are assumed to stand apart from subject matter. The aesthetic theory underlying abstract art maintains that beauty can exist in form alone, and no other quality is needed. Numerous painters have explored these approaches, and several subgroups such as de Stijl, Suprematists, Constructivists, and the Bauhaus painters have pursued its goals.

Piet Mondrian (1872–1944) believed that the fundamental principles of life consisted of straight lines and right angles. A vertical line signified active vitality and life, and a horizontal line signified tranquility, rest, and death. The crossing of the two in a right angle expressed the highest possible tension between these forces, positive

and negative. *Composition in White, Black, and Red* (Fig. 1.40) explores Mondrian's philosophy in a manner characteristic of all his linear compositions. The planes of the painting are close to the surface of the canvas, creating, in essence, the thinnest space possible, in contrast to the deep space of other styles. The palette is restricted to three hues. Even the edges of the canvas take on expressive possibilities as they provide additional points of interaction between lines. Mondrian believed that he could create "the equivalence of reality" and make the "absolute appear in the relativity of time and space" by keeping visual elements in a state of constant tension.

Georgia O'Keeffe (1887–1986), an American, proved to be one of the most original artists of our time. Her imagery draws on a diverse repertoire of objects abstracted in a uniquely personal way. She takes for example, an animal skull and transforms it into a form of absolute simplicity and beauty. In *Dark Abstraction* (Fig. 13.18) an organic form becomes an exquisite landscape which, despite its modest size, appears monumental. Her lines flow gracefully upward and outward with skillful blending of colors and rhythmic grace. Whatever the subject of the

13.18 Georgia O'Keeffe, *Dark Abstraction*, 1924. Oil on canvas, 24⅞ x 20⅞ ins (63.3 x 53 cm). Saint Louis Art Museum (gift of Charles E. and Mary Merrill).

13.19 Isamu Noguchi, *Kouros* (in nine parts), 1944–45. Pink Georgia marble, slate base, height c. 9 ft 9 ins (2.97 m). The Metropolitan Museum of Art, New York (Fletcher Fund, 1953 [53.87 a–i]).

painting, it expresses a mystical reverence for nature. O'Keeffe creates a sense of reality which takes us beyond our surface perceptions.

Isamu Noguchi (b. 1904), perhaps less concerned with expressive content than others, has continually experimented with abstract sculptural design since the 1930s. His creations have gone beyond sculpture to provide highly dynamic and suggestive designs for the choreography of Martha Graham, with whom he was associated for a number of years. Noguchi's *Kouros* figures (Fig. **13.19**) contain abstract relationships with archaic Greek sculpture and also exhibit exquisitely finished surfaces and masterly technique.

The original mobiles of Alexander Calder (1898–1976) (Fig. **2.17**) put abstract sculpture into motion. Deceptively simple, these colorful shapes turn at the whim of subtle breezes or by motors. Here is the discovery that sculpture can be created by movement in undefined space.

Objectivity returns in the unique approaches of Alberto Giacometti (1901–66). He was a surrealist sculptor in the 1930s but continued to explore the reality of the human figure and surface depiction and meaning, as can be seen in Figure **2.14**. Here form is reduced to its essence in a tortured fragmentation that appears to comment on the nature of humankind in the contemporary world.

W. H. Auden

Wystan Hugh Auden (1907–73), was an English poet whose work is an example of abstraction in poetry. His main concerns in the 1930s were for man and society, and he was influenced by Marx and Freud. His writings exhibit a strong desire for pattern and order. This early period represented his tendency toward discursiveness, the dialectic, and abstraction.

Overall, Auden's writing has been influenced by numerous factors, including Greek literature, Old English poetry, and the Icelandic sagas. His early poetry is marked by an emphasis on personal problems and social causes, although he appears to have become disenchanted with Marx and Freud in later works, which are marked by skepticism, irony, and a semireligious tone. *Poems* preceded his journey to Spain in 1936 to support the left-wing cause in the Spanish Civil War. From 1948 until the mid-1950s, Auden experimented with symbolic landscape poetry, characterized by a syllabically counted line. He remains one of the major influences in twentieth-century British and American poetry.

Musée des Beaux Arts

About suffering they were never wrong,
The Old Masters: how well they understood
Its human position; how it takes place
While someone else is eating or opening a window or just
walking dully along;
How, when the aged are reverently, passionately waiting
For the miraculous birth, there always must be
Children who did not specially want it to happen, skating
On a pond at the edge of the wood:
They never forgot
That even the dreadful martyrdom must run its course
Anyhow in a corner, some untidy spot
Where the dogs go on with their doggy life and the
torturer's horse
Scratches its innocent behind on a tree.
In Brueghel's *Icarus*, for instance: how everything turns away
Quite leisurely from the disaster; the ploughman may
Have heard the splash, the forsaken cry,
But for him was not an important failure; the sun shone
As it had to on the white legs disappearing into the green
Water; and the expensive delicate ship that must have seen
Something amazing, a boy falling out of the sky,
Had somewhere to get to and sailed calmly on.

In War Time

(For Caroline Newton)

Abruptly mounting her ramshackle wheel,
Fortune has pedalled furiously away;
The sobbing mess is on our hands today.

Those accidental terrors, Famine, Flood,
Were never trained to diagnose or heal
Nightmares that are intentional and real.

Nor lust nor gravity can preach an aim
To minds disordered by a lucid dread
Of seeking peace by going off one's head.

Nor will the living waters whistle; though
Diviners cut their throats to prove their claim,
The desert remains arid all the same.

If augurs take up flying to fulfill
The doom they prophesy, it must be so;
The herons have no modern sign for No.

If nothing can upset but total war
The massive fancy of the heathen will
That solitude is something you can kill,

If we are right to choose our suffering
And be tormented by an Either-Or,
The right to fail is worth dying for,

If so, the sweets of victory are rum:
A pride of earthly cities premising
The Inner life as socially the thing,

Where, even to the lawyers, Law is what,
For better or for worse, our vows become
When no one whom we need is looking, Home

A sort of honour, not a building site,
Wherever we are, when, if we chose, we might
Be somewhere else, yet trust that we have chosen right.

Two's Company

Again in conversations
Speaking of fear
And throwing off reserve
The voice is nearer
But no clearer
Than first love
Than boys' imaginations.

For every news
Means pairing off in twos and twos
Another I, another You
Each knowing what to do
But of no use.

Never stronger
But younger and younger
Saying good-bye but coming back, for fear
Is over there
And the centre of anger
Is out of danger.

The Composer

All the others translate: the painter sketches
A visible world to love or reject;
Rummaging into his living, the poet fetches
The images out that hurt and connect.

From Life to Art by painstaking adaption,
Relying on us to cover the rift;
Only your notes are pure contraption,
Only your song is an absolute gift.

Pour out your presence, O delight, cascading
The falls of the knee and the weirs of the spine,
Our climate of silence and doubt invading;
You alone, alone, O imaginary song,
Are unable to say an existence is wrong,
And pour out your forgiveness like a wine.

Voltaire at Ferney

Almost happy now, he looked at his estate.
An exile making watches glanced up as he passed,
And went on working; where a hospital was rising fast
A joiner touched his cap; an agent came to tell
Some of the trees he'd planned were progressing well.
The white alps glittered. It was summer. He was very great.

Far off in Paris, where his enemies
Whispered that he was wicked, in an upright chair
A blind old woman longed for death and letters. He would write
"Nothing is better than life." But was it? Yes, the fight
Against the false and the unfair
Was always worth it. So was gardening. Civilise.

Cajoling, scolding, scheming, cleverest of them all,
He'd led the other children in a holy war
Against the infamous grown-ups; and, like a child, been sly
And humble when there was occasion for
The two-faced answer or the plain protective lie,
But patient like a pheasant waited for their fall.

And never doubted, like D'Alembert, he would win:
Only Pascal was a great enemy, the rest
Were rats already poisoned; there was much, though, to be done,
And only himself to count upon.
Dear Diderot was dull but did his best;
Rousseau, he'd always known, would blubber and give in.

So, like a sentinel, he could not sleep. The night was full of wrong,
Earthquakes and executions. Soon he would be dead,
And still all over Europe stood the horrible nurses
Itching to boil their children. Only his verses
Perhaps could stop them: He must go on working. Overhead
The uncomplaining stars composed their lucid song.

Journey to Iceland

And the traveller hopes: "Let me be far from any
Physician"; and the ports have names for the sea,
    The citiless, the corroding, the sorrow;
    And North means to all: "Reject."

And the great plains are forever where the cold fish is
    hunted,
And everywhere; the light birds flicker and flaunt;
    In the abnormal day of this world, and a river's
    Fan-like polyp of sand.

Then let the good citizen here find natural marvels:
A horse-shoe ravine, an issue of steam from a cleft
    In the rock, and rocks, and waterfalls brushing the
    Rocks, and among the rocks birds.

And the student of prose and conduct places to visit:
The site of a church where a bishop was put in a bag,
    The bath of a great historian, the fort where
    An outlaw dreaded the dark;

Remember the doomed man thrown by his horse and
    crying,
"Beautiful is the hillside, I will not go,"
    The old woman confessing, "He that I loved the
    Best, to him I was worst."

For Europe is absent: this is an island and therefore
A refuge, where the fast affections of its dead may be
    bought
    By those whose dreams accuse them of being
    Spitefully alive, and the pale

From too much passion of kissing feel pure in its deserts.
Can they? For the world is, and the present, and the lie.
    The narrow bridge over the torrent,
    And the small farm under the crag

Are the natural setting for the jealousies of a province;
And the weak vow of fidelity is formed by the cairn;
    And within the indigenous figure on horseback
    On the bridle path down by the lake

The blood moves also by crooked and furtive inches,
Asks all our questions: "Where is the homage? When
   Shall justice be done? O who is against me?
   Why am I always alone?"

No, our time has no favourite suburb; no local features
Are those of the young for whom all wish to care;
   The promise is only a promise, the fabulous
   Country impartially far.

Tears fall in all the rivers. Again the driver
Pulls on his gloves and in a blinding snowstorm starts
   Upon his deadly journey, and again the writer
   Runs howling to his art.[9]

SURREALISM

Fascination with the subconscious mind, as popularized by the psychoanalyst Sigmund Freud, stimulated explorations in psychic experience. By 1924 a Surrealist manifesto had been put forward which tied the subconscious mind to painting. "Pure psychic automatism" described Surrealist works. Surrealism was seen by its advocates as a means for discovering the basic reality of psychic life through automatic association. A dream was supposedly capable of transference directly from the unconscious mind to canvas without control or conscious interruption by the artist.

Surrealism is probably more accurately described by the paintings of Salvador Dali. Dali (1904–89) called his works, such as *The Persistence of Memory* (Fig. **1.30**), "hand-colored photographs of the subconscious," and the high verisimilitude of this work, coupled with its nightmarish relationships of objects, makes a forceful impact. The whole idea of time is destroyed in these "wet watches" (as they were called by those who first saw this work) hanging limply and crawling with ants. And yet there is a strange fascination here, perhaps akin to our fascination with the world of our dreams. While the anti-art Dadaism of Max Ernst may seem repulsive, the irrationality of de Chirico and Dali can be entrancing. The starkness and graphic clarity of Figures **1.30** and **1.33** speaks of the unpolluted light of another planet, yet none the less reflects a world we seem to know.

REALISM

Pictorial objectivity was continued in the Realist tradition in the works of Grant Wood (1892–1942)—for example, *American Gothic* (Fig. **1.34**), a wonderful celebration of America's heartland and its simple, hardworking people. There is a lyric spirituality behind the façade of this down-home illustration. The upward movement of the elongated forms is pulled together at the top into a pointed arch which encapsulates the Gothic window of the farmhouse and escapes the frame of the painting through the lightning rod, in the same sense that the Gothic spire released the spirituality of the earth into heaven at its tip. Rural American reverence for home and labor is celebrated here with gentle humor. There is a capricious two-dimensionality to the picture plane. All objects, including the people, line up horizontally across the painting. We can see no linear perspective in the middle ground, and so the buildings appear pressed against the backs of the farmer and his wife.

Film

World War II and its aftermath brought radical change to the form and content of the cinema. A film came out in 1940 that stunned even Hollywood. Darryl Zanuck and John Ford's version of John Steinbeck's *The Grapes of Wrath* artistically visualized the social criticism of Steinbeck's portrayal of the Depression, through superb cinematography and compelling performances. Theme and social commentary burst forth again in 1941 with two outstanding works, *How Green Was My Valley*, which dealt with exploited coal miners in Wales, and *Citizen Kane*, about wealth and power, and thought by some to be the best film ever produced. The cinematic techniques of *Citizen Kane* forged a new trail. Orson Welles, director and star, and Greg Toland, cinematographer, brilliantly combined deep-focus photography, unique lighting effects, rapid cutting, and moving camera sequences.

But as the war ended and Italy revived from the yoke of Fascism, a new concept set the stage for the years ahead. In 1945 Roberto Rossellini's *Rome, Open City* graphically depicted the misery of Rome during the German occupation. It was shot on the streets of Rome using hidden cameras and mostly nonprofessional actors and actresses. Technically, the quality of the work was deficient, but the effectiveness of its objective viewpoint and documentary realism changed the course of cinema and inaugurated a style called Neorealism.

Theatre

Realism continued its strong tradition in the theatre throughout the post-war era and owed much of its strength to the works of Tennessee Williams (1912–83) and Arthur Miller (b. 1915). However, Realism has expanded from its nineteenth-century definition to include more theatrical approaches and devices such as fragmenting settings. Realism has also become more eclectic in its inclusion of many nonrealistic devices such as symbolism. Undoubtedly the theatre has concluded that stage realism and life's realism are two different concepts entirely. Tennessee Williams skillfully blended the qualities of Realism with whatever scenic, structural, or symbolic devices were necessary to meet his goals. His plays such as *The Glass Menagerie* deal sensitively and poignantly with the problems and psychology of everyday people. His character development is thorough and occupies the principal focus in his dramas as he explores the mental and emotional ills of our society. Arthur Miller probed the social and psychological forces that destroy contemporary men and women in plays such as *Death of a Salesman*.

ABSURDISM

A product of disillusionment, Luigi Pirandello (1867–1936) had lost faith in religion, realism, science, and humanity itself. Still searching, however, for some meaning or basis for existence, he found only chaos, complexity, grotesque laughter, and perhaps, insanity. His plays were obsessed with the question "What is real?" and he pursued that question with brilliant variations. *Right You Are If You Think You Are* presented a situation in which a wife, living with her husband in a top-floor apartment, is not permitted to see her mother. She converses with her daily—the mother is in the street and the daughter is at a garret window. Soon the neighbor's curiosity demands an explanation from the husband. A satisfactory answer is forthcoming, but the mother has an equally plausible, although radically different explanation. Finally, the wife, who is the only one who can clear up the mystery, is approached. Her response, as the curtain falls, is loud laughter! Pirandello cried bitterly at a world he could not understand, but he did so with mocking laughter directed at those who purported to have the answers or were sure that they soon would.

Pirandello's nonrealistic departures created the mold from which emerged a movement called Absurdism.

Existentialism, a philosophy which questioned the nature of existence, placing a meaningless present amid a guilt-ridden past and an unknowable future, also contributed to Absurdist style. From such antecedents came numerous dramas, probably the best known of which were written by the French philosopher and playwright Jean-Paul Sartre (1905–80). Sartre's Existentialism held that there were no absolute or universal moral values and that humankind was part of a world without purpose. Therefore, men and women were responsible only to themselves. His plays attempted to draw logical conclusions from "a consistent atheism." Plays such as *No Exit* (1944) translate Sartre's philosophies and Existential viewpoint into dramatic form.

Albert Camus (1913–60) was the first playwright to use the term "absurd," a state which he considered to be a result of the dichotomy between humankind's aspirations and the meaninglessness of the universe in which individuals live. Finding one's way in a chaotic universe, then, became the theme of Camus's plays, such as *Cross-Purposes* (1944).

After these two playwrights came a series of Absurdists who differed quite radically from both Sartre and Camus, both of whom strove to bring order out of absurdity. The plays of Samuel Beckett, Eugene Ionesco, and Jean Genet all tend to point only to the absurdity of existence and to reflect the chaos they saw in the universe. Their plays are chaotic and ambiguous, and the absurd and ambiguous nature of these plays make direct analysis purely a matter of interpretation. *Waiting for Godot* (1958), the most popular work of Samuel Beckett (1906–89), has been interpreted in so many ways to suggest so many different meanings that it has become an eclectic experience in and of itself. Beckett, like the Minimalist sculptors, left it to the audience to draw whatever conclusions they wished about the work confronting them. The works of Ionesco (b. 1912) are even more baffling, using nonsense syllables and clichés for dialogue, endless and meaningless repetition, and plots that have no development. He called the *Bald Soprano* (1950) an antiplay. The Absurdist movement had influenced other playwrights and production approaches, from Harold Pinter to Edward Albee.

ABSTRACT EXPRESSIONISM

The first fifteen years following the end of World War II were dominated by a style called Abstract Expressionism. Beginning essentially in New York, Abstract Expressionism spread rapidly throughout the world. Like most modern styles, which include great variation among individual artists, Abstract Expressionism is difficult to define in specific terms, although some scholars believe it to be self-explanatory. Two characteristics can be identified. One is a freedom from traditional use of brushwork, and the other is the exclusion of representational subject matter. Complete freedom of individual expression to reflect inner life gave rein to create works of high emotional and dynamic intensity. Absolute individual freedom of expression and freedom from rationality underlie this style. There appeared to be some relationship to the optimistic post-war sense of conquest over totalitarianism. By the early 1960s when life was less certain and the implications of the nuclear age had sunk in, Abstract Expressionism had all but ceased to exist.

The most heralded artist of this style was Jackson Pollock (1912–56). A rebellious spirit, Pollock evolved this approach to painting only ten years before his death. Although he insisted that he had absolute control, his compositions consisted of unfettered dripping and spilling of paint on to huge canvases placed on the floor. His work (Fig. **13.20**), often called action painting, elicits a sense of tremendous energy, actually transmitting the action of paint application to the respondent through a revolutionary concept of space, line, and form.

The Abstract Expressionist tradition continues in the work of Helen Frankenthaler (b. 1928). Her staining technique, as seen in *Buddha* (Fig. **13.21**), consists of pouring color across an unprimed canvas, creating amorphous shapes which seem to float in space. The image has infinite potential meaning, apart from that suggested by the title. The very freedom of the form symbolizes our freedom to choose its associations. However, we are directed by the sensual quality of the work. Its fluidity, and the nonlinear use of color, give it softness and grace.

Abstract Expressionism proved to be a uniquely American movement. Nowhere else did anything even remotely comparable emerge during this time. However, by the early 1960s the style seems to have reached its zenith. An entirely new perception of reality, one of consumerism and affluence, began to sweep the world.

After, and in some instances as a reaction against the emotionalism of Abstract Expressionism came an explosion of styles: Pop Art, Op Art, Hard Edge, Minimal Art, Post-Minimal Art, Environments, Body Art, Earth Art, Video Art, Kinetic Art, Photo Realism, and Conceptual Art. We have space to note only some of these.

13.20 Jackson Pollock, *Autumn Rhythm*, 1950. Canvas, 105 x 207 ins (267 x 526 cm). The Metropolitan Museum of Art, New York, George A. Hearn Fund.

13.21 Helen Frankenthaler, *Buddha*, 1988. Acrylic on canvas, 74 x 81 ins (188 x 206 cm). Private collection. Courtesy of André Emmerich Gallery, New York.

POP ART

Pop Art evolved in the 1950s, and concerned itself above all with image in a representational sense. Subjects and treatments in this style come from mass culture and commercial design. These sources provided Pop artists with what they considered to be essential aspects of today's visual environment. The Pop artists traced their heritage to Dada, although much of the heritage of the Pop tradition continues to be debated. However, Pop is essentially an optimistic reflection of the contemporary scene. The term "Pop" was coined by the English critic Lawrence Alloway and related to the images found in popular culture that marked this approach. Probably the compelling depictions of Roy Lichtenstein (b. 1923) are the most familiar (Fig. **13.23**). These magnified cartoon-strip details use the Ben Day screen of dots by which colored ink is applied to cheap newsprint. Using a stencil about the size of a coin, the image is built up into a stark and dynamic, if sometimes violent, portrayal.

Pop objects serve as source materials for Claes Oldenburg (b. 1929). *Dual Hamburgers* (Fig. **13.22**) presents an enigma to the viewer. What are we to make of it? Is it a celebration of the mundane? Or is there a greater

comment on our age implicit in these objects? Certainly Oldenburg calls our attention to the qualities of design in ordinary objects by taking them out of their context and changing their scale. The influence of the Pop Movement can also be seen in the plaster figures of George Segal (b.

13.22 Claes Thure Oldenburg, *Two Cheeseburgers, with Everything (Dual Hamburgers)*, 1962. Burlap soaked in plaster, painted with enamel, 7 x 14¾ x 8⅝ ins (17.8 x 37.5 x 21.8 cm). Collection, The Museum of Modern Art, New York (Philip Johnson Fund).

13.23 Roy Lichtenstein, *Whaam!*, 1963. Acrylic on canvas, 68 x 160 ins (173 x 405 cm). The Tate Gallery, London.

1924). Working from plaster molds taken from living figures, Segal builds scenes from everyday life with unpainted plaster images. These unpainted ghosts remove the sculptural environment from reality to a different plane altogether. Similar in a way, but in stark contrast, are the photorealistic sculptures of Duane Hanson (b. 1925), whose portrayals, including hair and plastic skin, are often displayed in such circumstances that the respondent does not know for sure at first sight if he or she is viewing a sculpture or a real human. Hanson's portrayals express a tragic quality and are an exposé of crassness and bourgeois tastelessness.

13.24 Frank Stella, *Tahkt-I-Sulayman I*, 1967. Polymer and fluorescent paint on canvas, 10 ft $\frac{1}{4}$ in x 20 ft $2\frac{1}{4}$ ins (3.04 m x 6.15 m). The Pasadena Art Museum, California (gift of Mr. and Mrs. Robert A. Rowan).

OP ART

Op Art concerns itself with optics and perception. Emerging from the 1950s, Op Art was an intellectually oriented and systematic style, very scientific in its applications. Based on perceptual tricks, the misleading images of these paintings capture our curiosity and pull us into a conscious exploration of what the optical illusion does and why it does it. Victor Vasarély (b. 1908) bends line and form to create a very deceiving sense of three-dimensionality. Complex sets of stimuli proceed from horizontal, vertical, and diagonal arrangements. Using nothing but abstract form, Vasarély creates the illusion of real space.

HARD EDGE

Hard Edge or Hard Edged Abstraction also came to its height during the 1950s. In this style, which the work of Ellsworth Kelly (b. 1923) and Frank Stella (b. 1936) best illustrates, flat color areas have hard edges which carefully separate them from each other. Essentially, Hard Edge is an exploration of design for its own sake. Stella often abandoned the rectangular format in favor of irregular compositions to be sure his paintings had no relationship to windows. The shape of the canvas was part of the design itself, as opposed to being a frame or a formal border within which the design was executed. Some of

13.25 Louise Nevelson, *Black Wall*, 1959. Wood, 112 x 85¼ x 25½ ins (264 x 216 x 65 cm). The Tate Gallery, London.

Stella's paintings have iridescent metal powder mixed into the paint, and the metallic shine further enhances the precision of the composition. *Tahkt-I-Sulayman I* (Fig. **13.24**) stretches 20 ft (6 m) across and intersperses wonderfully surging circles and half-circles of yellow, reds, and blues. The intensity of the surface counters the grace of its form with jarring fluorescence. The simplicity of these forms provides a deceptive counterpoint with the variety of their repetitions.

PRIMARY STRUCTURES

The Primary Structures movement pursues two primary goals: extreme simplicity of shape and a kinship with architecture. A space–time relationship distinguishes Primary Structures from other sculpture. The viewer is invited to share an experience in three-dimensional space by walking around and/or through the works. Form and content are abstracted to Minimalist qualities.

Louise Nevelson (1900–88), perhaps the twentieth century's first major woman sculptor, overcame the percep-tion that sculpture was a man's profession because of the heavy manual labor involved. In the 1950s she began using found pieces of wood to construct her own vision of reality. At first miniature cityscapes, her work grew to larger proportions—for example, *Black Wall* (Fig. **13.25**), a relief-like wall unit painted a monochromatic flat black. These pieces suggest the world of dreams, but their mean-ing and logic remain a puzzle with intense appeal to the imagination.

ENVIRONMENTAL ART

Environmental Art creates an inclusive experience and in Figure **13.26**, *Jardin d'Email* by Jean Dubuffet (b. 1901), we find an area made of concrete, which is painted with white paint and black lines. It is capricious in form and surrounded by high walls. Inside the sculptural environ-ment we find a tree and two bushes of polyurethane. We might conclude that Dubuffet has pushed the essence and the boundaries of art to their limits. He has consistently opted for chaos, for *art brut*—the art of children,

13.26 Jean Dubuffet, *Jardin d'Email*, 1973–74. Concrete, epoxy paint and polyurethane, 66 ft 8 ins x 100 ft (20 x 30 m). State Museum Kröller-Müller, Otterlo, The Netherlands.

psychotics, and amateurs. The *Jardin d'Email* is one of a small series of recent projects in which he has depicted the chaotic, disorienting, and inexplicable in three-dimensional form.

PHOTOREALISM & CONCEPTUALISM

Photorealism is an offshoot of Pop Art concerned with photographic images. Using photographic images as a basis, Photo-Realist works are usually extremely complex.

Conceptual Art challenges the relationship between art and life and, in fact, the definition of art itself. Essentially anti-art, like Dada, Conceptual Art attempts to divorce totally the imagination from aesthetics. It insists that only the imagination, not the artwork, is art. Therefore artworks can be done away with. The creative process needs only to be documented by some incidental means such as a verbal description or a simple object like a chair. The paradoxes of Conceptual Art are many, including its dependence on a physical something to bridge the gap between artist's conception and respondent's imagination.

ART NOUVEAU

The unique characteristic of Art Nouveau is the lively, serpentine curve known as the "whiplash." The style reflects a fascination with plant and animal life and organic growth. The influence of Japanese art is evident in the undulating curves. Art Nouveau incorporates organic and often symbolic motifs, and treats them in a very linear, relief-like manner.

Art Nouveau continued into the early years of the twentieth century, with one of its greatest exponents, Antoni Gaudí (1852–1926), designing town houses such as the Casa Batlló (Fig. **13.27**) in Barcelona.

13.27 Antoni Gaudí, Casa Batlló, Barcelona, 1905–7.

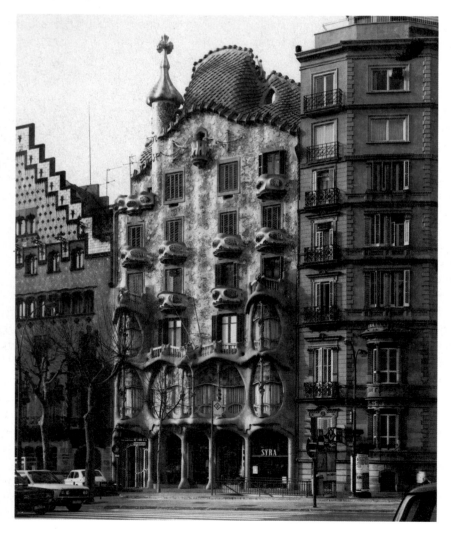

EXPERIMENTATION IN ARCHITECTURE

Structural expression and preoccupation with building materials dominated the early twentieth century, as it had dominated the nineteenth. Of vital importance to the new century and its approaches was reinforced concrete or ferroconcrete. Ferroconcrete had been in use as a material since around 1849, but it had taken nearly fifty years to emerge fully as an important architectural material. Auguste Perret (1874–1954) single-mindedly set about developing formulas for building with ferroconcrete, and his efforts were influential in the works of those who followed. We can grasp some of the implications of this approach in Perret's Garage Ponthieu (Fig. 13.28). The reinforced concrete structure emerges clearly in the exterior appearance. The open spaces were filled with glass or ceramic panels. The result achieved a certain elegance and logical expression of strength and lightness.

If Perret was single-minded in his approach to problems in structure and materials, his contemporary (and assistant to Louis Sullivan), Frank Lloyd Wright (1867–1959), was one of the most innovative and influential of twentieth-century architects. Perret summarized and continued earlier tradition, but Wright wished to initiate new ones. One manifestation of Wright's pursuits was the Prairie Style, developed around 1900 and drawing upon the flat landscape of the Midwest for its tone. The Prairie houses reflected Japanese influence in their simple horizontal and vertical accents. Wright was also influenced by Sullivan in his pursuit of form and functional relationships. Wright attempted to devise practical arrangements for his interiors and to reflect the interior spaces in the exterior appearance of the building. He also tried to relate the exterior of the building to its context or natural environment and took great pains to suggest an interrelationship of interior and exterior space (Fig. 7.36).

Wright also designed some of the furniture for his houses—comfort, function, and design integration were the chief criteria. Textures and colors in the environment were duplicated in the materials, including large expanses of wood both in the house and its furniture. He made a point of giving his furniture several functions—for example, tables that also served as cabinets. All spaces and objects were precisely designed to present a complete environment. Wright was convinced that houses profoundly influenced the people who lived in them, and he saw the architect as a "molder of humanity." Wright's works ranged from the simple to the complex, from the serene to the dramatic, and from interpenetration to

13.28 Auguste Perret, Garage Ponthieu, Paris, 1905–6.

enclosure of space. He always pursued experimentation, and the exploration of various interrelationships of spaces and geometric forms marks his designs.

Poured concrete and new concepts in design can also be seen in the works of Le Corbusier (1887–1965) in the 1920s and 1930s. The machine concept did not imply a depersonalization, as much machine-related art in the first half of the century did. Rather, it implied efficient construction from standard, mass-produced parts, logically designed for usage as the parts of an efficient house-machine. Le Corbusier had espoused a domino system of design for houses, using a series of slabs supported on slender columns. The resulting building was box-like, with a flat roof, which could be used as a terrace. The Villa

13.29 Le Corbusier, Villa Savoye, Poissy, France, 1928–30.

Savoye (Fig. **13.29**) combines these concepts in a design whose supporting structures freed the interior from the necessity of weight-supporting walls. In many ways the design of the Villa Savoye reveals Classical Greek inspiration, from its articulated columns and human scale to its precisely articulated parts and totally coherent and unified whole. The design is crisp, clean, and functional.

International and Corporate Architecture

Architecture affords no relief from the problem of trying to sample or overview an era still in the making. In a sense, the task is more difficult here, because the human element of artistic creation has been blurred by architectural corporations, as opposed to individual architects. There is also a tendency for the contemporary observer to see a sameness in the glass and steel boxes of the International Style that dominate our cities and to miss the truly unique approach to design that may comprise a housing project in an obscure locale.

World War II caused a ten-year break in architectural construction and, to a certain extent, separated what came after from what went before. However, the continuing careers of architects who had achieved significant accomplishment before the war bridged that gap. Geographical focus shifted from Europe to the United States, Japan, and even South America. The overall approach still remained modern or international in flavor, which helps us to select a few examples to illustrate general tendencies.

As a type, the skyscraper saw a resurgence of building in the fifties, in a glass-and-steel box approach that continues today. Illustrative of this type and approach is Lever House in New York City (Fig. **13.30**). A very important consideration in this design is the open space

surrounding the tower. Created by setting the tower back from the perimeter of the site, the open space around the building creates its own envelope of environment or context. Reactions against the glazed appearance of the Lever

13.30 Gordon Bunshaft (Skidmore, Owings and Merrill), Lever House, New York, 1950–52.

13.31 Mies van der Rohe and Philip Johnson, Seagram Building, New York, 1958.

13.32 Pier Luigi Nervi, Small Sports Palace, Rome, 1957.

Building have occurred throughout the last thirty years, with surfaces such as aluminum pierced by small windows, for example. In the same sense, an intensification of the glazed exterior has occurred, wherein metalized windows, rather than normal glass, have formed the exterior surface. Such an approach has been particularly popular in the Sun Belt, because metalized glass reflects the sun's rays and their heat. In any case, the functional plain rectangle of the International Style has continued as a general architectural form regardless of individual variation.

The rectangle, which has so uniformly and in many cases thoughtlessly, become the mark of contemporary architecture leads us to the architect who, before World War II, was among its advocates. Mies van der Rohe insisted that form should not be an end in itself. Rather, the architect should discover and state the function of the building. His pursuit of those goals and his honesty in taking mass-produced materials at face value—that is, bricks, glass, and manufactured metals—and outwardly expressing their shapes was the basis for the rectangularization that is the common ground of twentieth-century architecture. His search for proportional perfection can be traced, perhaps, to the German Pavilion of the Barcelona Exposition in 1929 and was expressed in projects such as New York's Seagram Building (Fig. 13.31).

Differing reflections in contemporary design have ultimately pursued the question formulated by Louis I. Kahn, "What form does the space want to become?" In the case of Frank Lloyd Wright's Guggenheim Museum (Fig. 7.36), space has become a relaxing spiral that reflects the leisurely progress one should make through an art museum.

The simple curvilinearity of the arch and the dome is the mark of two different and noteworthy architects. The unencumbered free space in their projects represents a contrast to the self-contained boxes of the International Style. Pier Luigi Nervi's Small Sports Palace (Fig. 13.32) and Richard Buckminster Fuller's Climatron (Fig. 7.20) illustrate the trend toward spansion architecture which stretches engineering to the limits of its materials, and which, in the case of the Kansas City Hyatt Regency Hotel, took design tragically beyond practicality.

Post-Modernist Architecture

Contemporary architecture also has turned in pluralistic directions. Post-Modern or Revisionist architecture puts new manifestations on past styles. The Spanish architect Ricardo Bofill (b. 1939) and the Italian Aldo Rossi both derive much of their architectural language from the past.

13.33 Ricardo Bofill, The Palace of Abraxas, Marne-la-Vallée, near Paris, 1978–83.

13.34 Michael Graves, Portland Public Office Building, Portland, Oregon, 1979–82.

As Bofill remarked, his architecture takes "without copying, different themes from the past, but in an eclectic manner, seizing certain moments in history and juxtaposing them, thereby prefiguring a new epoch." We see this eclectic juxtaposition in his public housing development called, with typical grandiosity, The Palace of Abraxas (Fig. **13.33**). Here columnar verticality is suggested by glass and by cornice/capitals, which dynamically exhibit the characteristics of Classicism. In Japan, Post-Modern architects such as Arata Isozaki portray in their buildings the restrained elegance and style of traditional Japanese art. In the United States, Michael Graves (b. 1934) has reacted to the repetitive glass, concrete, and steel boxes of the International Style, which dominates modern cities, by creating a metaphorical allusion to the keystone of the Roman arch (Fig. **13.34**). The bright red pilasters suggest

13.35 Renzo Piano and Richard Rogers, Pompidou Center, Paris, 1971–78.

fluted columns, and fiberglass garlands recall both Art Deco and the Rococo. Post-Modern architecture focuses on meaning and symbolism: The past and ornamentation are acceptable; functionalism no longer controls. The Post-Modernist seeks to create buildings "in the fuller context of society and the environment." Social identity, cultural continuity, and sense of place become foundations for the art.

In a clear repudiation of the glass and steel box of the International Style and other popular forms in mainstream architecture, the design for the Pompidou Center in Paris (Fig. **13.35**) turns the building inside out, externalizing its network of ducts, pipes, and elevators, while hiding the internal structure, which has no fixed walls; temporary dividers can be arranged in any desired configuration. The bright primary colors of the exterior combine with the serpentine, plexiglass-covered escalators to give a whimsical, lively appearance to a functional building. The Pompidou Center has become a tourist attraction rivaling the Eiffel Tower and, while controversial, has wide popular acceptance.

MODERN CLASSICAL MUSIC

Music took no less radical a path from its nineteenth-century heritage than did painting and sculpture. Nevertheless, contemporary concert programs illustrate for us the unique phenomenon that response to works of art is always in the present tense. Our own experiences with and responses to the meanings in works of art are those of today, whether the artwork was created this morning or 20,000 years ago. So we have the luxury of sharing experiences directly with Michelangelo, Shakespeare, Leonardo da Vinci, J. S. Bach, and the architects of Athens, as well as with those men and women of our own era who illuminate and comment upon the events and circumstaances surrounding us. Our contemporaries may and do choose to follow the traditions of the past or invent new ones.

Twentieth-century music took both paths. New directions differed from past essentially in three ways. The first was rhythmic complexity. Prevailing tradition since the Middle Ages emphasized grouping beats together in rhythmic patterns called meter. The characteristic accents of duple and triple meters helped to unify and clarify compositions, as well as to give them certain flavors. The modern composer did away with these patterns and regularity of accents, choosing instead to employ complex, changing rhythms in which it is virtually impossible to determine meter or even the actual beat.

The second change consisted of a focus on dissonant harmonies. Prior to the late nineteenth century, musical convention centered upon consonance as the norm to which all harmonic progressions returned. Dissonance was used to disturb the norm, so as to enable the music to return to consonance. The late nineteenth century witnessed significant tampering with that concept. By the twentieth century composers were using more and more dissonance, focusing on it, and refraining from consonant resolution.

The third major change from the past comprised the rejection of traditional tonality or sense of key altogether. Traditional thinking held that one note, the *do* or tonic of a scale, was the most important. All music was composed with a specific key in mind. Modulations into distant or related keys occurred, but even then the tonic of the key was the touchstone to which all progression related. Many composers rejected that manner of systematizing musical sound and chose, instead, to pursue two other paths. One was to reject any sense of tonal center and importance of one tone over the other. All twelve tones of the chromatic scale became equal. The systems that resulted from this path were called twelve-tone composition and serialism.

Transition from the nineteenth to the twentieth centuries rode primarily on the works of one major composer, the Impressionist Claude Debussy. Several other traditions were current. One, of German–Italian influence, built upon the works of Richard Wagner and was called the *cosmopolitan* style. The principal composer in this group was César Franck. A Classically oriented style came into the century in the works of Camille Saint-Säens.

Debussy's style linked him closely with the French composer Maurice Ravel (1875–1937), who began as an Impressionist but became more and more Classical in orientation as years went by. However, even in his earlier works, Ravel did not adopt Debussy's complex sonorities and modality. Ravel's *Bolero* (1928) exhibits strong primitive influences and the unceasing rhythm of Spanish dance music. More typical works of Ravel—for example, his *Piano Concerto in G*—use Mozart and traditional Classicism as their models. As a result of Ravel's tendencies and the similar concerns of other composers, the early twentieth century witnessed a Neoclassical

direction, which stayed completely within the established conventions of Western music but rejected both Romantic and Impressionistic developments.

Traditional tendencies continued throughout this period and can be seen in various quarters, one of which is the music of the American William Schuman in the 1930s and 1940s. His symphonies exhibit bright timbres and energetic rhythms and focus on eighteenth- and nineteenth-century American folklore. The eighteenth-century American composer William Billings figures prominently in the works of Schuman in the *William Billings Overture* (1943) and the *New England Triptych* (1956), based on three pieces by Billings. *American Festival Overture* (1939) is perhaps his most famous work. Traditional tonality can also be found in the works of Russia's Prokofiev. Notwithstanding traditional tonality, his *Steel Step* reflected the encroachment of mechanization of the 1920s. The machine as a symbol for tremendous energy and motion found its way into music, and in the *Steel Step* Prokofiev intentionally dehumanized the subject in order to reflect contemporary life.

Hindemith

Experimentation and departure from traditional tonality marked the compositions of Paul Hindemith (1895–1963). Concerned with problems of musical organization, he systematized his approach to these problems and theorized solutions in the *Craft of Musical Composition*. His work was extremely chromatic, almost atonal. His system of tonality was based on the establishment of tonal centers, but did not include the concepts of major and minor keys. He hoped that his new system would become a universal music language, but it did not. He was, however, extremely influential in twentieth-century music composition, both as a composer and a teacher. His works are broad and varied, encompassing nearly every musical genre, including ten operas, art songs, cantatas, chamber music, requiems, and symphonies.

Bartók

Another nontraditional approach to tonality was the unique style of the Hungarian composer Béla Bartók (1881–1945). He was interested in folk music and is often considered a representative of a nationalistic school of composition. Whether or not that is true, Bartók's interest in Eastern European folk music is significant, because much of that music does not use Western major/minor modality. So Bartók's interest in it and in nontraditional tonality in general went hand in hand. Bartók invented his own type of harmonic structure, which could accommodate folk melodies. As nontraditional as some of his work is, however, he also employed traditional devices and forms. His style was precise and very well structured. He often developed his works from one or two very short motifs. His larger works were unified by repetition of thematic material throughout. He even used sonata-allegro form. Textures in Bartók's works are largely contrapuntal, which gives them a melodic emphasis with little concern for harmony. Dissonances occur freely.

Rhythm was very important to Bartók. His works tended to focus on rhythmic energy, employing many different devices, such as repeated chords and irregular meters (always to generate dynamic rhythms). His use of polyrhythms—that is, various juxtaposed rhythms—created a nonmelodic counterpoint of unique quality. These qualities resulted from the subtleties of rhythms found in folk song and dance. His compositions exhibit a wonderfully spontaneous freshness.

Stravinsky

Nontraditionalism was followed in other quarters, and with *The Firebird* (1910) Igor Stravinsky (1882–1971) came to prominence. *The Rite of Spring* (1912–13) created an even greater impact. Both works were scores for ballets. *The Firebird* was a commission for the Russian impresario Diaghilev, and premièred successfully at the Paris Opéra, while *The Rite of Spring* caused a near riot and a great scandal because of revolutionary orchestrations and driving primitive rhythms. On the whole his works display a variety of styles and forms, but whatever their nature, he was a significant composer who was as prolific as he was diverse.

Schoenberg

The movement which drew the most attention in the first half of the twentieth century grew out of German Romanticism and took a radical turn into atonality. The composer at the root of the movement was Arnold Schoenberg (1874–1951). Between 1905 and 1912 Schoenberg turned away from the gigantic Post-Romantic works he had been composing to a more contained style, in works for small ensembles and in orchestral works, which treated instruments individually. In orchestral works his timbres alternate swiftly, contrasting with large blocks of tone color characteristic of earlier works. They also display rhythmic and polyphonic complexity fragmented melodies.

Although the word atonality (without tonality) is used to describe Schoenberg works, he preferred the term pantonality—that is, inclusive of all tonalities. His compositions sought freedom to use any combination of tones without the necessity of having to resolve chordal progressions. He called that concept "the emancipation of dissonance."

At times in their careers Schoenberg, Alban Berg, and Anton Webern represented Expressionism in music. Expressionism approached humanity in terms of its psychological relationship to the modern world. Humankind was helpless in a world beyond its control and governed by subconscious forces in rebellion against established order. *Erwartung*, in which Schoenberg utilized complex rhythms, dissonance, strange orchestration, and fragmented melodies, evokes great intensity of feeling. As with many of his works, it sought to portray complex thoughts and emotions relative to his subject matter.

By 1923 Schoenberg was composing in a twelve-tone or dodecaphonic technique, in which a row or series of the twelve tones in an octave was used in various ways—as melodies and harmonies, with rhythmic considerations, upside down, backward, upside down and backward, that is, in whatever predetermined form the composer desired. The logical structure of this technique is fairly mathematical and somewhat formalized, but it does maintain a balance between emotion, accident, and mechanization. The important thing for a listener to understand about these apparently strange works, or works which stand outside conventional tonal organization, is the fact that they contain specific organization and logical order. When the listener knows the guideposts to look for, Schoenberg's music progresses just as comfortably as does that of traditional tonality.

Berg

Alban Berg (1885–1935) was a close friend and disciple of Schoenberg, and his compositions are based on the serial technique. However, Berg's sense of lyricism means his works do not have the disconnectedness of much serial music. Many of the characteristics of his work can be found in his *Lyric Suite* (1927), a string quartet in six movements with a binary (AA) form. It is based on several different tone rows. Each *tone row* uses the twelve notes of the chromatic scale only once; the composer decides in which order the notes will occur. As a result, the harmonies of the piece are *atonal*. He is probably best-known for his opera *Wozzeck*.

Ives and Copland

Ives and Copland were both Americans with experimental and highly personal styles. Charles Ives (1874–1954) was so experimental and ahead of his time that many of his compositions were considered unplayable and did not receive public performances until after World War I. Content to remain anonymous, Ives went unrecognized for many years. His melodies spring from folk and popular songs, hymns, and other, often familiar, material, which he treated in most unfamiliar ways. His rhythms are hopelessly irregular and often without measure delineation except for an occasional bar line to indicate an accent beat. Textures involve such dissonant counterpoint that frequently it is impossible to distinguish one melodic line from another. Some of the tone clusters in his piano music are unplayable without using a block of wood to depress all the necessary keys at once. Ives's experiments, such as the *Unanswered Question* (1908), also employ ensembles placed in various locations to create stereophonic effects. For Ives all music related to life's experiences and ideas, some of which were consonant and some dissonant, and his music reflected that philosophy accordingly.

Aaron Copland (b. 1900) integrated national American idioms into his compositions. Jazz, dissonance, Mexican folk songs and Shaker hymns all appear. The latter figure prominently in Copland's most significant work, *Appalachian Spring* (1944). First written as a ballet, later it was reworked as a suite for symphony orchestra. Copland also used a variety of approaches, some reserved and harmonically complex, and some simple. He often used all tones in the diatonic scale, such as in the opening chord of the work. Despite a diversity of influences, he achieved a very personal and individual style, which is traditionally tonal. His unique manipulation of rhythms and chords has been highly influential in twentieth-century American musical composition.

SERIALISM

Post-Webern or post-war serialism reflects a desire to exert more control and to apply a predetermined hierarchy of values to all elements of a composition. Before the war, twelve-tone technique involved the creation of a set or row of twelve pitch classes arranged in a specific order. Although the order could be manipulated in a number of ways, certain relationships between the pitches of the tone-row were constant and provided the underlying structure and much of the flavor of this style. To a certain extent structural decisions were made before the composer actually began writing the composition itself. The composer was then subject to fairly strict limitations regarding the selection of pitches as the work progressed, since all pitch order was pre-established. Proponents of the technique argued that composers have always worked within limitations of some kind and that the discipline required to do so is an essential part of the creative problem-solving process. Opponents argued that writing music in this fashion was more a matter of mathematical manipulation and less the function of a composer's ear and basic musical instincts.

Three Compositions for piano (1947–48) by the American composer Milton Babbit is one of the earliest examples of serial technique applied to elements other than pitch. In this work, rhythm, and dynamics are also predetermined by serial principles.

IMPROVISATION

An open, improvisatory tradition was carried on by composers like Lukas Foss with the Improvisation Chamber Ensemble of which he was founder. A number of other improvisation groups, many funded by granting organizations and universities, sprang up in the United States during the 1960s along with the intense exploration of new sound possibilities from both conventional and electronic instruments.

MAINSTREAM

What is often referred to as a mainstream of musical composition also continued after the war. The source of much of this music is a combination of nineteenth-century Romantic tradition, the folk styles of Bartók and Copland, quartet harmonies of Hindemith, the modality of the Impressionists Ravel and Debussy, and the Neo-classicism of Prokofiev and Stravinsky. To some degree, both serialism and indeterminacy can be found here as well as popular or jazz elements. Many American and European composers belong to the so-called mainstream.

ELECTRONIC MUSIC

The development of the RCA synthesizer and the establishment of the Columbia-Princeton Electronics Music Center provided an opportunity for composers such as Milton Babbitt to pursue the application and further development of primarily serial techniques. Composers such as John Cage found electronics a logical means to achieve their musical goals of indeterminacy as in *Imaginary Landscape No. 5*. Mainstream and radical jazz composers were not seriously affected by the electronic medium until the 1960s.

We need to note that electronic production and alteration of sound does not imply, in itself, a specific musical style. However, electronic sound production led to two new approaches during the 1950s. First, *musique concrète*—the use of acoustically produced sounds, and, second, electronically generated sound. In recent times this distinction has become less meaningful due to the major advances in technology since that time.

ULTRARATIONALISM & BEYOND

The 1960s and early 1970s saw even further extremes in the "ultrarational" and "antirational" directions in addition to an even stronger desire constantly to create something new. At times this desire for newness superseded most other considerations. Stockhausen, for example, became more interested in the total manipulation of sound and the acoustic space in which the performance was to take place. His work *Gruppen* (1957) for three orchestras is an early example. As he became more and more interested in timbre modulation, his work encompassed a greater variety of sound sources both electronic and acoustic in an interesting combination of control and noncontrol. An example of this is *Microphonie I* (1964). Igor Stravinsky, one of the most influential composers of the early part of this century, developed his own serial art form in the late 1950s and early 1960s.

Elliott Carter, although not a serialist, developed a highly organized approach toward rhythm, often called metric modulation, in which the mathematical principles of meter, standard rhythmic notation, and other elements are carried to complex ends. The pitch content of Carter's music is highly chromatic and exact, and his music requires virtuoso playing both from the individual and the ensemble. Virtuoso playing produced an important composer–performer relationship in the 1960s, and many composers, such as Luciano Berio, wrote specifically for individual performers, such as trombonist Stewart Dempster. In the same vein percussionist Max Neuhaus was associated with Stockhausen, and pianist David Tudor, with John Cage.

Experimentation with microtones has been of interest to music theorists throughout history and many non-Western cultures employ them routinely. Microtones can be defined as intervals smaller than a half step. Our system divides the octave into twelve equal parts. There seems to be no reason why the octave cannot be divided into 24, 53, 95, or any number of parts. The possibilities are

limited, only by our ability to hear such intervals and a performer's ability to produce them. Alois Haba experimented in the early part of the century with quarter tones (24 per octave) and sixth tones (36 per octave), as did Charles Ives. A number of instruments were designed to produce microtones, and experimentation and composition has been carried out widely.

In an atmosphere of constant searching and experimentation, composers often questioned the validity of traditional concepts of art in general and specifically the limitations of the traditional concert hall. The earlier work by Cage and others led in a number of directions including theatre pieces, multimedia or mixed media, so-called danger music, biomusic, soundscapes, happenings, and total environments which might include stimulation of all the senses in some way. Thus the definition of a composer as opposed to playwright, filmmaker, visual artist, and so on was often obscured.

Since the early 1960s electronic instruments which could be used in live performance have been highly influential in music composition. Live performance mixed with prerecorded tape occurred in the 1950s, and by the 1960s it became common to alter the sound of live performers by electronic means. Computer technology has been added to the composition and performance of music, and the options available through computer application are now endless.

Theatre music, sometimes referred to as experimental music, ranges from relatively subtle examples of performers playing or singing notated music and moving to various points on the stage, as in Berio's *Circles* (1960), to more extreme examples, such as the works of La Monte Young, in which the performer is instructed to "draw a straight line and follow it" or react to the audience just as an audience was to react to the performers, that is, exchange places. A more active example is Nam June Paik's *Homage to John Cage* in which the composer ran down into the audience, cut off Cage's tie, dumped liquid over his head, and ran from the theatre, later to phone and let the audience know the composition had ended. Such compositions contain a high degree of indeterminacy.

Some works were never intended to be performed, but only conceptualized, such as Nam June Paik's *Danger Music for Dick Higgins*, which instructs the performer to "Creep into the vagina of a living whale," or Robert Moran's *Composition for Piano with Pianist*, which instructs the pianist to climb into the grand piano. There was also a return to minimal materials, exemplified by Stockhausen's *Stimmung (Tuning)*, dating from 1968, for six vocalists singing only six notes. Minimal music generally can be defined as music which uses very little musical material, but often for an extended length of time, such as *One Sound* for string quartet by Harold Budd and the electronic piece *Come Out* (1966) by Steve Reich.

Many mainstream composers continued writing throughout the 1960s and early 1970s. However, a noticeable element of controlled indeterminacy has found its way into the music of many of them. The late 1960s and 1970s brought greater tolerance and acceptance on the part of composers for each other's varying aesthetic viewpoints and musical styles, in a blending of avant-garde techniques with the mainstream.

Just as indeterminacy and aleatoric procedures had been developed during the 1950s by composers of the Western Europe music tradition, freedom from melodic, rhythmic, and formal restraints in jazz led to the free jazz art form of the 1960s. Saxophonist Ornette Colman was one of the earliest proponents of such freedom. Others, such as John Coltrane, developed a rhythmically and melodically free style based on more modal materials, while Cecil Taylor developed materials which were more chromatic. In the mid to late 1960s a mature blend of this freedom, with control and sophistication, was reached in Miles Davis's *Bitches Brew* album of 1967. A number of musicians who originally worked with Miles Davis became leading artists in the 1970s, developing a style called jazz-rock, or fusion.

Polish composer Krzysztof Penderecki (b. 1933) has striven to produce new sounds from traditional string instruments. He is widely known for both instrumental and choral works, including a major composition, the *Requiem Mass*, written 1985. Penderecki's *Polymorphia* (1961) uses twenty-four violins, eight violas, eight cellos, and eight double basses. Because of his experimentation with new techniques and sounds for strings, Penderecki had to invent a whole new series of musical markings, listed at the beginning of the score. In actual performance, the timings are measured by a stop watch and there is no clear meter. *Polymorphia* uses a free form with structure achieved from textures, harmonies, and string techniques. The piece is dissonant and remains atonal until the very end. It begins with a low, sustained chord in the bass. The mass of sound grows purposefully, with the entry of the upper strings, and then the middle register. Then comes a section of glissandos, which can be played at any speed between two given pitches or with what amounts to improvization. A climax occurs, after which the sound tapers off. Then a number of pizzicato effects are explored. Fingertips are used to tap the instruments, and the strings are hit with the palms of the hands. A second

climax occurs. After another section in which bowed, sustained and sliding sounds are explored, a third climax is reached. After all this atonality, the work ends with a somewhat surprising C major chord.

The post-war period has been one of rapid change due to the constant quest for something new. Whether it be new sounds, the application of new technology, new notation, new formal parameters, entirely new ways of presenting music, or combining music with visual and other stimuli, aesthetic viewpoints and styles have been both numerous and varied. Extremism and intolerance from both the conservative and avant-garde have not been uncommon. An insatiable appetite for something new has affected composers of almost all music styles since World War II. The influence of music composition for film and television has made the era an interesting one, bringing together varying styles for dramatic purpose and proliferating new sounds and applications to a wide audience.

There is no doubt that the extremism beginning after the war and culminating gradually during the 1970s has given way in the 1980s to a re-evaluation and acceptance of all styles as containing valid material upon which to draw for a composition.

MODERN DANCE

Romantic ballet had become conventional and static by the late nineteenth century. In revolution to traditional ballet came the remarkable Isadora Duncan (1878–1927). By 1905 she had gained notoriety for her barefoot and deeply emotional dancing. She was considered controversial among balletomanes and reformers alike.

Although an American, Isadora Duncan achieved her fame in Europe. Her dances were emotional interpretations of moods suggested to her by music or by nature. Her costume was inspired by Greek tunics and draperies and she danced in bare feet, a strictly unconventional and significant fact, which continues to be a basic quality of the modern dance tradition she helped to form.

Isadora Duncan's contemporary Ruth St. Denis, and her husband, Ted Shawn, were to lay more substantial cornerstones for modern dance. St. Denis's dancing began as a strange combination of exotic, oriental interpretations, and Delsartian poses. (Delsarte is a nineteenth-century system originated by François Delsarte as a scientific examination of the manner in which emotions and ideas were transmitted through gestures and posture. His system came from overzealous disciples who formed his findings into a series of graceful gestures and poses, which supposedly had specific denotative value).

St. Denis's impact on dance was solidified by the formation with her husband of a company and a school to carry on her philosophies and choreography. The Denishawn school and company were headquartered in Los Angeles and took a totally eclectic approach to dance. Any and all traditions were included, from formal ballet to Oriental and American Indian dances.

First to leave Denishawn was Martha Graham, probably the most influential figure in modern dance. Although the term modern dance defies accurate definition and satisfies few, it remains the most appropriate label for the nonballetic tradition Martha Graham has come to symbolize. Graham found Denishawn unsatisfactory as an artistic base, but her point of view, essentially, maintained that artistic individualism is fundamental. "There are no general rules. Each work of art creates its own code." Even modern dance has come to include its own conventions, however, principally because it tried so hard to be different from formal ballet. Ballet movements were largely rounded and symmetrical. Therefore, modern dancers emphasized angularity and asymmetry. Ballet stressed leaps and based its line on toework, while modern dance hugged the floor and dancers went barefoot. As a result, the early works of Graham and others tended to be rather fierce and earthy, as opposed to graceful. But beneath it all was the desire to express emotion first and foremost. The execution of conventional positions and movements, on which ballet is based, was totally disregarded. Martha Graham described her choreography as "a graph of the heart."

After the Depression, when social criticism formed a large part of artistic expression, Graham pursued topical themes (unusual for her) concerning the shaping of America, including her renowned work to the music of Aaron Copland, *Appalachian Spring* (1944). *Appalachian Spring* dealt with the effects of Puritanism and depicted the overcoming of its fire and brimstone by love and common sense.

Martha Graham's troupe produced a radical and controversial choreographer who broke with many of the traditions of modern dance (as flexible as those traditions have been). He incorporated chance or aleatory elements into his choreography and has often been associated with the composer John Cage. Merce Cunningham uses everyday activity as well as dance movements in his works. His concern is to have the audience see the dance in a new light, and, whatever the reaction may be, his choreography is radically different from anyone else's. His works show elegance and coolness, as well as a severely abstract quality. Works such as *Summerspace* and *Winterbranch* illustrate Cunningham's use of chance, or indeterminacy. He thoroughly prepares numerous options and orders for sets, which then (sometimes by flipping a coin) can be varied and intermixed in different order from performance to performance. The same piece may appear different from one night to the next. Cunningham also treats stage space as an integral part of the performance and allows focus to be spread across various areas of the stage, unlike classical ballet which tends to isolate its focus on center stage or downstage center alone. So Cunningham allows the audience member to choose where to focus, as opposed to forcing that focus. Finally, he tends to allow each element of the dance to go its own way. As a result, the direct, beat-for-beat relationship that audiences have come to expect between music and footfalls in ballet and much modern dance simply does not exist.

Since 1954, another graduate of Martha Graham's troupe (and also of Merce Cunningham's) has provided strong direction in modern dance. Paul Taylor's work has a vibrant, energetic, and abstract quality that often suggests primordial actions. Taylor, like Cunningham, often uses strange combinations of music and movement in highly ebullient and unrestrained dances such as *Book of Beasts*. Interestingly, Taylor's music often turns to traditional composers, such as Beethoven, and to specialized works like string quartets. The combination of such a basically esoteric musical form with his wild movements creates unique and challenging works for the viewer.

In a tradition which encourages individual exploration and independence, there have been many accomplished dancer/choreographers. Alwin Nikolais was among these. His works (he designs the scenery, costumes, and lights and composes the music, as well as the choreography) tend to be mixed-media extravaganzas, which celebrate the electronic age. Often the display is so dazzling that the audience loses the dancers in the lighting effects and scenic environment. Another figure of importance is Alvin Ailey, a versatile dancer whose company is known for its unusual repertoire and energetically free movements. Twyla Tharp and Yvonne Ranier have both experimented with space and movement. James Waring has incorporated Bach and 1920s pop songs, florid pantomimes and abstractions, as well as romantic point work.

FOOTNOTES

CHAPTER FOUR

1 August Wilson, *Fences*, in Lee A. Jacobus, *The Bedford Introduction to Drama* (New York: St. Martin's Press, 1989), p. 1055.
2 Pierre Corneille, *Le Cid*, trans. and ed. by John C. Lapp (New York: Appleton Century Crofts, 1955), pp. 36–37.

CHAPTER SIX

1 John Martin, *The Dance*, New York: Tudor Publishing Company, 1946, p. 26.

CHAPTER EIGHT

1 K. L. Knickerbocker and W. Willard Reninger, *Interpreting Literature*, New York: Holt, Rinehart and Winston, 1969, p. 218.
2 William Faulkner, "A Rose for Emily," in *American Poetry and Prose*, ed. Norman Foerster, New York: Houghton Mifflin Co., 1970, pp. 1562–67. Copyright © 1930 and renewed 1958 by William Faulkner. Reprinted from *Collected Stories of William Faulkner*, by permission of Random House Inc., and Curtis Brown Ltd.
3 Chaucer, *The Canterbury Tales*, translated by J. Nicolson, New York: The Crown Publishing Group, 1934, pp. 120–23. Used by permission of the publisher.
4 Robert Frost, "Stopping by Woods on a Snowy Evening," from *The Poetry of Robert Frost* edited by Edward Connery Lathem. Copyright 1923, © 1969 by Holt, Rinehart and Winston. Copyright 1951 by Robert Frost. Reprinted by permission of Henry Holt and Company, Inc.

5 W. H. Auden, "Musée des Beaux Arts." Copyright © 1940 and renewed 1968 by W. H. Auden. Reprinted from *W. H. Auden: Collected Poems*, edited by Edward Mendelson, by permission of Random House, Inc., and Faber and Faber Ltd.
6 John Wesley, *God Brought Me Safe*.
7 Oliver Goldsmith, "The Benefits of Luxury, in Making a People more Wise and Happy."

CHAPTER TEN

1 Revised Standard Version Bible.

CHAPTER ELEVEN

1 In each Greek tragic contest a playwright was required to present four plays in succession – three tragedies and a satyr play.
2 Peter D. Arnott, trans, in *An Introduction to the Greek Theatre*, Bloomington, IN: Indiana University Press, 1963, pp. 76–7.
3 The chorus was a distinctive feature of Greek drama, portraying the dual function (in the same play) of narrator and collective character responding to the actors.
4 Hugh Honour and John Fleming, *The Visual Arts: A History*, Englewood Cliffs, NJ: Prentice-Hall Inc., 1982, p. 96.
5 Virgil, *The Aeneid*, translated by Theodore C. Williams, New York: Houghton Mifflin Co., 1938, p.1.
6 John Garraty and Peter Gay, *A History of the World*, (2 vols), New York: Harper and Row, 1972, p. 209.
7 "Rings around the Pantheon," *Discover*, March 1985, p.12.

8 William MacDonald, *Early Christian and Byzantine Architecture*, New York: George Braziller, 1967, p. 32.

9 AOI: these three mysterious letters appear throughout the text. No one has ever adequately explained them, though every reader feels their effect.

10 *The Song of Roland*, translated by Frederick Goldin, New York: W. W. Norton and Co., Inc., 1978.

11 Boccaccio, *The Decameron*, translated by John Payne, New York: Stravon Publishers, 1957, pp. 15–24. Used by permission of the publisher.

12 H. W. Janson, *A Basic History of Art* (2nd edn.), Englewood Cliffs, NJ and New York: Prentice-Hall Inc., and Harry N. Abrams Inc., 1981, p. 452.

13 D. Redig de Campos (ed.), *Art Treasures of the Vatican*, Englewood Cliffs, NJ: Prentice-Hall Inc., 1974, p.7.

14 Lilian Hornstein et al, *World Literature* (2nd edn.), New York: Mentor, 1973, p. 155.

Chapter Twelve

1 Honour and Fleming, op. cit., p. 478.

2 Germain Bazin, *The Baroque*, Greenwich, CN: New York Graphic Society, 1968, p. 30.

3 Frederick Hartt, *Art* (2 vols), Englewood Cliffs, NJ and New York: Prentice-Hall Inc., and Harry N. Abrams Inc., 1981, p. 283.

4 Jonathan Swift, "A Modest Proposal," in *The Norton Anthology of English Literature* (vol. 1, 3rd edn.), New York: W. W. Norton and Co., Inc., 1974, p. 2094.

5 Frederick Hartt, *Art*, op. cit., pp. 292–3.

6 Oliver Goldsmith, "The Deserted Village."

7 Samuel Johnson, "Idler Essays" in *A Johnson Reader*, E. L. McAdams, Jr. and George Milne, eds., New York: Random House Inc., 1964, p. 199.

8 Dominique-Rene de Lerma, *Reflections on Afro-American Music* (Kent, Ohio: Kent State University Press, 1973), p. 162.

9 William Allen, Charles Ware, and Lucy Garrison, *Slave Songs of the United States* (New York: A. Simpson, 1867), p. 50; in George R. Keck and Sherrill V. Martin, *Feel the Spirit* (New York: Greenwood Press, 1988) p. 3.

10 Keck and Martin, pp. 4–5.

11 Keck and Martin, p. 12.

12 Keck and Martin, p. 10.

13 Bernard Katz, *The Social Implications of Early Negro Music in the United States* (New York: Arno Press and The New York Times, 1969), p. 26.

14 Katz, p. 14.

15 Henry Edward Krehbiel, *Afro-American Folksongs* (New York: G. Schirmer, n.d. [c. 1914]), p. 26.

16 Frederick J. Dockstader, *Indian Art of the Americas*, New York: Museum of the American Indian Heye Foundation, 1973; p. 14.

17 Ibid.

18 Susette la Flesche, "Nedawi." Copyright © 1989 The American Board of Regents. Reprinted from *The Singing Spirit*, edited by Bernd C. Peyer.

19 William Wordsworth, "Tintern Abbey," in *The Poetical Works of William Wordsworth*, New York: Houghton Mifflin Co., 1982, pp. 91–3.

20 Helen Gardner, *Art through the Ages*, New York: Harcourt, Brace, Jovanovich, 1980, p. 760.

Chapter Thirteen

1 Zitkala-Sa (Gertrude Bonnin), "The Soft-Hearted Sioux." Copyright © 1989 The Arizona Board of Regents. Reprinted from *The Singing Spirit*, edited by Bernd C. Peyer.

2 Paula Gunn Allen, "Recuerdo." Reprinted from Joseph Bruchac, *Survival This Way* (Tucson, AZ: University of Arizona Press, 1987), p. 3.

3 "Harlem Renaissance, Art of Black America," Exhibition book for the traveling exhibition under the auspices of the American Federation of Arts, 1989.

4 Ibid.

5 Ibid.

6 Ibid.

7 Langston Hughes, "Theme for English B," in *Selected Poems*. Reprinted by permission of David Higham Associates Ltd. Copyright © 1951 by Langston Hughes. Copyright renewed 1979 by George Houstan Bass. "Harlem" Copyright © 1951 by Langston Hughes. Reprinted from *The Panther and the Lash*, by permission of Alfred A. Knopf, Inc.

8 H. W. Janson, *A Basic History of Art*, op. cit., p. 682.

9 W. H. Auden, "Musée des Beaux Arts." Copyright © 1940 and renewed 1968 by W. H. Auden. Reprinted from *W. H. Auden: Collected Poems*, edited by Edward Mendelson, by permission of Random House, Inc. "In War Time," "Two's Company," "The Composer," "Voltaire at Ferney," and "Journey to Iceland" from *The English Auden* edited by Edward Mendelson. Copyright © 1977 by Edward Mendelson, William Meredith and Monroe K. Spears, as Executors of the estate of W. H. Auden. Reprinted by permission of Random House, Inc.

GLOSSARY

ABA. In music, a three-part structure that consists of an opening section, a second section, and a return to the first section.

a cappella. Choral music without instrumental accompaniment.

abacus. The uppermost members of the capital of an architectural column; the slab on which the architrave rests.

absolute music. Music that is free from any reference to nonmusical ideas, such as a text or program.

abstract. Nonrepresentational; the essence of a thing rather than its actual appearance.

abstraction. A thing apart that is removed from real life.

accelerando. In music, a gradual increase in tempo.

accent. In music, a stress that occurs at regular intervals of time. In the visual arts, any device used to highlight or draw attention to a particular area.

adagio. A musical term meaning slow and graceful.

additive. In sculpture, those works that are built. In color, the term refers to the mixing of hues of light.

aerial perspective. The indication of distance in painting through use of light and atmosphere.

aesthetic. Having to do with the pleasurable and beautiful as opposed to the useful.

aesthetics. A branch of philosophy dealing with the nature of beauty and art and their relation to experience.

affective. Relating to feelings or emotions, as opposed to facts.

aleatory. Chance or accidental.

allegretto. A musical term denoting a lively tempo, but one slower than allegro.

allegory. Expression by means of symbols to make a more effective generalization or moral commentary about human experience than could be achieved by direct or literal means.

allegro. A musical term meaning brisk.

alliteration. A sound structure in which an initial sound is repeated for effect.

altarpiece. A painted or sculptured panel placed above and behind an altar to inspire religious devotion.

alto. In music, the lowest female voice.

ambulatory. A covered passage for walking, found around the apse or choir of a church.

amphora. A two-handled vessel for storing provisions with an opening large enough to admit a ladle and usually fitted with a cover.

andante. A musical term meaning a medium leisurely, walking tempo.

andantino. A musical term meaning a tempo a little faster than andante.

appoggiatura. In music, an ornamental note or series of notes above and below a tone of a chord.

apse. A large niche or niche-like space projecting from and expanding the interior space of an architectural form such as a basilica.

aquatint. An intaglio printmaking process in which the plate is treated with a resin substance to create textured tonal areas.

arabesque. A classical ballet pose in which the body is supported on one leg, and the other leg is extended behind with the knee straight.

arcade. A series of arches placed side by side.

arch. In architecture, a structural system in which space is spanned by a curved member supported by two legs.

architrave. In post-and-lintel architecture, the lintel or lowest part of the entablature, resting directly on the capitals of the columns.

aria. An elaborate solo song found primarily in operas, oratorios, and cantatas.

art song. A vocal musical composition in which the text is the principal focus.

articulation. The connection of the parts of an artwork.

assemblé. In ballet, a leap with one foot brushing the floor at the moment of the leap and both feet coming together in fifth position at the finish.

assonance. A sound structure employing a similarity among vowels but not consonants.

atonality. The avoidance or tendency to avoid tonal centers in musical compositions.

avant-garde. A term used to designate innovators, "the advanced guard," whose experiments in art challenge established values.

balance. In composition, the equilibrium of opposing or interacting forces.

balletomane. A term used by ballet enthusiasts to refer to themselves. A combination of ballet and mania.

balloon construction. Construction of wood using a skeletal framework. See *skeleton frame*.

Baroque. A seventeenth- and eighteenth-century style of art, architecture, and music that is highly ornamental.

barre. A wooden railing used by dancers to maintain balance while practicing.

barrel vault (tunnel vault). A series of arches placed back to back to enclose space.

bas-relief. See *relief*.

basilica. In Roman times a term referring to building function, usually a law court, later used by Christians to refer to church buildings and a specific form.

battement jeté. A ballet movement using a small brush kick with the toe sliding on the floor until the foot is fully extended about two inches off the floor.

bearing-wall. Construction in which the wall supports itself, the roof, and floors. See *monolithic construction*.

beats. In music, the equal parts into which a measure is divided.

binary form. In music form consisting of two sections.

biography. A written account of a person's life.

biomorphic. Representing life forms as opposed to geometric forms.

bridge. A musical passage of subordinate importance played between two major themes.

buttress. A support, usually an exterior projection of masonry or wood, for a wall, arch, or vault.

cadence. In music, the specific harmonic arrangement that indicates the closing of a phrase.

cantilever. An architectural structural system in which an overhanging beam is supported only at one end.

capital. The transition between the top of a column and the lintel.

cast. See *sculpture*.

catharsis. The cleansing or purification of the emotions through the experience of art, the result of which is spiritual release and renewal.

cella. The principal enclosed room of a temple; the entire body of a temple as opposed to its external parts.

chaîné. A series of spinning turns in ballet utilizing a half turn of the body on each step.

changement de pied. In ballet, a small jump in which the positions of the feet are reversed.

character Oxfords. Shoes worn by dancers which look like ordinary street shoes but are actually specially constructed for dance.

chiaroscuro. Light and shade. In painting, the use of highlight and shadow to give the appearance of three-dimensionality. In theatre, the use of light to enhance plasticity of human and scenic form.

chord. Three or more musical tones played at the same time.

choreography. The composition of a dance work; the arrangement of patterns of movement in dance.

chromatic scale. A musical scale consisting of half steps.

cinematic motif. In film, a visual image that is repeated either in identical form or in variation.

cinéma verité. Candid camera; a televisionlike technique of recording life and people as they are. The hand-held camera, natural sound, and minimal editing are characteristic.

Classic. Specifically referring to Greek art of the fifth century BC.

Classical. Adhering to traditional standards. May refer to Greek and Roman art in which simplicity, clarity of structure and appeal to the intellect are fundamental.

coda. A passage added to the end of a musical composition to produce a satisfactory close.

cognitive. Facts and objectivity as opposed to emotions and subjectivity. See *affective.*

collage. An artwork constructed by pasting together various materials, such as newsprint, to create textures or by combining two and three-dimensional media.

collography. A printmaking process

utilizing assorted objects glued to a board or plate.

colonnade. A row of columns usually spanned or connected by lintels.

column. A cylindrical post or support which often has three distinct parts: base, shaft and capital.

complementary colors. Colors that lie opposite each other on a color wheel.

composition. The arrangement of line, form, mass, color, and so forth in a work of art.

compression. In architecture, stress that results from two forces moving toward each other.

conjunct melody. In music, melody comprising notes close together in the scale.

consonance. The feeling of a comfortable relationship between elements of a composition. Consonance may be both physical and cultural in its ramifications.

contrapposto (counterpoise). In sculpture, the arrangement of body parts so that the weight-bearing leg is apart from the free leg, thereby shifting the hip/shoulder axis.

conventions. The customs or accepted underlying principles of an art.

Corinthian. A specific order of Greek columns employing an elaborate leaf motif in the capital.

cornice. A crowning, projecting architectural feature.

counterpoint. In music, two or more independent melodies played in opposition to each other at the same time.

crescendo. An increase in loudness.

crosscutting. In film, alternation between two independent actions that are related thematically or by plot to give the impression of simultaneous occurrence.

cruciform. Arranged or shaped like a cross.

curvilinear. Formed or characterized by curved line.

cutting. The trimming and joining that occurs during the process of editing film.

cutting within the frame. Changing the viewpoint of the camera within a shot by moving from a long or medium shot to a close-up, without cutting the film.

decrescendo. A decrease in loudness.

demi-hauteur. A ballet pose with the leg positioned at a 45-degree angle to the ground.

demi-plié. In ballet, a halfbend of the knees in any of the five positions.

dénouement. The section of a play's structure in which events are brought to a conclusion.

design. A comprehensive scheme, plan or conception.

detachment. Intellectual as opposed to emotional involvement. The opposite of *empathy.*

diatonic minor. The standard musical minor scale achieved by lowering, by one half step, the third and sixth of the diatonic or standard major scale.

disjunct melody. In music, melody characterized by skips or jumps in the scale. The opposite of *conjunct melody.*

dissonance. The occurrences of inharmonious elements in music or the other arts. The opposite of *consonance.*

divertissement. A dance, or a portion thereof, intended as a diversion from the idea content of the work.

divisionism. The juxtaposition of tiny dots of unmixed paints, giving an overall effect of color when mixed optically by the viewer's brain.

documentary. In photography or film, the recording of actual events and relationships using real-life subjects as opposed to professional actors.

dome. An architectural form based on the principles of the arch in which space is defined by a hemisphere used as a ceiling.

Doric. A Greek order of column having no base and only a simple slab as a capital.

drypoint. An intaglio process in which the metal plate is scratched with a sharp needlelike tool.

dynamics. The various levels of loudness and softness of sounds: the increase and decrease of intensities.

eclecticism. In design, a combination of examples of several differing styles in a single composition.

editing. The composition of a film from various shots and sound tracks.

elevation. In dance, the height to which a dancer leaps.

empathy. Emotional and/or physical

involvement in events to which one is a witness but not a participant.

empirical. Based on experiments, observation, and practical experience, without regard to theory.

engaged column. A column, often decorative, which is part of and projects from a wall surface.

engraving. An intaglio process in which sharp, definitive lines are cut into a metal plate.

en pointe. See *on point.*

entablature. The upper portion of a Classical architectural order above the column capital.

entrechat. In ballet, a jump beginning from fifth position in which the dancer reverses the legs front and back one or more times before landing in fifth position. Similar to the *changement de pied.*

ephemeral. Transitory, not lasting.

epic. A long narrative poem in heightened style about the deeds and adventures of a hero.

esprit d'escalier. French, meaning "spirit of the stairs." Remarks, thought of after the fact, that could have been *bon mots* had they been thought of at the right moment; witty remarks.

essay. A short literary composition on a single subject, usually presenting the personal views of the author. Essays can be formal or informal.

etching. An intaglio process: lines are cut in the metal plate by an acid bath.

façade. The front of a building or the sides if they are emphasized architecturally.

farce. A theatrical genre characterized by broad, slapstick humor and implausible plots.

fenestration. Exterior openings, such as windows and archways, in an architectural façade.

ferroconcrete. Concrete reinforced with rods or webs of steel.

fiction. A literary work created from the author's imagination rather than from fact.

fluting. Vertical ridges in a column.

flying buttress. A semidetached *buttress.*

focal point (focal area). A major or minor area of visual attraction in pictures, sculpture, dance, plays, films, landscape design, or buildings.

foreground. The area of a picture,

usually at the bottom, that appears to be closest to the respondent.

form. The shape, structure, configuration, or essence of something.

form cutting. In film, the framing in a successive shot of an object that has a shape similar to an image in the preceding shot.

forte. A musical term meaning loud.

found object. An object taken from life that is presented as an artwork.

fresco. A method of painting in which pigment is mixed with wet plaster and applied as part of the wall surface.

frieze. The central portion of the entablature: any horizontal decorative or sculptural band.

fugue. Originated from a Latin word meaning "flight." A conventional musical composition in which a theme is developed by *counterpoint.*

full-round. See *sculpture.*

genre. A category of artistic composition characterized by a particular style, form or content.

geometric. Based on man-made patterns such as triangles, rectangles, circles, ellipses, and so on. The opposite of *biomorphic.*

Gesamtkunstwerk. A complete totally integrated artwork: associated with the music dramas of Richard Wagner in nineteenth-century Germany.

gestalt. A whole. The total of all elements in an entity.

glyptic. Sculptural works emphasizing the qualities of the material from which they are created.

Gothic. A style of architecture based on a pointed-arch structure and characterized by simplicity, verticality, elegance, and lightness.

gouache. A watercolor medium in which gum is added to ground opaque colors mixed with water.

grande seconde. Ballet pose with the leg in second position in the air.

grand jeté. In ballet, a leap from one foot to the other, usually with a running start.

grand plié. In ballet, a full bend of the knees with the heels raised and the knees opened wide toward the toes. May be done in any of the five positions.

grave. In music, a tempo marking meaning slow.

Greek cross. A cross in which all arms are the same length.

groin vault. The ceiling formation created by the intersection of two tunnel or barrel vaults.

harmony. The relationship of like elements such as musical notes, colors, and repetitional patterns. See *consonance* and *dissonance.*

Hellenistic. Relating to the time from Alexander the Great to the first century BC.

heroic. Larger than life size.

hierarchy. Any system of persons or things that has higher and lower ranks.

homophony. A musical texture characterized by chordal development supporting one melody. See *monophony* and *polyphony.*

horizon line. A real or implied line across the picture plane which, like the horizon in nature, tends to fix the viewer's vantage point.

hue. The spectrum notation of color; a specific, pure color with a measurable wavelength. There are primary hues, secondary hues, and tertiary hues.

icon. A Greek word meaning "image." Used to identify paintings which represent the image of a holy person.

idée fixe. A recurring melodic motif.

identification. See *empathy.*

impasto. The painting technique of applying pigment so as to create a three-dimensional surface.

improvisation. Music etc. produced on the spur of the moment, spontaneously.

intaglio. The printmaking process in which ink is transferred from the grooves of a metal plate to paper by extreme pressure.

intensity. The degree of purity of a hue. In music, theatre, and dance, that quality of dynamics denoting the amount of force used to create a sound or movement.

interval. The difference in pitch between two tones.

intrinsic. Belonging to a thing by its nature.

Ionic. A Greek order of column that

employs a scroll-like capital with a circular base.

iris. In film and photography, the adjustable circular control of the aperture of a lens.

isolation shot. In film, the isolation of the subject of interest in the center of the frame.

jamb. The upright piece forming the side of a doorway or window frame.

jeté. In ballet, a small jump from one foot to the other, beginning and ending with one foot raised.

jump cut. In film, the instantaneous cut from one scene to another or from one shot to another; often used for shock effect.

key. A system of tones in music based on and named after a given tone—the tonic.

kouros. An archaic Greek statue of a standing, nude youth.

krater. A bowl for mixing wine and water, the usual Greek beverage.

kylix. A vase turned on a potter's wheel; used as a drinking cup.

Labanotation. A system of writing down dance movements.

largo. In music, a tempo notation meaning large, broad, very slow, and stately movement.

Latin cross. A cross in which the vertical arm is longer than the horizontal arm, through whose midpoint it passes.

legato. In music, a term indicating that passages are to be played with smoothness and without break between the tones.

leitmotif. A "leading motif" used in music to identify an individual, idea, object and so on. Associated with Richard Wagner.

lekythos. An oil flask with a long, narrow neck adapted for pouring oil slowly; used in funeral rites.

lento. A musical term indicating a slow tempo.

libretto. The words, or text, of an opera or musical.

linear perspective. The creation of the illusion of distance in a two-dimensional artwork through the convention of line and foreshortening.

That is, the illusion that parallel lines come together in the distance.

linear sculpture. Sculptural works emphasizing two-dimensional materials.

lintel. The horizontal member of a post-and-lintel structure in architecture.

lithography. A printmaking technique, based on the principle that oil and water do not mix, in which ink is applied to a piece of paper from a specially prepared stone.

low relief. See *relief.*

magnitude. The scope or universality of the theme in a play or film.

manipulation. A sculptural technique in which materials such as clay are shaped by skilled use of the hands.

masonry. In architecture, stone or brickwork.

mass. Actual or implied physical bulk, weight, and density. Also, the most solemn rite of the Catholic liturgy.

medium. The process employed by the artist. Also, the binding agent to hold pigments together.

melodrama. A theatrical genre characterized by stereotyped characters, implausible plots, and emphasis on spectacle.

melody. In music, a succession of single tones.

metaphor. A figure of speech by which new implications are given to words.

mime. In dance or theatre, actions that imitate human or animal movements.

mise en scène. The complete visual environment in the theatre, dance, and film, including setting, lighting, costumes, properties, and physical structure of the theatre.

mobile. A constructed structure whose components have been connected by joints to move by force of wind or motor.

mode. A particular form, style, or manner.

modeling. The shaping of three-dimensional forms. Also the suggestion of three-dimensionality in two-dimensional forms.

modern dance. A form of concert dancing relying on emotional use of the body, as opposed to formalized or conventional movement, and stressing

human emotion and the human condition.

modulation. A change of key or tonality in music.

monolithic construction. A variation of *bearing-wall* construction in which the wall material is not jointed or pieced together.

monophony. In music, a musical texture employing a single melody line without harmonic support.

montage. The process of making a single composition by combining parts of others. A rapid sequence of film shots bringing together associated ideas or images.

monumental. Works actually or appearing larger than life size.

Moog synthesizer. See *synthesizer.*

motif (motive). In music, a short, recurrent melodic or rhythmic pattern. In the other arts, a recurrent element.

musique concrète. A twentieth-century musical approach in which conventional sounds are altered electronically on tape to produce new sounds.

nave. The great central space in a church.

Neoclassicism. Various artistic styles which borrow the devices or objectives of Classical art.

nonobjective. Without reference to reality; may be differentiated from "abstract."

nonrepresentational. Without reference to reality; including *abstract* and *nonobjective.*

novel. A prose narrative of considerable length which has a plot that unfolds by the actions, speech, and thoughts of the characters.

objective camera. A camera position based on a third-person viewpoint.

objet d'art. A French term meaning "object of art."

octave. In music, the distance between a specific pitch vibration and its double; for example, concert A equals 440 vibrations per second, one octave above that pitch equals 880, and one octave below equals 220.

on point. In ballet, a specific technique utilizing special shoes in which the dancer dances on the points of the toes. Same as *en pointe*.

opera buffa. A comic opera.

opus. A single work of art.

overtones (overtone series). The sounds produced by the division of a vibrating body into equal parts. See *sympathetic vibration*.

palette. In the visual arts, the composite use of color, including range and tonality.

pantheon. A Greek word meaning all the gods of a people.

pas. In ballet, a combination of steps forming one dance.

pas de deux. A dance for two dancers.

pathos. The "suffering" aspect of drama usually associated with the evocation of pity.

pavane. A stately court dance in $\frac{2}{4}$ time; usually follows a galliard.

pediment. The typically triangular roof piece characteristic of Classical architecture.

pendentive. A triangular part of the vaulting which allows the stress of the round base of a dome to be transferred to a rectangular wall base.

perspective. The representation of distance and three-dimensionality on a two-dimensional surface. See also *aerial perspective and linear perspective*.

photojournalism. Photography of actual events that have sociological significance.

piano. A musical term meaning soft.

pirouette. In ballet, a full turn on the toe or ball of one foot.

plan. An architectural drawing that reveals in two dimensions the arrangement and distribution of interior spaces and walls, as well as door and window openings, of a building as seen from above.

plasticity. The capability of being molded or altered. In film, the ability to be cut and shaped. In painting, dance, and theatre, the accentuation of dimensionality of form through *chiaroscuro*.

platemark. The ridged or embossed effect created by the pressure used in transferring ink to paper from a metal plate in the intaglio process.

poetry. A literary work designed to convey a vivid and imaginative sense experience through the use of condensed language selected for its sound and suggestive power and meaning, and employing specific technical devices such as meter, rhyme, and metaphor. There are three major types of poetry: narrative, dramatic, and lyric.

polyphony. See *counterpoint*.

polyrhythm. The use of contrasting rhythms at the same time in music.

port de bras. The technique of moving the arms correctly in dance.

post-and-lintel. An architectural structure in which horizontal pieces (lintels) are held up by vertical columns (posts).

post-tensioned concrete. Concrete using metal rods and wires under stress or tension to cause structural forces to flow in predetermined directions.

precast concrete. Concrete cast in place using wooden forms around a steel framework.

presto. A musical term signifying a rapid tempo.

prestressed concrete. See *post-tensioned concrete*.

proportion. The relation, or ratio, of one part to another and of each part to the whole with regard to size, height, width, length, or depth.

proscenium. A Greek word meaning "before the skene." The plaster arch or "picture frame" stage of traditional theatres.

prototype. The model on which something is based.

pyramidal structure. In film, and dance, the rising of action to a peak, which then tapers to a conclusion.

quadrille. (1) an American square dance; (2) a European ballroom dance of the eighteenth and nineteenth centuries.

Realism. A style of painting, sculpture, and theatre based on the theory that the method of presentation should be true to life.

recitative. Sung dialogue, in opera, cantata, and oratorio.

rectilinear. In the visual arts, the formed use of straight lines and angles.

reinforced concrete. See *ferroconcrete*.

relevé. In ballet, the raising of the body to full height or the half height during the execution of a step or movement.

relief. See *sculpture*.

relief printing. The process in printmaking by which the ink is transferred to the paper from raised areas on a printing block.

representational. Objects which are recognizable from real life.

requiem. A mass for the dead.

rhyme. A sound structure coupling words that sound alike.

rhythm. The relationship, either of time or space, between recurring elements of a composition.

rib. A slender architectural support in a vault system projecting from the surface.

ribbed vault. A structure in which arches are connected by diagonal as well as horizontal members.

ritardando. In music, a decrease in tempo.

rondo. A form of musical composition employing a return to an initial theme after the presentation of each new theme.

ronds de jambe à terre. In ballet, a rapid semicircular movement of the foot in which the toe remains on the floor and the heel brushes the floor in first position as it completes the semicircle.

rubato. A style of musical performance in which liberty is taken by the performer with the rhythm of the piece.

saturation. In color, the purity of a hue in terms of whiteness; the whiter the hue, the less saturated it is.

scale. In music, a graduated series of ascending or descending musical tones. In architecture, the mass of the building in relation to the human body.

sculpture. A three-dimensional art object. Among the types are (1) *cast*: having been created from molten material utilizing a mold, (2) *relief*: attached to a larger background, (3) *full-round*: freestanding.

serial music. A twentieth-century musical style utilizing the tone row and serialization of rhythms, timbres, and dynamics.

serigraphy. A printmaking process in which ink is forced through a piece of stretched fabric, part of which has been blocked out—for example, silk-screening and stencilling.

shape. A two-dimensional area or plane with distinguishable boundaries.

short story. Short fictional works of prose focusing on unity of characterization, theme, and effect.

silhouette. A form as defined by its outline.

skeleton frame. Construction in which a skeletal framework supports the buildings. See *balloon construction* and *steel cage construction.*

skene. The stage building of the Ancient Greek theatre.

song cycle. A group of art songs combined around a similar text or theme.

sonority. In music, the characteristic of texture resulting from chordal spacing.

staccato. In music, the technique of playing so that individual notes are detached and separated from each other.

static. Devoid of movement or other dynamic qualities.

steel-cage construction. Construction using a metal framework. See *skeleton frame.*

stereotype. A standardized concept or image.

strophic form. Vocal music in which all stanzas of the text are sung to the same music.

style. The identifying characteristics of a work of art which identify it with an artist, a group of artists, an era, or a nation.

stylization. Reliance on conventions, distortions, or theatricality; the exaggeration of characteristics that are fundamentally verisimilar.

stylobate. The foundation immediately below a row of columns.

substitution. A sculptural technique utilizing materials transformed from a plastic, molten, or fluid into a solid state.

subtractive. In sculpture, referring to works that are carved. In color, referring to the mixing of pigments as opposed to the mixing of colored light.

symbol. A form, image, or subject standing for something else.

symbolism. The suggestion through imagery of something that is invisible or intangible.

symmetry. The balancing of elements in design by placing physically equal objects on either side of a center line.

sympathetic vibration. The physical phenomenon of one vibrating body being set in motion by a second vibrating body. See also *overtone.*

symphony. A large musical ensemble; a symphony orchestra. Also, a musical composition for orchestra usually consisting of three or four movements.

syncopation. In a musical composition, the displacement of accent from the normally accented beat to the offbeat.

synthesis. The combination of independent factors or entities into a compound that becomes a new, more complex whole.

synthesizer (Moog synthesizer). An electronic instrument that produces and combines musical sounds.

tempera. An opaque watercolor medium, referring to ground pigments and their color binders such as gum, glue, or egg.

tempo. The rate of speed at which a musical composition is performed. In theatre, film, or dance, the rate of speed of the overall performance.

terracotta. An earth-brown clay used in ceramics and sculpture.

tessitura. The general musical range of the voice in a particular composition.

texture. In visual art, the two-dimensional or three-dimensional quality of the surface of a work. In music, the melodic and harmonic characteristics of the composition.

theatricality. Exaggeration and artificiality; the opposite of *verisimilitude.*

theme. The general subject of an artwork, whether melodic or philosophical.

timbre. The characteristic of a sound that results from the particular source of the sound. The difference between the sound of a violin and the sound of the human voice is a difference in timbre, also called color.

toccata. A composition usually for organ or piano intended to display technique.

tonality. In music, the specific key in

which a composition is written. In the visual arts, the characteristics of value.

tondo. A circular painting.

tonic. In music, the root tone (*do*) of a key.

tragedy. A serious drama or other literary work in which conflict between a protagonist and a superior force (often fate) concludes in disaster for the protagonist.

tragicomedy. A drama combining the qualities of tragedy and comedy.

transept. The crossing arm of a cruciform church, in contrast to the nave.

triad. A chord consisting of three tones.

trompe-l'oeil. "Trick of the eye" or "fool the eye." A two-dimensional artwork so executed as to make the viewer believe that three-dimensional subject matter is being perceived.

tunnel vault. See *barrel vault.*

tutu. A many-layered, stiff short skirt worn by a ballerina.

twelve-tone technique. A twentieth-century atonal form of musical composition associated with Schoenberg.

tympanum. The open space above the door beam and within the arch of a medieval doorway.

value (value scale). In the visual arts, the range of tonalities from white to black.

vanishing point. In linear perspective, the point on the horizon toward which parallel lines appear to converge and at which they seem to vanish.

variation. Repetition of a theme with minor or major changes.

verisimilitude. The appearance of reality in any element of the arts.

vivace. A musical term denoting a vivacious or lively tempo.

virtuoso. Referring to the display of impressive technique or skill by an artist.

waltz. A dance in $\frac{3}{4}$ time

woodcut. A relief printing executed from a design cut in the plane of the grain.

wood engraving. A relief printing made from a design cut in the butt of the grain.

BIBLIOGRAPHY

Abcarian, Richard and Klotz, Marvin (eds.). *Literature, the Human Experience*. New York: St. Martin's Press, 1986.

Anderson, Donald M. *Elements of Design*. New York: Holt, Rinehart, and Winston, 1961.

Anderson, Jack. *Dance*. New York: Newsweek Books, 1974

Andreae, Bernard. *The Art of Rome*. New York: Harry N. Abrams, 1977.

Arnheim, Rudolph. *Art and Visual Perception: A Psychology of the Creative Eye*. Berkeley: University of California Press, 1957.

Arnheim, Rudolph. *Film as Art*. Berkeley: University of California Press, 1967.

Arnott, Peter D. *An Introduction to the Greek Theatre*. Bloomington, IN: Indiana University Press, 1963.

Artz, Frederick. *From the Renaissance to Romanticism*. Chicago: University of Chicago Press, 1962

Bacon, Edmund N. *Design of Cities*. New York: Viking Press, 1967.

Baker, Blanche M. *Theatre and Allied Arts*. New York: H. W. Wilson Company, 1952.

Bataille, Georges. *Lascaux*. Switzerland: Skira, n.d.

Bates, Kenneth F. *Basic Design: Principle and Practice*. New York: Funk and Wagnalls, 1975.

Bawden, Liz-Anne (ed.). *The Oxford Companion to Film*. New York: Oxford University Press, 1976.

Bazin, Germain. *The Baroque*. Greenwich, CN: New York Graphic Society, 1968.

Beam, P. C. *Language of Art*. New York: John Wiley and Sons, 1958.

Bentley, Eric (ed.). *The Classic Theatre* (four vols.). Garden City, NY: Doubleday Anchor Books, 1959.

Bloom, Eric. *Grove's Dictionary of Music and Musicians* (5th ed.). New York: St. Martin's Press, 1959.

Bloomer, Carolyn M. *Principles of Visual Perception*. New York: Van Nostrand Reinhold Company, 1976.

Bobker Lee R. *Elements of Film*. New York: Harcourt Brace Jovanovich, 1969.

Booth, Michael. *Victorian Spectacular Theatre 1850–1910*. Boston: Routledge and Kegan Paul, 1981.

Bordwell, David and Kristin Thompson. *Film Art: An Introduction*. Reading, Mass.: Addison-Wesley, 1979.

Borroff, Edith. *Music in Europe and the United States: A History*. Englewood Cliffs, NJ: Prentice-Hall, Inc., 1971.

Brandon, S. G. F. *Religion in Ancient History*. New York: Charles Scribner's Sons, 1969.

Brindle, Reginald Smith. *The New Music: The Avant-Garde Since 1945*. London: Oxford University Press, 1975.

Brockett, Oscar G. *History of the Theatre*. Boston: Allyn and Bacon, Inc., 1968.

Brockett, Oscar. *The Theatre* (2nd edn). New York: Holt, Rinehart and Winston, 1969.

Campos, D. Redig de (ed.). *Art Treasures of the Vatican*. Englewood Cliffs, NJ: Prentice-Hall, Inc., 1974.

Canaday, John. *What Is Art?* New York: Alfred A. Knopf, 1980.

Cheney, Sheldon. *The Theatre: Three Thousand Years of Drama, Acting and Stagecraft* (rev. edn). New York: Longmans, Green, 1952.

Chujoy, Anatole. *Dance Encyclopedia*. New York: Simon and Schuster, Inc., 1967.

Clarke, Mary and Crisp, Clement. *Ballet*. New York: Universe Books, 1973.

Clough, Shepard B. *et al. A History of the Western World*. Boston: D. C. Heath and Co., 1964.

Coleman, Ronald. *Sculpture: A Basic Handbook for Students*. Dubuque, IA: William C. Brown Company, 1980.

Collier, Graham. *Form, Space, and Vision*. Englewood Cliffs, NJ: Prentice Hall, 1972.

Cook, David A. *A History of Narrative Film*. New York: W. W. Norton and Company, 1981.

Cope, David H. *New Directions in Music*. Dubuque, IA: William C. Brown and Co., 1981.

Corrigan, Robert. "The Search for New Endings: The Theatre in Search of a Fix, Part III," *Theatre Journal*, vol. 36, no. 2, May 1984, pp. 153–63.

Coryell, Julie and Friedman, Laura. *Jazz-Rock Fusion*. New York: Delacorte Press, 1978.

Crocker, Richard. *A History of Musical Style*. New York: McGraw-Hill, 1966.

Davis, Phil. *Photography*. Dubuque, IA: William C. Brown Company, 1979.

Dean, Alexander and Lawrence Carra. *Fundamentals of Play Directing* (rev. edn). New York: Holt, Rinehart, and Winston, 1965.

De Lerma, Dominique-Rene. *Reflections on Afro-American Music*. Kent, OH: The Kent State University Press, 1973.

Diehl, Charles. *Byzantium*. New Brunswick, NJ: Rutgers University Press, 1957.

Dockstader, Frederick J. *Indian Art of the Americas*. New York: Museum of the American Indian; Heye Foundation, 1973.

Drinkwater, John. *The Outline of Literature*. London: Transatlantic Arts, 1967.

Engel, Carl. *The Music of the Most Ancient Nations*. Freeport, NY: Books for Libraries Press, 1970.

Ernst, David. *The Evolution of Electronic Music*. New York: Schirmer Books. 1977.

Esslin, Martin (ed.). *The Encyclopedia of World Theatre*. New York: Charles Scribner's Sons, 1977.

Faulkner, Ray and Ziegfeld, Edwin. *Art Today* (5th edn). New York: Holt, Rinehart, and Winston, 1969.

Fleming, William. *Arts and Ideas*. New York; Holt, Rinehart, and Winston, 1980.

Frankfort, Henri. *Kingship and the Gods*. Chicago: University of Chicago Press, 1948.

Freedley, George and Reeves, John. *A History of the Theatre* (3rd edn). New York: Crown Publishers, 1968.

Fuller, B. A. G. *A History of Philosophy*. New York: Henry Holt and Company, 1945.

Fulton, Albert R. *Motion Pictures*. Norman, OK: University of Oklahoma Press, 1960.

Gardner, Helen. *Art Through the Ages*. New York: Harcourt, Brace, Jovanovich, 1980.

Garraty, John and Gay, Peter. *A History of the World* (2 vols.). New York: Harper and Row, 1972.

Gassner, John (ed.). *A Treasury of the Theatre*. New York: Holt, Rinehart, and Winston, 1967.

Gessner, Robert. *The Moving Image: A Guide to Cinematic Literacy*. New York: E. P. Dutton, 1970.

Giannetti, Louis. *Understanding Movies* (2nd edn). Englewood Cliffs, NJ: Prentice-Hall, Inc., 1976.

Gilbert, Cecil. *International Folk Dance at a Glance*. Minneapolis, Minn.: Burgess Publishing Company, 1969.

Gilbert, Creighton. *History of Renaissance Art Throughout Europe: Painting, Sculpture, Architecture*. New York: Harry N. Abrams, Inc., 1973.

Glasstone, Victor. *Victorian and Edwardian Theatres*. Cambridge, MA: Harvard University Press, 1975.

Goethe, Johann Wolfgang von. *Faust: Part I*, trans. Philip Wayne, Baltimore: Penguin Books, 1962.

Grabar, André, *The Art of the Byzantine Empire*. New York: Crown Publishers, Inc., 1966.

Graham, Peter (ed.). *Dictionary of the Cinema*. London: Tantivy Press, 1964.

Graziosi, Paolo. *Paleolithic Art*. New York: McGraw-Hill, 1960.

Griffiths, Paul. *A Concise History of Avante-Garde Music*. New York: Oxford University Press, 1978.

Grimm, Harold. *The Reformation Era*. New York: The MacMillan Co., 1954.

Groenewegen-Frankfort and Ashmole, Bernard. *Art of the Ancient World*. Englewood Cliffs, NJ and New York:

Prentice-Hall, Inc. and Harry N. Abrams, Inc. n.d.

Gropius, Walter (ed). *The Theatre of the Bauhaus*. Middletown, CN: Wesleyan University Press, 1961.

Gropius, Walter. *The New Architecture and the Bauhaus*, Cambridge, MA: M.I.T. Press, 1965.

Grout, Donald Jay. *A History of Western Music* (rev. edn). New York: W. W. Norton and Co., Inc., 1973.

Halliwell, Leslie. *The Filmgoer's Companion*. New York: Avon Books, 1978.

Hamilton, Edith. *Three Greek Plays*. New York: W. W. Norton and Co., 1965.

Hamilton, George Heard. *Nineteenth and Twentieth Century Art: Painting, Sculpture, Architecture*. New York: Harry N. Abrams, Inc. 1970

Hartt, Frederick. *Art* (2 vols.). Englewood Cliffs, NJ and New York: Prentice-Hall, Inc. and Harry N. Abrams, Inc., 1979.

Hartt, Frederick. *Italian Renaissance Art* (3rd edn). Englewood Cliffs. NJ and New York: Prentice-Hall, Inc. and Harry N. Abrams, Inc., 1987.

Hatlen, Theodore. *Orientation to the Theatre* (3rd edn). Englewood Cliffs, NJ: Prentice Hall, 1981.

Hawkes, Jacquetta, and Wooley, Sir Leonard. *History of Mankind: Prehistory and the Beginnings of Civilization*. New York: Harper and Row, 1963.

Heffner, Hubert. *The Nature of Drama*. Boston: Houghton Mifflin Company, 1959.

Held, Julius and Posner, D. *17th and 18th Century Art*. New York: Harry N. Abrams, n.d.

Helm, Ernest. *Music at the Court of Frederick the Great*. Norman, OK: University of Oklahoma Press, 1960.

Henig, Martin (ed.). *A Handbook of Roman Art*. Ithaca, NY: Cornell University Press, 1983.

Hewett, Bernard. *Theatre U.S.A.* New York: McGraw-Hill Book Company, 1959.

Heyer, Paul. *Architects on Architecture: New Directions in America*. New York: Walker and Company, 1966.

Hickok, Robert. *Music Appreciation*. New York: Appleton-Century-Crofts, 1971.

Hitchcock, Henry-Russell. *Architecture: Nineteenth and Twentieth Centuries*. Baltimore: Penguin Books, 1971.

Hofstadter, Albert and Kuhns, Richard. *Philosophies of Art and Beauty*. Chicago: University of Chicago Press, 1976.

Honour, Hugh and Fleming, John. *The Visual Arts: A History* (2nd edn) Englewood Cliffs, NJ: Prentice-Hall, Inc., 1986.

Hoppin, Richard. *Medieval Music*. New York: W. W. Norton and Co., Inc., 1978.

Hornstein, Lillian, Percy, G. D., and Brown, Sterling A. *World Literature* (2nd edn). New York: Mentor, 1973.

Hubatsch, Walther. *Frederick the Great of Prussia*. London: Thames and Hudson, 1975.

Hubert, J., Porcher, J., and Volbach, W. F. *The Carolingian Renaissance*. New York: George Braziller, 1970.

Jacobs, Lewis. *An Introduction to the Art of the Movies*. New York: Noonday Press, 1967.

Janson, H. W. *A Basic History of Art* (2nd edn). Englewood Cliffs, NJ and New York: Prentice-Hall, Inc. and Harry N. Abrams, Inc., 1981.

Jones, LeRoi. *Black Music*. New York: William Morrow and Company, 1967.

Jung, Carl G. *Man and His Symbols*. New York: Doubleday and Co., Inc., 1964.

Karsavina, Tamara. *Theatre Street*. New York: E. P. Dutton, 1961.

Kassler, Elizabeth B. *Modern Gardens and the Landscape*. New York: Museum of Modern Art, 1964.

Katz, Bernard. *The Social Implications of Early Negro Music in the United States*. New York: Arno Press and *The New York Times*, 1969.

Keck, George R. and Sherrill Martin. *Feel the Spirit*. Westport, CN: Greenwood Press, 1988.

Kepes, Gyorgy. *Language of Vision*. Chicago: Paul Theobald and Company, 1951.

Kernodle, George R. *Invitation to the Theatre*. New York: Harcourt Brace Jovanovich, 1967.

Keutner, Hubert. *Sculpture: Renaissance to Rococo*. Greenwich, CT: New York Graphic Society, 1969.

Kirby, F. E. *A Short History of Keyboard Music*. New York: Macmillan Company, 1966.

Kjellberg, Ernst and Saflund, Gosta. *Greek and Roman Art*. New York: Thomas Y. Crowell Co., 1968.

Knickerbocker, K. L. and Reninger, H. Willard. *Interpreting Literature*. New York: Holt, Rinehart, and Winston, 1969.

Knight, Arthur. *The Liveliest Art: A Panoramic History of the Movies* (rev. edn). New York: MacMillan, Inc., 1978.

Knobler, Nathan. *The Visual Dialogue*. New York: Holt, Rinehart, and Winston, 1967.

Kratzenstein, Marilou. *Survey of Organ Literature and Editions*. Ames, Iowa: Iowa State University Press, 1980.

Kraus, Richard. *History of the Dance*. Englewood Cliffs, NJ: Prentice-Hall, Inc., 1969.

Lange, Kurt and Hirmer, Max. *Egypt*. London: Phaidon, 1968.

Lawler, Lillian. *The Dance in Ancient Greece*. Middletown, CT: Wesleyan University Press, 1964.

Lee, Sherman. *A History of Far Eastern Art*. (4th edn). Englewood Cliffs, NJ, and New York: Prentice-Hall, Inc. and Harry N. Abrams, Inc., 1982.

Leish, Kenneth W. *Cinema*. New York: Newsweek Books, 1974.

Lippard, Lucy R. *Pop Art*. New York: Oxford University Press, 1966.

Lloyd, Seton. *The Archaeology of Mesopotomia*. London: Thames and Hudson, 1978.

Lommel, Andreas. *Prehistoric and Primitive Man*. New York: McGraw-Hill, 1966.

Maas, Jeremy. *Victorian Painters*. New York: G. P. Putnam's Sons, 1969.

MacDonald, William. *Early Christian and Byzantine Architecture*. New York: George Braziller, 1967.

Machiavelli, Niccolo. *The Prince*, trans. George Bull. Baltimore: Penguin Books, 1963.

Machlis, Joseph. *The Enjoyment of Music* (3rd edn). New York: W. W. Norton and Company, 1955.

Mango, Cyril. *Byzantium*. New York: Charles Scribner's Sons, 1980.

Marshack, Alexander. *The Roots of Civilization*. New York: McGraw-Hill, 1972.

Martin, John. *The Dance*. New York: Tudor Publishing Company, 1946.

Martin, John. *The Modern Dance*. Brooklyn: Dance Horizons, 1965.

Mathers, E. Powys. *The Thousand Nights and One Night*. New York: Dingwall-Rock, Ltd., 1930.

McDermott, Dana Sue. "Creativity in the Theatre: Robert Edmond Jones and C. G. Jung." *Theatre Journal*, May 1984, pp. 212–30.

McDonagh, Don. *The Rise and Fall of Modern Dance*. New York: E. P. Dutton, Inc., 1971.

McGiffert, Arthur. *A History of Christian Thought*. New York: Charles Scribner's Sons, 1961.

McLeish, Kenneth. *The Theatre of Aristophanes*. New York: Taplinger Publishing Co., 1980.

McNeill, William H. *The Shape of European History*. New York: Oxford University Press, 1974.

Miller, Hugh. *Introduction to Music*. New York: Barnes and Noble, 1961.

Montet, Pierre. *Lives of the Pharoahs*. Cleveland: World Publishing Co., 1968.

Moore, Douglas. *Listening to Music*. New York: W. W. Norton and Company, 1963.

Moortgat, Anton. *The Art of Ancient Mesopotamia*. London: Phaidon, 1969.

Munro, Thomas. *The Arts and Their Interrelationships*. New York: Liberal Arts Press. 1949.

Murray, Margaret, *Egyptian Sculpture*. New York: Charles Scribner's Sons, 1930.

Muthesius, Stefan. *The High Victorian Movement in Architecture 1850–1870*. London: Routledge and Kegan Paul, 1972.

Myers, Bernard S. *Art and Civilization*. New York: McGraw-Hill Book Company, Inc., 1957.

Nadel, Constance and Nadel, Myron. *The Dance Experience*. New York: Praeger Publishers, 1970.

Newman, William S. *Understanding Music* (2nd edn). New York: Harper and Row, 1961.

Nicoll, Allardyce. *The Development of the Theatre* (5th edn). London: Harrap and Co., Ltd., 1966.

Nyman, Michael. *Experimental Music: Cage and Beyond*. New York: Schirmer Books, 1974.

Ocvirk, Otto, Bone, Robert O., Stinson, Robert E. and Wigg, Philip R. *Art Fundamentals* (4th edn). Dubuque, IA: William C. Brown Company, 1981.

Oppenheim, A. Leo. *Ancient Mesopotamia*. Chicago: University of Chicago Press, 1964.

Ostransky, Leroy. *Understanding Jazz*. Englewood Cliffs, NJ: Prentice-Hall, Inc., 1977.

Parker, Oren W. and Smith, Harvey K. *Scene Design and Stage Lighting* (2nd edn). New York: Holt, Rinehart, and Winston, 1968.

Perkins, V. F. *Film as Film: Understanding and Judging Movies*. New York: Penguin Books, 1972.

Pfeiffer, John E., *The Creative Explosion*. New York: Harper and Row, 1982.

Pignatti, Terisio. *The Age of Rococo*. London: Paul Hamlyn, 1969.

Politoske, Daniel T. *Music* (3rd edn). Englewood Cliffs, NJ: Prentice-Hall, 1984.

Powell, T. G. E. *Prehistoric Art*, New York: Frederick Praeger Publishers, 1966.

Preble, Duane. *We Create, Art Creates Us*. New York: Harper and Row, 1976.

Purves, Frederick (ed.). *The Focal Encyclopedia of Photography*. London: Ford Press, 1965.

Raphael, Max. *Prehistoric Cave Paintings*. Washington, DC: Pantheon, 1946.

Rasmussen, Steen Eiler. *Experiencing Architecture*. New York: John Wiley and Sons, 1959.

Read, Benedict. *Victorian Sculpture*. New Haven: Yale University Press, 1982.

Read, Herbert E. *Art and Society* (2nd edn). New York: Pantheon Books, Inc., 1950.

Renner, Paul. *Color, Order, and Harmony*. New York: Van Nostrand Reinhold Company, 1965.

Rice, David Talbot. *The Art of Byzantium*. New York: Harry N. Abrams, n.d.

Richter, Gisela. *Greek Art*. Greenwich, CN: Phaidon, 1960.

Roberts, J. M. *History of the World*. New York: Alfred A. Knopf, Inc., 1976.

Robertson, Martin. *A Shorter History of Greek Art*. Cambridge, MA: Cambridge University Press, 1981.

Robinson, David. *The History of World Cinema*. New York: Stein and Day Publishers, 1973.

Roters, Eberhard. *Painters of the Bauhaus*. New York: Praeger Publishers, 1965.

Rotha, Paul. *The Film Til Now*. London: Spring Books, 1967.

Rowell, George. *The Victorian Theatre* (2nd edn) Cambridge University Press, 1978.

Sachs, Curt. *World History of the Dance*. New York: W. W. Norton and Co., 1937.

Sachs, Curt. *The Rise of Music in the Ancient World*. New York: W. W. Norton Company, 1943.

Salzman, Eric. *Twentieth Century Music: An Introduction*. Englewood Cliffs, NJ: Prentice-Hall, Inc., 1967.

Sandars, N. K. *Prehistoric Art in Europe*. Baltimore: Penguin Books, 1968.

Saylor, Henry H. *Dictionary of Architecture*. New York: John Wiley and Sons, 1963.

Schevill, Ferdinand. *A History of Europe*. New York, Harcourt Brace and Co., Inc., 1938.

Schneider, Elisabeth *et al.* *The Range of Literature*. New York: American Book Company. 1960.

Schonberger, Arno and Soehner, Halldor. *The Rococo Age*. New York: McGraw-Hill, 1960.

Seiberling, Frank. *Looking into Art*. New York: Holt, Rinehart, and Winston, 1959.

Sherrard, Philip. *Byzantium*. New York: Time Inc., 1966.

Sitwell, Sacheverell, *Great Houses of Europe*. London: Spring Books, 1970.

Smith, Hermann. *The World's Earliest Music*, London: W. Reeve, n.d.

Smith, W. Stevenson. *The Art and Architecture of Ancient Egypt*. Baltimore: Penguin Books, 1958.

Sorell, Walter. *Dance in its Time*. Garden City, NY: Doubleday Anchor Press, 1981.

Sorell, Walter. *The Dance Through the Ages*. New York: Grosset and Dunlap, Inc., 1967.

Southern, Richard. *The Seven Ages of the Theatre*. New York: Hill and Wang, 1961.

Sperry, Roger. *Science and Moral Priority: Merging Mind, Brain, and Human Values*. New York: Columbia University Press, 1983.

Spitz, Lewis (ed.). *The Protestant Reformation*. Englewood Cliffs, NJ: Prentice-Hall, Inc., 1966.

Sporre, Dennis J. *The Arts*. Englewood Cliffs, NJ: Prentice-Hall, Inc., 1985.

Sporre, Dennis J. *Perceiving the Arts*. Englewood Cliffs, NJ: Prentice-Hall, Inc., 1981.

Sporre, Dennis and Burroughs, Robert C. *Scene Design in the Theatre*, Englewood Cliffs, NJ: Prentice-Hall Inc., 1989.

Stamp, Kenneth M. and Wright, Esmond (eds.). *Illustrated World History*. New York: McGraw-Hill Book Company, 1964.

Stearns, Marshall and Marshall, Jean. *Jazz Dance*. New York: The Macmillan Company, 1968.

Steinberg, Cobbett. *The Dance Anthology*. New York: Times Mirror, 1980.

Strayer, Joseph and Munro, Dana. *The Middle Ages*. Pacific Palisades: Goodyear Publishing Company, 1970.

Styan, J. L. *The Dramatic Experience*. Cambridge: Cambridge University Press, 1965.

Tierney, Brian and Painter, Sidney. *Western Europe in the Middle Ages*. New York: Alfred A. Knopf, 1974.

Tirro, Frank. *Jazz: A History*. New York: W. W. Norton and Co., Inc., 1977.

Trythall, Gilbert. *Principles and Practice of Electronic Music*. New York: Grosset and Dunlap, 1973.

Ucko, Peter J. and Rosenfeld, Andree. *Paleolithic Cave Art*. London: World University Library, 1967.

Ulrich, Homer. *Music: A Design for Listening*. (3rd edn). New York: Harcourt, Brace and World, Inc., 1970.

Van Der Kemp, Gerald, *Versailles*. New York: The Vendome Press, 1977.

Wheeler, Robert Eric Mortimer. *Roman Art and Architecture*. New York: Praeger Publishers Inc., 1964.

Wigman Mary. *The Language of Dance*. Walter Sorrell, trans. Middleton, CN: Wesleyan University Press, 1963.

Wittlich, Gary E. (ed.). *Aspects of Twentieth Century Music*. Englewood Cliffs, NJ: Prentice-Hall, Inc., 1975.

Zarnecki, George. *Art of the Medieval World*. Englewood Cliffs, NJ: Prentice-Hall Inc., 1975.

INDEX

Aalta (Douglas) 352, 13.11
Abraham's Hospitality & the Sacrifice of Isaac (mosaic) 232, 11.45
Abstract Expressionism 366-7
abstraction 361-5
Absurdism 366
Achilles Painter: lekythos 201, 11.1
acrylics painting 30
Adams, Ansel 37
Adding Machine (Rice) 356
Aeneid, The (Virgil) 221, 222-4
Aeschylus 203-4
African art 211, 309; Benin style 213-14, 11.19, 11.20; Djenne style 212-13, 11.18; Nok style 211, 11.15
African-American style 310; music of Black America 310
Agamemnon (Aeschylus) 203-4
Aida (Verdi) 327
Ailey, Alvin 284, 355
Akhenaton (Amenhotep IV) 196-7
Alberti, Leon Battista 265
Allen, Paula Gunn 343-4; *Recuerdo* 344
Amenhotep III 194
American Gothic (Wood) 365, 0.6, 1.34
American, Native, art of 241, 11.58, 11.59; culture 199, 10.27
Amiens Cathedral, France 149, 7.31
Amorous Flea, The (Devine and Montgomery) 4.14
Angelico, Fra 254
Antony and Cleopatra (Shakespeare) 272
Apollodorus of Damascus: Trajan's Column 70, 314, 2.20
Apollo playing the lyre 57, 2.1
Apoxymenos (Scraper) (Lysippos) 208, 11.9
Apuleius: *Golden Ass* 224
Aqueduct, Pont du Gard, Nîmes, France 7.18
arcade 132, 7.8
Archaic art 183, 185
architecture 129; arch, styles of 131-2, 134; building materials 138; climate 148-9; context of 145-7; line, repetition and balance 141-3; scale and proportion 144-5; space 147-8; structure 130
Aristophanes 204: *The Birds* 16; *Lysistrata* 16
Aristotle 92, 99: *Poetics* 89, 201
Arnolfini Marriage, The (Van Eyck) 254, 11.71
Art Nouveau 372, 13.27
Ascension Meditations (Coltrane) 354
Ascension of Mohammed 237, 11.52
Aspects of Negro Life (Douglas) 351
Assumption of the Virgin, The (Rubens) 284, 12.14

Auden, W.H. 362-5: "Musée Des Beaux Arts" 166, *Poems* 362-5
Augustus 220-1, 11.29
Autumn Rhythm (Pollock) 367, 13.20

Babbitt, Milton 381
Bacchae, The (Euripides) 4.16
Bach, J.S. 77, 287: *Fugue in G Minor* 287, 12.18; *Jesu Joy of Man's Desiring* 77, 3.6
Bakota ancestor figure 60, 2.5
Balanchine, George 116, 127
Bald Soprano (Ionesco) 366
ballet 116, 117-19, 121-2
Ballet mécanique (Léger) 108, 5.1
Baltimore: Basilica (Latrobe) 321, 12.50
Banjo Lesson, The (Tanner) 332, 12.61
Baraka, Imamu Amiri (LeRoi Jones) 355
Barber of Seville (Rossini) 327
Barbershop Mirror (McIntyre) 1.10
Baroque style 281-9; aristocratic Baroque 283-5; Baroque music 286-7; bourgeois Baroque 285-6; Counter-Reformation Baroque 282-3; Court Baroque 287, 289
Barry, Charles 329; Houses of Parliament, England 329, 12.57
Bartók, Béla 379-80
Batman (Williams) 356, 13.14
Beckett, Samuel 366; *Waiting for Godot* 366
Beckmann, Max 356, *Christ and Woman Taken in Adultery* 356, 13.13
Beethoven, Ludwig van 308-9: *Piano Sonata in C Minor* 12.40; *Symphony No. 9* 73; *Symphony No. 6* 308
Begay, Harrison 344-5; *Women Picking Corn* 344-5, 13.2
Belamy Mansion, Wilmington 321, 12.51
Benedict, St. 228
Benton, Thomas Hart; *Cradling Wheat* 1.8
Berg, Alban 380; *Lyric Suite* 380
Berio, Luciano 382; *Circles* 382
Bernini, Gianlorenzo 283; *David* 283, 12.13
Bernward of Hildesheim 243-4
Bibiena, Giuseppi Galli de; *Scene design for an opera* 3.12
Bible, The 188-90
Billings, William 379
Birds, The (Aristophanes) 16
Birth of a Nation, The (Griffith) 5.3
Bison 10.2
Bizet, Georges; *Carmen* 3.11
Black Wall (Nevelson) 371, 13.25
Blue Nude (Souvenir de Biskra) (Matisse) 359, 13.16
Boccaccio, Giovanni 259; *The Decameron* 259-63
Boccioni, Umberto; *Unique Forms of*

Continuity in Space 361, 13.17
Bofill, Ricardo 376-7; Palace of Abraxas (Marne-la-Vallée) 377
Bologna, Giovanni; *Mercury* 2.7
Bonheur, Rosa 323; *Plowing in the Nivernais* 323, 12.53
Bonnin, Gertrude (Zitkala-Sa) 341-3; *Soft-Hearted Sioux* 341-3
Botticelli, Sandro 254, 256; *Spring* 256, 11.72
Boucher, François 54; *Venus Consoling Love* 1.42
Brahms, Johannes 82, 327: *Ein Deutsches Requiem* 82; *Symphony No. 3 in F Major* 327, 12.55
Bramante, Donato 270-1, 11.82
Brancusi, Constantin 349; *Mlle. Pogany* 349, 13.9
Brighton Beach Memoirs (Simon) 88
Broadway Bound (Simon) 88
Brunelleschi, Filippo 263, 265; dome of Florence Cathedral 265, 11.76, 11.77
Buckingham Palace, London 143, 7.24
Budd, Harold 383
Buddha (Frankenthaler) 367, 13.20
Buddhism 214, 216, 217, 11.24, 11.25
Buddhist Monastery by Stream and Mountains (Chü-jan) 47, 1.27
Bunnell, Rufus H. 321; Belamy Mansion, Wilmington 321, 12.51
Burghers of Calais, The (Rodin) 2.3
Burn This (Lanford Wilson) 92
buttress 132, 7.6-7.7
Byzantine art 230-4; Hieratic style 234; ivories 235

Cabaret 89
Cabinet of Dr. Caligari (Wiene) 356
Cage, John 382, 384
Calder, Alexander 362; *Spring Blossoms* 2.17
Calling of St. Matthew, The (Caravaggio) 283, 12.12
Camus, Albert 366; *Cross-Purposes* 366
Canova, Antonio 320; *Pauline Borghese as Venus Victrix* 320, 12.49
Canterbury Tales, The (Chaucer) 164-5: "The Cook's Tale" 164-5
cantilevers 137, 7.16-7.17
Caravaggio 283; *The Calling of St. Matthew* 283, 12.12
Carmen (Bizet) 3.11
Carter, Elliott 382
Casa Battló, Barcelona (Gaudi) 372, 13.27
Cause Célèbre (Rattigan) 92
cave painting 13; 0.2
Ceiling Ornament (Hopfer) 1.7
ceramic bowl, (Lewis) 344, 13.1
ceremonial mask (Native American) 314, 12.47
Cézanne, Paul 337; *Mont Sainte-Victoire* 337, 12.66

Chabanon, Michel Paul de 307
Chaplin, Charlie 113
Chardin, Jean-Baptiste Simeon 302; *Menu de Gras* 302, 12.34
Charlemagne, statuette of 2.8
Chartres Cathedral, France 65, 145, 150, 7.26; Jamb statues 252-3, 2.12, 11.68-11.70
Chaucer, Geoffrey *The Canterbury Tales* 164-5
Cheops, Great Pyramid (Egypt) 191, 193, 10.15, 10.16
chiaroscuro 49, 50, 1.29
Ch'ien Hsuan: *Doves and Pear Blossoms* 274-5, 12.1
Chikamatsu 291
Child with Cat (Zorach) 2.16
China: Ancient 197-8; Han dynasty painting 216, 11.23; Ming dynasty 273-7; philosophies 214; Sung dynasty painting 218, 11.27; terracotta warriors 215, 11.21, 11.22; theatre 218-19
Chopin, Frederic 326-7
Christ and the Woman Taken in Adultery (Beckmann) 356, 13.13
Christo 15: *The Umbrellas* 0.4A, 0.4B; *Running Fence ...* 62, 2.9
Chu Ta; *Lotus* 1.3
Chü-jan; *Buddhist Monastery by Stream and Mountains* 47, 1.27
Chujoy, Anatole 116
Church of Nikolai Khamovnik, Moscow, Russia 174, 177, 9.5, 9.6
Citizen Kane (Welles) 365
Climatron (Fuller), St. Louis, 7.20
Clodion (Claude Michel) 295; *Satyr and Bacchante* 295; 12.29
Cnidian Aphrodite (Praxiteles) 207, 11.8
Colman, Ornette 383
color 39-40
Colosseum, The, Rome 225, 11.32, 11.33
Coltrane, John 354, 383: *A Love Supreme* 354; *Ascension Meditations* 354
columns, styles of Greek 7.3
Company (Sondheim) 4.15
Composition (Miró) 1.12
Composition in White, Black and Red (Mondrian) 53, 361, 1.40
Composition: dynamics 51-2; perspective 46-7; subject matter 47; elements 37-41; principles 41-4
Conceptual art 372
Concerning Architecture (Alberti) 265
Concorde airliner 144
concrete, in building 140
Confucianism 214, 218
Constantine The Great 221; head of 221, 11.30
Convergence (Pollock) 0.1
Copland, Aaron 381, 384; *Appalachian Spring* 381, 384
Corot, Jean-Baptiste-Camille 171-2: *A View Near Volterra* 171-2, 1.26, 9.1

Courbet, Gustave 330; *The Stone Breakers* 330, 12.59
Coussutius 210
covered jar (mark of Wan Li) 276, 12.4
Cradling Wheat (Benton) 1.8
Creation of Adam, The (Michelangelo) 268, 11.80
Creation, The (Haydn) 307
Crosby, Bing 113
Cross-Purposes (Camus) 366
Crystal Palace, London 329-30, 12.58
Cubism 358-9, 13.15
Cunningham, Merce 128, 384
Cuvilliés, François de: The Pagondenburg 296, 12.31

d'Orbay, François 289
da Vinci, Leonardo 265, 266, 268: *Last Supper*, 266, 268, 11.78
Dadaism 372
Dali, Salvador 365; *The Persistence of Memory* 365, 1.30
dance 116; color 128; dynamics 128; folk 117; idea content 125; lighting 127; line, form and repetition 123; mime and pantomime 125; *mise en scène* 126, 128; modern 117, 383-4; rhythm 125; sign language 128; ballet *see* ballet
Dance mask (carved) of Inuit tribe 312-13, 12.44
Dancing royal couple carving (African) 346, 13.3
Dark Abstraction (O'Keeffe) 361, 13.18
David (Bernini) 283, 12.13
David (Donatello) 258, 11.75
David (Michelangelo) 269, 11.81
David Harping (from Oscott Psalter) 248, 11.64
David, Jacques-Louis 305; *The Oath of the Horatii* 305, 12.35
Davis, Miles 354, 383
de Chirico, Giorgio; *Nostalgia of the Infinite* 51, 1.31
Death of a Salesman (Miller) 366
Debussy, Claude 82, 334, 336: *Prélude à l'après-midi d'un faune* 82, 336
Decameron, The (Boccaccio) 259- 63
Déjeuner sur l'herbe, Le (The Picnic) (Manet) 331, 12.60
Della Magnificenza ed Architettura dei Romani (Piranesi) 305
Delmonico Building (Sheeler) 1.9
Delsarte, François 383
Demoiselles d'Avignon, Les (Picasso) 359, 13.15
Dempster, Stewart 382
Department Store, Chicago (Carson, Pirie & Scott) 339, 12.68
Deserted Village, The (Goldsmith) 302-3
Diskobolus (Discus Thrower) (Myron) 202-3, 11.3

Disney, Walt 114
Doctor Faustus (Tragical History of the Life and Death of) (Marlowe) 272
Dolce Vita, La (Fellini) 113
Dome of the Rock, Jerusalem, 238-9, 11.53, 11.54
domes 134, 137, 7.12, 7.14, 7.15
Donatello: 258; *David* 258, 11.75; *St. George* 258
Doryphoros (Lance Bearer) (Polyklitus) 202, 11.2
Douglas, Aaron 351-2; *Aspects of Negro Life* 351; *Aalta* 352, 13.11
Doves and Pear Blossoms (Ch'ien Hsuan) 274-5, 12.1
drawing 32
Dubuffet, Jean: *Jardin d'Email* 371-2, 13.26
Duck, Donald 114
Duncan, Isadora 383
Dürer, Albrecht; *Lamentation* 1.6
Dying Gaul, The 209, 11.11

Egypt, Ancient 190: sculpture 70, 190, 2.19; painting 193
Eisenstein, Sergei 108
elephant helmet mask (African) 348, 13.6
Embarkation for Cythera (Watteau) 294, 12.27
Emperor Justinian and his court (mosaic) 232, 11.44
Enemy of the People, An (Ibsen) 17
Enlightenment, the 293-309; Architectural Neoclassicism 305-6; Genre and Social Comment 302-5; Landscape and Portraiture 300; Musical Classicism 307-9; Neoclassicism 305
entertainer's disguise (African) 348, 13.7
Environmental Art 371-2, 13.26
Ephesus theatre 205, 11.4
Epidaurus theatre (Polykleitus the Younger) 205, 11.5, 11.6
Essai sur l'architecture (Abbé Laugier) 306
Ethiopia Awakening (Fuller) 352
Eumenides, The (Aeschylus) 4.5
Euripides 204
Europe, Medieval 241: Gothic cathedral 248-51; Gothic sculpture 251; Gothic style 247-8; Romanesque style 242-7
Execution of the Citizens of Madrid (Goya) 1.43
Experimental architecture 373-8
Expressionism 356
Eyck, Jan van: *The Arnolfini Marriage* 254, 11.71

Falconet, Étienne-Maurice 295; *Madame de Pompadour...* 295, 12.28
'Falling Water', Bear Run, Pennsylvania (Wright) 146-7, 7.28

Family Tree (Jazz dance) 6.15
Faulkner, William; "A Rose for Emily" 160-3
Fauvism 359, 361, 13.16
Fences (August Wilson) 90, 355
film 105-6; absolute 106; camera viewpoint 108-9; conventions in 107; crosscutting 112; cutting within frame 109; direct address 112; dissolves 109; documentary 106; editing 107-8; frame 105-6; magnitude of 107; movement 109, 111; narrative 106; objectivity 109; shot, the 109; structural rhythm 113-14; tension build-up and release 112
Florence: Baptistery 258, 11.74; Cathedral (Brunelleschi) 265, 11.77
For Unto Us a Child is Born (Handel) 286-7, 12.16, 12.17
form and line 39
Fort Apache (Ford) 114
Foss, Lukas 381
Franck, César 379
Frankenthaler, Helen 367; *Buddha* 367, 13.21
fresco painting 32
Frost, Robert; "Stopping By Woods on a Snowy Evening" 165
fugue 81; *Fugue in G Minor* (Bach) 287, 12.18
Fuller, Meta Vaux Warrick 352; *Ethiopia Awakening* 352
Fuller, Richard Buckminster 141, 7.20
Futurism 361, 13.17

Gainsborough, Thomas 300; *The Market Cart* 300, 12.33
Garage Ponthieu, Paris (Perret) 373, 13.28
Gates of Paradise, The (Lorenzo) 258, 11.74
Gaudi, Antonio: Casa Batlló (Barcelona) 372, 13.27
Gauguin, Paul 337; *The Vision after the Sermon* 337, 12.67
Geodesic dome, Climatron, St. Louis, 141, 7.20
Géricault, Théodore 322-3; *The Raft of the Medusa* 322-3, 12.52
Gero Crucifix 69, 2.18
Ghiberti, Lorenzo: 258; *The Gates of Paradise* 258, 11.74
Ghost Sonata (Strindberg) 356
Giacometti, Alberto 362: *Man Pointing* 65, 2.14
Giambologna; *Samson Slaying a Philistine* 59, 2.4
Gillespie, Dizzy 354
Giotto; *The Lamentation* 1.37
Girl before a Mirror (Picasso) 42, 1.21, 9.4
Girl with a Red Hat, The (Vermeer) 1.29
Giselle (Adam/Coralli) 328

Gislebertus: *Last Judgement Tympanum* 243, 11.62
Glass Menagerie, The (Williams) 366, 4.12
Godfather The, Part I 112
Goethe, J.W. von 26
Goldsmith, Oliver 302; "The Benefits of Luxury ..." 167-8; *The Deserted Village* 302-3
Gordonne, Charles 355; *No Place to Be Somebody* 355
Gospel Book of Godescale 44, 1.24
Gospel Book of St. Médard of Soissons 44, 1.24
Gothic style 247-8; architecture 149-50; cathedral 248-51; sculpture 251
gouache painting 32
Goya, Francisco de 54, 56; *Execution of the Citizens of Madrid* 1.43
Gozzoli, Benozzo 254
Gracian, Balthasar 282
Graham, Martha 117, 384
Grande Odalisque (Ingres) 319, 12.48
Grapes of Wrath, The (Ford) 114, 365
Grateful Dead, The 14
Graves, Michael 377; Portland Public Office Building, Portland 377, 13.34
Great Wave off Kanazawa, The (Hokusai) 293, 12.25
Greece, Classical 200: architecture 205-7; Hellenistic style 208-10; late style 207-8; sculpture 201-202; style of 200-202; theatre 203
Greek cross 0.5
Green Coca-Cola Bottles (Warhol) 0.3
Guardian figure (Kota tribe) 309, 12.41
Guernica (Picasso) 172, 1.31, 9.2
Guggenheim Museum, New York (Sullivan/Wright) 153, 376, 7.36

Haba, Alois 382
Hagia Sophia, Istanbul 233-4, 11.46-11.49
Halicarnassus, east frieze 2.2
Hallelujah Chorus (Handel) 286-7
Hamlet (Shakespeare) 91, 103, 4.7
Hampton Court Palace, England 142-3, 146, 7.22, 7.23, 7.27
Han dynasty painting 216, 11.23
Handel, George Frederick 286: *For Unto Us a Child is Born* 286-7, 12.16, 12.17; *Hallelujah Chorus* 286-7; *Messiah* 286-7
Hansen, Duane 369
Harbaville Triptych, The 235, 11.50
Hard Edge 370-1, 13.24
Hardouin-Mansart, Jules 289
Hardy, Oliver 113
Harlem (Hughes) 353
Harlem Foundation 350
Hayden, Palmer 350-1
Haydn, Franz Joseph 81, 307, 308: *The Creation* 307; *Symphony No. 94 in G Major* 81, 307, 12.37

Heiji Monogatori scroll 228, 11.40
helmet mask (African) 347-8, 13.5
Herculaneum: *Hercules and Telephos* 0.9
High Noon (Zinnemann) 114
highboy 145, 0.7
Hildesheim Cathedral, Germany, doors 243-4, 11.63
Hindemith, Paul 379
Hiroshige, Ando 293; *Maple Leaves at the Tekona Shrine* 293, 12.26
Hogarth, William 299; *The Rake's Progress* 299, 12.32
Hokusai, Katsushika 291, 293: *The Great Wave off Kanazawa* 293, 12.25; *Manga* 291, 293, 12.24
Holy Family Church, architecture 150, 7.32
Home (Samm-Art Williams) 355
Hope, Bob 113
Hopfer, Daniel: *Ceiling Ornament* 1.7
Horace 221
housepost (carved, Native American) 313, 12.45
Houses of Parliament, London (Barry/Welby) 329, 12.57
How Green Was My Valley 365
Hsia Kuei: *Twelve Views from a Thatched Cottage* 218, 11.27
Hughes, Langston 350, 353; *Harlem* 353, *Theme for English B* 353

Ibsen, Henrik 17
Idler Essays, The (Johnson) 303-5
Igbo-Ukwu, roped pot from 211-12, 11.16
Iktinos and Kallikrates: The Parthenon 11.7
Imari porcelain vase 291, 12.23
Imperial Palace, Peking 277, 12.5, 12.6
Importance of Being Earnest, The (Wilde) 4.13
Improvisation Chamber Ensemble 381
In the Dining Room (Morisot) 334, 12.64
Inca vessel 241, 11.59
Indian art; Akhbar & the Mughals 279; Arya, The 277-8; Mughal painting style 279; Muslim vs Hindu Architecture 280-1; Muslims, the 278; painting styles 279-80; Punjab painting style 281; Rajput painting style 279-80
Industrial age style 319-39: architecture 337, 339; classicism 319-21; impressionism 332-4, 336; Post-Impressionism 337; realism 330-2; romanticism 322-30
Ingres, Jean-Auguste-Dominique 319; *Grande Odalisque* 319, 12.48
ink painting 32
Interior of the Pantheon, The (Panini) 7.13
Intolerance (Griffith) 108, 114

Ionesco, Eugene 366; *Bald Soprano* 366
Islam 236: architecture 239-40; literature 238; visual art 236-7
Isozaki, Arata 377
Ives, Charles 381, 382
Izumo, Takeda 291

Japan 227: art 289-91, 293; Imari porcelain 291; Kabuki theatre 291; painting and sculpture 228, 290; printmaking 291, 293; theatre 229
Jardin d'Email (Dubuffet) 371-2, 13.26
Jaws (Spielberg) 91, 109, 112, 5.2
Jazz 353-4
Jefferson, Thomas (architect) 306; Monticello 306, 12.36
Jemaa, Head from 211, 11.15
Jerusalem: Temple of Solomon 188, 10.14
Jesu Joy of Man's Desiring (J.S. Bach) 3.6
Johnson, Samuel 303; *The Idler Essays* 303-5
Johnson, William Henry 352
Joplin, Scott 354
Julius II, Pope 270
juxtaposition 54, 1.41

Kaisersaal Residenz, Würzburg, Germany (Neumann) 150, 7.34
Kaufmann House, (Wright) 146-7, 7.28
Keaton, Buster 113
King Lear (Shakespeare) 91, 98, 4.10
Kleptomaniac, The (Porter) 114
Kota tribe 309, 12.41
Kouros (Noguchi) 362, 13.19
Kouros figure 65, 2.13
Krohne, G.H.: The Music Room 296, 12.30
Kuan-yin (Bodhisattva) 216, 11.24
Kumano Mandala, the 228, 11.39

La Flesche, Susette 315; *Nedawi* 315-19
Lamentation (Dürer) 1.6
Lamentation (Graham) 127
Lamentation, The (Giotto) 1.37
Laocoön and his Sons 210, 11.13
Lascaux, France; cave painting 13; 181-2, 0.2, 10.4
Last Supper, The (da Vinci) 266, 268, 11.78
Latrobe, Benjamin H. 321; Basilica of the Assumption, Baltimore 321, 12.50
Laugier, Abbé 306; *Essai sur l'architecture* 306
Laurel, Stan 113
Lawrence, Jacob 350; *One of the Largest Race Riots Occurred in East St. Louis* 350, 13.10
Le Cid (Racine) 90
Le Corbusier 148, 373-4, 7.29, 7.30: Villa Savoye (Poissy) 373-4, 13.29

Le Roy, Philibert 287, 289
Leoncavallo, Ruggiero 85, 86; *I Pagliacci* 85
Lever House, New York (Bunshaft) 374, 376, 13.30
Lewis, Lucy: ceramic bowl 13.1
Lichtenstein, Roy 368; *Whaam!* 368, 13.23
line 37-9
Lippi, Fra Lippo 254
literature 155: anecdotes 159; biography 156, 159; essays 156-7; fiction 155-6, 157-8; hagiography 156; novels 156; poetry 156, 158-9; quotations 159; short stories 156; drama *see* theatre
Little Night Music, A (Mozart) 89
Liurong Temple, Guangzhou, China 217-18, 11.26
Livy 221
Louis VI, King 248
Louis XIV, King 287, 289
Louis XVI, King 305
Love Supreme, A (Coltrane) 354
Lu Chi: *Winter* 275, 12.3
Luxor, Temple at (Egypt) 194, 10.19, 10.20
Lysippos: *Apoxymenos (Scraper)* 208, 11.9
Lysistrata (Aristophanes) 16

Madame de Pompadour as the Venus of the Doves (Falconet) 295, 12.28
Mlle. Pogany (Brancusi) 349, 13.9
Maderno, Carlo 271, 11.85
Madhu Madhavi Ragini Malwa, India 12.8
Magic animal carving (African) 346-7, 13.4
Maillol, Aristide; *The Mediterranean* 65, 2.11
male antelope mask (Africa) 348-9, 13.8
man from Brno (Czechoslovakia) 10.1
Man Pointing (Giacometti) 2.14
Manet, Edouard 331-2; *Le Déjeuner sur l'herbe* 331, 12.60
Manga (Hokusai) 291, 293, 12.24
Mannheim Orchestra 307
Manon Lescaut (Puccini) 3.10
Maple Leaves at the Tekona Shrine (Hiroshige) 293, 12.26
Maqamat al-Hariri (Al-Qasim ibn Ali al-Hariri) 237, 11.51
Marin County Courthouse, California (Wright) 114, 7.21
Market Cart, The (Gainsborough) 300, 12.33
Marlowe, Christopher 272: *Doctor Faustus* 272
Marriage of Figaro, The (Mozart) 307, 12.39
Mary, Mary (Kerr) proscenium stage setting 4.11
Masaccio 256: *The Tribute Money* 256, 257, 11.73

Mascagni, Pietro 86
Mask (from Bamenda area) 309, 12.41
Matisse, Henri 369; *Blue Nude (Souvenir de Biskra)* 359, 13.16
McIntyre, Nancy; *Barbershop Mirror* 1.10
Mediterranean, The (Maillol) 2.11
Menu de Gras (Chardin) 302, 12.34
Mercury (Bologna) 2.7
Mesopotamian art 182, 10.5
Messiah (Handel) 286-7
Michel, Claude *see* Clodion
Michelangelo 14, 32; 265, 268-9, 271, 11.79, 11.80, 11.83, 11.84: *David* 269, 11.81; Sistine Chapel 14, 32, 268, 11.79, 11.80
Miller, Arthur 88, 366: *Death of a Salesman* 366
Ming Dynasty; styles 273-5: Imperial Architecture 277; Sculpture and Ceramics 275-6
Minnesänger 244
Miró, Joan; *Composition* 1.12
Modest Proposal, A (Swift) 296-9
Momaday, Scott 343-4
Monadnock Building, Chicago (Burnham & Root) 138, 337, 339, 7.19,
Mondrian, Piet 361: *Composition in White, Black and Red* 53, 361, 1.40
Monet, Claude 332; *On the Seine at Bennecourt* 332, 12.62
monotheism 196-7
Mont Sainte-Victoire (Cézanne) 337, 12.66
Monticello, Charlottesville, Virginia (Jefferson) 306, 12.36
Moore, Henry; *Two Large Forms* 2.6
Moran, Robert 382; *Composition for Piano with Pianist* 382
Morisot, Berthe 334; *In the Dining Room* 334, 12.64
Mosque of Damascus, Great 239-40, 11.55, 11.56, 11.57
Moulin de la Galette (Renoir) 12.63
mozaics, Byzantine 232, 11.44, 11.45
Mozart, W.A. 14, 16, 81, 85, 307, 308: *The Marriage of Figaro* 85, 307, 308, 12.39; *Symphony No. 40 in G Minor* 307, 308, 12.38
Muro-Ji, Kondo of 227, 11.37
music: cantata 73; concert overture 73; concerto 73; duration 75; electronic 381; harmony 77; improvisation 381; intensity 75; mainstream 381; mass 73; melody 77; meter 79; modern classical 379-81; motet 74; notation 75, 77, 3.3; opera 73, 82-6; oratorio 73; orchestra 3.4; pitch 74-5, 3.1; rhythm & beat 79; scales 75, 3.2; serialism 381; sonata 72-3; structure 80; suite 73, symphony 73; tempo 80; texture 79; timbre 75; tonality 78; tone 74-5; ultrarationalism 382-3

Myron 201, 202-3, 11.3

Nameless Hour (Jazz dance) 6.14
Nash, John 328-9; Royal Pavilion, Brighton 328, 12.56
Native American art 312-19: Inuit 312-13; literature 315-19; Northwest Coast tribes 312-13
Nedawi (La Flesche) 315-19
Nefertari, tomb of 195-6, 10.21, 10.22
Nervi, Pier Luigi: Small Sports Palace (Rome) 376, 13.32
Neuhaus, Max 382
Neumann, Balthasar, Kaisersaal Residenz, 150, 7.34
Nevelson, Louise 371; *Black Wall* 371, 13.25
Night Watch, The (Rembrandt) 285-6, 12.15
Nijinsky, Vaslav 23
Nike of Samothrace 209-10, 11.12
Nikolais, Alwin 384
No Exit (Sartre) 366
No Place to be Somebody (Gordonne) 355
Nofretete, Queen (Nefertiti) 197, 10.23
Noguchi, Isamu 362; *Kouros* 362, 13.19
Notre-Dame-du-Haut, France (Le Corbusier) 148, 149, 7.29, 7.30

O'Keeffe, Georgia 361-2; *Dark Abstraction* 361, 13.18
Oath of the Horatii, The (David) 305, 12.35
Oedipus The King (Sophocles) 87-8, 91
oil painting 29-30
Old Ship of Zion 311, 12.43
Oldenburg, Claes 368; *Two Cheeseburgers with Everything* 368, 13.22
On the Seine at Bennecourt (Monet) 332, 12.62
One of the Largest Race Riots Occurred in East St. Louis (Lawrence) 350, 13.10
Op Art 370
openwork bird jar 241, 11.58
Otello (Verdi) 327

Paik, Nam June 382; *Danger Music for Dick Higgins* 382
Palace of Abraxas, Marne-la-Vallée, France (Bofill) 377, 13.33
Palace of Versailles, France 143, 145, 287, 289, 7.25, 12.19, 12.20, 12.21; Hall of Mirrors 150, 7.35
Paleolithic art 179-82, 10.1
Pampapati temple, Vijayanagar, India 281, 12.11
Panini, Giovanni Paolo; *The Interior of the Pantheon* 7.13
Pantheon, The, Rome 140, 226-7, 11.35, 11.36
Parker, Charlie 354, 13.12

Parthenon, The Greece 63, 206-7, 7.2, 11.7; Dionysus 63, 0.10; *Fates* 2.10
Paul III, Pope 271
Pauline Borghese as Venus Victrix (Canova) 320, 12.49
Peer Gynt (Ibsen) 103, 4.8
Penderecki, Krzysztof 383; *Polymorphia* 383
Pericles 200
Perkins, Tony 112
Perret, Auguste 373; Garage Ponthieu (Paris) 373, 13.28
Persistence of Memory (Dali) 365, 1.30
Phantom of the Opera 89
Photorealism 372
Photography 36-7, 1.11
piano, the 74, 3.1
Piano Lesson, The (Wilson) 355
Piano Sonata in C Minor (Beethoven) 12.40
Piano/Rogers: Pompidou Center (Paris) 378, 13.35
Picasso, Pablo 31, 172, 358-9: *Les Demoiselles d'Avignon* 359, 13.15; *Girl before a Mirror* 1.21; *Guernica* 172, 1.31, 9.2
Pirandello, Luigi 366; *Right You Are If You Think You Are* 366
Piranesi, Giambattista 306; *Della Magnificenza ...* 305
Pittman, Hobson; *Violets No. 1* 1.4
Plowing in the Nivernais (Bonheur) 323, 12.53
Pluralism; African-American 350-5; Native American 340-5; African influence 349; African style 345-50
Poems (Auden) 362-5
Poetics (Aristotle) 89
poetry *see* literature
Pollock, Jackson 12, 367; *Convergence* 0.1; *Autumn Rhythm* 367, 13.20
Polyklitus 201-2, 11.2
Polymorphia (Penderecki) 383
Pompidou Center, Paris (Piano/Rogers) 378, 13.35
Pont du Gard, Nîmes, France 7.18
Pop Art 368-9
Portland Public Office Building, Portland (Graves) 377, 13.34
Portrait of an Unknown Roman 220, 11.28
Post-Modernist Architecture 376-8
Praxiteles: *Cnidian Aphrodite* 207, 11.8
Prélude à l'après-midi d'un faune (Debussy) 336
Primary Structures 371, 13.25
prints and printmaking 33: aquatint 33; collograph 32, 33; drypoint 33, 34; etching 33, 34; intaglio 32, 33, 34, 35; linoleum cut 32; lithography 33, 35; planography 33, 35; relief 32; silk screening 35, 36; stenciling 33, 35; wood

engraving 32, 33; woodcuts 32, 33
Psalms (22, 130, 132) 188-90
Psycho (Hitchcock) 112, 113-14
Ptolemy 106
Puccini, Giacomo 86: *Manon Lescaut* 3.10

Quiet Man, The (Ford) 115

Raft of the Medusa, The (Géricault) 322-3, 12.52
Rahotep, Prince, and Nofret (sculpture) 190, 10.17
Rainier, Yvonne 384
Rake's Progress, The (Hogarth) 299, 12.32
Rameses II 194
Rape of the Daughters of Leucippus (Rubens) 1.32
Raphael 265, 271
Ravel, Maurice 379
Realism 365-6; in art 365, 1.34; in film 365, in theatre 365
Recuerdo (Allen) 344
Reich, Steve 383
Rembrandt 285-6; *The Night Watch* 285-6, 12.15
Renaissance, the 253; architecture 263; Flemish painting 254; high, in Rome 265-6, 268-71; late, in England 271-2; literature 259; painting in Florence 254; sculpture in Florence 256
Renoir, Pierre Auguste 333: *Moulin de la Galette* 333, 12.63
Revolt in the Harem (Taglioni) 328
Rice, Elmer 356; *Adding Machine* 356
Richard II (Shakespeare) 4.6
Right You Are If You Think You Are (Pirandello) 366
Rite of Spring (Stravinsky) 23
Rococo style 293-9
Rodin, Auguste 323-4; *The Burghers of Calais* 2.3; *The Thinker* 324, 12.54
Rohe, Mies van der 376; Seagram Building (New York) 376, 13.31
Roland, The Song of 244-7
Romance of Amir Hamza (Mughal) 279, 12.7
Rome, Open City (Rossellini) 365
Rome: architecture 224-7; Imperial Classicism 219: style 219-21
Rossini, Gioacchino 327; *The Barber of Seville* 327
Royal Pavilion, Brighton, England (Nash) 328, 12.56
Rubens, Peter Paul 284-5: *Assumption of the Virgin* 284, 12.14; *Rape of the Daughters of Leucippus* 51, 1.32
Running Fence ... (Christo) 2.9

Saarinen, Eero 148
St. Alban's Cathedral, England 131, 7.5
St. Denis, Abbey Church of 248

St. Denis, Ruth 383-4
St. George (Donatello) 258
St. Médard of Soissons, Gospel Book of: St. Mark 44, 1.25
St. Paul's Cathedral, England 137, 7.12, 7.15
St. Peter's (Rome) 269-71, 11.82-11.85
St. Sernin, Toulouse, France, 242-3, 11.60, 11.61
Saint-Säens, Camille 379
Salisbury Cathedral 249, 251, 11.65, 11.66, 11.67
Samson Slaying a Philistine (Giambologna) 2.4
San Vitale, Ravenna 231-4, 11.42, 11.43, 11.44, 11.45
Sargon II 186-7, 10.11, 10.12, 10.13
Sartre, Jean-Paul 366; *No Exit* 366
Satyr and Bacchante (Clodion) 295, 12.29
Schoenberg, Arnold 78, 380
Schuman, William 379
sculpture 57: articulation 67; color 68-9; dynamics 69; environment 71; ephemeral 62; focal area 68; found 62; lighting 71; line and form 70; linear 59; manipulation 62; mass 70-1; relief 59; texture 68
Seagram Building, New York (Mies van der Rohe) 376, 13.31
Sears Tower, Chicago (Skidmore, Owings & Merrill) 154, 7.37
Segal, George 368-9
Seurat, Georges 337; *Sunday Afternoon ...* 337, 12.65
Seven Jupiter Trees (Wen Cheng-Ming) 275, 12.2
Shakespeare, William 271-2: *Antony and Cleopatra* 272; "The Seven Ages of Man" 164; *The Tempest* 271
Shang Dynasty art 198-9, 10.25
Shaw, Bernard 105
She Wore a Yellow Ribbon 115
Sheeler, Charles; *Delmonico Building* 1.9
Shiva & Devi on Gajasura Hide (Gajahamurti) (Basohli) 280, 12.9
Sistine Chapel, Vatican, Rome (Michelangelo) 11.79, 11.80
Small Sports Palace, Rome (Nervi) 376, 13.32
Smith, Bessie 353
Soft Hearted Sioux, The (Bonnin) 341-3
Solomon, Temple of 188, 10.14
Sophocles 13, 204
Sotatsu, Nonomura 290; *The Zen Priest Choka* 290, 12.22
Sphinx, the (Egypt) 191, 193, 10.18
Spring (Botticelli) 256, 11.72
Spring Blossoms (Calder) 68, 2.17
Stagecoach (Ford) 109
Star-Spangled Banner, The 77, 3.5
Starlight Express 89

Starry Night, The (Van Gogh) 172, 174, 337, 9.3
steel, in building 140-41
Stella, Frank 370-71; *Tahkt-I-Sulayman I* 371, 13.24
Stockhausen, Karlheinz 382
stone, in building 138
Stone Breakers, The (Courbet) 330, 12.59
Stonehenge, England 7.1
Stravinsky, Igor 380, 382
Streetcar Named Desire, A (Williams) 99
Strindberg, August 356; *Ghost Sonata* 356
style, analysis of artworks 171-2, 174, 177-8
Suessula Painter 208, 11.10
Suger, Abbot 248
Sullivan, Louis 153, 339; 7.36: Department Store, Chicago 339, 12.68
Sumerian art 182-3, 10.6
Sunday Afternoon on the Island of Grande Jatte (Seurat) 337
Sung dynasty painting 218, 11.27
Surrealism 365, 1.30
Swan Theatre, London 272, 11.86
Swift, Jonathan 296; *A Modest Proposal* 296-9
Symphony No. 3 in F Major (Brahms) 327, 12.55
Symphony No. 6 (Beethoven) 308
Symphony No. 40 in G minor (Mozart) 307, 308, 12.38
Symphony No. 94 in G Major (Haydn) 307, 12.37

Taglioni, Filippo 328; *Revolt in the Harem* 328
Tahkt-I-Sulayman I (Stella) 371, 13.24
Taj Mahal, Agra, India (Lahori) 280-81, 12.10
Tanner, Henry O. 332; *The Banjo Lesson* 332, 12.61
Taoism 214
Tartuffe (Molière) 25; 0.12

Taylor, Cecil 383
Taylor, Paul 384; *Book of Beasts* 384
Tchaikovsky, Peter 327: *Violin Concerto in D Major* 327
Tell Asmar statues 186, 1.7
tempera painting 30
Tempest, The (Shakespeare) 271
Temple of Fortuna Virilis, Rome 224-5, 11.31
Temple of Olympian Zeus, The (Athens) 210, 11.14
terracotta warriors 215, 11.21, 11.22
Tharp, Twyla 384
theatre; actors 99; comedy 88; costume design 97-8; denouement 91; dynamics 99; Greek Classical tragedy 88; lighting design 96; melodrama 88-9; plays 87; plot 90; properties 98; scene design 94, 96; script 89-90; tragedy 88; tragicomedy 88; verisimilitude 99-103
Theban rock tombs 195
Theme for English B (Hughes) 353
Thinker, The (Rodin) 324, 12.54
Tintern Abbey (Wordsworth) 324-6
Titus, Arch of, Rome 225-6, 11.34
Tom Jones (film) 112
Tomb of Shirvanshah, Baku, Azerbaijan 177, 9.7, 9.8
Torroja, Eduardo; Grandstand at Zarzuela Race Track, Madrid 154, 7.17
Totem poles of the Tlingit 313-4, 12.46
Trajan's Column: Apollodorus of Damascus 70, 2.20
Trans-World Airline Building, New York (Saarinen) 148
Traviata, La (Verdi) 327
Tree Spirit (Central Indian figure) 67, 2.15
Tribute Money, The (Masaccio) 256, 257, 11.73
trompe l'oeil 53
troubadours 244
Tudor, David 382

Tutankhamun, King 197, 10.24
Twelfth Night (Shakespeare) 4.9
Twelve Views from a Thatched Cottage (Hsia Kuei) 218, 11.27
Two Cheeseburgers with Everything (Oldenburg) 368, 13.22
Two Large Forms (Moore) 2.6

Umbrellas, The (Christo) 0.4A, 0.4B
Uncle Tom's Cabin (Stowe) 89
Unique Forms of Continuity in Space (Boccioni) 361, 13.17
United States Capitol Building, Washington, D.C. 150, 152, 7.33
Unkei: *Nio* 228, 11.38

van Gogh, Vincent 29-30, 172, 174: *The Starry Night* 172, 174, 1.1, 9.3
Vanni, Giovanni 29; *Holy Family with St. John* 1.2
Vasarély, Victor 370
Vatican, The (Rome) 269-71, 11.82, 11.83, 11.84, 11.85
vaults and vaulting 132, 7.9, 7.10, 7.11
Venus Consoling Love (Boucher) 1.42
Venus figures 181
Verdi, Giuseppi 327: *Aida* 327; *Otello* 327; *La Traviata* 327
Vermeer, Jan; *The Girl with a Red Hat* 1.29
View Near Volterra, A (Corot) 171-2, 9.1
Villa Savoye, Poissy, France (Le Corbusier) 373-4, 13.29
Violin Concerto in D Major (Tchaikovsky) 327
Virgil 221; *The Aeneid* 222-224
Vision after the Sermon, The (Gauguin) 337, 12.67
Volkswagen Beetle 0.8

Wagner, Richard 86, 327-8: *Art and Revolution* 327, *Opera and Drama* 327
Waiting for Godot (Becket) 23, 366, 0.11

Warhol, Andy 13, 14; *Green Coca-Cola Bottles* 0.3
Waring, James 384
watercolor painting 30
Watteau, Antoine 294: *Embarkation for Cythera* 294, 12.27
Welby, Augustus 329; Houses of Parliament, England 329, 12.57
Wen Cheng-Ming: *Seven Jupiter Trees* 275, 12.2
Wesley, John "God Brought Me Safe" 166-7
Westside Story 89
Whaam! (Lichtenstein) 368, 13.23
Wiene, Robert 356; *Cabinet of Dr. Caligari* 356
Williams, Samm-Art 355; *Home* 355
Williams, Tennessee 366; *The Glass Menagerie* 366
Williams, William T. 356; *Batman* 356, 13.14
Wilson, August 355; *The Piano Lesson* 355; *Fences* 355
Winter (Lu Chi) 275, 12.3
Wolsey, Cardinal Thomas 142
Woman from Willendorf, The 181, 10.3
Women Picking Corn (Begay) 344-5, 13.2
wood, in building 140
Wood, Grant 365; *American Gothic* 51, 365, 0.6, 1.34
Wordsworth, William 324-6; *Tintern Abbey* 324-6
Wren, Christopher 142, 7.15
Wright, Frank Lloyd 141, 146-7, 153, 373, 7.21, 7.28
Wyeth, Andrew 30

Young, La Monte 382
Your Darn Tootin' (Kennedy) 5.5

Zarzuela Race Track Grandstand, Madrid (Torroja) 154, 7.17
Zen Priest Choka, The (Sotatsu) 290
Zitkala-Sa *see* Boonin, Gertrude
Zola, Emile 322
Zorach, William; *Child with Cat* 2.16